W9-AUS-600

Dimitri Obolensky is Professor of Russian and Balkan History in the University of Oxford and a Student of Christ Church. He served as General Secretary of the xɪɪɪth International Congress of Byzantine Studies at Oxford in 1966. His published works include *The Bogomils*, *The Christian Centuries*, Vol. 2: *The Middle Ages* (with David Knowles), *The Penguin Book of Russian Verse* (which he edited), and *Byzantium and the Slavs: collected studies*.

FROM THE LIBRARY OF
Saint Michael
Ukrainian Orthodox Church
74 Harris Avenue
Woonsocket, RI 02895-1843

THE BYZANTINE COMMONWEALTH

Eastern Europe, 500-1453

Dimitri Obolensky
Professor of Russian and Balkan History
University of Oxford

St. Vladimir's Seminary Press
575 Scarsdale Road
Crestwood, New York 10707

Library of Congress Cataloging in Publication Data

Obolsensky, Dimitri, 1918-
The Byzantine Commonwealth, Eastern Europe, 500-1453.

Reprint. Originally published: London : Sphere Books, 1974.

Bibliography: p.
Includes index.
1. Byzantine Empire—Civilization. 2. Europe, Eastern—
Civilization—Byzantine influences.

I. Title.
DF521.026 1982   949.5   82-16970

THE BYZANTINE COMMONWEALTH
Eastern Europe, 500-1453

© Copyright 1971 by Dimitri Obolensky

ALL RIGHTS RESERVED

First published in Great Britain by
Weidenfield & Nicholson Ltd. 1971,
and in 1974 by Sphere Books Ltd.

ISBN 0-913836-98-2

Printed in the United States of America by Eastern Press,
New Haven, CT.

CONTENTS

Τιμὴ σ' ἐκείνους ὅπου στὴν ζωήν των
ὅρισαν καὶ φυλάγουν Θερμοπύλες.

CONSTANTINE CAVAFY

Πέφτουν ὁλοένα σήμερα νομίσματα πάνω στὴν πολιτεία
ἀνάμεσα σὲ κάθε κόμπο σὰ μιὰ σταλαματιὰ στὸ χῶμα
ἀνοίγει μιὰ καινούργια χώρα . . .

GEORGE SEFERIS

LIST OF ILLUSTRATIONS

LIST OF MAPS

ABBREVIATIONS

Cross   *The Russian Primary Chronicle*, translated and edited by S. H. Cross and O. P. Sherbowitz-Wetzor (Cambridge, Mass., 1953).

DAI   Constantine Porphyrogenitus, *De administrando imperio*, i, Greek text edited by Gy. Moravcsik, English translation by R. J. H. Jenkins, 2nd ed. (Washington, 1967); ii, Commentary, edited by R. J. H. Jenkins (London, 1962).

DOP   *Dumbarton Oaks Papers* (Cambridge, Mass., 1941–).

FHB   *Fontes historiae Bulgaricae* (Sofia, 1954–).

MGH   *Monumenta Germaniae historica* (Hanover, 1826–).

PG   J. P. Migne, *Patrologiae cursus completus. Series graeca* (Paris, 1857–1936).

PL   J. P. Migne, *Patrologiae cursus completus. Series latina* (Paris, 1844–).

Povest'   *Povest' Vremennykh Let* [The Russian Primary Chronicle], ed. D. S. Likhachev and V. P. Adrianova-Peretts, 2 vols. (Moscow–Leningrad, 1950).

FOREWORD

In a work which was planned and written over a period of years, I owe a considerable debt to many friends, teachers and colleagues whose ideas and writings have influenced my views. Their names recur frequently in the notes and the bibliography at the end of the volume. Professor A. Gieysztor kindly agreed to read an early draft of the typescript, and Professor I. Dujčev generously undertook to read the proofs. To them, as well as to Professors R. Auty and A. Soloviev, to the Rev. Gervase Mathew, to the Very Rev. Kallistos T. Ware, to Dr. W. H. Parker and to my pupil Mr. J. Shepard, who read various sections, I am grateful for perceptive and vigilant criticism. On particular points, I owe much to discussions with the Rev. Professor F. Dvornik, the late Romilly Jenkins, Dr. G. S. R. Kitson Clark, Professor I. Ševčenko and Dr. P. Sherrard. None of these scholars is responsible for whatever errors of fact or interpretation may be found in this book. My wife typed the whole manuscript twice, and I have relied on her judgment at many points.

It is a particularly pleasant duty to thank those friends who provided me, while this book was being prepared, with congenial surroundings for periods of uninterrupted work. I would like specially to mention Marcelle Uxkull von Gyllenband and Philip and Anna Sherrard, whose hospitality and kindness enabled me to complete much of the first draft in Greece during 1965 and 1968, and also my colleagues at the Dumbarton Oaks Center for Byzantine Studies in Washington.

The exacting task of assembling the photographs for the illustrations fell to Mrs. Pat Hodgson, to whom I offer my warm thanks. Many friends and colleagues, in addition, gave me valuable help in obtaining photographs. They include Mr. J. Beckwith, Mr. J. Blankoff, Miss Susan Boyd, Professor Kh. Danov, the Rev. Professor J. Gill, Mrs. Anne Kindersley, Professor V. Lazarev, Professor D. Likhachev, Mrs. Mabel Nandris, Professor G. Ostrogorsky, Dr. Anne Pennington, Professor I. Ševčenko, Dr. D. Stefanović and Professor D. Talbot Rice.

My long-suffering publishers have endured my protracted labours with great patience, and I am especially grateful for the help and unfailing kindness of Mr. Julian Shuckburgh and Miss Mary O'Connell.

A note is needed about the transliteration and forms of names. In the absense of a commonly accepted uniform system of transliteration for Greek and Slavonic personal and place names, I have endeavoured to use the spelling most familiar to the English reader. I have applied the same common-sense procedure, at the risk of incurring the charge of historical inconsistency, when selecting one of several existing forms of some place names. The more important alternative forms have been entered in the index, in the hope that appropriate cross-references will facilitate identification.

D.O.

Oxford,
21 March 1971

INTRODUCTION

This book is concerned with two themes. The first, a multiple and largely narrative one, is the history of Byzantium's relations with the peoples of Eastern Europe. These relations—political, diplomatic, economic, ecclesiastical and cultural—will be considered both in the light of the Byzantine Empire's foreign policy, and from the point of view of the East European peoples who, whether on their own initiative or in response to impulses emanating from Byzantium, were drawn into its orbit. The second theme is more unitary and synoptic. Through the relations established by these peoples with the empire during the Middle Ages, their ruling and educated classes were led to adopt many features of Byzantine civilization, with the result that they were able to share in, and eventually to contribute to, a common cultural tradition. This tradition was compounded of diverse elements. Among them were a common profession of Eastern Christianity; the recognition of the primacy of the Constantinopolitan Church; the acknowledgement—at least tacit—that the Byzantine emperor was endowed with a measure of authority over the whole of Orthodox Christendom; the acceptance of the norms of Romano-Byzantine law; and the belief that the literary standards and artistic techniques cultivated in the empire's schools, monasteries and workshops were of universal validity and worthy of imitation. The Byzantine heritage of these East European countries was, I believe, a significant enough component of their medieval tradition to justify the view that, in some respects, they formed a single international community.

In attempting to write the history of this community I have encountered a number of difficulties. In the first place, the geographical area inhabited by the European "heirs of Byzantium" altered in the course of time, expanding in some regions, contracting in others. Its heartland was the Balkan peninsula, the home of the Greeks, the Bulgarians, the Serbs and the Albanians. In the ninth and tenth centuries it came to include Russia, and in the late Middle Ages the Rumanian lands as well. For several centuries, moreover, Byzantine civilization had some impact on both sides of the middle Danube, and thus influenced the early medieval culture of the Moravians, the Czechs and the Hungarians. The notion of "Eastern Europe", used in this book to cover all these regions, is little more than a loose empirical category, obtained by combining a geographical with a cultural criterion. It thus excludes Poland, whose culture since the early Middle Ages has depended on the Latin world, as well as Sicily, Venice and the Caucasian lands which, though they lay for centuries within the Byzantine cultural orbit, will for geographical reasons be given no more than cursory consideration. The fact that the frontiers of Eastern Europe were shifting and impermanent imposes some limitation on a continuous study of its history.

A further difficulty lies in the fact that, to judge from the extant documents, the East Europeans of the Middle Ages were only fitfully and imperfectly aware of the nature of this international community. Its size and complexity, the subtlety of the bonds that kept its component parts together, as well as the slowness of its growth, no doubt imposed too great a strain on men's imagination. Most obvious and easiest to comprehend was its religious aspect. When they thought of this community as a whole, the East European peoples mainly conceived it as the body of Orthodox Christendom of which the Church of Constantinople was the acknowledged head and administrative centre. Its political, juridical and cultural features were less clearly perceived. Though their rulers recognized that the Byzantine emperor wielded much power over the church to which they belonged, that he was the ultimate source of law and that his authority transcended the political boundaries of the empire, they were so anxious to vindicate their own claims to national sovereignty that they probably found it unnecessary, even undesirable, to define their relationship to him with any precision. The Byzantines, for their part, believing that the political organization of this world was part of the divine order, do not seem to have felt the need to reflect deeply on the

14

actual mechanism of international society. Most of them took for granted the idea that their emperor's authority was universal. Nor did they have a special word for the whole community of their satellite peoples. "Barbarians" before their conversion to Christianity, they were supposed, on their baptism, to become subjects of the emperor of East Rome. With characteristic semantic ambiguity, the Byzantines applied the terms used to describe their own state—*basileia* ("empire"), *oikoumene* ("the inhabited universe"), *politeuma* ("government, community")—to the group of nations over which they claimed sovereignty. The word "commonwealth", likewise ambiguous, is used in this book as a rough equivalent of at least the last of these Greek terms. No precise constitutional significance should be ascribed to it, nor is its purpose to suggest any modern parallel. It is offered as a convenient and, it is hoped, not inappropriate description of a society whose structure and bonds were seldom wholly visible to men of the Middle Ages, but which the historian today, with his greater awareness of the unifying effect of culture on human institutions, values and behaviour, can perceive more clearly.

For this was a real society, not a mere intellectual abstraction. In recent years several distinguished Byzantinists have focused attention upon it, by studying the motive forces behind the empire's claim to universal hegemony. Their work—particularly the writings of George Ostrogorsky, Franz Dölger and André Grabar—has widened and deepened our understanding of international relations in medieval Eastern Europe. But they wrote primarily from the vantage-point of Byzantium: it was not their purpose to consider the cultural bonds of this community nor the contribution made to its life by the non-Byzantine peoples of this area. To the native scholars of Eastern Europe, specialists in the medieval history of their own countries, we owe a considerable debt. However, with comparatively few exceptions—that of the Rumanian historian Nicholas Iorga is outstanding—they have tended to write from an ethnocentric, if not nationalistic, point of view. Much has certainly been gained by their willingness to concentrate on the national elements in their countries' past. But there is danger for the medievalist in the temptation to equate national unity with unity of culture. And to view the association of the East European countries with Byzantium as a struggle between Byzantine "imperialism" and local national aspirations, is to miss something of that rich cosmopolitan experience which these countries enjoyed during much of their medieval history.

The problem of nationalism will be discussed several times in this book. Traces of it will be found in several East European countries of the Middle Ages. But by comparison with Western Europe it was muted and slow to develop. Byzantium retained a towering prestige, and its religious, cultural and political leadership was not denied. For all the irritation provoked by the "superbia Graecorum", there is no real analogy in medieval Eastern Europe to John of Salisbury's defiance of twelfth century Hohenstaufen imperialism: "Who appointed the Germans to be judges over the nations?" In the last resort, the fact that so long as the empire existed no single nation of Eastern Europe successfully challenged its religious and cultural supremacy, nor its claims to embody the Roman tradition of universality, is the clearest proof that the Byzantine Commonwealth was no mere figment of men's imagination. Sprawling between shifting boundaries, divided into ethnic groups and warring national states, increasingly threatened with disruption by centrifugal forces, this commonwealth, born in the travails of the barbarian invasions, achieved enough vitality and coherence to survive as a discernible entity from the mid-ninth to the mid-fifteenth century. It was finally destroyed by the Ottoman conquest of Constantinople in 1453, though its influence lived on in parts of Eastern Europe until the late eighteenth century. How it came to endure for so long is a question to which this book may suggest an answer.

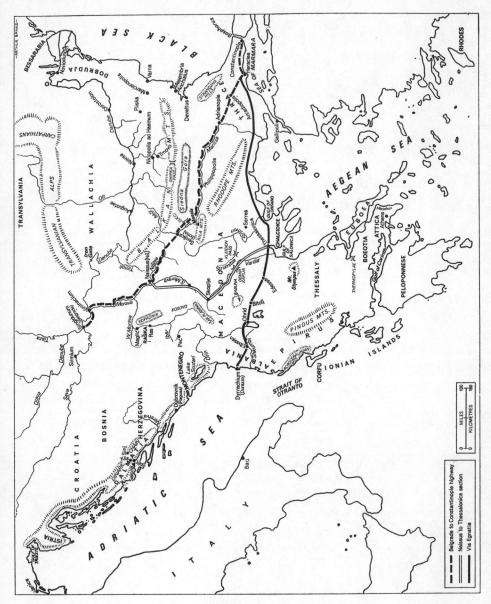

Map 1   The Balkans

I

The Geographical Setting

I THE BALKANS

The movement of men, goods and ideas across the Balkan peninsula in the Middle Ages was greatly affected by the features of its physical geography. Three of these features had a lasting effect upon the history of the Balkan lands. In the first place, the peninsula, itself predominantly mountainous, opens funnel-wise at its northern end into a vast plain, some 1,200 kilometres long, which is traversed by the Danube and its tributaries, the Sava and the Drava, and which—save for the low-lying plateau surrounding the Iron Gate and forming the southern extremity of the Transylvanian Alps—is barred by no physical obstacle. Communications were consequently easy between the peninsula and the lands of Central and Eastern Europe; and the Balkans lay open to the invasions of peoples from beyond the Danube, especially from the Hungarian plain and the South Russian steppe. Secondly, the mountainous nature of the peninsula and the fragmentation of its landscape, caused by its multiple ranges and isolated valleys, have deprived it of a commanding geographical centre. Its principal cities—Constantinople and Thessalonica—occupied a peripheral position; Constantinople, the capital of the Byzantine Empire, succeeded at times in enforcing its sovereignty over all or most of the Balkans; but these periods of Byzantine hegemony were few and brief. After the partition of the Roman Empire in 395, on three occasions only was the peninsula politically united under the sovereignty of Constantinople: between about 538 and 602, under Justinian and his three immediate successors; between 1018 and about 1070, as the result of the conquests of Basil II; and, for the last time, between 1172 and

19

1180, in the closing years of the reign of Manuel 1. During most of its medieval history, the Balkan peninsula had no single political centre. The most centrally situated of its large cities is Skopje in Macedonia; and on one occasion, in the middle of the fourteenth century, it seemed that this city, then the political centre of the Serbian realm, might become the capital of a united Balkan empire; but the eastern, southern and northern regions of the peninsula remained outside the medieval Serbian kingdom, and this last attempt to unite the peninsula under a single Christian ruler ended with the death of Stephen Dušan in 1355. Thirdly, the medieval history of the Balkans bears the mark of a peculiar relationship between its three most distinctive geographical features—the mountains, the plains and the sea.

The mountain is the most immediately striking feature of the Balkan landscape. Indeed, *balkan* is a Turkish word for "mountain chain"; and this name, applied by the Turks and by modern geographers to the range known to classical and Byzantine authors as Haemus, which lies south of the lower Danube, was extended by nineteenth century writers to the whole peninsula. Along the Adriatic coast and in parts of Greece, these mountains form rocky limestone ridges that gleam white in the sun; and in the central and northern areas of the peninsula, covered with forests that have greatly dwindled since the Middle Ages and whose humidity made them sometimes more attractive to settlers than the more arid lowland sites, they have directed movements of population, determined areas of settlement and formed the background for much of the human drama in the history of the Balkans. Judged by Alpine standards, none of them is very high: the loftiest summit in the peninsula, Musala in the Rila massif in Bulgaria, is slightly below 3,000 metres. On the whole, the mountain ranges of the peninsula have not proved insuperable obstacles to the movement of men: the Dinaric mountain chain, which runs parallel to the Adriatic coast, did not prevent the Slav invaders from crossing its massive limestone ranges in order to capture and destroy the cities of Roman Dalmatia; nor were these invaders halted, for any considerable time, by the Pindus range in their migrations further south which led them to occupy and colonize the greater part of Greece and of the Peloponnese. The Haemus, or Balkan range, proved even less of an obstacle to invaders from the north: the terrain shelves gently upwards from the Danube plain, and falls more steeply on the southern side of the mountains; the range itself is of medium height and, although it is traversed by only one river, the Iskŭr, it has a number of negotiable passes: six of them were used by the Romans, and at least nine in the Byzantine period. These passes played a notable role in the medieval history of Eastern Europe: providing a link between the Danube valley and the lowlands of Thrace, they served for successive invaders from the north as signposts on the road to Constantinople. They played this role for the thousand years which all but cover the life-span of the Byzantine Empire: Huns and Avars, Bulgars and Russians, Pechenegs and Cumans, Uzes and Mongols, all crossed these mountain passes in their attacks on the European provinces of Byzantium.

The extent to which the mountains of the Balkan peninsula were an effective barrier to cultural diffusion is harder to assess. At times, no doubt, they did slow down, halt for centuries, and even obstruct altogether the spread of ideas and institutions. The influence of Byzantine civilization spread northward from Constantinople and Thessalonica most easily across the plain of Thrace and up the valley of the Vardar. But in the hamlets and pastures of the Rhodopes—the most impenetrable range of the peninsula—in the highlands of Šar and Babuna that surround the Macedonian lakes, and in the Pindus, Byzantium remained for centuries, and perhaps always, a shadowy power and an ineffectual master, whose provincial governors and tax collectors could be largely ignored, and whose Christian missionaries, if they ever got so far, contended vainly against paganism and heresy. The reconquest and re-Hellenisation of the largely mountainous Peloponnese proved a formidable undertaking, and was never wholly achieved by the Byzantines. Perhaps the most striking instance of a barrier offered by a mountain range to the diffusion of culture is the Dinaric chain which follows the Adriatic coast from the Gulf of Trieste to the mouth of the Drin in Northern Albania. The height of the mountains, the ruggedness of the relief and the barrenness of this *karst* area isolated in antiquity and in the Middle Ages the inland regions from the narrow coastal fringe of Dalmatia. This fringe, with its Mediterranean climate and close connection with Italy, was successively colonized by the Greeks, dominated by the Romans and controlled by the Byzantines. In the late Middle Ages it became the preserve of Venetian civilization.

This natural barrier between the coastal plain and the ultramontane interior was not, of course, an absolute one. Merchants crossed it in places by mule; and through two gaps which break its continuity—the lower Neretva valley and the basin round Lake Scutari—trade routes joined the coast to the interior. It is true none the less that the Dinaric range contributed to the isolation of Bosnia and the inland regions of Herzegovina and Montenegro from the cultural influence of Venice and the civilization of the Mediterranean world.

The mountains of the Balkan peninsula have also helped to determine the rhythm of ethnic migrations. Islands of security in times of danger, retreats for defeated peoples who vanished for centuries beyond the historian's horizon, these mountains, in other circumstances, have unloaded their inhabitants over large areas of the peninsula. The Slav invasions of the sixth and seventh centuries destroyed the Roman and the Christian culture in the greater part of the Balkans. No records have survived to tell us what happened to the autochthonous inhabitants, Illyrians and Thracians, who managed to survive this destructive flood. Some of these natives, partly or wholly Romanized, probably retreated before the Slavs into the mountains. In tenth and eleventh century documents two peoples make their first appearance in the Balkan peninsula: the Vlakhs and the Albanians. Their origin has been the subject of much controversy. Most scholars today regard the Vlakhs as the descendants of the semi-Romanized natives of the Balkans, who were pushed into the mountains by the Slav invaders. In the Middle Ages they emerged as nomadic, Romance-speaking shepherds from their mountain retreats, from the Haemus, the Rhodopes and the Pindus, and descended into the lowlands of Thrace, Macedonia and Thessaly. The early history of the Albanians, though equally obscure, can also serve to illustrate this rhythmical pulse of the mountain, which both absorbs and disgorges large groups of men. Probably descended from the ancient Illyrians, the Albanians are believed to have retreated before the Slav invaders into the highlands which they still occupy; there, having exchanged the life of farmers for that of shepherds, they survived until the late Middle Ages. Then suddenly, in the fourteenth century, the Albanians began to descend from their mountainous homeland; in a great movement of expansion which has been compared in its scope and impetus to the earlier Slav invasions, they spread eastward and southward. By the following century we find them thick on the ground, in Thessaly, Attica, Boeotia, Euboea and the Peloponnese, colonizing and farming the countryside, moving as nomadic shepherds across the land, or serving as soldiers in the armies of the local Greek and Frankish lords.

It is not surprising that the mountains of the Balkan peninsula have in many ages provided refuge for dissident and freedom-loving minorities who have sought to resist the empire builders of the plains. In a Greek folk-song glorifying the military deeds of the *klephts*, the irregular fighters against the Turks, the proud boast that the mountain is the stronghold of liberty is uttered by Mount Olympus:

I am the ancient Olympus, famed throughout the world; I have forty-two summits and sixty-two springs: on every summit stands a flag, on every branch sits a klepht. And when the spring comes and the branches open up their leaves, the mountains are filled with klephts, and the valleys with slaves.[1]

These examples may suffice to illustrate the role, manifold and vital, played by the mountain in the medieval history of the Balkans: retreat of the fugitive, the have-not and the outlaw; stronghold of political liberty, racial seclusion, ancient customs, social individualism and religious dissent; land of scattered hamlets whose inhabitants, living on the margin of recorded history, remained for centuries refractory to the more advanced civilization of the plains; often presenting a barrier to the diffusion of culture; economically linked with the lowlands by the seasonal migrations of nomadic shepherds and their flocks; home of barbarians and a source of constant anxiety for the farmer who feared for the safety of his cornfields, vineyards and olive groves; recruiting ground for soldiers, often the finest in the peninsula; refuge of peoples who in their later migrations appeared as land-hungry highlanders occupying large tracts of the peninsula and who permanently affected its demographic features: the mountain, in its human as in its physical aspect, forms an ever-present background to the history of the Balkans.

"The mountains look on Marathon and Marathon looks on the sea": these words of Byron illustrate the proximity and intimate relationship between the mountainous skeleton of the Balkan peninsula and the seas which bathe it from all but the northern side and in places—the gulfs of Salonica and Corinth are the most notable examples—penetrate deep into the interior. It is this age-long intercourse of mountain and sea that has enabled the Balkan peninsula to share, throughout its history, in the common life of the Mediterranean. Like the mountain, the sea and the unknown world beyond could be a source of danger to the centres of agricultural and urban settlement. Some of Byzantium's most dangerous foes—the Arabs in the seventh and eighth centuries, the Russians in the ninth and tenth and the Normans in the eleventh and twelfth—attacked or invaded the Balkans from the sea.

Two of the seas which encompass the peninsula—the Black Sea and the Adriatic—played a particularly important role in its history. Flanking it to the north-east and the north-west, forming two gulfs by which Mediterranean waters penetrate deepest into the European continent, they provided highways of trade, channels of empire building, and routes for the diffusion of Byzantine civilization.

The earliest connections between the Black Sea and the Balkan peninsula go back to antiquity. The colonies set up by the Greeks on the western and northern coasts of the Black Sea in the seventh century B.C. and after, played a major role in the economic and cultural history of the ancient world: these trading factories, some of which grew into flourishing and autonomous city states on the north-eastern fringe of the Hellenic world—Tyras at the mouth of the Dniester, Olbia in the estuary of the Bug, Chersonesus, Theodosia and Panticapaeum in the Crimea, Tanaïs at the mouth of the Don and Phanagoria by the estuary of the Kuban'—exported to their mother cities in Greece the raw materials obtained from the natives of the North Pontic coast—fish, salt and especially grain—and sold to the rulers of South Russia the industrial and artistic products of the Greek world. And so, with the articles of gold and silver and together with some of the craftsmen who made them, the arts of Greece came to South Russia. Thus economically and culturally the Greek cities on the northern coast of the Black Sea became, in classical and Hellenistic times, intermediaries between the steppes of Western Eurasia and the Greek world of the Mediterranean. For the Scythian and the Sarmatian rulers of South Russia, they provided an outlet for their export trade and an access to the industrial markets of the Greek world. To the Greeks, and later to the Romans and the Byzantines, they appeared as outposts of Hellenism on the fringe of the mysterious "Scythian" steppes—"the hem of Greece", as Cicero described the Greek colonies, "sewn on to the fields of the barbarians".[2]

By the end of antiquity most of these North Pontic cities had lost their importance. Two of them, however, Chersonesus and Panticapaeum, survived into the medieval period and continued to play the traditional role of economic and cultural intermediaries between Byzantium and South Russia. This role will be more fully discussed later. For the present we must be content to note the following facts: the export of corn from South Russia greatly diminished after the barbarian invasions of the fourth and fifth centuries; when the trade between Byzantium and Eastern Europe began to revive five hundred years later, it was no longer the corn from the coastal regions but commodities obtained in the forests further north—furs, wax, honey and slaves—that were regularly shipped across the Black Sea to Constantinople; and when, in the late Middle Ages, the North Pontic steppes became once again essential suppliers of food to Constantinople and other Balkan cities, this was due to the trading activities of the Genoese and the Venetian colonies in the Crimea. As late as the sixteenth century the Black Sea was still an important channel for the provisioning of Constantinople.

The role played by the Adriatic in the medieval history of the Balkans was no less important. It was essentially an artery of East-West communications. At its southern extremity, the Straits of Otranto, between the coasts of Apulia and Albania, are at their narrowest point only 72 kilometres wide, a distance which even in antiquity, given a favourable wind, could be covered in one day. Across these straits the Byzantine government maintained contact with its possessions in South Italy until the capture of Bari by the Normans in 1071; and successive masters of South Italy, Normans in the eleventh and twelfth centuries and Angevins in the thirteenth, used the same route to establish on the Albanian coast bridgeheads for the conquest of the Balkan possessions of Byzantium. The other trans-Adriatic route followed the longitudinal axis of that sea: it led from Venice to the eastern shores of the Mediterranean, and thus served to link Central Europe with the Levant. Like the Black Sea, the Adriatic is famed for its winter storms; when the fearsome *bora* blew down the Balkan coastline, Byzantine and Venetian ships often sought the safety of the narrow channel between the coast and the islands which form a roughly parallel line to it from Istria to Dubrovnik. Further south, after an interval marked by the mountainous coast of Montenegro and the low-lying coastline of Albania, lie the Ionian islands; of these the most important in the Middle Ages was Corfù, the natural stepping-stone on the way from Brindisi to Epirus, the guardian of the southern entrance into the Straits of Otranto, and the key to the Adriatic sea route. The strategic importance of this island made it a prize for which the dominant powers of the Balkan and the Italian peninsulas—Byzantium, the principality of Epirus and the Ottoman Empire on the one hand, Venice, the Normans and the Angevins on the other—competed from the late eleventh century. The struggle, and coexistence, of the Greek and Italian traditions have left a permanent mark upon the cultural history of Corfù. In 1386 the island came under Venetian sovereignty and remained so for the next four centuries; the impressive fortifications which still dominate its principal port are evidence of the care which Venice lavished upon Corfù, the vital link in her trade route to Crete, Cyprus and Syria.

The importance which the Byzantines ascribed to the Adriatic sea route is apparent in the efforts they made to retain control of the coastal cities of Dalmatia and of the off-shore islands. These efforts, which will be described in a later chapter, were largely successful until the late twelfth century. By the early thirteenth Venice had established her supremacy in the Adriatic and over most of Dalmatia; and although this supremacy was challenged by the Hungarians in the second half of the fourteenth century, and was limited by the autonomy of the merchant republic of Ragusa (Dubrovnik), it was not without reason that the Venetians in the late Middle Ages proudly called the Adriatic Sea "our gulf".

The words of Byron quoted above evoke not only the close relationship of mountain and sea which is so characteristic a feature of the historical geography of the Balkans. The narrow vale of Marathon, which "looks" on both, brings to this relationship a third element whose contribution to the landscape of the peninsula must now be considered: the plains.

A study of the larger lowlands of the peninsula will suggest that they performed three main functions: they were sources of agricultural wealth, supplying the cities of the Balkans with foodstuffs; centres of military power and civil administration; and highways of communication, providing routes of invasion and channels for the diffusion of culture. The economic, political, military and cultural role of the plains may best be illustrated by three examples: the lower Danubian plain, between the Transylvanian Alps, the Balkan range and the Black Sea; Thrace, which lies between the mountain ranges of the Sredna Gora and the Rhodopes, extends east to the Black Sea and south-east to the Sea of Marmara, and is traversed by the valley of the Maritsa; and the "Campania", situated between the Aegean Sea, the Rhodopes and the Macedonian highlands, whose principal line of inland communication is the lower Vardar and whose main city is Thessalonica.

The basin on both sides of the lower Danube is, historically and geographically, a zone of transition between the Balkan Peninsula and the South Russian steppe. North of the river, in present day Rumania, lies the province of Wallachia; its western part, after Trajan's campaigns of A.D. 101–5, was incorporated into the Roman province of Dacia. The River Olt, which flows from the Carpathians down to the Danube, was then a major route of communication between the Balkan provinces of the Roman Empire and Transylvania, the centre of Roman Dacia. But in 272 Dacia was evacuated by the Romans, and the lower Danube became once again the northern boundary of the empire. The river's northern bank is flanked by a broad belt of marsh which extends to the delta, while its higher southern bank, dominated by Roman fortresses, guarded the entrance to the Balkans against invaders from South Russia and Central Europe. The lower Danube retained its traditional role as *limes Romanus* in the early Byzantine period; yet even then it seldom proved an insuperable obstacle to a determined invader from the north: Goths in the fourth century and

Huns in the fifth were able to cross the river, in order to occupy or to devastate imperial lands in the Balkans. During the next seven centuries much of the fate of South-Eastern Europe was decided on the banks of the lower Danube. The principal stages of Byzantium's struggle to hold, or reconquer, the Danubian *limes* will be described later: they were marked by Justinian's efforts to build a network of fortresses against barbarian attacks from the north; the collapse of this defensive line under the blows of the Slavs and Avars in the early seventh century; the Byzantine victories at the turn of the tenth century, which restored the empire's northern frontier to the Danube; and the final ruin of Byzantine hegemony in the Northern Balkans in the late twelfth century.

In the area, roughly rectangular in shape, bounded by the Black Sea and by the lower reaches and the delta of the Danube, lies the Dobrudja. In the Middle Ages it was a land of passage as well as a palimpsest of immigrants from beyond the Danube; for the swamps, channels and lagoons that surround the Danube delta, and the narrow confines of this land, tended to isolate the Dobrudja and to create on its territory ethnographic pockets, in which diverse populations lived for centuries side by side; on the other hand, the low-lying plateau that occupies most of this land is a southward extension of the great Eurasian steppe which in the Middle Ages covered the whole of South Russia and stretched across western and central Asia. The Dobrudja, aptly called "Little Scythia" by the Romans, who annexed it in the reign of Augustus, was thus a desirable goal for many nomadic peoples who, driven from their homes in South Russia by enemy pressure or economic want, longed to leave the hazards of the open steppe for the relative security of the lands to the south of the Danube, and to exchange the uncertainties of a nomadic existence for a more settled agricultural way of life. But the Dobrudja was not only a home of many races and tongues: for a determined aggressor, it pointed the way to the heart of the Balkans; and the most ambitious of these invaders from South Russia soon discovered that a direct route led along the Black Sea coast from the Danube delta to Constantinople.

The southern part of the lower Danubian plain is a platform, gently sloping upwards from the river to the Balkan range. This was the Roman province of Lower Moesia; and the richness of this country, and the even greater wealth of the lands further south, which could be reached by crossing the mountain passes, attracted many an invader from the north. The barbarian invasions of the third century made this area one of the storm centres of the Balkan peninsula; the Visigoths were allowed to settle here, as Roman *foederati*, in 382; in the sixth and seventh centuries Slavs and Avars passed through Moesia on their way south, destroying the Roman cities, and the Slavs settled in this area; by 681 the land was in the hands of the Bulgars, a Turkic people from the Eurasian steppe. The two successive kingdoms which they founded in the Balkans (681–1018 and 1187–1393) made the Moesian plain one of the main centres of political and military power in the peninsula. It was also a region of considerable economic importance: for the Moesian plain, watered by numerous rivers flowing north into the Danube and covered in large part by fertile loess, is particularly suited to agriculture. It was famed as a grain producing country as early as the first century of our era; and the corn grown in the hinterland of Varna increased in value in the late thirteenth and the fourteenth centuries, when the Black Sea was opened to Italian trade, and the Venetians and the Genoese shipped Bulgarian grain to Constantinople and Italy.

The suggestion, made above, that the plains of the Balkan peninsula performed in the Middle Ages the threefold role of suppliers of food, centres of power and highways of communication, can be further substantiated by considering the largest of them—the plain of Thrace. The south-bound traveller, after crossing the Balkan range, is faced with a much lower chain of hills, the Sredna Gora, over which he must pass before emerging into the plain, bounded in the south by the Rhodopes and traversed by the valley of the Maritsa. This river (the Hebrus of the ancients) springs out of the Rila Mountains south of Sofia and drains most of the Thracian plain, before flowing into the Aegean Sea. The northern limit of the olive tree runs through the centre of Thrace, whose southern regions have a pronounced Mediterranean climate. Two of the foremost cities of the Balkans, Philippopolis and Adrianople, stand on the Maritsa. The latter town, at the point of intersection of routes from the Aegean, the Sea of Marmara and the Black Sea, was the main fortress guarding the northern approaches to Constantinople, and was hence in the

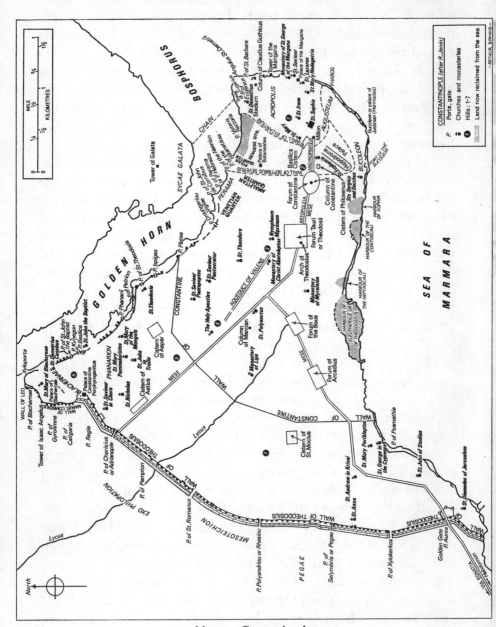

Map 2.   Constantinople

Middle Ages a key to military hegemony in the peninsula. The site of several memorable battles—the most famous being the defeat of the Emperor Valens by the Goths in 378 and the victory of the Bulgarians over the armies of Baldwin I, the Latin emperor of Constantinople, in 1205—Adrianople was a prize for which Byzantines and Bulgarians fought many times during the Middle Ages. And the city's strategic importance was demonstrated once again about 1365 when, as the first decisive step in the Turkish conquest of the Balkans, the Sultan Murad I set up his capital there.

From Adrianople the main highway led south-eastwards, past the Strandzha hills whose forest supplied wood for Byzantine ships, through the corn growing steppe of Eastern Thrace, to Constantinople. The remarkable position of the city, on a hilly promontory which juts out of the eastern extremity of Thrace to where the waters of the Bosphorus flow into the Sea of Marmara, has been described and extolled by many writers. In a book whose main theme is the encounter between Byzantium and the peoples of Eastern Europe, an encounter in which the empire, at first on the defensive, succeeded in the end in taming and civilizing its northern neighbours, two features of Constantinople's site deserve special mention: its role as a natural, and as a man-made, citadel; and its position as a centre of international communications.

Although surrounded on all but one of its sides by water, the city was virtually impregnable to attacks by sea. The rapid current which flows from the Bosphorus into the Sea of Marmara, the harbour chain which, in times of danger, barred the entrance into the Golden Horn, and the powerful sea-walls, combined to defend Constantinople during many naval assaults: some of these, like the Avaro-Slav attack of 626, the great Arab sieges of 674–8 and 717–18, and the Russian raid of 860, rank among the most memorable episodes of Byzantine history. The only successful naval assault on Constantinople occurred in 1204, when Venetian ships breached the walls on the Golden Horn, thus enabling the armies of the Fourth Crusade to capture the city. Very different, however, was the defensive position of Constantinople on the land side: for here the city lay open to invasion across the lowlands of Thrace. This was observed, as early as the second century B.C., by the Greek historian Polybius: and his remarks on the tragic ex-

31

posure of the ancient Greek city of Byzantium to attacks from the north-west are worth quoting, for they offer a vivid and accurate foretaste of the military problems that faced the East Roman statesmen in their relations with their Balkan neighbours during the Middle Ages.

As Thrace [Polybius writes] surrounds the territory of the Byzantines on all sides, reaching from sea to sea, they are involved in an endless and troublesome war against the Thracians; for it is not feasible, by making preparations on a grand scale and winning one decisive victory over them, to get rid once for all of their hostilities: the barbarous nations and dynasts are too numerous. If they overcome one, three more worse than the first arise and advance against their country. Nor can they gain any advantage by submitting to pay tribute and making definite contracts; for if they make any concession to one prince, such a concession raises up against them five times as many foes. For these reasons they are involved in a never-ending and troublesome war. For what is more dangerous than a bad neighbour, and what more dreadful than a war with barbarians? And besides the other evils that attend on war, they have to undergo (to speak poetically) a sort of Tantalean punishment, for when they . . . have been rewarded by the production of an abundant and surpassingly fine crop, then come the barbarians, and having reaped part of the fruits to carry off with them, destroy what they cannot take away. The Byzantines can only murmur indignantly, and endure.[3]

If for Polybius' invading Thracians we substitute the northern foes of the Byzantine Empire—Goths, Huns, Avars, Slavs, Bulgars, Magyars, Pechenegs, Russians and Cumans—and if to the patient endurance of the ancient Byzantines we add the capacity for military resistance displayed by their East Roman successors in the city of Constantine, we shall have an overall picture of the struggle, which lasted throughout the Middle Ages, between the empire and its northern neighbours for military hegemony over the Balkans.

The outcome of this struggle, on which the continued existence of the Byzantine Empire not infrequently depended, was decided more than once before the land walls of Constantinople. These fortifications, four miles long, which stretched from the Sea of Marmara to the Golden Horn and are still, despite their ruined condition, the most impressive secular monument to have survived from the Byzantine Empire, bear witness to the constant challenge that faced the Byzantines from across the plain of Thrace. Built in 413 and extended in depth in 447, in the reign of Theodosius II, they formed a triple line of fortifications: an inner wall, eleven metres high, an outer one, eight metres high, each supported by numerous towers, and an external moat eighteen metres broad, with a breastwork along its inner side. These Theodosian walls, frequently restored in the Middle Ages, remained impregnable for a thousand years. They were stormed on 29 May 1453 by the armies of Mehmet II: on that night the last emperor of East Rome died fighting by the breach made by the Turkish cannon, and the Byzantine Empire fell with him.

Constantinople's position at the southern outlet of the Bosphorus, commanding both the land route from Europe to Asia and the waterway between the Black Sea and the Mediterranean, equipped the city for its role as the centre of a world empire. Blessed with one of the best natural harbours in the world—the Golden Horn—it could hardly fail to become an international emporium and a port of call for ships from three continents. Until the late eleventh century, so long as Byzantium was mistress of the seas, her fleet could support the empire's political and military action in areas as remote as Venice and the Crimea; exert pressure on hostile Balkan tribes by policing the lower reaches of the Danube; maintain communications between the imperial capital and the ports on the Aegean and Ionian coasts; and ensure a continued Byzantine presence in Dalmatia. Constantinople's position as a focus of international communications was enhanced by the fact that it was the terminus, and point of origin, of several continental routes that crossed the Balkan peninsula. These routes were not only highroads of invasion, providing access to the cities and the heartland of the peninsula for barbarians from across the Danube: they were also, particularly from the ninth century onwards, regularly used by East Roman merchants, ambassadors and missionaries who acted as agents for the diffusion of Byzantine civilization throughout the Balkans, to Central Europe, Rumania and distant Russia. The most important of these routes was the highway from Constantinople to Belgrade which traversed the plain of Thrace and followed the Morava river to the Danube; the Via Egnatia, which linked Constantinople with Thessalonica and, across the Macedonian highlands, with the Adriatic port of Dyrrachium; and the roads which led across Thrace and over the passes of the Balkan Mountains to the lower Danube.

The role played by Thrace as a channel of communication between the empire and its northern neighbours was matched by that of a third, smaller, plain, the South Macedonian "Campania". It is bounded by the southern spurs of the Rhodopes, the peninsula of Chalcidice, and the highlands of South-Eastern Macedonia. Its axis is the alluvial basin of the lower Vardar (the Axios), and its political and economic centre is Thessalonica. The position of Thessalonica, the second most important city of the Byzantine Empire, was in several respects comparable to that of Constantinople: a wealthy port standing at the head of a well-protected gulf dominating the north Aegean, it was the principal target for the barbarians thrusting southward from the central Balkans and from beyond the Danube towards the warm sea. Though it proved less impregnable than Constantinople—it was captured by the Arabs in 904, by the Sicilian Normans in 1185, and by the Turks in the late Middle Ages—it was a citadel of no mean stature. Its massive fortifications, which crowned the hills surrounding the city from the north, enabled it to withstand, during the early Middle Ages, successive attacks by Goths, Slavs, Avars and Bulgars. Like Constantinople Thessalonica provided an outlet for the export of raw materials from the Balkan interior to the principal ports of the Mediterranean. It, too, stood at the south-eastern terminus of a great land route which cut across the peninsula: the route followed the valleys of the Vardar and the Morava and led to Belgrade, the middle Danube, and Central Europe. No less than the Constantinople-Belgrade road up the Maritsa, it provided a channel for the northward spread of Byzantine civilization. Its existence, as well as the brilliance of Thessalonica's cultural life, explains the fact that Macedonia was, next to Thrace, the Balkan area most deeply influenced by this civilization during the Middle Ages.

Mountains, seas and plains, the geographical environment which nature has imposed upon the Balkan peoples, are the natural framework within which their history has developed. At all times, however, man has sought to escape from the pressure of his immediate environment, to tame and transform it, and to exploit it for his own advantage. To achieve these aims, he must have freedom of movement. To cultivate the soil on which he lives, to extract mineral wealth from the earth, to trade, travel and build

34

states, he must overcome his isolation and enlarge his horizons, physical and mental. In order to enjoy the fruits of civilization, and often indeed to survive, human communities must build roads, and learn to use and maintain them. In the Balkans, particularly since Roman times, the roads have played an important historical role. Traversing plains or using river valleys, circumventing or crossing mountains, starting or ending in cities by the sea, they have given a man-made unity to the fragmented landscape of the peninsula. This unity was limited by the fact that the great Balkan routes, like the motorways of today, often ran through many miles of open country, by-passing villages. Yet they seldom avoided the major towns; and, except for periods of violent unrest—such as the Hunnic and Gothic invasions of the fifth century and the Slavonic occupation of the seventh—the history of the Balkan peninsula in late antiquity and in the Middle Ages bears the imprint of the double network of roads and cities.

Some of these major roads have already been mentioned. It may be useful, however, to describe them here in greater detail, and to consider their interconnection: for, no less than the physical features of the Balkan landscape, these man-made lines of communication formed the setting in which the encounter between Byzantium and many peoples of Eastern Europe took place.

The most important of these trans-Balkan routes was the Belgrade-Constantinople highway. From its construction by the Romans, probably in the first century of our era, down to modern times when it provided a railway track for the Orient Express, it has served as the main continental route linking Central Europe with Constantinople. As the *via militaris* of the Roman legions, as the *tsarski put* pointing to the Balkan Slavs the "imperial way" to Byzantium, or as the principal road of the Ottoman Empire in Europe, it retained this unique importance.

We may picture some of the features of this road by following the footsteps of an imaginary traveller bound for Constantinople in the middle of the sixth century. A Byzantine officer, returning home from his frontier command on the Danube, or an envoy to Constantinople from one of the barbarian peoples north of the river, would have been struck by the road's military character. The whole of its northern section showed signs of the activity of Justinian's engineers, who, to guard the empire against the mounting pressure of the Slavonic tribes from beyond the Danube, were hastily rebuilding the cities and fortresses which the Hunnic and Gothic invasions of the previous century had crippled or destroyed. One of them was the northern terminus of the road—the city of Belgrade, known to the Romans as Singidunum, which occupied at the confluence of the Danube and the Sava a crucial position in the northern defences of the empire. From there, a two days' journey along the right bank of the Danube brought a slow-moving traveller to Viminacium, the capital of the Roman province of Upper Moesia. There the road left the Danube and, turning south, penetrated into the interior of Moesia. Following more or less the Morava valley, it entered the province of Dacia Mediterranea, and on the seventh day of the journey the traveller reached the great city of Naissus (Niš), the birthplace of Constantine the Great and a point of intersection of routes leading north to the Danube, south-east to Constantinople, south to Macedonia and the Aegean, and westwards to the Adriatic. After Niš the road left the Morava valley, turned south-eastward and, following the course of the Nišava, began to climb through the mountains which today form the frontier between Yugoslavia and Bulgaria. After crossing three mountain passes, the traveller on the eleventh day of his journey saw to his left the Haemus, or Balkan range, and beneath him an oval-shaped basin with the city of Serdica (Sofia), overtopped by Mount Vitosha. A flourishing Roman city since the fourth century, recently rebuilt after being burned by the Huns, Serdica held next to Adrianople and Philippopolis the most important strategic position in the interior of the Balkan peninsula. By its proximity to the Iskŭr (Oescus), which flows a few miles east of the city, and the Struma (Strymon) which springs from Mount Vitosha, it dominated the water-shed between the Black Sea and the Aegean; and roads leading to the Danube, to Thrace, to Macedonia, and to the Adriatic met within its walls. Three days beyond Sofia, on the fourteenth day of the journey, the traveller reached the most spectacular landmark of the entire itinerary. Having climbed on the previous day to the pass of Vakarel, 840 metres above sea level (the highest point of the journey), he now negotiated another pass which led into a defile known to the Romans as Succi (or *Succorum angustiae*). The entrance to the defile was barred by a high wall with a stone gateway flanked by two forts and perpetually guarded. These were the famous "Gates of Trajan", often described by travellers (until their demolition by the Turks in 1835), the scene of many a battle for the mastery of the Balkans. This awesome fortress stood on the boundary between Dacia and Thrace, and between the Latin and Greek-speaking halves of the Balkan peninsula. Here, too, was the half-way point on the journey from Belgrade to the Sea of Marmara.

On emerging from the Succi pass the traveller beheld a remarkable view: to his left stretched the low-lying hills of Sredna Gora, and in the distance further north the more imposing summits of the Balkan range; to his right rose the Rila Mountains, seldom free of snow, and the densely wooded Rhodopes. Beneath him the lowland of Thrace extended to the horizon, and in the distance loomed the three cone-shaped hills of Philippopolis (Plovdiv). The road now descended into the plain and followed the meandering course of the Maritsa through Philippopolis to Adrianople (Edirne), the capital of the province of Haemimontus; the journey so far had lasted twenty-one days. A further six days' trek, through Arcadiopolis (Lüleburgaz) and across flat country still studded at that time with tall forests, brought our traveller to the Sea of Marmara, which he reached at Heraclea. Three or four days later, depending on whether he followed the coastal route through Selymbria or an alternative inland road, he reached Constantinople. The length of the whole journey from Belgrade—thirty to thirty-one days—has been calculated with a fairly leisurely traveller in mind. An imperial courier, and other fast-moving traffic, could doubtless have covered the distance in half that time.

The later history of this road is obscured by the devastations caused by the Avaro-Slav invasions: for two and a half centuries after the death of the Emperor Maurice (602) not a single Balkan city north of Serdica is so much as mentioned in contemporary documents. And when, in the ninth century, the darkness begins to lift from the peninsula the Roman place names have mostly vanished, superseded or transformed by a new Slav nomenclature. In the eleventh and twelfth centuries the road became once again a major international highway. During most of this period the Byzantines controlled, as they did in the sixth century, its entire stretch; and between 1096 and 1189 it was well known throughout

37

Europe as the main land route of the Crusaders. Peter the Hermit and Godfrey of Bouillon in 1096, Conrad III and Louis VII in 1147, and Frederick Barbarossa in 1189 all passed with their armies along this road on their way to the Holy Land. In the contemporary accounts of the first three Crusades a theme that recurs with particular insistence—next to the complaints about the unfriendliness of the local inhabitants—is the extreme difficulty of crossing the "Bulgarian forest" between Belgrade and Niš; William of Tyre, the historian of the First Crusade, accused the "miserable Greeks" of deliberately keeping this section of the road as wild and overgrown as possible, and of relying on the immense forests and impassable shrubbery to discourage foreign invaders. This area, known to the Serbs as the Šumadija—today largely open country—was until the early nineteenth century famed for its vast oak forests.

The eleventh and twelfth centuries marked the heyday of the road's international importance. The rivalry between the Balkan powers in the late Middle Ages, coupled with the Turkish invasion, reduced most of it by the mid-fifteenth century to a parlous state. With the capture of Belgrade by the Turks in 1521, the entire road came, for the third and last time in its history, under the control of a single power.

The role played by the Constantinople-Belgrade road as a highway of invasion, trade and cultural diffusion was enhanced by its connections with other Balkan land routes. Not least of these were the roads linking the lower Danube, across the passes of the Balkan range, with Thrace and Constantinople. Two of them deserve special mention. The first followed the Black Sea coast from the mouth of the Danube, through Varna, Mesembria and Anchialus to the Byzantine capital. The second led from Novae on the Danube through Nicopolis and Haemum, over the famous Shipka pass and across the Valley of the Roses and the Sredna Gora hills, into the plain of Thrace: a popular route at all times, it became in the late Middle Ages the main road from Trnovo, the Bulgarian capital, to the south.

Through these north-south roads the southern section of the Belgrade-Constantinople route was linked to the lower Danube, and to the Rumanian and Russian lands that lay beyond. Similarly, its northern sector, between Belgrade and Niš, followed the

38

itinerary of another major highway which traversed the Balkan peninsula—the Morava-Vardar route from the middle Danube to Thessalonica. The depth with which the Gulf of Thessalonica penetrates inland and, at the other end, the advance of the middle Danube to the southernmost extremity of the Pannonian basin, have combined to make this the shortest north-south route across the Balkan peninsula. Between Belgrade and Thessalonica—a distance of some 700 kilometres—a series of depressions cutting through the mountains of Serbia and Macedonia have traced a natural furrow. It is followed by the Morava and the Vardar, whose headstreams are barely separated by a low-lying water shed at the southern end of the plain of Kosovo. Along this furrow the Romans built a road, with garrisons in Singidunum, Naissus, Justiniana Prima and Thessalonica. In the Middle Ages the main road deviated in places from the river valleys, to avoid a series of defiles, dangerous for marching armies. Thus, to circumvent the Vardar gorge at Demir Kapija, it took off from the river near Skopje and followed the low-lying basins of Ovče Polje, Štip and the Strumica. From the Strumica one branch of the road rejoined the Vardar in the plain, another led through the pass appropriately known as Kleidion, "the key" (where, in one of the famous battles in the history of the Balkans, Basil II defeated the Bulgarians in 1014), across the Strymon valley to Serres and the sea. The Morava-Vardar route, now followed by the Belgrade-Thessalonica railway, occupies a crucial position in the Balkan peninsula: it forms the natural dividing line between its eastern and western halves; and it is, apart from the region between the lower Danube and the Haemus, the only Balkan area naturally suited to form the backbone of a geographically viable state. The only attempt in the Middle Ages to create such a state in this area was made by the Serbs. Their starting point, however, was not the Morava valley, but a roughly parallel furrow further west, formed by the valley of the Ibar and the plain of Kosovo. There, along a narrow north-south depression between the fortress of Maglić (near Kraljevo) and Kosovo Polje, lay the land of Raška, the nucleus of the medieval Serbian kingdom. In the late thirteenth century the Serbs began to expand from this region towards the south-east in an attempt, which almost succeeded in the mid-fourteenth, to control the entire Morava-Vardar route, and to build a

39

multinational Balkan Empire as a stepping-stone to the conquest of Thessalonica and Constantinople.

The network of communications in the eastern part of the Balkans combined, we have seen, a longitudinal route—the Belgrade-Constantinople highway—with a number of intersecting transverse roads connecting the lower Danube with Thrace. A similar pattern can be observed in the western part of the peninsula, where the Morava-Vardar line played the role of a longitudinal line, and the transverse links were provided by several roads striking eastward and north-eastward from the Adriatic coast.

The Via Egnatia was, until the early thirteenth century, the most important of these. Its starting point was the fortress of Dyrrachium on the coast of Albania, one of the pivots of Byzantine power in the Western Balkans and on the Southern Adriatic in the early Middle Ages. It dominated the plain—the largest on the western seaboard of the peninsula—between Lake Scutari, the Albanian highlands, and the Acroceraunian Mountains. In the Middle Ages, before the malaria-infested swamps of the coastal fringe forced the Albanian towns to move into the higher interior, this plain was a rich supplier of corn. From Dyrrachium the Via Egnatia passed through Elbasan up the Shkumbi valley and led through Ohrid, Bitolj and Edessa to Thessalonica and thence to Constantinople. For the Romans, who built it soon after their conquest of Macedonia, it was the shortest land route to their Asian territories. The Byzantines valued it as the most direct means of access to their outposts on the Adriatic, to their possessions in South Italy and to Rome.

In the later Middle Ages the growth of the Serbian and Bosnian kingdoms and the development of a mining industry in the central and western areas of the Balkans increased the importance of other transverse routes, connecting the Adriatic coast with the interior. One of them passed along the northern shore of Lake Scutari and led, across the mountains of Montenegro, to Peć and thence, through the Kosovo plain, to Niš. The Venetians and the Ragusans, who used this route for their trading operations in Serbia and Bulgaria, called it Via de Zenta, after the name of Zeta, the earliest Slavonic realm on the Adriatic seaboard. It played an important cultural role in bringing the centres of inland

Serbia into regular contact with the Latin-speaking cities on the Adriatic coast, and through them with Venice. Serbian connections with the West were also maintained by a second route, which led from Ragusa through the heartland of Serbia to the mining districts of Kopaonik and Niš. The Ragusan merchants, who made great use of this route, acted as middlemen in the export of corn, livestock, silver and iron from Serbia and Bulgaria to Italy. Two other routes, further to the north-west, led from the coast into the interior of Bosnia: one of them followed the canyon-like gorges of the Neretva; the other, starting from Split, crossed the Dinaric chain through the fortresses of Klis and Sinj.

The medieval routes of the Balkan peninsula belonged, we have seen, to two types; longitudinal and transverse. The relative importance of these types depended on the shifting balance of political power and on the location of the centres of wealth and culture within the peninsula. The Slav peoples who built their states in the interior of the peninsula used both kinds of route: the Bulgarians advanced over the Balkan passes to annex Northern Thrace, and down the Belgrade-Constantinople highway to attack the Byzantine capital. The Serbs took advantage of the Morava-Vardar furrow to expand into Macedonia towards Thessalonica, and of the transverse routes to the Adriatic to trade with Ragusa and Venice. But the history of the Balkan routes was influenced more lastingly by the great imperialist powers whose centres were located on the periphery of or outside the peninsula. The Romans, who used all the main natural highways and built the principal roads in the Balkans, seem to have given pride of place to the transverse routes: this, perhaps, partly explains the fact that Roman civilization (as distinct from military occupation) was largely confined to the Adriatic coast and to the valleys of the Sava and the Danube. By contrast, Byzantine civilization expanded northward most effectively along the longitudinal highways, the Maritsa and the Vardar. When Byzantine control over the Northern Balkans loosened in the twelfth century, and the powers of Western Europe—Normans, Crusaders, Neapolitan Angevins—sought ways to strike at the empire's heart, the transverse routes, above all the Via Egnatia, acquired military importance for a time. In the thirteenth century the temporary collapse of the

41

Byzantine Empire which followed the Fourth Crusade gave Venice commercial mastery in South-Eastern Europe, and Venetians and Ragusans began increasingly to use the transverse routes which led from the Adriatic coast into the interior of the peninsula. These routes retained their importance until the close of the Middle Ages. However, though they performed an important function in linking the interior of Serbia to the Latin culture of the coastal cities, they did not to any significant extent facilitate the spread of Venetian civilization, which in the North-West Balkans remained largely confined to the narrow coastal strip of Dalmatia. In the last resort, the more important role was played by the great longitudinal roads. They linked together the major cities of the peninsula; they served as channels for the transmission of Byzantine civilization to the nations of South-Eastern Europe; and most of the crucial events of Balkan history took place on them or in their vicinity.

2 THE AREA NORTH OF THE BLACK SEA

The lower Danube played in the Middle Ages a two-fold geographical role. It provided, for migrating peoples who came from the north, access to routes which radiated across the Balkan peninsula towards the great cities on the Black Sea, the Marmara, the Aegean and the Adriatic; and, at least until the late twelfth century, it marked in the eyes of the Byzantines the effective limits of the direct political sovereignty which, whether or not they actually controlled the river, they claimed over their northern provinces. Beyond this *limes Romanus* lay a vast and imperfectly known country bounded by the northern coast of the Black Sea and extending across plains, rivers and forests to the limits of the geographical horizon of the Byzantines. This country was peopled with a large and ever-growing number of tribes and nations whose movements caused much anxiety to the authorities in Constantinople: for they knew from long and painful experience that the peoples who dwelt beyond the Danube and the Black Sea were often attracted by the prospect of invading imperial territory and settling in the Balkans. Nomadic tribes pushed along the Pontic coast by successive invaders from Asia; splintered fragments of

42

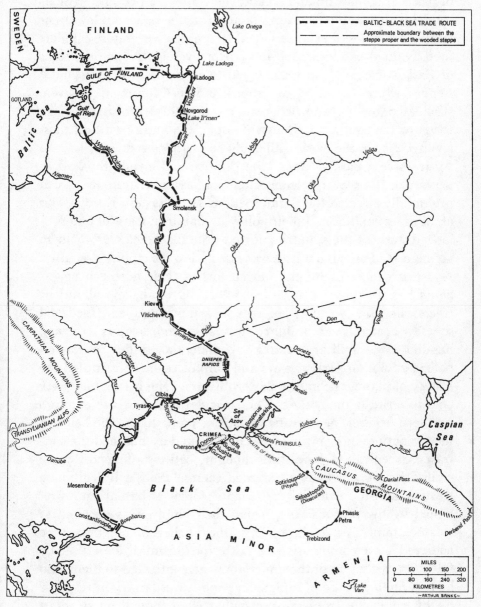

Map 3   Russia and the North-Pontic area

Eurasian empires driven by economic want or the fear of their eastern neighbours to exchange the hazards of the open steppe for the relative security of the Balkans; nascent nations emerging out of pastoral nomadism and seeking lands for a settled and agricultural life; parasitical hordes craving for the richer and warmer lands of the Mediterranean world; prospective empire-builders fired by the dream of establishing their sovereignty upon the ruins of East Rome; and, in general, all those denizens of the Pontic steppes whose curiosity, ambitions and lust for conquest were stimulated by the knowledge that the natural terminus of the roads to the south was Constantinople, the wealthiest and most civilized city in the world—all could be expected sooner or later to try to force a passage across the Danube and invade the Balkan peninsula. This ever-present threat of invasion from the north profoundly affected the Byzantines' image of Eastern Europe, and at all times conditioned their policy in that area. Careful and prolonged study of the countries north of the Black Sea was for them no mere academic pursuit: it was essential to the empire's security. And this concern with the movements of their northern neighbours has, fortunately for the modern historian, left abundant traces in the writings of the Byzantines; their medieval sources—accounts of military missions, ambassadors' reports, handbooks of military strategy, confidential guides to foreign policy, ethnographical surveys and chronicles—have recorded the history of many a people of Eastern Europe long before they were able to write it themselves. The struggle to defend the empire's northern frontiers against the barbarian strengthened the belief of the Byzantines in its providential destiny and exemplified the contrast, so central to Byzantine thought, between Graeco-Roman civilization of which they regarded themselves as sole legitimate trustees, and the external and chaotic forces of barbarism represented by the pagan *ethne*, whom their empire was destined to subdue, tame and civilize. This, they believed, could best be achieved by a combination of faith and technical expertise: by fidelity to the vision of the imperial mission entrusted to them, and by the intelligent use of diplomacy; and it was largely in response to this challenge from the north that were forged, by steadfast faith and lucid thinking, by careful study and observation, by trial and error, the traditions of Byzantine foreign policy which con-

44

tributed so much to the preservation and spread of civilization in Eastern Europe.

What was the role played by the physical environment and by lines of communication in the encounter between Byzantium and the peoples of Eastern Europe in this area? In the middle of the tenth century an important and confidential document of state was compiled in Constantinople under the personal direction of the ruling emperor, Constantine VII Porphyrogenitus. A treatise on statecraft addressed to Constantine's son, the future Emperor Romanus II, it was primarily intended as a guide to foreign policy in the area which at the time presented the most serious challenge to Byzantium: the lands to the north of the Black Sea. The *De Administrando Imperio*, as this treatise has been named by modern scholars, contains, alongside a historical and geographical survey of most of Byzantium's neighbours and much useful advice about how best to deal with them, a chapter (the forty-second) devoted to a geographical description of the area beyond the empire's northern borders.[4] It is written in the form of an itinerary, and was probably based on a topographical report of an imperial envoy. The starting point of this journey is Thessalonica, whence the envoy travelled north-westward, probably up the Vardar–Morava road: "From Thessalonica to the river Danube where stands the city called Belgrade, is a journey of eight days, if one is not travelling in haste but by easy stages." From Belgrade the route followed the Danube to its estuary. From the mouth of the Danube the itinerary describes a semi-circle, fetching a compass round the northern shores of the Black Sea. We are taken, probably by ship, along the coast, past the mouth of the Dniester and thence along the "gold coast" to the estuary of the Dnieper. Here we are given a glimpse into the interior of the country, across the steppe, as far as the East European forest belt: "On the higher reaches of the Dnieper live the Russians, and down this river they sail and arrive at the Romans." From the mouth of the Dnieper the sea route turned south-eastward and, after following the West Crimean coast, reached Cherson. "From the Dnieper river to Cherson is three hundred miles, and between are marshes and harbours, in which the Chersonites manufacture salt." The Southern Crimea was then under Byzantine sovereignty, and the next section of the itinerary, from Cherson to Bosporus, was protected by im-

45

perial garrisons stationed along the coast. Bosporus stood on the European side of the Straits of Kerch (the Cimmerian Bosporus), near the entrance into the Sea of Azov, which is here given its classical name: "The Lake of Maeotis, which for its size everybody calls a sea." At this point the author allows himself another digression into the northern hinterland, which, no less than his previous detour into the interior of Russia, can be explained by the contemporary political interests of his government. He takes us up the Tanaïs River (the Don) into territory subject to the Khazar realm, as far as the fortress of Sarkel on the left bank of the lower Don. His digression concluded, he proceeds from Bosporus to the city of Tamatarcha on the eastern shore of the Straits of Kerch, and follows the north-eastern coast of the Black Sea, past the lands of the Zichians, the Circassians and the Abasgians, as far as the city of Sotirioupolis (Pityus, modern Pitsunda), the end of the journey. A last digression, brief though politically significant, takes us over the Caucasus to the country of the Alans on the upper Terek: the Alans had long been esteemed in Byzantium as the empire's most useful ally in the North Caucasian area.

This historico-geographical description of the lands to the north of the Black Sea no doubt largely reflects a mid-tenth century picture; the many ethnic and political changes that took place in that area before and later, and the re-adjustments of Byzantine foreign policy to the shifting balance of power in the steppes, scarcely permit us to use the forty-second chapter of the *De Administrando Imperio* as a blueprint for the whole of the Middle Ages. Yet, given the constancy with which this policy adjusted itself to the geopolitical realities of the area, it is possible to use this account as a reliable starting point for a description of its historical geography. It will be observed that the region included in the account can be divided into three sub-areas, defined by two roughly concentric semi-circles. The first follows the outline of the Black Sea, from the mouth of the Danube to the slopes of the North-Western Caucasus; the second is bounded by the Carpathian Mountains and the lower Volga, extends over the lower courses of the great rivers which flow into the Black Sea and the Sea of Azov, and comprises the South Russian steppe land; beyond this second semi-circle, which bisects the Dnieper at the forty-ninth parallel, began the wooded steppe, which merged some three

46

hundred miles further north into the great forest belt stretching north-eastward across the plain of European Russia. Each of these three zones had its own distinct geographical features; each made its separate contribution to the medieval history of Eastern Europe; each, for different reasons, was of vital concern to the statesmen of Byzantium.

The first of these zones had as its pivot the southern coast of the Crimea. The Crimean peninsula is a land of geographical and cultural contrasts. Three quarters of its area, with a semi-arid climate, consisted in the Middle Ages of pasture land and formed part of the South Russian steppe. A low-lying isthmus, joining the peninsula to the mainland, offered easy transit to invaders from the north. The situation of the Northern Crimea explains the double role it played as a target for invaders and as a relatively well-protected pocket within which relics of earlier masters of the South Russian steppes—the Cimmerians and Scythians, for example—survived for centuries after memories of them had vanished from their homelands further north. The southern part of the Crimea, on the other hand, is dominated by a series of parallel mountain ranges, partly wooded, the highest of which rises in places to 1,500 metres. The southernmost range, which runs parallel to the coast and is geologically an extension of the Caucasus, falls steeply down to a narrow, fertile coast, studded with natural harbours, with a picturesque scenery reminiscent of the French and Italian Riviera. Protected by the mountain screen, this coast enjoys a climate of the Mediterranean type, and the olive and the vine, introduced by the Greek colonists in antiquity, ensured a mode of life familiar to Greek, Roman and Byzantine, and strikingly different from the pastoral existence of the continental nomads beyond the mountains. The contrast between the semi-arid steppe, the rain-absorbing mountains, and the lush seaboard, provided the natural setting to the medieval history of the Crimea, full of variety and rich in drama. This coastal fringe is too narrow, and the bounty of its orchards and vineyards too precarious, for economic self-sufficiency; and this remote outpost of the Mediterranean world can live only by constant contact with its environment: with the sea whose trade routes radiated southward to the Balkans, Asia Minor and the Caucasus; and with the open spaces that lie beyond the mountains, menacing because of the barbarians who periodically descended from them, yet life-giving too, owing to the foodstuffs and other raw materials which they provided. Thus were the basic features of the Crimean landscape—the sea, the mountains and the plains—combined in a typically Mediterranean relationship; and they ensured that the southerners who settled on the coastal fringe—Greeks, Romans, Byzantines and later Italians—became middlemen between the Mediterranean world and the steppes of Eurasia.

The cities of Cherson and Bosporus stood at the two extremities of this coastal fringe, the latter on its furthermost eastern projection, the former on the south-western tip of the Crimea, on a secondary limestone peninsula. Both were protected by hills, yet each stood sideways from the main range, thus communicating more easily with the land routes of the interior than the coastal towns between them which nestled at the foot of the mountains. Both were blessed with excellent harbours. Bosporus, on the site of ancient Panticapaeum, was in the early Byzantine period an important centre of Greek and Christian civilization. The imperial government attached great value to the city as a diplomatic and missionary outpost and as a land-terminus of the silk route from China. Its position, however, was too exposed to attacks by nomads of the Eurasian steppe, and after the sixth century Byzantium was seldom able to maintain effective authority in Bosporus for more than relatively brief periods. Its statesmen were thus forced to rely increasingly, as a platform for their diplomatic activity in the steppes, on the political loyalty of Cherson.

The position of Cherson (the ancient Chersonesus), two miles from present-day Sebastopol (founded by the Russians in 1784) had several advantages: of all the major Crimean ports it was the nearest to Asia Minor; it lay on the direct sea-route from the lower Danube to the West Caucasian seaboard; it was less vulnerable than Bosporus to attacks from the steppes; and the deep Quarantine Bay provided an admirable harbour. Its monumental land walls, first erected in the Hellenistic period, were rebuilt several times by the Byzantines: once by the Emperor Zeno, about 488, and again by Justinian. On both occasions they were erected to protect the city against groups of Huns who, after the break-up of Attila's Empire, had occupied the steppes of the Northern Crimea. Justinian not only restored the walls of Cherson and Bosporus, but also constructed between these two cities a line of forts along the coast, including Alousta (Alushta) and Gorzovium (Gurzuf), and built another line of fortifications in the mountains further inland, to defend the passes against attacks from the north. Thus a regular military frontier was drawn in the sixth century across the Southern Crimea, and Justinian's *limes Tauricus*, which coincided with the natural boundary between the Mediterranean and the Eurasian sections of the peninsula and probably followed the old fortified line built by the Romans against the Scythians, increased the security of Cherson and of the other Byzantine possessions on the coast. Some of Justinian's fortifications were probably still standing when William of Rubruck, the Franciscan friar, passed through the Crimea on his way to Mongolia in 1253, and must have formed part of the forty castles which, he tells us, then guarded the southern coast of the peninsula.[5]

But the Byzantine statesmen, true to the time-honoured methods of Roman diplomacy, were not content to entrust the defence of the Crimean *limes* solely to walls and fortifications. By the late fifth century they had secured, to counterbalance the pressure of the Huns and other steppe barbarians, the alliance of the Crimean Goths. These remnants of the mighty Ostrogothic state which once comprised much of Southern Russia had, after its destruction by the Huns in A.D. 370, retired to the safety of the Crimean mountains. Their principal city, Doros, probably stood on the site of Mankup-Kale, a fortress perched on rocky cliffs in the mountains, about twenty kilometres east of Cherson. The Crimean Goths became close friends of Byzantium in the reign of Justinian; their loyalty to the empire was strengthened by the fact that they had been Christians since the fourth century and, unlike the Arian Goths who settled in Western Europe, always remained Orthodox; and for four centuries they played a useful role in guarding the northern approaches to the Byzantine possessions in the Crimea. Until the thirteenth century, when they were lost by the empire, these possessions were of considerable value to it. This was partly due to economic reasons: for the Crimea provided Byzantium, as it had supplied the cities of ancient Greece, with the raw materials of the hinterland: fish from the estuaries of the Russian rivers, salt from the Sea of Azov and the coast of

49

the Western Crimea, furs, honey, wax and slaves from the forests further north. Politically, Cherson and the southern coastline, known to the Greeks as the *Klimata*, "the Regions", were an invaluable observation post, a watch-tower surveying the fringe of the barbarian world of South Russia which Byzantine diplomatists were ever anxious to study, influence and control. From these outposts in the Crimea the imperial government could follow the moves of the nomadic tribes who roamed the steppes between the Don and the Dnieper, and often, by a timely bribe or by fomenting internal strife among them, ward off their attacks from the Balkans. From these advanced positions in the north the Byzantines were thus able to pursue towards the nations of the steppes the traditional Roman policy of "divide and rule", or at least, when this was impossible, "weaken and watch".[6] The security of the empire's Balkan provinces frequently depended on the watchfulness of its agents in the Crimea. It is no wonder that Byzantium hung on to its Crimean outpost with grim determination, struggling to preserve it from the domination of Turkic tribes encamped between the lower Volga and the Sea of Azov, attempting—not always successfully—to channel into lawful forms the traditions of Greek municipal autonomy which were always strong in Cherson.

The Crimean peninsula retained its two faces, the one looking northward to the steppes, the other southward across the Black Sea towards the Mediterranean, until the late Middle Ages. But the patterns of its political and commercial life were no longer, in that period, influenced by decisions taken in Constantinople. The Mongol overlords of Russia, who gained control over the peninsula in the second half of the thirteenth century, and the Genoese and Venetian merchants who settled on its coastal fringe in the same period, now determined between them the fate of the Crimea. Cherson and Bosporus sank into insignificance and obscurity. In their place, Italian trading colonies arose along the coast: the more important were in Caffa (on the site of the ancient Greek Theodosia) and in Sugdaia (called Soldaia by the Italians and Surozh by the Russians) further west. For two hundred years they purveyed to Constantinople and Italy corn and salt from South Russia, and silk from Central Asia and China. Their history, which survived the Ottoman conquest, illustrates the remarkable continuity in the economic history of the Black Sea. This continuity rested on three factors: on the presence in South Russia of politically stable societies, capable of ensuring peace and of appreciating the advantages of foreign trade; on the survival on the South Crimean coast of communities specializing in transit trade, linked by culture and political loyalties to their Mediterranean or Balkan homes, yet adaptable to conditions of life on the fringe of the Eurasian steppe; and on the ability of Mediterranean powers to absorb the surplus produce of the Pontic steppe, to provide in exchange its inhabitants with the products of their own industry, and to control the trade routes that led across the Black Sea through the Bosphorus and the Dardanelles. The Mongols of the Golden Horde, who inherited the commercial traditions of their Scythian, Sarmatian, Gothic and Khazar predecessors in the steppe; the Genoese and Venetians, who stepped into the shoes of the Greek and Byzantine merchants in the Crimea; and their parent cities in Italy, which built their commercial empires in the Eastern Mediterranean on the ruins of Byzantine thalassocracy: these late medieval powers restored to the Black Sea the role it had played in antiquity and in the early Middle Ages—that of a major highway of world trade.

The last segment of the north Pontic itinerary described in the *De Administrando Imperio* followed the eastern coast of the Black Sea from the Straits of Kerch to the city of Sotirioupolis. This coast, which includes the low-lying Taman′ peninsula, traversed by the delta of the Kuban′, extends southward over a series of narrow and lush valleys dominated by the wooded north-western spurs of the Caucasus, and ends in the rich and warm plain of Mingrelia, the Colchis of the ancients. Tradition dates the earliest connections between this region and the Greek world back to the voyage of the Argonauts; and in the classical period the eastern coast of the Black Sea was studded with Greek cities—Phasis, Dioscurias, Pityus were the most important—whose founders had been drawn to this region by the gold mines of the Caucasus. Strategic and economic factors made this coast of great importance to the Byzantine Empire. Its curved outline and pronounced south-easterly direction facilitated contact with the interior and provided a springboard for the defence of the whole Caucasian isthmus. The defence of this isthmus was of vital concern to By-

51

zantium for three reasons: its northern extremity opened funnel-
wise into the Eurasian steppe and on to the highway of invasion
used by the nomads heading for the Black Sea and the Danube;
the passes of the Central Caucasus offered these same nomads a
direct route that led to Byzantine Asia Minor; and further south
the lands of Transcaucasia presented to the great powers of the
Middle East—the Persians, the Arabs, and the Turks—a tempting
springboard for their attacks on Asia Minor, the Bosphorus and
Constantinople. To guard against these dangers, Byzantine diplomacy sought to build a favourable balance of power in the Caucasian sector; this, in political terms, meant creating a chain of
allied or vassal states from the lower Volga and the Sea of Azov to
Lake Van in Armenia. The role played in this defensive imperialism by the peoples who dwelt on the eastern coast of the Black
Sea depended, of course, on their geographical position and military resources; but all of them, provided they were friendly, could
at least enable the Byzantine navy to operate safely in Caucasian
waters. In the northern sector of this coast lived the Zichians. The
strategic importance of their country lay in its proximity to the
Byzantine colonies in the Crimea and to the lower Don, a notoriously insecure area in the history of the steppe. Zichia's loyalty to
the empire was promoted by its local church, whose archbishop
played a leading role in the early Middle Ages in Byzantine ecclesiastical policy on the borders of the steppe. In the tenth century, to judge from the *De Administrando Imperio*, the Zichians
were regarded in Constantinople, in terms of their usefulness to
the empire, on a par with the Russians and the Khazars. Not the
least token of their usefulness was the fact that their country
abounded in wells yielding naphtha, a substance which formed the
basis of Byzantium's secret weapon, the "Greek fire".[7]

South of Zichia, on the southern slopes of the Caucasus and
along the coast, lay Abasgia (Abkhazia). The remoteness of this
country, covered with dense forests, enabled the Abasgians of the
interior to maintain a semi-independent existence for centuries;
but in the coastal cities, Sotirioupolis and Sebastopolis (Sukhumi),
Byzantine control was usually effective until the late eleventh century. Apart from their military usefulness as allies against the Persians and the Arabs, the Abasgians were expected to guard the
relevant section of the silk route from China, which skirted the

northern shores of the Caspian, crossed the Central Caucasus range, reached the Black Sea coast of Abasgia and continued by sea via Phasis (Poti) to Trebizond.

In the south Abasgia bordered on Lazica, the most important of the Byzantine colonies on the eastern shores of the Black Sea. The country of the Lazes, traversed by the Phasis river, lay on the south-eastern curve of the coast and extended inland within striking distance of the Darial pass in the Central Caucasus. This gave Lazica a key position in the defence of Transcaucasia against attacks from the north; while its rugged terrain and thick forests were a barrier to Persian ambitions in the Black Sea region. The coastal cities of Lazica—Phasis, and especially Petra which had been powerfully fortified by Justinian—helped to keep the country under Byzantine control until the Arab invasion of the late seventh century. "Our Lazica", as Justinian described the country in an official document,[8] carried on a lively trade with Byzantium, exporting furs, skins and slaves, and importing salt, wine and corn. The Lazes, as well as the Abasgians and the Zichians, were converted to Christianity in the sixth century by Byzantine missionaries, and the ecclesiastical organization set up in their lands proved a powerful means of keeping them within the political orbit of East Rome; while the roads and the fortresses which the Byzantines built in these countries were the material counterpart of the flattering if less tangible links which their rulers were induced to cement with the imperial court of Constantinople.

From these client states on the coast Byzantium deployed its influence inland, in an effort to beget more marchland wardens to serve its interests in the Caucasus. The Iberians, or Georgians, were wooed from neighbouring Lazica; the Alans in the central Caucasus, described in the sixth century by Procopius as "friends of the Romans from of old",[9] stood guard over the Darial pass and could check attacks of the steppe nomads against the Crimea; and further north the Hunnic Sabiri, who lived between the upper Kuban′ and the lower Terek, were used by the Byzantines in the sixth century to guard the approaches to the "Caspian Gates", the pass of Derbend which controlled a main route of invasion from the steppes to Transcaucasia.

The second of the three North Pontic zones, mentioned above,

53

lay between the coastal fringe and the forest zone. Much of this area is covered with "black earth" (*chernozem*), a fertile soil rich in humus and overspread with feather grass before the coming of the plough. The northern part of this area merges into the wooded steppe whose soil, combining open grassland with extensive tracts of woodland, was cultivated in the Middle Ages by a predominantly settled, farming population. Further south lay the belt of the open steppe. From time immemorial it has offered pasture lands to the sheep-rearing, horse-riding nomads moving westward from their homes in Central Asia, through this funnel-shaped corridor between the Black Sea coast and the wooded steppe, towards the Carpathians and the middle Danube. Some of them were content to remain in proximity to the warm and fertile plains bordering on the sea and to the coastal cities which offered prospect of plunder or trade. Others, driven by economic necessity, by bottlenecks of fresh invaders further east, or by military ambition, followed the "steppe corridor" to its end, through the narrow passage between the Danube delta and the arc of the Transylvanian Alps, into the Wallachian plain: from there they could either press on across the passes of the mountains of the Banat into the plain of Hungary, or else cross the lower Danube into the Balkans. The prime motive behind these periodic migrations was probably economic: for the steppe, despite its rich soil, was subject to spells of terrible aridity. On its western fringes, however, the more abundant rainfall made agriculture possible. This impelled the Eurasian nomad to rely for his subsistence not only on pasture land, but also on ready supplies of agricultural produce: these he could obtain both from the farming population of the wooded steppe and from the coastal cities; these cities also provided him with fixed bases for empire building. The tendency of the nomad to shift towards an agricultural mode of life brought the steppe of Eurasia into an intimate relationship with the wooded steppe and the Black Sea coast, comparable to that which prevailed between nomad and farmer elsewhere on the fringes of the Mediterranean world, in the Sahara and the Syrian desert. And the resultant interest, compounded of envy and contempt, which the Eurasian nomad showed for the farmer and merchant, underlies much of the human drama in the medieval history of Eastern Europe. The longing felt by so many nomads for a settled agricultural existence and for the higher standards of living which Byzantine civilization could provide is poignantly illustrated by the following episode. The Emperor Justinian had been playing off one against the other two Hunnic tribes, the Kutrigurs and the Utigurs, who lived in the steppes respectively west and east of the Don. In 550, as a reward for their services to the empire, Justinian allowed two thousand Kutrigurs to settle in Thrace. This aroused the indignation of the khan of the Utigurs, who sent an envoy to Constantinople to protest against the favouritism shown to their rivals. This oral remonstration—the Huns were illiterate—was recorded, and perhaps improved upon, by Procopius:

I know [said the khan] a certain proverb which I have heard from my boyhood, and if I have not forgotten it, the proverb runs somewhat as follows. That wild beast, the wolf, might, they say, possibly be able to change in some degree the colour of his fur, but his character he does not transform, nature not permitting him to change this. ... And I know something else which I have learned from experience, one of those things which it would be natural that a rough barbarian should learn: the shepherds take dogs when they are still suckling and rear them with no lack of care in the house, and the dog is an animal grateful to those who feed it and most mindful of kindness. Now this is obviously done by the shepherds with this purpose, that when the wolves attack the flock at any time, the dogs may check their attacks, standing over the sheep as guardians and saviours. And I think that this takes place throughout the world ... and that even in your empire, where practically everything is found in abundance, including doubtless even impossible things, there is not the slightest variation from this rule. ... But if these things are by nature everywhere fixed, it is not, I think, a fair thing for you to receive hospitably the nation of the Kutrigurs, inviting in a foul set of neighbours, and making people at home with you now whom you have not endured beyond your boundaries. ... While we eke out our existence in a deserted and thoroughly unproductive land, the Kutrigurs are at liberty to traffic in corn and to revel in their wine cellars and to live on the fat of the land. And doubtless they have access to baths too, and are wearing gold— the vagabonds—and have no lack of fine clothes embroidered and overlaid with gold.[10]

The fact that the steppe was an open road connecting the Black Sea coast and the lower Danube with Mongolia and China weighed heavily on the life of medieval Europe. The tactical superiority of the mobile archer from Asia, which Europeans came to fear so much, was ended only by the invention of gunpowder. And the first stage in the victory of Europe over Asia was achieved in 1552 by the Russian sovereign Ivan iv, whose cannons blasted the walls of the Tatar stronghold of Kazan' and dispersed the remnants of the Golden Horde.

It would be a mistake, however, to regard these invaders of the steppe merely as a recurrent military scourge, or as human material for the exercise of Byzantine diplomacy. Some of them made a lasting contribution to the cultural history of Southern Russia. The distinctive and cosmopolitan culture, which flourished in that land in the classical and Hellenistic periods and survived into the early Middle Ages, was compounded of elements from Iran and Mesopotamia, from the Balkans and Asia Minor, and from Central and Northern Europe. It was sustained by international trade and by the commercial routes which converged on Southern Russia from Central Asia and Western Siberia, from the southern coast of the Black Sea, and from the northern forests. Yet, for all its international connections, the South Russian steppe was, both in antiquity and in the Middle Ages, mainly an oriental land, the westward projection of the Eurasian steppe; and its culture, unlike that of the Greek coastal cities and of the Slav communities to the north of the steppe belt, was largely Asian in origin. To identify the carriers of these cultural traditions is no easy task, for the picture we obtain from the written sources is that of a bewildering procession of tribes and nations which every few centuries succeed one another in the steppes, only to sweep each other off the map: Cimmerians, Scythians, Sarmatians, Goths, Huns, Avars, Bulgars, Khazars, Magyars, Pechenegs, Cumans and Tatars emerge and vanish in turn on the historian's horizon. Modern scholarship has done much to modify this over-simplified picture. It has taught us to read the political history of the steppe no longer as a kaleidoscope of successive populations, but primarily as a sequence of conquering minorities, each of which imposed its political authority and often its name on the earlier inhabitants, without wholly displacing or absorbing them. What changed in each case was the ruling race and the designation of its conquered subjects, not the basic ethnographic substratum. The ethnic continuity in the history of the Pontic steppes is apparent in the enduring importance of Iranian, and later Turkic, peoples in Southern Russia. The Iranians (Scythians, and later Sarmatians) who dominated this region between about 600 B.C. and A.D. 600,

56

and their successors, the Turkic Khazars, Pechenegs and Cumans who in turn lorded it over the steppe until the early thirteenth century, left a lasting imprint upon the economic and political history of the North Pontic area. And the principal aims of these Asian tribes—the exploitation of the East European river routes, the urge to reach the Black Sea and the Mediterranean world beyond it, and the promotion of trade relations with Western Asia—were taken over in the ninth and tenth centuries by Kievan Russia, that joint creation of the Eastern Slavs and of Scandinavian Vikings, which inherited commercial traditions established from time immemorial in the steppes of Southern Russia.

At the eastern extremity of the South Russian steppe, between the Sea of Azov, the Caspian and the Caucasus, lay a region of peculiar strategic importance. Conveniently framed by seas and rivers, it offered a natural halting-place to many a nomadic people who had come from Asia across the gap between the Caspian and the Ural mountains. The Byzantine statesmen were quick to appreciate the need to secure a strong ally in this sector, politically the least unstable in the Pontic steppes: for the peoples who dwelt there, if they were friendly and sufficiently powerful, could be counted upon to guard the eastern extremity of the European steppe corridor and, generally, to help preserve the balance of power along the whole length of the empire's northern front. On several occasions Byzantine diplomacy achieved success in this area. In the early seventh century it actively contributed to the growth of the Turkic kingdom of "Old Great Bulgaria", which for some fifty years guarded the empire's interests north of the Black Sea; during the following two centuries it was the turn of the Khazars, who replaced the Bulgars in this area, to enjoy imperial support. The Khazar alliance served the empire in good stead: in the eighth century it probably did much to save Byzantium from the Arab menace, for if the Khazars had not halted the northward thrust of Islam in the Caucasus, the Arabs might well have invaded the steppes of South Russia, appeared on the lower Danube, and thus outflanked the whole Byzantine system of defence. Once again, in the second half of the thirteenth century, the steppes to the north of the Caucasus played their part in the balance of power which the Byzantine statesmen sought to build up in the steppes. The alliance then concluded between Byzantium and the Tatars of the Golden Horde helped to relieve the pressure exerted by the enemies of the empire upon its Balkan provinces.

The North Pontic itinerary described in the *De Administrando Imperio* contains, it will be remembered, a brief but significant parenthesis. On reaching the estuary of the Dnieper, we are told that its higher reaches are inhabited by the Russians, who sail down the river towards Byzantium. The term "Russians" was in the mid-tenth century still an ambiguous one: it could mean either the Eastern Slavs, or their Viking overlords, or both. But the word "Russia", when used in a geographical sense, designated the territory occupied by the Eastern Slavs. This territory embraced the western and part of the central areas of what we today call European Russia. The approximate boundary extended in the north to the region of Lake Ladoga, crossed the Western Dvina and the Niemen, turned eastward on the slopes of the Carpathians, and reached the Dnieper about a hundred miles south of Kiev; from there it ran north-eastward up the Psiol River, crossed the upper Don, reached the upper Volga not far from its confluence with the Oka, followed the Volga upstream and then cut north-westward to Lake Ladoga. In the south the Eastern Slavs were cut off from the Black Sea by a broad belt of steppe land, except at the estuaries of the Bug, the Dniester and the Prut, which they had occupied by the sixth century and over which they still maintained a precarious hold. In geographical terms, "Russia" in the tenth century was restricted to that part of the East European forest zone which extends between the twenty-second and the forty-third meridians and the sixtieth and the forty-third parallels. It formed the last, and most northerly, of the three North Pontic zones. Its western section had belonged to the Eastern Slavs from time immemorial; they occupied the remainder during the early centuries of the Christian era. Except for their later colonization of the lands inhabited by Finnish tribes to the north and north-east, the Eastern Slavs remained confined to their tenth century habitat during the greater part of the Middle Ages. The forest zone, with spruce and pine predominating in the north, and oak in the south, was the natural setting within which Slavonic tribes and communities, living in forest clearings and river valleys, were united in the ninth century within the medieval Russian state. The vast and in many places still primeval forests supplied them with animal furs, fuel and unlimited timber for building; in the clearings and on the fringes of the steppe, rye, barley and wheat were sown; and the rivers offered great possibilities for trade.

The rivers of European Russia, with their sinuous courses and far-flung basins, form a network of waterways unique in Europe. Their head waters are very nearly contiguous: thus the sources of the Volga, of the Dnieper, and of the Western Dvina are separated by a narrow watershed extending over the low morainic Valdai hills and offering easy portages from one river to the other. Furthermore, the Don through its upper reaches is closely linked with the basin of the Oka, and its middle basin comes within about twenty-five kilometres of the Volga. Not only did these rivers serve to connect the different parts of the forest and the steppe areas of European Russia: each of them had in the Middle Ages an international significance, as a route linking the country of the Eastern Slavs with ancient centres of civilization: the Volga, through the Caspian Sea, with the Caucasus, Iran and Mesopotamia; the Don, with the Kuban' delta and the Crimea; the Dnieper, across the Black Sea, with Constantinople. And all three of these south-flowing rivers allowed, across the portages that led from their upper reaches to the Western Dvina and to the Lovat'-Volkhov system, easy access to the Baltic, and thus to Scandinavia and Germany. It is no wonder that the earliest groupings of the Eastern Slavs took shape along the rivers. The river deserved the respect and the affection lavished upon it by the Russian: it directed his movement of colonization, welded his scattered communities into a geographically viable state, taught him trade and the other arts of peace and, at the dawn of his nation's history, brought him out of the restrictive grasp of the forest on to the highroads of the world.

Of all the Russian river routes the most important, at least in the early Middle Ages, led from the Baltic to the Black Sea. Three factors caused it to become, between 850 and 1100, a major highway of international communication. The Swedish Vikings, or Varangians, used it as their main route to the spoils and luxury markets of Byzantium; it was the geographical backbone of the earliest Russian state; and it linked Western Europe with the Levant at a time when trans-Mediterranean trade was on the de-

59

cline. For these reasons the "way from the Varangians to the Greeks", as the Russians called this river route, played a decisive role in the history of Russo-Byzantine relations. This fact warrants a description of its main topographical landmarks.

We possess several medieval descriptions of this route. The most informative are to be found in the *Russian Primary Chronicle*,[11] compiled in the eleventh and early twelfth centuries, and in the *De Administrando Imperio*.[12] The two accounts conveniently supplement each other, the former concentrating on the northern section of the route, from the Baltic to Kiev, the latter dealing mainly with the itinerary from Kiev to Byzantium. The chief starting points were the coastal areas of South-Eastern Sweden, Upland and Södermanland, and the island of Gotland. The route from Scandinavia across the Baltic and into the interior of Russia divided into two main branches. The first led into the Gulf of Riga and thence, up the Western Dvina, to the watershed between that river and the upper Dnieper. The other branch followed a northerly itinerary, across the Gulf of Finland and up the Neva into Lake Ladoga; from there the Swedes sailed up the Volkhov to Ladoga (the Aldegjuborg of the Islandic sagas), an ancient fortress and a major trading centre. Here, perhaps, the Northmen exchanged their Viking ships for smaller dug-out canoes, made from hollowed-out tree trunks supplied by the local Slav population. These enabled them to negotiate the dangerous rapids of the Volkhov which began upstream from Ladoga and extended for nineteen kilometres. The next halt was in Novgorod (the Hólmgardr of the sagas) near the banks of Lake Il'men', an emporium for the fur trade and the centre of an important Scandinavian colony as early as 860. From Novgorod the route continued due south, across Lake Il'men' and up the Lovat'. By the head stream of that river began the celebrated watershed between the Western Dvina, the Volga, and the Dnieper, known to the Russians as "the Great Portage". The area is criss-crossed by many small tributary rivers, over which Vikings and Slavs sailed, pulled or punted their boats; when this was impossible, they dragged or carried them overland. The main route led from the Lovat' into the Western Dvina, where it joined the other branch from the Gulf of Riga, and, over a further series of portages, debouched into the Dnieper by Smolensk. The next stretch, from Smolensk to Kiev down the

Dnieper, was generally easy and uneventful. In Kiev, Russia's capital city, whenever the object of the expedition was trade, elaborate preparations were made for the journey south. During the month of April, when the ice on the Dnieper melts, *monoxyla* (dug-out canoes) converged on the city from the towns on the river route that lay upstream. There they were dismantled, refitted with oars and rowlocks, and loaded with goods—mainly furs, honey, wax and slaves. In June the convoy of boats set out from Kiev on the "Greek route" to Constantinople. A halt of two or three days was called at Vitichev, some fifty kilometres downstream from Kiev, where it was joined by a further contingent of boats. The flotilla proceeded down the Dnieper to the point, about 450 kilometres downstream from Kiev, where the river abruptly altered course from a south-easterly direction to cut due south through a belt of crystalline rocks, forming a series of nine rapids. This, the most perilous part of the entire journey, is vividly described in the *De Administrando Imperio*. The first rapid gave the travellers a sombre foretaste of what lay ahead:

> In the middle of it are rooted high rocks, which stand out like islands. Against these, then, comes the water and wells up and dashes down over the other side, with a mighty and terrific din. Therefore the Russians do not venture to pass between them, but put in to the bank hard by, disembarking the men on to dry land but leaving the rest of the goods on board the *monoxyla*; they then strip and, feeling with their feet to avoid striking on a rock, pass through. This they do, some at the prow, some amidships, while others again, in the stern, punt with poles; and with all this careful procedure they pass this first barrage, edging round under the river-bank. When they have passed this barrage, they re-embark the others from the dry land and sail away.

But the largest rapid, whose name in Slavonic means "insatiable", had to be circumvented by land: for six miles the goods were carried, "the slaves in their chains" conducted on foot, and the boats partly dragged, partly carried on men's shoulders, while the military escort kept vigilant watch for a possible enemy attack. This danger was always acute in the area of the rapids: for here the steppe nomads would lie in ambush, drawn by the prospect of loot and encouraged by the relative defencelessness of the slow-moving and earth-bound caravan. "It is at this point," our Byzantine writer tersely observes, "that the Pechenegs come down and attack the Russians." If all went well during the passage of the rapids, the flotilla reassembled downstream on the island of St. Gregory (the modern Khortitsa), where the pagan Russians expressed their relief by sacrificing live cocks to their gods beneath a huge oak-tree. Four days' sailing then brought them to the mouth of the Dnieper. There, on the island of St. Aitherios (Berezan'), they spent two or three days resting and preparing for the sea voyage by equipping their boats with sails, masts and rudders. Out in the Black Sea the convoy took care to hug the coast, putting in to shore at frequent intervals. At Mesembria they entered Byzantine territorial waters, which carried them into the Bosphorus to Constantinople, journey's end. The whole voyage from Kiev probably lasted, under favourable conditions, about six weeks.

The nature and extent of the Russo-Byzantine trade carried by the Baltic-Black Sea waterway will be discussed in a later chapter. What should be emphasized here is the importance which this arterial route possessed in the eyes of the Russians, and the difficulties they encountered in keeping it open. Its importance was due to their need to trade with the countries around the Black Sea, to the military ambitions of the rulers of Kiev, and to their and their subjects' desire to acquire the fruits of Byzantine civilization. The main difficulty was the one so vividly evoked in the ninth chapter of the *De Administrando Imperio*: the nomads of the steppe threatened to intercept the Russian trading caravans and to cut off the route of the lower Dnieper.

It may be said that the historical geography of Russia was shaped in the Middle Ages by a peculiar relationship between two features of the country's physical environment: the rivers and the steppe. Between the rivers, which opened for the Russians avenues of trade and access to the civilization of the Mediterranean world, and the steppe which spelled danger of foreign invasion, there was mostly in this period irreconcilable opposition. It is significant that the north–south line described by the principal river route of early medieval Russia and the east–west road represented by the steppe, intersect not far from Kiev, which was at once a frontier fortress and the capital of the Russian realm. In this simple geographical fact lies much of the drama of early Russian history. For the Russians knew well that by resisting the pressure of the steppe nomads they were fighting to preserve their state, their culture and their religion. And, as their powers of resistance gradually weakened with the waning of the twelfth century, it became increasingly apparent that not the least of their motives in fighting a national crusade had been to keep open at all costs Russia's economic lifeline, the water route to Byzantium.

NOTES

1. N. G. Polites, Ἐκλογαὶ ἀπὸ τὰ τραγούδια τοῦ ἑλληνικοῦ λαοῦ, 3rd ed. (Athens, 1932), no. 23, p. 40.

2. Cicero, *De Re Publica*, ii, 4, ed. C. F. W. Mueller (Leipzig, 1898), p. 309.

3. Polybius, *Historiae*, iv, 45, ed. T. Büttner-Wobst, ii (Leipzig, 1889), pp. 57–8; transl. J. B. Bury, *A History of the Later Roman Empire from Arcadius to Irene*, ii (London, 1889), pp. 11-12.

4. *DAI*, pp. 182–9.

5. *The Texts and Versions of John de Plano Carpini and William de Rubruquis*, ed. C. R. Beazley (London, Hakluyt Society, 1903), pp. 146, 187.

6. M. Rostovtzeff, *Iranians and Greeks in South Russia* (Oxford, 1922), p. 153.

7. *DAI*, ch. 53, p. 284.

8. *Novella 28, praefatio: Corpus Iuris Civilis*, ed. R. Schoell and G. Kroll, iii (Berlin, 1904), p. 212.

9. Procopius, *De bellis*, ii, 29, ed. J. Haury, i (Leipzig, 1962), pp. 291–2; English transl.: *History of the Wars*, H. B. Dewing, i (London, 1914), p. 533.

10. Procopius, *De bellis*, viii, 19; ed. J. Haury, ii, pp. 587–9; *History of the Wars*, transl. Dewing, v (1928), pp. 247–51.

11. *Povest'*, i, pp. 11–12; Cross, p. 53.

12. *DAI*, ch. 9, pp. 56–63; commentary by D. Obolensky, *DAI*, ii (London 1962), pp. 16–58.

2

Barbarians in the Balkans

The disintegration of the kingdom of the Huns after Attila's death in 453 transformed the balance of power in the lands beyond the northern borders of the Byzantine Empire. On the ruins of a realm which had stretched from the Caspian to the Rhine and had pressed down upon and in places overrun the Byzantine frontier on the Danube, a motley collection of emancipated peoples, each struggling to assert its newly-won independence, now stand exposed to the historian's view. In the steppes of Southern Russia there emerged, by the late fifth century, a group of tribes composed in part of Huns who had moved eastward after the dissolution of Attila's empire, and whom the Byzantines called Bulgars. On the middle Danube two Germanic peoples, the Gepids and the Lombards, respectively east and west of the Tisza, were beginning to contend for the Pannonian plain, once the centre of the Hunnic realm. More significantly still, the northern bank of the Danube, from Belgrade to the estuary, was by the year 500 occupied by the Slavs.

For some time past these Slavs had been moving southward from their earliest European home. The location of this home has provoked much controversy, and its precise boundaries are still in some measure open to question. However, the evidence available today testifies with overwhelming weight against the view, popular fifty years ago and still repeated in some current textbooks, that the Slavs were originally confined to the dreary and narrow precincts of the Pripet marshes in Polesie. There can no longer be any doubt that their original home covered a considerable area of the East European plain, between the lower Vistula and upper Niemen in the north and the Carpathians in the south. It extended eastward at least as far as the middle Dnieper; its western bound-

64

ary is generally placed on the Oder or the Elbe. We still do not know when and in what circumstances the Slavs began their migration to the south; the earliest unambiguous evidence comes from the mid-fifth century, when a Slavonic population was settled on the middle Danube and on the Tisza, in present-day Hungary, as subjects of the Huns. It is probable that the Slavs moved southward along two ancient trans-continental routes: the first passed through the "Moravian Gate", formed by a depression between the Sudetes and the Carpathians and leading from the headstreams of the Oder and the Vistula to the valley of the Northern Morava (not to be confused with the Balkan river of that name) which flows into the Danube on the western borders of present-day Slovakia; this thoroughfare, along which amber from the Baltic coast had been carried south from prehistoric times, connected the North European lowlands with the Pannonian plain of present-day Hungary; and Pannonia offered access to Italy, and, across the Danube, to the Balkans. The second route led southeastward across the low-lying plateau of Galicia and Podolia, outflanked the Carpathian Mountains, skirted the south-western margin of the steppe, and, following the valleys of the Dniester and the Prut, reached the Black Sea. This, too, was an ancient amber route, along which this commodity was brought from the Baltic to the Black Sea and the Aegean; and it was used by the Goths in their migration to South Russia. From Southern Bessarabia, the steppe land between the lower courses of the Dniester and the Prut, further roads opened to the Slav immigrants: southwestward, into the plain of Wallachia, and southward, across the Danube delta, into the Dobrudja.

Of the circumstances in which the Slavs established themselves on the northern banks of the Danube we know nothing; but it may be assumed that, in their desire to cross the river and settle in the Balkans, they began to exert a mounting pressure on the Byzantine frontier after the collapse of the Hunnic Empire. It is only in the mid-sixth century that the darkness begins to lift over the lower Danube. The Slavs whom the Byzantines came to know by personal and often exceedingly painful experience belonged to two main groups. The first, called the Sclavini, were stationed along the whole length of the lower Danube and as far north as the Dniester; they seem to have been particularly numerous in Wallachia. The second group, known to the Byzantines as Antes (or Antai), appears to have occupied a considerable area of the South Russian steppes, from Bessarabia to the Donets. Whatever their exact origin (they may well have once formed a confederation of partly non-Slavonic tribes, ruled by the Iranian Sarmatians in Southern Russia) the Antes were regarded in the sixth century as Slavs, closely related to the Sclavini. The distinction between the Sclavini and the Antes must be borne in mind, for their geographical distribution in the sixth century leaves no doubt that the former were the ancestors of the Balkan Slavs, while the latter, at least in the area between the Danube delta and the Dnieper, formed part of the community of the Eastern Slavs, who were later to be known as Russians.

The history of the Mediterranean lands in the sixth century is dominated by the conquests of Justinian. The restoration of Roman power in Italy, Southern Spain, North Africa and in Sicily, Sardinia and Corsica, made Byzantium for a time the unchallenged mistress of the Inner Sea. On its eastern fringes a long succession of wars with Persia which continued through the century kept virtually unaltered the balance of strength between the two foremost powers of the earth. Justinian's immediate successors witnessed the ruin of his design to restore the ancient *Imperium Romanum*, especially in Italy. Yet so compelling was the force of this imperial dream that the prosecution of war on the western and eastern fronts remained the main military task of Byzantine governments in the second half of the sixth century. The educated Byzantine was deeply aware of his Graeco-Roman inheritance: the war with Persia which evoked memories of Marathon and Salamis, and the maintenance of imperial authority in Rome and in Carthage, bespoke the historic mission of his empire and promised a return to the glories of antiquity. Such, it seems, was the belief of Justinian; and few of his contemporaries appear to have challenged this view, and seen clearly how dangerous for the security of their empire was this obsession with classical reminiscences. For already in Justinian's reign (527–65) it became apparent that a menacing storm-centre was building up on the empire's Danubian frontier. Yet soldiers and money could ill be spared for a protracted and unspectacular border warfare against miserable barbarians. Justinian and his successors paid a heavy

66

price for their inability, or unwillingness, to adequately defend the northern border. For it was on the Danube, not on the Euphrates or on the Po, that the fate of the medieval Byzantine Empire was to be decided during the fifty years that followed Justinian's death.

The earliest well-attested inroads of the Slavs into Byzantine territory occurred in the reign of Justin I (518–27). It was not, however, until the beginning of Justinian's reign that these attacks assumed masive proportions. Their regularity and depth of penetration may be judged from these often quoted words of the contemporary Byzantine historian Procopius:

> Illyricum and all of Thrace, that is, from the Ionian Gulf to the suburbs of Constantinople, including Greece and the Chersonese [i.e. the Gallipoli peninsula], were overrun by the Huns [i.e. the Bulgars], Sclavini and Antes, almost every year, from the time when Justinian took over the Roman Empire; and intolerable things they did to the inhabitants.[1]

The area here described by Procopius covers the greater part of the Balkan peninsula; however these annual razzias undertaken for loot, after which the barbarians retired across the Danube, were at first largely confined to the countryside and as yet led to no permanent settlements of Slavs in the Balkans. By 550, however, the picture had begun to change: the duration of the raids became longer, and the Slavs were emboldened to attack Byzantine fortresses and towns, some of which they succeeded in taking and holding for several years. The growing effectiveness of these incursions may in part have been due to the military expertise of the Bulgars, who had been raiding the Balkans since the late fifth century, and who often led or supported the Slavonic invasions of Justinian's reign. These Bulgars, known as Kutrigurs, had emerged as the major military power in the steppes to the west of the Don. In 540 the Kutrigurs, probably allied with the Slavs, delivered a shattering attack on the Balkans, capturing thirty-two fortresses in Illyricum and plundering the countryside as far as the suburbs of Constantinople. Henceforth, save for a brief period of relative calm between 552 and 558, the rhythm of invasions scarcely ever abated. To mention only the most memorable: in 545 the Slavs plundered Thrace; repulsed by Narses, Justinian's famous general, they were back in the Balkans in 548, reaching the outskirts of Dyrrachium; in 550 a great horde of Sclavini penetrated to the environs of Niš and thence, presumably along the Belgrade-Constantinople highway, advanced to within some forty miles of the capital, defeating a Byzantine army near Adrianople: repulsed before the Long Wall which formed the outer defences of Constantinople, they retired beyond the Danube. The most formidable invasion of Justinian's reign took place in 559. In March a Kutrigur army, with detachments of Sclavini, crossed the frozen Danube and marched across Moesia over the Balkan passes into Thrace. There it divided into three sections: one advanced through Macedonia and Thessaly as far as the defile of Thermopylae, where it was halted by the Byzantine defences; the second attacked the Gallipoli peninsula, at the entrance to which it, too, was defeated; the third group marched towards Constantinople, forced the defences of the Long Wall and laid waste the suburbs. At this moment of acute peril the emperor summoned the aged veteran Belisarius. He forced the barbarians to retire beyond the Long Wall, and simultaneously reinforced the Byzantine fleet on the Danube to cut off their retreat. This strategy, which the Byzantines were often to repeat, proved effective: caught between two fires, the Kutrigurs sued for peace and returned to their homes in the steppe. Never again did they present so deadly a menace to the empire.

The successful repulse of the Kutrigur invasion shows that at moments of supreme danger Byzantium could still defend its Balkan provinces by force of arms. The extent to which Justinian neglected their military defence should not be exaggerated. A list of over six hundred fortresses which he is said to have built or restored in the peninsula is given by Procopius.[2] Some were probably not much more than fortified watch towers; other items of this remarkable engineering programme may have remained largely or wholly on the drafting-board. Yet even allowing for this, the achievements of Justinian's builders were impressive. In contrast to the old Roman fortified *limes* which was built along the Danube, his fortifications formed a system of roughly parallel belts, disposed in depth: this provided some insurance against marauding bands of Slavs and Bulgars who had penetrated into the interior of the peninsula, and a refuge for the local villagers in time of war. This network, broadly speaking, consisted of three fortified zones. The first followed the old Roman frontier from Belgrade to the mouth of the Danube. It comprised Roman cities on the southern bank of the river, including Singidunum, Viminacium, Augustae, Novae, Dorostolon, Noviodunum, all of which were refurbished by Justinian. Further south stood the second fortified line: it stretched from west to east across the Roman provinces of Upper Moesia (which coincided with the Šumadija region of Northern Serbia), Dacia Ripensis (bisected by the valley of the Timok), Lower Moesia (the North Bulgarian plain) and Little Scythia (the Dobrudja). Eighty strongholds in the two latter provinces, and twenty-seven in the Timok region, were built or restored in Justinian's reign. The southern boundary of this fortified line was formed by the Balkan Mountains: the northern entrances to the two main passes that led over them were commanded by the great fortresses of Nicopolis ad Haemum and Marcianopolis. The third fortified zone reached deep into the interior of the peninsula. It guarded the provinces of Haemimontus and Thrace, relieving the pressure on Adrianople and Philippopolis; covered Dacia Mediterranea (present-day Eastern Serbia and Western Bulgaria) whose principal fortresses were Naissus and Serdica, and Dardania, which was traversed by the upper courses of the Morava and the Vardar; reached the Adriatic coast of Epirus, strengthening the network of fortifications based on Dyrrachium and Valona; and extended south through Macedonia and Thessaly as far as Thermopylae and the isthmus of Corinth. The fact that Justinian's military constructions were particularly numerous along the Belgrade-Constantinople road suggests that it was one of the major highways of invasion; and it is significant that many of them appear to have been built or planned after the Kutrigur invasion of 540.

The efficacy of this elaborate system of fortifications is open to doubt. The suspicion that, like so much else in the military programme of Justinian, his fortresses were not built to last is confirmed by the growing tempo and success of the barbarian invasions in the second half of the century. Neither man-power nor money was available for their adequate defence; and it seems significant that while the topography of the Balkans has preserved to the present day the memory of several great imperial builders—Constantine, Hadrian, and especially Trajan—many of

Justinian's fortresses were obliterated and forgotten so completely that their very location poses difficult problems to modern scholars.

The inability of his armies and fortifications to prevent the Slavs and the Bulgars from invading the Balkans forced Justinian to resort to other means of defending the Danube frontier. Byzantine statesmen had already, in the fourth and fifth centuries, resorted in this sector to the tried methods of Roman diplomacy in order to curb the invasions of the Goths. These methods were perfected by Justinian's government. It was he above all who developed and bequeathed to his successors that conception of diplomacy as an intricate science and a fine art, in which military pressure, political intelligence, economic cajolery and religious propaganda were fused into a powerful weapon of defensive imperialism. The main lines and the principles of this diplomacy will be discussed later. We may note now, however, some of the diplomatic measures taken by Justinian to relieve the pressure on the lower Danube. In 530 a certain Chilbudius, a Slav chieftain of outstanding ability who had been enticed into Byzantine service, was appointed supreme commander on the Danube, which he successfully defended for several years against Kutrigurs, Antes and Sclavini.[3] In 545 Justinian offered the Antes a considerable sum of money, lands on the northern bank of the lower Danube, and the status of imperial *foederati*, on condition that they guarded the river against the Bulgars.[4] The time-honoured art of stirring up strife among the barbarians was practised by the emperor with characteristic duplicity in his dealings with the Kutrigurs and the Utigurs: in 551, as the Kutrigurs were plundering the Balkans, he bribed the Utigurs to cross the Don and attack them in the rear; he then informed the Kutrigurs of this attack upon their homes, hastened their retreat across the Danube by a gift of money, concluded a pact with them and allowed a group of them to settle in Thrace.[5] The resultant indignation of the Utigurs found expression in the protest addressed to Justinian by their khan Sandilkh, part of which was quoted in the preceding chapter. The Byzantine government must have succeeded in appeasing the anger of the Utigurs, for a few years later they were serving again as allies of the empire in the steppe. Their usefulness, and gullibility, were demonstrated again in 559, during the great Kutrigur invasion of the Balkans: as the Kutrigurs were retreating towards the Danube, Justinian sent a message to Sandilkh urging him, by arguments that combined flattery with bribery, to lead his nation against the Kutrigurs. The Utigur chieftain was impressed by these blandishments: and the resultant war between the two nations, so insidiously planned by the Byzantine diplomats, fatally undermined them both.[6]

The elaborate game of chess which Justinian's government played with the Utigurs and the Kutrigurs shows how closely the protection of the Danube frontier was bound up with the need to build a favourable balance of power in the South Russian steppes. There is no doubt that Justinian's diplomacy was to a marked degree responsible for the fact that the lower Danube, however frequently overrun by Bulgars and Slavs, remained during his reign an effective political boundary. One of the imperial Novels made the following not wholly idle boast: "Now, with the aid of God, the public territory is increased, and both banks of the Danube are occupied by towns subject to Our Empire."[7] Several of Justinian's contemporaries, such as the historians Agathias and Menander, clearly realized how much this was due to the emperor's diplomacy; which they characteristically praised for its "foresight", "prudence" and "shrewdness"—qualities always highly prized by the Byzantines. Menander even claimed that "without war, by his prudence alone, he would have destroyed the barbarians, had he lived long enough".[8] This claim, however, was hardly supported by the facts: for the emperor's diplomacy in the north was afflicted by two weaknesses which greatly undermined its effectiveness. On the one hand, the vast sums of money which the Byzantine government regularly disbursed to the barbarians to stave off their attacks were a ruinous drain on the already depleted imperial exchequer, and led to widespread discontent among its subjects: many of them bitterly resented the fact that the empire was so humiliatingly held up for ransom by border bandits. On the other hand, these same barbarians were encouraged by Justinian's largesses to raise their price and return for more tribute or lands. The self-defeating effect of this diplomacy inadequately backed by force was exposed with bitter irony by Procopius:

For these barbarians, having once tasted Roman wealth, never forgot the road that led to it. ... Thus all the barbarians became masters of all the

71

wealth of the Romans, either being presented with it by the emperor, or by ravaging the Roman Empire, selling their prisoners for ransom, and bartering for truces.[9]

Justinian's reign ended in 565 with the Slavs still maintaining their pressure on the lower Danube. Soon, however, a chain of events set in motion a few years earlier in the Pontic steppes further weakened the empire's position in the north. In 557 the Byzantine agents in the Caucasus were suddenly faced with a fresh problem. The imperial commander in Lazica received, through the good offices of the king of the Alans, a request for alliance and protection from the Avars. This nomadic people, consisting, it seems, of Mongol and Turkic tribes, had just arrived in the area north of the Caucasus, having fled across the steppes from their enemies, the Central Asian Turks. The message was promptly relayed to Constantinople, and the next year an Avar embassy was received by Justinian in the Byzantine capital. Its citizens were accustomed to the sight of exotic barbarian envoys, yet the appearance of the Avars, with their long plaited hair hanging down their backs, and their swaggering behaviour, created a mild sensation. Their requests were the usual ones: precious gifts, an annual pension, and fertile lands on which to settle. The last request was ignored by the imperial government; nevertheless the Avars, placated by presents of gold-encrusted chains, saddles, bridles, couches and silken robes, concluded a treaty with the empire and promised to fight its enemies. Justinian could not but welcome this opportunity of securing an ally in the South Russian steppes, believing, as Menander saw it, that "whether the Avars are victorious, or whether they are defeated, in either case the Romans will profit".[10] The Avars played their role of imperial *foederati* only too thoroughly: by 561 they were on the lower Danube, having subjugated in their westward advance the Sabiri, the Utigurs, the Kutrigurs, and the Antes of Bessarabia. Their relations with Byzantium now entered a new and more critical phase. Their territorial ambitions now centred on the Dobrudja, which promised them security from the vengeance of their enemies in the steppe and could also be used as a gateway to the rich pasture lands of Thrace. But the Byzantine government had no intention of allowing Avars to cross the Danube; and their frustrated ambitions created before long an explosive situation on the empire's northern frontier.

In 565, a few days after his accession, Justin II received an Avar embassy in his palace. Corippus, the emperor's court poet, wrote an account of this interview, at which he appears to have been present. Written in flowery Latin hexameters, it gives a picture, seen through Byzantine eyes, of the reaction of barbarians to the ordeal of an imperial audience. As they were conducted through the vestibules that led to the audience chamber, the envoys, we are told, admired with trepidation the huge stature of the guards with their gilded shields and lances and their purple-crested helmets, and supposed that the imperial palace was another heaven (*et credunt aliud Romana palatia caelum*). Yet they were visibly pleased to be gazed at, and walked, the poet tells us, like Hyrcanian tigers when they are let out of their cages in the circus, proud to feel the eyes of the Roman people round the arena fixed upon them. As a curtain was drawn aside in front of the imperial chamber, they looked up to the richly gilded ceilings and beheld the emperor seated upon his raised throne, clothed in purple and with a glittering diadem upon his head. The leader of the embassy then bent the knee three times, and prostrated himself before the emperor. His companions followed suit, and as the Avar envoys lay with their faces on the floor, the carpets were covered by their long flowing hair.[11]

The emperor, determined to put a stop to his predecessor's humiliating policy of buying off the northern barbarians, haughtily rejected the Avars' request for tribute. In the meantime they had become embroiled in the struggles for Central Europe: allied with the Lombards, the Avars defeated the Gepids and seized their lands in Dacia and Eastern Pannonia (567). Two events of grave consequence to the empire resulted from this move. The Lombards, evidently threatened in their turn by the new invader, migrated to Italy (568), a large portion of which they soon wrested from Byzantine control. And in the same year the Avars moved into the territory vacated by the Lombards, thus occupying the entire plain of present-day Hungary. The establishment of the Avars as the dominant power in Central Europe, masters of an empire that stretched from Bohemia to the lower Danube and, like Attila's realm, was centred on the Tisza valley, transformed the balance of power along Byzantium's northern borders. During the next three decades the Avars formed the spearhead of the barbarian attacks on East Roman territory, determined the rhythm of the Slav migrations into the Balkans and the pattern of Byzantine policy on the Danube, and were an almost constant threat to the empire's security in that sector. The supreme ruler of the Avars, the Khagan Bayan, ruthless conqueror and a subtle diplomatist, soon showed where his true ambitions lay. His immediate objective was the Roman city of Sirmium on the lower Sava (on the site of the present-day Sremska Mitrovica), a key to the Byzantine strategic position in the Northern Balkans. For the moment, however, the fortress was impregnable, and Bayan was impelled to conclude a treaty with the empire (574). This arrangement was for a time beneficial to both sides: for the Sclavini, massing for another major attack across the Danube, were becoming increasingly restive under Avar control. In 578 an Avar army of 60,000 horsemen was ferried across the Danube by the Byzantines, marched along the Roman road that followed the south bank of the Danube, reached the Dobrudja, and crossed the river into Wallachia to chastise the Sclavini. Bayan hoped to find in their land vast stores of gold looted during their raids on the Balkans; in the event the Avars liberated several thousand Byzantine citizens, captives of the Sclavini.

But Bayan, always a treacherous ally, soon showed his hand. With the forced help of Byzantine architects whom the emperor had sent to build him a palace and some baths, he constructed a bridge across the Sava downstream from Sirmium. With the city now cut off from Singidunum and the other Byzantine strongholds on the Danube, the Avars were in a position to demand its surrender. The Emperor Tiberius declared that he would sooner give one of his daughters to the khagan than abandon the fortress of his own free will. But Bayan, who knew that the emperor's hands were full with the Persian war, was not to be bluffed; and after a siege of two years, Sirmium, inadequately defended and provisioned, was surrendered to the Avars (582). The strategic key to the North-Western Balkans was now in Avar hands; the first of the great Roman fortresses in the northern part of the peninsula had fallen to the barbarians; and today little remains of this great metropolis except some excavated ruins and a pitiful inscription in ungrammatical Greek, probably dating from the days of Sirmium's last agony: "Lord Christ, help the city and smite the Avars and watch over Romania and the writer. Amen."[12]

The whole of the peninsula seemed during that terrible decade to be sinking under a deluge of savagery and extermination. In 581, while Sirmium was besieged, the Slavs launched a massive attack on the Balkans. A Syriac historian, John of Ephesus, writing four years later, describes it as follows:

> That same year, being the third after the death of King Justin, was famous also for the invasion of an accursed people, called Slavonians, who overran the whole of Greece, and the country of the Thessalonians, and all Thrace, and captured the cities, and took numerous forts, and devastated and burnt, and reduced the people to slavery, and made themselves masters of the whole country, and settled in it by main force, and dwelt in it as though it had been their own without fear. And four years have now elapsed, and still, because the king is engaged in the war with the Persians, and has sent all his forces to the East, they live at their ease in the land, and dwell in it, and spread themselves far and wide as far as God permits them, and ravage and burn and take captive. And to such an extent do they carry their ravages, that they have even ridden up to the outer walls of the city [i.e. the Long Wall of Constantinople], and driven away all the king's herds of horses, many thousands in number, and whatever else they could find. And even to this day ... [584] they still encamp and dwell there, and live in peace in the Roman territories, free from anxiety and fear, and lead captive and slay and burn: and they have grown rich in gold and silver, and herds of horses, and arms, and have learnt to fight better than the Romans, though at first they were but rude savages, who did not venture to shew themselves outside the woods and the coverts of the trees; and as for arms, they did not even know what they were, with the exception of two or three javelins or darts.[13]

Two features of this account are especially significant: the Slavs are described as expert soldiers, having the necessary instruments and technique—both no doubt acquired partly from their Avar masters and partly from their Byzantine opponents—for conducting siege operations; and in the second place, they no longer appear as transient interlopers who, their raids completed, returned to their homes across the Danube: indeed in the opinion of many scholars this passage of John of Ephesus provides an early instance of permanent Slavonic settlements in Thrace, Macedonia and Greece. Avars and Slavs, not always distinguished from each other in contemporary accounts, continued to spread havoc in the Balkans during the 580s. In 586 they besieged Thessalonica; the

75

next year they invaded Epirus, Thessaly, Attica and Euboea and occupied parts of the Peloponnese.

The events of the past ten years had demonstrated to the Byzantines that a policy of military defence on their northern border, supplemented by efforts to buy and play off the barbarians, could no longer hold the Danube. Only a determined attempt to crush the Avars and the Slavs in their own homes could put an end to their periodic invasions of the Balkans, during which the defenceless Byzantine population was indeed reduced, in Polybius' phrase, to "murmur indignantly, and endure". Yet so long as the bulk of the imperial troops was engaged in trying to save the remnants of Justinian's conquests in Italy from the Lombards and in fighting Persia, no active policy on the Danube was possible. In the early 590s, however, the situation changed. The Byzantines consolidated their hold on the Po valley, and, more importantly, the successful completion of the Persian war (591) enabled the Emperor Maurice to transfer his seasoned troops from the eastern front to the Balkans. Priscus, his ablest commander, was entrusted with the double duty of holding the lower Danube and of asserting the emperor's authority on its northern bank. Though he was not immediately successful in either task, the tide gradually began to turn. In 596 he recaptured Belgrade. In 600 a treaty between Byzantium and the Avars fixed the empire's frontier on the Danube, Maurice undertaking to increase the annual tribute which he and his two predecessors had periodically paid them. But in 601 Priscus was across the river, carrying the war into the enemy's territory. Defeated several times by the Byzantines, Bayan retreated northward to the Tisza valley, where his forces were again routed by Priscus. Not since the days of Trajan and Marcus Aurelius had Roman power asserted itself so effectively north of the Danube.

Maurice's victories, which seemed to promise the Balkans some respite from Avaro-Slav attacks, proved ephemeral. In 602 the emperor's order that the troops were to winter north of the Danube provoked a mutiny. The rebellious army marched on Constantinople, where it overthrew Maurice and proclaimed emperor their leader Phocas. During his disastrous reign (602–10) the Danube frontier, which had been held, however precariously, throughout the sixth century, finally broke down, and Slavs and Avars surged over the Balkans. It is worth noting that these early decades of the seventh century, which saw the occupation of the greater part of the peninsula by the Slavs, also witnessed, in the opinion of many scholars, the death of the late Roman Empire and the beginnings of the process which led to the emergence of the medieval Byzantine world.

The occupation of the Balkan peninsula by the Slavs seems to have taken place mainly during the reign of Phocas and the early years of the reign of Heraclius (610–41). Its history is obscure: and, so far as we can legitimately argue from the silence of the sources, we can perhaps assume that in the countryside it proceeded slowly and followed no systematic plan. But whenever the Slavs attacked important cities, and were led or supported by the Avars, the pattern was that of a military conquest. The Avaro-Slav invasions developed into a three-pronged attack: south-westward to the Adriatic, southward to the Aegean, south-eastward to the Bosphorus. The great metropolis of Salona on the Adriatic, the capital of Roman Dalmatia, was sacked between 612 and 615; the lands south of the Sava were occupied by the Slavs, and Byzantine authority on the Adriatic coast was reduced to a few cities, such as Iader (Zadar), Tragurium (Trogir), Spalatum (Split), Ragusa (Dubrovnik), Acruvium (Kotor), Butua (Budva), Lissus (Lješ) and Dyrrachium, and to some off-shore islands. Thessalonica was attacked several times by the Slavs and Avars during the first quarter of the seventh century; and in 626 Constantinople lived through the most dangerous siege it had yet endured. While the emperor was in eastern Asia Minor, preparing an attack on Persia, the Avar khagan at the head of a large army of Avars, Slavs, Bulgars, and Gepids appeared on 29 July before the Byzantine capital; simultaneously a Persian army which had marched across Asia Minor was encamped near Chalcedon on the Asiatic side of the Bosphorus. The danger which Byzantium's arms and diplomacy always sought to avert had at last materialized: its northern and eastern foes had coordinated their efforts and launched a concerted attack on Constantinople. The khagan's forces are said to have numbered 80,000 men—probably three or four times the number of soldiers the Byzantines could muster. His strategic plan was to breach the land walls by an infantry assault between the Gates of Pempton and Polyandriou, half-way between the Golden

77

Horn and the Sea of Marmara; to deploy as a supporting force the Slav *monoxyla*, or dug-out canoes, which were to sail from the upper end of the Golden Horn and attack the city from the north; and to use some of these Slav boats to transport the Persian army across the Bosphorus. The land attack was supported by elaborate siege engines which the Avars had brought with them: catapults that hurled stones, battering rams covered by "tortoises" or protective shields, and wooden towers which were advanced against the city walls. Though the Avar cavalry succeeded in storming part of the Blachernae quarter near the Golden Horn, which lay outside the main fortifications, the Byzantines under the command of the *magister* Bonus repulsed the infantry assaults on the land walls. Fortunately for them, the imperial fleet consisting of seventy *dromons*, swift-moving warships, was stationed in home waters, and was able to prevent the link-up between the Avars and the Persians. The decisive phase of the battle was fought on 7 August. The Byzantine navy, aware of the khagan's plan, intercepted the Slavonic *monoxyla* in the northern part of the Golden Horn and destroyed them. The slaughter was so great that the water became red with the blood of the Slav sailors. The same night the khagan raised the siege, and the Avars began to withdraw to Pannonia. Never again were they able seriously to threaten Byzantium. The Persian troops, which had remained throughout passive spectators of the siege, returned home in the spring of the following year. The empire had been saved by the land walls of Constantinople, its overwhelming naval superiority and the efficiency of its military intelligence.

Another important factor in the Byzantine victory of 626 was morale. In the absence of Heraclius, the citizens of Constantinople were inspired during the siege with civic and religious fervour by the Patriarch Sergius, the head of the Byzantine Church. He, no less than his sovereign, instilled a fresh spirit of resistance into the people of Byzantium, and provided this resistance with a new spiritual and moral foundation. The belief that the empire was divinely protected, and that its victories were those of the Christian religion, was not new in Byzantium; but it acquired a more compelling force in the reign of Heraclius, whose victories over the Persians, the Avars, and the Slavs were hailed as the triumph of Christ and His Church over the forces of pagan barbarism. This conviction that the empire's wars were holy wars, so characteristic of medieval Byzantium, sustained the citizens of Thessalonica and Constantinople during the sieges of their cities by the Avaro-Slav hordes in the early seventh century; and it led them to ascribe the salvation of their cities to the personal intervention of their supernatural defenders, St. Demetrius, the patron saint of Thessalonica, and the Mother of God, the heavenly protectress of Constantinople. Nowhere is this belief in the heavenly protection vouchsafed to the empire more eloquently expressed than in the words of the *Akathistos* Hymn still in current use in the liturgy of the Orthodox Church:

> To thee, the invincible Captain, do I, thy City, freed from danger, dedicate the thanksgiving for victory, O Mother of God; but, since thou hast power irresistible, free me from all kinds of peril, that I may cry out to thee: Hail, Bride unbrided.[14]

It is now believed that the *Akathistos* was composed in the sixth century, and that these celebrated words of the *prooemium* which now forms part of it were later added after one of the sieges of Constantinople. However, whether they were written by the Patriarch Sergius after the Avars retreated from Constantinople, or by the Patriarch Germanus when the Arab siege was lifted in 718, they are an eloquent expression of the feelings of triumph and gratitude which the Byzantines felt at the salvation of their city in the summer of 626.

But outside Constantinople and Thessalonica and the few cities on the Adriatic coast to which the Byzantines managed to cling, nearly the whole of the Balkan peninsula was lost. The Slavs, freed from Avar domination after 626, continued to occupy the countryside and the inland cities, probably including Niš and Sofia, and to push southward across Thessaly and Epirus into the Peloponnese. They had, moreover, taken to the sea, pillaged the Aegean islands and even raided Crete (623). We may assume that they used the Belgrade-Constantinople highway as well as the roads over the Balkan passes to move into Northern Thrace, and the Morava-Vardar route to push into Macedonia and towards Thessalonica. They entered the Peloponnese probably both by the land route over the Isthmus of Corinth and, in their *monoxyla*, across the Gulf of Patras.

The results of the Slav invasions of the Balkans is a subject that has provoked much controversy, due partly to the paucity of the evidence, written and archaeological, relating to the seventh and eighth centuries which form one of the darkest periods in the history of the peninsula. The ethnographic situation can, however, be described with a fair degree of accuracy. Virtually all the northern and central regions of the Balkans, north of the fortieth parallel, from the Alps to the Black Sea and from the Adriatic to the Aegean, were occupied by the Slavs. Only in some coastal areas and in the more inaccessible mountains of the interior was the pre-existing population able to maintain itself and to seek refuge: the cities on the Adriatic seaboard, largely Latin-speaking, and the Greek cities which studded the Black Sea coast from the Danube to the Bosphorus, remained under Byzantine authority; while some of the autochthonous Illyrians and Thracians retreated into the Dinaric chain, the Albanian highlands, the Pindus, the Rhodopes and the Balkan mountains. Thessalonica and Constantinople stood out as impregnable fortresses; but the first city was all but ringed by Slavonic territory, while the Byzantine capital maintained, at least until the end of the seventh century, only a precarious hold on Eastern Thrace. In the southern regions of the peninsula the situation was not radically different. Thessaly, Epirus, and the western districts of the Peloponnese were densely Slavicized. But the cities which could be relieved by sea—Athens, Corinth, Patras, Monemvasia—seem to have maintained Byzantine garrisons for at least part of the time, and on the rugged eastern coast of the Peloponnese the Greek population held its ground. The rest of the Peloponnese was for nearly two centuries outside effective Byzantine control. Contemporary accounts, scarce though they are, testify unanimously to the fact that the Slavicization of the southern part of the Balkan peninsula was widespread and thorough. Isidore of Seville could write with scarcely any exaggeration that at the beginning of Heraclius' reign "the Slavs took Greece from the Romans".[15] Between 723 and 728 the pilgrim Willibald, on his way from Western Europe to Palestine, stopped at Monemvasia on the south-eastern tip of the Peloponnese, a town which, his biographer informs us, lay "in the land of the Slavs".[16] And Constantine Porphyrogenitus, writing soon after 934 and describing the Peloponnese, states that after the great plague of 746–7 "the whole country was Slavicized and became barbarian".[17]

How long the Slavs remained the dominant population in Greece and the Peloponnese; how permanently their colonization affected the ethnic landscape and cultural life of these areas; how successful were the attempts of the Byzantine authorities to absorb and Hellenize them: these controversial questions will be considered in the next chapter. Here an attempt must be made to assess the more immediate effects of their invasions. These, at first, were wholly destructive. It is essential to realize that, despite the temporary agreements concluded by Byzantium with the Slavs in the sixth century, the latter, unlike the Germans, occupied Roman provinces not as *foederati*, seeking a legitimate and subordinate place within the empire, but as invaders bent on conquest. The destruction wrought by the Slavs in the Balkans was extensive and thorough. The cities of the interior were sacked; large areas of the countryside were laid waste and were turned, in the words of Procopius, into a "Scythian wilderness"; the Roman and Byzantine administrative machinery totally collapsed; the network of bishoprics established since the fourth century in the principal cities of Illyricum was almost wholly uprooted, and the once flourishing Christianity of this region extinguished for several centuries; whole stretches of the countryside were emptied of their inhabitants who, when they escaped the slaughter, either fled or were deported in thousands to regions north of the Danube; and the ethnographic map of the Northern Balkans was permanently transformed.

It seems unlikely, however, that this wholesale destruction, mournfully described by contemporary authors and strikingly confirmed by recent archaeological work at Athens and Corinth, wholly precluded any peaceful relations between the Slav invaders and their victims. These relations must have become more constructive as the Slavs began to settle on and cultivate the soil which they occupied. In the third quarter of the seventh century we hear of a certain Perbundus, chieftain of a tribe of Macedonian Slavs, who lived in Thessalonica, wore Byzantine dress and spoke fluent Greek.[18] In general, however, our knowledge of the culture of the Slavs is too scanty to allow any clear picture to be drawn of its encounter with Byzantine civilization in this early period. To judge from the brief reports of Byzantine authors of the sixth and seventh centuries, the Slavs practised an agricultural and pastoral economy, living in small rural settlements, and were grouped within a tribal society based on kinship. Their religion was monotheistic, but included the belief in secondary divinities. According to Procopius, the Slavs "believe that one god, the maker of lightning, is alone lord of all things and they sacrifice to him cattle and all other victims. . . . They reverence, however, rivers and nymphs and some other spirits, and they sacrifice to all these also, and they make their divinations in connection with these sacrifices."[19] Tribal societies are usually marked by the weak development of political institutions and by the prevalence of "primitive democracy": and Procopius, in fact, states that the Slavs "are not ruled by one man, but they have lived from of old under democracy, and consequently everything which involves their welfare, whether for good or for ill, is referred to the people".[20] By contrast the political institutions of the Slavonic Antes in South Russia appear to have been more centralized, with kings wielding authority over unions of tribes. The monarchical structure of the Antic society may well have developed as a result of Sarmatian influence.

With the sole exception of the plain between the lower Danube and the Balkan Mountains, where the Slavs were incorporated in the late seventh century into the Bulgar kingdom, the Slavonic communities in the peninsula seem to have remained for long in the tribal stage. Certainly no developed political institutions and nothing that could be properly termed a state can be detected among the Balkan Slavs—with the above-mentioned exception—until the ninth century. Herein lies a basic difference between the Slavonic and the Germanic invasions of Roman imperial territories. The Slavs were far slower than the Germans in appreciating the advantages to be derived from political association with the empire, from the acceptance of Roman laws and institutions, and from the prestige their chieftains could gain by becoming the subjects and vicegerents of the emperor in Constantinople. No Clovis or Theoderic arose among the Slavs, during the first two centuries of their sojourn in the Balkans, to mould their scattered communities into a nation or state and to enable their barbarian culture to achieve peaceful and profitable symbiosis with the Graeco-Roman civilization of Byzantium. Perhaps the invading Slavs had destroyed too much for any such cultural assimilation to be possible as yet. It seems significant that the only clear evidence of Byzantine influence upon the Slavs at the time of their invasions relates to military technique, and is exemplified in the above-quoted judgement of a contemporary that they had "learnt to fight better than the Romans".[21] Another reason for the cultural backwardness of the Balkan Slavs in the seventh and eighth centuries lies in the fact that—again in contrast to the Goths and the Franks—they remained in the period of their migrations and settlement largely impervious to the influence of Christianity. Political, military and religious factors thus combined in this period to isolate the Slavs from their more civilized neighbours in the Balkans. The Byzantines called their tribal communities *Sklaviniae* (sing. *Sklavinia*), a term of central importance in the early medieval historical geography of the Balkans. Scattered throughout the peninsula, the *Sklaviniae* were regions which usually possessed a geographical unity and were often centred on river valleys, after which their inhabitants were named: thus the Timochane lived on the Timok, the Moravane on the Morava, the Strimoniti on the Struma and the Narentani on the Narenta (Neretva). Politically, the *Sklaviniae* designated areas occupied by the Slavs, over which Byzantium had lost all effective control but which had acquired no alternative form of central administration. Their status is succinctly defined by the Greek *Chronicle of Monemvasia*, probably composed in the ninth or the early tenth century: the Peloponnesian Slavs were, it states, "subject neither to the emperor of the Romans nor to anyone else".[22]

The Slavonic invasions of the Balkans had several long-term effects on the history of Eastern Europe, two of which may be mentioned here. Illyricum, the Roman prefecture which covered the entire Balkan peninsula with the exception of Thrace, had for centuries provided some of the best soldiers for the armies of Byzantium. The Avaro-Slav invasions, which resulted in the slaughter, deportation or flight into the mountains of great numbers of autochthonous Illyrians and Thracians, all but eliminated Illyricum as a source of conscripts. In search of new recruiting grounds, the Byzantines turned to the region of the Caucasus, and especially to Armenia; the important role played in the early Middle Ages by Armenians in the armed forces and in the government of the empire dates from the late sixth century, and was an indirect result of the Slavonic invasions of the Balkans. Furthermore, these invasions contributed to the estrangement between the Greek and the Latin halves of Christendom. So long as Illyricum contained a sizeable Latin-speaking population, peacefully intermingling with the Greeks, and the trans-Balkan routes between Constantinople and Rome remained open, the Balkan peninsula formed a bridge between the Byzantine and the Latin worlds. The Slavonic invasions largely removed the Latin-speaking elements of Illyricum, and interposed a barrier of pagan barbarism which for more than two centuries made any movement across the Balkans exceedingly hazardous. This continental obstacle contributed, at least as much as the Arab domination over the Mediterranean, to the growing cultural rift between Eastern and Western Europe. Latin, hitherto the official language of the Byzantine Empire, was replaced by Greek in the first half of the seventh century and soon largely forgotten. The depth of this cultural schism should not be exaggerated: the Roman traditions, at least in the realms of law, government and political thought, remained strong in Byzantium; the consciousness of a still united Christendom survived in Eastern and Western Europe at least until the thirteenth century; and the physical barrier to trans-Balkan communications was to some extent removed in the ninth century, when most of the Balkan Slavs were converted to Christianity and entered the civilized community of Europe. Yet it remains true that the Slavonic occupation of the Balkans, by blocking and partially destroying a vital channel of communications between Greeks and Latins, contributed to their mutual estrangement in the seventh and eighth centuries, a decisive period during which political and religious factors were pulling the Byzantine and the Roman Churches increasingly apart. As for the Avars, the long-term effects of their invasions were mainly on the development of the Empire's military tactics. It was above all from the Avars that, in the sixth and seventh centuries, the Byzantines borrowed the techniques, used against their northern and eastern enemies, of rapid manoeuvres, feigned retreats, ambushes and traps. In these new tactics of guerrilla warfare the decisive role was played by the light-armed cavalry, formed of carefully trained archers. The importance ascribed to this cavalry in successive manuals of military instruction, issued to imperial commanders from *c*. 600 to the late tenth century, as well as their armies' adoption of the tactics of "dogging and pouncing"[23], are striking instances of the influence exerted by the Eurasian nomads on the Byzantine conduct of war in the early middle ages.

There was little the Byzantines could do to halt the spread of the Slavs over the Balkans during the seventh century, and the proliferation of independent *Sklaviniae*. Only the main coastal cities were able to withstand the Avaro-Slav onslaughts. After 626 Constantinople was not besieged again by invaders from the north until the early ninth century; but Thessalonica remained under pressure from the Slavs throughout much of the seventh: and it was probably to relieve this threat that Constans II in 658, and Justinian II in 688-9, campaigned against the Slavs of Macedonia; on the latter occasion the emperor entered Thessalonica in triumph, where he offered solemn thanks to St. Demetrius for having once again saved his city. These are the only recorded examples of a successful Byzantine counter-offensive against the Slavs between 626 and the late eighth century.

The only other weapon left to the Byzantines was diplomacy. Fortunately for the empire, the traditions of Justinian's foreign policy were revived with considerable success by Heraclius. The main achievements of his policy in the north, aimed at the prevention of further Avar invasions, were three. About 623, the Slavs of Bohemia, Moravia and Slovakia revolted against the Avars with the help of Samo, a Frankish merchant, and founded under his leadership a short-lived kingdom which extended from the upper Elbe to the middle Danube. It is likely that Samo's rebellion was instigated by Heraclius' diplomacy; and there is no doubt that the rise of his realm, by weakening the power of the Avars on the eve of their assault on Constantinople, served the interests of Byzantium. Of more lasting importance were the measures taken by the emperor, probably soon after 626, to relieve the Avar pressure in Illyricum and on the middle Danube. Constantine Porphyrogenitus relates in the *De Administrando Imperio* how Heraclius enlisted against the Avars the aid of another ally. These were the Croats, who lived at that time in "White Croatia" north of the Carpathians, in present-day Galicia, Silesia and Eastern Bohemia. A group of them, invited into the Balkans by the Byzantine government, defeated and expelled the Avars from Illyricum, and were then settled by order of the emperor in the lands between the Drava and the Adriatic which they had liberated. A little later the Serbs, a people closely related to the Croats, also sought Byzantine protection; and in similar circumstances some of them migrated from "White Serbia" north of the Carpathians (present-day Saxony) to the Balkans, where they were settled by Heraclius in their present home, east of Croatia. On their arrival in the Balkans, the Croats and the Serbs became subjects of Byzantium, and were converted to Christianity by missionaries sent from Rome at the emperor's request.[24] The reliability of this story has often been doubted by scholars; at least one of its elements, however—the existence of a White Croatia north of the Carpathians—is corroborated by the independent testimony of medieval Arab geographers[25] and of King Alfred of England;[26] and most modern historians, while recognizing that it contains legendary features, regard Constantine's account of the migrations of the Croats and Serbs to the Balkans as substantially true. The ethnic origin of the Croats and the Serbs has also provoked some scholarly controversy: but whether we regard them as Slavs, and their migration as the last wave of the Slavonic invasions of the Balkans, or as alien people, possibly of Caucasian origin, they were absorbed in the course of time by the Slavs who had preceded them a generation or so earlier, and to whom they gave their ethnic names. Their conversion by Roman missionaries—their new homes in Illyricum were then within the jurisdiction of the Latin Church—was doubtless superficial and impermanent, for the Christianization of Serbia and Croatia had to be carried out afresh in the ninth century; nor should we ascribe too literal a significance to Constantine's assertion that the Serbs and the Croats were, from the time of their arrival in the Balkans, "in servitude and submission" to the emperor of Byzantium[27] – an assertion that betrays the imperial claims of the mid-tenth century, when the De Administrando Imperio was compiled. There is no doubt, however, that these new settlers, subjected in some degree to Byzantine suzerainty and, at least at first, to the civilizing influence of Christianity, provided a measure of stability in the chaos which the Avaro-Slav invasions of the preceding sixty years had brought to the Balkans.

A significant feature of Heraclius' relations with the Croats and Serbs was his use of Christianity as a means of restraining the warlike instincts and of ensuring the loyalty to the empire of his new subject-allies. According to Constantine:

> after their baptism the Croats made a covenant, confirmed with their own hands and by oaths sure and binding in the name of St. Peter the Apostle, that never would they go upon a foreign country and make war on it, but rather would live at peace with all who were willing to do so.[28]

The intermingling of religious and political motives, and the close association of church and state in the common task of extending the hegemony of the Christian Empire, are constant and characteristic features of Byzantium's relations with the peoples of Eastern Europe. They are already apparent in the missions of Justinian's reign: of which two examples may be cited. The first, from the religious point of view, was a failure. In 527–8 a certain Gordas, King of the Huns (probably either the Utigurs or the Onogurs), who lived in the neighbourhood of the Crimean city of Bosporus, came to Constantinople and was baptized there. His sponsor was Justinian himself. Loaded with presents, Gordas was sent back to his own country where, as godson and subject-ally of the emperor, he was expected to guard the interests of Byzantium in the Crimean sector. His more specific task was to provide military aid to the Byzantine garrison in Bosporus in the event of enemy attack. But the imperial diplomats had played their cards too hastily: most of Gordas' subjects disliked both Christianity and the Byzantine protectorate; and when their king started to convert them by force, and had the nation's idols of silver and electrum melted down and minted into coin, they rose in revolt, murdered Gordas and set up his pagan brother in his place. The rebellious Huns then seized Bosporus and slaughtered its garrison. The imperial government, unwilling to accept the loss of its strategically important Crimean colony and to endure this affront to the empire's prestige, reacted vigorously. It dispatched a fleet and an army to the Crimea. The latter marched through Bessarabia and along the northern coast of the Black Sea—a noteworthy event, for this is the only recorded instance of an invasion of South Russia by Byzantine armed forces. The Huns retreated from Bosporus, and the empire's authority was restored in the city.

After this painful episode Justinian had the walls of Bosporus rebuilt and the fortified line in the Southern Crimea strengthened.[29]

The second example is that of another mission to the Huns, almost contemporary with Gordas' baptism. It was accomplished in the North Caucasian sector. About the year 535 an Armenian bishop by the name of Kardutsat went, accompanied by seven priests, from Arran (Caucasian Albania) to the land of the "Huns" (probably the Sabiri), who lived in the steppes to the north of the Caucasus, to comfort some Byzantine captives and to preach the Gospel. He stayed in his missionary diocese for seven years, baptized many Huns and translated some books—doubtless the Scriptures and the liturgy—into their language. When the emperor learnt of the missionaries' achievements, he sent them a convoy of thirty mules loaded with flour, wine, oil, linen cloths and ecclesiastical vessels. Kardutsat was succeeded as the head of the Hunnic Christian community by another Armenian bishop, Maku. This remarkable missionary, we are told by a contemporary Syriac writer, "built a brick church and planted plants and sowed various kinds of seeds and did signs and baptized many".[30] Here, condensed into a vivid miniature, are all the essential features of a successful Byzantine-sponsored mission to the nations of the steppe: the eagerness to preach the Gospel to pagan barbarians; the use of vernacular translations of the Scriptures and the liturgy in order to facilitate their conversion; the support, political and economic, given to the mission by the imperial government; the missionaries' efforts to convert the nomads to a settled, agricultural way of life, and thus to provide a stable framework for the religious and cultural growth of their community; their willingness to place their technical expertise—in this case their architectural and botanical skill—at the service of their flock; and the shrewd flexibility of imperial diplomacy (for the Armenian clerics who worked to promote the interests of the Orthodox Empire among the Huns were, in all probability, Monophysites): this picture is an epitome of many a later Byzantine mission to the nations of Eastern Europe.

It was in this same area, north of the Caucasus, that Heraclius' policy of neutralizing the Avar attacks on the Balkans achieved its third and greatest triumph. In 619 the Byzantine court and government were hosts to a party of "Huns" who had arrived in Constantinople together with their ruler. The visitors were baptized in the capital, the emperor becoming godfather to the Hunnic monarch, and the noble lords and ladies of Byzantium standing sponsors to his retainers and their wives. The distinguished guests were rewarded with presents, and their ruler before his return home was granted the title of *patricius* of the Roman Empire.[31] The details and chronology of the ensuing events are confused and in part controversial; but the following reading of the facts is not inconsistent with the evidence of the sources. The "Huns" in question were the Onogurs, a people of West Siberian origin, belonging to the Bulgaric (West Turkic) linguistic group and related to the Kutrigurs and the Utigurs. Since the second half of the fifth century they had lived on the eastern coast of the Sea of Azov and in the Kuban' valley. The Onogur ruler who came to Constantinople in 619 was called Organa; and with him was his nephew Kovrat, who was later to become the architect of his nation. Kovrat, according to a seventh century Egyptian chronicler, was baptized in Constantinople in his childhood, was brought up in the imperial palace and was united to the Emperor Heraclius by a close friendship which lasted until the latter's death. "After he had been baptized with life-giving baptism he overcame all the barbarians and heathens through virtue of holy baptism."[32] In 619, however, Kovrat's victories were in the future: his people were still under Avar rule. However, the Byzantine alliance promised the Onogurs a mitigation of this yoke; and Heraclius, by this diplomatic masterstroke, secured in the North Caucasian sector a subject-ally who could be counted upon to counteract the Avar threat to his Balkan provinces and to protect at the same time the empire's northern flank against Persia.

Kovrat must have assumed supreme power over his people some time between 619 and 635. Towards the end of this period he led a successful revolt against the Avars and expelled them from his country; he then sent an embassy to Constantinople, confirmed the Onogur-Byzantine alliance, and was in his turn elevated to the rank of *patricius*.[33] The imperial diplomatists and missionaries were more successful with the Onogurs than they had been a century earlier with the Crimean Huns. Kovrat's loyalty to Heraclius and the spell cast upon him by his early memories of Constantinople served the empire in good stead. His kingdom, known to the Byzantines as "Old Great Bulgaria", undoubtedly built with East Roman support, and extending from the Caucasus to the Don and probably as far as the lower Dnieper, acted until his death in 642 as the guardian of Byzantium's interests in the North Caucasian area and in the South Russian steppes.

The Onogur-Byzantine alliance seems to have come to a sudden end soon after Kovrat's death. Towards the middle of the century Old Great Bulgaria broke up under the blows of a new invader from Asia, the Khazars, who struck westward from the lower Volga. In the scattering of tribes that followed, one of the branches of the Onogur people suddenly emerged as a menacing cloud on Byzantium's northern horizon. Led by Kovrat's son Asparuch, a horde of considerable size moved westward across the steppe and, probably soon after 670, arrived on the delta of the Danube. Like so many of their predecessors who had reached this terminal point on the historic highway of Eurasia—most recently the Avars—the Onogurs longed to cross the Danube, partly to escape from the hazards of the steppe, partly, no doubt, because, being then in a transitional stage between pastoral nomadism and an agricultural economy, they sought for lands to colonize and cultivate. And so, from their grazing grounds in Southern Bessarabia and from the natural stronghold they had occupied probably to the north of the Danube delta, Asparuch's hordes began, in the 670s, to push southward into the Dobrudja. It was the traditional policy of Byzantium to welcome potential allies on the northern bank of the Danube, but to oppose by every means their attempts to cross the river: so in 680 a large squadron of Byzantine warships, under the personal command of the Emperor Constantine IV, sailed up the Black Sea coast and disembarked north of the Danube estuary; simultaneously a detachment of cavalry was rushed across Thrace to the river. But the Bulgars—as the Balkan Onogurs were to be known henceforth to the Byzantines—taking advantage of the terrain, avoided battle and retired behind the swamps and lagoons of the delta. The emperor, stricken by gout, retired to Mesembria, and his forces, having achieved nothing, were obliged to withdraw. While they were crossing the Danube they were attacked by the Bulgars and driven back, suffering many losses. The victorious Bulgars advanced to the neighbourhood of Varna and occupied the Dobrudja. The empire was in no position to expel the invaders: the Bulgars had come to stay. In 681 Constantine IV concluded peace with Asparuch and undertook to pay an annual tribute to his people. Thus was Byzantium forced to acknowledge the existence of an independent barbarian state on imperial territory. The extent of this disaster may not have been immediately apparent to the Byzantines: for the area occupied by the Bulgars south of the Danube had to all intents and purposes been lost to the empire after the Slav invasions. Yet the *Sklaviniae*, here as elsewhere in the Balkan peninsula, were loose tribal associations, lacking any clearly defined political structure, and over them the fiction of Byzantine sovereignty could still be maintained. The Bulgars, whose political institutions and military organization had developed long before they came to the Balkans, were a different matter. Asparuch had carved himself a powerful kingdom on Byzantine soil. For the first time in its history the empire was compelled formally to relinquish sovereignty over a significant fragment of the Balkan peninsula. The peace treaty of 681 was indeed, in the words of a medieval Byzantine chronicler, "a disgrace to the Romans".[34]

Asparuch's realm extended on both sides of the lower Danube, from the mouth of the Dniester to the Balkan Mountains. It comprised Southern Bessarabia, some of the Wallachian plain, the whole of the Dobrudja, and the province of Lower Moesia between the Black Sea coast and the Timok river. The latter region became the political and economic kernel of the country henceforth to be known as Bulgaria. It was in Eastern Moesia that Asparuch established his capital, Pliska, a fortress which inherited the strategic position of the Roman Marcianopolis, guarded the southern approaches to the Dobrudja, and controlled the northern sector of the road linking the Danube, across one of the Balkan passes, with Anchialus and Constantinople.

The Bulgars' new home in the Balkans had, during the past eighty years or so, been colonized by the Slavs. There is no doubt that the Moesian Slavs were subjugated by Asparuch's horde. However, in his subsequent treatment of his Slavonic subjects Asparuch showed himself a statesman as well as a conqueror. He first settled them on the periphery of his kingdom, as guardians of its military frontiers: thus the tribe of the Severi was transferred from its home by the Veregava pass in the Balkan Mountains to the eastern borders of Bulgaria, which it was expected to defend against the attacks launched by the Byzantines from the cities they still held on the Black Sea coast; while another group of Slavs, collectively known as "the Seven Tribes", was established by Asparuch along the southern frontier and also on the western borders, where his realm abutted on the lands of the Avars. Gradually some of the Moesian Slavs appear to have agreed to collaborate politically with the Bulgars, whose growing hegemony in the North-Eastern Balkans promised their subjects a permanent relief from Avar attacks and the prospect of further territorial aggrandizement at the expense of Byzantium. This symbiosis probably saved the Slavs in this area from losing their ethnic identity: for, had they not been incorporated into the Bulgar kingdom, they would doubtless have been as thoroughly Hellenized in the course of time as the Slavs in Greece. In fact, during the next two centuries, they became an increasingly important partner, and eventually the dominant element, in the medieval Bulgarian state. For some time to come Byzantine writers continued to differentiate between Bulgar and Slav inhabitants of this realm. But the assimilation of the Turkic Bulgars by the far more numerous Slavonic population gathered momentum; recent archaeological discoveries suggest that this fusion had advanced considerably by the ninth century;[35] and by the tenth century Bulgaria was to all intents and purposes a Slav country.

The Bulgars had not long been established in the Balkans before their realm began to play a significant role in Byzantine politics. The Emperor Justinian II, as the result of a revolution in Constantinople, had been deposed and exiled to Cherson in 695. Pursued by the vengeance of his enemies in the capital, he fled from the Crimea to the Khazar-controlled city of Phanagoria, at the mouth of the Kuban', and thence to the estuary of the Danube. There he appealed for help to the Khagan Tervel, Asparuch's successor. The Bulgar ruler seized this golden opportunity to intervene in the internal affairs of the empire: in 705 his army of Bulgars and Slavs appeared before the walls of Constantinople. The fortifications once again proved impregnable, but Justinian crawled through a pipe of the aqueduct into the city during the night, and in the ensuing panic regained his throne. The timely, if hardly disinterested, services of the Bulgar khagan were duly rewarded. Tervel was invested by the emperor with the dignity of Caesar.[36] Like Asparuch, Tervel was a pagan; yet he could now glory in a title more resounding than the one which his Christian ancestor Kovrat had obtained from the empire: for the rank of Caesar was, next to the imperial dignity, the highest in the hierarchy of Byzantium. No barbarian ruler had ever risen so high, and the Bulgarians were not soon to forget that their khagan had received, as an associate of the emperor, the homage of the people of East Rome. The Byzantines, however, viewed the ceremony of 705 with different eyes: Tervel's title, which carried no power, could be regarded as a sign of his recognition of the emperor's supreme authority.

The treaty of 705, even more than that of 681, ensured Bulgaria's position as a rising power in the Balkans. The Byzantine authorities had every reason to feel alarmed by the presence of this vigorous alien body on a territory which, despite the treaties signed with Asparuch and Tervel, they persisted in regarding as belonging by right to the empire. The Bulgars had in 705 their first taste of the riches of Constantinople: it was a heady experience; and Tervel showed no signs of behaving as a vassal of the empire. In 712, a year after the death of Justinian II, he invaded Thrace, marched unopposed to the walls of Constantinople and devastated the surrounding country. In 716, as the Arabs were preparing to lay siege to Constantinople, the Emperor Theodosius III concluded a treaty with the Bulgarians. Two of its clauses are of special importance. The frontier between the empire and Bulgaria was fixed along a line running through Northern Thrace, probably from the Gulf of Burgas to a point on the Maritsa about half-way between Philippopolis and Adrianople: this shows that the Bulgarian realm had started to expand into the plain of Thrace, had advanced its frontier to within striking distance of the Byzantine ports of Mesembria and Anchialus, and had reached at one point the Belgrade-Constantinople highway.

The ports and the highway had a commercial as well as a strategic importance, and it is noteworthy that another clause of the treaty provided for regular state-controlled trade between the two countries. It was probably in 716 that the Bulgarians began to play

93

an active part in the export of Thracian corn to the Byzantine cities on the Black Sea coast and in the import of manufactured goods from Constantinople and the Mediterranean world through these same towns into the interior of the Balkans. Thus through trade, diplomacy and military expansion, the young Bulgarian state was gradually anchored in the Balkans and brought into closer relationship with the cities of the Byzantine Empire.

The three peace treaties which Byzantium had concluded with the Bulgars were little more than desperate expedients, devised by the imperial diplomats to confine the invaders to the area north of the Balkan Mountains. The territorial arrangements of 716 showed, however, that this policy of containment could not be successful for long. The Bulgarian khagans and many of their *boyars*, the Turkic warrior aristocracy, were consistently hostile to the empire, and could be expected to pursue a policy of further expansion into Thrace. Only a determined attempt to stamp out the parasitical kingdom and to throw the Bulgars back beyond the Danube could, in the view of the Byzantine government, bring permanent relief to the northern frontier. Yet, as the campaigns of the Emperor Maurice had so clearly demonstrated, only when the seasoned imperial troops were transferred from the eastern front to Europe could Byzantium hope to conduct a successful offensive in the Balkans. By the mid-eighth century the victories of Constantine v in Syria, Armenia and Mesopotamia had temporarily removed the Arab menace in the east, and the emperor could turn to what he regarded as the main military and political task of his life—the annihilation of Bulgaria. For some twenty years (756–75) Constantine v devoted his considerable talents as a soldier and diplomatist to this objective. He very nearly succeeded. He took advantage of the political instability which overcame Bulgaria in the third quarter of the eighth century by kindling the latent antagonism between the Bulgar aristocracy and the Slavs; and in a series of nine campaigns, mostly successful, which usually combined—in what was now traditional Byzantine strategy—land attacks across Thrace with naval expeditions to the Danube estuary, he routed the Bulgarian armies again and again. But even his victory by Anchialus in 763, the greatest of his reign, did not subdue the country. Constantine's death on his last campaign (775) left the empire stronger in the Northern Balkans than it had

94

been since the reign of Maurice. But Bulgaria, though exhausted and crippled, was still on the map, its ruling classes more united than ever in their hatred of Byzantium.

The vitality of the Bulgarian state, and the danger which its military recovery could present to the empire, were dramatically demonstrated when Krum, the mightiest of its early rulers, became Sublime Khagan in the early years of the ninth century. The destruction of the Avar Empire by Charlemagne had enabled the Bulgarians to annex Transylvania and the eastern part of present-day Hungary, where many Bulgars lived, thereby vastly increasing the territory, the economic resources and the military potential of their state; and Krum became the sovereign of a kingdom which stretched from Northern Thrace to the Carpathians and from the lower Sava to the Dniester, and adjoined the Frankish Empire on the Tisza. He was soon to prove as great a scourge to the Byzantines as Constantine v had been to the Bulgars. A strong line of imperial fortresses, which had probably been restored by Constantine, extended in a semi-circle south of the Balkan Mountains, barring the Bulgarian advance on central Thrace and Macedonia; its key points were Serdica, Philippopolis, Adrianople and Develtus. During the five years that followed Krum's first major onslaught on Byzantine territory (809), every one of these cities was captured by the Bulgars. Even Mesembria, whose position on a small peninsula at the northern end of the Gulf of Burgas, joined to the mainland by a narrow isthmus, made it almost impregnable, was stormed by Krum after a two weeks' siege (812). Apart from large hoards of gold and silver, the Bulgars gained possession in that city of a supply of Greek fire, the celebrated secret weapon of the Byzantines; and, a fact which illustrates even more clearly the military expertise the Bulgars had acquired, Krum could now rely, when he besieged imperial cities, on the technical advice of the distinguished engineer Eumathius, who had deserted from Byzantine service after the fall of Serdica (809). Despite occasional Byzantine successes, such as the capture and sack of the Bulgar capital of Pliska by the Emperor Nicephorus I, the war was disastrous for the empire. In July 811 Krum gained his most celebrated triumph: a Byzantine army was trapped by the Bulgars in a defile of the Balkan Mountains and slaughtered almost to a man. Nicephorus himself perished in the fray; and from his skull Krum made a goblet, encrusted with silver, out of which he made his *boyars* drink. This was a terrible blow to the empire's prestige: not since the death of Valens on the field of Adrianople (378) had an emperor fallen in battle against the barbarians. Equally dramatic was the appearance in July 813 of Krum's army at the gates of Constantinople. But the land walls proved too strong even for him, and the Bulgars had no fleet: so the khagan offered peace terms. In the meeting which followed with the Emperor Leo v on the shore of the Golden Horn, Krum barely escaped a Byzantine plot to murder him; breathing vengeance, he laid waste the environs of the city, and stormed Adrianople. But the following spring, as he was preparing a huge assault on the Byzantine capital, Krum suddenly died (April 814).

Krum's death removed from Constantinople a danger as acute as that which had faced it during the Avaro-Slav siege of 626. But the balance of power in the Balkans had radically altered. Bulgaria, a country which fifty years before had seemed on the verge of extinction, was now one of the great military powers of Europe. About 816 the Khagan Omurtag made a peace treaty with Byzantium; the frontier between the two realms was to run along the so-called "Great Fence", cutting across Northern Thrace from Develtus by the Gulf of Burgas to Makrolivada near the Maritsa, and thence northward to the Balkan Mountains: it thus coincided with the boundary of 716. The peace between Byzantium and Bulgaria was not to be seriously disturbed until the end of the century. But, although the great fortresses captured by Krum were returned to the empire, the stabilization of its frontier in the Northern Balkans was more apparent than real: Adrianople and Mesembria, it is true, were heavily fortified after 815; but Serdica and Philippopolis, whose fortifications had been dismantled by Krum, were left undefended—a constant encouragement for the Bulgarian state to expand towards the south.

Elsewhere in the Balkans, the situation in the early years of the ninth century was still far from favourable to Byzantium: in the north-west its authority was confined to the main cities on the Adriatic; in the interior, the Serbs had shaken off the shadowy dependence imposed upon them by Heraclius; the Croats in Dalmatia and north of the Sava were subjects of the Frankish Empire;

the central and southern regions of the Balkans were studded with independent *Sklaviniae*, over which the Byzantine administration, operating from the few coastal cities which had escaped the Slavonic occupation, had as yet little or no control. But the ethnic and political map of the Balkans, so fluid and confused during the period of the barbarian invasions and settlements, was gradually becoming stable; and in the course of the ninth century, during which Byzantium made a determined and largely successful effort to regain its power and influence over South-Eastern Europe, the Balkan peninsula began to emerge from its Dark Ages and to assume, in broad outline, the features it was to retain during much of its medieval history.

NOTES

1. Procopius, *Historia arcana*, ch. 18, ed. Haury (Leipzig, 1963), p. 114; English transl.: *Secret History*, R. Atwater (Ann Arbor, 1961), p. 91.
2. Procopius, *De aedificiis*, bk. iv, ed. Haury (Leipzig, 1964), pp. 102–49; English transl.: *The Buildings*, Dewing (London, 1954), pp. 219–315.
3. Procopius, *De bellis*, vii, 14, ed. Haury, ii, pp. 353–4; *History of the Wars*, Dewing, iv, pp. 263–5.
4. *De bellis*, ibid., p. 359; *History of the Wars*, pp. 273–5.
5. *De bellis*, viii, 19, ed. Haury, ii, pp. 584–9; *History of the Wars*, v, pp. 243–51.
6. Agathias, *Historiae*, v, 24–5, ed. R. Keydell (Berlin, 1967), pp. 195–7.
7. *Novella 11: Corpus Iuris Civilis*, ed. R. Schoell and G. Kroll, iii (Berlin, 1904), p. 94.
8. Menander, *Excerpta de legationibus*, ed. C. de Boor, i (Berlin, 1903), p. 283. Cf. Agathias, loc. cit.
9. Procopius, *Historia arcana*, ed. Haury, pp. 51, 123; *Secret History*, pp. 40–41, 97.
10. Menander, *Excerpta de legationibus*, ed. C. de Boor, i, p. 443.
11. Corippus, *In laudem Iustini*, lib. iii: *MGH, auctor. antiquiss.*, iii, 2, pp. 143–4.
12. J. Brunšmid, 'Eine griechische Ziegelinschrift aus Sirmium', *Eranos Vindobonensis* (Vienna, 1893), pp. 331–3.
13. *The Third Part of the Ecclesiastical History of John, Bishop of Ephesus*, transl. R. Payne Smith (Oxford, 1860), pp. 432–3.
14. *The Akathistos Hymn*, introduced and transcribed by E. Wellesz (Copenhagen, 1957) (*Monumenta Musicae Byzantinae*, ix); E. Wellesz, "The 'Akathistos': A study in Byzantine Hymnography", *DOP*, ix–x (1956), pp. 141–74.
15. Isidore of Seville, *Chronicon*, *PL*, 83, col. 1056.

16. *Vita S. Willibaldi, MGH, Script.*, xv, 1, p. 93.

17. *De thematibus*, ed. A. Pertusi (Vatican, 1952), p. 91.

18. A. Tougard, *De l'histoire profane dans les Actes grecs des Bollandistes* (Paris, 1874), pp. 148–57.

19. Procopius, *De bellis*, vii, 14, ed. Haury, ii, pp. 357–8; *History of the Wars*, iv, pp. 270–1.

20. *De bellis*, ibid., p. 357; *History of the Wars*, pp. 268–9.

21. See above, p. 75.

22. P. Charanis, "The Chronicle of Monemvasia and the Question of the Slavonic Settlements in Greece", *DOP*, v (1950), pp. 147–8.

23. A. Toynbee, *Constantine Porphyrogenitus and his World* (London, 1973), pp. 282–322.

24. *DAI*, ch. 30, 31, 32, pp. 138–60.

25. See F. Dvornik, *The Making of Central and Eastern Europe* (London, 1949), pp. 270–1.

26. J. Bosworth, *A Literal English Translation of King Alfred's Anglo-Saxon Version of the Compendious History of the World by Orosius* (London, 1855), p. 37.

27. *DAI*, ch. 31, 32, pp. 150, 160.

28. Ibid., ch. 31, p. 148.

29. Theophanes, *Chronographia*, ed. C. de Boor (Leipzig, 1883), pp. 175–6.

30. *The Syriac Chronicle of Zachariah of Mitylene*, transl. by F. J. Hamilton and E. W. Brooks (London, 1899), pp. 329–31.

31. Nicephorus Patriarcha, *Opuscula historica*, ed. de Boor (Leipzig, 1880), p. 12.

32. *The Chronicle of John, Bishop of Nikiu*, transl. R. H. Charles (London, 1916), p. 197.

33. Nicephorus, *Opuscula historica*, p. 24.

34. Theophanes, *Chronographia*, p. 359.

35. See Zh. Vŭzharova, "Slavyani i prabŭlgari v svetlinata na arkheologicheskite danni", *Arkheologiya* (Sofia), 1971, 1, pp. 1–22 (with a summary in French).

36. Nicephorus, *Opuscula historica*, p. 42.

3

The Balkans in the Ninth Century: the Byzantine Recovery

The ninth century was a turning point in the history of the Balkans. The attacks by the empire's northern neighbours subsided after Krum's death in 814. In the central and southern regions of the peninsula the Slavs began to fall under the military and political control of Byzantium. Further north, the consolidation of the Bulgarian realm and the emergence of new centres of political life in Serbia and Croatia caused the Slav communities to gravitate towards one or the other of these emerging nations. As the latter acquired more developed institutions and a more distinctive group consciousness, their leaders began to reach out for the fruits of Byzantine civilization. This movement of the Balkan Slavs into the empire's political and cultural orbit gathered momentum in the relatively peaceful conditions of the second half of the ninth century, continued through the storms which swept over the peninsula in the tenth, and was completed by about the year 1000. By that time most of the Balkan peoples formed part of the medieval community of East European nations which may be termed the Byzantine Commonwealth.

The earliest and most decisive stages of this movement were the result of a remarkable political and cultural revival which the Byzantine Empire underwent in the middle of the ninth century. Signs of this recovery had appeared earlier: the economic situation within the empire began to improve at the beginning of the century; domestic and foreign trade—the latter directed more and more to the countries of Eastern Europe—was increasing; the main

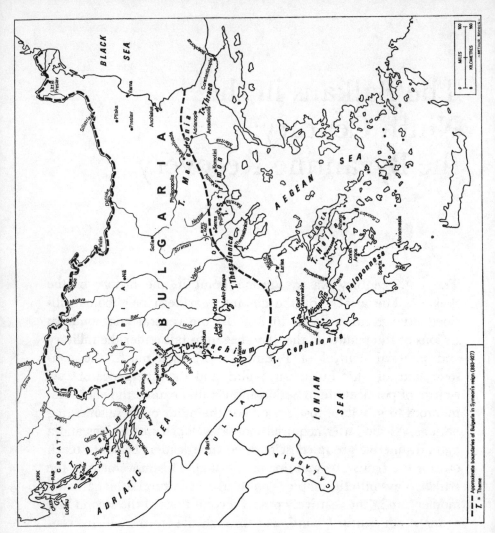

Map 4   The Balkans, *c.* 900

cities of the Balkan peninsula, which the Slav invasions had isolated from the surrounding countryside, began to recover their
former importance; while large numbers of Slav immigrants, their
destructive force now spent and with their man-power absorbed
into the depleted communities of Byzantine farmer-soldiers and
free peasants, contributed materially to the revival of agriculture
in the provinces. The military situation in the Balkans, as the wars
with Bulgaria had demonstrated, was still precarious; but the

empire's northern borders in Thrace and Macedonia, stabilized after 815, were re-enforced by garrisons of soldiers transferred from the Asian provinces.

A new age of recovery and expansion dawned for the empire in the fifth decade of the century. It was inaugurated by four events: the removal of the Arab threat from the eastern frontier; the defeat of Iconoclasm; the revival of secular education; and the resurgence of the missionary energies of the Byzantine Church.

For more than two centuries Byzantium had been waging a defensive war against the Arabs. In the first phase of this conflict, which ended in 718, the empire had fought for its survival. The Umayyad Khalifate, whose capital was Damascus, held sway over the former imperial provinces of Syria, Mesopotamia, Palestine, Egypt and North Africa, and enjoyed supremacy in the Mediterranean; on two occasions, moreover, in 674–8 and 717–18, its forces besieged Constantinople by land and sea. It was only with the greatest difficulty that the Byzantines were able to save their city and their empire—on the first occasion largely owing to the timely invention of Greek fire, in the second case, partly thanks to Bulgarian support. The second phase of the Byzantine-Arab struggle lasted for the next century and a half: though less critical for the empire, it was marked by an almost ceaseless border warfare in Asia Minor, in which the Abbasid Khalifate, whose capital was Baghdad, frequently had the upper hand. In 842, however, the power of the khalifate began to decline, and although the Arabs retained a strong position in the Mediterranean by holding Crete and pursuing their conquest of Sicily, the initiative on the eastern frontier now passed to the Byzantines. In 863 they defeated the Arabs in a major battle in Northern Anatolia. This victory inaugurated the third phase in the war between Byzantium and Islam: henceforth, until the Seljuq successes of the mid-eleventh century, the empire was, on the whole, able to pursue an offensive policy in Asia.

The defeat of Iconoclasm was brought about by men who drew their inspiration from the resistance of a section of the Byzantine Church and society to the attempts of the Iconoclast emperors (726–87 and 813–43) to stamp out the veneration of sacred images. The defenders of the icons, led by St. John of Damascus and later by the monastery of Studios in Constantinople, defended their veneration in writings which came to enjoy great authority not only in Byzantium but throughout Eastern Europe as a whole. These works, in theology, hagiography and hymnology, were widely diffused after the condemnation of Iconoclasm and the restoration of the veneration of images, proclaimed in March 843 by a synod in Constantinople. Its decisions, which ended a crisis which for over a hundred years had divided the church, convulsed the political and social life, exhausted the cultural energies and crippled the foreign policy of the Byzantine Empire, proved a turning point in the history of Eastern Europe. The termination of the Iconoclast controversy was a prime cause of the new vigour and initiative which the empire's foreign policy, now linked more closely than ever to the missionary programme of its church, displayed in the second half of the ninth century: it was then that Byzantine civilization, spreading far beyond the empire's northern frontiers, gained the allegiance of a substantial part of the Slav world. This achievement will be described in a later section of this book; it may be noted here that an important role in this process of diffusion was played by those elements in Byzantine culture which had been accentuated by the defeat of Iconoclasm. Thus the new pattern of church decoration which expressed the cult of the icons, the renewed prestige of monasticism whose representatives had borne the brunt of the Iconoclast persecutions, and the liturgy and hymnography of Byzantium, revised, enlarged and codified by St. John of Damascus and the Studite monks, were all transmitted after 843 by the empire's missionaries to the nations of Eastern Europe.

The Byzantine cultural revival was not confined to the field of religion. A renaissance of secular learning, particularly of classical studies, had begun in the reign of the Emperor Theophilus (829–42). Two of its notable features were the gradual substitution of the minuscule for the uncial writing—a reform which for its cultural significance has been compared to the later invention of printing—and the increase in the number of *scriptoria* which served as workshops for the copying of manuscripts; of these that of Studios was the most important. Theophilus restored the university of Constantinople and appointed as its principal teacher the celebrated scholar Leo the Mathematician. The early history of this university, founded in the reign of Constantine the Great, enlarged and reorganized by Theodosius II in 425 and which survived until the fall of Byzantium in 1453, is in some respects obscure; and the question as to whether it had a continuous existence between the fourth and the ninth centuries remains an open one. Higher education had certainly declined in Byzantium during the eighth century, except for the study of theology which was then concentrated in the patriarchal school. The revival of classical studies and the prestige of secular learning, already apparent in Theophilus' reign, gathered strength after the defeat of Iconoclasm. During the following decade a remarkable group of scholars were assembled in Constantinople: among them were Leo the Mathematician, a man of encyclopaedic knowledge whose interests, apart from mathematics, were focused on natural science and mechanics; Photius, the greatest theologian and philosopher of his age, who played the leading role in this intellectual movement; and Constantine (Cyril), the future apostle of the Slavs. These men had close personal links with each other: Photius and Constantine were probably both pupils of Leo; and although the traditional view that Photius, before he became head of the imperial chancery, had been formally connected with the university has recently been challenged, there seems no reason to doubt that Constantine at least was appointed professor of philosophy. Whether or not Photius ever held an academic post, the mutual relationship and careers of these three scholars illustrate the central role played by the university of Constantinople, reorganized again in 863, not only in the revival of learning, but also in the missionary achievement and in the cultural expansion of ninth century Byzantium: Photius, appointed patriarch of Constantinople in 858, planned during the 860s the missions to Moravia, Bulgaria and Russia; Constantine, after taking part in an embassy to the Arabs (probably in 855–6) and heading another to the Khazars (860–1), led, together with his brother Methodius, the Moravian mission (862–3), which brought Byzantine cultural influence to the lands on both sides of the middle Danube. It seems likely that the training-ground for those who planned and carried out the Byzantine missions to the peoples of Central and Eastern Europe in the third quarter of the ninth century was the university of Constantinople, of which Leo the Mathematician was appointed rector in 863. It was there, in all probability, that the new generation of missionaries and diplomatists acquired not only the necessary expertise in the fields of theology, foreign politics and ethnography, but also two special qualities which they displayed in this period: the tendency to preach the Christian faith on missions abroad not merely by appealing to the Gospel, but by conducting high-level theological and philosophical debates with the more educated of their intended proselytes; and secondly, their awareness that they represented not only the Christian Church, but the prestige of Byzantine civilization and the power and majesty of the emperor of East Rome. Both these traits are exemplified in Constantine's missionary activity: during his disputations with the Arabs and the Khazars he assured the former that all the arts come from Byzantium, and to the latter made this profession of faith:

> Our empire is that of Christ, as the prophet said, "the God of heaven shall set up a kingdom, which shall never be destroyed; and the kingdom shall not be left to other people, but it shall break in pieces and consume all these kingdoms, and it shall stand for ever".[1]

It was not only in the field of foreign missions that the Byzantine recovery of the ninth century affected the future history of the Eastern Empire. By the early years of the century the Byzantine authorities were able to devise and implement a programme whose aims were the recovery of imperial lands occupied for the past two hundred years by the Slavs, and the reduction and assimilation of these barbarian invaders. This was a slow and gradual process, less spectacular than the contemporary achievements of Byzantium abroad, and—owing to the paucity of the sources—far less easy to trace in detail. Yet it resulted, in little more than a hundred years, in the transformation of the political and cultural landscape of the central and southern regions of the Balkan peninsula.

The areas which the Byzantines sought to reclaim first of all and in which they met with particular success were the plains that lie along the Aegean, Adriatic and Ionian seaboards, and are situated, except for Dalmatia, south of the forty-second parallel. Their climate and vegetation are Mediterranean, unlike those of the North Balkan areas and of the Pindus range which belong to the continental, Central European type. These plains form a fringe round the Balkan peninsula: the most important were Thrace, the North

Aegean seaboard, the Macedonian "Campania", Thessaly, Boeotia and Attica, the Peloponnesian coast, Southern Epirus, Western Albania and Dalmatia. Several of these plains penetrated up river valleys deep into the interior, forming "gulfs" of Mediterranean influence; thus the valleys of the Maritsa and the Vardar brought this influence as far north as Philippopolis and Veles; here, in the neighbourhood of the forty-second parallel, the natural boundaries between the Mediterranean and the continental zones are the hills of Sredna Gora on the one hand, and the mountains of Skopska Crna Gora and Šar Planina on the other. The terrain, the climate and the vegetation of these coastal plains sustained a culture very different from the agricultural and pastoral way of life of the interior. A largely Greek population, only temporarily submerged during the Slav invasions; the presence of ancient cities from which imperial power had never wholly vanished; the proximity of the sea which brought relief to their beleaguered garrisons, trade to their merchants in times of peace, and which fostered an outward-looking and cosmopolitan mentality; a diet whose basic ingredients were supplied by the olive, the vine and fish: these conditions, which prevailed in the maritime plains, forced the Slavs who came down from the mountains to adapt themselves to a new way of life, and—whenever they succeeded in surmounting the harsh contrasts of the Mediterranean climate and the unfamiliar perils of wine and malaria—hastened their absorption by the local Greek population.

Physiological and economic factors could not by themselves, of course, ensure the effective assimilation of the Slavs. Before they could be absorbed into the Greek village and urban communities, Byzantium had to assert its political authority and impose its administrative order over the territories which they occupied. In the late eighth century most of this work of reconquest still remained to be done. Macedonia, Northern and Central Greece, and the greater part of the Peloponnese were still dotted with independent *Sklaviniae*. Earlier attempts by Constans II and Justinian II to subdue the Slavs of Macedonia had no lasting results. More effective were the victories gained in 782-3 over the Slavs near Thessalonica, in Central Greece and in the Peloponnese by the Empress Irene's chief minister Stauracius. But in 799 the Slavs of

Thessaly were able, albeit for a short time, to revolt against the Byzantine government.

However, the tide in the Balkans was now gradually turning against the Slavs. In several parts of the peninsula the empire still possessed strongholds which could be used as bridgeheads for the reconquest: the coastal cities—Thessalonica, Athens, Corinth, Patras, Monemvasia—were by now strongly garrisoned and could be supplied by sea; while the eastern coast of the Peloponnese, from Corinth to Cape Malea, had always remained free of Slav invaders. In the reign of Nicephorus I (802–11) the Peloponnesian Slavs revolted and attacked the city of Patras. The rebellion was put down on the emperor's personal orders; whereupon Nicephorus delivered the rebels in bondage to the city's ecclesiastical authorities and, in order to keep the Slavs under control, had colonies of Christians from different parts of the empire forcibly transferred to the Balkans. In their new homes they were granted lands and had to undertake military service.[2] Byzantine writers considered that the defeat of the Slavs at Patras marked the end of the Slav occupation of the Peloponnese. This was an over-optimistic view, for the Peloponnesian Slavs revolted again several times; and on the slopes of Mount Taygetus Slav tribes retained until the Turkish conquest of the fifteenth century their language, their ethnic identity, and a tradition of insubordination to the imperial government. Nevertheless, Nicephorus I's victory over the Slavs at Patras marked a decisive stage in the restoration of Byzantine authority in the southern part of the Balkan peninsula.

Military reconquest was followed by the resorption of the *Sklaviniae* into the empire's administrative structure. Between the seventh and the eleventh centuries the basic units of Byzantine provincial administration were the themes. These were districts in which soldiers were settled on small farms which they held on condition of hereditary military service, and whose governors (usually called *strategoi*, "generals") exercised, under the direct control of the emperor, the supreme military and civil command. Each theme was thus, under the authority of the *strategos* and the indirect sovereignty of his imperial master, a miniature state with its own army, police and civil administration. The theme system did much to strengthen the armed forces and increase the economic resources of the empire, first in Asia Minor and, from the end of the seventh century, in its European provinces as well. It was introduced, slowly and with difficulty at first, then on an increasing scale after 800, into those areas of the Balkans where the Byzantine authorities succeeded in establishing direct political control over the Slavs. The location of these Balkan themes shows how deeply the facts of geography influenced the master-plan conceived by the strategists of Constantinople for the reduction and assimilation of the Slav invaders, and illustrates at the same time the changing fortunes of this Byzantine counter-offensive: for, although it is not always possible to decide with certainty whether the creation of a particular theme reflected the fear or the confidence of the imperial government, it is broadly speaking true that the gradual introduction of the theme system into the Balkans signposts the successive stages in which Byzantine control and administration were re-established in the peninsula.

It is a remarkable fact that every one of the ten themes established in the Balkans between the late seventh and the late ninth century was situated in a coastal plain; all of them lay within the zone of Mediterranean climate; their administrative centres were mostly located in ancient cities whose municipal and cultural traditions went back to Greek and Roman times; and the majority of these cities were seaports which, in periods when Byzantium controlled the Aegean, Ionian and Adriatic seas, could be supplied and garrisoned from Constantinople.

The two earliest Balkan themes were created in the late seventh century. The theme of Thrace, comprising the eastern part of the Thracian plain, nearest to Constantinople, is first mentioned in 687. Its chief city was probably Arcadiopolis. It was presumably set up as a means of defence against the Bulgars who had recently invaded the Balkans. A few years later there arose the theme of Hellas, first mentioned in 695. It was confined to Attica and Boeotia, whose plains open upon the Saronic Gulf and the Straits of Euboea; its administrative centre was Athens, one of the few Balkan cities to have partially escaped the ravages of the Slavs.

For the next hundred years no further themes were set up in the Balkans. This does not mean that Byzantine authority was confined in this period to the themes of Thrace and Hellas. Imperial sovereignty was also maintained, precariously at times, in some of the larger coastal cities of the Peloponnese. Yet it remains true that a regular pattern of Byzantine provincial administration covering a distinct geographical area is attested in this period only in the two peninsulas which project south-eastward from Arcadiopolis to the Bosphorus and from Mount Parnassus to Cape Sounion.

The next theme, that of "Macedonia", was created between 789 and 802. Its name, geographically misleading, expressed no more than the intention of the Byzantine government to use this area as a springboard for the recovery of Macedonia proper, then still in the hands of the Slavs. The theme comprised the central and western part of the Thracian plain; its capital was Adrianople, and its second city Philippopolis.

The process of absorbing the *Sklaviniae* into the network of Balkan themes was accelerated in the early ninth century. The Peloponnesian theme, centred on Corinth, appears at that time (its actual foundation may go back to the late eighth century). Of special importance was the creation, in the same period, of the two themes of Thessalonica and Dyrrachium. These two fortresses, the main bases of Byzantine seapower in the Aegean and the Adriatic, were thus strengthened and, by the addition of the coastal plains that lie behind them, enabled to extend the influence of the empire over the Slavs of the interior. The Thessalonican theme, which comprised the valley of the lower Vardar and probably extended as far north as the gorges of the river, was later to play an important role in the diffusion of Byzantine civilization to the Slavs of Macedonia and Serbia.

The importance attached by the Byzantines to their strongholds on the western seaboard of the Balkan peninsula, which could be used both to police the Ionian and the Adriatic Seas and to subdue the Slav tribes on the coast and in the interior, was further exemplified by three other themes, also founded in the ninth century. The theme of Cephalonia, consisting of the Ionian Islands, was in existence by 809. The coastal plain of Southern Epirus, encircling the gulf of Amvrakia, was organized into a theme in the second half of the century. It was called after its chief city, Nicopolis, which dominated the peninsula of Preveza. The strategic importance of this area went back to ancient times; and the city was founded by the Emperor Augustus to commemorate the battle of Actium which was fought in its immediate vicinity in 31 B.C. Finally, between 868 and 878 the Byzantine possessions in Dalmatia, which since the early seventh century had been reduced to the main coastal cities and the offshore islands, were formed into a theme. In addition to Zadar, its capital, the theme comprised the cities of Trogir, Split, Dubrovnik and Kotor, and the islands of Krk, Cres, Rab and Lošinj. The theme of Dalmatia proved valuable to the empire for several reasons. In the first place it provided a series of bases for the protection of the sea route to Venice, which was then a Byzantine dependency, and for the defence of the empire's naval hegemony in the Adriatic against the Arabs: it was certainly no coincidence that the theme was set up soon after a Byzantine naval squadron had forced the Arab fleet to raise the siege of Dubrovnik (868). Secondly, it supplied the empire with a springboard to subdue the Slav tribes between the Neretva River and Lake Scutari and to extend its influence into Croatia. Thirdly, it was a convenient stepping-stone for the reconquest of Southern Italy, which had recently been lost to the Arabs. The recapture of Bari by the Byzantines (876) proved the first step in their recovery of Apulia and Calabria, achieved in the 880s.

One further Balkan theme, that of Strymon, was probably created in the ninth century: it lay in the Eastern Macedonia, between the southern spurs of the Rhodope Mountains and the North Aegean coast, and comprised the lowlands between the lower courses of the Strymon and the Nestos. Ancient and famous cities, such as Philippi and Neapolis (on the site of Kavalla) stood on this plain; the Via Egnatia, connecting Rome with Constantinople, traversed it; and its strategic significance was due to the gorges of the Strymon and the Nestos which formed the last line of defence against invaders from the north, thrusting towards the Aegean. The Rupel defile of the Strymon, which since the late seventh century had formed the nucleus of a Byzantine *kleisoura*, or fortified mountain march, was one of the gateways to Northern Greece. The principal city of the theme of Strymon was Serres. It is likely that the region situated immediately to the east of this theme was at first administratively attached to it: it comprised the coastal plain between the lower Nestos and the hills which project from the Rhodopes to the sea west of Alexandroupolis; its main cities, Xanthea (Xanthi) and Mosynopolis (Komotini), guarded the southern approaches to the Eskeje and the Turesi passes in the Rhodopes, which were repeatedly used by invaders from Bulgaria. Not later than the eleventh century, this region was raised by the Byzantines to the status of a separate theme, under the name Boleron.

Thus, by the end of the ninth century, the Byzantines had succeeded in establishing administrative control over a string of themes which formed an almost continuous edging around the Balkan peninsula. In some of these districts, notably in Thrace and in Southern Macedonia, Byzantine power extended far inland. In other parts of the interior the situation was different. Broadly speaking, south of a line drawn from Thessalonica to Dyrrachium, the inland *Sklaviniae* were by the year 900 well on the way to being reduced to political dependence on the empire and absorbed into the theme system. By contrast, the *Sklaviniae* of the interior situated north of this line remained—except in Thrace and Southern Macedonia—beyond the reach of Byzantine administration, and in the course of the ninth century were merged into the Slav states of Bulgaria, Serbia and Croatia. Only in the eleventh century, following the conquests of Basil II, was the Byzantine theme system introduced into the North Balkan area.

We know little of the methods used by the Byzantine authorities to bring the Slavs under their administrative control. No doubt they varied from place to place, as did the dues and services to which the Slav communities were subjected. In the tenth century the Slavs of the themes of Thessalonica and Strymon lived under the authority of officers appointed by the *strategoi*, or provincial governors. The Slavs in the region of Patras, after their subjugation in the early ninth century, became serfs of the local bishop and, in addition to the ordinary taxes, were obliged to maintain a lodging house in the city for the free entertainment of the provincial governors, imperial agents and foreign envoys. The Melingoi and the Ezeritae, two Slavonic tribes who lived in Laconia in the Southern Peloponnese, were compelled in the tenth century to accept a headman appointed by the provincial governor, to perform military service under him, and generally to carry out the public duties incumbent on crown peasants.[3]

The incorporation of the *Sklaviniae* into the administrative structure of the themes went together with a determined effort to advance their cultural assimilation. The most effective way of achieving this end was to convert the Slavs to Christianity. No sooner had imperial officials gained a foothold in their communities than the Byzantine authorities applied themselves with vigour to this task. In the coastal regions, and in much of the interior south of the Thessalonica-Dyrrachium line, the work of Christianization began on a large scale in the early ninth century, and was largely completed by the end of the tenth. During these two hundred years the work of the Christian missionaries, supported by the provincial governors and often by the central authorities in Constantinople, was marked by the same interplay of religious and political motives which we have observed in the history of Byzantine missions abroad. The conversion of these Slav subjects had two aspects, the one public and official, the other more spontaneous and less organized.

The public aspect is, not unnaturally, the better documented. Its main feature was the establishment, and in some cases the reconstitution, of a network of bishoprics directly dependent on local metropolitanates which, in their turn, owed allegiance to the patriarchate of Constantinople. Some of these metropolitanates—Philippopolis, Thessalonica, Dyrrachium, Larisa, Athens and Corinth—were ancient sees, most if not all of which had survived the Slavonic invasions. Others, such as Patras and Naupactus-Nicopolis, were former bishoprics which were promoted to metropolitan rank after 800 in order to direct and organize the conversion of the Slavs. By the late ninth century these metropolitan sees were supported by a large number of recently created suffragan bishoprics, some of which, notably in Macedonia and Thessaly, appear to have been set up specifically to minister to the local Slav communities. Though precise information is often lacking, we may assume that many of these Slavonic bishoprics were created in the reign of Basil I who, in association with the Patriarch Photius, planned and directed the conversion of the empire's Slav subjects and was responsible for the re-Christianization of much of the Balkan peninsula.

While this reorganization of the Balkan dioceses was being carried out, a less conspicuous, but perhaps even more effective campaign to convert the pagan Slavs was launched in the lower echelons of the Byzantine Church. Many episodes of this campaign, whose principal agents were local missionaries, monks and parish priests, have remained unrecorded. Its results, however, belong to the outstanding achievements of medieval Greek Christianity. In something like two centuries the Gospel was carried over the length and breadth of the Balkan peninsula, and by the year 1000 the evangelization of the Slav subjects of Byzantium was, though not complete, at least more than partially achieved. A particularly determined effort was made in the Peloponnese, where the restoration of Byzantine authority and the rebuilding of the roads were followed in the late ninth and in the tenth century by a remarkable revival of religious life. The main centres of missionary activity in this region were Patras, Corinth, Argos, Sparta, Monemvasia and the Mani peninsula, which was evangelized by the most famous of the Peloponnesian missionaries, St. Nikon the Penitent (died *c.* 998).

The effectiveness of Orthodox Christianity as a means of achieving the cultural assimilation of the Slavs was enhanced, in the Balkan provinces of the empire, by the deliberate use of Greek as a liturgical language. By contrast with the Slav lands that lay beyond the empire's borders, where, through a combination of linguistic tolerance and tactful diplomacy, the Byzantines encouraged the propagation of Christianity in the Slavonic vernacular, their policy towards the Slav colonists at home was Hellenization through Christianization. In the Slavonic lands now reintegrated into the framework of the Byzantine provincial administration, Greek was not only the idiom of the church but the language of a civil service, of the armed forces and of polite society; a knowledge of Byzantine Greek became henceforth the necessary key to social status and a successful career. Whatever view we may hold of the ethnic origin of the inhabitants of modern Greece, and whatever stand we may take in the passionate and still unresolved debate aroused by the claim made in the 1830s by the German scholar Fallmerayer that the Greeks of today are predominantly of Slav and Albanian stock, this surely is beyond dispute: the Slavonic tribes which in the early Middle Ages had colonized virtually the whole of continental Greece and the Peloponnese began to lose their political independence and ethnic identity in the ninth century; their assimilation was caused by their incorporation into the Byzantine theme structure, by their acceptance of Greek Christianity, and by the spell cast over them by the superior prestige of Byzantine power and Hellenic culture. Despite the continued resistance of isolated pockets of Slavs—particularly in the mountainous areas of the Peloponnese—the movement of assimilation never lost its momentum after the middle of the ninth century. First subdued, then converted and finally civilized by Byzantium, the Slavs of the central and southern areas of the Balkan peninsula became Greeks. The three stages in this process of absorption are well illustrated in a Byzantine text of the early tenth century, in which the Emperor Leo VI paid tribute to the achievement of his predecessor, Basil I (867–86):

> Our father of blessed memory, Basil, the emperor of the Romans, prevailed upon them [the Slavs] to renounce their ancient customs and, having made Greeks of them and subjected them to governors according to the Roman model and bestowed baptism upon them, he freed them from bondage to their own rulers and taught them to make war on the nations that are hostile to the Romans.[4]

With the exception of Dalmatia and parts of North-Western Thrace, the *Sklaviniae* which the empire had successfully reclaimed were situated south of the forty-second parallel. The lands to the north of this line remained until the early eleventh century, with these two exceptions, beyond its administrative control. A number of factors prevented the extension of direct Byzantine rule to these areas in the ninth century: the remoteness of these lands from the centres of imperial power, and the resultant difficulty of deploying troops from the coastal themes into the mountainous interior; the existence of the Bulgarian state, which presented a barrier to Byzantine expansion north of the Thracian plain; the rival ambitions of the Carolingian Empire which, as a result of Charlemagne's conquest of the Avars (791–6), controlled the north-western part of the Balkan peninsula; and the fact that in the northern areas of the Balkans, Byzantine imperialism was faced, not as in Greece and the Peloponnese, with largely inchoate Slavonic tribes, but with ethnic groups of substantial size and stability, with a growing social and political cohesion and governed by native princes.

And yet, despite these obstacles, the Byzantines succeeded during the ninth century in extending their empire's cultural influence over a considerable part of the Northern Balkans. In so doing they brought the nascent Slav states in these areas permanently or for a time into the orbit of its civilization. The objects of their efforts were the Bulgarians, the Serbs and the Croats. This struggle to ensure the political loyalty and the religious allegiance of these peoples to the empire must be considered in some detail, for its outcome determined the subsequent pattern of Balkan history until the end of the Middle Ages, and proved decisive in the destinies of the Byzantine Commonwealth.

The "Thirty Years' Peace", concluded by Omurtag with the empire in about 816, could not fail to bring the Bulgarian state, now anchored in the Balkans for nearly a century and a half, into a more intimate relationship with Byzantium. During the next fifty years, however, this relationship remained tense and ambivalent. On the one hand, the Bulgarian khans—following Tervel's example—were keenly aware of the towering prestige of Byzantium and of the advantages they could gain in relation both to their own subjects and to foreign countries, by adopting the trappings of its civilization. On the other hand, the wars of Constantine v and Krum were still a living memory; the khans could not allow themselves to forget that, in the eyes of the Byzantines, the Bulgars were alien intruders in the Balkans, whose realm, if it could not be wiped off the face of the earth, might at least be brought into political subjection to the emperor; an influential section of the Bulgarian people, above all the descendants of the *boyar* aristocracy who had crossed the Danube with Asparuch, still regarded Byzantium as the hereditary foe; finally, the Bulgarians were still pagans: their religion, which they had brought with them from the steppes of South Russia, and which combined a belief in a supreme God, the glorification of war and the cult of ancestors, remained in the eyes of their rulers a means of maintaining their cultural identity and independence in a world where the spread of Christianity could be expected to lead to Byzantine political control. This ambiguous attitude to Byzantium underlay the policy of Omurtag (*c.* 814–31) and of his immediate successors.

There can be no doubt that Byzantine influence grew stronger in Bulgaria in this period. Evidence of this is provided partly by the buildings, some of them palaces, erected by the khans to commemorate their military and other achievements. These exploits are described in inscriptions on columns and tombstones, a large number of which date from the reign of Omurtag. A few of them attempt to transcribe the Old Bulgar language with Greek characters; but the great majority are in Greek, the spoken Greek vernacular of the time. It is true that the Bulgars had no script of their own, and that some knowledge of Greek must have survived the barbarian invasions in this north-eastern corner of the Balkans. Yet it remains a striking proof of the continued appeal of Byzantine civilization in this area that Greek was used as the official written language of the Bulgarian state in the first half of the ninth century. The content of these inscriptions, moreover, suggests that some of the traditions of the Byzantine chancellery were then being imitated at the court of Pliska: the most striking example is the use of the term "ruler by God's authority" (*ho ek theou archon*) in the khan's titles.[5] Its Christian connotations were doubtless not taken too seriously; and there are no explicit traces of Christian belief in these simple but moving words which Omurtag had inscribed on a column when he caused his own tomb to be built:

> Man dies, even though he lives nobly, and another is born; and let the latest born, seeing this, remember him who made it. The name of the prince is Omurtag, the Sublime Khan. God grant that he live a hundred years.[6]

Omurtag's policy was in fact overtly and at times violently anti-Christian. The growing success of Byzantine Christianity in his realm no doubt alarmed him for political reasons. The principal agents of this proselytism were the many thousands of prisoners whom Krum had taken from the Byzantine cities in Thrace (ten thousand, a contemporary source tells us, from Adrianople alone) and deported to Bulgaria. Attempts to make them renounce their religion failed, at least in some cases, and a number of them were put to death by order of the khan. The most distinguished of these martyrs was Manuel, metropolitan of Adrianople. Before long Christianity gained a convert in the khan's own family: Omurtag's son and successor Malamir (831–6) was forced to execute his own brother Enravotas, who had been baptised under the influence of a Greek captive from Adrianople.

115

The first recorded encounter between Bulgarian paganism and Byzantine Christianity, spreading northward across Thrace and the Balkan Mountains, had several features of more than local interest and suggests a cultural pattern which, to some extent at least, was to be reproduced in other countries of Eastern Europe. In the first place, though our knowledge of Bulgarian paganism is scanty, it seems to have been then in a state of decline. The migration of the Bulgars to the Balkans, the dislocation brought about in their realm by the growing importance of the Slavs, the abandonment of their former nomadic life, and the need to adapt themselves to a predominantly agricultural economy, these factors created a new situation for which their social and religious traditions, which had developed in the steppes of South Russia, must have been ill-prepared. Secondly, though we must be careful not to read too much into the scanty evidence of the sources, we may surmise that the Slavs in Bulgaria were at that time more receptive to Christianity than their Bulgar overlords: a fact no doubt due partly to the earlier contacts of the Slavs with Byzantine communities in the Balkans, and partly to the greater social and political cohesion of the Bulgar clans. Finally, it is in the first half of the ninth century that Bulgarian paganism first appears as an aggressive, actively anti-Christian, force. This feature, which it retained during the decades that followed the country's official conversion to Christianity, was scarcely fortuitous. A hostile attitude to Christianity as certainly linked with the fear of Byzantine imperialism, which the Bulgars had displayed ever since they came into the Balkans. But it is equally true that the paganism of their ruling clans became more self-conscious and aggressive at the very time when it was nearing its dissolution. A similar phenomenon can be observed in the following century in Scandinavia and in Russia, where the dying paganism of their rulers erupted for a while into overtly anti-Christian movements.

This fear and distrust of Byzantium partly accounts for the relations established by the Bulgarians with the East Frankish part of the Carolingian Empire. The two realms had a common frontier along the middle Danube and the Tisza. These relations, which began in Omurtag's reign, led to the conclusion of a peace treaty between the Franks and the Bulgarians in 845. By the time Boris 1 became ruler of Bulgaria (852) the country's foreign policy seemed firmly set on a pro-Frankish, Western, course. Here too, no less than in the relations between Bulgaria and Byzantium, political and religious factors were intermingled: for the Carolingian and the Byzantine Empires were then competing for the religious, as well as the political, allegiance of the Balkan peoples. And behind the Frankish Empire stood the Church of Rome, distrustful at times of the tendency of Germanic rulers to regard churches as the private property of their secular founders, yet anxious to take advantage of Frankish missionary zeal to extend the boundaries of Western Christendom. Boris' mercurial relations with Byzantium, Rome and the Franks were, in the next two decades, to determine the religious and cultural future of his country.

In the early 860s Boris reaffirmed his country's alliance with Louis the German and, it seems, promised to accept Christianity at the hands of the Frankish clergy. The danger of Carolingian influence spreading as far as Thrace, within striking distance of Constantinople, seriously alarmed the Byzantines. The Emperor Michael III decided on a military demonstration: in 864, in accordance with the usual tactics, he moved an army to the Bulgarian frontier and sent his fleet along the western coast of the Black Sea. Boris, whose military position was precarious and whose country was suffering from famine, capitulated at once. He promptly sent an embassy to Constantinople, promising to accept Byzantine Christianity and to renounce the Frankish alliance. Soon afterwards—probably in September 865—Boris was baptized by a bishop dispatched to Bulgaria by the Byzantine authorities, and a number of his prominent subjects likewise accepted Christianity.

It is significant that several Byzantine authors, writing in the following century, assert that on becoming Christians the Bulgarians acknowledged the sovereignty of the Byzantine emperor;[7] and this claim is also mentioned, with patent disapproval, by Pope Nicholas I in a letter addressed to Hincmar, archbishop of Rheims.[8] This claim was not incompatible with Leo VI's statement that the Bulgarians and the East Romans "are brothers in virtue of having one faith"[9]; and it fully accords with a basic tenet of Byzantine political philosophy, according to which a nation, having accepted the empire's Christian faith, became thereby subject to the authority of the emperor, who was held to be the sole legitimate sovereign of the Christian world. A sign of this subordination was the spiritual relationship that bound henceforth the ruler of the newly converted nation to the person of the emperor: the degree of this relationship, which varied from country to country, was supposed to define the exact status occupied by this nation in the international community of Christian states of which the emperor was, in the eyes of the Byzantines, the supreme head. Bulgaria's position within the Byzantine Commonwealth was expressed symbolically by the rank bestowed upon Boris on his baptism: christened Michael, he became the spiritual son of the Emperor Michael III. How far these Byzantine claims to sovereignty over Bulgaria were accepted by Boris is hard to discover: in his subsequent policy he certainly showed no signs of acting as the emperor's subject: yet there is reason to believe that he valued his spiritual adoption by the emperor, which increased his authority at home and prestige abroad, and that neither he nor his successors ever challenged the Byzantine doctrine of the one, universal empire whose overlord was the *basileus* in Constantinople. But, though unchallenged in theory, this doctrine, with its corollary that Bulgaria occupied a subordinate place in the Byzantine Commonwealth, did in practice generate grave internal tensions in the Bulgarian state and society. These tensions are worth examining for several reasons: the immediate results of Boris' conversion are unusually well documented; Bulgaria was the first large and well-organized state in Eastern Europe to accept Byzantine Christianity; and several of the more acute problems posed by this conversion were later to reappear in other countries which experienced the impact of Byzantine civilization.

Boris' conversion was followed by a nation-wide revolt, fomented by the leaders of the Old Bulgar clans. Its aims were the assassination of Boris and the restoration of paganism. It very nearly succeeded. Boris was able to rally a group of faithful supporters and, by an intervention so timely that later writers called it miraculous, crushed the rebellion. His counter-measures were ruthless: fifty-two of the ringleaders, together with their children, were put to death. Boris was later to regret the cruelty of this punishment, which he seems to have imputed to the influence of the Greek clergy at his court. There is no doubt, however, that by the virtual elimination of the pagan party of opposition the deadly threat to the future of the Byzantine mission in the country was temporarily removed.

Meanwhile the Byzantine authorities were working to consolidate their hold over Bulgaria. Soon after Boris' baptism and probably before the revolt of the *boyars*, or at least before news of it reached Constantinople, the Patriarch Photius, head of the Byzantine Church, sent a letter to the Bulgarian ruler.[10] Photius was one of the greatest Byzantine scholars of all time, and an accomplished stylist and rhetorician. His epistle is redolent of these qualities. In ample and learned phraseology, it expounds the doctrines of the church as defined by the oecumenical councils, demonstrates the superiority of Christianity over paganism, and, tempering classical wisdom with orthodox theology and ethics, paints an ideal portrait of a Christian philosopher-ruler, master of himself and mindful of the welfare of his subjects. As a literary exercise whose manifest aim was to overwhelm a barbarian ruler with the wisdom and splendour of the Christian tradition of East Rome, Photius' letter is not unimpressive; but much of the patriarch's scholarship and dialectical skill was, we may suspect, wholly lost upon Boris, whose knowledge of Greek could scarcely have been adequate to enable him to understand the lengthy admonitions without the help of a translator, and who was mainly interested in the practical applications of his new religion in the moral, social and political fields. Of these worldly considerations Photius' letter bears almost no trace. There is, it is true, a passing reference to the "concord" (*homonoia*) which a Christian ruler should strive to establish among his subjects[11]—an ideal which Boris, faced in his own country with the ethnic dualism of Bulgar and Slav and with the religious antagonism of pagan and Christian, could not fail to view with approval; a cursory, and uncomplimentary, allusion is made to polygamy[12]—a practice that was widespread among the pagan Bulgars; and, with what was doubtless a fine sense of the diplomatic value of silence, nowhere in his letter does Photius refer to the Byzantine emperor, Boris' new spiritual father; he does, however, flatter the Bulgarian ruler by comparing him, on account of his evangelical zeal, with Constantine the Great.[13]

Despite these perfunctory concessions to his practical pre-occupations and susceptibilities, it is unlikely that Boris found much satisfaction in Photius' letter. The future of his country's relations with the empire must have seemed to him fraught with dangerous pitfalls. The widespread hostility to Byzantium that existed in his country had been dramatically demonstrated by the *boyar* revolt; and the Greek clergy, now active in Bulgaria, combined their missionary work with political loyalty to their imperial master. In order to safeguard the independence of his country while continuing to reap the benefits of his new association with the empire, it was essential to build up, with Byzantine approval, a separate, and if possible autonomous, ecclesiastical organization in Bulgaria. Boris knew that according to the theory of the pentarchy, which was then widely accepted in Byzantium, the supreme government of the Christian Church is jointly vested in the five patriarchs—those of Rome, Constantinople, Alexandria, Antioch and Jerusalem. The idea of acquiring a separate patriarchate for Bulgaria may well have occurred to Boris at the time of his baptism; it was certainly in his mind by the summer of 866. But the Byzantines, who regarded Bulgaria as their own missionary preserve, were unlikely to accede to such a request; and Photius in his letter to Boris was ominously silent on all matters concerned with the status and organization of the new Bulgarian Church.

Frustrated in his plans of ecclesiastical autonomy, and probably disappointed in the Greeks who seemed to be treating him as a poor barbarian, Boris decided to renew his former links with the West. In the summer of 866 he sent an embassy to the court of Louis the German at Regensburg, requesting Frankish missionaries for his country; simultaneously he dispatched envoys to Rome to ask the Pope for a patriarch and priests. Pope Nicholas I, who claimed spiritual jurisdiction over the whole of Christendom and was determined to reimpose the direct authority of the Roman Church over those areas of the Eastern Balkans which had been annexed by the patriarchate of Constantinople in the eighth century, was naturally delighted by Boris' *volte-face*. He promptly sent two bishops to Bulgaria, and composed a long and careful reply to a list of 106 questions which Boris had sent him.[14] The pope's letter to Boris is in several respects a remarkable document: it exemplifies the universalist claims of the medieval papacy; it casts light on the outlook and ambitions of the Bulgarian ruler; it reveals the roots of the conflict between the Byzantine and the Western Churches for the spiritual allegiance of the Bulgarian people, a rivalry which Boris was fully prepared to exploit in order to increase the independence and status of his own church; finally, this shrewd and eminently practical document shows that for the time being at least the pope understood the mentality of the Bulgarian ruler better than the patriarch of Constantinople.

For our present purpose it will be sufficient to consider Nicholas' letter from two more particular points of view. In the first place it provides evidence of the methods used by the Byzantine missionaries in Bulgaria, and of the doubts—amounting at times to animosity—which some of these methods aroused in the minds of Boris and his subjects. Secondly, Boris's questions, which have survived embedded in the pope's reply, illustrate vividly the strains and tensions produced in Bulgaria's social and political life by the encounter between the old pagan ethos and the teaching of Christianity.

Many of Boris' questions will strike the modern reader as exceedingly trivial. To judge from the pope's reply, not a single theological issue was raised in them. The Bulgarian ruler may have felt that he had had enough theology from Photius; and he probably believed that there was no fundamental doctrinal difference between the Latin and the Greek Churches: a belief that was largely correct, for of the two basic questions over which the two churches separated in the Middle Ages—the addition of the word *filioque* to the Western Creed, and papal supremacy—the first did not become a vital issue until the following year (when it was raised by Photius, who accused the Latin clergy of teaching this heretical doctrine in Bulgaria), while the papal claims were then regarded by the Byzantines as a matter of jurisdiction, not of doctrine. Boris' questions were concerned with behaviour, not with belief. Were the Byzantines right, he asked the pope, in forbidding the Bulgarians to have baths on Wednesdays and Fridays,[15] to take communion without wearing their belts,[16] or to eat the meat of animals killed by eunuchs?[17] And were they justified in claiming that no layman may conduct public prayers for rain[18] or make the sign of the cross over a table before a meal,[19] and in insisting that people should stand in church with arms crossed over their breasts?[20] The pope's answer to all these questions were, predictably, in the negative. Indeed, one cannot avoid the suspicion that Boris expected that this would be so, and that the Bulgarians had been adversely struck by the formalistic ritualism of the Byzantine missionaries and by their attempts to ensure for the clergy a dominant position in the country's social life. At least on one occasion the Greek clergy seem to have exerted political pressure on Boris: his question as to whether they were right in refusing to accept the repentance of some of the pagan rebels—also answered in the negative by the pope[21]—implies that the Byzantine clergy in Bulgaria were in part responsible for his decision to deal harshly with the ringleaders of the revolt.

Three of Boris' questions referred specifically to Byzantine ecclesiastical claims. His inquiry as to "how many true patriarchs there are"[22] was no doubt intended to sound the pope on the Greek theory of the pentarchy; and his question as to which of them came second in Christendom after the bishop of Rome[23] was clearly designed to test Nicholas' opinion on the Byzantine view that it was the patriarch of Constantinople. Nicholas' reply to both questions showed scant regard for the Byzantine position. He admitted that there were five patriarchates in all; but he strongly denied that Constantinople was second among them, declaring that this city, though it called itself "the New Rome", was neither an apostolic foundation nor a see that deserved, on other than political grounds, to rank as a patriarchate. It is clear that the pope's answers flatly contradicted the idea, which the Byzantine clergy had no doubt impressed on the Bulgarians, that Constantinople enjoyed ecclesiastical hegemony in Eastern Europe. The third of Boris' questions on these jurisdictional matters implies that in one field the Byzantines were claiming an even wider authority: were they right, Boris inquired, in asserting that the holy chrism, used in the sacraments of the church, was produced only in their empire and from there distributed throughout the world?[24] This statement, which the pope dismissed contemptuously, seems to echo, in an ecclesiastical context, the universal pretensions of the Byzantine Empire.

Boris' interest in patriarchs was, of course, prompted by more than a desire to test the validity of contemporary Greek ecclesiology. For reasons that have already been explained he badly wanted one for himself. His request for a patriarch was, however, nimbly side-stepped by the pope. For the present, Boris was politely but firmly told, he would have to be content with a bishop; the future would depend on the report of the legates whom Nicholas was sending to Bulgaria.[25]

Boris' irritation at some of the rules of behaviour which the Byzantine missionaries were trying to impose on the newly converted Bulgarians; his resentment of their interference in the political life of his country; and his awareness that the supremacy claimed by the patriarchate of Constantinople over Eastern Europe undermined his hopes of securing an autonomous church—these facts, which may be inferred from the pope's replies, help to explain his overtures to Rome and to the Franks. Apart from these grievances, many of Boris' questions reveal his preoccupation with the particular problems created by the impact of Christianity on the still largely pagan society and on the traditional institutions of the Bulgarians. Most of these problems, of course, had arisen as the result of the importation of Byzantine culture into Bulgaria. The changes and innovations brought by this alien culture produced dislocations and resistances which are often encountered whenever a more advanced culture-pattern is introduced into a backward country. This phenomenon is clearly of the greatest interest to the student of cultural diffusion. The preservation of the letters addressed almost simultaneously to Boris by the Byzantine patriarch and by the pope, and the fact, equally fortunate for the historian, that Boris endeavoured to play off the one against the other, have ensured that this process is more fully documented with regard to ninth century Bulgaria than in any other East European land over which Byzantine civilization became dominant.

Several of Boris' questions reveal the same perplexity about Christian ritual observances which, we have seen, appeared in those parts of his letter to Nicholas in which he referred to the Byzantine clergy. In general terms he asked the pope how many days one should fast in the year,[26] at what time one may breakfast in the morning on non-fasting days,[27] whether sexual intercourse is permissible on Sundays,[28] whether communion may be taken every day in Lent,[29] what animals and birds a Christian is allowed to eat,[30] whether a woman should have her head covered in church,[31] and whether one may work on Sundays and on certain feastdays.[32] The triviality of some of these questions should not blind us to their underlying significance: the little we know about Bulgarian paganism suggests that it attached great importance to religious observance; the problem of replacing one set of ritualistic rules by another could not fail to have far-reaching social implications; finally, both the Byzantine and the Latin Churches were themselves, by modern standards, highly ritualistic (though, to judge from the pope's replies, the latter was then rather less so): and the difference in rites and ecclesiastical discipline which already then divided the two churches must have increased Boris' perplexity.

Nicholas' letter also reveals that the Bulgarian ruling class was preoccupied by the problem of reconciling Christianity with the traditions of their militaristic society in which great emphasis was laid on the cultivation of warlike virtues and the glorification of military success. Cases could easily occur when the need to attend to Christian duties interfered with the efficient pursuit of war. What is one to do, Boris asked the pope, when a military campaign coincides with Lent,[33] or when the news of an enemy attack is received during prayer time?[34] And how are soldiers, besieged in a military camp, to perform their devotions in a fitting manner?[35] More perplexing still was the inherent contradiction between the Christian insistence on charity and mercy and the need for a ruler, if he is to be effective, to deal harshly with criminals or with those who fail in their military duty. Must one then forgive murderers, thieves and adulterers?[36] Can confessions be extracted without the use of torture?[37] Can a criminal be granted the right of asylum in a church?[38] And how is one to treat soldiers who run away in battle or disobey orders to march against the enemy?[39] Is there any alternative to imposing the death sentence on frontier guards who let fugitives slip across the state border,[40] or on a soldier whose weapons and horse cannot pass inspection before battle?[41] And behind these concrete questions loomed a larger and even more difficult one, which Boris also put to the pope: is the existence of criminal law, with its system of punishments, compatible with Christian ethics?[42] It seems unlikely that Nicholas' replies to these questions, in which, reasonably enough, he advised Boris to temper justice with mercy, differed very substantially from the attitude taken in these matters by the Byzantine clergy in Bulgaria, except for their refusal to forgive the repentant survivors of the pagan rebellion, a severity which, we have seen, was censured by the pope.

This last matter raised, in a particularly acute form, the problem of how a Christian state is to deal with religious dissent. Boris' predecessors had persecuted the Christians of their realm. The situation was now reversed: how, he asked the pope, should one treat inveterate worshippers of pagan idols? Should they be forced to accept Christianity?[43] The pope's advice to use methods of gentle persuasion and, if these failed, to have no social contact with the heathens, would no doubt have been given by Photius too, had his views been sought on the matter. We may suspect, however, that the Byzantine missionaries who were working "in the field" were sometimes less scrupulous, and were apt to turn a blind eye to the use of more forceful measures by the Bulgarian authorities. Boris' uncertainty as to the proper way of dealing with pagans was not confined to the home ground: several of his questions show that he was concerned at the possible effects of Christianity upon his country's foreign policy. What, he asked, was the right way of concluding an alliance with a friendly nation? What should one do when a Christian state breaks a solemn treaty it has signed with one's own country? And is it permissible for a Christian realm to conclude a treaty with a pagan one?[44] The pope's replies to these questions, though somewhat hesitant, were clearly designed to reassure Boris: the nature of international treaties must depend on the customs of the countries concerned; in difficult cases advice should be sought from the Church; alliances with pagan countries are permissible, provided that the Christian partner genuinely seeks to convert its heathen ally.

A final group of questions concerned various traditional customs to which the Bulgars seem to have been strongly attached. It seems that most, if not all of them, had been reprobated by the Byzantine missionaries; and Boris may well have hoped that the pope would show himself more lenient. Several pertained to military ritual: the use of a horse's tail as a banner;[45] the seeking of auguries, the casting of spells and the performance of ceremonial songs and dances before battle;[46] the taking of oaths on a sword.[47] These practices were no doubt deeply rooted in the Old Bulgar pagan tradition, and Boris must have been disappointed by Nicholas' disapproval of them. Others implied the belief that inanimate objects could possess magical powers: the Bulgarians, the pope was hopefully told, sought cures from a miraculous stone,[48] and wore amulets round their necks as a protection against sickness.[49] These customs were much too redolent of paganism for the pope to tolerate them. The same was true of polygamy, which was castigated by Nicholas as severely as Photius had done in his letter to Boris.[50] An important feature of Bulgarian paganism seems to have been the cult of ancestors; on this point, too, the pope proved uncompromising: the Bulgarians should not, he declared, pray for their deceased parents if they had died as pagans.[51] On the other hand, he was prepared to allow them to retain their eating habits: he raised no objection to their custom of eating animals and birds slaughtered without their blood being shed[52]—a practice of which, we know from other sources, the Byzantine clergy greatly disapproved; as for their ruler's custom of eating alone, seated at a raised table, it was not irreligious, even if it was rather bad manners.[53] The Bulgarians were free to dress as they liked: and Boris' question as to whether the wearing of trousers is permissible was dismissed rather testily by the pope as "supervacuum".[54]

To sum up, Boris' questions to the pope suggest that in 866 he hoped that by renouncing Byzantine jurisdiction and submitting to Rome he would solve two basic problems which his country faced after its conversion to Christianity: the first arose from the need to ensure that the acceptance of the new religion did not undermine the social cohesion and military efficiency of his realm; the second was inherent in Boris' determination to see that Christian Bulgaria did not become a mere political satellite or cultural dependency of the Byzantine Empire. Internal unity and the maintenance of his country's autonomy were his two basic aims. Both were reflected in the specific requests he made to the pope: he asked for a code of secular laws,[55] for a manual of canon law,[56] for liturgical books[57] and for an autonomous patriarch.[58]

There is no doubt that for the next year or so Boris remained convinced that he had got the better deal out of Rome. He swore fidelity to the see of St. Peter, welcomed the papal mission which arrived in Bulgaria late in 866, and expelled the Greek clergy from his country. The Byzantine authorities, however, soon recovered from this blow. Their reaction was vigorous. In the following spring the Patriarch Photius sent an encyclical letter to the leaders of the other Eastern Churches. Much of its contents was devoted to the recent events in Bulgaria. After alluding to the original conversion, when that barbarous nation "renounced their ancestral demons and orgies", he unleashed a flow of passionate rhetoric on the subject of their recent apostasy. The Latin missionaries now working in the country he describes as "impious and execrable" men risen from the darkness of the West, and compares them to a thunderbolt, to violent hail and to a wild boar savagely trampling on the Lord's vineyard. Passing from metaphors to doctrine, he lists the more disreputable customs and false teachings imposed by the wicked Latins on the unfortunate Bulgarians: they include the practice of fasting on Saturdays and shortening Lent by a week, the condemnation of married priests, and the insistence that only bishops may administer the sacrament of confirmation. Some of these differences, which were then becoming controversial issues between the Byzantine and the Roman Churches, may seem of minor importance: but Photius is at pains to remind his Eastern colleagues that "even the smallest neglect of the traditions leads to the complete contempt for dogma". More serious still, he pointed out, was the fact that the Latin clergy in Bulgaria was propagating the dogma of the Double Procession of the Holy Spirit ("the *filioque*"): this was downright heresy. Photius assured the other patriarchs that he would do everything in his power to bring the Bulgarian Church back to Orthodoxy, and urged them to send representatives to a synod, to be convened in Constantinople in order to condemn the Latin errors.[59]

The Bulgarian question was but one factor, though an important one, in the growing tension between the Byzantine and the Roman Churches. Since 863, when the pope, claiming direct jurisdiction over all Eastern Christendom, excommunicated and deposed Photius, a state of open schism existed between them. The pope's decisions were ignored in Constantinople, and in 867 on Photius' initiative a synod, presided over by the emperor, deposed and excommunicated Nicholas I, and condemned the *filioque* and other Latin usages. Later in the year, however, the situation was transformed by a palace revolution in Constantinople. Michael III was assassinated, and his successor and murderer, Basil I, compelled Photius to resign. Ignatius, the new patriarch, was *persona grata* with the pope, and his appointment restored communion between Constantinople and Rome.

If the new pope, Hadrian II (who succeeded Nicholas in December 867), hoped that the end of the schism would cause the Byzantines to renounce their claim over Bulgaria, he was mistaken. By the end of 867 opinion in Bulgaria appears to have started to swing in favour of the Greek Church. Boris, whose hopes of securing a patriarch must have worn thin by then, was showing increasing impatience at Rome's refusal to let him appoint a person of his choice as archbishop of Bulgaria. Both Nicholas I and Hadrian II were determined to show him that the decision in this matter rested with the Holy See. The former, in the closing days of his life, complained that the Bulgarians were falling prey to Byzantine propaganda and were cold-shouldering the Latin clergy; and the pope's librarian Anastasius noted with alarm that the Greeks were using large-scale bribery and ingenious sophistries in an endeavour to detach Boris from Rome.[60] It is clear that the full resources of imperial diplomacy were being marshalled to bring Bulgaria back into the Byzantine fold.

In February 870 a council of the universal church, convened in Constantinople to judge the rival claims of Photius and Ignatius, was ending its sessions. Its last plenary meeting was attended by Bulgarian delegates who brought an urgent message from their sovereign. Three days later the council was hastily re-convened on the emperor's orders to consider Boris' communication: to which church, he disingenuously inquired, should his country belong—to the Roman or to the Byzantine? An acrimonious debate ensued, with the papal legates taking one side and the Byzantines and the representatives of the Eastern patriarchs, the other. Both sides appealed to historical precedent. The former urged that Bulgaria was part of the ecclesiastical province of Illyricum, which had once been under Roman jurisdiction; the Greeks and the Easterners retorted that this territory had formerly belonged to the Byzantine Empire. It was a foregone conclusion: the pope's representatives were in a minority; and the council decided that Bulgaria should henceforth be under the jurisdiction of the patriarchate of Constantinople.

The decision was implemented forthwith: it was now the turn of the Latin clergy to be expelled from Bulgaria; Greek priests returned, and an archbishop, appointed by Patriarch Ignatius, was sent to take charge of the Bulgarian Church. The Byzantine authorities were careful in 870 to avoid the mistake which four years earlier had thrown Boris into the arms of the pope: the archbishop of Bulgaria, though canonically dependent on Constantinople, was granted a degree of autonomy, and a rank superior to that of the majority of the bishops of the Byzantine Church.

The relations between Bulgaria and the empire now seemed set on a smooth course. The Bulgarian Church was divided into dioceses, headed by bishops, most of whom were presumably sent from Constantinople. Through them, and through the clerics and secular agents who accompanied them, the further diffusion of Byzantine culture to Bulgaria seemed assured. Young Bulgarians, destined for high office in their church, were sent to Constantinople to be trained in the monastic life, where they attended a school under the direction of the abbot Arsenius.[61] Among them was Prince Symeon, Boris' son. Symeon, as we shall see, was to acquire in Constantinople not only a religious training, but a solid grounding in Greek secular education. Yet behind this picture of peaceful cultural penetration an underlying *malaise* persisted. The tensions caused by the impact of Byzantine patterns upon a rapidly changing and still partly pagan Bulgarian society, and so vividly illustrated by Boris' correspondence with Nicholas I, could not be removed in a few years. Moreover, the remnants of the old Bulgar clans, crippled though they were by Boris' harsh measures after their revolt, were gathering strength in the new generation, their traditional dislike of Byzantium undiminished. We lack detailed information on the difficulties which the Bulgarian nation was experiencing in adapting itself to the cultural changes that resulted from its new relationship with the empire during the two decades following Boris' final acceptance of Greek Christianity; but there is no doubt that these difficulties were enhanced by two factors: the continued ethnic dualism between Bulgar and Slav, and the fact that Byzantine Christianity was preached in a language unintelligible to the great majority of Boris' subjects.

The Slavs, who at first were little more than subject tribes, supplying their Bulgar masters with food and other economic necessities, began to play an increasing role in the social and political life of the country during the first half of the ninth century. The process of assimilation of the Bulgars by the Slavs cannot, for lack of evidence, be traced in detail. It must have been accelerated by intermarriages, by economic and political cooperation, by the territorial expansion of the Bulgarian state south-westward into Macedonia, and by the growing contact between the Bulgarians and the Serbs. By the middle of the ninth century much of Central and Southern Macedonia, around Lakes Ohrid and Prespa, with its predominantly Slav population, had been annexed to the Bulgarian state. The Macedonian Slavs had for long been exposed to Byzantine influence, spreading from Thessalonica up the Vardar; and it is natural to suppose that by the mid-ninth century some of them had already become Christians. It is likely that Christianity continued to gain more converts among the Slavs than among the Bulgars, and that Boris was increasingly driven to rely on the cooperation of the former to achieve the two aims of his internal policy: the consolidation of the Bulgarian Church and the promotion of social and political unity within his realm. In one sense these two aims were interrelated: for his Slavonic subjects seem to have accepted, far more readily than the Bulgar aristocracy, the new patterns of Byzantine culture. In another respect, however, they were still difficult to reconcile: the clergy working in Bulgaria were, at least in the higher ranks of the hierarchy, for the most part Byzantine missionaries, few of whom could have had an adequate command of the Slav language; the church services were celebrated in Greek, of which many of the native priests were largely ignorant. Christianity thus suffered from the grave disability of appearing in Bulgaria in an alien garb, and its leading representatives, though they doubtless enjoyed considerable social prestige and are known in some cases to have displayed a praiseworthy missionary zeal, laboured under the disadvantage of being foreigners, whose means of communication with their flocks were at best imperfect. It did not take Boris long to realize that only by acquiring a native clergy and by solving the linguistic problem could his people safely continue to accept Byzantine civilization without risk of losing their cultural independence.

A means of solving this problem was suddenly offered to Boris in 885. Reference has already been made to the mission of the two brothers Constantine and Methodius to the Slavs of Moravia. This mission, organized by the Byzantine authorities in 862–3, was made possible by the invention by Constantine of a Slavonic alphabet, by means of which the Byzantine liturgy and the Christian Scriptures were translated from Greek into the Slav language. The work of Constantine and Methodius, which proved of immense importance in transmitting Byzantine Christianity and civilization to the Slavs, will be discussed in a later chapter. It should be noted here that in the space of some twenty years it laid the foundation of a Slav vernacular literature and brought into being a Slav-speaking clergy capable of preaching Byzantine Christianity to the Slavs in their own idiom. On the organizational level, this mission was evidently wrecked by the hostility of the Frankish clergy in Central Europe, and on Methodius' death in 885 several of his principal disciples were exiled from Moravia.

Whether Boris ever had any personal contact with Constantine and Methodius is uncertain; but he undoubtedly realized that the Slav vernacular Christianity which they and their pupils had been creating under Byzantine auspices was just what he needed to ensure a desirable balance between the cultural influences from Byzantium and the native Slavo-Bulgarian traditions. Methodius' exiled disciples must have been aware of his interest in their work: they travelled down the Danube, reached Bulgarian territory at Belgrade, and were sent on by the governor of that city to Boris' court at Pliska. There they received a warm welcome. Two leading members of the group, the priests Clement and Naum, held daily consultations with Boris. Clement's medieval biographer seems to hint at a certain secrecy surrounding these discussions:[62] it is indeed probable that the Bulgarian ruler wished to decide on the main lines of his future policy without antagonizing the Bulgar aristocracy (which was suspicious of anything that would strengthen the hand of the Byzantines or the Slavs) and possibly the Greek clergy as well, which may have resented the appearance of this distinguished band of rival missionaries. About 886 Clement was sent to Macedonia, with the task of baptizing those who were still pagans, celebrating the liturgy in the Slavonic language, translating Greek religious writings, and training a native clergy. The centre of his activity was first the region of Devol (in present-day Albania) between Lake Ohrid and the Adriatic and later, after his appointment as bishop in 893, the area round Ohrid. Thanks to St. Clement's labours in these districts which continued for thirty years, Macedonia, and notably Ohrid, one of its main cities, became a leading centre of Slavonic Christian culture in early medieval Europe. Meanwhile Clement's companion Naum remained in North-Eastern Bulgaria where, both in Pliska and in the royal monastery of St. Panteleimon near Preslav, he helped to found another school of Old Slavonic literature, under the patronage of Boris and Prince Symeon, who had returned home after completing his education in Constantinople. In 893 St. Naum was transferred to Macedonia to help St. Clement in his missionary and educational work.

Whatever doubts the Greek clergy in Bulgaria may have had about these Slav cultural activities, the work of Methodius' disciples in that country enjoyed the support of the state authorities in Constantinople. The role which Byzantine policy played in the creation and development of the Slav vernacular tradition will be discussed later. A significant episode must, however, be mentioned here. Soon after Methodius' death an envoy of the Emperor Basil I, visiting Venice, noticed a group of slaves, offered for sale by Jewish merchants. On inquiry, he discovered that they were disciples of Constantine and Methodius, whom the Moravians had sold as heretics. He redeemed them and sent them to Constantinople. Some of them, doubtless supplied with Slavonic liturgical books, were later sent to Bulgaria to join their exiled colleagues.[63]

In 889 Boris abdicated his throne. He had done much to implant Byzantine Christianity firmly in his country, and the sincerity of his Christian beliefs are beyond question. He decided to spend the rest of his days as a monk. But he made one grave miscalculation. The Bulgar aristocratic party had been cowed and silenced by the repressions that followed its abortive revolt. But now that Boris' firm hand was removed, they struck again. The new ruler Vladimir, Boris' eldest son, proved a pliant tool in their hands. In behaviour and in policy he was the exact opposite of his father: he led a dissolute life, abandoned the Byzantine alliance for a pact with King Arnulf of Germany, encouraged a revival of paganism and began a persecution of the clergy. For four years Bulgaria remained in the throes of this pagan and anti-Byzantine reaction. At last, aware of this threat to his life-work, Boris emerged from his monastic retreat and appeared at Pliska. He rallied the faithful, re-assumed power, and had Vladimir blinded and imprisoned. He then summoned in 893 a general assembly of the land which ratified the following decisions: Boris' third son Symeon became ruler (conveniently renouncing the monastic vows he had taken earlier), Slavonic replaced Greek as the official language of the country, and the capital was transferred from Pliska (where paganism, as recent events had shown, was still a strong force) to Preslav.

We do not know whether the Byzantines played any part in the suppression of this pagan revival. In the event, this proved the last attempt of the votaries of the old Bulgar religion to seize power in the Bulgarian state. The authorities in Constantinople, as well as the Greek clergy in Bulgaria, could well feel gratified by the events of 893. Boris, as he returned to his monastery (where he died in 907), had also grounds for satisfaction; his son Symeon was firmly in the saddle, and under his patronage the work of adapting Byzantine civilization to the needs of the Slavonic-speaking Bulgarians was resumed in the churches, monasteries and literary schools of the land.

Bulgaria's entry into the political orbit of Byzantium was due in no small measure to the energetic policy of the Emperor Basil 1 (867–86). Its range and resourcefulness recalled, and possibly excelled, the achievements of Justinian 1 and Heraclius in the field of external affairs; and for the next century and a half it remained, with its characteristic blend of adroit diplomacy, Christian missionary activity and military force, a model which successive emperors of the Macedonian dynasty, founded by Basil, strove to imitate. One of the prime objects of this policy was to restore Byzantine hegemony over the Balkans, and particularly over the Slavs in the central and western areas of the peninsula. Here, no less than in Bulgaria, Basil 1 met with a large measure of success.

The western borders of the Bulgarian realm abutted on the land of the Serbs. They lived in scattered communities called *županije* or *župe*, mostly situated in the valleys of the mountainous region watered by the upper Drina, the Piva, the Tara, the Lim, the Ibar and the upper course of the Western Morava. The area of their original settlement in the Balkans—known in the Middle Ages as Raška—lay immediately to the north of the watershed between the Danube and Adriatic; it was separated from the sea by the mountains of Montenegro and by a number of kindred tribes inhabiting the coastal regions and inland districts between the Drin and the Neretva rivers, over whom the Serbs gradually extended their authority during the ninth and tenth centuries. These were the Diocleians, between the lower Bojana and the Bay of Kotor; the Terbouniotes and Kanalites, who lived respectively in the areas of Trebinje and Konavlje, between Kotor and Dubrovnik; the Zachlumi, between Dubrovnik and the lower and middle course of the Neretva (their country was known in successive periods as Hlm, Hum and Herzegovina); and the Narentani who inhabited the coast between the Neretva and the Cetina rivers, as well as the islands of Mljet, Korčula, Hvar, and Brač. Over all these tribes—the Serbs of the interior and the Slavs on the seaboard of Montenegro and Southern Dalmatia—the Byzantines seem to have retained a largely nominal sovereignty until the reign of Michael II (820-9) when, in the words of Constantine Porphyrogenitus, they "shook off the reins of the empire of the Romans and became self-governing and independent, subject to none".[64] About 850 we hear of a Serbian prince Vlastimir, who successfully defended his country against a Bulgarian invasion. Under his leadership, the Serbs appear to have made a notable stride towards nationhood. Most of them had relapsed into paganism since the days of Heraclius, aiming, Constantine tells us significantly, to renounce "every pledge of friendship for and enslavement to the Byzantines".[65] Yet, like Boris of Bulgaria, their rulers must have come to realize that, in the international Balkan world of the time, their paganism was an obstacle to political and cultural progress. It was at the beginning of Basil I's reign that the Serbs decided to seek admittance into the civilized world of Christendom. The event was described by Basil's grandson, Constantine Porphyrogenitus:

> They sent envoys to the emperor ... requesting that they might be placed under the humane yoke of Roman authority and under that of its supreme pastor [i.e. the Byzantine Patriarch]. ... The emperor, like the humane father who received his senselessly rebellious son who repented and returned to the fold, received and accepted them, and straightway sent them priests together with a diplomatic agent. ... When they had all received divine baptism and returned to the Roman allegiance, the emperor's authority was fully restored over their country ... and he wisely determined that they should be governed by princes [of their own nation], chosen by them.[66]

This, of course, is a typically Byzantine reading of the facts, and it may not have wholly accorded with the political interpretation which the Serbs themselves placed on their action. Yet, allowing for this, we may safely draw the following conclusions from Constantine's account: the Serbian embassy to Constantinople was empowered, in requesting Greek missionaries, to offer their ruler's political allegiance to the empire; the Byzantines, in sending to Serbia an embassy whose aims were both religious and political, took the view—identical with the one they had taken when they dispatched a mission to Bulgaria in 864-5—that the Serbs, by accepting Christianity from Constantinople, had become subjects of the emperor. But, whereas the Bulgarians remained after their conversion politically independent of the empire in all but theory, the Byzantine government felt strong enough to impose on the still inchoate Serbian nation a real political vassalage, and to insist that their elected rulers be confirmed in office by the authorities of Constantinople. This exchange of embassies between Serbia and the empire, and "the final conversion" of the Serbs, probably took place between 867 and 874. We do not know whether the acceptance of Byzantine Christianity and imperial suzerainty produced in Serbia any social or political tensions comparable to those which occurred in Bulgaria after 865. If there were any, they were probably far less intense and disruptive, for the Serbs, unlike the Bulgarians, lacked an alien aristocracy with a tradition of hostility to the empire. The only known example of a militantly anti-Christian tribe in that area were the Narentani on the Adriatic coast, who were then outside Serbian control. Notorious pirates, they were a constant threat in the first half of the ninth century to communications between Byzantium and Venice. In vain did the Venetians seek to convert them, in the hope of curbing their piracy. Their warlike spirit seems to have made them for long refractory to Christian influences: known as "Pagani" to the inhabitants of the Dalmatian cities, they were the last tribe in the north-western Balkans to accept Christianity: they were finally converted by Byzantine missionaries later in Basil's reign.[67]

The conversion of the Narentani was one of a series of events of Basil 1's reign which greatly strengthened the empire's position in the Adriatic; the other important landmarks in this process—the Byzantine naval victory over the Arabs at Dubrovnik and the establishment of the theme of Dalmatia—have already been noted. But the Dalmatian theme, though it ensured Byzantine supremacy in the principal cities of the coast for the next two centuries, did not form a continuous territory. The Byzantine strongholds were few and far between, and all around them on the coast and further inland were Slav communities over which the empire could seldom claim control. Beyond the Cetina, as far as Istria in the north-west, extending north to the lower course of the Vrbas and north-east probably as far as the River Bosna, lay the country of the Croats. Their political life began to develop rather earlier than that of the Serbs, in two different areas, situated south and north of the Sava. Dalmatian Croatia and Pannonian Croatia, as these nascent states are known to modern historians, both attracted in the ninth century the interest of Byzantine diplomatists and missionaries. Their relations with the empire were closely bound up with the changing pattern of Byzantine power on the Adriatic coast; for this reason the two areas must be considered together.

The first stirrings of political life among the Croats were the result of the eastward expansion of the Frankish Empire. The Pannonian Croats accepted the rule of Charlemagne in the closing years of the eighth century, and the Franks thus became masters of the land between the Drava and the Sava, as far as the middle Danube. Dalmatian Croatia exchanged a nominal Byzantine overlordship for Frankish supremacy in 803 and, except for the coastal cities and the offshore islands, was formally ceded by the Byzantines to the Franks at the Treaty of Aachen in 812. The Croats, however, soon grew restive under Frankish control; and their attempts to shake it off were supported—possibly in Pannonian Croatia, certainly in Dalmatian Croatia—by Byzantine diplomacy. In 819 Ljudevit, prince of the Pannonian Croats, revolted against

136

the Franks; but his attempt to rally his Slav neighbours proved a failure, and in 822, after his flight to Serbia, Frankish rule was reimposed over his country. In Dalmatian Croatia the movement for independence developed more slowly. The local bishoprics seem to have remained in this period under papal jurisdiction. But the empire's political presence in the coastal cities was having its effect; and it was probably to secure closer collaboration with the Byzantines that Mislav, prince of the Dalmatian Croats (c. 835–45), transferred his residence to Klis, a fortress with a fine strategic position, dominating the mountain pass leading from the interior to the coast, fourteen kilometres north of Split.

Byzantine influence in this area further increased as a result of Basil I's Adriatic policy: in 878 the supreme power in Dalmatian Croatia was seized by a local prince, Zdeslav, a tool of Byzantium. Zdeslav promptly acknowledged the political sovereignty of the emperor and the ecclesiastical jurisdiction of the see of Constantinople. This was something of a triumph for the empire, whose political and religious dominion now showed promise of spreading as far as Istria and across the Dinaric Mountains towards the valley of the upper Sava. Not since the Avaro-Slav invasions of the early seventh century had Byzantium been able to make its presence felt so far to the north-west in the Balkan peninsula.

Yet this Byzantine success proved ephemeral. Croatia had a strong rival party, supported by the Roman clergy and led by the bishop of Nin, a see probably founded by Pope Nicholas I in 860. The very next year (879) the pro-Roman faction struck. A revolution broke out, Zdeslav was assassinated, and Branimir, the new ruler, pledged his country's loyalty to the pope. Croatia remained under the spiritual jurisdiction of Rome and became, until its union with Hungary in 1102, to all intents and purposes a sovereign country. This was not the end of Byzantine hegemony in the north-western Balkans. Imperial sovereignty was maintained, more or less effectively, over the cities and islands of Dalmatia until the late twelfth century. In Croatia itself, despite the independent policy pursued by its kings, Byzantine political influence was strong enough in the mid-tenth century to provoke the admittedly over-sanguine claim of the *De Administrando Imperio* that "the prince of Croatia has from the beginning ... been in servitude and submission to the emperor of the Romans".[68] As late as the eleventh century the Croats acknowledged for a time the nominal suzerainty of the emperor. Nevertheless the events of 879 marked a turning point in their country's relations with the empire. It proved to be the first and decisive event in a process that was to fix the north-western boundary of the Byzantine Commonwealth on the borders between Serbia and Croatia.

NOTES

1. *Vita Constantini*, vi, 53, x, 52–3: *Constantinus et Methodius Thessalonicenses. Fontes*, ed. F. Grivec and F. Tomšič (Zagreb, 1960) (Radovi Staroslavenskog Instituta, 4), pp. 105, 116–17; French transl. F. Dvornik, *Les Légendes de Constantin et de Méthode vues de Byzance* (Prague, 1933), pp. 349–93. Cf. Dan. ii, 44.

2. *DAI*, ch. 49, pp. 228–32.

3. Ibid., ch. 50, pp. 232–4; cf. A. Bon, *Le Péloponnèse byzantin* (Paris, 1951), p. 63 and map, pp. 40–1.

4. Leo VI, *Tactica*, xviii, 101, *PG*, 107, col. 969.

5. V. Beševliev, *Die protobulgarischen Inschriften* (Berlin, 1963), pp. 156, 164, 216, 260, 277.

6. Ibid., p. 247; transl. S. Runciman, *A History of the First Bulgarian Empire* (London, 1930), p. 84.

7. Theophanes Continuatus, *Chronographia*, iv, 15, ed. I. Bekker (Bonn, 1838), pp. 164–5; Georgius Monachus Continuatus, ibid., p. 824.

8. Nicholas I, Epistola 100, *MGH, Epistolae Karolini Aevi*, iv (Berlin, 1925), p. 601.

9. Leo VI, *Tactica*, xviii, 44, *PG* 107, col. 957.

10. Photius, ep. 8, *PG* 102, cols. 628–96.

11. Ibid., col. 677.

12. Ibid., col. 688.

13. Ibid., col. 660.

14. *Responsa Nicolai ad consulta Bulgarorum*, *PL* 119, cols. 978–1016.

15. *Resp.* 6, col. 982.

16. *Resp.* 55, col. 1000.

17. *Resp.* 57, col. 1001.

18. *Resp.* 56, col. 1001.

19. *Resp.* 53, col. 1000.

20. *Resp.* 54, col. 1000.

21. *Resp.* 78, col. 1008.

22. *Resp.* 92, cols. 1011–12.
23. *Resp.* 92, col. 1012.
24. *Resp.* 94, col. 1012.
25. *Resp.* 72, col. 1007.
26. *Resp.* 4, cols. 980–1.
27. *Resp.* 60, cols. 1002–3.
28. *Resp.* 63, col. 1004.
29. *Resp.* 9, cols. 983–4.
30. *Resp.* 43, cols. 996–7.
31. *Resp.* 58, cols. 1001–2.
32. *Resp.* 10, 11, cols. 984–5.
33. *Resp.* 46, col. 998.
34. *Resp.* 74, cols. 1007–8.
35. *Resp.* 38, col. 994.
36. *Resp.* 27, 28, 31, 32, col. 992.
37. *Resp.* 86, col. 1010.
38. *Resp.* 26, cols. 991–2.
39. *Resp.* 22, 23, col. 991.
40. *Resp.* 25, col. 991.
41. *Resp.* 40, cols. 994–5.
42. *Resp.* 83, cols. 1009–10.
43. *Resp.* 41, cols. 995–6.
44. *Resp.* 80, 81, 82, cols. 1008–9.
45. *Resp.* 33, cols. 992–3.
46. *Resp.* 35, cols. 993–4.
47. *Resp.* 67, col. 1005.
48. *Resp.* 62, cols. 1003–4.
49. *Resp.* 79, col. 1008.
50. *Resp.* 51, cols. 999–1000.
51. *Resp.* 88, col. 1011.
52. *Resp.* 90, col. 1011.
53. *Resp.* 42, col. 996.
54. *Resp.* 59, col. 1002.
55. *Resp.* 13, col. 986.
56. *Resp.* 37, col. 994.
57. *Resp.* 76, col. 1008.
58. *Resp.* 72, col. 1007.
59. *PG* 102, cols. 721–41.
60. *PL* 129, col. 20.
61. Photius, ep. 95, *PG* 102, cols. 904–5.

62. *Vita S. Clementis*, xlix: A. Milev, *Grötskite zhitiya na Kliment Okhridski* (Sofia, 1966), p. 122.

63. *Vita S. Naoum*, ed. M. Kusseff, *The Slavonic and East European Review*, xxix (1950–1), p. 142.

64. *DAI*, ch. 29, p. 124.

65. Theophanes Continuatus, v, 52, pp. 288–9.

66. Ibid., v, 54, pp. 291–2.

67. *DAI*, ch. 29, p. 126, ch. 36, p. 164.

68. *DAI*, ch. 31, p. 150.

4

The Balkans in the
Tenth Century:
the Crisis of Imperialism

In the year 900 the Byzantine government must have viewed the situation in the Balkans with some satisfaction. The theme structure, imposed during the preceding two centuries on the coastal fringes of the peninsula and in the interior of Greece, ensured direct imperial control over the greater part of Thrace, Eastern and Southern Macedonia, Thessaly, Boeotia, Attica, the Peloponnese and the Ionian and Adriatic seaboards from the Gulf of Patras to the confines of Istria. Outside the borders of the empire, the Serbs and the kindred tribes of Montenegro and Southern Dalmatia had accepted Byzantine suzerainty, and in token of their loyalty had recently sent troops to help the Byzantines to recover South Italy from the Arabs; even the Croats, though they had rejected this suzerainty in 879, were not averse to enjoying the prestige that came from a state of dependence, however theoretical, on the emperor in Constantinople. Further to the north-west, Venice, whose culture was deeply influenced by Byzantium and whose fleet could be counted on to police the Adriatic, was still among the most loyal of the empire's vassals. In Greece and the Peloponnese the Slavs were well on the way to being Christianized and absorbed by the Greek population. Further north, it is true, the Bulgarian state had annexed, at the empire's expense, Northern Thrace and much of Central and Western Macedonia: its borders now ran south-westward from the Gulf of Burgas, crossed the Rhodope Mountains and the plain to the north of Thessalonica, cut across the Pindus range to a point just south of Jan-

141

nina, turned north over the Albanian Mountains to Lake Scutari, and, skirting the eastern frontier of Serbia, reached the Danube slightly west of Belgrade. The fact that in two hundred years the Bulgarians had more than doubled the size of former Byzantine territory which they held, might well, it is true, have seemed ominous. But the East Roman government could at least find comfort in the thought that Symeon, the new Bulgarian ruler, had been educated in Constantinople. His ability and the eagerness with which he imbibed Byzantine culture had greatly impressed his tutors who, as Liutprand of Cremona was later informed by his contacts in Constantinople, nicknamed him "the half-Greek" on account of his proficiency in "the rhetoric of Demosthenes and the syllogisms of Aristotle".[1] Furthermore, the Bulgarian Church, governed by a prelate who owed obedience to Constantinople, could be expected to keep its flock on the straight path of loyalty to the empire.

Seventeen years later there was little left of this hopeful picture. The imperial hegemony which Basil I had done so much to build up in the Balkans had been shattered. The Byzantines, routed in battle, were fighting for the survival of their empire; and the victorious Bulgarians, as in the days of Krum, looked like becoming the masters of the whole peninsula. This conflict between the empire and Bulgaria is the main theme in the history of the Balkans during the first quarter of the tenth century. It was in several respects unlike all the previous wars which the Byzantines had fought to defend their territory and interests in the peninsula; and it introduced into the empire's relations with its northern neighbours a new, ideological, factor which was to loom large in the later history of the Byzantine Commonwealth.

At the turn of the ninth century the literary activity inaugurated by Boris and the disciples of Constantine and Methodius in Pliska and in Macedonia was in full swing. This work of adapting Byzantine culture to the educational needs of the Bulgarians enjoyed the full support of Symeon, who combined a devotion to Greek literature with an enthusiasm for the Slavonic vernacular tradition. While the work of Clement and Naum in Macedonia was undermining paganism, increasing literacy and filling the ranks of the Slavonic-speaking clergy, it was in the new capital of Preslav, and especially in the royal monastery of St. Panteleimon near by, that this literary movement thrived during the next decades. The priest (later bishop) Constantine translated homilies of the Greek Fathers, notably (*c.* 907) St. Athanasius' *Discourse against the Arians*; John the Exarch, a leading member of this school, wrote versions of several works of St. John of Damascus and an adaptation of the *Hexaemeron* of St. Basil the Great; Symeon himself supervised the translation of selections from the works of St. John Chrysostom; a treatise on poetics by the Byzantine grammarian George Choeroboscus was also translated at the time. This literature, of which only a few leading instances have been cited, was mainly one of translation and adaptation; but some original works were produced in the Slavonic language, such as the first grammar of that tongue (by John the Exarch), and an apologia for the Slav letters (by the monk Khrabr). The linguistic basis, literary qualities, and historical significance of this movement, which has caused Symeon's reign to be known as "the golden age of Bulgarian literature", will be discussed in a later chapter; three of its features, however, may be noted here: it produced, in several successive generations, a group of scholars, mostly churchmen, who were linked to each other by a common devotion to the memory of Constantine and Methodius, whose disciples they considered themselves to be; it enjoyed the continued patronage of the Bulgarian royal family—first of Boris, then of Symeon and of Boris' brother, the monk Duks; and it rapidly assumed an international character, spreading through Eastern Europe and fostering for many centuries the cultural life of the nations which found themselves in the orbit of Byzantium.

It may seem paradoxical that at the very time when this Slav vernacular literature was producing its first fruits in Bulgaria under Greek auspices, and the country's autonomy and favoured status within the Byzantine Commonwealth seemed assured, the empire and Bulgaria found themselves locked in bitter conflict and engaged in prolonged war. This paradox can be partly explained by the mentality and ambitions of Symeon. His early years in Constantinople had given him some grounding in the education, at once Christian and classical, which the Byzantine authorities dispensed so willingly to the sons of neighbouring princes. In his later years his spoken Greek caused raised eyebrows among the linguistic pundits in Constantinople; yet he must have felt flattered by the epithet "the half-Greek" which his complaisant mentors had bestowed upon him. Symeon remained all his life under the spell of Byzantine civilization and, like so many other East European rulers of the Middle Ages, could never bring himself to forget that Constantinople was, in wealth, culture and international prestige, the first city in Christendom. Hence, like his father Boris, he felt impelled to imitate in his own country the works of Byzantium. He wished his capital of Preslav to be a second Constantinople and strove to copy, in the outward trappings of his power, the glory that radiated from the emperor's sovereignty. The builders and artists he and his father had imported from Byzantium helped him in this task. A contemporary Bulgarian observer, John the Exarch, has left us an account of the royal palace at Preslav, whose splendour, he claims, defied description, in which sat Symeon, "in a garment woven with gold, a golden chain round his neck, girt with a purple girdle, his shoulders adorned with pearls, and wearing a golden sword".[2]

In modern times a situation in which the ruler of a relatively backward country, having received his education in a foreign land that claims supranational sovereignty and a monopoly of culture, resolved on his return home to adopt its customs and institutions, might well have led sooner or later to a nationalistic revolt of his subjects against that land's pretensions to hegemony. But in the ninth century, nationalism, as we know it today, did not yet exist; political thought, at least in Eastern Europe, was dominated by the idea of the one universal empire, whose centre was in Constantinople. This empire was, by definition, a unique and all-embracing institution. And so Symeon, impelled by restless ambition, convinced of the innate superiority of all things Byzantine, and well-grounded as he was in East Roman political philosophy, was driven to the only course of action he could logically adopt: to try to make himself master of an enlarged Byzantine Empire, which would include Bulgaria. To achieve this he needed to capture Constantinople and to seat himself on the imperial throne.

The immediate cause of the first war that broke out between Symeon and Byzantium was economic: in 894, as the result of a court intrigue, two Greek merchants secured the monopoly of the Bulgarian trade and transferred the market from Constantinople to Thessalonica, where they imposed heavy taxes on Bulgarian goods. Symeon promptly protested to the Emperor Leo vi; but the speculators enjoyed the protection of their government, and the Bulgarian representations were ignored. Symeon invaded Thrace, defeated a Byzantine army and advanced towards Constantinople.

Symeon's grievance was real enough. Since the early eighth century the Bulgarians had attached great importance to their trade with the empire: corn and cattle, linen and honey were exported from the khan's dominions in Moesia and Northern Thrace to Constantinople and the cities on the western coast of the Black Sea; in exchange the Bulgarians obtained from Byzantium manufactured goods, among which dyed silken robes were especially prized. By the middle of the ninth century, as the Bulgarian realm expanded into Macedonia, Thessalonica became another outlet for its foreign trade. However, the Morava-Vardar trade route, which led to that city, passed through the western periphery of the khan's domains, and was therefore of secondary importance. The main commercial highways were in the central and eastern parts of the country, and they led to Constantinople: they included the sea route from South Russia, which hugged the Bulgarian coast; the overland roads which led from the lower Danube across the passes of the Balkan range; and above all the Belgrade-Constantinople thoroughfare. The merchants and travellers who used them journeyed through the main cities of Bulgaria—Silistria, Varna, Pliska, Preslav, Niš, Sofia, Philippopolis—and, like the tourists of today, could be expected to leave some of their currency in local shops and markets. It is not surprising that the transfer of the Bulgarian market to Thessalonica, and the consequent shift of the export and transit trade from the centre to the periphery of the land, quite apart from the heavier duties now imposed on Bulgarian goods, were regarded by Symeon as a severe blow to his country's economic interests.

Symeon's invasion of Thrace was a serious threat to the empire, whose best troops were away in Asia, fighting the Arabs. The Emperor Leo vi was forced to resort to diplomacy. Early in 895 he sent an embassy to the Magyars, who were then encamped north of the Danube estuary, in the plain of Bessarabia. This Finno-Ugrian nomadic people, by then considerably mixed with Turkic elements, had probably formed part of Kovrat's "Old Great Bulgaria"; during the ninth century they moved westward across the Don and the Dnieper. The imperial ambassadors succeeded in bribing them to attack Symeon in the rear: ferried across the Danube by the Byzantine fleet, the Magyars invaded the Dobrudja, advanced to the neighbourhood of Preslav, and inflicted several defeats on the Bulgarian armies. Symeon, precariously enclosed in Silistria, sued the Byzantines for peace.

The events of the next few years were to demonstrate how adept Symeon could be in imitating the techniques of Byzantine diplomacy and in outplaying his teachers at their own game. The emperor sent the distinguished diplomat Leo Choerosphactes to parley with him. No sooner had he arrived in Bulgaria than he was arrested on Symeon's orders; from the fortress in which he was imprisoned he was reduced to negotiating by correspondence. The fourteen letters which he exchanged with Symeon in 895–6 show that the Bulgarian ruler was trying to gain time by sidetracking the Byzantine envoy into an inconclusive discussion about an exchange of prisoners and by entangling him in a mock-serious argument about semantics and punctuation.[3] He raised no objection to Leo's repeated references to the emperor as Symeon's "father"; but on all the other points at issue he was in turn truculent, sarcastic and cunning. He could now afford to show his hand more openly: his southern frontier secure, he turned against the Magyars and drove them back across the Danube; about the same time, mindful of the lessons he had learned from the Byzantines in the art of diplomacy, he sent an embassy to the Magyars' eastern neighbours, the dreaded Pechenegs, and persuaded them to attack the Magyars in the rear. The Pechenegs, a Turkic people who lived in the steppes on both sides of the Dnieper, promptly invaded Bessarabia and occupied the Magyars' homes. The latter, deprived of their territory, were forced to migrate: so they moved westward, crossed the passes over the Carpathians, and entered the Pannonian plain (896). A few years later they founded in that area the kingdom of Hungary. The rise of this medieval realm was thus the direct result of the rival diplomatic intrigues of Symeon of Bulgaria and the Byzantine government in the steppes of South Russia. Symeon, meanwhile, had invaded Thrace and again routed a Byzantine army. Peace was then concluded (896), and the empire undertook to pay the Bulgarians an annual subsidy.

For the next seventeen years the empire and Bulgaria remained formally at peace. This did not prevent Symeon from making a bid to seize Thessalonica and, when this attempt failed, from advancing Bulgaria's frontier to within about twelve miles of that city. But the true goal of his ambitions was Constantinople. The situation in Byzantium soon reached a stage that seemed to call for his intervention. In 912 the Emperor Leo VI died, leaving the empire, weakened abroad and rent by the internal dissensions provoked by his fourth, uncanonical, marriage, in the hands of his worthless brother Alexander. Alexander's only noteworthy act of foreign policy was to insult the envoys sent by Symeon to renew the treaty of 896, and to refuse the agreed tribute. By the time of Alexander's death on 6 June 913, Symeon had obviously resolved on war. The internal situation in the empire was everything he could wish for. The legitimate emperor, Constantine VII Porphyrogenitus, was a sickly boy of seven; the government, in the hands of a regency council dominated by the Patriarch Nicholas Mysticus, was not yet firmly in the saddle; and an uprising against the young emperor, fomented immediately after Alexander's death by the commander-in-chief, Constantine Ducas, had narrowly failed, leaving an aftermath of bitterness and disaffection. Symeon, at the head of a large army, marched into Thrace and, in August 913, invested Constantinople along the whole length of the land walls, from the Golden Horn to the Sea of Marmara. Strategically he now found himself in the same position as his predecessor Krum, exactly a century earlier: in full control of all the approaches to the city by land, yet unable to breach its fortifications, and lacking the necessary instrument for storming it from the sea—a navy. So Symeon in his turn was driven to negotiate.

The course and outcome of these negotiations, which were to determine the development of Balkan history during the next fourteen years, shed some light on Symeon's ambitions, the methods of East Roman diplomacy and the view currently held by the Byzantines on the structure of international society. On the Byzantine side one man stood out, embodying with vigour and subtlety the imperial claims to world dominion: the Patriarch Nicholas Mysticus. During his first tenure of the patriachate (901–7) this prelate, inflexibly opposed to Leo VI's fourth marriage, had the courage, on Christmas Day 906, to close the gates of the church of St. Sophia in the emperor's face. During his second tenure of the office (912–25), and as president of the regency council in 913–14, he had the prime responsibility for negotiating with the Bulgarians; in this task he displayed, most of the time, the same mixture of firmness and moderation which, in the empire's heyday, so often distinguished its foreign policy.

We possess twenty-six letters, written by Nicholas to Symeon between 912 and 924.[4] They are the principal source of our knowledge of Byzantine-Bulgarian relations in this period. One of the most revealing was written in early July 913, just as Symeon was embarking on his invasion of the empire. The patriarch implores him to desist from "tyrannical" attack on the child-emperor, and threatens him with excommunication should he persist in his criminal venture. Nicholas makes it quite clear that Symeon's professed intention was to obtain the Byzantine throne: "Are you not afraid," he wrote, "of God's judgement? Are you not afraid to harbour the design of seizing that imperial authority which Christ has exalted on earth?"[5] Repeatedly in this letter Nicholas castigates Symeon's design as "tyranny" (*tyrannis*) which, in medieval Greek, meant an unlawful revolt of a subject against the sovereign emperor. The patriarch's strong language is understandable: Byzantium had many times been threatened by alien foes, and rebellious subjects of the emperor had even usurped his throne; but never before had a Christian prince, whose country was part of the Byzantine Commonwealth, claimed the supreme rank in the "oecumenical" society of nations whose legitimate head was the emperor in Constantinople.

Having failed to stave off Symeon's invasion, Nicholas could at least, now that his enemy was at the gates of Constantinople and amenable to talks, try to induce him to take his army home. As head of the regency government, the patriarch was empowered to offer favourable terms. They proved so acceptable that Symeon raised the siege and returned to Bulgaria. The nature of these concessions, never explicitly mentioned (and for good reason) by Byzantine writers, can be inferred from subsequent events. It is virtually certain that Symeon was promised that one of his daughters would be allowed to marry the Emperor Constantine, and that on the same occasion, in September 913, he was crowned by the patriarch as "Emperor of the Bulgarians". The matrimonial promise was calculated to appeal to Symeon's ambitions: recent precedent suggested that the status of father-in-law to the emperor could carry great power in Constantinople. Even if Constantine survived his delicate childhood, there seemed every hope that Symeon would be formally associated before long with the imperial throne. The title of "Emperor of Bulgaria" (*basileus Boulgarias*), it is true, fell short of Symeon's dream of securing the *imperium* of the Romans. Yet it greatly increased his international prestige; and he must have realized that in the matter of titles the Byzantine government was not, at least for the present, prepared to go further. So long as Constantine was the legitimate emperor, he alone had the right to the title of *basileus tôn Rhomaiôn*. From the Byzantine standpoint the restriction of Symeon's imperial title to Bulgaria seemed to offer some hope that he would not reiterate his former exorbitant claims; the simple title of *basileus*, which was far from implying equality of status with the East Roman emperor, had already been granted in 812 by the Byzantine government to Charlemagne. In these circumstances, there seemed no compelling reason to refuse it to Symeon. It looked as though Nicholas' diplomacy had, by these concessions, adroitly averted the Bulgarian peril.

Symeon, for his part, also seemed reasonably satisfied by the agreement of 913. Though he had failed in his immediate plans to capture Constantinople and secure the Byzantine throne, the empire, he had reason to hope, would soon fall into his hands like a ripe plum. Before returning home he had a cordial meeting with the patriarch and assured him of his firm intention to live henceforth at peace with Byzantium.

But Nicholas and Symeon had both made a miscalculation. The patriarch, deluded perhaps by that arrogant sense of superiority which Byzantine statesmen so often displayed in their dealings with "barbarians", doubtless believed that Symeon would be suitably impressed by his new title of "Emperor of the Bulgarians". Symeon, for his part, overestimated the strength of the patriarch's influence. Zoe, the empress-mother, whom Nicholas had forced to take the veil, had still a powerful following in Constantinople. Early in 914 she seized control of the regency government. Nicholas, whose political power was now drastically reduced, was unable to prevent the new government from repudiating the concessions he had made to Symeon in the previous year. It was probably then that a curious story began to circulate in Constantinople. It provides a diverting example of that mixture of ingenuity, arrogance and naïveté with which public opinion in Byzantium often sought to interpret in a manner flattering to its vanity the empire's relations with other countries. Symeon's coronation by the patriarch, the story went, was quite invalid, for Nicholas, during the ceremony, had placed on the head of the Bulgarian ruler not the imperial crown, but his *epirrhiptarion*, the piece of black material which covered his monastic hat; and Symeon, because he had bowed his head before the patriarch, failed to notice the cunning substitution and, in his barbaric simple-mindedness, was tricked by Nicholas into believing that he had been lawfully crowned. The blatant improbability of this tale, which is told by the tenth century chronicler Symeon the Logothete,[6] needs no demonstration. But this brazen attempt to justify, perhaps with the connivance of the patriarch himself, the decision of Zoe's government to repudiate the agreement with Symeon is an interesting addition to the storehouse of the empire's political mythology; and the contrast, so disingenuously drawn, between the diplomatic cunning of the Byzantines and the artlessness of the Bulgarian monarch must have caused much self-satisfied amusement in Constantinople.

Before long, however, Symeon learned to his fury that the new Byzantine government had dishonoured its predecessor's obligations, and that the Empress Zoe had no intention of allowing her son Constantine to marry his daughter. He invaded Thrace and captured Adrianople (September 914). Zoe's government took energetic counter-action: an experienced diplomat, John Bogas, military governor of Cherson, was sent to the Pechenegs in South Russia to persuade them to cross the Danube with the help of the Byzantine fleet, and to invade Bulgaria. In vain did Symeon try to counter-bribe his former allies of the steppe: he was, for the time being, caught between two fires. It was probably then that, frustrated in his ambition to become the *basileopatôr*, the emperor's father-in-law, he reiterated his earlier demand: that the Byzantines recognize him as their sovereign. Once again Nicholas Mysticus rejected this offer with horrified indignation: though he strongly disapproved of the new aggressive policy towards Bulgaria and tried to appease Symeon by openly blaming Zoe's government in his letter, he refused to betray the basic tenet of Byzantine political philosophy: in a letter written in the summer of 914 he countered the latter's "tyrannical" claims by solemnly reminding him that "the emperor's authority stands above all earthly authority, and alone on earth was established by the King of all".[7]

The Byzantine government was now determined to crush Symeon. A large army commanded by Leo Phocas marched across Thrace, while the fleet, under the command of the Admiral Romanus Lecapenus, sailed to the Danube to ferry the Pechenegs across. But these fickle allies refused to cross the river; and at Achelous, in the neighbourhood of Anchialus, on 20 August 917, the Byzantine army was routed by Symeon. The Bulgarians swept into Thrace and, at the approaches to Constantinople, gained another victory.

As soon as the news of the disaster at Achelous reached the capital, the patriarch wrote a long and carefully worded letter to Symeon.[8] Despite some turgid rhetoric and an occasional touch of special pleading, it is, on the whole, a dignified and impressive document. He admitted that the Byzantine government was wrong to attack Bulgaria, but asserted that Symeon, by invading imperial territory in Thrace, Macedonia and on the Adriatic seaboard, and by his deceitful attempts to gain the alliance of the Pechenegs, shared the responsibility for this deplorable war between Christians. All the patriarch's eloquence and diplomacy were, however, wasted on Symeon: his reply was to accuse Nicholas of stupidity, an insult which prompted the patriarch in his next letter to give him a lesson in history: the Bulgarians, he wrote, who had once been slaves of the Avars, ought not now to seek dominion over those who, by teaching them the Christian faith, had brought them freedom.[9]

Nicholas' admonitions were clearly proving of no avail. Zoe's government, however, had another and more effective card to play. In 917, shortly before the battle of Achelous, the military governor of Dyrrachium was sent to Dalmatia to confer with Prince Peter of Serbia, who was well known for his loyalty to Byzantium. But Peter's attack on Bulgaria failed to materialize. Symeon, too, had his agents in Dalmatia: Michael, prince of Zachlumia, who was probably jealous of Peter's newly acquired sovereignty over the Narentani, promptly informed the Bulgarian monarch that his country faced the danger of military encirclement. Symeon's reply was to invade Serbia and carry off its prince to a Bulgarian prison (918).

During the next five years Symeon was virtually master of the Balkans. His armies marched through Thrace with devastating regularity, often reaching the environs of Constantinople; punished the Serbs for their willingness to stir up trouble against him in the interests of Byzantium; and on one occasion (probably in 918) invaded Greece as far as the Gulf of Corinth. But he was still unable to force the defences of the capital; and meanwhile events within the city were spelling the doom of his ambitions. On 25 March 919 the Admiral Romanus Lecapenus seized power in Byzantium; in May 919, by the marriage of his daughter to Constantine VII, he became the emperor's father-in-law; and on 17 December 920 he was crowned co-emperor. The way to the imperial throne—the very one he had planned to use—was now closed to Symeon. With impotent rage he now demanded the deposition of Romanus in favour of himself. His communications to the Byzantine court became even more insulting in tone. The fresh batch of letters written to Symeon between 919 and 924 by the Patriarch Nicholas[10] (who, until his death in 925, remained the emperor's principal adviser in foreign affairs) show that Romanus' government was prepared to go as far as it could to appease the Bulgarian monarch. In turn conciliatory and firm, pleading and dignified, bland and menacing, Nicholas suggested that he and Symeon should meet; implored him to end the bloodshed between two Christian peoples; repeatedly condemned the aggressive policy of Zoe's now defunct government; ominously mentioned Romanus' military preparations; conjured up the menace of a vast anti-Bulgarian coalition of northern peoples, Magyars, Pechenegs, Russian and Alans, raised up by imperial diplomacy; proposed a marriage alliance—now quite harmless to Byzantium —between the families of Romanus and Symeon; and offered the latter money, silken robes of state and imperial territory in exchange for peace. But on the only matter that really interested Symeon, the patriarch was as adamant as ever: the idea that the Bulgarian monarch should seat himself on the imperial throne was unthinkable; and it is worth noting that Nicholas justified his rejection of Symeon's imperialist ambition by the argument that the entire Balkan peninsula lay by right under the sovereignty of Byzantium: "Dominion over the whole of the West", he asserted, "belongs to the empire of the Romans".[11] But Symeon remained unmoved by these threats and blandishments, and Nicholas' last letters to him reveal an understandable bitterness, doubtless due to his awareness that his policy of appeasement had failed.

In the autumn of 924 Symeon's army appeared for the last time before Constantinople. He was now expecting the help of the Egyptian Fatimid navy, but his alliance with the African Khalife was wrecked at the last minute by Romanus' diplomacy. Once again he was forced to negotiate. The Patriarch Nicholas came out to see him; but Symeon demanded to see the emperor himself. The meeting took place on a pier specially built out into the Golden Horn, under the curious eyes of the senate, assembled on the city walls. Symeon is said to have spoken first, in a Greek disfigured by numerous solecisms.[12] Romanus' speech which followed may well have been composed by Nicholas. It was designed to remind the Bulgarian ruler of his station and duties:

> I have heard [said the emperor] that you are a religious man and a true Christian, but I see that your acts do not accord with your words: a religious man welcomes peace and love, for God is love, as it is said, but it is an impious and irreligious man who delights in slaughter and in the unjust shedding of blood. If then you are a true Christian—and we have been informed that you are—cease your unjust slaughter and the criminal shedding of blood, and make peace with us Christians, since you call yourself a Christian. . . . You are a mortal man; you await death and resurrection and judgement and retribution; today you live, and tomorrow you are dust; one fever will quench your pride. What answer will you give to God for your unrighteous slaughter, when you come before Him? How will you face the terrible and just Judge?[13]

It is quite likely that Symeon was impressed by Romanus' words, which echoed the august and confident traditions of the Christian Empire of which he had once been the devoted pupil. But in the field of practical politics his bid for world hegemony had only too patently failed. On his return to Bulgaria, his pent-up resentment burst out afresh. During the winter of 924-5 he proclaimed himself "Emperor of the Bulgarians and the Romans".

The Byzantine government must have realized by then that the acute peril which it had faced during the past thirteen years from Bulgaria was receding; and there was evidence that Symeon's subjects were becoming tired of these endless wars. The growing confidence of the authorities in Constantinople is apparent in the three letters which the Emperor Romanus wrote to Symeon in 925 and 926.[14] Their firm and authoritative tone is more reminiscent of Romanus' speech of the autumn of 924 than of the suppliant and occasionally lachrymose passages of the Patriarch Nicholas' letters to Symeon. The emperor's terms are set out in peremptory manner: all the lands and fortresses seized by Symeon since 913 must be returned to the empire; his assumption of the title of "Emperor of the Romans" is a grotesque usurpation of what does not belong to him; why not then style himself, Romanus inquired sarcastically, Lord of the Whole World, or Emir of the Saracens? If it came to appropriating empty titles, it was rather he, Romanus, who could claim with better reason to be "Emperor of the Bulgarians", for Symeon's forbears had, regrettably, been allowed to settle on Byzantine territory.[15] In fact Romanus did concede to Symeon this restricted title, which the regency government, we have seen, had granted him in 913. And, by addressing him as his "spiritual brother", he tactfully underlined that Symeon's title of *basileus* of Bulgaria conferred upon his nation a loftier status within the Byzantine Commonwealth than the one it had been accorded under Boris, who had been content to be counted among the emperor's "spiritual sons". But this status was still a subordinate one, and spiritual brotherhood implied not political equality, but merely a common profession of the Christian faith.

After 924 Symeon never invaded Eastern Thrace again. But his armies could still harass the empire in the central region of the Balkans, where the Serbs retained, albeit unsteadily, their traditional loyalty to Byzantium. The Serbian prince Zacharias, who had been educated in Constantinople, was appointed ruler of his country by the Emperor Romanus, probably in the winter of 920–1. But, defeated by the anti-Byzantine party in Serbia, he was carried off to a Bulgarian gaol. Three years later he was reimposed on the Serbs, this time by Symeon. His natural sympathies, however, lay with Byzantium, and no sooner was he restored to his native throne than he broke with the Bulgarians and reaffirmed his allegiance to the empire. Symeon decided to teach the Serbs a lesson. In two campaigns he devastated their country so thoroughly that Serbia became a deserted wilderness for a whole decade. After Zacharias had sought refuge in neighbouring Croatia, a Bulgarian army invaded that country (926), where it was defeated by the Croatian King Tomislav. Symeon never recovered from this blow. On 27 May 927 he died of a heart attack. His death transformed the balance of power in the Balkan peninsula. Its southern provinces devastated by a war that had lasted almost without interruption for more than a decade, its economy in ruins, its army decimated in distant adventures, its aristocracy seething with humiliation and its peasantry with discontent, Bulgaria ceased for half a century to play an active part in the politics of Eastern Europe.

A study of the conflict between Symeon and Byzantium leads to several conclusions which may help us to understand better the nature of the empire's relations with the countries of Eastern Europe. In the first place, one is struck by the role played in this conflict by the problem of titles. Symeon's claim to the imperial title—whether restricted to his own land or, increasingly as the conflict unrolled, coming to include the words "and of the Romans"—was the main cause of a war that was fought for the best part of a generation, and in which provinces and cities were devastated and countless lives lost. Symeon's demands, and the Byzantine reaction to them, were both based on the doctrine, commonly accepted in Eastern Europe in the Middle Ages, of the single and unique Christian Commonwealth, whose centre was in Constantinople and which, outside the borders of the empire proper, comprised a hierarchy of subordinate nations owing an ecclesiastical and in some degree political allegiance to Byzantium. The particular place assigned to each nation in this "oecumenical" society depended on several factors: on the extent to which it had absorbed Byzantine civilization, on the political and military power possessed by its ruler, and on the value of the services which he and his subjects could render to the empire. A sign of how high a given nation had risen in this international hierarchy was the title granted to its monarch by the East Roman government. The title of emperor (*basileus* in Greek, *imperator* in Latin, *tsar* in Slavonic), either unqualified or applied to a particular country, bespoke the highest subordinate rank in the Byzantine Commonwealth. This was the title which Symeon sought, and legally obtained, in 913. Above it there was only the supreme rank, that of the emperor in Constantinople, who alone, as head of the commonwealth, had the right to style himself *basileus* (and, from the early tenth century, also *autocrator*) of the Romans. By soliciting and later assuming this title—to which he had no legal or historical right—Symeon was claiming in effect that a ruler of a subordinate nation could usurp the prerogatives of his overlord. His aim was not to establish a Bulgarian *basileia* of his own, nor to rival or supplant the Byzantine Empire, but to set himself up as Roman Emperor in Constantinople. Nicholas Mysticus and Romanus Lecapenus understood clearly that his ambitions threatened the very foundations of the commonwealth, whose survival was essential for Christendom and mankind. The Byzantine Empire could not accept Symeon's demands without committing political suicide. It might be objected that Symeon, with his Hellenic education, could have played the role of emperor of Byzantium at least as effectively as Romanus, who was the son of an Armenian peasant; that, had he captured Constantinople, he might—as other usurpers of the throne—have been acceptable to the Byzantine ruling circles; and that, in this case, he would probably have been able to bring Bulgaria into the Empire's political fold. But, whatever the Byzantine theory, he was in fact the sovereign of an independent and hostile state: and no foreign monarch had yet succeeded in seizing the imperial throne. Moreover, as Nicholas' letters so clearly show, Symeon's claim to the title of *basileus* of the Romans directly threatened the position of Constantine Porphyrogenitus, and was consequently regarded as a "tyrannical" challenge to the legitimate Macedonian dynasty, which was attracting the growing loyalty of the Byzantines in the tenth century. It will later be shown that this problem of titles bedevilled the relations of Byzantium with other nations of Eastern Europe, notably with the Russians and the Serbs; for the rulers of these countries, no less than the Bulgarian monarchs, considered that this problem was of central importance in their political designs.

In the second place, Symeon's relations with the empire show that a country could be at war with Byzantium while continuing to absorb the fruits of its civilization. The fact that Symeon was at the same time fighting and copying the empire, devastating Byzantine territory and sponsoring the translation of Greek literature into Slavonic, can, we have seen, be partly explained by the nature of his ambitions: a Bulgarian prince who coveted the imperial throne of Constantinople would obviously wish to identify himself with the cultural traditions of Byzantium, especially when he was already "half-Greek" by education. But in a wider sense this paradox had its roots in the situation which was to confront the ruling classes of every country that entered the Byzantine orbit. The more educated they became, the more they strove to absorb the attractive and exportable features of the empire's civilization: its religion, its law, its literature and its art. At the same time, as that country acquired more developed institutions, its rulers became increasingly anxious to safeguard and increase the cultural and political autonomy of their realm. The difficulty lay in reconciling the universalist claims of Byzantium with its satellite's desire for independence. It is not surprising that this problem proved to be, in Eastern Europe in the Middle Ages, recurrent and intractable. And, as we shall see, it was responsible for the rise, in the lands of the Byzantine Commonwealth, of an attitude to the empire at once complex and ambiguous, in which attraction and repulsion were at times evenly balanced.

Finally, the outcome of Symeon's wars with Byzantium proved once again that, in the existing state of Constantinople's defences, the city could not be taken by a continental power which lacked a navy. The Bulgarians, like so many nations which came from the Eurasian steppes, retained in the Middle Ages a curious aversion to the sea. The peoples who came nearest to capturing Constantinople in the early Middle Ages were those who had mastered the seafaring technique: the Slavs, the Arabs and the Vikings. So long as the Byzantines kept control of the waters that bathed the Thracian coast—the western seaboard of the Black Sea, the Bosphorus, the Sea of Marmara and the Dardanelles—Constantinople, and therefore the empire, was safe. It was not until the second half of the twelfth century that they finally surrendered their maritime supremacy to the Italians; and in this same period the empire lost for ever its political control over the northern and central parts of the Balkan peninsula.

In October 927 a peace treaty was signed between the empire and Bulgaria. At first sight its terms seem remarkably favourable to Bulgaria. Peter, Symeon's son and successor, was married to Maria Lecapena, the granddaughter of the Emperor Romanus, and was acknowledged by the Byzantine government as "Emperor (*Tsar*) of Bulgaria"; and *post-factum* recognition was also given to Symeon's illegitimate act, performed in the last years of his reign, of raising the archbishop of Bulgaria to the rank of patriarch. These flattering concessions, however, could not conceal the fact that Romanus had gained a signal diplomatic victory over Symeon's mild and saintly son. The patriarch of Bulgaria was independent of his colleague in Constantinople only in name; and the Byzantines, it seems, insisted that his see be located not at Preslav, where he might be subjected to undesirable pressures from the Bulgarian government, but in distant Silistria on the Danube. Yet Peter's marriage to a princess of the imperial blood was a boost to Bulgaria's international prestige; and as such it was frowned upon by the racial purists in Constantinople, such as Constantine Porphyrogenitus, who greatly disapproved of the practice of giving Byzantine brides to foreign monarchs: a conduct which he reprobated (except for marriages with Frankish rulers) as strongly as the indiscriminate selling of state robes and diadems to barbarians, or the surrender of the Greek fire to potential enemies of the empire.[16] Maria's marriage could, however, be defended on political grounds: for the Byzantine *tsaritsa* of Bulgaria, now renamed Irene in symbol of the peace that would reign henceforth between her husband and her grandfather, ensured the continued influence of Constantinople over the court of Preslav. As for Peter's title of "Emperor of Bulgaria", it was no more than the Byzantines had, admittedly under duress, already conceded to his father. The rank which it denoted in the hierarchy of the commonwealth was, we have seen, a subordinate one, and it implied that its holder owed allegiance to the emperor in Constantinople. Such at least was the Byzantine theory; and its relevance to the status of Bulgaria after 927 appears very clearly in the protocols of the *Book of Ceremonies*, compiled in the mid-tenth century by Constantine Porphyrogenitus. In this manual of Byzantine court ceremonial we find, graded with the utmost precision, the formulae of address used by the emperor in his correspondence with

158

foreign rulers.[17] It has been demonstrated that these formulae conform to a definite political pattern, and define the different ranks ascribed to their addressees in the international hierarchy of states by the Byzantine protocol. In this list the Bulgarian ruler occupies an honourable, but by no means exalted, place: higher than the client princes of the Caucasus and the nations who lived north of the Danube, the Russians, the Pechenegs and the Magyars; yet lower than the Frankish rulers, and the Khalife of Baghdad. It is also significant that he is described in the list as the emperor's "spiritual son"; this shows that Bulgaria had descended a rung in the hierarchical ladder. Now that the country had ceased to be a military threat to the empire, the spiritual "brotherhood" bestowed on Symeon could be withdrawn; Peter had to be content with his title of Tsar of Bulgaria, and the spiritual "sonship" which now bound him to Romanus, as it had bound Boris to Michael III, symbolized unequivocally the allegiance he and his subjects owed to Byzantium.

The Bulgarian peace treaty of 927 was celebrated in an oration delivered in the same year in the palace, probably by Theodore Daphnopates, a high imperial official and the author of Romanus' letters to Symeon. It provides an interesting comment on the attitude to Bulgaria which then prevailed in official circles in Constantinople. The author mentions the "community of brotherly love and concord" which now binds that country to the empire; alludes to Symeon's coronation as "Emperor of the Bulgarians" in 913 with a "makeshift diadem"; refers indignantly to the "insurrection" and "apostasy" of which he was guilty by usurping the imperial crown of the Romans, an act that "discrowned Europe", i.e. brought disaster on the Balkans; praises the diplomacy of the Patriarch Nicholas, by which he "cunningly mastered and restrained" this "wild boar"; describes Symeon's meeting with Romanus in 924; and rejoices in the knowledge that thanks to Romanus' understanding with Peter the Bulgarians are no longer called Scythians or barbarians, since God has "healed the parts of the *oikoumene* that were split apart and thus brought them together in wholeness and continuity".[18]

With Bulgaria reduced to the status of a docile satellite, the empire quickly restored its authority over the Serbs. Shortly after Symeon's death, the Serbian prince Časlav escaped from Bulgaria, where he had been held a captive. It seems likely that his flight was engineered by the Byzantines, for on his return home he hastened to pay homage to the empire: an allegiance which he maintained throughout his reign (i.e. at least until 950), and which partly jutifies Constantine Porphyrogenitus' claim that Serbia "is, as before, in servitude and subjection to the emperor of the Romans".[19]

How heavily imperial sovereignty weighed on the Serbs during the remaining part of the tenth century we do not know. All the evidence we have regarding the impact of Byzantium on the Balkan Slavs in this period concerns Bulgaria; and much of it is highly revealing.

Bulgarian society in the reign of the Tsar Peter (927–69) reflected in several ways the new political relations with the empire. There was still an anti-Byzantine party at the Bulgarian court: as early as 928 its leaders—"Symeon's nobles", as the contemporary Byzantine chroniclers call them[20]—staged an abortive revolt against the tsar. But the old Bulgar nobility, who formed the nucleus of this war party, were fast losing their ethnic identity and becoming absorbed by the Slavs; and the country as a whole, exhausted by Symeon's wars, was no longer capable of a sustained military effort. Nor is there any evidence that the remnants of this military aristocracy still retained their ancestors' pagan beliefs. Christianity had made considerable progress in Bulgaria during the past half century, and its impact had been much strengthened by the fact that it was now being preached in a Slavonic vernacular dress. It found its leading champion in the tsar, for Peter was a man of deep and zealous piety. During his reign a number of monasteries were established in Bulgaria, some royal or aristocratic foundations, others, particularly in the mountain retreats of Rila and of the Rhodopes, and in remote Macedonia, hermitages founded by solitary ascetics, who were later joined by disciples and pilgrims from all over the country. Within these monasteries, whose religious and cultural role will be examined in a later chapter, the traditions of Byzantine asceticism and spirituality became accessible to Bulgarian Christians.

The growth of monasteries in so many parts of the Bulgarian realm did much to bring Christianity to the country districts and thus to broaden the range of its social impact. At first the Byzantine missionaries seem to have worked mainly in the cities and among the ruling classes. It was only gradually, probably not much before the turn of the ninth century, that the new religion began to have a perceptible influence on the peasantry, owing to the increasing use of Slavonic in the liturgy and to the activity of men like St. Clement of Ohrid. In the tenth century this work of the country clergy received the support of provincial monasteries, some of which became centres of pilgrimage for the village people. Nevertheless the cities and the educated classes of society remained for a long time the main strongholds of the new faith.

Some historians have looked for evidence of the "Byzantinization" of Bulgarian society in the economic changes of the tenth century, particularly in the growth of large landed estates at the expense of the small holdings and in the increasing tendency of the peasants to seek the patronage of the territorial magnates. Both these phenomena were certainly widespread in the tenth century Byzantine Empire, and successive governments, not least that of Romanus I, took energetic steps to protect the small freeholders against the encroachments of the provincial aristocracy. But it is dangerous to assume that these trends towards "feudalization" were equally pronounced in tenth century Bulgaria, and even more hazardous to ascribe them to deliberate imitation of Byzantine models. The little evidence we have suggests that the rise of large estates, the economic dependence of the peasants on the magnates, and the immunities from taxation and public duties secured by the latter, are phenomena which were not encountered on a large scale in Bulgaria before the second half of the eleventh century. Nevertheless, at least the first two may well have begun to appear already in the tenth century in the north-eastern part of the country, between the Danube and the Balkan Mountains, where the geographical and economic conditions were more favourable than elsewhere to the growth of large landed estates. This tendency was probably accelerated by the economic misery resulting from Symeon's wars, and by the famine and plague in the Balkans which followed the exceptionally severe winter of 927–8 and which, in many parts of the empire, caused the starving peasantry to sell their land to the magnates at low prices or in exchange for food.

These social and economic developments may not have been

161

linked directly with the importation of Byzantine practices and institutions. But the two phenomena were not wholly unconnected: for the new patterns in the country's social structure and distribution of wealth were the cause of widespread misery among the Bulgarian peasantry, which in the middle of the tenth century erupted in a powerful movement of revolt against the authorities of church and state, a movement whose anti-Byzantine overtones are clearly apparent. Its essentially popular nature shows that militant opposition to the imported Byzantine culture had shifted since the days of Boris from the military aristocracy to the Bulgarian peasantry. The origins and early history of this movement must now be considered.

Some time between 933 and 956 the Tsar Peter received a letter from the patriarch of Constantinople, Theophylact Lecapenus. This prelate, who was a son of the Emperor Romanus, merely signed the epistle: its author, the manuscript tells us, was the chief secretary of the patriarchate. It is clear from its contents that the Bulgarian ruler had earlier appealed to the patriarch for guidance on the proper manner of dealing with a heresy which had recently appeared in his country; that a written reply had been sent to him from the patriarchate; and that Peter, finding its contents obscure, had written back, requesting a clearer and fuller explanation. He was doubtless as mystified as Boris had been when trying to unravel Photius' epistle, with the tortuous rhetoric affected by the patriarchal chancellery. In his new letter the patriarch addressed Peter as "Emperor of Bulgaria", tactfully alluded to their relationship by marriage, and praised him for his orthodox zeal. In reply to the tsar's question as to whether "the secular laws of Christians" should be applied against the heretics, Theophylact stated that for those who persist in their evil ways the rightful punishment was death; though he urged Peter to avoid excessive severity and to make every effort to secure their conversion by gentler arguments. As for ecclesiastical sanctions, the patriarch prescribed the use of solemn anathema against the obdurate heretics; in the formulae which he recommends for this purpose their principal errors are listed: they include the belief in two eternal principles, the one good, the other evil, the first of whom created light and the invisible world, the second, darkness, matter and the human body; the rejection of the Old Testament, as belonging to the realm of darkness; the disbelief in the physical reality of Christ's incarnation; and the assertion that marriage and the reproduction of the human species should be condemned as a law of the devil. The patriarch describes this heresy as both "ancient" and "newly appeared" and defines it as "Manichaeism mixed with Paulicianism".[21]

It seems unlikely that Peter found the patriarch's second letter much more enlightening than the first: its abstract terminology, its tendency to describe the heresy in terms of its doctrinal ancestry, its fondness for heresiological clichés, and its almost total lack of practical advice, all this was not very helpful in the concrete predicament that faced the Bulgarian ruler. But the patriarch, or more probably his theological advisers, had at least succeeded in identifying to their own satisfaction the component parts of the new Bulgarian heresy. His reference to Paulicianism is particularly significant. The Paulician sect arose in Armenia, and enjoyed considerable success there and in Asia Minor during the eighth and ninth centries. Its votaries were frequently persecuted by the Byzantine authorities not only on account of their heretical teachings, but also because they were unruly frontiersmen and, often allied with the Arabs, a chronic nuisance on the empire's eastern border. In the second half of the ninth century their military power became so great that they were able, from their strongholds on the upper Euphrates, to thrust westward as far as the Aegean coast and to demand the surrender of the whole of Asia Minor. In 872, however, Basil 1's armies invaded their homes in Armenia and brought them to heel. Their main doctrines (except for the condemnation of marriage, to which they did not subscribe) were indeed those enumerated by Theophylact. Zealous proselytizers, they had long regarded the Balkans as a profitable missionary field: an enterprise in which, oddly enough, they received the involuntary help of the Byzantine government. In 757 the Emperor Constantine v, in an attempt to strengthen the empire's northern frontier against the Bulgarians, garrisoned a number of fortresses in Thrace with Armenian and Syrian colonists whom he had transported from Erzerum and Melitene; among them were Paulicians who, we are told by a ninth century Byzantine chronicler, were responsible for spreading their heresy in Thrace. From this Thracian borderland, which was continually changing hands during the Bulgaro-Byzantine wars, and through the many prisoners whom Krum had deported from this area to various parts of his realm, Paulicianism spread to Bulgaria. The earliest definite evidence of the sect's proselytism in the country dates from the second half of the ninth century; but it must have begun earlier. We may assume that the Christian elements in their teaching—they had a special devotion to St. Paul, and claimed that their doctrines were based on the Gospels—enabled the Paulicians to compete with the Greek and Latin missionaries in Bulgaria on their own ground; while their bitter and long-standing hostility to Byzantine Christianity made their sect a rallying point for those Bulgarians who opposed everything that came from Constantinople.

The Paulicians, however, suffered from one disability which prevented them from becoming the real leaders of a popular anti-Byzantine movement. For all their successful proselytism, they remained in the early Middle Ages largely a body of foreign immigrants in the Balkans. This was doubtless the main reason why their communities were unable fully to identify themselves with, and to act as a channel for, the local groundswell of religious dissent and social revolt. This role was assumed by another sectarian movement, native to the Balkans—the "ancient" and "newly appeared" heresy whose growth caused the Tsar Peter such alarm that he appealed for help to Constantinople.

Defined by the patriarch as a mixture of Manichaeism and Paulicianism, the new movement did indeed bear some resemblance to the latter. As for the term "Manichaeism", it could scarcely have referred with any historical precision to the Manichaean movement which had flourished between the third and the seventh centuries in the Near East and in the Mediterranean world and had, indeed, given birth to Paulicianism: for, as far as we know, by the tenth century there were no more Manichaeans proper in the Balkans. But the term "Manichaeism", when used, as it frequently was by Byzantine churchmen, in an abstract and generic sense, could be made to cover a fair number of kindred teachings: and it seems likely that Theophylact used this word to describe the extreme moral rigorism which he imputed, quite correctly, to the Bulgarian heretics.

The new heresy which the patriarch defined, somewhat inadequately, solely by reference to its antecedents, was Bogomilism. This movement of dissent, the most powerful in the medieval history of Eastern Christendom, derived its name from its founder, the priest Bogomil (Theophilus), who was a contemporary of the Tsar Peter (927–69) and probably taught in the early years of his reign.

No comprehensive account of the doctrines and history of the Bogomil sect can be given here. Our attention must be confined to those aspects of Bogomilism which are relevant to the subject of this book: it will be considered primarily as an example—the most strikingly successful in the whole of the Middle Ages—of a spontaneous and popular movement of resistance to the patterns of Byzantine culture which were being imposed upon their subjects by the ruling classes of a country within the empire's orbit. The success of this movement was due mainly to the fact that its leaders were not attempting (as did the Bulgarian *boyars* in the ninth century) to restore the old, pagan way of life, nor to resist alien domination by violent methods (as the Bulgarian insurgents against the empire attempted to do in the eleventh and twelfth centuries), but fought Byzantine Christianity on its own ground and with its own weapons: these, derived from the moral teaching of the Gospels, were a thirst for personal righteousness, a desire for social justice and pity for innocent suffering.

Bogomilism, however, was far from being a simple attempt to reform the Orthodox Church by an appeal to evangelical ideals. All the contemporary evidence, the bulk of which, it is true, comes from their enemies, shows that the Bogomils preached a cosmological dualism akin to that of the Paulicians. The Bulgarian priest Cosmas, who in about 970 wrote a detailed, vivid and first-hand account of the movement,[22] stated this very clearly: "They say that everything exists by the will of the Devil: the sky, the sun, the stars, the air, man, churches, crosses; all that comes from God they ascribe to the Devil; in brief, they consider all that moves on earth, animate and inanimate, to be of the Devil".[23] Unlike the Paulicians, who believed in two eternal principles, parallel and coeval, the Bogomils recognized that the Devil is inferior to and ultimately dependent on God, who is the creator of the invisible world and of man's soul. But Bogomils and Paulicians were at one in postulating a radical opposition between God and the principle

165

of Matter, and in believing that this opposition is reflected in the nature of man, whose soul is of divine origin and whose body the domain of the Evil One. Historically, Bogomilism thus appears as an offshoot of the Dualist movement which, through its Paulician and Manichaean manifestations, goes back at least as far as Gnosticism. Dualism, which seeks to explain the orgin of evil by tracing it to a principle contrary to God, has always been opposed to the Judaeo-Christian tradition, which posits an ontological link between the infinite and the finite (cemented by the divine act of Creation and, in Christianity, also by the Incarnation) and holds that evil is due to man's disobedience to God's will.

The dualistic cosmology of the Bogomils and the Paulicians was regarded by their Orthodox opponents as an absurd delusion. In the abundant polemical literature which the latter have left us there is only one example of a writer who, despite his violent dislike of the Bogomils, seems aware that behind their fanciful metaphysics there lurked a human problem of singular poignancy. The church teaches that God is the source of all perfection and that the whole world, visible and invisible, is His creation. Yet one does not need to be a philosopher to observe that in this world of ours moral and physical evil—suffering, cruelty, decay, death—is abundantly present. How then can God, the Supreme Good, be the cause of suffering and evil? Must He be held responsible for wars, epidemics, the oppression of the poor by the rich? Cosmas tells us that such questions were frequently raised, and not only in heretical circles, in tenth century Bulgaria: "many of our people [i.e. the Orthodox]", he wrote, "are heard to say: 'why does God allow the Devil to assail man?'" Cosmas may dismiss this question as the product of "a childish and unhealthy mind";[24] yet, to judge from his words, it was one to which few parish priests of his time and country were capable of giving a satisfactory reply. To put the question in this form was already to advance a step towards heresy; for the Bogomils had an answer which was at least logical and consistent: evil and pain are inherent in this world, because this world is the creation of the Evil One. Cosmas' brief statement, apart from its human interest, has a further significance: it shows that Bogomilism was capable of appealing to the simple folk—the first, but not the only, sign that it had become in tenth century Bulgaria a popular, peasant movement.

This may seem at first sight surprising: for Christianity had by that time made considerable inroads into the Bulgarian countryside; and its doctrines were patently incompatible with the dualistic cosmology of the Bogomils. Equally obvious, even to the most ignorant of the Orthodox, was the incongruity between the teaching of the church and the other tenets of the sectarians, which were a logical consequence of this cosmology: holding matter and the human body to be creations of the Devil, the Bogomils were led to deny the physical reality of the Incarnation, to reject all the sacraments of the church, to condemn the veneration of the cross, of icons and relics and to shun all buildings used for Christian worship.

And yet, even on this doctrinal plane, there were points of contact between Orthodoxy and Bogomilism which must have smoothed the path that led from the former to the latter. The Bogomils claimed to base their teaching on the New Testament, which they accommodated to their own dualistic and anti-sacramental views by an ingenious use of allegory. Thus, according to Cosmas, they held that the two brothers in the parable of the prodigal son were Christ and the Devil, and that the words of institution used by Christ during the Last Supper referred not to His body and blood, but to the Gospels and the Acts of the Apostles.[25] This method of "double-think", and the ingenuity with which Christian Scriptures were interpreted, suggest that the doctrines of the sect had an outward and an inward esoteric aspect, and that the latter was communicated only to a relatively small group of initiates. This occultism which the Bogomils shared with other dualistic sects made the task of detecting and identifying them very difficult, and consequently frightened and angered their Orthodox opponents. It implies, furthermore, that though the Bogomil rank and file were probably mostly people of humble station, peasants, artisans and merchants, their leaders must have been educated, in some cases indeed accomplished, theologians. It seems likely that these were mostly drawn from the lapsed clergy and monks of Bulgaria.

It was, however, in the field of ethics and behaviour that the blurred outlines that so often separated Orthodoxy from heresy caused the greatest irritation and concern to the "representatives of order" in church and state. The moral teaching of the Bogomils was as consistently dualistic as their theology: if the material world is the creation and realm of the Evil One, it naturally follows that, in order to escape from his grasp and to be united with God, man must avoid as far as possible every contact with the world of the flesh, through which the Devil seeks to gain mastery over his soul. Hence the Bogomils imposed on their followers (in fact, only on the "elect" minority of initiates) total abstinence from sexual intercourse, meat and wine. This rule seems to have been fairly strictly obeyed throughout the greater part of the sect's long history, and it is with some reason that the Bogomils have been called "the greatest puritans of the Middle Ages". It was here, perhaps, that the Greek and the Bulgarian clergy, faced with the evangelical appeal of Bogomilism, felt that the greatest danger lay. For, on the one hand, the medieval church, in its struggle against different forms of dualism, always found it hard to distinguish in practice between true and false asceticism, between the legitimate wish to discipline the body and an ontological hatred of matter. On the other hand, we know from the evidence of Cosmas that in his time the boundary between these two types of asceticism was often slender; and he inveighs with some bitterness against those monks of his country who assert that salvation is impossible for those who marry and live in the world: this, he protests, is "nothing but a heretical thought".[26] The sense of alarm which the moral austerity of the Bogomils stirred up in their Orthodox opponents is vividly conveyed in Cosmas'. ironical portrait:

> In appearance the heretics are lamb-like, gentle, modest and silent, and pale from hypocritical fasting. They do not talk idly, nor laugh loudly, nor give themselves airs. They keep away from the sight of men, and outwardly they do everything so as not to be distinguished from Orthodox Christians. ...The people, on seeing their great humility, think that they are Orthodox and able to show them the path of salvation: they approach and ask them how to save their souls. Like a wolf that wants to seize a lamb, they first cast their eyes downwards, sigh and answer with humility. ... Wherever they meet any simple or uneducated man, they sow the tares of their teaching, blaspheming the traditions and rules of holy church.[27]

This accusation of hypocrisy was constantly made against the Bogomils by the Orthodox. It was based partly on the existence within the sect of a secret current of esoteric doctrine, and partly on the fact that the Bogomils claimed that they alone had the right to the name of Christians. The official church hierarchy, they contended, had forfeited this right because of their un-Christian behaviour: according to Cosmas, the heretics accused the Orthodox clergy of idleness, drinking and robbery.[28] In pointed contrast, the Bogomil preachers passed from village to village, carrying, he tells us, the book of the Gospels in their hands,[29] and with it their message of evangelical poverty, purity and asceticism.

The Bogomil movement thus acquired in the early stage of its history two main features: on the one hand, its doctrines were rooted in a dualistic cosmology, imported into the Balkans from the Near East through the Paulicians; on the other, its ethical teaching, based on the New Testament, embodied the ideal of a "reformed" Christianity, free from the abuses of the institutionalized and worldly church of Byzantium, and seeking to return to the purer and more heroic virtues of the apostolic age. And, at least in tenth century Bulgaria, it had a third aspect which must have further increased its popular, revolutionary appeal. A movement which not only rejected the basic doctrines of the Orthodox Church, but also denounced the ecclesiastical hierarchy and, by condemning marriage, undermined the very foundations of family life, inevitably became, in a medieval society, a revolt against the secular laws. Cosmas rebukes the Bogomils for teaching "that it is unbecoming for man to labour and to do earthly work", and accuses them of a crime even more serious: "They teach," he writes, "their own people not to obey their lords, they revile the wealthy, hate the tsar, ridicule the elders, condemn the *boyars*, regard as vile in the sight of God those who serve the tsar, and forbid every servant to work for his master".[30] This brief but explicit statement provides the final proof that the Bogomils were not only in revolt against the authorities of the church and the hierarchical structure of Bulgarian society but, by preaching and practising civil disobedience, urged the people to rebel against the established political order.

Unfortunately neither Cosmas nor any other medieval writer has anything definite to say about the practical results of the Bogomils' social and political anarchism. There is no reason to believe that they preached anything but a passive resistance to the state. The practice of violence was incompatible not only with their evangelical ideals, but also with their dualistic theology: for Satan can never be defeated with the material weapons which he has himself fashioned to enslave man's soul. In the view of the Bogomils the material world is irredeemable: they wished not to transform it, but to escape from it. Their espousal of social equality and their championship of the poor against the rich and powerful were not a programme of revolutionary political action, but rather a reflection in the realm of human society of their belief in the cosmic struggle between good and evil.

The danger which the sect presented to the authorities of church and state was increased by the courage and tenacity of its votaries. Theophylact's advice to use methods of persuasion against the heretics proved impracticable. Cosmas, who knew them better, asserts that they are incapable of being converted. The Bulgarian government was forced to resort to persecution, which seems to have been violent. But Cosmas was honest enough to admit that this merely increased their popular appeal, since many "do not know what this heresy is, and imagine that they suffer for righteousness and wish to receive rewards from God for their chains and imprisonment".[31]

The subsequent history of the Bogomil movement will be mentioned only intermittently on the pages of this book. We must note here that from its original home, which was probably in Macedonia, it later spread to many areas of the Byzantine Empire, enjoyed a brief though spectacular vogue in Constantinople at the turn of the eleventh century, survived in Bulgaria (alongside the largely separate Paulician sect) until the late Middle Ages, spread westwards to Serbia and Bosnia and, in the second half of the twelfth century, exerted a powerful influence upon the Patarene and Cathar (or Albigensian) movements in Italy and Southern France.

The success enjoyed by Bogomilism in medieval Bulgaria shows that the impact of Byzantine culture and institutions upon a country that had moved into the empire's orbit could, in certain circumstances, be withstood and repelled with the very weapons which the Byzantines used to extend their hegemony. Three examples may help to illustrate this point. In the first place, the most effective carriers of Byzantine influence to a recently converted country were the clergy, Greek and native, who could usually be relied upon to instil into their flocks a loyalty to the mother church of Constantinople. The Bulgarian clergy were no exception: their leader, the Bulgarian patriarch, was in theory autonomous, but even he owed a measure of allegiance to the Constantinopolitan see, and some of his bishops were probably Byzantine citizens. Cosmas, who cannot be suspected of anti-clerical bias, paints a gloomy picture of the state of his country's clergy. Not a few of the bishops, it seems, were wealthy landowners, and had lost that close contact with their flocks which had been the strength of such men as St. Clement of Ohrid. The parish priests, we have seen, were charged by the Bogomils with sloth, drunkenness and peculation; and Cosmas, who had probably been one of them himself, admitted that these accusations were true. Indeed he went so far as to place the main responsibility for the spread of heresy in Bulgaria on the clergy: "whence", he wrote, "arise these wolves, these wicked dogs, these heretical teachings? Is it not from the laziness and ignorance of the pastors?"[32] By the same token the Bogomils, by the austerity of their lives, their intimate knowledge of the Gospels, their resolute proselytism and courage in persecution, seemed to many of their compatriots to be the bearers of true Christianity.

In the second place, monasticism, which developed rapidly in tenth century Bulgaria, also proved a two-edged weapon in Byzantine hands. Undoubtedly the monks made a notable contribution to the cultural life of the country, especially in and near the capital, and, particularly in the southern and western areas, did much to evangelize the pagans. But the overall picture of contemporary Bulgarian monasticism was not an edifying one. Cosmas tells us of monks who, ignoring their vows, live unchastely, engage in trade and business, indulge in endless gossip or, like the *gyrovagi* of Western Europe, wander about on the excuse of some pilgrimage. Not a few of them, moreover, by accepting the "Manichaean" belief that the human body is evil and that marriage is an obstacle to salvation, were playing into the hands of the heretics. This could not fail to lead to the contamination of Orthodoxy by dualist doctrines; and it is significant that Cosmas' treatise was written both against the Bogomils and the abuses of contemporary monasticism. Thus did a religious institution imported from Byzantium become in the hands of the dualist sectarians a weapon used with some effect against the Byzantine

Orthodox tradition.

Thirdly, the Bogomils used their religious convictions and their reputation for holiness to discredit the Byzantine tradition in the sensitive field of political theory. Central to this theory was the idea of the monarch who rules by God's authority. The supreme example of such a monarch was the emperor, God's vicegerent on earth. But the Byzantines were willing to concede that a measure of divine sanction endorsed the authority of those East European sovereigns whose realms lay within the commonwealth, and who were supposed to reign over their respective countries as deputies of the emperor in Constantinople. This theory of the divine origin of the king's power was regarded in Byzantium as a useful reminder to the satellite rulers of their religious and political obligations towards the empire. The Bulgarians had long been accustomed to think of their monarch in these terms: already Omurtag had styled himself in his inscriptions "ruler by God's authority". After Bulgaria's conversion to Christianity the Byzantines from time to time reminded its rulers that they held their power by divine decree. Thus the Patriarch Theophylact, in his letter to the Tsar Peter about Bogomilism, stated that his realm was "governed by God".[33] This association of Orthodox Christianity with the theory of divine monarchy was attacked by the Bogomils with particular vehemence: by denouncing the belief that man-made institutions may be sanctified by divine warrant, they were led "to regard as vile in the sight of God those who serve the tsar". And in the face of this rejection by the Bogomils of both spiritual and temporal authority, Cosmas felt obliged to remind them of the church's traditional teaching on the source of earthly power: "the tsar and the *boyars*", he wrote, "are established by God".[34]

We have little information on the political relations between the empire and Bulgaria in Peter's reign, except in its last years. In the latter part of the tenth century and until 1018, Bulgaria once again loomed large on Byzantium's northern horizon. The relations between the two were then, as in the days of Symeon, dominated by war. These wars, chronicled at length in medieval sources, have been frequently described by modern historians. For this reason, and also because they do not provide much evidence on the impact of Byzantium on Bulgaria in any but the military field, a brief account of them will suffice. They culminated in a remarkable military effort which has been aptly termed "the Byzantine epic" and which, in the space of some fifty years, led to the Byzantine reconquest of the Northern Balkans.

In 965, soon after the death of his Byzantine wife, the Tsar Peter, perhaps under pressure from the old Bulgarian war party, sent an embassy to Constantinople to demand the next instalment of the "tribute" due under the treaty of 927. The empire had just embarked on the period of the greatest military successes in its history. The new emperor, Nicephorus Phocas, who had recently captured Crete, Cyprus and Cilicia from the Arabs and was soon to achieve the reconquest of Antioch, was not in the habit of concealing his conviction that the empire was superior to all the nations of the earth. The Bulgarian envoys were ignominiously dismissed with a message in which their tsar was described as "a prince clad in leather skins" who, instead of demanding tribute, should acknowledge the emperor as his lord and master. Nicephorus then moved his troops to the Bulgarian frontier. Reluctant, however, to invade a country where the armies of his predecessors had so often come to grief in the mountainous interior, particularly since his forces were still engaged in Asia, he resorted to the traditional methods of Byzantine diplomacy: he sent an embassy to Russia, with a vast sum of money and instructions to bribe its ruler Svyatoslav to attack Bulgaria in the rear. The prince of Kiev proved only too willing: in 967, at the head of a large army, he crossed the Danube—without Byzantine help, for the Russians possessed an excellent fleet—and occupied the Dobrudja. The Bulgarian army, overwhelmingly defeated, retired to Silistria.

It was not long before the emperor realized that his diplomatic coup had misfired. Kalokyros, his ambassador, had turned traitor and, no doubt with Svyatoslav's connivance, was known to harbour imperial ambitions. As for the prince of Kiev, his behaviour showed that he had no intention of playing the role of the emperor's hireling. As a military commander he was Nicephorus' match. Alarmingly, his ambitions were now centred on the Balkans. The springboard for his southward advance was to be Little Preslav, near the Danube delta. According to a medieval Russian source, he intended to make this city the capital of his realm: for "there", he is said to have declared, "all the good things converge: gold, precious silks, wine and fruit from Byzantium, silver and horses from Bohemia and Hungary, furs, wax, honey and slaves from Russia."[35]

The Russian ruler's interest in the commercial amenities of the lower Danube region suggest that he now regarded the Balkans as something more than an arena for a passing military adventure: soon his eyes would be cast in the direction of Constantinople. The Emperor Nicephorus, aware that his diplomacy had conjured up a monster he could no longer control, promptly made peace with the Bulgarians. Fortunately for both sides, Svyatoslav was summoned home during the winter of 968-9 by the news that the Pechenegs were besieging Kiev. It is hard to avoid the suspicion that these steppe nomads had been called in either by the Bulgarians or by the Byzantines. By the following summer, having defeated the Pechenegs, he was back in Bulgaria. His ambitions were now firmly fixed on Byzantine territory. Marching south, he captured Preslav, the Bulgarian capital, and stormed Philippopolis. By the end of 969 the whole of Eastern Bulgaria was in Russian hands, and Svyatoslav, at the head of a large army of Vikings and Slavs and allied with the Pechenegs and Magyars, was planning to descend on Constantinople. The new emperor, John Tzimisces, attempted to negotiate Svyatoslav in reply demanded an enormous ransom for the Byzantine prisoners and territory he held, and ended his provocative message with these words: "If the Romans do not want to pay, let them withdraw from Europe, which does not rightly belong to them, and retire to Asia; otherwise there will be no peace between the Russians and the Romans."[36] Not since the days of Symeon had a barbarian ruler dared to address the emperor of Byzantium in such outrageous terms.

The imperial government was no longer content, as it had been in the days of Romanus 1, to pursue a defensive policy in Thrace and to rely on the impregnable walls of Constantinople. Happily for the Byzantines John Tzimisces was as great a military leader as his predecessor. By the spring of 971 he had completed his preparations for a campaign to drive the Russians from the Balkans. His strategic plan, though conventional, relied on the elements of speed and surprise: the land army, led by the mail-clad cavalry and supported by elaborate siege artillery, was to march from Adrianople across Thrace and force the passes of the Balkan Mountains before the Russians had time to fortify them; simultaneously, a fleet of more than three hundred ships, some of them armed with Greek fire, sailed to the mouth of the Danube to cut off their retreat. This pincer movement was brilliantly successful. The army crossed an unguarded Balkan pass and descended into the plain surrounding Preslav. In April the Bulgarian capital, furiously defended by the Russians, was stormed by the imperial forces. From Preslav Tzimisces marched north to Silistria on the Danube, where Svyatoslav had entrenched himself. A great battle was fought at the approaches to the city, in which the Russians, fighting on foot, were put to flight by the Byzantine heavy cavalry. The siege of Silistria lasted for three months: in the end the Russians, exhausted by famine and by the desperate fighting, and aware that their retreat was sealed off by the Byzantine fire-shooting ships which guarded every crossing of the Danube and which, a contemporary Byzantine writer asserted, were capable of turning the very stones to cinders, sued for peace. Svyatoslav undertook to leave Bulgaria, and solemnly pledged himself never again to attack the empire or its possessions in the Crimea; in return he asked for some food for his starving men, a safe-conduct through the Byzantine naval blockade, and a promise that the emperor would prevail on his Pecheneg allies not to attack him on his way back to Kiev. Tzimisces accepted these terms, and confirmed the trading privileges which the Russian merchants had formerly enjoyed in Constantinople. After a brief meeting on the banks of the Danube, the two monarchs left for their respective homes: Svyatoslav was ambushed beside the Dnieper rapids by the Pechenegs, who had refused the emperor's request to let the Russians through, and was killed by them (972). Tzimisces' entry into Constantinople followed the traditional pattern of an emperor's return from a victorious campaign against barbarians, and was imbued with the religious and political symbolism so beloved by the Byzantines on great occasions of state. At the gates of the city he was met by the highest dignitaries of church and empire, who sang hymns of praise in his honour and offered him a crown and a sceptre, made of gold and precious stones. On a gilded chariot drawn by four white horses and normally ridden by the emperor was placed instead an icon of the Mother of God, which he had brought from

175

Bulgaria, and beneath it lay the purple robes and diadems of the Bulgarian tsars. Behind the chariots, as the procession entered the city, rode the emperor in full regalia on a white charger, followed on foot by the tsar of Bulgaria, Boris II, whom Tzimisces had captured in Preslav. In the church of St. Sophia the emperor laid the splendid crown of Bulgaria upon the high altar, as a token of thanksgiving and the first spoils of war. Then, in front of the crowd assembled in the main forum, he bade the Bulgarian tsar divest himself of his insignia of sovereignty and bestowed on him the Byzantine court title of *magister*. In a single year (971) John Tzimisces had achieved a military feat unparalleled in the medieval annals of the Balkans. He had removed the Russian threat which imperilled the empire's survival in Europe, restored its northern frontier to the Danube, and recovered the territory which Asparuch's Bulgars had wrested from Byzantium three centuries earlier.

During this savage war the Bulgarians had watched helplessly the two greatest military powers of Eastern Europe fighting for their land. We know little of the measures taken by John Tzimisces in 971 to incorporate Bulgaria into the administrative structure of the empire. It seems that there was no complete military occupation and that the Byzantines confined themselves to fortifying and garrisoning the main cities of Eastern Bulgaria. In the west, in the hills and isolated valleys of Macedonia, where neither the Russians nor the Byzantines had set foot during the fighting, imperial rule was largely nominal, and the political traditions of the defunct Bulgarian state lived on. It was there that, on Tzimisces' death in 976, the four sons of a provincial Macedonian governor raised the standard of revolt. Samuel, the youngest, taking advantage of the civil wars in Byzantium that followed the death of John Tzimisces, gradually built up a kingdom whose capital was first on an island in Lake Prespa and later in Ohrid, and which by the end of the century comprised most of the former Bulgarian lands between the Black Sea and the Adriatic, with the addition of Serbia up to the lower Sava, Albania, Southern Macedonia, Thessaly and Epirus. The origin of Samuel's kingdom has provoked a lengthy debate which has sometimes been befogged by anachronistic arguments. Whatever role we ascribe in its creation to local "Macedonian" elements, there can be no doubt that Samuel deliberately identified himself with the political and religious traditions of the empire of Symeon and Peter. This continuity was particularly evident when Samuel, in the closing years of the tenth century, proclaimed himself tsar and restored the Bulgarian patriarchate which had been abolished by John Tzimisces. Although there is no evidence that he considered himself as anything more than emperor of the Bulgarians, his act was regarded in Byzantium as a rebellion. A contemporary Byzantine writer refers to him as "the Bulgarian tyrant",[37] implying that he was on a par with the arch-rebel Symeon.

It was some time before the Byzantine government, busy suppressing a series of revolts by factious generals and intermittently occupied with the Arab war in Asia, was able to give its full attention to Bulgarian aggression, before which all the achievements of John Tzimisces in the Balkans were gradually crumbling. The danger, it is true, may have seemed less immediate than in Symeon's time: for Symeon, from his strongholds in the North-Eastern Balkans, had continually led his armies across Thrace against Constantinople; the centre of Samuel's kingdom was remote from the Byzantine capital, and its natural lines of expansion were eastward to the Aegean, westward to the Adriatic and southward into Greece. Yet Samuel's conquests in these areas were alarmingly easy: in the closing years of the century he marched unopposed up the valley of the Tempe and across Thessaly, Boeotia and Attica to the Isthmus of Corinth, over which he crossed into the Peloponnese. A Byzantine army, it is true, defeated him near Thermopylae (997). But in the same year the Bulgarians captured Dyrrachium: their seizure of this fortress and their subsequent advance to the Dalmation coast threatened the Byzantine strategic position in the Adriatic. On the North Aegean seaboard Samuel was less successful; though his repeated attempts to capture Thessalonica were ominous enough.

The first major Byzantine counter-offensive took place in 986. It ended in disaster. The Emperor Basil II marched with a large army up the Roman highway through Adrianople and Philippopolis, and reached the walls of Serdica. But his siege of the city was unsuccessful, and as his army was retreating the Bulgarians rushed down the mountains and, by the "Gates of Trajan" in the Succi Pass, gained a total victory. The sorry remnants of the Byzantine army, having lost its cavalry and all its baggage, were pursued by Samuel back to the borders of the empire.

It was not until the very end of the century that Basil II was able to concentrate all his energy and military resources on what he came to regard as the main task of his reign—the final subjugation of Bulgaria. To this task he now applied the powers of mind and character, nurtured by the political and military trials of his youth, and that meticulous attention to detail which have earned him a place among the greatest generals in Byzantine history. His strategy aimed at the systematic conquest of the two regions which the empire had to control in order to dominate the northern part of the Balkan peninsula: the plain between the Balkan Mountains and the Danube, and the highlands of Macedonia. In this he was served by admirably equipped and disciplined troops, and by commanders fully aware of the dangers which the treacherous mountain passes presented to an army marching northward from Thrace or from the Aegean coast. Basil's conquest of Northern Bulgaria was achieved between 1000 and 1004 by the capture, after carefully planned campaigns, of Vidin, Pliska and Great and Little Preslav. The crucial battle for Macedonia was fought on 29 July 1014, in the pass of Kleidion which overlooks the plain of Campu lungu traversed by the Strumitsa. Samuel's army, which had blocked the pass, was surprised in the rear by a Byzantine force which the emperor had sent over the Belašica Mountains, south of the pass. Though Samuel himself escaped, much of his army was butchered. Basil's savage reprisal has made this battle one of the most memorable in the history of the Balkans. He had all the Bulgarian captives—numbering, it was said, fourteen thousand—blinded, save for one in every hundred who was left with one eye to guide his comrades back to the Bulgarian tsar. At the sight of the gruesome procession, Samuel fell to the ground in a fit. Two days later, on 6 October 1014, he was dead.

The end of the Bulgarian state was now in sight. In vain did Samuel's two ephemeral successors offer their allegiance to the emperor: Basil pursued his methodical conquest of Macedonia. In 1018, at the gates of Ohrid, he received the submission of the late tsar's family. After a last tour of his conquered territory, his work completed, the "Bulgar-slayer" (thus known henceforth to his subjects) paid a visit to Athens where, before the more solemn triumph that awaited him in Constantinople, he offered thanks for his victory to Our Lady of Athens in her church, the Parthenon.

The state which Asparuch and his Bulgars had founded in the Balkans over three centuries earlier and which on several occasions, under Krum, Symeon and Samuel, had challenged Byzantium for political hegemony in the peninsula, was no more. Its autonomous church was abolished and its territory incorporated into the structure of the empire's provincial administration. Further to the north-west, the Serbs, the Croats and the Slav tribes on the Adriatic now acknowledged, under their native princes, the emperor's overlordship. The loyalty of the Dalmatian cities to the empire seemed assured. Thus, for the first time since the barbarian invasions of the late sixth century, the entire Balkan peninsula lay in the unchallenged possession, or under the sovereignty, of Byzantium.

NOTES

1. Liutprand, Bishop of Cremona, *Antapodosis*, iii, 29: *MGH, Scriptores in usum scholarum* (Hanover and Leipzig, 1915), p. 87; English transl. F. A. Wright, *The Works of Liutprand of Cremona* (London, 1930), p. 123.

2. John the Exarch, *Shestodnev*, ed. R. Aitzetmüller, *Das Hexaemeron des Exarchen Johannes*, 1 (Graz, 1958), p. 195.

3. G. Kolias, *Léon Choerosphactès* (Athens, 1939) (Texte und Forschungen zur byzant.-neugriechischen Philologie, xxxi) = *FHB*, viii (1961), pp. 175–84.

4. *PG* 111, cols. 40–89, 97–196 = *FHB*, viii, pp. 186–188, 191–223, 229–97.

5. Ep. 5, ibid., cols. 45–56.

6. Leo Grammaticus, *Chronographia*, ed. I. Bekker (Bonn, 1842), p. 292; Theophanes Continuatus, vi, 5, p. 385.

7. Ep. 8, col. 64.

8. Ep. 9, cols. 68–80.

9. Ep. 10, cols. 80–4.

10. Ibid., cols. 84–9, 97–196.

11. Ep. 27, col. 176.

12. R. J. H. Jenkins, "The Peace with Bulgaria (927) celebrated by Theodore Daphnopates", *Polychronion. Festschrift Franz Dölger zum 75. Geburtstag* (Heidelberg, 1966), pp. 292, 296.

13. Theophanes Continuatus, vi, 15, pp. 405–9.

14. Romanus Lecapenus, *Epistolae*, ed. I. Sakkelion, Δελτίον τῆς ἱστορικῆς καὶ ἐθνολογικῆς ἑταιρίας τῆς Ἑλλάδος, i (1884), pp. 658–66, ii (1885), pp. 38–48 = *FHB*, viii, pp. 298–314.

15. Ibid., i, p. 659.

16. *DAI*, ch. 13, pp. 66–77.

17. Constantine Porphyrogenitus, *De cerimoniis*, ii, 48, ed. J. J. Reiske (Bonn, 1829), pp. 686–92; cf. G. Ostrogorsky, "Die byzantinische Staatenhierarchie', *Annales de l'Institut Kondakov*, viii (1936), pp. 49–53.

18. Jenkins, *The Peace with Bulgaria*, pp. 289–97.

19. *DAI*, ch. 32, p. 160.

20. *Theophanes Continuatus*, vi, 28, p. 419.

21. I. Dujčev, "L'epistola sui Bogomili del Patriarca Costantinopolitano Teofilatto", *Studi e Testi*, 232 (1964), pp. 88–91.

22. M. G. Popruzhenko, *Kozma Presviter, bolgarsky pisatel' X veka* (Sofia, 1936) (*Bŭlgarski Starini*, xii): French transl. H.-C. Puech and A. Vaillant, *Le Traité contre les Bogomiles de Cosmas le Prêtre* (Paris, 1945).

23. Popruzhenko, p. 26; Puech and Vaillant, p. 77.

24. Popruzhenko, p. 24; Puech and Vaillant, p. 75.

25. Popruzhenko, pp. 26, 10; Puech and Vaillant, pp. 62, 77.

26. Popruzhenko, p. 58; Puech and Vaillant, p. 106.

27. Popruzhenko, p. 3; Puech and Vaillant, pp. 55–6.

28. Popruzhenko, pp. 4, 13; Puech and Vaillant, pp. 57, 64–5.

29. Popruzhenko, p. 25; Puech and Vaillant, p. 76.

30. Popruzhenko, p. 35; Puech and Vaillant, p. 86.

31. Popruzhenko, p. 22; Puech and Vaillant, p. 74.

32. Popruzhenko, p. 75; Puech and Vaillant, p. 124.

33. Dujčev, "L'epistola", p. 88.

34. Popruzhenko, p. 35; Puech and Vaillant, p. 86.

35. *Povest'*, p. 48; Cross, p. 86.

36. Leo Diaconus, *Historiae*, vi, 10, ed. B. G. Niebuhr (Bonn, 1828), p. 105.

37. *Cecaumeni Strategicon*, ed. B. Wassiliewsky and V. Jernstedt (St. Petersburg, 1896), p. 65.

1 *The Land Walls of Constantinople*. The parallel lines of the fifth-century fortifications are here clearly visible: the moat (in the foreground), the low crenellated breastwork, the external *peribolos*, the outer walls and, separated from them by the internal *peribolos*, the great inner wall.

he Walls of Thessalonica, prob-
built in the late fourth century
ur era, on the site of the earlier
lenistic walls, dominate the hills
he city's northern side. They
e frequently rebuilt in the Byzan-
period, notably after the Avaro-
sieges of the sixth and seventh
uries.

3 *The Turkish siege of Belgrade, 1456*. This contemporary Turkish drawing—the earliest known plan of Belgrade—shows Mehmet II's fleet attacking the city from the north, and the Serbian cannon on the walls. Belgrade was relieved on this occasion by John Hunyadi, and was captured by the Turks in 1521.

4 *Golubac*. This castle, on a steep cliff overlooking the right bank of the Danube, some 80 kilometers above the Iron Gate, was protected by six towers and a tall keep. First mentioned in 1337, it was captured by the Turks after the battle of Kosovo, and was granted in fief by the Sultan to the rulers of northern Serbia. It really fell to the Turks, in 1458.

St Sophia, Constantinople. For the peoples of Eastern Europe, Justinian's Church of The Holy
Wisdom, built between 532 and 537, was the spiritual centre of Christendom. Its incomparable
ome (reconstructed in 558), which appears to be floating above the radiance diffused by the cor-
na of forty windows at its base, was seen by the Byzantines as though 'suspended from heaven'. The
inting of the vaults, the inscription in the dome, the four great medallions in the choir, the pulpit
d tribune on either side of the apse, the railings and the chandeliers, are all of Turkish origin.

6 *Studios* was one of the leading monasteries of the Byzantine Empire, and the constitutions of many coenobitic houses in Eastern Europe were modelled on its Rule. Its colonnaded basilica, completed about 463 and now in ruins, is one of the earliest surviving church buildings in Constantinople.

7 Rebuilt in the first half of the eleventh century, after Basil II's conquest of Macedonia, St Sophia became the cathedral of the archdiocese of Ohrid. Its Byzantine structure, with three naves and three apses, and its monumental cycle of paintings, express the will of the church and government of Constantinople to impose their authority over the newly-acquired Bulgarian territory. The exonarthex, in the foreground, was added in 1314.

Reconstructed model of St Sophia, Kiev The outward shape of Yaroslav's great cathedral, with thirteen cupolas disposed in a pyramid and rich polychromatic surfaces, is no longer recognisable since it was rebuilt between 1685 and 1707 in the style of the Ukrainian Baroque. Its foundation stone was laid in 1037. Until the sack of Kiev by the Mongols in 1240 its architecture and decoration provided the most tangible evidence of Russia's cultural links with Byzantium.

9 *The Rila Monastery* Founded in the first half of the tenth century by St John of Rila, it was the leading monastery of medieval Bulgaria. It was rebuilt in the fourteenth century on its present site (probably a few miles to the west of the original one) beneath the pine-covered slopes of the Rila Mountains. The central tower alone is medieval; the remaining buildings were erected between 1834 and 1837.

10-11 *The Cathdral of St Dimitri, Vladimir* (10-below) Built between 1194 and 1197, as the palace church of Prince Vsevolod III, it contained several relics of St Demetrius brought from Thessalonica. Its compact majesty suggests the glorification of the ruler's power. The celebrated stone relief carvings on its facades were perhaps influenced by native traditions of wood carving. (11-right) The world of animals and plants, sculptured on the facades, is given unity and purpose by the seated figure of King David who is probably inviting them to glorify their Creator (Ps. 148).

12-14 Mount Athos
(12) The summit of
Athos, the Holy Moun-
tain of Byzantine
Monasticism, is in the
distance; in the fore-
ground is the Monas-
tery of Stavronikita,
founded in the mid-
twelfth century.
(13) The Monastery of
Docheiariou, an elev-
enth century founda-
tion on Mt. Athos.
(14) The Serbian mon-
astery of Chilandar,
founded on Athos *c.*
1198 by Stephen
Nemanja and St Sava,
played a major role in
cementing cultural
links between Byzan-
tium and the peoples
of Eastern Europe. The
present church was
built in 1303; the tow-
ers and part of the
walls also date from
Milutin's reign
(1282-1321).

15-16 *Sucevița* Rumanian church architecture reached the peak of its development in the sixteenth century in Bucovina (northern Moldavia), in the foothills of the Carpathians. The Moldavian monasteries of this period had the form of a walled quadrangle, with the church standing isolated in the middle. (16-below) They were centres of learning and are with close contacts with Mount Athos. The present church was built in 1582-5. The most remarkable and original feature of these churches are the paintings on their exterior walls. (15-left) Those of Sucevița, which date from *c.* 1595, are the best preserved.

17 *Studenica* (below), built between 1183 and 1191, was the greatest of the foundations of Stephen Nemanja and the leading monastery of medieval Serbia. While the cupola of the Church of the Virgin is essentially Byzantine, its white marble facades, the sculptured portals and the windows are in the Romanesque tradition, which came to Serbia from the Dalmatian coast. The exonarthex and side chapels (on the right in the picture) were added *c.* 1230.

5
Byzantium and East-Central Europe

The northern frontier of the Byzantine Empire in Europe, as established by 1019 after the conquests of Basil II, followed the Danube upstream as far as its confluence with the Drava, and then ran parallel to the lower and the middle course of the latter. North of this line, from the arc of the Transylvanian Alps to Lake Balaton, lay territory which the Byzantines never succeeded in annexing, but which, at least in the early Middle Ages, they regarded as falling within their sphere of influence. In modern terms, it comprised the Transylvanian province of Rumania, the Vojvodina region of Yugoslavia and the greater part of Hungary. Further north, beyond the curve of the middle Danube, in Slovakia and Moravia, lay territory in which the Byzantine statesmen of this period showed a keen interest, and over which they also succeeded for a while in imposing the cultural influence of the empire. The reason for this interest was part ideological, part political. The rulers of Byzantium, who regarded themselves as the successors of the Roman Caesars, were not likely to forget that the latter had once held sway over Pannonia and Transylvanian Dacia, and that in the second century of our era the Roman legions had entered Slovakia and pushed northward as far as the foothills of the Carpathians. But Byzantium's trans-Danubian policy was also influenced by more urgent and practical considerations. Since the third century and until the empire's recovery in the ninth, the lands beyond the Danube had been a seething cauldron of hostile tribes pressing down on the imperial *limes*. Goths and Huns and Slavs in turn overran it to plunder the Balkans. To study these peoples, to forestall their attacks by the use of dip-

Map 5   East-Central Europe in the early Middle Ages

lomacy and to tame their instincts by bringing them under the
influence of its civilization—this for the empire was a matter not so
much of imperialist ambition, as of simple survival. Moreover, the
Balkan peninsula had from time immemorial been linked with the
lands beyond the Danube by trade, and the invasion routes that
led from Central and Northern Europe to the Bosphorus, the
Aegean and the Adriatic were also commercial highways. In these
circumstances, it is not surprising to find evidence of fairly close
contact between Byzantium and Central Europe at least as far
back as the fifth century. The later history of these contacts falls

into three phases. The first, which covers the period from 550 to 650, was overshadowed by the military problem posed to the empire by the settlement of the Avars in Pannonia. The second, which spans the last four decades of the ninth century, was marked by the mission of Constantine and Methodius to Moravia. The third and final phase extends approximately from 900 to 1200: its main theme is the relations between Byzantium and the Magyars.

We know least about the first of these phases. It is clear, however, that the coming of the Avars to Pannonia in 567–8 led to closer contact between Byzantium and Central Europe. In an attempt to ward off the Avar attacks on the Balkans, which became particularly dangerous after the fall of Sirmium in 582, to tame and civilize them, and to keep open the trade routes to the Middle-European plain, the Byzantine government repeatedly sent embassies to Pannonia. The envoys were sometimes accompanied by architects and craftsmen, and probably by Christian missionaries as well. Archaeological finds in present-day Hungary indicate that there was a fairly brisk trade between the empire and the Avars in the seventh century, that imperial coinage was in current use in their realm in the sixth, and that Byzantine craftsmen, working in their country, were adapting their techniques to the tastes of their Avar patrons. Byzantine merchants and artisans were no doubt attracted to Pannonia by the quantities of gold which circulated there and which the empire had paid Attila in tribute. Byzantium's diplomatic effort in that area met with some success. Heraclius' network of alliances with Kovrat's Onoguric kingdom, with the Croats and the Serbs, and probably with Samo as well, were notable achievements which may well have contributed to the defeat of the Avars before Constantinople in 626. Yet the empire was not able to maintain its influence in Pannonia, to Christianize the Avars, nor to save its northern frontiers from being overwhelmed by the Avaro-Slav hordes. For two centuries, between 650 and 850, Central Europe lay outside the orbit of Byzantium.

It was in the second half of the ninth century that the empire's foreign policy achieved its greatest success in Central Europe. The

183

beginnings of this operation were modest and unspectacular; its long-term effects were of momentous importance for the future relations between Byzantium and the peoples of Eastern Europe. In 822 we first hear of the existence, north of the middle Danube, of a Slav state called Moravia. Its founder, Prince Mojmir, expanded its original nucleus on the middle and lower Moravia southward to the territory between the Dyje and the Danube, and eastward into Western Slovakia. Nominally a subject of the Frankish Empire, he accepted the German missionaries who had been sent to evangelize his country. His two successors, Rastislav (846–70) and Svatopluk (870–94), gradually built up a realm that extended from Southern Poland and the upper Oder to the Danube (and for a time as far as the Drava), and from Bohemia to Eastern Slovakia, and was known to the Byzantines as "Great Moravia".

Frankish overlordship, and the growing influence of the missionaries from Salzburg and Passau, encountered resistance in the young Moravian state. By the middle of the ninth century Rastislav, whose realm had expanded eastward as far as the Bulgarian frontier on the Tisza, was able from the hillforts that dotted his country to challenge Frankish hegemony. His bid for independence provoked swift reaction from the Franks; and it was partly to curb Rastislav's insubordination that Lois the German concluded in the early 860s the alliance with Boris of Bulgaria which has been mentioned in an earlier chapter (p. 117). The Moravian prince, faced with the danger of military encirclement, reacted with equal promptness. In 862 he sent an embassy to Constantinople. It is at least probable that his envoys were instructed to seek a political alliance with the empire. Michael III's government which, we have seen, felt equally threatened by the *rapprochement* between Bulgaria and the Franks, responded to Rastislav's offer by concluding a treaty with Moravia. This treaty, which clasped Bulgaria within a pincer-grip, strengthened the hand of the Byzantine government two years later when, by a show of force, it compelled Boris to renounce the Frankish alliance and to accept Christianity from Constantinople.

These political negotiations between Byzantium and Moravia are not explicitly mentioned in any contemporary document. But the international alignment of forces at the time, as well as subsequent events, make it virtually certain that these negotiations were consummated by a formal alliance between the two powers. Medieval writers were interested in another aspect of Rastislav's embassy to Byzantium; which indeed was to prove of more lasting significance than the political one. Rastislav requested the emperor to send the Moravians a Christian missionary acquainted with their own Slavonic language. It is clear that in so doing he was moved by the awareness that the German priests working in Moravia were acting as agents of Frankish imperialism, and by the hope that a Slav-speaking clergy owing allegiance to Constantinople would help him to increase his country's cultural autonomy.

The emperor's choice of ambassadors to head the return mission to Moravia fell on two brothers from Thessalonica, Constantine and Methodius. Some reference has already been made to the career of the former, to his intellectual distinction, to his personal links with the leading Byzantine scholars of his time, and to the role played by the university of Constantinople in training him as a missionary and a diplomatist. The two brothers came from a family with a tradition of public service: their father had worked on the staff of the *strategos* of the theme of Thessalonica. Methodius, the elder, had held a high administrative post, possibly that of governor, in one of the Slav provinces of the empire. He and his brother were thus, by birth and training, part of the Byzantine "establishment", while their education placed them in the mainstream of the tradition of scholarship and letters which was then actively sponsored by government circles in Constantinople. Both entered the ranks of the clergy: Constantine was ordained deacon, and Methodius became a monk in the great monastic foundation of Mount Olympus in Asia Minor. Their ability and experience were highly valued in Constantinople: in 860, for instance, they were entrusted by the Emperor Michael III and the Patriarch Photius with an important political and religious mission to the realm of the Khazars, north of the Caucasus. When they were chosen to head the Moravian embassy, Methodius was abbot of one of the monasteries of Mount Olympus, while Constantine was teaching philosophy at the patriarchal school attached to the church of the Holy Apostles in Constantinople.

On linguistic grounds as well Constantine and Methodius were admirably equipped to lead a mission, one of whose aims was to preach Christianity to the Moravians in the Slavonic language. Thessalonica, their native town, was in the ninth century a bilingual city: the presence of numerous Slavs living within its walls, and the close contact between its citizens and the Slav communities in the surrounding countryside, explain the intimate knowledge of their language which they acquired in their childhood. Methodius' ninth century biographer tells us that the emperor, in urging them to go as his envoys to Moravia, adduced the following argument: "you are both natives of Thessalonica, and all Thessalonians speak pure Slav".[1]

The success of the Moravian mission depended not only on the ability of its members to preach Christianity in the local language by word of mouth; it was also necessary to provide the Moravians with Slavonic translations of the Scriptures and of the Christian liturgy. This problem had for some time been exercising the minds both of the Frankish and the Byzantine missionaries who worked among the Slavs. The Franks, during the first half of the ninth century, had translated for the benefit of their Moravian converts a few Christian texts from Latin into Slavonic, and transcribed them in Latin characters; among them were formularies of baptism and confession, the Creed and the Lord's prayer. The Byzantines, it seems, had made similar efforts during their missionary work among the Slav subjects of the empire, transcribing Slavonic religious terms (if not whole texts) by means of the Greek alphabet, doubtless in the expectation of the day when these alien settlers on their territory would be sufficiently Hellenized to understand the Greek Scriptures and liturgy. Outside the borders of the empire, however, the problem was more complicated. Apart from the fact that a number of sounds in the Slavonic language could not be adequately rendered by means of the Greek alphabet, the new Slav nations that were emerging in the ninth century beyond the Empire's northern borders were developing a degree of political and cultural self-awareness which made their leaders desire to obtain proper translations of the Scriptures and the liturgy into their own language. Such, at least, seems to have been the express wish of Rastislav of Moravia. And this presupposed the existence of a Slavonic alphabet.

The Byzantine authorities had been aware of this need for some time. Michael III admitted to Constantine in 862 that his two immediate predecessors, Theophilus and Michael II, had tried in vain to invent a Slavonic alphabet.[2] This task was now undertaken, and successfully accomplished, by Constantine. Medieval writers describe this invention as rapid, and state that it was made for the specific needs of the Moravian mission and as a result of Constantine's appeal for divine help. His early career certainly shows that he was an outstanding linguist; yet we also know that he had collaborators and disciples who helped him in this task; and it seems likely that both he and Methodius, whose interest in missionary work among the Slavs must have developed well before 862, had been working to compose a Slavonic alphabet for some years before Rastislav's embassy arrived in Constantinople. The alphabet which Constantine invented before leaving Moravia was, not surprisingly in view of his birthplace and childhood environment, adapted to a Slavonic dialect of Southern Macedonia, from the neighbourhood of Thessalonica. It should be noted that in the ninth century the various languages of the Slavonic world were far from having their present degree of differentiation: their close similarity in vocabulary and syntax ensured that the spoken tongue of the Macedonian Slavs was fully intelligible to those of Moravia.

The nature of Constantine's alphabet has provoked much controversy. The oldest Slavonic manuscripts that have come down to us are written in two different scripts, the Glagolitic and the Cyrillic. Which of the two did he invent? This complex and technical philological problem cannot be adequately discussed here. It should be said, however, that, in the virtually unanimous belief of present-day scholars, the alphabet invented by Constantine was the Glagolitic, while the so-called Cyrillic script, which bears his later monastic name of Cyril, is the result of an attempt by Methodius' disciples, probably in Bulgaria, to adapt Greek uncial writing of the ninth century to the phonetic peculiarities of the Slavonic tongue. Of the two, Glagolitic is the more complicated. Many philologists now believe that one of its sources was the Greek minuscule script; though some of its letters have been held to be adaptations from Semitic, and perhaps the Coptic, alphabets. But, viewed as a whole, Glagolitic is a highly distinct and original creation. Cyrillic, on the other hand, is, except for half a dozen letters, little more than an adaptation of the Greek alphabet. Its comparative simplicity, and its close resemblance to the Greek script, whose range and prestige were unequalled in Eastern Europe, invested it with far greater historical importance. To the present day, the church books of the Orthodox Slavs—the Bulgarians, the Serbs and the Russians—are printed in a slightly simplified form of Cyrillic, and the modern alphabets of these three peoples are based upon it. The Rumanians also adopted this alphabet in the Middle Ages, and their liturgical books were written and printed in it until the late seventeenth century. Yet the invention of Glagolitic which, for all its greater complexity, was well adapted to the qualities of the Slavonic tongue, was undoubtedly the work of a linguist of the very first order, and Constantine deserves to rank among Europe's greatest philologists.

Before leaving Constantinople, he translated, with the help of his new alphabet, a selection of lessons from the Gospels, intended for liturgical use. In the Byzantine Church the lectionary begins with the opening verses of the first chapter of the Gospel of St. John, which are read during the Easter liturgy: "In the beginning was the Word, and the Word was with God, and the Word was God." Their symbolic relevance to the impending task of evangelizing the Slavs in their own language was, we may be sure, lost neither on Constantine nor on his medieval biographer.

In the autumn of 863 the Byzantine mission arrived in Moravia, and was warmly welcomed by Prince Rastislav. Its immediate tasks were two. The first was a religious and cultural one: Constantine and Methodius had to build the foundations of a Slav vernacular church by translating the essential liturgical and scriptural texts and training a native clergy. The second problem was political and diplomatic: as envoys of the Byzantine emperor, they needed to come to terms with the Frankish clergy who had been working in Moravia for at least half a century, and with the secular and ecclesiastical powers which supported them: with the Frankish Empire which claimed political authority over Rastislav's domains; and with the Roman Church, which exercised spiritual jurisdiction over Moravia. In the first of these tasks they achieved rapid success. The liturgical offices had so far been celebrated in Latin, a language with which the Moravians were almost wholly unfamiliar. In a short time Constantine, in the words of his contemporary biographer, translated into Slavonic "the whole ecclesiastical office, matins, the hours, vespers, compline and the Mass".[3] There is little doubt that Constantine's Slavonic liturgy was, at least originally, based on the current Greek rite, and that the Mass which he translated was the Byzantine liturgy of St. John Chrysostom. At some later date, it seems, the Latin Mass was also translated into Slavonic for the use of the Cyrillo-Methodian mission, though in what circumstances we know not: the history of the Slavonic Roman rite in Central Europe is very obscure.

Constantine' translation of the liturgical offices and of the Gospel lectionary laid the foundations of a new literary language, based on the spoken dialect of the Macedonian Slavs, modelled on Greek, and mainly ecclesiastical in character. It is known to modern scholars as Old Church Slavonic. In the course of time its grammatical range was broadened and its vocabulary enriched by further translations of the Christian Scriptures, of Greek patristic and theological writings and of Byzantine legal texts, carried out by Constantine and Methodius and their disciples, as well as by the composition of original works in this language. However, in terms of linguistic accuracy and literary quality, the earliest phase in the development of Old Church Slavonic was the most successful. Constantine's own translations were above all distinguished by their scholarly accuracy and poetic insight. And because he was so successful in rendering the rich variety of the Greek vocabulary and syntax without doing violence to the genius of Slavonic, and because the various Slav peoples still spoke at that time a relatively uniform tongue, Old Church Slavonic became the third international language of Europe and the common literary idiom of those East European peoples, the Bulgarians, the Russians, the Serbs and the Rumanians, who gained entry into the Byzantine Commonwealth. Constantine was not only, with his brother Methodius, the greatest of all the Byzantine missionaries who worked among the Slavs; he was also the founder of a cultural tradition, at once religious, literary and intellectual, in which Byzantine and native Slav elements were in some degree blended. This composite Graeco-Slav culture, whose nature and role will be discussed in a later chapter, was to provide a channel for the transmission of Byzantine civilization to the medieval peoples of Eastern Europe.

The second problem that faced the Byzantine mission, posed by

189

the presence in Moravia of an active Frankish clergy, jealous of its prerogatives, was a more delicate one. Constantine and Methodius had come as envoys of their emperor to a country to which Byzantium could lay no convincing political or ecclesiastical claim. They had come, it is true, at the invitation of the Moravian ruler; but the latter, for all his bid for independence, was still under strong Frankish pressure. Indeed in 864, the year following the arrival of the Byzantine missionaries, the armies of Louis the German invaded Moravia, eventually forcing Rastislav's submission. The Frankish clergy, not without reason, regarded Constantine and Methodius as trespassers on their own missionary field. Furthermore, the Slavonic liturgy which the Greeks were implanting in the country, no doubt with the support of the Moravians themselves, was a challenge to the liturgical monopoly, based on the Latin Mass, which the Franks had hitherto enjoyed in the country. The latter must have known that the Byzantine Church recognized, at least in theory, that the Greek liturgy could be lawfully translated into foreign languages. But Moravia was part of Western Christendom; and in the Western Church Latin had for long been recognized as the only legitimate idiom for public worship. It is hardly surprising that the Frankish clergy, whose position had been strengthened by Louis the German's show of force, viewed the missionary activity and the liturgical experiments of Constantine and Methodius with profound suspicion.

It was clear that the Byzantine mission in Moravia could survive only if it secured the protection of some power able to support it against the Franks. The Byzantine Empire, geographically remote and occupied at the time with its dispute with the Roman Church and with the conversion of Bulgaria, could not be expected to intervene effectively. Prince Rastislav did everything he could to assist the work of Constantine and Methodius; but his freedom of action was severely limited by the military strength of Louis the German. There was only one power able to interfere authoritatively in the ecclesiastical affairs of Moravia and sufficiently interested at the same time in reducing the influence of the local Frankish clergy. This was the papacy. The eastward expansion of the Frankish missions and the manifest intentions of the bishops of Salzburg and Passau to build a powerful Germanic Church in

Central Europe were arousing the suspicions of Pope Nicholas I. Knowing the insubordinate tendencies of the Frankish episcopate, he considered that their policy threatened the superior rights of the Roman see. In 867 he sent an invitation to Constantine and Methodius to visit him in Rome.

The two brothers received the invitation in Venice. They had left Moravia several months earlier, in order to have some of their disciples ordained to the priesthood. It is a moot point whether they originally intended to travel to Constantinople or to Rome. On their way south, they stayed for some months at the court of the Slav prince Kocel near Lake Balaton in Pannonia. Although Kocel owed political fealty to Louis the German and spiritual allegiance to the archbishop of Salzburg, he welcomed the Byzantine missionaries with the same enthusiasm as Rastislav. He and some fifty of his subjects were instructed by them in the Slavonic alphabet. Like his Moravian colleague, Kocel obviously hoped to replace the Frankish hierarchy by a Slav-speaking clergy owing a more or less tenuous allegiance to the Byzantine patriarchate.

In Venice Constantine and Methodius had their second encounter with an organized group of Latin clerics strongly opposed to the Slavonic liturgy. Constantine's biographer seems to suggest that this opposition was fiercer and more articulate than the resistance they had encountered in Moravia. The local bishops, priests and monks, he tells us, fell upon Constantine "like ravens upon a falcon", arguing that it is permissible to celebrate the divine office only in three languages—Hebrew, Greek and Latin. Constantine retorted by denouncing this doctrine as "the three languages' heresy", a name which his disciples later adopted as a polemical term to describe their opponents' views, and in an ensuing debate with his adversaries propounded with great eloquence his conviction that all languages are equally valid and acceptable in the sight of God. In support of his position he cited the fourteenth chapter of St Paul's First Epistle to the Corinthians. The following verses were to provide valuable ammunition to his followers in their defence of the Slavonic liturgy:

He that speaketh in an unknown tongue edifieth himself; but he that prophesieth edifieth the church. . . . For if the trumpet give an uncertain sound, who shall prepare himself to the battle? So likewise ye, except ye utter by the tongue words easy to be understood, how shall it be known what is spoken?

for ye shall speak into the air. There are, it may be, so many kinds of voices in the world, and none of them is without signification. . . . For if I pray in an unknown tongue, my spirit prayeth, but my understanding is unfruitful. . . . Yet in the church I had rather speak five words with my understanding, that by my voice I might teach others also, than ten thousand words in an unknown tongue.[4]

In the winter of 867–8 Constantine and Methodius arrived in Rome and were received by the new pope, Hadrian II. They could hardly have chosen a more propitious moment to plead their cause before the Holy See. The papacy had recently gained the spiritual allegiance of Boris of Bulgaria, whose realm bordered on Moravia. It was not unreasonable to hope that the whole Slavonic world might soon be brought under its direct authority. The two brothers, furthermore, had come to Rome under the most favourable auspices: they had brought with them from the Crimea the relics, then believed to be genuine, of St. Clement, pope and martyr; their missionary work among the Slavs had, during the past four years, proved remarkably successful; their personal reputation as evangelists and scholars stood high in many parts of Christendom; and they were strongly backed by the Slav rulers of Central Europe, by Rastislav of Moravia, and Kocel of Pannonia. Yet the fact that they celebrated the divine offices in Slavonic and not in Latin, as the Western custom now required, placed the pope in an awkward dilemma. To sanction this departure from the established practice might encourage centrifugal forces within the Western Church; yet to disown the work of the two brothers was to risk surrendering the effective control of Moravian and Pannonian Christianity to the Frankish clergy. Hadrian II's decision showed the same foresight and practical sense that had distinguished the Slavonic policy of his predecessor Nicholas I. He gave his full support to the work of Constantine and Methodius, and by a special bull solemnly authorized the use of the Slavonic liturgy.

Constantine did not long survive this crowning achievement of his missionary career. After a brief illness, he died in Rome on 14 February 869. A few weeks before his death he became a monk under his now more familiar name of Cyril. At his brother's request he was buried in the church of San Clemente. On his deathbed St. Cyril had implored his brother to resist the temptation to return to his monastery in Asia Minor, and urged him to continue their common work for the Slavs. Methodius remained loyal all his life to his brother's last wish. Hadrian II, after consulting Prince Kocel, appointed him archbishop of Pannonia and papal legate to the Slavonic nations, reviving for this purpose the long defunct diocese of Sirmium, and granting him jurisdiction over Pannonia, Moravia, Slovakia and perhaps part of Croatia. At that very moment, however, the political situation in Central Europe took a critical turn which placed in jeopardy the whole future of the Slavonic Church as planned by the pope, Methodius, Rastislav and Kocel. In 870 Rastislav's nephew Svatopluk seized power in Moravia, had his uncle imprisoned and acknowledged the supremacy of Louis the German. Methodius, on arriving in his new missionary diocese, thus found himself deprived of one of his main supporters. The Frankish and Bavarian clergy, who considered that their prerogatives in Pannonia and Moravia had been violated by Methodius' new jurisdiction, secured his arrest. Condemned as a usurper of episcopal rights by a synod of bishops probably held in Regensburg, he was imprisoned for two and a half years in Swabia. It was not until 873 that the new pope, John VIII, having learnt at last of Methodius' plight, compelled Louis the German and the Bavarian bishops to release him.

During the next twelve years Methodius worked to build up his Slavonic Church in Central Europe. His position was a singularly difficult one. He had to contend simultaneously with three main problems, caused by the Franks, the Moravian government and the papacy. The Frankish clergy did everything possible to undermine his authority: their resentment of his archiepiscopal powers and their dogged opposition to the Slavonic liturgy now combined with a theological grievance, which they loudly voiced both in Moravia and in Rome. The Frankish Church was now firmly committed to the doctrine of the *filioque*, according to which the Holy Spirit proceeds not from the Father alone (as is stated in the Nicene Creed), but from the Father and the Son. The Church of Rome, though it did not formally accept this doctrine until the early eleventh century, had already begun to adopt it unofficially. The Byzantine Church strongly objected to the *filioque*, partly on the grounds that any alteration to the Creed had been expressly forbidden by the oecumenical councils, and partly because it believed it to be theologically erroneous. Methodius, who, despite his position as papal legate, remained a Byzantine in outlook, could not fail to regard this doctrine, accepted by his Frankish subordinate clergy, as heretical. The *filioque* was to become the basic theological issue in the medieval controversies between the Byzantine and the Roman Churches. It had already arisen in 867, when, it will be remembered, the Patriarch Photius denounced the Latins for spreading this doctrine in Bulgaria. Now in Moravia, between 879 and 885, it flared up afresh, embittering the last years of Methodius' life.

Secondly, Methodius was handicapped by the lukewarm support accorded him by Prince Svatopluk. The new Moravian ruler, after revolting against Louis the German and even defeating his troops in battle, began to lean increasingly on the Frankish clergy. His annexation of a large part of Pannonia suggests that he may have entertained the ambition to supplant the Franks as the main political power in Central Europe; he certainly had no use for the pro-Byzantine policy pursued by his predecessor.

Thirdly, Methodius came to realize in those years that Rome was losing interest in the Slavonic liturgy. It seems that the papacy was becoming more and more unwilling to risk, for the sake of this liturgy, a major conflict with the Frankish Church. But John VIII, though he imposed a temporary ban on the Slavonic liturgy, continued to support Methodius. In 880, in a letter to Svatopluk, he vindicated the liturgical use of the vernacular as firmly as Constantine had done in his disputation with the protagonists of the "three languages' heresy" in Venice:

> It is certainly not against faith or doctrine to sing the Mass in the Slavonic language, or to read the Holy Gospel or the divine lessons of the New and Old Testaments well translated and interpreted, or to chant the other offices of the hours, for He who made the three principal languages, Hebrew, Greek and Latin, also created all the others for His own praise and glory.[5]

This, however, proved to be the last papal pronouncement in medieval times in favour of the Slavonic liturgy. John VIII's successors, turning their back on the policy inaugurated by Nicholas I and Hadrian II, banned its use.

In his growing loneliness, Methodius now turned for help to his Byzantine fatherland. His enemies in Moravia were vindictive enough to try to isolate him from this last source of support. According to Methodius' biographer, they spread alarming rumours, alleging that he was in disgrace in Constantinople. "The emperor," they said, "is angry with him, and if he lays his hands upon him, he will not escape alive."⁶ It is possible that Methodius' acceptance of a high ecclesiastical office from the papacy may have impaired his relations with the Byzantine authorities, particularly between 870 and 877, a time when the churches of Rome and Constantinople were still locked in conflict over the pope's refusal to recognize the appointment of Photius to the patriarchate. In the event, however, the rumours put about by the Franks proved false. In 881 Methodius travelled to Constantinople at the invitation of Basil I. It is quite possible that his journey was undertaken with the approval of Pope John VIII, who was now fully reconciled with the Byzantine Church. His biographer tells us that he was warmly received by the emperor and the Patriarch Photius, and that before returning to his Central European diocese he left behind in Constantinople two of his disciples, a priest and a deacon, supplied with church books translated from Greek into Slavonic. Methodius' visit to Constantinople—his first since he and his brother had left for their Moravian mission twenty years earlier—may well have been due to the desire of the Byzantine authorities to discuss with him the problem of evangelizing the Slav neighbours of the empire. Both Basil I and Photius were deeply concerned with this problem, and favoured the use of the Slavonic liturgy in missionary enterprises beyond the empire's northern borders. Methodius' gift of two pupils and of Slavonic liturgical books to his sovereign, and the dispatch to Constantinople a few years later of another group of his disciples redeemed from slavery in Venice by Basil I's ambassador,⁷ provide positive evidence that the Byzantine government was then assembling Slav-speaking priests and stockpiling Slavonic books with the intention of using them in Bulgaria, and probably in Serbia and Russia as well.

After his return to Moravia, Methodius devoted the last years of his life to the work of translation. He had already helped Constantine to render into Slavonic the Greek liturgical offices and the New Testament. Now, with the assistance of his disciples, he translated the canonical books of the Old Testament, selected writings from the Greek Fathers, and the *Nomocanon*, a Byzantine manual of canon law and of imperial edicts concerning the church. The latter usefully supplemented the adapted translation, attributed by some scholars to Constantine, of the *Ecloga*, a Byzantine manual of private and criminal law. Thus, in the space of some twenty years, Constantine and Methodius had provided the new Slavonic Church in Central Europe not only with vernacular versions of all the main ecclesiastical offices and of the Christian Scriptures, but also with translations and adaptations of Byzantine juridical texts, religious and secular.

In 885 St. Methodius, harassed by the intrigues of the Frankish clergy, Svatopluk's unconcern, and the indifference of Rome, died in Moravia. After his death his principal disciples, Gorazd (a Moravian Slav, whom he had appointed as his successor), Laurence, Clement, Naum and Angelarius, were imprisoned by the Moravian authorities. The last three were then exiled from the country.

It must have seemed to the followers of Cyril and Methodius, during that tragic winter of 885–6, that their masters' life-work lay in ruins, and that the Slavonic liturgy and the new Slavo-Byzantine culture which they had brought into being were doomed to extinction. Yet it took more than two centuries for the results of their work to be wiped out in Central Europe—a sure sign of its vitality and popular appeal. Outlawed in Moravia, the Slavonic liturgical and literary tradition probably found refuge in remote monasteries in the Moravian and Bohemian forests. The destruction of the Moravian state by the Magyars early in the tenth century dealt this tradition a further blow; though there is some evidence that it survived for some time in parts of the new Hungarian kingdom. In Bohemia, which had formed part of Svatopluk's realm and which after his death became subject to the Frankish Empire and, about 926, to the dukes of Saxony, Old Church Slavonic literature and the Slavonic liturgy of the Roman rite continued to flourish alongside Latin Christianity for two centuries. According to a reliable Czech tradition, the first known Christian duke of Bohemia, Bořivoj, was baptized by Methodius himself. He, his wife Ludmila and their grandson St. Wenceslas, Duke of Bohemia (920–9), are believed to have patronised Slav-speaking priests and the vernacular liturgy. A leading centre of this Slavo-Byzantine tradition was, in the eleventh century, the Benedictine abbey of Sázava near Prague. It was a religious and cultural foundation of international standing, maintaining close links with monasteries in Hungary and Russia. Not till the late eleventh century did the Roman policy of centralization and linguistic uniformity succeed in uprooting this cultural tradition in the Czech lands. It remains a notable achievement of the Cyrillo-Methodian mission that it brought Bohemia for some two centuries into the orbit of the new Graeco-Slavonic culture, thus enabling Byzantine civilization to reach the furthest point of its northerly expansion west of the Carpathians.

The penetration of the Cyrillo-Methodian tradition to the lands north and south of the former Moravian state is less clearly attested. Attempts have been made to prove that it survived until the eleventh century in Southern Poland, in the region of Cracow and on the upper Vistula, which had formed part of Svatopluk's realm. The evidence, however, remains inconclusive, and though it is possible that the Slavonic liturgy and the influence of Greek Christianity endured there for some time after the destruction of the Moravian state, we are not entitled to affirm this positively. We are not much better informed about the impact of this tradition on Croatia and Dalmatia. However, the substantial traces of it which we find on the Dalmatian coast in the tenth and eleventh centuries suggest that it may have spread southward across the Drava and the Sava at the time of the Moravian mission, and that some of Methodius' disciples may have fled to Croatia after their master's death. This, however, is no more than a hypothesis. In the Western Balkans, the Slavonic liturgy and the Glagolitic script seem to have been confined at first to the territory of the Byzantine theme of Dalmatia; and they may equally well have been brought there from Macedonia. In 925 the Dalmatian clergy, gathered in a synod at Spalatum (Split), issued at the request of the pope a decree forbidding the use of the Slavonic liturgy except in those districts which lacked an adequate supply of Latin-speaking priests.[8] The view of earlier Croat historians, who saw in the Slavonic liturgy a symbol of their people's national resistance to Latinization, is increasingly challenged today; and the legendary figure of Bishop Gregory of Nin, who took part in the Synod of Spalatum and whom popular tradition has, mistakenly it seems, built up into a champion of the Glagolitic tradition, is beginning to assume more plausible proportions. It seems likely that the Dalmatian clergy either ignored the papal prohibition, or at least interpreted it fairly liberally: more than a century later the Slavonic liturgy was still celebrated for the benefit of the local Croat population. A further ban issued by another Synod of Spalatum (c. 1060) against the ordination of Slavs to the priesthood, "unless they have learned Latin letters", does not appear to have been more effective. In 1069 Byzantium ceded administrative authority (though not its sovereignty) over Dalmatia to the Croat kingdom; and the Slav Glagolitic tradition thus became a cultural heritage of the Croatian people. It bore rich fruit between the fourteenth and the sixteenth centuries, and is still not extinct: the Slavonic liturgy of the Roman rite is celebrated today in the coastal towns of Poreč, Pula, Rijeka, Senj, Zadar, Šibenik and Split, and on the offshore islands of Krk and Hvar. Missals printed in the Glagolitic alphabet were in general use in churches of these dioceses until 1927. Today the knowledge of this script has declined so much that the text of the Mass, except for the Canon, is transliterated into the Latin alphabet.

The persistence of the Cyrillo-Methodian tradition in Bohemia and Dalmatia is, however, of marginal importance from the standpoint of this study. The main task of salvaging Slavonic vernacular Christianity, it will be recalled, was performed by the Bulgarians who, by granting asylum in their country to some of the leading disciples of Methodius and by supporting the work of Clement and Naum and their collaborators in Macedonia and Preslav, were able to enrich this cultural heritage and to transmit it to the other nations of Eastern Europe.

A further contribution made by the Bulgarians to this tradition should be mentioned here. The Moravian mission had used the Glagolitic alphabet invented by Constantine-Cyril. At the general assembly of the Bulgarian land, convened in 893, it was decided to adopt officially the new "Cyrillic" script. It had recently been invented, probably in Bulgaria, by one or several of Methodius' disciples; and it had the double advantage of being simpler than Glagolitic and of closely resembling the Greek alphabet with which the Bulgarians were far more familiar than the Moravians. To abandon Glagolitic altogether was, however, hardly feasible: it carried the prestige of its creator, Constantine, whose memory was held in deep veneration by his disciples; and, by having served as the medium for the translation of the Scriptures and the liturgy, it had acquired a sacred character which it seemed essential to preserve in order to ensure God's blessing upon the Slavonic letters. This is doubtless why the Glagolitic alphabet survived for several centuries in the Balkans alongside the Cyrillic. And it is significant that, whereas after 893 Cyrillic was adopted by the government and court schools of Preslav, Glagolitic was mainly cultivated—at least until the end of the twelfth century—in the geographically remote and culturally more conservative Macedonian school founded by Clement.

Two general questions relating to the Cyrillo-Methodian mission may be asked in conclusion: why did the impact of Byzantine civilization upon the lands which comprised "Great Moravia"—essentially Bohemia, Moravia, Slovakia, and Western Pannonia—prove to be of relatively short duration? How far was the work of this mission actively supported by the Byzantine authorities? To the first question there are doubtless several answers. Geographically, Moravia was remote from the centres of the empire, and hence the Byzantine statesmen could have maintained the necessary pressure upon that country only with the connivance of the Moravian rulers. The only one of them who actively collaborated with Byzantium, Prince Rastislav, was deposed in 870. The destruction of the Moravian state by the Magyars and their settlement in Pannonia, by inserting a wedge of alien origin deep into what had been Slavonic territory stretching continuously from Poland and Bohemia to the Balkans, further isolated the empire from the surviving centres of Cyrillo-Methodian activity in Central Europe. Furthermore, the balance of political power in that area, after Rastislav's defeat by Louis the German in 864, was increasingly unfavourable to Byzantium. Rastislav's successors proved unable to withstand the Frankish bid for hegemony over the Slavs on the middle Danube, and Bohemia, which might have maintained contact with the Greek Church through its centres of Cyrillo-Methodian learning and spirituality, was forced into the orbit of the duchy of Bavaria and later into that of the Saxon Kings of Germany. By the middle of the tenth century the

Byzantines appear to have lost interest in the Slav lands north of Pannonia and the middle Danube: in the *De Administrando Imperio*, which contains so much accurate information on the empire's northern neighbours, past and present, Constantine Porphyrogenitus devotes only a brief and vague chapter to Moravia; virtually the only precise knowledge he was able to impart is that Prince Svatopluk "was valiant and terrible to the nations that were his neighbours", and that the Magyars "utterly ruined them [i.e. the Moravians], and possessed their country".[9] This apparent indifference to the lands that had once formed a distant, though important, outpost of Byzantine missionary activity can also be explained by the pressure of more urgent preoccupations on the empire's northern front: between 913 and 927 Byzantium was engaged in a life-and-death struggle with Bulgaria; later in the century its statesmen were gravely concerned at the recurrent Magyar raids into the Balkans; and, as we shall see, much of the effort expended by the empire's northern diplomacy in the tenth century was aimed at securing the alliance of the nomadic tribes in the steppes bordering on the Black Sea, and averting the danger of the Russian invasions.

The gradual weakening of the cultural ties between Bohemia and Byzantium raises the problem, implicit in our second question, of how far the imperial authorities were prepared to go in their support of the Slavonic liturgy. It may be helpful to put the problem in a more general context, by asking ourselves what attitude towards the work of Cyril and Methodius was adopted by the government, church and public opinion in Byzantium.

There is no doubt that the aims of the Moravian mission were wholly in accord with the foreign policy of the emperors Michael III (842–67) and Basil I (867–86). They and their governments were vitally interested in the Slav world that lay beyond the empire's northern borders, and were willing, in support of their policy in this area, to harness the dynamic forces in Byzantine society which the recent conclusion of the Iconoclast crisis had released. The church had also gained strength and unity from the solution of this crisis; and its missionary activity, now linked more closely than ever to the aims of East Roman diplomacy, embarked on a period of unprecedented vigour. The 860s were in this respect a period of astonishing achievement: in a single decade the

Khazar ruler in South Russia was induced, through the good offices of a Byzantine embassy, to follow a policy of toleration towards the Christians of his realm; Constantine and Methodius were sent to Moravia; Bulgaria was converted to the Christian faith; the evangelization of the Serbs was initiated; and the Patriarch Photius, the organizer of all these missions, was able to announce in 867 that the Russians had exchanged paganism for Christianity and had recently accepted a bishop from Constantinople. The Slav vernacular liturgy became an instrument of great efficacy in these missionary enterprises. Michael III was fully aware of its potentialities: in a letter written to Rastislav of Moravia, which he probably entrusted to Constantine and Methodius before they left Constantinople, he wrote, with reference to the newly-invented Slavonic letters: "Accept a gift greater and more precious than gold or silver or precious stones or transient riches ... so that you also may be numbered among the great nations which render glory to God in their own languages."[10] Basil I was equally alive to the value of this vernacular tradition: evidence has been cited which shows that he actively supported both Methodius and his disciples.

This "Slavophile" policy, pursued by the imperial government in the second half of the ninth century, is often cited as evidence of the linguistic liberalism and cultural tolerance of Byzantine Christianity; qualities which recent historians have compared favourably with the uniform imposition of Latin upon Western Christendom by the Roman Church in the Middle Ages. There is certainly much to be said for this view. In principle, the Byzantines, citizens of an empire that claimed to be universal, recognized the right of every nation to celebrate the divine office in its own tongue. Thus St. John Chysostom, in a sermon preached in Constantinople, expressed his joy at the fact that the city's Gothic community chanted the liturgy in its own language, and proclaimed the right of every barbarian nation to become a member of the great Christian family: "The teaching of fishermen and tent-makers," he triumphantly announced, "shines in the language of barbarians more brightly than the sun."[11] This sermon of the Christian Father was not forgotten in Byzantium; and it may well be that its text was in Constantine-Cyril's mind when he made this plea for the equality of all languages before the opponents of the

Slavonic liturgy in Venice: "Does not the rain that comes from God fall equally upon all men? Does not the sun shine upon all? Do we not all equally breathe the air?"[12] The Byzantine churchmen knew well, and from time to time publicly acknowledged, that the legitimacy of non-Greek liturgical languages had long been recognized in Eastern Christendom; and Constantine was certainly justified in citing in his Venetian speech the example of several nations which, in the words of his biographer, "know the letters and glorify God, each in its own language".

Yet when all has been said in praise of the Byzantines for their willingness to admit non-Greek languages into the company of sacred liturgical tongues, it must be conceded that there is another side to the picture. Despite their conviction that their empire was supranational and universal, they were acutely and arrogantly conscious of the gulf between themselves and the "barbarians". They may have genuinely recognized, or sometimes paid lip-service to the belief, that these "lesser breeds without the law" who dwelt in outer darkness beyond the confines of the *oikoumene* ceased to be barbarians the moment they became Christians and accepted the emperor's sovereignty. Yet they never wholly lost the mental attitude, inherited from the ancient Greeks, which associated the concept of "barbarian" with alien tongues, evil-sounding and incomprehensible. The inherent superiority of Greek over all other languages was axiomatic to most educated Byzantines; and with characteristic and repulsive snobbery, writers who prided themselves on the elegance of their prose, such as the Princess Anna Comnena of the Archbishop Theophylact of Ohrid, thought themselves obliged to ask their readers' forgiveness for having to mention from time to time some proper name of "barbarian" origin. Even the Latin tongue incurred at times the scorn of the linguistic purists: thus the Emperor Michael III, the very man who sent Constantine and Methodius to Moravia, declared in a letter to the pope that Latin was "a barbarous and Scythian tongue";[13] and at the beginning of the thirteenth century, Michael Choniates, the learned metropolitan of Athens, averred that asses would sooner perceive the sound of the lyre, and dung-beetles perfume, than the Latins apprehend the harmony and grace of the Greek language.[14]

This attitude to non-Greek languages, which recurs though not always in so blatant a form in the works of other Byzantine authors, must have made it difficult for some of the compatriots of Cyril and Methodius to wholly approve of their championship of the Slavonic tongue. There is indeed evidence to suggest that at the very time when the Slav alphabet was invented some influential persons in Constantinople looked askance at this linguistic and liturgical experiment. According to Constantine's biographer, the Emperor Michael considered the translation of the Byzantine liturgy into a foreign language as a departure from recent tradition, and Constantine himself feared that in putting his invention to practical use, he might be accused of heresy.[15] This implies that public opinion in Byzantium was at that time divided, perhaps sharply, on this issue. The emperor, the Caesar Bardas (his uncle and chief adviser), a number of high officials, the Patriarch Photius, as well as Constantine and Methodius and their disciples, believed that the Slavonic alphabet offered the best hope of evangelizing the Slavs beyond the empire's borders and of attaching them by firmer bonds of loyalty to the Byzantine Church and state. They were opposed, it seems, by a group of persons whom Constantine's biographer, perhaps for reasons of prudence, does not identify, but who must have belonged to the clergy of Constantinople. Doubtless they based their opposition to the Slavonic liturgy on the belief—also held, we have seen, by the Frankish and Venetian clergy—that the divine office should be celebrated only in Hebrew, Greek or Latin. A few decades later we find probable evidence of "the three languages' heresy" among the Greek missionary clergy in Bulgaria. In the late ninth or early tenth century an anonymous Bulgarian monk, writing under the pseudonym of Khrabr (which means "brave" in Slavonic), composed a fervent apologia of the Slavonic alphabet.[16] He was bold enough to opine that this alphabet was superior to the Greek one, and he supported his view by an argument calculated to appeal to his medieval Slav readers: the Greek alphabet was created in several stages by pagans; the Slavonic, by contrast, was invented in a short time by one man, Constantine the Philosopher, who was a great Christian saint. Khrabr's treatise is a polemical work, aiming to exalt the deeds of his master Constantine and to demonstrate that the Slavonic letters enjoy divine favour. It was obviously directed against the proponents of "the three languages' heresy", with

203

whom its author appears to have had acrimonious disputes; and it is hard to avoid the conclusion that his nameless opponents belonged to the Byzantine clergy in Bulgaria.

It seems, therefore, that there existed in Byzantine society, at least in the ninth and tenth centuries, two contrary attitudes to the Slavonic liturgy. The champions of this liturgy, who were drawn from government circles and the higher ranks of the ecclesiastical hierarchy, were doubtless moved by a mixture of political and religious motives: the Slav vernacular tradition, in their eyes, was a useful instrument of imperial diplomacy as well as a reminder that in the Christian dispensation, which has abolished the distinction between Greek and Gentile, all languages are equally acceptable in the sight of the Lord. Their opponents, who belonged mainly to the more conservative circles of the metropolitan and missionary clergy, were probably swayed partly by the conviction that Greek was inherently superior to all other languages, and partly by professional jealousy and exclusiveness: the Slavonic liturgy broke with established tradition, endangered their monopoly of liturgical expertise, and added to the practical difficulties of their missionary work. It is probable that these opposing parties were never rigidly distinct, and that they overlapped in some degree. Yet it also seems likely that the liberal and the rigorist groups which disputed over the legitimacy of the Slavonic liturgy had some connection respectively with the "moderate" and the "extremist" parties which collided so often in Byzantium over matters of ecclesiastical policy. Be that as it may, we can accept that the two opposing attitudes to the Slavonic liturgy existed side by side, and sometimes clashed, both at home and abroad. In the final analysis, this ambivalent attitude to the work of Cyril and Methodius reflected a tension between the Greek classical tradition and the doctrines of Christianity which was never wholly resolved in Byzantine society.

The Magyars, or Hungarians, who began to settle in the Pannonian plain in the closing years of the ninth century, cut off the centres of Cyrillo-Methodian culture in Central Europe from their Byzantine fountainhead, and thus contributed to their eventual decline and extinction. At the same time, by occupying a region which had lain for several decades within the empire's sphere of influence, they could hardly fail to enter into direct contact with its civilization. The third phase in the empire's relations with the lands of East-Central Europe is the story of the Magyars' relations with Byzantium, and of its impact upon their culture and institutions.

In the course of the ninth century the Magyars moved westward across the steppes of South Russia. Some of them, probably forward detachments, had reached the mouth of the Danube by 837, when their first hostile encounter with the Byzantines was recorded. Towards the end of the century (but before 895) their main horde was encamped in the lowlands north of the Danube estuary. However, their earliest contacts with Byzantium almost certainly go back much further in time. There is every reason to believe that the Magyars, who once lived between the Don and the Caucasus, were in touch with the Byzantine centres in the Crimea as early as the sixth century, and that Greek missionaries had attempted to convert them to Christianity. They cannot have been very successful, and when the Magyars began to loom on the political horizon of the Byzantines (who usually called them "Turks") they appeared as typically pagan and nomadic tribes from the Pontic steppes. This was in 895 when, it will be recalled, an embassy from the Emperor Leo VI persuaded them to cross the Danube as imperial auxiliaries and attack the Bulgarians in the rear. This characteristic piece of "steppe-diplomacy" was foiled by Symeon of Bulgaria who unleashed the Pechenegs against the Magyars, thus causing the latter to migrate. Under the leadership of their ruler Arpád they moved westward and north-westward, some of the tribes crossing the Carpathian passes, others circumventing the mountains by crossing the Galician and Podolian plateaux or by passing through the Iron Gate, and occupied Transylvania and the plain between the Tisza and the Danube.

Thus, as a result of its diplomacy in the Pontic steppes, the empire was confronted at the turn of the ninth century by a new situation north of the Danube whose ominous overtones recalled the events of 567–8, when the same lands were seized by the Avars. Within a few years the Magyars occupied the whole of the Pannonian plain and, with the help of the Germans, destroyed the remnants of the Moravian state. Their wars in the west are not the concern of this book. It is worth noting, however, that the raids they carried out on the Balkan provinces of the Byzantine Empire during the tenth century were hardly less destructive than the more amply chronicled campaigns which they waged in Germany, Italy and France, until their defeat by Otto I on the Lechfeld (955). Between 934 and 961, except during the personal reign of Constantine Porphyrogenitus (945–59) when they seem to have lived at peace with the empire, they ravaged Thrace and Macedonia with fearful regularity; Bulgaria lay helpless across their invasion routes to the south; in 934 and 959 they reached the walls of Constantinople, and in 936 one of their bands penetrated as far as Attica. On their fast-moving horses, employing the tactics of the rapid thrust which they had learnt in the steppes, the Maygars were well trained for plunder and the taking of prisoners; but they do not seem to have been interested in settling in the Balkans, and they were incapable of storming Byzantine cities. This perhaps explains the comparative coolness with which the Byzantines reacted to these raids: there is no sign in their medieval chronicles of the terror which the Magyars provoked in Western Christendom.

The Byzantines, moreover, disposed of other weapons to deal with their new neighbours. Constantine Porphyrogenitus tells us that a certain "cleric Gabriel" was sent on a mission to the Magyars with a message from the emperor ordering them in peremptory tones to take possession, on his behalf, of the land of the Pechenegs. The date of this embassy is uncertain; it was probably dispatched soon after 927. This attempt to remind the Magyars of their former status of imperial auxiliaries was rebuffed: they were still much too afraid of the Pechenegs ("a bad lot", as they described them to the emperor's envoy) to fall in with the Byzantine plot.[17] Gabriel's clerical status suggests that part of his brief was to preach Christianity to the Hungarians. We do not know how successful he was in this; perhaps it was his work that bore fruit about 948, when several important Hungarian visitors were received in Constantinople. The first to arrive were the chieftain Bulcsu, leader of one of the Maygar clans, and Termács, Árpád's great-grandson. Bulcsu was baptized, Constantine Porphyrogenitus standing as his sponsor and godfather, and, before returning home laden with gifts, received the title of *patricius*. The event, described by the eleventh century Byzantine chronicler

John Scylitzes,[18] had all the elements of a well-rehearsed pageant: the baptism in Constantinople of a foreign ruler, his acceptance of the emperor's spiritual paternity, his investiture with an imperial court title, and his incorporation thereby into the hierarchy of the Byzantine Commonwealth, were all by now part of a recognized pattern. By a fortunate chance the scene of Bulcsu's baptism is depicted in one of the miniatures of the medieval manuscript of the chronicle, preserved in the National Library in Madrid, which shows the Hungarian leader sitting in the baptismal font with a bishop (probably the patriarch) laying his hands upon the convert's head, and the emperor himself waiting to raise him up after the ceremony.[19] The victory of church and empire over pagan barbarism which this scene so neatly illustrates proved illusory: on his return to Hungary Bulcsu renounced his Christian faith, made war on Byzantium, and, after a series of victorious campaigns in Germany which made his name an object of terror throughout Western Europe, was captured at the battle on the Lechfeld and executed at Regensburg. The Byzantines were more successful with another high-ranking Hungarian visitor who came to Constantinople about 952. This was Gyula, chief of one of the Magyar clans of Transylvania. He too was baptized and was raised to the rank of *patricius*. On his homeward journey he took with him the monk Hierotheus, whom the patriarch Theophylact had consecrated as "bishop of Hungary" (*episkopos Tourkias*). The successful work of this Byzantine missionary is recorded by Scylitzes: "And when he came to Hungary, he converted many from their barbarous delusions. And Gyula remained firm in the faith, undertook no raids against Byzantine territory and cared for Christian prisoners."[20]

Hierotheus' diocese seems to have covered all the territory on which the Magyars had settled. It thus included Pannonia which, a little more than fifty years earlier, had formed part of Methodius' Slavonic archdiocese. It is tempting to speculate whether there was any historical continuity between the two. Some elements of the Cyrillo-Methodian tradition must have survived in the Pannonian region of the Hungarian state. The numerous Slavs who lived there, and who had been converted to Christianity by the Franks or by the Byzantine mission to Moravia, may well have played some part in the conversion of their new overlords. The

Magyars, moreover, had almost certainly come into close contact with Slavonic Christianity before their migration to Central Europe; thus, in the opinion of many philologists, the Hungarian word *kereszt* ("cross"), which is of Slav origin, was borrowed at the time the Magyars were moving westward across Southern Russia: and Methodius is said to have had a friendly meeting with a Hungarian king, who was probably the leader of a clan which had made an early foray across the Carpathians.[21] The tradition of Slav vernacular Christianity survived in Hungary for at least two centuries: for when the monks of the Slavonic abbey of Sázava were expelled from Bohemia *c.* 1055, they found refuge in a Hungarian monastery.[22]

Hierotheus' mission, supported by Gyula's political power, enabled Christianity to take roots in the lowlands east of the Tisza and in Transylvania during the second half of the tenth century. It is worth remembering that this first successful attempt to evangelize the Hungarians was made by the Byzantines. Their conversion to Christianity was undoubtedly hastened by the economic and social changes which they were undergoing in their new environment. The Magyars had brought with them from South Russia a way of life and an outlook common to all the Eurasian nomads: an economy based on the rearing of horses, used for their far-flung military expeditions and for the mares' milk which, together with the produce of hunting and fishing, provided them with their basic food; and a distrust of, and contempt for, the farmer settled on the margins of the steppe. In their new home in Central Europe their traditional way of life seems to have persisted for the first fifty years; but after their defeat on the Lechfeld and the almost simultaneous baptism of Gyula in Constantinople, a gradual change seems to have set in: their warlike instincts began to diminish; in the Pannonian plain, on whose empty spaces they had settled their numerous captives who were made to cultivate the land, and in parts of which the Slavs had been living as farmers for centuries, they came into increasing contact with agriculture; and under the influence of their subjects they too began to take an interest in farming. These changes in the economic life of the Maygar society were accomplished by a gradual transformation of its political structure. This at first was loose and decentralized. The Emperor Leo VI noted that they were divided into "many tribes":[23] a fact which he must have viewed with satisfaction, for it made it easier for Byzantine diplomacy to foment internal strife among them; and fifty years later his son, Constantine Porphyrogenitus, observed the same disunity in their political organization.[24] It is true that shortly before their migration to Central Europe the Magyars elected Arpád as ruler over all the tribes. But neither he nor his immediate successors were able to enforce their authority over the whole Hungarian people. It was only in the second half of the tenth century that Arpád's dynasty gained effective hegemony over the country, and the former clan and tribe structure was replaced by a strong central authority. This event, which marked the birth of the Hungarian nation, is associated with the reign of Prince Géza (c. 970–97) and especially with that of his son St. Stephen, Hungary's first king (1000–38).

The growth of agriculture at the expense of pastoral nomadism, and the increasing political centralization, certainly facilitated the task of the Christian missionaries in Hungary, who sought to evangelize the country by working through the state authorities and by building up a parish structure in the villages. But an essential problem still remained unsolved. Hungary at the turn of the tenth century was, like Bulgaria had been in the 860s, at the crossroads between Western and Eastern Christendom, between the Latin-Germanic and the Graeco-Slav spheres of influence. In the eastern part of the country, between the Tisza and the Carpathians, a Byzantine mission, planted in the mid-tenth century, was operating successfully. West of the Tisza lay territory which had for long been the preserve of the Frankish clergy. In the 970s a missionary from Passau baptized Prince Géza and his son Vajk, the future St. Stephen. The latter took the decision which officially and finally brought Hungary into the sphere of Western culture and into the orbit of the Roman Church. He placed himself and his realm under the spiritual jurisdiction of the papacy, and in the year 1000 received, in token of his new status in Western Christendom a royal crown from Pope Sylvester II.

Yet this formal adoption of Latin Christianity by the Hungarian state in the early years of the eleventh century did not sever the religious and cultural links that bound the country to Byzantium. It may be doubted whether it even weakened them. For over two hundred years after the conquest of Bulgaria by John Tzimisces, from 971 to 1185, Hungary and the empire had a common frontier along the middle Danube and the Sava. As a result, political and diplomatic relations between them were close during most of that period, particularly in the twelfth century when Hungary played a vital role in the empire's foreign policy. Across the frontier cultural influences from Byzantium continued to flow. Recent research has shown that the impact of Byzantine Christianity upon Hungary in the eleventh century was far more powerful than was formerly supposed. Above all this was true of the lands east of the Tisza. In that area Prince Ajtony, whose domains stretched from the Körös to the Danube and from the Tisza to Transylvania, was in the early years of the eleventh century baptized in Vidin according to the Greek rite. In Marosvár, his residence, he founded a monastery dedicated to St. John the Baptist, which he made over to Byzantine monks. It is believed that on the occasion of his baptism Ajtony paid allegiance to the Emperor Basil II, who had recently captured Vidin from Samuel of Bulgaria. Later defeated and subjected by St. Stephen, this Hungarian vassal of Byzantium was buried in his Greek monastery.

Nor was the impact of Byzantium confined to the eastern districts of Hungary. At St. Stephen's court the traditions of Eastern and Western Christianity, and the influences of the Byzantine and the German empires, met and were fairly evenly balanced. The medieval Hungarian kingdom, by its very geographical position, could not fail to be closely involved in the politics of the Balkan peninsula. Thus Stephen concluded an alliance with Bazil II against Bulgaria, and in 1004 Hungarian troops helped the Byzantines to capture Skoplje from Samuel. Despite his recognition of papal authority, Byzantine Christianity held a strong appeal for Stephen. He caused a church to be built in Constantinople, and endowed it lavishly; the churches he erected in his own realm display, to judge from their remains, the influence of contemporary Byzantine architecture; many members of his family had Greek Christian names; knowledge of Greek was common at his court. The charter by which he established in Veszprém a convent dedicated to the Virgin is written in the popular Greek language of the time. Throughout the eleventh century there is much evidence of Byzantine influence on Hungarian Christianity:

several Greek monasteries are attested in this period on Hungarian soil, and there must have been others whose names have not come down to us; the Byzantine theological and spiritual tradition which they cultivated has left a mark on the writings of the Hungarian bishop St. Gerard of Csanád, and the traces of Greek ritual and disciplinary rules which we find in early Hungarian Christianity can partly be attributed to the influence of these monasteries. The veneration of Greek saints was widespread, not least that of St. Demetrius, patron saint of Thessalonica, the birthplace of whose cult was probably Sirmium, a city which in the eleventh and twelfth centuries changed hands several times between Hungary and Byzantium; his cult was fostered in the monastry of Szávaszentdemeter in Sirmium, which was founded in the eleventh century and was inhabited by Greek, Hungarian and Slav monks; it was then under the direct jurisdiction of the patriarch of Constantinople, and was in the hands of Greek monks until the early years of the fourteenth century, when it became the property of the Benedictines.

On the political plane, the most striking evidence of the close relations that existed between Byzantium and the Hungarian realm in the eleventh century is provided by two crowns which were preserved in Hungary. The first is the so-called Crown of Constantine Monomachus; its fragments, which were found in Hungary during the last century by a peasant ploughing, are now in the Hungarian National Museum. They consist of seven gold and *cloisonné* enamel plaques representing, according to the inscriptions upon them, the Emperor Constantine ix Monomachus, the two empresses who reigned jointly with him—his wife Zoe and his sister-in-law Theodora—, two allegorical female figures, and the Apostles St. Peter and St. Andrew. The plaques must have been made between 1042 and 1050, when all three imperial personages were on the throne together. It is generally believed that they formed a crown, sent as a gift from the imperial house of Byzantium to King Andrew i (1046–60) or to his wife. Andrew was a curiously cosmopolitan figure, with close contacts with both the Slav and the Byzantine worlds. He was baptized in Kiev and married a daughter of the Russian sovereign Yaroslav. He seems to have done much to strengthen Byzantine influence in Hungary, founding a Greek monastery near Visegrád, dedicated to his patron saint, where Byzantine monks were still living in the early thirteenth century. It is probable that he acknowledged in some degree the supremacy of the Byzantine emperor: for the crown to which the surviving plaques bear witness was of the kind which the emperor bestowed on the highest dignitaries of the empire, as well as on foreign princes whom he wished to honour and reward by his personal patronage; while the plaque depicting Constantine IX in full regalia belongs to the type of imperial portraits habitually sent to the rulers of lands which were considered to form part of the Byzantine Commonwealth, in order to remind them in a visible and quasi-sacramental form of the presence of the supreme monarch in Constantinople and of their duty to serve his interests.

The second crown illustrates the Byzantine theory of the hierarchical dependence of the Hungarian king on the emperor of Byzantium even more clearly. The lower part of "the Holy Crown of Hungary", used in the coronation rites of Hungarian kings, is a Byzantine diadem of the "open" type, with a number of enamel portraits. Most scholars believe that it was sent by the Emperor Michael VII Ducas to King Géza I of Hungary (1074-7), probably soon after the latter's accession. Like Andrew I, Géza was known for his pro-Byzantine sympathies. About 1075 he married the niece of the future emperor Nicephorus III Botaneiates, thus becoming a relation by marriage of Michael VII. Even before his accession, he had proved himself a useful ally of Byzantium; and it is understandable that Michael, who came to the throne in the months following the defeat of the Byzantines by the Seljuq Turks at Manzikert (1071), and who had reason to fear that the empire's power might crumble in the Northern Balkans, looked with gratitude to his Hungarian ally. The crown, which came to be known in Hungary as the *corona graeca*, is an object of some splendour. On the obverse side at the top is the seated figure of Christ the All-Ruler; below Him stand the Archangels Michael and Gabriel, flanked by St. George and St. Demetrius, and these by St. Cosmas and St. Damian. On the reverse side, on the same level as the picture of Christ, is a portrait bust of the Emperor Michael VII, wearing his crown of state; below him are two other personages: the first is named Constantine, and he must be one of the two co-emperors of that name, either Michael's son or his brother; the other portrait has a Greek inscription which reads "Géza, the faithful king of Hungary (*Krales Tourkias*)". The relative status of the three figures is differentiated with a care which bears every mark of the political ideas cultivated in the Byzantine chancellery; the crown looks indeed like a pictorial rendering of some passages from Constantine Porphyrogenitus' *Book of Ceremonies*: the sovereign emperor, earthly counterpart and vicegerent of Christ Pantokrator, superior in rank to his junior colleague and to the Hungarian king, invests them with some of the political authority which he derives from God; his head, and that of his co-emperor, are circled with a nimbus, and their names and titles are inscribed in red, a colour reserved in Byzantine documents for the imperial signature. By contrast Géza, whose figure stands beneath the emperor, his eyes turned towards the co-emperor, has no nimbus, is clothed in a more humble attire, and the inscription identifying him is not red, but blue. In the whole of Byzantine art there is no more vivid illustration of the theory of the hierarchy of states and nations, gravitating in obedient harmony round the throne of the universal monarch in Constantinople. The lower part of the "Holy Crown" provides conclusive evidence of the honourable, though subordinate, position which the medieval Hungarian kingdom occupied in the Byzantine Commonwealth.[25]

The relations between Hungary and Byzantium became still more intimate in the twelfth century. In 1104 Piroska, the daughter of King Ladislas I, was married to John Comnenus, the son of the reigning Emperor Alexius. When her husband ascended the throne in 1118, this Hungarian princess became empress of Byzantium. Renamed Irene, she bore her husband eight children, one of whom was the future Emperor Manuel I. After her death in 1134 she was canonized by the Byzantine Church.

The fact that Manuel Comnenus was Hungarian on his mother's side may explain in some measure the crucial role which Hungary played in the politics of the empire during his reign (1143–80). But the principal reason was a political one. Manuel inherited from his father an uneasy relationship with the Hungarian kingdom, which sometimes supplied the empire with auxiliary troops, but also waged war against Byzantium. The main cause of these hostilities was the repeated attempts of the Byzantine government to intervene in the country's internal affairs by supporting and giving refuge in Constantinople to seditious members of the Árpád dynasty. Manuel at first continued this policy, which led him to invade Hungary no less than ten times in twenty-two years. His political programme was far-reaching: its purpose was to restore Byzantium's hegemony over the West and to revive the empire of Justinian. To the realization of this universalist scheme the German Empire of Frederick Barbarossa was the principal obstacle, and Manuel saw in Hungary, with its strategic position on the eastern borders of Germany and its permeability to Byzantine influence, a valuable base for his imperialist designs in Central Europe. His aim was no less than the complete incorporation of Hungary into the Byzantine Empire. He strove to achieve it by two methods: first by military campaigns followed by diplomatic negotiations; and, when it became apparent that these were failing to achieve his end of total annexation, he devised a plan for a personal union between Hungary and the empire which, from the Byzantine standpoint, had no precedent in the history of the commonwealth.

The last of Manuel's Hungarian campaigns ended with a Byzantine victory near Belgrade in 1167. By the ensuing peace treaty the city of Sirmium, as well as Dalmatia and Croatia, were recognized as parts of the empire, and the Hungarian kingdom acknowledged Byzantine suzerainty. The title *Oungrikos*, which Manuel had assumed not later than 1166, thus proved to be no empty boast. Until the end of his reign the Hungarian monarchy appears to have accepted its subordinate position within the Byzantine Commonwealth.

A few years earlier Manuel had put his alternative plan into operation. In 1163 Prince Béla, the son of the former Hungarian King Géza II, was brought to Constantinople, where he was betrothed to the emperor's daughter Maria. He became a member of the Greek Church, under the name of Alexius, was granted the newly created title of *despotes*, and was proclaimed by his prospective father-in-law heir to the Byzantine throne. The dream cherished by Symeon of Bulgaria of using an imperial marriage in order to seat himself upon the throne of Byzantium and incorporate his own realm into the empire of the *Rhomaioi* seemed about to be realized two and a half centuries later by a prince of another country within the commonwealth, this time with the

214

full agreement of the Byzantine government. Béla's hopes, however, proved equally short-lived. In 1169 a son was born to the Emperor Manuel. A native *porphyrogenitus* was deemed more suitable as heir to the throne; the project of a personal union between Hungary and the empire was dropped; Manuel broke off Béla's engagement to his daughter and married him to his sister-in-law, the Princess Anne of Châtillon; and the unfortunate Hungarian prince was stripped of his rank of *despotes*.

The shabby treatment meted out to Béla did not destroy his loyalty to Byzantium. The ten years which he spent in Constantinople left a permanent mark on his subsequent career. In a medieval Hungarian chronicle he is termed "Graecus".[26] In 1172 he became king of Hungary, and before leaving the Byzantine capital he swore fealty to Manuel, pledging himself always to hold before his eyes "the interests of the emperor and of the Romans".[27] Béla III was, at least towards Manuel, as good as his word: at the battle of Myriocephalon, where the Byzantines were routed by the Seljuq Turks (1176), Hungarian troops fought on the side of the former.

The plan of a union between Byzantium and Hungary under the joint rule of Béla III was revived after Manuel's death. In 1182 Andronicus Comnenus seized power in Constantinople, and before long most of the members of Manuel's family, including his son and successor Alexius II, were murdered on his orders. Béla now took up arms against the usurper. Allied with the Serbs, he advanced into the Balkans, capturing Belgrade, Niš and Sofia. Once again he laid claim to the Byzantine throne, in accordance with Manuel's original plan. When his wife died in 1184 he demanded the hand of Manuel's sister Theodora. Although she had taken monastic vows, Béla's chances of gaining his objective seemed good: his armies were poised for an entry into Constantinople, and he had friends in the city who shared his hatred of the tyrant Andronicus. For the second time, however, an unexpected event in the capital robbed the Hungarian ruler of his prize. In 1185 Andronicus fell victim to a popular revolt, and Isaac II Angelus was raised to the throne. In the new situation the Constantinopolitan Synod refused to release Theodora from her vows, and Béla had to return to Hungary, in the knowledge that his matrimonial and imperial ambitions had suffered final shipwreck.

During the remaining years of his reign his kingdom was still closely linked to Byzantium. His daughter married the Emperor Isaac. The Byzantine gold sovereign was legal tender in his realm, and the imperial double cross was introduced by him into the coat-of-arms of the Hungarian monarchy. But these visible signs of Byzantine influence could no longer mask the increasing tendency of the court and society to seek for models in Western Europe. In 1186 Béla married Margaret Capet, the daughter of Louis VII of France. Western influences grew stonger still under his successors. Béla III's death in 1196 may be said to mark the end of the period of two hundred and fifty years during which Hungary, despite her formal affiliation to Latin Christendom, belonged in several respects to the Byzantine Commonwealth of nations.

NOTES

1. *Vita Methodii*, iv, 8, ed. Grivec and Tomšič, p. 155; Dvornik, *Les Légendes ·de Constantin et de Méthode vues de Byzance* (Prague, 1933), p. 386.
2. *Vita Constantini*, xiv, 10, ibid., p. 129; Dvornik, p. 372.
3. *Vita Constantini*, xv, 2, p. 131; Dvornik, p. 373.
4. *Vita Constantini*, xvi, 21–58, pp. 135–6; Dvornik, pp. 375–8.
5. *PL*, 126, col. 906.
6. *Vita Methodii*, xiii, 1, p. 163; Dvornik, p. 390.
7. See above, p. 132.
8. D. Farlati, *Illyricum sacrum*, iii (Venice, 1765), pp. 93–7.
9. *DAI*, ch. 41, p. 180.
10. *Vita Constantini*, xiv, 16, 18, p. 129; Dvornik, p. 373.
11. *Homilia* viii, *PG* 63, col. 501.
12. *Vita Constantini*, xvi, 4, p. 134; Dvornik, p. 375.
13. Nicholas I, ep. 88, *MGH, Epistolae Karolini Aevi*, iv, p. 459.
14. Michael Choniates (Acominatus), *Works*, ed. Sp. Lambros, ii (Athens, 1880), p. 296.
15. *Vita Constantini*, xiv, 11, p. 129; Dvornik, p. 372.
16. I. Ivanov, *Bŭlgarski starini iz Makedoniya*, 2nd ed. (Sofia, 1931), pp. 442–6.
17. *DAI*, ch. 8, p. 56.
18. Scylitzes-Cedrenus, *Synopsis historiarum*, ed. I. Bekker, ii (Bonn, 1839), p. 328.
19. S. C. Estopañan, *Skyllitzes Matritensis*, i (Barcelona–Madrid, 1965), p. 337.

20. Scylitzes-Cedrenus, ii, p. 328; *DAI*, ch. 40, p. 178.
21. *Vita Methodii*, xvi, p. 165; Dvornik, p. 392.
22. *Vita S. Procopii: Fontes Rerum Bohemicarum*, i (Prague, 1873), pp. 365–6.
23. Leo vi, *Tactica, PG* 107, col. 961.
24. *DAI*, ch. 40, pp. 174–8.
25. The traditional view that these enamel portraits were part of a crown sent by Michael vii to Géza i has been challenged by several scholars, most recently by J. Deér (*Die Heilige Krone Ungarns. Denkschriften der Öster-reichischen Akadeime der Wissenschaften*, vol. 91, 1966). He believes that they were originally fixed to some other object sent by Michael vii to the Hungarian king, and were transferred in the last quarter of the twelfth century to a crown which King Béla iii (1172–1196) caused to be manu-factured for his queen. Deér's arguments, though they have re-opened the question of the origin of the lower part of the "Holy Crown", hardly affect the political interpretation of the portraits: for, as he himself admits, whatever the object on which they were first placed, their iconography and disposition were clearly intended to illustrate the Byzantine claims to hege-mony over Hungary.
26. Simonis de Keza *Gesta Hungarorum*, ed. A. Domanovszky: *Scriptores rerum Hungaricarum*, ed. E. Szentpétery, i (Budapest, 1937), p. 183.
27. Cinnamus, *Historiae*, ed. A. Meineke (Bonn, 1836), vi, p. 287.

6

The Black Sea Coast, the Eurasian Steppe and Russia

The area within which the encounter took place between Byzantium and the people who lived on and beyond the northern coast of the Black Sea has been described in an earlier chapter. This area, it was suggested, can be divided into three zones, clearly differentiated by their geographical features, and bounded by two roughly concentric semi-circles. The first zone comprised the narrow coastal fringe from the mouth of the Danube to a point on the east coast of the Black Sea approximately half-way between the Straits of Kerch and the present-day port of Batumi. It included two regions of crucial importance to the empire: the southern coast of the Crimea, between Chersonesus and Bosporus, and the equally narrow seaboard at the foot of the North-Western Caucasus, from the mouth of the Kuban' to Sotirioupolis. The geo-political reasons for which the Byzantines were interested in these regions—an interest which they inherited from the ancient Greeks and Romans—have already been noted. They are sufficient to explain the considerable efforts made by the empire to maintain its presence and consolidate its influence there in the early Middle Ages. These efforts, we shall see, were on the whole successful: for although its influence in these regions declined between the late seventh and the early ninth century, when it was fighting for survival in the Balkans and in Asia Minor, Byzantium never lost for long the bridgeheads built on the Black Sea coast by Justinian I; and the revival of its military power and foreign policy in the ninth century enabled it to assert its presence with renewed vigour all along this coast.

The second zone comprised the South Russian steppe. Between

Map 6   The North-Pontic area in the ninth and tenth centuries

the late sixth and the early thirteenth century it was occupied by nomadic or semi-nomadic peoples, mainly of Turkic origin, who had come from Asia along the "steppe corridor", either to settle on the north-eastern confines of the Black Sea or to move further west towards the lower Danube. The threat which their invasions presented to the empire's dependencies or possessions in Transcaucasia and the Balkans led its statesmen, we have seen, to develop that intricate "steppe diplomacy" which operated from two pivotal areas—the Byzantine cities on the Crimean coast and the lowlands between the Caspian, the Northern Caucasus and the Sea of Azov. The successful implementation of this diplomacy, notably by Justinian I and Heraclius, has underlined two facts of crucial importance in the pattern of Byzantine policy in the area north of the Black Sea: the close link that always existed between the imperial bridgeheads on the coast, particularly in the Crimea, and the barbarian world of the steppe; and the awareness of the statesmen in Constantinople that their programme of defensive imperialism, pursued along the whole length of the West Eurasian steppe, from the Volga to the Danube, was ultimately aimed at protecting the empire's possessions in the Balkans. Both these points will be further illustrated in the present chapter which, so far as the steppe zone is concerned, will deal mainly with Byzantium's relations with the two major powers which occupied the South Russian steppes between about 700 and the early eleventh century: the Khazars and the Pechenegs.

The last of our three zones comprised the forest area, approximately north of the fiftieth parallel. It was traversed by the middle and upper course of the Dnieper and its affluents, and stretched northward as far as the Gulf of Finland and north-eastward to the basin of the upper Volga. The arrival of the Vikings in this area in the eighth and ninth centuries, as we shall see, gave a strong southward impetus to the commercial and political life of the Eastern Slavs, and brought them into closer contact with the Black Sea coast and the Byzantine world. In the second half of the ninth century, the Russians—a name first applied to the Swedish Varangians and later to their Slav subjects as well—began to loom large on the empire's horizon. Their relations with Byzantium will be discussed in the latter part of this chapter. The history of Russia in the ninth and tenth centuries cannot be entirely isolated from that of the Black Sea coast and the Pontic steppe; but, whereas the two latter zones were so closely interconnected that they must be considered together, the history of Russia's relations with Byzantium in this period is singular and complex enough to merit separate treatment.

Of the two coastal regions the more important to the empire in the period under review was the Southern Crimea. Justinian's fortifications, as well as the continued loyalty of the Crimean Goths, enabled Byzantium to retain its hold over the area, with one relatively brief exception, during the whole of the sixth century. This exception was due to one of the most curious episodes in the history of the empire's relations with the peoples of the Eurasian steppe. In 568 there arrived in Constantinople an embassy from the Turks of Central Asia, whose empire stretched from Mongolia to Turkestan and was now expanding westward towards the Caspian Sea. They had recently rebelled against their masters, the Avars, forcing a group of them to migrate to South Russia and thence to Pannonia, a migration whose dire effects upon Byzantium's position on the Danube and in the Balkans have already been noted. The envoys brought Justin II the offer of an alliance from their sovereign Silzibul, khan of the western branch of the Central Asian Turks. The purpose of this alliance was to promote the silk trade. This was a matter of considerable interest to both parties. The Turks and their vassals, the Sogdians, controlled the eastern sector of the silk route which led from China to Europe, through the oases of Chinese Turkestan, Kashgar, Bactria, Ecbatana, across the Euphrates to Antioch and thence to Byzantium. Its middle section crossed Persian territory. The Persians, usually hostile both to the Turks and to the Byzantines, took advantage of this fact to raise the customs dues on this transit trade. And so both the Turks, who seem to have aspired to the role of commercial intermediaries between China and Byzantium, and the Byzantines, who were interested in obtaining a regular supply of silk which played an important role in the ceremonial and liturgical life of their empire, sought a means of circumventing the Persian control of the silk route, which in the past had made both of them economically dependent on their traditional enemy. Hence the agreement concluded in Constantinople between Justin II's government and the Turks provided, next to a clause regulating the silk trade, for a military alliance against Persia. "It was thus," the sixth century Byzantine historian Menander observed, "that the Turkish nation became friends of the Romans."[1] During the next few years their relations remained close, to judge from the numerous embassies—no less than seven Byzantine ones in eight years—that travelled between Constantinople and the Turkish capital, which was situated to the south of Lake Balkhash, near the present town of Alma Ata in Kazakhstan. To avoid crossing Persian territory, the silk was carried from Central Asia to Byzantium by a circuitous northerly route: its two main branches—the one leading down the valley of the Jaxartes (Syr Daria) past the northern shore of the Aral Sea, the other following the Oxus (Amu Daria) and passing south of the sea—met somewhere near the mouth of the Ural River. The route then skirted the head of the Caspian, crossed the Caucasus over the Darial Pass and led to Trebizond, whence the precious commodity was conveyed by sea to Constantinople. But in 576 the situation altered dramatically. When the Byzantine envoys, headed by Valentinus, presented their credentials to the Khan Tourxath, Silzibul's successor, they were met with an explosion of rage. Placing his fingers in his mouth in symbolic illustration of his point, the Turkish sovereign exclaimed:

> Are you not those Romans, who have ten tongues, but one deceit? . . . As my ten fingers are now in my mouth, so you use many tongues: with one you deceive me, with another the Avars, my slaves. You flatter and deceive all peoples with the artfulness of your words and the treachery of your thoughts, indifferent to those who fall headlong into misfortune, from which you yourselves derive benefit.

"It is strange and unnatural," he added in stinging rebuke, "for a Turk to lie." And, passing from general insults to concrete grievances, he went on:

> Your emperor will answer to me for his behaviour, he who speaks to me of friendship and at the same time concludes an alliance with the Avars, slaves who have run away from their masters. . . . Why, O Romans, do you always conduct my envoys across the Caucasus when they travel to Byzantium, and assure me that there is no other route for them to take? You do this in the hope that I might forbear, because of the roughness of the ground, from invading Roman territory. But I know exactly where flow the Dnieper and the

Danube, and indeed the Maritsa. I am not ignorant of the extent of your forces: for the whole earth is subject to my dominion, from the first ray of the sun to the limits of the West.[2]

This alarming audience almost cost the Byzantine envoys their lives; the Turko-Byzantine alliance, which had lasted for eight years, was abruptly terminated; and in the same year (576) a Turkish army, marching westward from the shores of the Caspian, captured Bosporus, invested Cherson and threatened the empire's whole position in the Crimea.

How can this dramatic *volte-face* be explained? Several clues are contained in Tourxath's speech, as it is cited by Menander, whose text may well be based on the report of the Byzantine envoys. The khan's evident obsession with the Avars must have been aggravated by the fact that two years earlier Byzantium had concluded an agreement with their leader Bayan, directed against the Danubian Slavs; this alliance with their hated enemies the Turks chose to regard as a hostile act. In the second place, Tourxath's anger at the thought of his envoys to Constantinople being regularly escorted over the Caucasus, instead of being allowed to take the easier route across the steppes of South Russia, and his ominous allusion to his knowledge of the latter route, can perhaps be explained by a recent shift in the empire's policy between the lower Volga and the Sea of Azov. It is probable that the choice of the trans-Caucasian route by the Byzantine authorities was more than a matter of routine security, and that the khan's suspicions that they were trying to conceal military and political secrets from him were not unfounded. We may surmise that by 576 the Byzantines were losing interest in their distant Turkish allies and had decided to transfer their patronage to the Onogur Bulgars, with whose help they were soon to build a new balance of power in the West Eurasian steppe.

Finally—and this is perhaps its most interesting feature—the Turkish khan's speech provides a vivid example of the distrust and contempt which Byzantium's over-subtle and unscrupulous diplomacy must have often provoked among its victims in the Eurasian steppe. Save for their greater dignity and self-confidence, his words are reminiscent of the message, recorded by Procopius, sent by the khan of the Utigurs to Justinian, protesting against the latter's insidious policy towards his people.[3] Certainly the moral indignation, and the mordant sarcasm, are the same. It may be that both Procopius and Menander over-dramatized the facts, in order to make more vivid the contrast between the sophisticated and double-faced policy of their compatriots and the artless candour and simple moral virtues of their nomadic dupes: their contempt for barbarians did not prevent the Byzantines from occasionally idealizing the life of the nomad, the "noble savage" of both the ancient and the medieval Greek. Yet we should not be over-sceptical of Menander's frank report; and there is no doubt that the picture he draws of this encounter between the Byzantine and the Turkish ways of life is substantially accurate. The sixth century Turks adorned their Central Asian capital with a luxury that surprised even the Byzantine ambassadors; yet they were capable of rejecting what they regarded as the evils of civilization: when the Chinese tried to make them adopt some of their customs, their khan proudly replied: "We have had our habits for a long time, and we cannot change them".[4]

Modern historians have sometimes judged the Byzantines harshly for their failure to maintain their alliance with the Turks. It is hard to see how they could have done so, for all their interest in obtaining silk at cheaper rates. The sheer distance between Constantinople and Central Asia made the exchange of embassies a strenuous and costly business, and Menander's description of the hardships of the journey across mountain and desert is striking proof of this; the Turkish alliance would have almost certainly involved the Byzantines in a war on two fronts—against the Avars in Europe and the Persians in Asia—a task which exceeded the military resources of the empire in the reigns of Justinian's two immediate successors; above all, the Avar menace weighed heavily on its Balkan frontier, and Sirmium was already under severe pressure: it is hardly surprising that the imperial government preferred between 574 and 576 to placate the Avars at the risk of incurring the enmity of their distant ally in Central Asia.

It is possible nevertheless that, by sacrificing the Turkish alliance to the more urgent preoccupations of their Danubian frontier, the Byzantines missed something of an opportunity. Had their relations with the Turks developed further, they would have gained a powerful ally whose realm was expanding towards the Caspian and the Caucasus, and it is arguable that the political and cultural influence of Byzantium would have spread, like that of the Russian Empire in more recent times, through the steppes of Central Asia to Manchuria and the Pacific. By the second half of the sixth century, Christianity, admittedly in Nestorian garb, had made many converts in several regions of the Turkish Empire, notably in Khorasan, Afghanistan and the area round Bokhara and Samarkand. Byzantine missionaries, by entering this field, might conceivably have gained a vast new territory for their church.

In the event, things turned out very differently. In the early eighth century the western part of the Turkish Empire was conquered by the Arabs. Christianity, which its rulers might have been induced to accept in the late sixth century, gave way before the victorious advance of Islam. And when the Byzantines and the Turks next met each other face to face it was on the eleventh century battle-fields of Asia Minor.

How long the city of Bosporus remained in Turkish hands after 576 is unknown. It would seem that Byzantine authority was restored over the southern part of the peninsula between 581 and 587; Cherson was certainly in Byzantine hands in the middle of the following century, when Pope Martin I was exiled there (654) by order of the Emperor Constans II. Martin, who died in Cherson in the following year, paints a sombre picture of the economic conditions in this city where bread, usually imported from the southern coast of the Black Sea, "is only spoken of but never seen".[5] The empire's position in the Crimea was threatened once again in the late seventh century by the westward advance of the Khazars, who crossed the Straits of Kerch and occupied Bosporus.

The turn of the seventh century was a period at once crucial and dramatic in the history of the Crimea. Between 695 and 711 the Khazars were the dominant force in the politics of the peninsula; the South Crimean cities became involved in a burst of diplomatic activity which spread over the northern coast of the Black Sea and affected the two other principal sectors of Byzantium's northern front, the Balkans and the North Caucasian area; finally, events that took place in Cherson during these years had a direct effect on the fate of Constantinople.

The fate of Pope Martin suggests that the East Roman government regarded Cherson as a conveniently distant place of exile for its more distinguished and dangerous opponents. It was to that city that the dethroned Emperor Justinian II was banished in 695. A few years later, having learnt that his intrigues to regain his throne had made the Chersonites, fearful of the vengeance of the Emperor Tiberius II, decide either to kill or extradite him to Constantinople, he fled to Doros, the mountain fastness of the Crimean Goths. From there he sent a message to the Khazar ruler, asking for political asylum. The khagan, who controlled a considerable part of the Crimea, received Justinian with honour, married him to his sister, and assigned to him the city of Phanagoria on the eastern shore of the Straits of Kerch. But the long arm of Byzantine diplomacy pursued the exiled emperor to his new residence in Khazaria. Strong pressure from Constantinople was exerted on the Khazar ruler to deliver up Justinian, dead or alive. The latter's Khazar wife, who on her marriage had been baptized Theodora (with pointed reference to her celebrated namesake, Justinian I's consort), warned him that her brother the khagan planned to have him assassinated. Once again the exiled emperor had to flee for his life. He appeared at the mouth of the Danube, and with the assistance of the Bulgarian ruler Tervel regained Constantinople and his throne (705).

Justinian II never forgave the Crimean cities for his humiliating experiences. From Constantinople he sent three punitive expeditions against Cherson. The first resulted in a large-scale massacre in the town; the second made the Crimean cities rally to the cause of the Armenian Bardanes, who proclaimed himself emperor; the third led to Justinian's downfall: his army and fleet, with orders to raze Cherson to the ground and kill all its inhabitants, deserted to the cause of Bardanes who then resided at the Khazar court; the rebellious fleet, with the new emperor (renamed Philippicus) at its head, sailed to Constantinople and entered the city, encountering no resistance. Justinian II, abandoned by all, was assassinated (711).

The interest shown by medieval Byzantine chroniclers in these colourful adventures of Justinian II is responsible for the fact that the almost impenetrable darkness that covers the history of the Crimea during much of the seventh and eighth centuries lifts a little towards the middle of this period. Justinian's intrigues and his savage reprisals against Cherson threw the Byzantine possessions in the peninsula into the arms of the Khazars: Cherson, still part of the empire in 695, was governed some ten years later by an official appointed by the khagan; the Gothic communities of the peninsula had probably accepted Khazar sovereignty somewhat earlier; while the Khazars themselves, now the dominant power in the Crimea, were able, by supporting the revolution of 711 against Justinian II, to intervene decisively in the empire's internal affairs.

The struggle between Byzantium and the Khazars for the South Crimean coast came to an end soon afterwards. The Byzantines reestablished their authority over Cherson. The Khazars, on the other hand, retained control over the northern and central areas of the peninsula. This political division of the Crimea, maintained until the early tenth century, corresponds to the geographical distinction between the pasture lands which occupied most of the peninsula and were an extension of the South Russian steppe, and the narrow coastal fringe, with its Mediterranean climate and its southward orientation, across the Black Sea, towards the Greek-speaking world. In fact compelling circumstances were drawing Byzantium and the Khazars closer together. The Byzantines had long ago realized that they could be useful in the empire's strategy on the North Caucasian front. Heraclius, on the eve of his great offensive against the Persian Empire in 627, had concluded in Lazica a military agreement with them. Fifty years later the Khazars, owing to their conquest of "Old Great Bulgaria", that client kingdom of Byzantium, were masters of the area between the lower Volga, the Sea of Azov and North Caucasia. It was not long before the Byzantine statesmen, mindful of the importance of this area for the empire's security in the north, transferred their support to the newcomers. And in the first half of the eighth century another factor—the common threat of Islam—finally cemented that alliance between Byzantium and the Khazars which was to remain the guiding principle of the empire's policy in this area for the next two hundred years.

The Khazars, a Turkic people, had emerged in the steppes to the north of the Caucasus towards the end of the sixth century. During the following few decades they were associated with, and probably subject to, the empire of the Central Asian Turks. By the middle of the seventh century, now fully independent and a considerable military power, they began their westward expansion which brought under their sway the steppe lands between the Volga and the Dnieper, as well as the southern fringe of the forest belt of Central Russia as far as the upper Oka. During its heyday in the eighth and ninth centuries their kingdom, whose capital was Itil' in the estuary of the Volga, comprised a variegated population of Turks, Caucasian tribes, Jews, Arabs, Slavs and Finno-Ugrians, and grew rich from the international trade which the caravan road from Central Asia to the Black Sea and the water route down the Volga and across the Caspian brought to its principal cities. The main contribution of the Khazars to world history was their success in holding the line of the Caucasus against the northward onslaught of the Arabs. For a hundred years the issue was in suspense, each power repeatedly crossing the mountains to invade the other's territory without, however, succeeding in holding it for long. The supreme trial of strength came in 737, when the Arabs marched up the Volga, destroyed the Khazar army, but were compelled to retreat south of the Caucasus. Five years earlier Charles Martel had, by his victory at Poitiers, halted the Arab thrust against Western Christendom on the line of the Pyrenees. The achievement of the Khazars in holding the Caucasus was of comparable importance. Had they failed in this task, there is little doubt that the armies of Islam would have appeared on the Don, the Dnieper and the lower Danube. One may speculate about the effect this would have had on the history of Byzantium and Russia. No wonder that the Byzantine statesmen attached such importance to their alliance with the Khazars. During the eighth and ninth centuries the relations between the two powers, despite occasional clashes in the Crimea, remained close and friendly. In 733 Leo III married his son, the future Emperor Constantine V, to the khagan's daughter; christened Irene, the Khazar princess introduced her national dress, the *tzitzakion*, into the court of Constantinople—a curious, but by no means isolated, instance of "barbarian" influence upon the material culture of the Byzantines. In the middle of the tenth century, as is shown by the terminology prescribed in the *Book of Ceremonies* for the emperor's correspondence with foreign princes, the Khazar khagan ranked among the non-Christian rulers in the diplomatic protocol of Byzantium second only to the khalife of Baghdad.[6]

The Byzantines would have been false to the time-honoured traditions of their empire's diplomacy if they had not sought to consolidate this alliance by converting the Khazars to Christianity. This task was all the more urgent as two rival religions, Judaism and Islam, were making some progress in Khazaria during the eighth century. In 737–8, as a result of his defeat by the Arabs, a Khazar khagan was induced to accept the Muslim faith. The prospect of his subjects following suit, and of the Khazar realm becoming, through official acceptance of Islam, a dependency of the Umayyad Khalifate whose fleet only twenty years earlier had narrowly failed to storm Constantinople, must have seemed a daunting one to the statesmen in Byzantium. More than ever before the empire's security now depended on the success of its Christian missions between the Sea of Azov, the Caspian and the Caucasus. Their future, in the eighth century, was not unpromising. The Khazars wielded much influence on the north-east coast of the Black Sea, where a network of Byzantine bishoprics formed the ecclesiastical provinces of Zichia and Abasgia. These bishoprics, which kept in touch across the sea with Constantinople, continued to be active in this period. According to a medieval Georgian source, there were many Christian towns and villages in Khazaria in the eighth century.[7] But it was mainly on the Crimean Church that the Byzantines pinned their hopes of evangelizing the Khazars. Crimean Christianity, which had flourished in the fourth century and had been reinforced by Justinian I's policy in the peninsula, seems to have lost ground in the troubled times of the seventh. In the eighth century it revived with some power. This was due in part to the Iconoclast movement. The persecution of the iconophiles, especially violent under Constantine v (741–75), caused many of them, especially monks, who were among the staunchest defenders of the veneration of icons, to emigrate from Constantinople and the central provinces to the outlying regions of the empire. The *Life of St. Stephen the Younger*, written in the early ninth century, relates how the saint, who in 767 was martyred for his loyalty to the icons, advised his monastic disciples to flee from persecution to those regions of the empire which remained faithful to Orthodoxy: apart from Southern Italy, Southern Asia Minor, Cyprus, Syria and Palestine, he recommended as a desirable refuge the northern shores of the Black

Sea, particularly the diocese of Zichia, the coastal area between Cherson and Bosporus and the land of the Crimean Goths. The monks followed his advice. The pious biographer of the saint was no doubt justified in complaining that "the monastic order was, as it were, led away into captivity",[8] but Byzantium's loss was a gain for the Crimea. The refugee monks, by settling in Cherson, Bosporus and "Gothia", where they founded many new monasteries, strengthened the influence of Byzantine culture in the peninsula and enhanced its role as a missionary outpost on the fringe of the steppe. During the greater part of the Iconoclast crisis the Crimean Church seems to have remained faithful to the veneration of icons; this is especially true of the Crimean Goths, whose bishop, St. John of Gothia, was a prominent member of the iconophile party in the second half of the eighth century, and maintained contact with his supporters in Georgia, Jerusalem and Constantinople. About 787 John organized an unsuccessful revolt against the Khazars; imprisoned by them, he escaped by sea to Amastris, where he died soon after.

There is no evidence that the Byzantine authorities, who were actively and at times violently implementing their iconoclast programme between 726 and 787, attempted to stop the emigration of iconophile monks to the northern coast of the Black Sea. They seemed quite content, while persecuting the defenders of the images nearer home, to use them, in the interests of the empire's foreign policy, to propagate Christianity among the peoples of the north. A fourteenth century Greek manuscript has preserved a list of eight bishoprics, subject to the patriarchate of Constantinople, forming the ecclesiastical province of Gothia, and administered by the metropolitan of Doros.[9] Scholars have long argued about the date of composition and the reliability of this document. It is fairly generally believed today that the list is a trustworthy source, and that it was drawn up during the eighth century, perhaps between 733 and 746. It seems that all the bishoprics of this "Gothic" province were situated on Khazar territory. Several of the places and peoples to which they refer have not been identified with certainty; but there is little doubt that these bishoprics formed a network with a coherent geographical pattern covering a large part of the territory occupied by the Khazars in the eighth century: starting from Doros in the Crimean mountains, the list takes us eastward to the Khazar capital of Itil' on the lower Volga; from there we move south over the steppes bordering on the western coast of the Caspian, to the Terek River, and thence westward to the valley of the Kuban', ending our journey in the town of Tamatarcha, on the eastern shore of the Straits of Kerch. Several of these sees were urban ones: Doros, Itil', Tamatarcha; others were missionary dioceses serving the needs of nomadic peoples subject to the Khazars, such as the Huns and the Onogurs. The vastness of the territory covered by this "Gothic" province, and the fact that with the exception of Doros and Tamatarcha none of its bishoprics is mentioned again in any medieval document, have caused some historians to doubt whether this ecclesiastical network was ever put into operation. Their scepticism seems unfounded, and there are no convincing reasons for believing that this Byzantine project to set up a missionary church over the length and breadth of the Khazar realm remained simply on paper.

It is probable, however, that, at least in this extended form, this chain of bishoprics was short-lived, and that the progress of Judaism in Khazaria soon imposed on the Byzantines a policy of retrenchment. The history of the conversion of the Khazars from their earlier shamanistic religion to Judaism bristles with obscurities. Medieval Hebrew sources, whose reliability is still a matter of dispute, date its first success in Khazaria to about 730–40, when some Jewish beliefs are said to have been adopted by the Khagan Bulan. While recognizing the controversial nature of the problem, the present writer believes that the conversion of the ruling circles of Khazaria to Judaism took place in gradual stages, and that their final acceptance of the Mosaic law was delayed until the second half of the ninth century. In preferring the Jewish religion both to Christianity and to Islam, they were probably moved by the desire to remain politically and culturally independent both of Byzantium and of the Arab Khalifate.

The failure to convert the Khazars to Christianity did not substantially affect the friendly relations between Byzantium and its northern ally. In the ninth century the value which both parties placed on this alliance was demonstrated repeatedly. About the year 833 the Khazar khagan sent an embassy to the Emperor Theophilus, asking for engineers to build him a fortress on the Don. The request was prompted by the pressure of hostile barbarians, probably either the Magyars or the Vikings, on Khazar territory. Theophilus, whose constant wars with the Arabs required a stable position north of the Caucasus, acceded to this request. A high official by the name of Petronas Camaterus, escorted by a squadron of the imperial navy, went on his orders to Khazaria by way of Cherson. After building for the Khazars the brick fortress of Sarkel on the left bank of the lower Don, he returned to report to the emperor on the political situation in the Crimea. This he had found distinctly alarming: Cherson and the other towns on the south coast were visibly restless under Byzantine control, and the loyalty of their locally elected magistrates was open to grave doubts: if the empire were not to lose control over its outpost in the north, the traditions of municipal autonomy, which in the Crimean cities went back to classical times, had to be diverted into lawful channels. On his envoy's advice, Theophilus reorganized the whole administrative structure of Byzantine Crimea, creating out of it the theme of Cherson and appointing Petronas its military governor, directly responsible to the emperor and with authority over the local magistrates.[10] This act of administrative centralization brought Southern Crimea (including Gothia) into line with the other imperial provinces which had been, or were to be, erected into themes. It is worth observing that the theme of Cherson shared a number of geo-political features with the themes set up between the late seventh and the late ninth century in the Balkan peninsula: it too was situated in a coastal plain with seaports which could be supplied and defended by the Byzantine navy; it lay within the zone of Mediterranean climate; and it included several ancient cities with municipal traditions going back to antiquity. It is probable that the creation of the theme of Cherson was directly linked with the building of Sarkel, and that both were conceived as a defensive measure against the attacks of Magyars or Vikings. The Cherson-Sarkel axis, which may well have included a chain of fortifications up the Don, thus served both as inner line of defence for the Khazar realm, and as a pivot of Byzantium's strategic position in the steppes of South Russia. Common problems of military security had once again confirmed the traditional alliance between Byzantium and the Khazars.

This alliance was reaffirmed, in new and even more urgent circumstances, in the reign of Michael III. Probably at the end of 860 an embassy left Constantinople for Khazaria, headed by Constantine, the future apostle of the Slavs, who was accompanied by his brother Methodius. Following the usual route, it travelled by sea to Cherson; there the Byzantine envoys spent the winter, and Constantine prepared for his mission by learning Hebrew. At the khagan's summer residence in the foothills of the Caucasus (possibly at Samandar on the lower Terek, more probably at Derbent) he held theological disputations with Jewish rabbis, whose influence was powerful at the Khazar court. Yet the Jewish religion, though dominant by then in the country's ruling class, was still competing both with Christianity and Islam for the allegiance of the Khazars; and the choice of Constantine as head of the mission suggests that the Byzantines had not lost hope of achieving their conversion. His ninth century biographer, while depicting the Khazars as monotheists and people of the Book, implies that they had not yet accepted all the tenets of Rabbinic Judaism. The earliest unambiguous reference to their observance of the Mosaic law dates from about 864–6, and for this reason Constantine's embassy must be reckoned a failure on the religious plane, despite some two hundred conversions and an equivocal declaration of sympathy for Christianity which he obtained from the khagan.[11]

Unfortunately Constantine's biographer shows virtually no interest in the other, political, aim of the Khazar mission. Yet it must have been at least as important as the religious one, and on this plane, it seems, the Byzantine envoys achieved their object. At least the alliance between Byzantium and the Khazars was confirmed, for the khagan wrote to Michael III in the following terms: "We are all of us friends and allies of your empire, and ready to serve you in whatever place you may need us."[12] The nature of these "services" which the empire required from the Khazars in 860–1 is nowhere specified, but we may safely assume that they were connected with a new danger that threatened both powers from the north. In the summer of 860 Constantinople had been attacked by a powerful Viking fleet from Russia; and the same Vikings, a few years earlier, had driven the Khazars out of Kiev. There can be little doubt that Constantine's mission to Khazaria was undertaken with the aim of concerting on common action against the new Scandinavian overlords of the middle Dnieper.

The usefulness of the Khazars in the empire's strategy north of the Black Sea did not outlive the ninth century. By the first half of the tenth their realm was on the decline; and the emergence of the Pechenegs as a major power in the Pontic steppes forced the Byzantines to readjust their policy. And just as they had once, in their search for a reliable ally in this sector, abandoned the Turks for the Bulgars, and later these for the Khazars, so now they hastened to build up a new balance of power on the northern coast of the Black Sea. The elaborate structure of the ecclesiastical province of Gothia had collapsed long before the year 900. A list of bishoprics subject to the patriarchate of Constantinople, compiled in the reign of Leo VI (886–912), shows that the Byzantine Church in the North Pontic area had been compelled to retreat to the area immediately bordering on the coast: the bishoprics in question are the Crimean sees of Cherson, Bosporus, Gothia (now limited to the mountainous zone of the peninsula), Sugdaia and Phoullae, as well as Sebastopolis on the eastern shore of the Black Sea.[13] As for the see of Tamatarcha, on the Taman' peninsula, it is not mentioned after the eighth century until the 970s, when it was identified with the former bishopric of Zichia.

Yet, despite this policy of retrenchment, the Byzantine Church continued to deploy its missionary forces on the Black Sea coast. Indeed the Patriarch Photius, in a letter to the archbishop of Bosporus, expressed with characteristic regard for the niceties of language his gratification at the thought that the Black Sea, formerly so inhospitable (*axeinos*), was now becoming not merely hospitable (*euxeinos*), but also pious (*eusebes*).[14] Nor was this an empty boast: Cherson, we shall see, continued in the tenth century to be an important channel for the northward spread of Greek Christianity. On the West Caucasian seaboard, the Abasgian Church remained a vigorous missionary outpost, with close links across the sea with Constantinople. In the tenth century Abasgia was a valued client state of Byzantium, and in the *Book of Ceremonies* its ruler is dignified with the title of *exousiates*,[15] a kind of imperial viceroy. The empire's confidence in the Abasgian kingdom was not misplaced: in the early tenth century it made an important contribution to the conversion of the Alans to Byzantine Christianity. Since the sixth century the Alans had been loyal satellites of the empire in the region immediately to the north of the Central Caucasus. Constantine Porphyrogenitus pointed out their usefulness in checking possible Khazar attacks on the Crimea.[16] Their ruler, who also held the title of *exousiastes*, occupied in the Byzantine hierarchy a rank higher than that of the king of Abasgia, and was indeed in the mid-tenth century one of the three imperial vassals honoured with the title of the emperor's "spiritual son" (the two others were the tsar of Bulgaria and the Armenian king).[17] The earliest evidence of Christianity in Alania dates from the turn of the ninth century, when the monk Euthymius from the Bithynian Mount Olympus began the evangelization of the country. The work seems to have been long and laborious; and the conversion of its king in the opening years of the tenth century marked an important stage in the process. This conversion was the joint achievement of the Patriarch Nicholas Mysticus and of his nominee, Peter, the first archbishop of Alania. Peter seems to have been hampered by the remoteness of his diocese, by his disputes with Euthymius and by the continued attachment of his flock to their pagan customs. Nicholas wrote him encouraging letters,[18] assuring his impatient subordinate that he was not forgotten in Constantinople, urging him to keep the peace with his missionary colleague, and advising him to be tactful: strictness, he pointed out, was all very well when applied to the simple folk of his diocese, but the greatest caution was necessary in enforcing the rules of Christian marriage on the king and the nobles.[19]

If, in the tenth century, the Alans replaced the Khazars as the guardians of the Empire's interests in the North Caucasian sector, this role in the steppes of South Russia now devolved upon the Pechenegs. This Turkic nomadic people has already made more than one appearance on the pages of this book. By the late ninth century, pushed westward by other Eurasian tribes, they had become the dominant power between the Don and the lower Volga, forcing the Magyars to migrate to Pannonia. Stepping into the shoes of the Khazars, they soon occupied the pasture lands of the Northern and Central Crimea, and began to raid Cherson and other Byzantine dependencies in the peninsula.

The imperial statesmen met this new challenge from the north

235

by a re-alignment of their forces in this area. After Symeon's death in 927 and the consequent decline of Bulgarian power, the buffer which had long protected the empire's Balkan provinces from raids across the Danube was removed, and the defence of its northern frontier came to depend more and more on diplomatic expertise. It was fortunate for the empire that the reign of Romanus I (920–44) and the personal reign of Constantine VII (945–59) proved to be one of the most successful periods in the history of Byzantine diplomacy. The achievements in Hungary and in the North Caucasian area have already been noted. The success in the Crimean sector was no less remarkable. At no other time was Byzantium's traditional policy of hanging on to the Crimea more brilliantly vindicated. For it was from Cherson and other Byzantine possessions on the south coast that the imperial statesmen could most effectively adjust their northern strategy to the changes which the coming of the Pechenegs had brought to the steppes. By the middle of the tenth century alliance with the Pechenegs had become the cornerstone of the empire's policy in the north. Of this new and urgent preoccupation there is no more striking memorial than the first eight chapters of the *De Administrando Imperio*. For, as Constantine VII is at pains to explain to his son, if this alliance is kept, Byzantine Crimea is safe, trade with Russia can flourish, and the empire's potential enemies in the north, Bulgarians and Magyars and Russians, who tremble with fear before the Pechenegs, will not dare to attack:

> I conceive then [the emperor writes] that it is always greatly to the advantage of the emperor of the Romans to be minded to keep peace with the nation of the Pechenegs and to conclude conventions and treaties of friendship with them and to send every year to them from our side a diplomatic agent with presents befitting and suitable to that nation.[20]

These chapters provide a wealth of information on Byzantium's northern policy in the tenth century and on the means used to implement it. The day-to-day business of negotiating with the Pechenegs was the responsibility of the governor of Cherson; but the special embassies mentioned by Constantine, whose duty was to conduct high-level diplomatic discussions with them, were sent from Constantinople. They either travelled via Cherson, or met the Pechenegs at the mouth of the Danube; and they were led by important officials, termed *basilikoi*, who were generally high-ranking diplomats and members of the Byzantine intelligence service. The Crimean cities, as well as the central government, could hope to reap benefit from these embassies; for, as Constantine points out, the Pechenegs "perform services" for the Chersonites and for the emperor "in Russia and Khazaria and Zichia and all the parts beyond".[21] Cherson, we note from his account, also purveyed Byzantine articles of luxury to the nomads of the steppe: the Pechenegs, he tells us, receive from the Chersonites in respect of their services "a prearranged remuneration ... in the form of pieces of purple cloth, ribbons, loosely woven cloths, gold brocade, pepper, scarlet or 'Parthian' leather, and other commodities which they require". Their appetite for these goods, he noted disapprovingly, was insatiable. Whether the influence of Byzantium on the Pechenegs extended in this period beyond material objects is not known for certain; but we may surmise that the Pecheneg hostages who were regularly taken to Constantinople and there lodged under the charge of an official of the foreign affairs' ministry, were not always immune to the Christian and imperial propaganda disseminated by their hosts.

It is hard to believe, moreover, that the imperial *basilikoi* who periodically visited the Pecheneg horde in the mid-tenth century were not accompanied by missionaries, who could have come from either Constantinople or Cherson. Yet we know nothing of any Byzantine endeavour to convert the Pechenegs at this time. St. Bruno of Querfurt, the distinguished German missionary who spent five months among them in 1008 with little success, described them as "omnium paganorum crudelissimi".[22] The earliest evidence of Greek Christianity among them comes from the mid-eleventh century and from the Balkan peninsula, where some of them were allowed to settle by the Byzantine government. The Byzantines came to realize before long that their pagan and nomadic allies in the steppe could not be permanently trusted to render "services" to the empire. Indeed by 969–70 the Pechenegs had joined Svyatoslav's anti-Byzantine coalition. When faced with a real or potential enemy on the borders of their empire, the statesmen in Constantinople usually sought, by what was probably inbuilt political instinct, to neutralize this threat by an alliance with some nation that lived in its rear. The only people in the tenth century who could effectively counterbalance the Pechenegs were the Russians. They could also, it is true, present a threat to Byzantium far greater than the Pechenegs; yet the imperial statesmen had reason to believe that they were not impervious to the influence of its civilization and might be brought in their turn into the fold.

The term "Russians" is derived from the name of a people who, in the ninth and tenth centuries, were called *Rus'* by the Slavs, *Rhos* by the Greeks, and *Rūs* by the Arabs. The name Rus' still had at that time three different, though occasionally overlapping, meanings. It designated the Swedish Vikings, or Varangians, who used the Volga and later the Dnieper for their trading expeditions to the south, and who gained control towards the middle of the ninth century over the greater part of the Baltic-Black Sea river route; it occasionally referred both to the Varangians and to their East Slavonic subjects who, it will be recalled, then occupied the western and some of the central areas of what is termed today European Russia; and it gradually acquired a geographical connotation, designating the territory in question (inhabited by Finnic tribes as well as by the Eastern Slavs), over which the Vikings held sway. This is not the place to discuss the complex and still controversial problem of the respective roles played by the Scandinavians and the Slavs in the creation of the ninth century Russian state. The following points, however, deserve to be stressed: the Russian state, whose capital was in the second half of the ninth century fixed in Kiev, was not born *ex nihilo* with the advent of the Varangians; its economic and social foundations were laid in the preceding centuries, during which the Slavs in the Dnieper basin played, notably under the aegis of the Khazars, an active part in the commercial life of the West Eurasian steppe; a native Slavonic merchant class, and perhaps a land-owning aristocracy, played a vital economic and social role in Kievan Russia under its Viking overlords; and the latter, always a relatively small minority, were in the course of some two centuries absorbed by their Slav subjects. It is in this writer's view equally undeniable that the Scandinavian invaders united the scattered tribes of the Eastern Slavs into a single state, geographically and economically based on the Baltic-Black Sea waterway, a state to which they gave their "Russian" name. This process is described in the *Russian Primary Chronicle*, the earliest native historical source, compiled in the late eleventh and early twelfth centuries. It was marked by three stages. Towards the middle of the ninth century a group of Varangians from Scandinavia seized control over the cities of northern Russia, thus conquering a territory, inhabited by Slav and Finnic tribes, which stretched from Lake Ladoga and Beloozero to the middle course of the Western Dvina and to the lower Oka. According to the chronicle they were led by three brothers, of whom the eldest, Ryurik, established himself in Novgorod.[23] The second stage was achieved soon after, when two Viking earls, Askold and Dir, sailed down the Dnieper and captured Kiev from the Khazars.[24] Finally, about 882, Oleg, a relative of Ryurik, incorporated Novgorod and Kiev within a single realm, thus completing the political unification of the greater part of the Baltic-Black Sea river route, from the Gulf of Finland to a point on the Dnieper some hundred miles north of the rapids. He made Kiev the capital of his kingdom, declaring, in the chronicler's words, that it would be henceforth "the mother of the Russian cities".[25]

The earliest recorded relations between the Russians and the Byzantine Empire go back to the first half of the ninth century. In 839, we learn from the Frankish *Bertinian Annals*, a group of foreigners collectively answering to the name *Rhos* were sent by the Byzantine Emperor Theophilus to the Western Emperor Louis the Pious with the request that they be helped to return to their own country across Frankish territory, as their direct homeward route was barred by hostile barbarians. Under interrogation the strangers revealed that they were Swedes. Louis, whose northern coasts were then being plundered by the dreaded Norsemen, had the *Rhos* arrested.[26] Their ultimate fate is unknown; but it is clear from this story that a group of Viking "Russians", possibly diplomatic envoys but more probably merchants, had appeared in Constantinople by 839. By that time, or perhaps a little earlier, the Byzantines had come to know the Russians as dangerous pirates and raiders. Two medieval documents, whose reliability has been suspected or denied, but whose evidence is now accepted by a growing number of scholars, describe two attacks carried out by them on Byzantine territory in the first half of the century. In one of them the Russians are said to have captured Sugdaia in the Southern Crimea and plundered the coast between Cherson and Bosporus. The other document describes an attack delivered by them against the town of Amastris on the northern coast of Asia Minor.[27]

It was not until 860, however, that the Byzantines encountered their new enemy at close quarters on the home front. On 18 June of that year a fleet of two hundred Russian ships, having slipped unnoticed into the Bosphorus, turned against Constantinople and invested the city from the sea. The attack had been timed with a remarkably accurate knowledge of Byzantium's military position: the imperial fleet was in Mediterranean waters, fighting the Arabs; the army, commanded by the emperor, was on its way to the Asia Minor frontier. The Byzantines were taken completely by surprise. The suburbs of the city, the shores of the Bosphorus and the Princes' Islands were defenceless before the savage depredations of the barbarians. In the emperor's absence the duty of defending the capital and encouraging its citizens fell to the prefect of the city and to the Patriarch Photius, head of the Byzantine Church. In the cathedral of St. Sophia, the spiritual heart of the empire, Photius addressed the frightened people, urging them to take courage and repent of their sins. The text of his sermon has been preserved, and for all its rhetorical embellishments we can sense in his words something of the terror that gripped Constantinople at the sight of these savage strangers beneath its walls:

What is this? What is this grievous and heavy blow and wrath? Why has this dreadful bolt fallen on us out of the farthest north? ... A people has crept down from the north, as if it were attacking another Jerusalem ... the people is fierce and has no mercy; its voice is as the roaring sea. ... Woe is me, that I see a fierce and savage tribe fearlessly poured round the city, ravaging the suburbs, destroying everything, ruining everything, fields, houses, herds, beasts of burden, women, children, old men, youths, thrusting their sword through everything, taking pity on nothing, sparing nothing. ... O city reigning over nearly the whole universe, what an uncaptained army, equipped in servile fashion, is sneering at thee as at a slave![28]

This attack, which Photius compares for its suddenness and rapidity to a thunderbolt from heaven, does not seem to have lasted long. The Russians probably raised the siege even before

240

Michael III, warned by the prefect of the city, hastened back with his army from Cappadocia. But the Byzantines ascribed their salvation to a force greater than armies and fortifications. The patriarch, in another sermon delivered after the end of the siege, relates that one of Constantinople's most hallowed relics, the robe supposed to have belonged to the Virgin, was solemnly carried in procession round the city walls: whereupon, as suddenly as they had appeared, the enemy withdrew.[29]

This first Russian attack on Constantinople stirred the Byzantines deeply: the people and the statesmen of East Rome never forgot, it seems, how narrow had been their escape. The dramatic words of their patriarch, uttered at an anxious moment in the empire's history, made a lasting impression: so lasting in fact that in 1422, when Constantinople was besieged by the Turks, a bishop preached a sermon to its citizens made up entirely of passages taken from Photius' two homilies on the Russian attack of 860.[30] For more than a century the Russians held a prominent position in the chamber of horrors created by the fertile imagination of the Byzantine folk. They were supposed, in the popular belief, to be none other than the fabulous and destructive people of Gog and Magog who, as everyone knew, had been enclosed in the Caucasian mountains by Alexander the Great. Had not Ezekiel prophesied their invasion from the north? These words of his were doubtless much quoted in Constantinople during the summer of 860: "And the word of the Lord came unto me, saying: Son of man, set thy face against Gog and the land of Magog, the prince of Rosh" (Ez. xxxviii, 1-2, Septuagint version). Was not this dreadful people of "Rosh" the same as the Rhos, these new northern invaders whom Photius described as obscure and unknown? And the statesmen of Byzantium, without necessarily believing these fables, reacted in their own characteristic manner to the Russian attack. A sense of urgency pervaded the government circles: rapid measures were required to prevent further attacks by the Russians. It was probably before the end of 860 that the embassy headed by Constantine left Constantinople for Khazaria; its political aim, as we have seen, was probably to conclude a military alliance against Askold and Dir, the Viking rulers on the middle Dnieper who had launched the naval attack on Byzantium.

This diplomatic encirclement of Kiev was followed up by an

attempt to convert the Russians to Christianity. Soon after 860 ambassadors from the *Rhos* were baptized in Constantinople,[31] and Photius in his encyclical of 867 addressed to the eastern patriarchs proudly announced that the Russians, who formerly surpassed all nations in cruelty, were now living under the spiritual authority of a Byzantine bishop, as "subjects and friends" of the empire.[32] The choice of these two terms (*hypekooi* and *proxenoi*), which go back to classical antiquity, is significant: the former designated the subject-allies of Athens, while the latter was applied to persons who had been nominated by a foreign state to be its "friends", its honorary citizens, as it were. The pattern which we have seen operating so often in the conversion of barbarian peoples to Byzantine Christianity was thus repeated in the case of the Russians: in Photius' eyes their acceptance of the Christian religion and of a bishop from Constantinople made them, however independent their rulers may have been in practice, citizens of the Byzantine Commonwealth and thus subjects of the emperor. These religious and political links were further strengthened about 874, when the Russians concluded a formal treaty with Byzantium and accepted an archbishop, sent to their country by the patriarch Ignatius.[33]

The status and prerogatives of this prelate are unknown, but it may be assumed that they were comparable to those enjoyed by the archbishop whom the same Ignatius some four years earlier had dispatched to head the Bulgarian Church. It is natural to assume that he resided in Kiev where, if the Russian chronicle can be trusted, Askold and Dir ruled jointly at that time. Whether one or both of these princes formally accepted Christianity is also unknown. Nor can we follow, in the absence of reliable evidence, the fate of this first Byzantine ecclesiastical organization on Russian soil: most probably it was submerged, later in the century, by a wave of paganism which swept away the pro-Christian rulers of Kiev and replaced them by a rival group of Scandinavians from North Russia, headed by Oleg. Yet, as we shall see, this bridgehead which Byzantine Christianity had secured on the middle Dnieper was probably never wholly destroyed, for a Christian community survived and even increased, at least in Kiev, during the fifty years before Russia's final conversion in the late tenth century.

By the year 900 the state known to modern historians as Kievan Russian was firmly anchored on the Baltic-Black Sea river route. Yet Oleg and his immediate successors seem to have regarded their new capital as a stepping-stone on the road to more inviting horizons. The Viking appetite for military adventure and the longing for the rich and warm lands of the south were not without effect on their foreign policy. Constantinople, the still fabulous Mikligard of the Northmen, remained as desirable an objective as it had been in 860: five times during the tenth century the Russians went to war with the empire; on at least three occasions their campaigns were aimed at the capital. In 907 Oleg sailed with a large fleet to Constantinople. According to the *Russian Primary Chronicle*, the unique source of our knowledge of this expedition, the Russians started to destroy the palaces and churches of the suburbs and to slaughter the inhabitants. Then, seeing that the Byzantines had barred the entrance to the Golden Horn by means of a chain, they placed their boats on wheels, equipped them with sails and, with the help of a favourable wind, conveyed them overland towards the city. The Byzantines, awestruck by this sight of a fleet sailing over dry land, promptly sued for peace. Oleg extracted from them an astronomically high tribute and, before returning home with his armada, fixed his shield to the gate of Constantinople, as "a sign of victory".[34] The story is a curious one, and less fictitious than some of its details would suggest. The chronicler, who was almost certainly a Russian monk writing at least a century and a half after the event, seems to have been poorly acquainted both with the topography of Constantinople and with military affairs. Yet his account was probably based on a Viking saga in which the facts, though embroidered with poetic licence, were genuine enough. Oleg obviously placed his boats "on wheels" and transported them over dry land not in order to overawe the Byzantines by this prodigious spectacle (as the chronicler seems to believe), but to circumvent the chain which barred the entrance to the Golden Horn: the Vikings were skilled in the art of dragging their boats overland from river to river; and there can be little doubt that Oleg resorted to the same stratagem which was used on 22 April 1453 by the Sultan Mehmet II who, being unable to force the boom, had part of his fleet dragged overland (also with sails hoisted) across the Galata peninsula, from the Bosphorus into

243

the Golden Horn. The episode of Oleg's shield may also reflect an authentic event whose significance was misunderstood by the Russian chronicler. The Norsemen in Western Europe were accustomed to raise their shields, or to fix them in conspicuous places, as a ritual gesture announcing the end of war; by the same token, it is probable that Oleg hung his shield on the gates of Constantinople not as an insulting symbol of victory, but to signify his intention of concluding peace with Byzantium. A treaty was indeed concluded between the Russians and the empire soon afterwards: its terms were certainly favourable to the Russians, but not so favourable that they could have been imposed by a conqueror. The chauvinistic bias which the Russian chronicler so often displays in his accounts of his compatriots' wars with the empire supports the conclusion that the expedition of 907, though moderately successful from the Russian point of view, was not, as he would have us believe, an overwhelming triumph.

On 2 September 911 a treaty was signed in Constantinople between the envoys of Oleg and the Byzantine government. Its text is reproduced, in a Slavonic version, in the Russian chronicle, which also cites the clauses of what appears to have been a preliminary agreement concluded immediately after the end of the 907 war.[35] The treaty is mainly concerned with trade and with the legal problems posed by the presence of Russian merchants in Constantinople. These were given preferential treatment: they were granted total exemption from customs, were allotted a special residence in the suburban quarter of St. Mamas (the present-day Beşiktaş, on the European shore of the Bosphorus), and received free board for six months, a period twice as long as the normal limit of residence then allowed to foreign merchants in the city. A special clause stipulated that they were to have as many baths as they wished: this was doubtless agreed on the insistence of the Novgorodians who, to the ironical astonishment of their South Russian compatriots, to say nothing of the Byzantines, were addicted to the North European equivalent of Turkish baths. Several articles of the treaty prescribed the measures to be taken in the case of personal clashes between Russians and Byzantines, fixing appropriate penalties for murder, bodily injury and theft; and each contracting party undertook to help the shipwrecked merchants of the other. Another clause affirmed (or perhaps reiterated) the right of the Russians to serve as mercenaries in the emperor's armed forces: a stipulation that may well be related to the fact that seven hundred Russian sailors took part in the large, but unsuccessful, naval expedition launched in 911 against Crete by the Byzantine Admiral Himerius.

Although the Russian merchants who in the early tenth century resided for months at a time in Constantinople no doubt included some Slavs, the majority were probably Scandinavians. The Byzantines, though anxious to trade with them, knew from bitter experience the wisdom of keeping these bellicose Northmen at arm's length. Thus a clause was written into the treaty, requiring the Russians to enter Constantinople through one gate only, unarmed and never more than fifty at a time, escorted by an imperial officer.

As to the nature of the Russo-Byzantine trade of the time, the Russian chronicle confines itself to the statement that Oleg brought home from Constantinople "gold, silk fabrics, fruit, wine and all manner of finery".[36] Except for gold, which was doubtless exacted as the price for a partial victory, the other commodities were indeed the staple articles of Byzantine export to Russia and other countries of Eastern Europe. All of them articles of luxury, they were intended for the ruling classes of these lands who had learned to appreciate the sartorial and culinary delights of Byzantine civilization. The nature of the goods shipped from Russia to Constantinople is known from other sources: they included slaves, as well as furs (beaver, sable, ermine, black fox and squirrel), wax and honey obtained from the forests of the central and northern regions of the country.

The treaty of 911 was the first of several commercial and political agreements concluded between Byzantium and Russia in the tenth century. It is thus an important landmark in the history of their relations. It did not end the hostilities between Kiev and Constantinople. But it does show that the Varangian masters of Russia and their Slav subjects were, through trade, diplomacy and human contact, being drawn ever closer into the economic and political orbit of Byzantium. These contacts could not fail to stimulate cultural intercourse: for Russian merchants and mercenaries, and diplomatic envoys from both countries, constantly travelling between Kiev and Constantinople, acted as carriers of ideas, beliefs and fashions; and on the other hand, the Byzantine statesmen had compelling reasons for wishing to use their relations with the Russians to bring this barbarian and still largely pagan people under the double control of the church and the empire of East Rome. The year 911 has, from this standpoint, a further significance in European history: in the same year the French king Charles the Simple granted the Norman duke Rollo, at the treaty of St. Clair-sur-Epte, the nucleus of the future duchy of Normandy, an event which heralded the assimilation of the Norsemen into the world of Western Christendom; and the English, having in the previous year won a decisive victory over the Danes near Tettenhall in Staffordshire, occupied London and Oxford as a preliminary to the reconquest of the Danelaw. This coincidence shows that the Viking tide was ebbing simultaneously on the Dnieper, the Seine and the Thames, and serves to underline the similar pattern followed by the Scandinavian invasions in Eastern and Western Europe.

The treaty concluded by Oleg with the empire appears to have been observed for thirty years. It is not until 941 that we hear of another war between the Russians and Byzantium. This, like the campaigns of 860 and 907, was another Viking expedition in the grand style. Igor, Oleg's successor, suddenly appeared with a fleet in the Bosphorus and began to ravage the approaches to the Golden Horn. Once again the Russians had carefully timed their attack: the imperial forces were engaged elsewhere—the navy in the Aegean, the army in Armenia. Both were hastily recalled, and the duty of defending the empire was entrusted by Romanus I to two outstanding commanders, his chief minister Theophanes and John Curcuas, the legendary hero of the Arab wars. Driven out of the Bosphorus, the Russians landed on the coast of Bithynia and plundered the country from Nicomedia to Heraclea. As they were withdrawing, their ships were attacked by the Byzantine navy under Theophanes. The Russian armada was all but annihilated. The terrifying memories of the Greek fire, which decided the issue of the battle, long haunted the survivors: the bewildered report which, on their return home, they made to their compatriots has been preserved in the Russian chronicle: "The Greeks," they said, "have something which is like lightning from heaven, and, discharging it, they set us on fire: that is why we did not defeat

246

them."[37] In 944, at the head of a large amphibious army of Varangians and Slavs, Igor set off from Kiev to avenge his defeat. An embassy from the Emperor Romanus · succeeded, however, in buying off the Russians and their Pecheneg allies on the Danube. Then, as in 941, the Byzantines were forewarned of the danger by the intelligence service of the military governor of Cherson. "Behold," the Chersonites informed the emperor, "the Russians are coming in countless ships, and their ships have covered the sea."[38]

At the end of 944, after two Byzantine embassies had travelled to Kiev and a Russian one to Constantinople, Igor concluded a treaty with the empire. Its clauses, which are cited in the Russian chronicle, show how greatly the balance of power between the two countries had altered since 911. The victorious empire could now impose more stringent terms on its ally and trading partner. The Russian merchants were no longer exempted from customs duties, and were now expressly forbidden to buy large silk fabrics higher in price than fifty sovereigns, and to winter in St. Mamas. The prince of Kiev undertook to keep his hands off Cherson and the other Byzantine possessions in the Crimea, and to prevent his subjects from spending the winter on the island of Berezan' at the mouth of the Dnieper on their return journey from Constantinople, or from interfering with the Chersonite fisheries in this area:[39] a sure sign, this, that the interests of Byzantium and Russia were beginning to clash on the northern coast of the Black Sea. Despite its restrictive clauses, the treaty of 944 shows that both countries still greatly valued their trade connections; and its importance as a historical document is further enhanced by the fact that it is exactly contemporary with the detailed account of the Russian trading expeditions to Constantinople, contained in the ninth chapter of the *De Administrando Imperio*. It is indeed likely that the material for this chapter was compiled by one of the *basilikoi* whom the Emperor Romanus sent to Kiev in 944 to ratify his treaty with the Russians.

A notable feature of this treaty is the evidence it provides of the growing influence of Christianity upon the ruling circles of Kievan Russia. Some of the envoys who signed the treaty in Constantinople were Christians, and the Russian chronicle mentions a Christian church, ministering to a large community of Varangians and Khazars, in Kiev at that time.[40] There is no proof that this community had existed continuously since the second half of the ninth century. But the likelihood that Christianity never wholly died out in Kiev after 867 is increased by the following story told by the Russian chronicle: when the envoys of Oleg came to Constantinople in 911 to ratify the treaty with Byzantium, the Emperor Leo VI appointed some officials to show them the sights of the city; they were taken to see palaces, filled with objects of beauty and luxury, and churches containing the most famed relics in Christendom, their guides losing no opportunity "to teach them their faith and instruct them in the true religion".[41] And we may be sure that the highlight of this conducted tour was the church of St. Sophia, beneath whose vaults, as we know from a variety of sources, many a barbarian mind was overwhelmed by the beauty and majesty of Christian Rome, and the conversion of more than one pagan nation was initiated. St. Sophia had recently been decorated with a series of splendid mosaics; it is not hard to imagine the impression produced on the Russian envoys by one of the finest of these, high up in the narthex, depicting their host, the Emperor Leo the Wise, in an attitude of adoration before Christ the All-Ruler who is seated on the throne of majesty and holds an open Gospel book inscribed with the words: "I am the light of the world". Gradually this Christian and imperial propaganda, both in Constantinople and Kiev, was breaking down the cultural isolation of the Russian ruling classes. And in 957 Byzantine Christianity gained its most illustrious Russian convert to date: Igor's widow, the Princess Olga, regent of the realm, went on a mission of peace to Constantinople; there she was received in audience by the emperor and the empress and—either before or after her visit to the Byzantine capital—became a Christian adopting the name, symbolic of her new spiritual and political relationship with the imperial house, of the reigning Empress Helen, the wife of Constantine VII. Olga, on her return to Russia, proved unable to impose her religion on her subjects at large; her role was to pave the way for the final triumph by Byzantine Christianity in Russia in the reign of her grandson.

Olga's reception at the imperial court is described in the *Book of Ceremonies,* compiled by her host, Constantine VII Porphyrogenitus.[42] Two formal audiences, at which she was received, standing, first by the emperor and then by the empress, were followed by a more familiar meeting when she sat in the company of the imperial couple and their children, speaking, on the emperor's command, "of whatever she wished". Later that day a banquet was held in her honour, at which she was invited to sit at the empress' table together with the highest ranking ladies-in-waiting, each of whom had the title of *zôste patrikia* ("girded patricia", a rough equivalent of "mistress of the robes"). The privilege of sitting at the imperial table was at that time confined to those who held the first six ranks in the court hierarchy. After the banquet, dessert was served on a golden table, at which Olga sat in the company of the emperor and his family. These various functions, stage-managed with that precise attention to symbolical detail which Constantine strove to impart to all the ceremonies of the court, graphically expressed Olga's new relationship to the rulers of Byzantium. Her seat at the *basilissa*'s table alongside the ladies-in-waiting, her peers, bespoke her willingness to become the empress' spiritual daughter and to acknowledge Constantine VII's supreme authority. At the same time the unusual honours so pointedly accorded to her signified that she, and by extension her country, were now granted a high rank in the family of rulers and nations over which the emperor presided. Russia, if only provisionally, had entered the Byzantine Commonwealth by the main door.

Byzantium, however, was not the only goal of Olga's ecclesiastical policy. We learn from a contemporary Western chronicle that in 959 envoys from the "queen of the Russians"—she was, in fact, acting as regent during the minority of her son Svyatoslav—came to Germany, to the court of Otto I, with the request that a bishop and priests be ordained for her country. The king (soon to be emperor) of Germany was then embarking on his career of expansion, whose aim was the incorporation of Eastern Europe into his empire. Two years later a German bishop was dispatched to Kiev: but Russia was then in the throes of a pagan reaction, and the unwanted missionary was obliged to return home.[43]

We do not know the reasons that prompted Olga to ask for a German hierarchy barely two years after her journey to Constantinople. The Russian chronicle, whose account of her sojourn in that city is loaded with improbable and at times humorous

249

details probably borrowed from some Varangian saga, intimates that her return to Kiev was followed by a cooling-off in her relations with Byzantium. The emperor is said to have protested at her failure to keep her promise of sending him mercenary troops, as well as slaves, wax and furs; Olga, in reply, is alleged to have complained at her treatment by the Byzantine government, which had made the Russian fleet that escorted her stand at anchor in the Golden Horn for some time before admitting her into the city.[44] These facts are quite possibly genuine: it is not improbable that the imperial authorities enforced strict security measures against her numerous retinue, and that this irked the proud princess. It is also possible that, following the example of Boris of Bulgaria, she hoped to secure for her future church greater freedom from Byzantine control than the emperor was prepared to grant, and in her disappointment turned to the West. Be that as it may, Olga was no doubt the first Russian ruler to realize that Christianity could help her country to gain a place among the civilized nations of Europe: and, by making the Christian religion the guiding thread of her foreign policy, she brought it a step forward on the way to integration into the Christian community. Yet the duality of her religious policy shows that a major problem remained unsolved: the world of Christendom stood before Russia in the guise of two empires—the Byzantine and the German—both seeking the allegiance of this powerful country. The Western Empire, recently restored and organized by the Saxon kings of Germany, was then embarking on a career of expansion in Central, Northern and Eastern Europe; in the second half of the tenth century its spiritual partner, the Roman Church, scored some remarkable triumphs: the Christianization of the Baltic Slavs, the foundation of the bishopric of Prague, the conversion of Poland, the spread of Christianity to Scandinavia—Western Christendom seemed to be advancing victorious on Russia, in the wake of the German *Drang nach Osten*. The Eastern empire held undisputed sway in Eastern Europe, where it had converted the Balkan Slavs and part of the Hungarian nation, and had made several attempts to evangelize the Russians. Between these two Christian empires, Russia in the middle of the tenth century stood at the crossroads, at a vital moment of her history: was Byzantium or Rome to claim her final allegiance?

The answer to this question was postponed for a further thirty years. This delay was due partly to the strongly anti-Byzantine policy of Olga's son Svyatoslav, whose wars against the empire have been described in an earlier chapter, and partly to the influence of paganism which, to judge from the meagre evidence of the sources, seems to have recovered strength in Russia between 960 and 985.

The motive force behind this revival of paganism cannot be identified with certainty, though there are reasons for seeking it at least partly in the Varangian retinue of the princes of Kiev. We must beware, however, of oversimplifying the picture: there is no evidence that the Varangians as a body formed an organized anti-Christian and anti-Byzantine party in Russia, as the leaders of the Old Bulgar clans did in ninth century Bulgaria. In fact, as we have seen, by the mid-tenth century many Russian Varangians had accepted Christianity and, by their journeys to and from Constantinople, were acting as carriers of Byzantine civilization to Russia. Yet some of their Kievan compatriots were undoubtedly strongly attached to their pagan beliefs. It was they who secured an influence over so typical a Viking ruler as Svyatoslav.

This anti-Byzantine Varangian faction, reinforced by pagan mercenaries from Scandinavia, seems to have been the dominant force in Russia early in the reign of Svyatoslav's son Vladimir. About 980, shortly after he became prince of Kiev, Vladimir set up on a hill near his palace a galaxy of pagan idols whose names (listed in the Russian chronicle) and functions have long been discussed by linguists and historians. This pantheon was presided over by the statue of Perun, the god of thunder and lightning (whose attributes may have combined those of a Slavonic deity and of the Scandinavian Thor), made of wood, with a silver head and a golden moustache. Human beings were sacrificed to these idols.[45] It seems significant that this earliest evidence of an organized pagan cult in Russia comes from a period immediately preceding its formal suppression: a few years later, Christianity was declared the official religion of the Russian state. There is probably a valid analogy here with the situation in ninth century Bulgaria where, as has already been noted, paganism became consciously and aggressively anti-Christian at the very time when it was already on the decline. The analogy may be strengthened by observing that in both countries the Indian summer of paganism coincided with a persecution of Christians. The Russian chronicler relates that a Christian Varangian was lynched by an irate mob in Kiev for refusing to allow his son to be sacrificed to the pagan idols. This earliest known Russian martyr had come from Byzantium.[46]

The story of Russia's final conversion is told by the *Russian Primary Chronicle*. Fact and fiction (the latter probably enhanced by later manuscript interpolations) are curiously intermingled in this account. Stylistically, too, the story is a peculiar blend of straightforward narrative, prolix theological exegesis, and racy and ironical drollery. In 986, the story goes, Prince Vladimir was visited in Kiev by missionaries from foreign lands. First came envoys from the Bulgars on the middle Volga who were Muslims. "You are a wise and prudent prince," they told him, "but you have no religion; believe in our religion, and revere Muhammad." But when Vladimir learnt that Islam forbade its votaries to drink wine, he showed himself less than enthusiastic: "Drinking," he said—in words which the chronicle puts into verse—"is the joy of the Russians; we cannot exist without it." The Bulgars vanish from the scene, and are replaced by envoys from the pope. For reasons that are far from clear, their doctrines are rejected, and they are dismissed from the presence. Next there arrived ambassadors from the Khazar khagan, missionaries of Judaism. The Russian prince trapped them into admitting that the Jews have no country of their own, and have been scattered among the Gentiles "because of their sins". "Do you want us to share the same fate?" Vladimir inquired rhetorically. That, presumably, was the end of the Khazar mission. At last there came a Greek "philosopher", an envoy from Byzantium. He confutes the doctrines of Rome and of the Jews, grossly lampoons those of Muhammad, and in reply to Vladimir's theological questions, delivers a speech of about five thousand words. Curiously enough, after this learned, if in places oddly unorthodox, exposition of the tenets of Byzantine Christianity, Vladimir still appears hesitant and, on the advice of his counsellors, decides to send emissaries abroad to find out more about all these religions. On their return to Kiev, the envoys reported on their tour of inspection as follows:

The Bulgars bow down and sit, and look hither and thither, like men possessed; and there is no joy among them, but only sorrow and a dreadful stench. Their religion is not good. Then we went to the Germans, and we saw them celebrating many services in their churches, but we saw no beauty there. Then we went to the Greeks [i.e. to Byzantium], and they led us to the place where they worship their God; and we knew not whether we were in heaven, or on earth: for on earth there is no such vision nor beauty, and we do not know how to describe it; we know only that there God dwells among men.

This glowing testimonial to the liturgical expertise of the Byzantines is preceded by a passage in which the chronicler describes the reception of Vladimir's envoys in Constantinople. The Emperor Basil II, we are told, received them in audience and, on learning the purpose of their visit, bade the patriarch don his vestments and celebrate a religious service for their edification. The Russians were taken into a church, almost certainly the cathedral of St. Sophia, where they were made to stand "in a wide space" (i.e. probably in the area beneath the central dome), admiring the liturgical display and the singing.

One would expect the report of his envoys to have decided Vladimir and his advisers to accept Christianity from Byzantium. This event may well have formed the climax of the story in the original version of the chronicle. But in the extant one, which probably dates from the second half of the eleventh century, the prince's baptism is once again delayed, and for the last act of the drama the scene shifts to the Crimea. Vladimir marched with his army on Cherson. The Russians succeeded in cutting the city's water supply and forced its surrender. Vladimir then sent an embassy to Basil II, demanding his sister Anna in marriage and threatening, if this was refused, to deal with Constantinople as he had dealt with Cherson. The emperor was forced to comply, and the unwilling princess, sacrificed to the interests of imperial diplomacy, was dispatched by sea to the Crimea. There she was married to the Russian ruler, after the latter, in accordance with the terms imposed by the Byzantines, was baptized by the bishop of Cherson. Vladimir and his imperial bride then travelled to Kiev, where Vladimir had the Kievan population baptized in the Dnieper and the pagan idols overthrown. The gaudy statue of Perun was tied to a horse's tail and, to the accompaniment of blows delivered by twelve men armed with sticks, was ignominiously

253

dragged down to the river and set afloat. In the place of idols, churches were set up in Kiev and other Russian cities, and Christianity, fostered by the priests who had come with Princess Anna from Constantinople and by the clerics whom Vladimir had brought back from Cherson, was declared the religion of the realm.[47]

Such is the traditional story of Russia's conversion, as told in the Russian chronicle. It is the principal source of our knowledge of this event, on which all contemporary Byzantine writers are strangely silent. Obviously not all the elements of this story can be accepted at their face value. In attempting to examine it critically, two features of the chronicle should be borne in mind. Firstly, this document consists of several layers, written at different times in the eleventh and early twelfth centuries by authors who sometimes held widely different views on the events they described. Thus the transparent devices by which Vladimir's conversion is delayed until his capture of Cherson and his marriage to Anna strongly suggest the work of a later editorial hand. In the second place, the successive compilers of the chronicle, most of whom were Russian monks, were working on literary material and oral traditions of heterogeneous origin; in order to overcome the discrepancies in this source material, and to make their narrative as edifying and dramatic as possible, they were apt to resort to the method of analogy, merging together similar but not contemporary events, and transposing details of one story into another: the result is often a narrative based on fact, but stylized and conventional.

This is certainly true of the account of the foreign missionaries at Vladimir's court. That they held with the prince the dialogues which are cited in the chronicle is incredible; that all of them—Bulgars, papal envoys, Khazars and a Byzantine—should have arrived in Kiev one after the other, like suitors in a fairy tale, is most unlikely. Yet the story has no doubt a sound core of truth: we may be sure that Vladimir had occasion to listen to preachers of different religions, who must have been anxious to convert the ruler of a country whose power and international prestige had grown steadily throughout the tenth century. The account of the Russian embassies abroad is also highly stylized: *pace* a number of modern writers who seem to believe that the medieval Russian approach to religion was primarily aesthetic, we may find it hard to accept that Vladimir decided in favour of Greek Christianity solely because of what his envoys told him of the beauty of the Byzantine ritual. Yet here again the kernel of the story is sound enough; it illustrates the powerful impact which the splendours of Constantinople had on the minds and imagination of the Russian people, and expresses in a poetic form what it was that so impressed and moved them in Byzantine Christianity: that ancient liturgy, which kept the Russian envoys in St. Sophia spellbound with wonder, which so inspired the eleventh century chronicler that he attributed his country's conversion to its beauty, and which still remains Russia's most vital and lasting inheritance from Byzantium.

In the second part of the narrative, which describes Vladimir's capture of Cherson, his marriage and his conversion, the true facts are easier to reconstruct, with one important exception: the date and place of his baptism. The chronicle gives the main credit for the latter event to the Crimean clergy and to his Byzantine bride. It is possible that this part of the story goes back to a local Cherson patriot anxious to extol the role played by his city in the conversion of Russia. As for the rest of the chronicle account, it can be checked and supplemented by the independent evidence of an almost contemporary Arab historian, Yahya of Antioch,[48] and of a few other non-Greek sources. The events may be reconstructed as follows.

At the beginning of 988 Byzantium was in grave peril. The rebellious general Bardas Phocas, master of all Asia Minor, had proclaimed himself emperor and marched on Constantinople; the usurper's army was encamped on the eastern shores of the Bosphorus, threatening the capital. Basil II, foreseeing this danger, had, probably earlier that winter, sent an embassy to Kiev with an urgent request for help. By the terms of the treaty concluded between Svyatoslav and the empire in 971, the Russians were bound to give the Byzantines military assistance in case of need. Vladimir promptly sent a corps of six thousand Varangians. This expeditionary force, which arrived in Constantinople in the spring of 988, tipped the scales in favour of Basil II, who defeated his rival at the battles of Chrysopolis (988) and Abydus (989), and thus saved his throne. These Russian mercenaries, their mission completed, continued to play a role in Byzantine history: some of them at

255

least remained in Constantinople and became members of the Varangian Guard, the emperor's personal bodyguard who defended the palace and were sometimes enrolled in the field armies of Byzantium.

Vladimir was in a position to demand an exceptional reward for his services. In return Basil II promised him the hand of his sister Anna, imposing only one condition: his future brother-in-law must become a Christian. To this Vladimir agreed, probably during the winter of 987-8. Whether he became a Christian in Russia, on the conclusion of this agreement with Byzantium, as some Russian sources seem to imply, or whether, as the *Russian Primary Chronicle* relates, he was baptized a year or two later in Cherson before his marriage, is a question which—in the present writer's opinion—cannot be answered with certainty, in view of the conflicting nature of the evidence. The two versions could perhaps be reconciled if we supposed that Vladimir, before his Crimean campaign, gave a preliminary, and possibly ceremonial, undertaking to become a Christian, and that the full sacrament of baptism was later administered to him in Cherson. This acceptance of Christianity in two stages, a preliminary and a final one, might also explain the discrepancy we find in the documents regarding the time and circumstances of Olga's baptism: she too, it may be, underwent a preliminary ceremony of reception into the Christian community in Kiev, postponing her final christening until her visit to Constantinople. Such conversions in two stages were not unknown among the Scandinavians at that time: converts some time before their formal baptism, went through an introductory rite which allowed them, as catechumens, to consort with Christians and which the documents call *prima signatio*.[49]

It is necessary to know something of the matrimonial customs of the ruling house of Byzantium to appreciate what it meant to the emperor to consent to his sister's marriage to Vladimir. A fictitious but convenient tradition, which was supposed to go back to Constantine the Great, forbade the offspring of the imperial family to marry "barbarians". Only recently the Emperor Constantine VII, in a chapter of great political weight which he wrote for the *De Administrando Imperio*, had explicitly repeated this prohibition, excepting only the Frankish rulers and warning his son to resist any "monstrous demand" for a marriage alliance from the "shifty and dishonourable tribes of the north". The arguments by which he saw fit to justify this doctrine of ethnic exclusiveness, characteristic though they are of the arrogance so often shown by the Byzantines towards foreigners, may sound strange coming from a monarch who affected to believe in the universality of the empire over which he ruled:

> For each nation has different customs and divergent laws and institutions, and should consolidate those things that are proper to it, and should form and develop out of the same nation the associations for the fusion of its life. For just as each animal mates with its own tribe, so it is right that each nation also should marry and cohabit not with those of other race and tongue but of the same tribe and speech. For hence arise naturally harmony of thought and intercourse among one another and friendly converse and living together; but alien customs and divergent laws are likely on the contrary to engender enmities and quarrels and hatreds and broils, which tend to beget not friendship and association but spite and division.[50]

Constantine, of course, knew very well that such marriages had been condoned by several of his predecessors for reasons of political expediency. Not so long ago, he admitted, Romanus I had given his granddaughter to the tsar of Bulgaria; but this *mésalliance* he viewed with unconcealed distaste: Romanus was "a common, illiterate fellow", who should have known better than to flout "the Roman national customs". In this case at least there was a mitigating circumstance: the Byzantine princess who in 927 had married the Bulgarian ruler was not a *porphyrogenita*. The title of *porphyrogenitus* ("born in purple") was given to all children born to a reigning sovereign of Byzantium; they were objects of special veneration in the empire. When a foreign ruler presumed to ask for the hand of a *porphyrogenita* princess, he was apt to receive a haughty refusal: as Liutprand, bishop of Cremona, soon found out, when he came to Constantinople in 968 as ambassador from Otto I to negotiate an imperial marriage for the German emperor's son. "It is an unheard of thing", he was told by the government of Nicephorus II, "that a daughter born in the purple of an emperor born in the purple should marry a foreigner."[51] But Anna, Vladimir's bride, was the daughter of the Emperor Romanus II, born while her father was on the throne, and was thus a *porphyrogenita*. It is obvious that Basil II must have been in desperate straits, and Vladimir able to exert the strongest diplomatic pressure, for the royal family of Kiev to be accorded this signal honour, which twenty years earlier had been refused to the German emperor who stood far above him in international status and power.[52]

Having accepted, or undertaken to accept, Christianity, and thus fulfilled his part of the bargain, Vladimir awaited his bride in Kiev. But Anna showed no signs of arriving, and he probably soon began to suspect that Basil II, now that the danger to his throne presented by Bardas Phocas' rebellion had been removed, was at least in no hurry to honour his promise. Hence he decided to force the emperor's hand. To launch an attack on Constantinople was a risky and costly undertaking, so he resolved to strike nearer home, at the Byzantine possessions in the Crimea. Thereafter the sequence of events followed the course described in the Russian chronicle: Vladimir's capture of Cherson (989), his ultimatum to Basil II, the sending of Anna to the Crimea, the baptism of the Russian ruler (assuming he had not already been baptized at home) and his marriage in Cherson to his Byzantine bride. Thus, whatever view we may hold on the time and place of Vladimir's baptism, the role played by this Crimean city in the conversion of Russia will appear decisive; and it may truly be said that Cherson, so long a centre of Byzantine missionary work among the pagans north of the Black Sea, took her captor captive: for Vladimir and his bride were escorted from the Crimea to Kiev by members of the local clergy, who at least in the early stages played a leading role in building up the new Russian Church; while, in an elegant gesture of reconciliation and goodwill, Vladimir returned Cherson to the emperor, as the traditional gift of the bridegroom to his wife's family.[53]

The circumstances and immediate results of Vladimir's conversion raise a number of controversial problems which must be briefly examined. His motives in becoming a Christian were doubtless mixed, and it is scarcely possible to classify them in order of importance. The Russian chronicle sees this event primarily as the miraculous effect of divine grace, working on his receptive mind and soul. It draws a vivid, if implausible, contrast between the cruelty and incontinence of his life as a pagan, and the unmitigated piety and generosity which marked his career as a Christian ruler. The hagiographical tradition of the Russian Church, which raised him to the rank of a saint "equal to the apostles", endorsed this view. Probably all that the student of history can do is to record that there is no evidence to suggest that his conversion was anything but sincere; and that, through the influence of his grandmother Olga, by whom he was brought up, and of his several Christian wives, he must have come to know the Christian community in Kiev long before he resolved to renounce paganism. Other, non-religious, considerations no doubt also weighed heavily in his decision: the opportunity of marrying the emperor's sister "born in purple", of thus increasing his and his country's international prestige, of developing still further Russia's commercial, diplomatic and cultural links with Byzantium, and, last but not least, of consolidating his own political power over a Slavo-Varangian realm united by a common loyalty to a church of which he would be the secular guardian: these, too, must be reckoned important reasons for his decision to embrace what the Russian chronicler calls "the Greek religion".

Until his death in 1015 Vladimir superintended the building of churches and the establishment of bishoprics in the main cities of his realm. Most of these bishoprics were set up on or near the Baltic-Black Sea river route, which thus became as important in Russia's ecclesiastical history as it had been for so long in the country's economic and political life. There can be little doubt that, at least during his reign, they were staffed mostly by clerics from Constantinople and Cherson. Attempts have been made to prove that Vladimir's Church was under the jurisdiction of the Bulgarian patriarch of Ohrid, subject to Rome, or independent. None of these theories can stand the test of objective criticism. Contemporary documents are admittedly either silent or singularly imprecise on this matter. But circumstantial evidence shows beyond reasonable doubt that from the time of Vladimir's conversion the Russian Church was placed under the authority of the patriarchate of Constantinople. The statement of Yahya of Antioch that Basil II sent Vladimir bishops who baptized him and his people; the role played by the Crimean clergy in the Christianization of Russia; the building of his first stone church in Kiev by Byzantine architects; his marriage to the emperor's sister; and his assumption at baptism of the name Basil, in honour of his imperial godfather: these facts point clearly to the same conclusion.

Another problem is that of the language in which the services of the Russian Church were celebrated, not only immediately after Vladimir's conversion, but also during the preceding period of a hundred and twenty-five years when a Christian community had, continuously or with brief interruptions, existed in Kiev. Was this language Greek or Old Church Slavonic? No certain reply to this question can be given before the time of Vladimir. But we can go some way towards answering it with the help of circumstantial evidence. The beginnings of Russian Christianity go back to the sixties of the ninth century, and thus coincide in time with the Moravian mission of Constantine and Methodius and with the conversion of Bulgaria. In the tenth century Russia had fairly close political relations with Bohemia and Bulgaria; and it is natural to suppose that these links, as well as the common linguistic and ethnic ties between the Eastern Slavs on the one hand, and the Western and Southern Slavs on the other, facilitated the spread of Slavonic books to Kiev either from the former territories of Great Moravia, or else from Bulgaria. Some of these books and the priests who used them may also have come from Constantinople where, as we have seen, the Byzantine authorities built up in the ninth century a centre of Slav vernacular Christianity for the needs of missionary enterprises beyond the empire's northern borders. There is, it is true, no direct evidence to show how far the Byzantine missionaries in Russia deliberately encouraged the Slavonic vernacular tradition; however, its rapid spread in the country after 989, to the virtual exclusion of Greek from the liturgy—and this at a time when the Russian Church was governed by prelates appointed by Constantinople—strongly suggests that, whatever doubts some Byzantines may have privately entertained on the subject, the imperial authorities acknowledged that the vernacular tradition of Cyril and Methodius, which had already yielded such rich dividends in Bulgaria, was the only one that could reasonably be imposed on their powerful and distant northern proselyte.

It is surprising, in these circumstances, that the traces of Slav vernacular writing between 867 and 988 which have been found in Russia are either singularly meagre or are derived from documents of questionable authenticity. Yet it can scarcely be doubted that the Christian community in Kiev, which survived as a going concern during the whole or most of that time, was provided with an effective clergy, intelligible Scriptures, and a liturgy capable of satisfying the needs of the Slavonic and Slav-speaking Varangian converts to the Christian religion. In other words, it is very likely that well before Vladimir's conversion, by the mid-tenth century at the latest, this community was familiar with the Slavonic liturgy, with Slavonic translations of parts of the Scriptures, and with Slav-speaking priests. It would be unwise to ascribe to this vernacular tradition an exclusive position before the late tenth century: Greek was doubtless used, alongside Slavonic, in the Kievan liturgy, at least before the time of Vladimir. It was only after Russia's official conversion that the task of building up a Slavophone Church became really urgent. This task was undertaken by Vladimir himself. The Russian chronicle tells us that as soon as the citizens of Kiev had been baptized the prince "sent round to assemble the children of noble families, and gave them to be instructed in book learning".[54] It is impossible to believe that the teaching in these earliest known Russian schools was conducted in Greek; some knowledge of the language was doubtless imparted to those members of Vladimir's *jeunesse dorée* who were singled out for high office in the Russian Church. But it is clear from the context of this passage that by "book learning" the chronicler meant literary instruction in Slavonic. The brighter of these *alumni*, who must have become adults by the year 1000 at the latest, formed the nucleus of the country's first educated Christian élite; during the next fifty years they were to produce the earliest works of Russian literature.

A final question must be raised here: what were the effects of Vladimir's conversion on the political relations between Russia and Byzantium? Or, to put it in another form: what status did Christian Russia come to occupy within the Byzantine Commonwealth of nations? A comprehensive reply to this question, which anticipates a knowledge of Russo-Byzantine relations from the year 1000 to 1453, must be postponed to a later chapter; but a few preliminary remarks are called for here. Before 989, except for the period when Olga ruled in Kiev as a Christian (957–69), there is no doubt that the country's princes regarded themselves as

261

wholly independent in every sense: the treaties they signed with the empire during the tenth century are clear evidence of this. Nor did the Byzantines claim any jurisdiction, ideal or actual, over pagan Russia: by the middle of the tenth century the former "subjects and friends" of the empire, who could be dignified by these names in 867 on the morrow of their first conversion, were considered in Byzantium to have relapsed into paganism. At the most—so long as the hope of their return could be entertained—they were regarded as potential members of the commonwealth. In the *Book of Ceremonies* the Russians are placed in the same class as the Magyars and the Pechenegs, and their ruler is given the paltry title of *archôn*; protocol required that the communications which he received from the empire be officially described as "letters", in contrast to the "orders" which were received from Constantinople by the Christian clients of Byzantium in the Caucasus, "the most honorable *kouropalates* of Georgia" and "the illustrious *exousiastes* of Abasgia".[55] Olga's conversion, and her recognition of the emperor's universal sovereignty, restored Russia to membership of the commonwealth for some twelve years. After her death in 969, however, paganism and an anti-Byzantine policy were adopted once more by the ruling classes in Kiev. Vladimir's acceptance of Byzantine Christianity and his marriage to the emperor's sister placed him and his country in a new relationship to the empire. By marriage the emperor's brother-in-law, he became by baptism, at which he was christened Basil, his spiritual son. Vladimir's status in the hierarchy of Christian rulers was thus similar to that achieved in 927 by Peter of Bulgaria. Yet it was more lofty by virtue of his marriage to a *porphyrogenita* princess. It is tempting to inquire whether the Russian sovereign's new rank was formally acknowledged by the bestowal upon him of a Byzantine title, by analogy with Peter of Bulgaria who was recognized as *basileus* or tsar on his marriage with Maria Lecapena. Contemporary sources are silent on this point, but according to a late medieval Russian tradition, Vladimir was indeed granted the title of tsar by the Byzantine emperor. The evidence on this point, though not incredible, is inconclusive. There is no doubt, however, that Russia after 989 was accorded a high status within the East European community. Though high, this status was of course a subordinate one; and it will be suggested in a later chapter that, although Vladimir and his medieval successors were wholly independent of Byzantine control in political matters, they all, with one temporary exception, recognized that the emperor, as the head of the Orthodox Christian community, possessed by divine right a meta-political jurisdiction over Russia. The Byzantines, for their part, could regard the conversion of Russia as a considerable achievement. It had taken more than a century to accomplish; but in the end the East Roman missionaries and diplomatists had gained for the Byzantine Commonwealth and for Christendom a territory which in size exceeded the empire itself.

NOTES

1. Menander, *Excerpta de legationibus*, 1, p. 452.
2. Ibid., pp. 205–6.
3. See above, p. 55.
4. Cited in E. H. Minns, *Scythians and Greeks* (Cambridge, 1913), p. 95.
5. Ep. 16, *PL* 87, col. 202.
6. Constantine Porphyrogenitus, *De cerimoniis*, ii, 48, p. 690; cf. G. Ostrogorsky, *Die byzantinische Staatenhierarchie*, p. 50.
7. P. Peeters, "Les Khazars dans la Passion de S. Abo de Tiflis", *Analecta Bollandiana*, lii (1934), p. 25.
8. Stephanus Constantinopolitanus Diaconus, *Vita S. Stephani Junioris*, PG 100, col. 1120.
9. G. I. Konidares, Αἱ μητροπόλεις καὶ ἀρχιεπισκοπαὶ τοῦ οἰκουμενικοῦ πατριαρχείου καὶ ἡ «τάξις» αὐτῶν (Athens, 1934), p. 100.
10. *DAI*, ch. 42, pp. 182–4.
11. *Vita Constantini*, xi, 41–4, p. 124; Dvornik, p. 370.
12. *Vita Constantini*, xi, 44, p. 124; Dvornik, ibid.
13. H. Gelzer, "Ungedruckte und ungenügend veröffentlichte Texte der Notitiae episcopatuum', *Abhandlungen der philos.-philol. Classe der König. Bayerischen Akademie der Wissenschaften*, xxi (1901), p. 551.
14. *PG*, 102, cols. 828–9.
15. *De cerimoniis*, ii, 48, p. 688.
16. *DAI*, ch. 11, p. 64.
17. *De cerimoniis*, ii, 48, p. 688.
18. *Epistolae*, 52, 118, 133, 134, 135, *PG* 111, cols. 244–8, 336–7, 352–60.
19. *Ep.* 52, ibid., cols. 245–8.

20. *DAI*, ch. 1, p. 48.

21. *DAI*, ch. 6, p. 52.

22. *Epistola Brunonis ad Henricum regem, Monumenta Poloniae Historica*, i (Lwów, 1864), p. 224.

23. *Povest'*, p. 18; Cross, pp. 59–60.

24. *Povest'*, p. 18–19; Cross, p. 60.

25. *Povest'*, p. 20; Cross, p. 61.

26. *Annales Bertiniani, MGH, Scriptores*, i, p. 434.

27. V. G. Vasil'evsky, *Zhitiya svv. Georgiya Amastridskogo i Stefana Surozhskogo; Trudy*, iii (St. Petersburg, 1915).

28. Photius, *De Rossorum Incursione, Homilia* I, *Fragmenta Historicorum Graecorum*, ed. C. Müller, v (Paris, 1870), pp. 162–7; English transl. C. Mango, *The Homilies of Photius, Patriarch of Constantinople* (Cambridge, Mass., 1958), pp. 82–95.

29. *Homilia* II, ibid., pp. 169–70; Mango, pp. 102–3.

30. Kh. Loparev, "Tserkovnoe slovo Dorofeya, mitropolita Mitilinskogo", *Vizantiisky Vremennik*, xii (1906), pp. 166–71.

31. Theophanes Continuatus, iv, 33, p. 196.

32. *PG* 102, cols. 736–7.

33. Theophanes Continuatus, v, 97, pp. 342–3.

34. *Povest'*, pp. 23–5; Cross, p. 64.

35. *Povest'*, pp. 25–9; Cross, pp. 65–8.

36. *Povest'*, p. 25; Cross, p. 65.

37. *Povest'*, p. 33; Cross, pp. 71–2.

38. *Povest'*, p. 34; Cross, pp. 72–3.

39. *Povest'*, pp. 34–9; Cross, pp. 73–7.

40. *Povest'*, p. 39; Cross, p. 77.

41. *Povest'*, p. 29; Cross, pp. 68–9.

42. *De cerimoniis*, ii, 15, pp. 594–8.

43. *Continuatio Reginonis, MGH, Scriptores Rerum Germanicarum in usum scholarum*, pp. 170, 172.

44. *Povest'*, p. 45; Cross, p. 83.

45. *Povest'*, p. 56; Cross, pp. 93–4.

46. *Povest'*, pp. 58–9; Cross, pp. 95–6.

47. *Povest'*, pp. 59–81; Cross, pp. 96–117.

48. *Histoire de Yahya-ibn-Sa'īd d'Antioche*, transl. I. Kratchkovsky and A. Vasiliev, *Patrologia Orientalis*, xxiii, p. 423.

49. See W. Lange, *Studien zur christlichen Dichtung der Nordgermanen* (Göttingen, 1958), pp. 179–81.

50. *DAI*, ch. 13, p. 74.

51. Liutprand, *Relatio de Legatione Constantinopolitana*, xv, ed. J. Bekker, *MGH, Scriptores Rerum Germanicarum in usum scholarum*, p. 184; English transl., Wright, p. 244.

52. Whether Vladimir was the first foreign ruler to marry a porphyrogenita is a moot point. See G. Ostrogorsky, *History of the Byzantine State* (Oxford, 2nd ed., 1968), pp. 296–7, n. 2, and 304; R. Jenkins, *Byzantium, The Imperial Centuries, AD 610–1071* (London, 1966), pp. 293–5.

53. *Povest'*, p. 80; Cross, p. 116.

54. *Povest'*, p. 81; Cross, p. 117.

55. *De cerimoniis*, ii, 48, pp. 687–91.

7

The Bonds of the Commonwealth

This book has so far been planned on a regional pattern. The encounter between the empire and the peoples of Eastern Europe has been separately considered within three geographical areas: the Balkan peninsula; the lands of East-Central Europe, bounded in the south by the Danube and the Sava, in the east by the Carpathians and the Transylvanian Alps, and in the north by the Sudetes and the Erzgebirge; and finally the far more extensive territory whose limits were the northern coast of the Black Sea, the Caucasus range, and two lines drawn approximately from the Gulf of Finland to the lower Volga on the one hand, and to the Danube estuary on the other. A separate treatment of these three areas was required not only by the varieties of their physical landscape, economic conditions and political history, but also by the widely differing circumstances in which their inhabitants came into contact with the Byzantine Empire. In respect of two of these areas our narrative has brought us approximately to the year 1000: Basil II's conquest of the Balkans, completed in 1018, and Russia's final conversion to Christianity, achieved in 989 during the reign of the same emperor, were significant landmarks in the historical process with which this book is concerned. In the case of East-Central Europe, our account has covered a further two hundred years: for it seemed scarcely profitable to discuss the fate of the Cyrillo-Methodian tradition in Bohemia, or the impact of Byzantine civilization upon the culture of medieval Hungary, without taking the story down to about 1100 in the first case, and about 1200 in the second. It is nevertheless true that within each of these three areas the years immediately preceding and following A.D. 1000 mark, in the history of the empire's relations with its northern neighbours, a major turning point.

It will not have escaped the reader's notice that the histories of these three regions not infrequently overlap. To take three examples: the movement of the nomads across the steppes of South Russia spelled danger to the empire's Balkan provinces whenever the lower Danube frontier was vulnerable to attack; this forced the Byzantine diplomatists, operating in the North Caucasian and Crimean sectors, to have the defence of the Balkans as their ultimate concern. Secondly, the Moravian mission of Cyril and Methodius was also closely connected with events in the Balkans: it was launched partly to counteract the threat to Byzantium of Frankish influence spreading to the eastern regions of the peninsula, and it led to the rise of Slavonic vernacular Christianity in Bulgaria. Thirdly, the same Cyrillo-Methodian tradition was, no doubt with Byzantine approval, adopted by Russia and thus cemented a link between that country on the one hand and Bohemia and Bulgaria on the other.

These three examples suggest that the connection between our three areas were not only "external" and contingent on the movement of peoples, individuals and ideas from one sector of the empire's northern front to another: they also had an "organic" aspect, since these movements were often caused either by the ambition of the northern tribes and nations to invade Byzantine territory, or by the desire of the statesmen in Constantinople to control and subdue these real or potential enemies, sometimes indeed by both factors together. In either case, the movements of peoples and the resultant regional interconnections cannot be understood without reference to Byzantium. Our three areas developed still more organic links with each other when the nations that dwelt within them accepted Byzantine culture and became members of an international commonwealth, presided over by the emperor of East Rome.

As far as Eastern Europe is concerned, this commonwealth achieved its greatest territorial extent in the early eleventh century. By the year 1000 there had come into being a community of states and nations, extending from the Gulf of Finland to the Southern Peloponnese, and from the Adriatic to the Caucasus, all of which in varying degrees owed allegiance to the Byzantine

Map 7   The Byzantine Commonwealth in the eleventh century

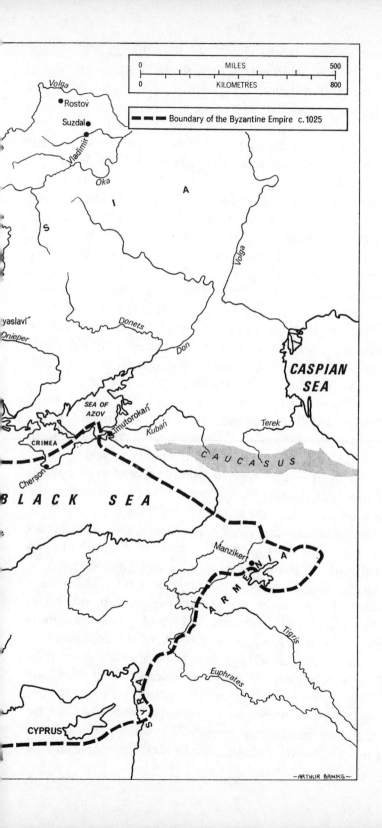

MILES
0   500

KILOMETRES
0   800

▬ ▬ ▬ Boundary of the Byzantine Empire c.1025

Volga

● Rostov

Suzdal ●

● Vladimir

Oka

Volga

I

A

S

...yaslavl´

Dnieper

Donets

Don

CASPIAN
SEA

SEA OF
AZOV

Tmutorokań

Kuban´

Terek

CRIMEA

C A U C A S U S

Cherson ●

B L A C K   S E A

Manziker...

A N I A

A R M

Tigris

Euphrates

S Y R A

CYPRUS

~ARTHUR BANKS~

Church and empire. It was then, too, that this East European community acquired a hitherto unprecedented cultural and political cohesion. And although its political bonds were seriously loosened in the second half of the twelfth century and relaxed almost to the point of severance in the late thirteenth, its cultural unity not only survived the catastrophic events of 1180–1240, but acquired a new content and strength in the late Middle Ages.

The emergence, in the early eleventh century, of the Byzantine Commonwealth in Eastern Europe as a recognizable cultural and political entity will, it is hoped, justify the new method adopted henceforth in the arrangement and treatment of our material: in the remaining part of the book, the approach to our subject will be global rather than regional, synoptic rather than fragmentary. In the interests of clarity, the empire's relations with the various peoples of Eastern Europe will still be discussed, in this and the following chapter, under separate headings. No attempt will be made, moreover, to underestimate the differences—political, social and to a lesser degree cultural—which existed, and in some areas increased, within the East European community. Yet the nature of our subject will increasingly demand a proper emphasis on those unifying factors which, despite many strains and disruptive tendencies, enabled the Byzantine Commonwealth to survive until the end of the Middle Ages as a more or less coherent society.

It may be helpful at this stage to attempt a brief geographical and ethnic survey of Eastern Europe during the first quarter of the eleventh century. By 1018 the whole of the Balkan peninsula, as far as the lower and middle Danube, the Drava, the eastern foothills of the Slovenian Alps and the confines of Istria, had been incorporated into the Byzantine Empire. These imperial lands in Europe (Apulia, Calabria, Eastern Sicily and Crete, which were also then part of the empire, are outside the scope of this book) were inhabited by five different races. Two of them, the Greeks and the Slavs, who together formed the bulk of the population of the Balkans, had already made significant contributions to the political and cultural history of medieval Europe. The third, the Latin-speaking citizens of the Dalmatian cities, still proudly conscious of their Roman origin, were gradually being absorbed by the Slavs of the surrounding countryside. The other two, the Albanians and the Vlachs, were about to make their first unmistakable appearance in the medieval annals of the Balkans. The Albanians, probably descended, as we have seen, from the ancient Illyrians, were still enclosed in their highland retreats which formed the nucleus of the Byzantine theme of Dyrrachium. The Vlachs, whose Romance dialect, akin to modern Rumanian, points to their descent from the aboriginal population of South-Eastern Europe which was partly Romanized when Rome held sway over this area, appear in the Byzantine sources of the eleventh and twelfth centuries in much the same guise as today: transhumant shepherds, moving their flocks of sheep and goats between their winter settlements in the plain of Thessaly and their summer pastures in the Pindus and Grammos Mountains. Their seasonable migrations are later attested in other parts of the Balkan peninsula. The Byzantines knew them mostly for their cheese and home-spun coats, much prized by the poorer classes in Constantinople, for their dislike of paying taxes, and for their incurable insubordination: the Jewish traveller Benjamin of Tudela, who visited Greece in the second half of the twelfth century, describes the Vlachs of Thessaly as follows: "They are as swift as hinds, and they sweep down from the mountains to despoil and ravage the land of Greece. No man can go up and do battle against them, and no king can rule over them. . . . They are altogether lawless".[1]

Beyond the empire's northern borders dwelt a number of peoples who in the early eleventh century were associated with the empire by culture or religion. The most tenuous of these links with Byzantium were those maintained by the Czechs. They were mostly indirect links, created by the Cyrillo-Methodian tradition which was still a living force in eleventh century Bohemia. But the channels of communication between Bohemia and the Byzantine Empire, though still open through Hungary, were gradually closing up. And although in the middle of the twelfth century Vladislav, king of Bohemia, acknowledged himself the vassal (*lizios*) of the Emperor Manuel Comnenus,[2] the religious and political life of the Czechs had for some time already been steered in the direction of Germany and Rome.

South-east of Bohemia, the Hungarian kingdom was still strongly influenced, in its cultural and religious life, by the civilization of Byzantium. This influence was widespread in the eastern part of the country, between the Tisza and the Carpathians;

but it was still far from negligible in the court circles, and at least two eleventh century kings of Hungary seem to have acknowledged the supremacy of the Byzantine emperor. The greater part of Eastern Hungary consisted of Transylvania. Much of the early history of this province is obscure. Between A.D. 106 and 271 it formed the kernel of the Roman province of Dacia; occupied by the Magyars at the time of their migration to Central Europe, it was annexed to the Hungarian crown in the eleventh century. During the thousand years that followed the evacuation of Dacia by the Romans, a process took place in Wallachia, Moldavia and Transylvania, in circumstances obscure and controversial, which led to the rise of the Rumanian people. This is not the place to summarize this notorious controversy, marked by strong political and nationalistic overtones, in which modern Rumanian and Hungarian historians have been the main protagonists. It can scarcely be doubted that the Rumanians, who—like the Vlachs of the Balkans—speak a Romance language, owe their origin in part to the Roman colonists who came to their country in the second and third centuries, and in part to the earlier Dacian population. These Romanized Dacians retreated into the remoter areas of the Carpathians after the Roman legions were withdrawn south of the Danube, and there, in their mountain refuge, preserved their language and—despite a later admixture of Slav blood—their ethnic identity. Part of the Rumanian people seem to have been converted to Christianity by the Bulgarians, probably in the late ninth or in the early tenth century, and to have borrowed from them the Slavonic liturgy and the Cyrillo-Methodian literary tradition. This conversion, however, appears to have been superficial, and it is not until the fourteenth century that any organized political life is reliably attested in the two Rumanian principalities of Wallachia and Moldavia. It was then that the church and culture of Constantinople became dominant in those lands, and the Rumanians made their belated entry into the Byzantine Commonwealth of nations.

Moving eastward from the Rumanian lands, we come to the North Pontic area. The Greek, or at least Greek-speaking, cities of the South Crimean coast and the Gothic settlements in the mountains further north were during the eleventh century still part of the empire. Immediately to the east of the Crimea, on the other side of the Straits of Kerch, was a small Russian principality centred on the city of Tmutorokan'. This city, whose eccentric position, uncertain past and sudden rise to prominence in the eleventh century have exerted a strange fascination upon Russian historians, is first mentioned under its Greek name Tamatarcha in the eighth century list of Byzantine bishoprics in Khazaria. Though it was separated from Kievan Russia by a wide expanse of steppe land, Tmutorokan' seems to have been one of the main points of direct contact between the Russians and the Byzantines in the eleventh century. By 1118 at the latest the city, and doubtless its hinterland as well, were under imperial sovereignty. As for Kievan Russia, neither its territory nor its mixed Slav, Finnic and Scandinavian population had altered much since the late ninth century. Still the great river route from the Baltic to the Black Sea, fiercely defended against the mounting pressure of the steppe nomads, served as the political backbone and the economic life-line of the young Russian state, directing its commercial interests and cultural aspirations southward to Constantinople.

All the peoples enumerated above shared a common characteristic: they were either citizens of the empire, or else, through the influence exerted by it upon their religion, culture and institutions, they formed part of the Byzantine Commonwealth. Their citizenship of, or association with, the empire did not always begin or end at the same time, though they came nearest to forming a single community in the eleventh and first half of the twelfth century. The Czechs, however, had dropped beyond the Byzantine horizon by 1100 except for a brief period in the mid-twelfth century, and the Rumanians, though they came under the influence of Byzantine Christianity in the tenth century, did not become closely associated with the empire until the mid-fourteenth. To illustrate the different types of relationship that bound the peoples of Eastern Europe to Byzantium in the eleventh and twelfth centuries it may be helpful to consider the five following examples: the assimilation of the Slav settlements in Greece; Bulgaria's forced incorporation into the empire by conquest; the more tenuous, yet still tangible, subjection of the Serbian lands to Byzantium; the largely theoretical dependence of the Russian state of Kiev on the Byzantine emperor; and the status of the empire's Varangian mercenaries.

The main stages by which the Slavs, who had settled in large numbers in Epirus, Hellas and the Peloponnese, were first reduced and then civilized by the Byzantine authorities during the ninth and tenth centuries have been sketched in an earlier chapter. By the first half of the eleventh century the imperial policy of settling Byzantine peasant-soldiers in the *Sklaviniae*, of setting up an extensive network of bishoprics and parish churches in the southern part of the Balkan peninsula, and of insisting on the use of Greek in the church, the army and the local administration, had been remarkably successful. The Byzantinization of the Slavs in Greece was now virtually complete. Only in the remoter areas of the Southern Peloponnese did Slav tribes retain their language and their sense of ethnic distinction until the end of the Middle Ages: these recalcitrants were the Melingoi, on the slopes of the Taygetus Mountains, and the Ezeritai, who lived on the northern and eastern coast of the Gulf of Laconia, from Gytheion to Vatika Bay near Cape Malea. Both tribes revolted several times against Byzantine rule, and in the second half of the thirteenth century were granted local autonomy and the right of bearing arms. But this was an exception. Apart from these two isolated pockets the Slav language was probably extinct in Greece by the late twelfth century. Christianity and the prestige of Byzantine civilization had together succeeded in absorbing and Hellenizing the Slavs. It is probable that the Slav racial stock, later supplemented by the Albanian, has remained to the present day a strong component of the population of Greece; but this hypothesis, however likely, is scarcely susceptible of rigorous proof. Today all that remains in Greece as evidence of the ethnic predominance of the Slavs in the seventh and eighth centuries is the relatively large number of place names of Slavonic origin. For the rest, the rapid assimilation of the Slavs is eloquent testimony to the vitality and prestige of Greek Byzantine civilization. It has rightly been said that for the barbarians of the West the empire was "not an enemy but a career":[3] this is equally true of the Slavs in Greece after the year 800.

By 1018 the whole of Samuel's Bulgarian realm had, through Basil II's conquests, been incorporated into the Byzantine Empire. The newly annexed territory was parcelled out into themes, on a par with the other imperial provinces. The kernel of Samuel's empire, Macedonia, now became the theme of Bulgaria, centred on Skoplje. The lands between the lower Danube and the Balkan Mountains formed the theme of Paristrion or Paradunavon: recently discovered evidence suggests that this theme, whose main city was Silistria, was in fact set up after John Tzimisces' conquests of 971 and that its continuous history was only briefly interrupted by the Bulgarian victories of the late tenth century.[4] A third theme, that of Sirmium, was probably created further west, on the middle Danube and the lower Sava. These administrative measures were supported by other steps which show that Basil II intended to keep a firm hand on the conquered country: most of the surviving male members of Samuel's family and some of the Bulgarian aristocracy were brought to Constantinople, married to Byzantines and then conveniently dispatched to distant military posts in Asia Minor and Armenia; the patriarchate of Ohrid, that religious symbol of Bulgaria's independence, was degraded to the rank of an archbishopric. The ruthless power of the "Bulgar-slayer" is vividly portrayed in the eleventh-century illuminated Venetian psalter of Basil II, in which the emperor, in ceremonial armour, stands surrounded by saints and archangels and receiving a crown from Christ, while at his feet in humble submission Bulgarian chieftains grovel in the dust.[5]

Now that Bulgaria's powers of resistance were crushed, the emperor could afford to be generous. According to an eleventh century Byzantine chronicler he wished the Bulgarians to retain the administrative system by which they had been governed in the days of Samuel. Unfortunately the chronicler confines himself to a single example: the Bulgarian peasants were allowed to continue to pay their taxes in kind; they had to supply the government with a yearly measure of corn, millet and wine, and were thus freed from the obligation imposed on the population of other Byzantine provinces of paying their taxes in money.[6] We know more, on the other hand, about the ecclesiastical arrangements devised by Basil

II for Bulgaria. In three charters he declared the archbishopric of Ohrid to be autocephalous, i.e. independent of the jurisdiction of the patriarch of Constantinople, and placed under its authority all the bishoprics, not a few of them Byzantine ones, which had belonged to the empires of Peter and Samuel.[7] Its incumbent, who was granted a number of privileges, was to be appointed by the emperor himself. The latter stipulation, of course, shows how extensive was the control acquired by Byzantium over the Bulgarian Church after the conquest. In the circumstances, however, it was intended as a concession to local susceptibilities. Ohrid's autocephalous status was supposed to safeguard the Bulgarian Church against direct interference by the patriarch; its archbishop ranked high in the hierarchy of the Byzantine Church, and was given (and retained for several centuries) a dominant position in the Central and Northern Balkans; and the appointment, immediately after the conquest, of a native Bulgarian to this see shows how far Basil II was prepared to go towards granting a measure of local autonomy to his new Bulgarian subjects.

The emperor's decision to allow the Bulgarians to preserve, within the administrative framework of the empire, some of their most cherished national institutions was an act of statesmanship. This policy of moderation, had it been followed by his successors, might conceivably have led to the country's complete assimilation; and it may be that modern Bulgarian historians of the nationalistic school, in deploring the subsequent reversal of Basil's policy, have been somewhat inconsistent: for it is arguable that without this reversal there would have been no large-scale revolts of the Bulgarians against Byzantine rule, and hence no revival of their country's independence in the later Middle Ages.

It should be noted, however, that the policies pursued by successive Byzantine governments towards Bulgaria in the eleventh century were closely bound up with the political, economic and military situation within the empire. The reign of Basil II marked a high point of Byzantine power: by 1025, the year of his death, the empire's frontiers seemed impregnable to foreign attack; the aristocracy, whose greed for land and chronic insubordination had caused his predecessors so much trouble, was held in check by legislation and the emperor's authority; the state treasury was full; and the empire's clients and satellites, both within and beyond its frontiers, had been pacified by the power and the liberalities of the emperor, and drawn into the orbit of Byzantium by the prestige and appeal of its civilization. Basil's policy towards Bulgaria, was after 1018, pursued from a position of strength.

Fifty years later the picture had altered beyond recognition. The imperial defences in Europe and Asia had broken down; the empire was on the verge of economic bankruptcy; and the subject peoples in the Balkans, their loyalty to Byzantium gravely undermined, had revolted several times and were in a state of ferment. This situation was brought about by an acute military, economic and social crisis which overwhelmed the empire between 1025 and 1081. The causes of this crisis have recently been much debated by historians. Among the more important were a decline in the rural population, accentuated by several severe droughts and famines, and a resultant fall in agricultural production; a neglect of the armed forces by successive governments who favoured the civil nobility of Constantinople against the military aristocracy of the provinces; and the emperors' growing tendency to grant rights of immunity to landowners, which undermined the system of military holdings that had previously been a major source of the empire's strength. Nowhere was the combined effect of these factors more baneful than in Byzantium's Bulgarian provinces.

To meet the economic crisis a ruthless policy of taxation was pursued. The Bulgarian peasantry was particularly hard hit by this policy, not only because the Byzantine tax collectors resorted to extortionist methods in the newly conquered territory, but also because the frequent wars and invasions imposed extra financial burdens on the population. In 1040 by order of John the Orphanotrophus, the all-powerful minister of Michael IV, the Bulgarians were deprived of their privilege of paying taxes in kind; Bulgaria was thus absorbed into the fiscal system of the empire. This measure provoked a major revolt in the Northern Balkans. Peter Delyan, who was probably Samuel's grandson, was proclaimed tsar of Bulgaria in Belgrade. In a short time the insurgents captured Niš, Skoplje, Dyrrachium, Nicopolis and Serdica, and thrust deep into Thessaly, as far as Demetrias (Volos). Their attempt to seize Thessalonica failed, however, and in 1041 the rebellion, which suffered from a lack of unity among its leaders, was suppressed by the Byzantines. It was an ominous sign of the growing disaffection of the Balkan peoples, and proved to be the first crack in the edifice which Basil, barely twenty years earlier, had built up in the northern part of the peninsula. The Bulgarian insurgents had been joined by Albanians and Greeks, and the rebellion enabled the Serbs on the Adriatic coast to assert their independence soon afterwards. The Serbs played an active part in another Bulgarian revolt which broke out in 1072. It too was put down by force of arms. The empire was still capable of holding down the subject peoples of the Balkans; but the Slavs in the peninsula were showing an increasing unwillingness to be ruled by local governors or indigenous princes owing allegiance to Constantinople.

The military situation in the Balkans during the eleventh century is epitomized in the chequered history of the strategically crucial area which lay between the lower Danube and the Balkan Mountains. The conquests of John Tzimisces and Basil II, by obliterating Bulgaria, had removed a buffer which had impeded, if it did not wholly prevent, the nations of the steppe from invading the Balkans. The security of the peninsula now depended on the military potential of the Byzantine province of Paristrion. The lower Danube had been heavily fortified by John Tzimisces after his victory over Svyatoslav in 971, to guard against the possibility of further Russian attacks across the river. The excavations recently carried out in the Dobrudja by Rumanian archaeologists have revealed the impressive scale of these fortifications: not only were the old Romano-Byzantine fortresses near the mouth of the Danube—Dinogetia, Carsium, Capidava—rebuilt and garrisoned by John Tzimisces; a new stronghold was built as a naval base on Păcuiul lui Soare, an island in the Danube, eighteen kilometres to the east of Silistria. We do not know what happened to this elaborate system of fortifications in the closing years of the tenth century, when much of the lower Danube area was controlled by the Bulgarians; but by 1000 or soon after, these forts were once more in Byzantine hands. The work of archaeologists has revealed that at least one of them, Păcuiul lui Soare, was then transformed by Basil II's engineers from a naval base into a land fortress: this change was caused by a new military situation on the lower Danube in the opening years of the eleventh century. The empire was no longer threatened in this area by the naval power of the Russians, but by the nomadic and land hungry Pechenegs.

The Pecheneg raids into the Balkans became frequent and dangerous after 1034. It was not before 1047, however, that the weakness of the empire's *limes* on the lower Danube became apparent. During the next six years the Pechenegs ravaged Thrace with fearful regularity, and on one occasion reached the environs of Constantinople. The Byzantine government attempted to deal with this menace by the time-honoured method of diplomacy: taking advantage of an internecine strife between Tyrach and Kegen, the leaders of two Pecheneg hordes, the Emperor Constantine ix allowed the latter to settle with his subjects on Byzantine territory, allotted him three fortresses on the southern bank of the Danube on condition that he guard the river against the attacks of his rival and compatriot, bestowed on him the rank of *patricius*, and persuaded him to accept Christianity. The empire's new subject-allies were baptized by the monk Euthymius. After a fresh bout of fighting between Kegen and Tyrach, the Byzantine authorities invited Tyrach in his turn to come into the Balkans, and settled large numbers of his men in the plains round Serdica and Niš. The Pecheneg chieftain and his retinue were invited to Constantinople and were baptized in the city.[8]

This belated attempt to deal with the Pechenegs in the manner prescribed in the *De Administrando Imperio* failed to bring the empire even temporary relief. Other Pecheneg hordes were continually pressing on the lower Danube, and their invasions of Thrace continued in the 1050s. The rare victories gained over them by the Byzantines were due not to imperial policy, so deficient at this time in military matters, but to the local initiative of provincial governors and field commanders. In 1064 a fresh disaster overtook the Balkans: the Uzes, another Turkic nomadic people from the South Russian steppe, who had cut their way through the Pecheneg lands to the Danube, swept over Bulgaria, Thrace, Macedonia and even Greece. So great was the anguish caused by their ravages that the local population was tempted to emigrate. Fortunately for the empire, their horde, said to have numbered 600,000 men, was decimated by plague. Those Uzes who did not either perish or retreat across the Danube were settled on imperial lands in Macedonia and, in the words of a contemporary writer, "became allies and subjects" of Byzantium.[9]

In the early 1070s the empire seemed on the verge of total military collapse. The simultaneous disasters of Manzikert and Bari (1071) resulted in the loss of most of Asia Minor and of its last possessions in South Italy. The next year the Bulgarians and the Serbs were in revolt, and the commanders of the theme of Paristrion, incensed by the government's decision to make the corn trade a state monopoly, declared their independence. In the words of a recent historian, the empire had been deprived of its two wings—Asia Minor and Italy—and was threatened in its very heart, the Balkan Peninsula.[10]

In some respects the situation in these dark days resembled that of the early seventh century. As far as the empire's northern frontier was concerned the crisis of the 1070s was at once less and more ominous. This frontier did not, as it had done at the time of the Avaro-Slav invasions, totally collapse. On the contrary, by a remarkable military and diplomatic effort Byzantium was able during the next two decades to retrieve the situation, and to hold the Danube as an effective *limes* for a further hundred years. Much of the credit for this must go to the Emperor Alexius Comnenus (1081–1118), whose able generalship and astute foreign policy did much to rebuild the shattered structure of the empire. Yet the internal resources and the political resilience which in the seventh and the eighth centuries had enabled it to overcome the gravest crisis of its early history were now lacking. The further decline of the military small-holdings, the growing tendency to grant rights of immunity to private landowners, the persistent financial crisis, and the ever-increasing role which the Italian maritime republics were playing in Byzantine trade—these factors, whose combined effects became only too evident in the twelfth century, made any lasting reconstruction of the fabric of the empire impossible. Alexius, it is true, dealt successfully with the three major calamities of his realm: the Norman invasion, the First Crusade and the attacks of the Pechenegs. The latter, who had been at war with the empire almost uninterruptedly since 1086, reached the walls of Constantinople in 1090. The emperor appealed for help to the Turkic Cumans, the latest nomadic inhabitants of South Russia, who then occupied the steppes between the Don and the lower Danube. In a battle fought with singular ferocity on 29 April 1091 by Mount Levunion near the mouth of the Maritsa the Pechenegs were routed and virtually wiped out by the Byzantines and their Cuman allies. The gravest threat from the North which the empire had faced during the eleventh century was thus removed in a single day. The simultaneous re-establishment of imperial authority in Paristrion inaugurated a period—the last—when the lower Danube as well as the Northern Balkans were effectively controlled by Byzantium.

The emergence of a system of political and economic relations which gradually came to resemble West European feudalism is traceable in Bulgaria, as in other parts of the Byzantine Empire, from the second half of the eleventh century. Its characteristic feature was the *pronoia*, a method of tenure whereby property (most frequently land) was handed over by the government to secular magnates, usually in return for military service, together with its entire revenue and with rights of administration. The holders of these estates were often granted privileges and immunities exempting them from taxes and other public obligations. In Bulgaria, alongside the great ecclesiastical estates with their dependent peasants (those of the archbishop of Ohrid and of the monastery of Bachkovo in the Rhodopes were among the largest), secular *pronoiai* administered by members of the Byzantine aristocracy were widespread in the late eleventh and in the twelfth centuries, particularly in Thrace and Macedonia. It is not easy to gauge the effect of this development on the attitude of the Bulgarians towards their Byzantine masters. At first those peasants who in times of hardship renounced their independence to become the tenants or serfs of some territorial magnate no doubt regarded their new status, which at least preserved them from starvation, with some relief. But in the unsettled conditions of the eleventh century their economic plight worsened steadily in many districts, particularly in view of the central government's policy of farming out taxes and giving the landlords virtually unrestricted jurisdiction over their peasants. To them and to other classes of Bulgarian society the Byzantine *pronoiarioi* must have often appeared as alien exploiters.

It is natural to inquire how far these anti-Byzantine sentiments were exploited by the dualist heretics in Bulgaria, the Bogomils and the Paulicians. Modern historians are all but unanimous in their belief that the Bulgarian Bogomils instigated, or at least participated in, the revolts of the eleventh century, and that they supported the Pechenegs in their attacks on the empire. It is difficult to subscribe to this view. It is true, as we have already seen, that the Bogomils preached a doctrine of civil disobedience, directed against the established order in church and state. Their movement, moreover, acquired a new impetus in the eleventh century and, now unrestricted by state frontiers, spread over the entire south-eastern part of the Balkan peninsula. In the last quarter of the century the sect gained a foothold in Constantinople itself, and the trial and public burning in the Hippodrome of its leader Basil *c.* 1110 was a *cause célèbre* of the time. But it must be recalled that the Bogomils' social anarchism was an expression of their religious and moral convictions, not a political programme; and that violence and the shedding of blood were incompatible both with their belief in the inherent wickedness of the material world and with their ideal of evangelical poverty. We may accept that the Bulgarian Bogomils continued in the eleventh and twelfth centuries to oppose the established Orthodox Church and the hierarchical structure of a society dominated by the Byzantine masters of their country, without thereby subscribing to the view that they fought with man-made weapons in defence of their ideals. The Paulicians, however, were a different matter. Settled mainly in Thrace, and especially numerous in and around Philippopolis (Anna Comnena, the Emperor Alexius' daughter, asserted that at the turn of the century they formed almost the entire population of that city),[11] they had probably lost by then many of their Armenian characteristics and become mixed with Greeks and Slavs. They still retained, however, their warlike spirit and their willingness to rise at the slightest provocation against the Byzantine overlords. Several times in the second half of the eleventh century we find them in revolt, allied with the Pecheneg and Cuman enemies of the empire. Some of them were converted to Orthodoxy in 1114 after strenuous theological disputations with the Emperor Alexius, of which his daughter has left us a pious and probably overcoloured account. On the whole, however, the readiness with which the Paulicians fought against Byzantine domination illustrates the failure of the imperial policy of garrisoning the Thracian fortresses with heretics transported from Asia.

One final problem must be considered in this survey of Byzantine rule in Bulgaria. Did the occupying power pursue a policy of cultural assimilation? And if so, with what success? The evidence provided by medieval documents on this matter is disappointingly slender and equivocal, and it is not surprising that the views of modern historians conflict. The majority seem convinced that the Byzantines made a determined and systematic attempt to destroy Bulgaria's national traditions, and in particular to eradicate the Slavonic language from the liturgy of the Bulgarian Church. There is certainly no doubt that the Byzantine authorities did all they could to absorb Bulgaria into the empire's administrative structure. The division of the country into themes was followed by the appointment of Byzantine officials to the higher military and civilian posts in the land. These measures were clearly aimed at forestalling separatist movements; and those which did break out were ruthlessly suppressed. These efforts at political assimilation were designed to be supported by the work of the archbishopric of Ohrid. The appointment by Basil II of a native Bulgarian to this post proved an ephemeral measure. After 1037 all his successors were Greeks. Of these prelates' cultural activity we have no precise knowledge. It is often assumed that they pursued in their archdiocese the same deliberate policy of fostering Greek as the official language which the Byzantines had imposed so successfully on their Slav subjects in Greece. It is indeed likely that they encouraged the liturgical use of Greek in the Bulgarian Church: their own prejudices in its favour were doubtless reinforced by arguments of prestige. But there is no evidence whatever to show that the archbishops of Ohrid attempted to extirpate the Slavonic liturgical tradition. To do so in the eleventh century would scarcely have been possible. Nor is there any reason for regarding these prelates as devoid either of elementary common sense or of a modicum of concern for the spiritual welfare of their flock. There are, on the contrary, some grounds for believing that the literary tradition of Clement and Naum and of their masters, Cyril and Methodius, was cultivated in Bulgaria with at least the tacit approval of its Greek archbishops. Thus a comparatively large number of well-known Old Church Slavonic manuscripts, probably copied in the eleventh (in some cases the twelfth) century, have been attributed by philologists either to Macedonian or to

East Bulgarian *scriptoria*. Among them are the Glagolitic *Codex Assemanianus, Psalterium Sinaiticum, Euchologium Sinaiticum* and *Rila Fragments,* and the Cyrillic *Codex Suprasliensis, Savvina Kniga* and *Codex Eninensis* (the last was discovered in 1960). The subsequent flowering of Church Slavonic literature in Bulgaria in the late Middle Ages is hardly intelligible unless we admit some continuity in this cultural tradition during the period of Byzantine rule.

The view that the archbishopric of Orrid, while acting as a channel for the diffusion of Byzantine culture in the central and northern areas of the Balkans, was not a centre of deliberate anti-Slav activity, finds some support in the one detailed document we possess on the state of the Bulgarian Church in this period. The voluminous correspondence of Theophylact, archbishop of Ohrid from *c.* 1090 to *c.* 1109, paints a vivid picture of the trials that faced these Greek prelates in their day-to-day task of administering their vast and ethnically alien diocese.[12] This remarkable man, born in Euboea, had studied in Constantinople under the famous philosopher Michael Psellus, had been tutor to the heir-presumptive to the throne, and retained close connections with the Byzantine court. A theologian of no mean stature, he wrote in about 1090, at a time when the disputes between the Roman and the Byzantine Churches were often acrimonious, a treatise in which he severely criticized his Greek colleagues for slandering the customs of Latin Christianity.[13] The circumstances of his appointment to the see of Ohrid are unknown, but we may safely assume that he did not view it with unmitigated pleasure. His letters, many of which are addressed to high officials in Constantinople, are full of intemperate and lachrymose complaints at being relegated to this dreary outpost of the empire. In one of them he laments the necessity of living among "unclean barbarian slaves who smell of sheepskin", and compares himself to Zeus' bird, the eagle, condemned to spend its life among frogs. His Bulgarian diocese he describes as "a filthy marsh", and its inhabitants as "monsters".[14] This scarcely suggests a zealous pastor or a benevolent *Kulturträger.* But we must beware of judging Theophylact too hastily. Such sentiments were part of the conventional rhetoric of many a Byzantine mandarin impelled by the rigours of provincial life to contrast his rude surroundings with the distant delights of Constantinople or Thessalonica. In the late twelfth century Michael Choniates, the learned metropolitan of Athens, mortified at the discovery that the miserable and demotic-speaking peasants who constituted his flock fell short of his shining vision of the ancient Greeks, wrote these remarkable words: "I am becoming a barbarian by living for a long time in Athens."[15] It seems unlikely that Theophylact's attitude to his Bulgarian fold was quite as fastidious as he pretended in his letters to the court. He defended them—and himself—with considerable vigour against the exactions of the local Byzantine tax collectors, and complained in his letters of the intolerable behaviour of these "robbers".[16] He was far-sighted enough to realize that, if provoked too frequently, the Bulgarian peasants would revolt; and he urged the authorities in Constantinople to treat them with caution and restraint, "lest the patience of the poor be finally exhausted".[17] Still more remarkable is the fact that this Byzantine prelate who professed such contempt for his Slavonic flock wrote a biography of Clement of Ohrid, based in part on an earlier Slav *Vita* of the saint, in which he lavished enthusiastic praise on Ss. Cyril and Methodius.[18]

This fact alone should be sufficient to put us on our guard against the popular picture of Theophylact as a fanatical enemy of Slavonic culture. An unbiased study of his activity in Ohrid seems to bear out the little we know from other sources about Byzantine policy in Bulgaria between 1018 and 1185. The evidence suggests that the authorities in Constantinople and their local agents in the field, while aiming at the total assimilation of Bulgaria into the empire's political structure, did not carry this policy as far as a systematic attempt to subvert the culture of the Bulgarian people by outlawing their language and literature. The role played by Ohrid in transmitting Byzantine civilization to the Balkan Slavs during the Middle Ages would hardly have been so great had the two literary traditions, the Greek and the Slav, not continued to exist side by side in the country's schools and monasteries and to interact in a bilingual milieu.

On the political plane the attempt to absorb Bulgaria into the empire proved in the end a total failure. The often arbitrary acts of local Byzantine officials, the extortionist fiscal policy, the misery of the peasants in many parts of the country, increased by foreign invasions, and the popularity of the dualist sectarians, all these factors provoked a growing resentment against Byzantine rule. The comparative ease with which the Bulgarians regained their independence in 1187 showed up the bankruptcy of the empire's efforts to hold down the Slav states in the Balkans by force of arms. On the cultural plane the Byzantines were more successful. It is largely due to the archbishops of Ohrid that Macedonia became for several centuries a leading centre of Byzantine civilization in the peninsula. Many Bulgarians, after a century and a half of alien rule, must have strongly disliked the "Greeks" and much of what they stood for. But in their educated and socially privileged classes there were certainly some who had come to accept the patterns of thought and behaviour brought from Constantinople. In the first half of the thirteenth century, according to a contemporary Byzantine writer, a Bulgarian nobleman from Philippopolis urged the citizens of Melnik in North-Eastern Macedonia to submit to the emperor of Nicaea by using the following argument, admittedly based on the fact that the latter's son had married the Bulgarian tsar's daughter:

> The emperor [he said] has long had authority over us, since our land belongs to the Byzantine Empire. ... And all of us, natives of Philippopolis, are pure Byzantines by race. The Byzantine emperor, however, would still truly have the right to rule over us even if we were Bulgarians.[19]

In 1185 the two brothers Peter and Asen, who probably belonged to a Vlakh (or perhaps Cuman) family in the Byzantine service, raised a revolt in Northern Bulgaria. In the ensuing war against the imperial forces (1186–7) the rebels were eventually victorious, and the Emperor Isaac Angelus was forced to recognize the existence of an independent Bulgaria between the Balkan Mountains and the lower Danube. Byzantine dominion over this area, which had lasted for 169 years, was at an end. The Second Bulgarian Empire, as this Balkan state is known to modern historians, claimed to be the legitimate heir of the realm of Boris, Symeon and Peter. In defiance of the ecclesiastical rights of both Ohrid and Constantinople, an independent archbishopric was established in Trnovo, the new capital, and Asen was crowned tsar by its first incumbent.

Soon after Basil II's conquest of Bulgaria a number of independent Slav countries and principalities in the north-western and central areas of the Balkans made their submission to the empire. These were Croatia, Bosnia, Zachlumia, Dioclea and Raška. Sandwiched between the Byzantine themes of Sirmium, Dalmatia, Dyrrachium and Bulgaria, they were not formally annexed, but were allowed to keep their native princes who acknowledged the emperor's suzerainty. This suzerainty was most nominal and tenuous in the case of the Croats, who often showed scant regard for the emperor's political interests and intervened on their own account in the affairs of Byzantine Dalmatia. The empire, faced with the rising power of Venice in the Adriatic—the Republic of St. Mark still recognized theoretically the sovereignty of Byzantium—was obliged in 1069 to cede effective power over its Dalmatian possessions to the Croat king, while retaining nominal supremacy over them. But Croatia was too far from Constantinople, its kings' capacity for independent action too great, and their loyalty to the Roman Church too secure, for Byzantine suzerainty to be much of a reality. The coronation of its ruler Demetrius Zvonimir by the legates of Pope Gregory VII in 1075, and the acquisition of the Croatian throne by the kings of Hungary, in 1102, set the final stamp on Croatia's orientation to Central and Western Europe, and removed the country for all time (except for a brief interlude in the second half of the twelfth century) from Byzantium's sphere of influence.

The Bosnians and the Zachlumi were more obedient clients of the empire during much of the eleventh century. Byzantine control was usually exercised over them through the Serbian principalities further east. The Zachlumi of Herzegovina had been within the Byzantine sphere of influence since the second half of the ninth century, except for a brief period when they owed allegiance to Symeon of Bulgaria. To the north of Zachlumia, between the upper Neretva, the Drina and the Sava, lay the land of Bosnia. First mentioned in the *De Administrando Imperio* as a separate district of the Serbian realm,[20] its history in this period is obscure. In the late Middle Ages the Bosnians were to build up a powerful kingdom; for the present, enclosed in their mountains and high valleys, they played a shadowy and peripheral role in the Byzantine Commonwealth through their commercial and political relations with the Serbs on the Adriatic coast.

The Serbs in this period were much the most important, and insubordinate, of the empire's subjects in the Western Balkans. During the first half of the eleventh century the first Serbian realm to achieve international status arose in the coastal area round Lake Scutari and the Gulf of Kotor, extending along the coast as far as the Pelješac peninsula and into the North Albanian and Montenegrin mountains of the interior. It was known first as Dioclea and later as Zeta. Three of its successive rulers proved a severe trial to Byzantium. It was in Zeta, no less than in Bulgaria, that the Slav movements of resistance to imperial rule originated. In 1042 the prince of Zeta, Stephen Vojislav, after an abortive attempt a few years earlier to shake off imperial control, defeated an army commanded by the military governor of Dyrrachium by the same methods of mountain warfare which were later used so successfully by his Montenegrin successors against the Turks. His independence secured, he proceeded to annex the neighbouring lands of the Terbouniotes and the Zachlumi. His son Michael (c. 1052–81) dealt a further blow to the influence of Byzantium on the South Adriatic seaboard. The spearhead of this influence hitherto had been the Greek metropolitanate of Dyrrachium, whose incumbents had played the leading part in the Christianization of Dioclea and were beginning to assume ecclesiastical control over the whole country. Michael counteracted the claims of Dyrrachium by persuading the pope to raise the Latin see of Antibari (Bar) on the coast to the rank of an archbishopric, and to grant it jurisdiction over the other bishoprics of his realm. His anti-Byzantine policy was consummated and the political independence of his realm was secured in 1077 when, following the example of King Demetrius Zvonimir of Croatia, he received a royal crown fom Gregory VII and thus became a papal vassal. Michael's son Constantine Bodin joined the Bulgarian insurrection of 1072, and was proclaimed tsar of Bulgaria in Prizren. After the suppression of the rebellion he spent some time in Byzantine captivity, eventually escaped, and returned to rule over his country (c. 1082). He continued his predecessors' policy of territorial expansion at the expense of the empire and of close relations with Rome. Raška and Bosnia were now annexed to the kingdom of Zeta, and Bodin was described by the pope as *"filius noster ... rex Sclavorum gloriosissimus"*.[21]

Zeta's heyday, however, was almost over. The victories of the Emperor Alexius over the Norman invaders in Albania and on the Ionian Sea re-established Byzantine power in this area. Between 1085 and 1090 Bodin was defeated and captured by Alexius' troops, and the empire's sovereignty over his country was restored. In the early twelfth century Zeta fell into political anarchy, and the leadership over the medieval Serbian people soon passed to the rulers of Raška.

The geographical position of Raška, the original nucleus of Serb settlement in the Balkans, has already been described. It derived its name, rendered as Rascia in medieval Western sources, from the name of an affluent of the Ibar on which, near the present town of Novi Pazar, stood the capital of this principality, the fortress of Ras. It was the residence of the Grand Župans, the princes of Raška who had gradually asserted their power over the local chieftains, or župans. From the late eleventh century until 1180 they were mostly subjects of the emperor, though fitfully and increasingly rebellious. Taking advantage of the wars between Byzantium and Hungary, they began in the twelfth century to expand the frontiers of their realm eastwards towards Niš and south-eastward towards Macedonia. This movement, whose amplitude was to increase during the next two centuries, brought the medieval Serbian realm into closer contact with the centres of Byzantine administration and culture in the Balkans. The rulers of Raška in this period were appointed and deposed by the imperial government and were required to provide the empire with auxiliary troops. Their revolts against Byzantium were regarded as treason and treated accordingly: the most famous instance occurred in 1172, when the Grand Župan Stephen Nemanja, defeated in battle by Manuel Comnenus, appeared before the emperor barefooted and bareheaded, with a rope round his neck, and holding his sword in his left hand; he handed his sword to the emperor, then threw himself on the ground at his feet.[22] This theatrical display of imperial omnipotence was followed by Nemanja's forced participation, as a defeated rebel, in Manuel's triumphant entry into Constantinople. These symbolical acts backed by the use of force, had their desired effect: after his return to Raška the Serbian ruler remained the emperor's obedient vassal.

Like the Bulgarians, the Serbs repudiated direct Byzantine rule soon after the death of the Emperor Manuel (1180). Taking advantage of the Hungarian and Norman attacks on imperial territory, Stephen Nemanja annexed part of the Dalmatian coast, including the city of Kotor which belonged to Byzantium. His anti-Byzantine designs were further manifest in his support of the Bulgarian rising and in the friendly reception he gave in Niš to the Emperor Frederick Barbarossa (1189) who with his German troops was on the way to the Third Crusade. On this occasion the Bulgarians as well as the Serbs offered the Western Emperor their allegiance and military help against Byzantium. Frederick, however, was unwilling to be side-tracked from his main purpose and responded to these overtures with considerable reserve.

In 1190, with the German crusaders safely across the Bosphorus, the Byzantines were able to make one last attempt to regain the Northern Balkans. The Emperor Isaac Angelus, using the time-honoured strategic plan, sent his fleet to the lower Danube and led his army from Mesembria to Northern Bulgaria. After a brief and abortive siege of Trnovo, the Byzantine forces were surprised during their retreat and largely destroyed in a pass of the Balkan mountains. In the same year the emperor marched against the Serbs, with greater success. Nemanja was defeated on the Morava river and forced to make peace. Its terms were more favourable to the Serbian ruler than might have been expected: he was allowed to retain a considerable part of the Byzantine lands he had annexed, and the treaty he concluded with the emperor implied that the latter recognized Serbia's existence as an autonomous state. For the first time in history a marriage alliance was concluded between the ruling families of Byzantium and Serbia: Nemanja's son Stephen married Eudoxia, the niece of the Emperor Isaac. A few years later Stephen was given the rank of *sebastocrator*, one of the highest in the Byzantine hierarchy, which was reserved for members of the ruling family and carried the privilege of being addressed as "Imperial Majesty". This title, no less than the marriage alliance, symbolized Serbia's incorporation, at the turn of the twelfth century, into the Byzantine Commonwealth.

Raška's ties with Byzantium were further strengthened by the bishopric of Ras, founded in the tenth century and since 1018 canonically dependent on the archbishopric of Ohrid. Yet the influence of the Roman Church, spreading inland from the Latin sees on the Adriatic, remained strong in the country throughout the twelfth century. Nemanja's double baptism, first by a Latin priest in his native Zeta and later by the Orthodox bishop of Ras, illustrates this ecclesiastical dualism. However, Byzantine Christianity was gaining ground. How strong was its appeal is shown by the decision of Nemanja's youngest son Rastko to run away secretly from his father's court to Mount Athos where, in the Greek monastery of Vatopedi, he became a monk under the name Sava. Nemanja's own religious instincts, which had been nurtured by the bishop of Ras, were soon stirred by his son's example: in 1196 he abdicated in favour of his other son, the Sebastocrator Stephen, and entered his own monastic foundation of Studenica. Symeon, as he was now to be called in religion, soon decided to join Sava on Mount Athos. There father and son performed an act which was to have far-reaching consequences for the history of their country, and indeed of Eastern Europe. In this international centre of Orthodox Christianity they founded the Serbian monastery of Chilandar, which soon became an important focus of medieval Serbian literature and spirituality and a place of encounter between Byzantines and Slavs.

4 RUSSIA AND THE EMPIRE IN THE ELEVENTH AND TWELFTH CENTURIES

Russia's relationship to the empire was at once simpler and more complex than the ties of dependence which in this period bound the Serbian principalities to Byzantium. In the late tenth and the first half of the eleventh century Russia was a considerable military power, expanding westward and capable of holding at bay and eventually defeating (in 1036) the Pechenegs, who thereafter directed their attention to the Balkans, with such disastrous effects for Byzantium. It is obvious that the princes of Kiev, whose realm was separated from Byzantine territory by hundreds of miles of sea and steppe, could not be forced to accept in any meaningful sense the emperor's direct overlordship. And when, after 1054, the Russian realm began to display the fissiparous tendencies which in the following century caused it to break up into several virtually autonomous principalities, some of these were powerful enough to maintain a sovereign existence and to pursue an independent foreign policy. The Russian princes, furthermore, claimed legal foundation for their authority not in any fictitious prerogative delegated to them by the emperor, but solely on two grounds: their membership of the ruling family, descended from St. Vladimir (and through him from Ryurik), in which the rights of political sovereignty were collectively and exclusively vested; and a direct mandate from God. And yet the relations between the princes of Russia and the emperors of Byzantium were not, and could not be, relations between equals. On the ideal, "meta-political", plane the Russian princes, the *archontes Rhosias*, as they styled themselves in Greek on their seals, continued to acknowledge the emperor's supreme position in Christendom, which was at least tacitly recognized by Vladimir after his baptism. This recognition is implied in the distinction made in the *Russian Primary Chronicle* between the *prince*, i.e. the local national ruler, whose authority is confined to his own realm, and the *emperor* who alone possesses jurisdiction over all Christian peoples: "The Most High appoints emperor (*tsesarya*) and prince (*knyazya*), and gives authority to whomsoever He wishes. ... Thus did Isaiah say: 'They have sinned from head to the foot', that is from the emperor to the common people."[23] The doctrine of the emperor's universal sovereignty was, it seems, accepted without demur by the educated classes in Kievan Russia. As we shall see, it was enunciated in the code of Byzantine canon law which served as the official constitution of the Russian Church; and it was stated with equal clarity and explicitness in another Byzantine text which, in its Slavonic version, enjoyed a wide currency in Eastern Europe during the Middle Ages, and was known in Russia as early as the eleventh century. This work, a didactic treatise written in the sixth century by the deacon Agapetus for Justinian I, describes the emperor as "the lord of all men" and defines his prerogatives as follows: "In the substance of his body, the emperor is like any man, but in the power of his office he is like God, the Master of all men: for there is on earth no higher than he."[24] Overt acknowledgement of the emperor's supremacy, it will later be shown, was made by several Russian rulers in the late Middle Ages. In the eleventh and twelfth centuries the evidence is admittedly less explicit; but not, as will be argued below, wholly nugatory.

Direct contact between the Russians and the Byzantines was maintained in the eleventh century through the Russian colony in Constantinople, the Byzantine metropolitans of Kiev and their staffs, the architects, painters and merchants who came to Russia from Byzantium, the cities of Cherson and Tmutorokan', and Mount Athos which was then becoming a leading centre of East Christian monasticism and pilgrimage. Trade continued, as in the tenth century, to play a large part in these relations. Among articles of export from Byzantium to Russia the documents mention fabrics, jewellery, ceramics, glassware, pepper, olive oil, wine, fruit, icons and objects intended for liturgical use: mostly things designed to gratify the luxurious tastes of the ruling classes or to meet the needs of the church. Slaves, furs, wax and honey remained as before the staple Russian exports to Byzantium. The empire's commercial policy towards Russia thus remained basically "colonialist" in character.

Trade relations were not always, however, conducive to good neighbourly relations; and a brawl between Russian and Byzantine merchants in Constantinople in which a prominent Russian was killed seems to have been the immediate cause of the last major war between Russia and the empire, fought with great ferocity in 1043. Psellus, the scholar and statesman who observed its first battle from his vantage point by the emperor's side and described it as "the rebellion of the Russians", attributed it to the "rage and fury" which this "barbarian race" had always felt for "the hegemony of the Romans";[25] though some historians have taken the Greek word *hegemonia* to mean in this context no more than "empire", it is quite possible that Psellus was alluding to the traditional Byzantine claim to political sovereignty over Russia. A fleet of four hundred ships, commanded by the prince of Novgorod, was sent by his father, the Kievan ruler Yaroslav, to attack Constantinople. Troops had been levied for this purpose in Scandinavia, and the attack thus assumed the fearsome features of an old-style Viking raid. Taking the Byzantines by surprise, the Russians appeared at the northern entrance to the Bosphorus. Hastily assembling a fleet, the Emperor Constantine IX sailed up the straits to meet them. A major clash now was inevitable. As a measure of precaution the emperor ordered the arrest and deportation of every Russian merchant in Constantinople and of all the Varangian mercenaries stationed in the capital, who were suspected of sympathy for, if not collusion with, the invaders. In a naval battle fought near the entrance to the Bosphorus, the Russians were defeated by the combined effect of the Greek fire and of a timely storm. The slaughter was immense, and the numerous Russian prisoners had their right hands cut off; these gruesome objects were exposed to public view on the walls of Constantinople. A subsequent victory gained by the remnant of the Russian fleet over a Byzantine squadron off the coast of Thrace had no effect on the outcome of the war. The bulk of the invading forces, attempting to return home overland, were cut to pieces by an army commanded by the military governor of Paristrion. Some eight hundred of them were taken to Constantinople where they were blinded—a traditional punishment reserved in Byzantium for rebels against the state. The war was followed by negotiations which seem to have been protracted: in 1046 the remaining Russian prisoners were released, and a peace treaty was concluded: either then or a little later it was agreed that a Byzantine princess, almost certainly the daughter of Constantine IX Monomachus, was to marry a younger son of Prince Yaroslav of Kiev.

The child of this marriage, born in 1053, is a distinguished figure in Russian history. Called Vladimir, he inherited his imperial grandfather's surname which the Russians rendered as Monomakh. Equally outstanding as a statesman, a general, a writer and a man, Vladimir Monomakh has been compared to King Alfred of England. In his reign as prince of Kiev (1113–25) Russia regained for a while some of the power and stability she had lost during the preceding half-century owing to the princes' internecine strife and the attacks of the steppe nomads. His family tree is striking evidence of the matrimonial ties which, prior to the Mongol invasion of the thirteenth century, bound the Russian ruling house to the reigning dynasties of Europe: his mother was a Byzantine princess; one of his uncles married the daughter of the king of Poland; of his three aunts, one married the king of

Norway, another married Henry I of France, a third became the wife of the king of Hungary. Vladimir's own wife was the daughter of King Harold of England; his eldest son married the daughter of the king of Sweden, his daughter married the king of Hungary; and his granddaughter married into the imperial family of the Comneni.

Several marriages took place between members of the Byzantine and the Russian reigning houses; most of them were concluded in the twelfth century, when the empire was ruled by the Comnenian dynasty. It is noteworthy, however, that in the pre-Mongol period the Russian princes contracted more marriage alliances with the countries of Central, Northern and Western Europe than with Byzantium or the Balkan Slav lands. This was especially the case in the eleventh century, when few Russians were as yet conscious of the growing rift between Eastern and Western Christendom. Of the nine marriages mentioned above only two were with Byzantine princes or princesses: a proportion fairly representative of the pre-Mongol period as a whole. Yet the commercial, diplomatic and cultural contacts which the Russians maintained in this period with Central and Western Europe, however close, were less intimate and continuous than their relations with Byzantium. The extent to which Russia was gradually permeated by Byzantine civilization will be discussed in a later chapter. We may pause, however, to note a curious instance of the impact of Byzantium on the consciousness of the Russians. In 1069 Prince Izyaslav of Kiev, who had been driven out by a popular revolt, was about to force his way back into his capital with the help of a Polish army. The assembly of the citizens appealed to the prince's brothers for protection, and threatened, if they were left undefended, to burn their city and "depart to the land of the Greeks".[26]

The Russians' loyalty to the empire was above all safeguarded by the metropolitans of Kiev who not only represented the spiritual authority of the patriarchs of Constantinople, but also, when they were Byzantine citizens, served the political interests of their imperial masters. Subject only to pressures from the local princes—these admittedly were sometimes strong—they exercised control over the whole Russian Church. In the second half of the eleventh century, it is true, their jurisdiction appears to have been circumscribed by the creation of the titular metropolitanates of

Chernigov and Pereyaslavl', directly subject to Constantinople. This division of the Russian Church may well have been inspired, or accepted, by the Byzantine authorities in order to satisfy the separatist proclivities of the princes of these two South Russian cities. But these concessions, if they were made, were effective only for a few decades: by 1100 at the latest the whole country was once more united under the ecclesiastical authority of the metropolitan of Kiev. His influence in political matters was often considerable; there are many examples of metropolitans and their subordinate clergy—the bishops and the abbots of the more important monasteries—intervening vigorously to settle interprincely discords, to promote the unity of the realm and to reconcile city factions. The local ruler, it is true, was usually acknowledged to possess a general right to protection and supervision over the church of his realm. But in matters of doctrine and of private and public behaviour the clergy's authority was undisputed. More than one primate of Russia must have had occasion to admonish the princes of the land with the same authority with which St. Theodosius, abbot of the Russian monastery of the Caves in the second half of the eleventh century, spoke to a prince whom he had condemned for usurping his brother's throne: "My good lord, it is our duty to rebuke you and to say whatever bears upon the salvation of your soul, and it is your duty to listen."[27]

The Russian primates were in most cases appointed directly by the patriarch of Constantinople; sometimes, however, the patriarchate (and the emperor, who in fact exercised considerable power over the nomination) seem to have been content to ratify the choice of a candidate made by the Russians themselves. The circumstances in which they were appointed are seldom known; but the evidence we have suggests that the Byzantine authorities, while insisting on retaining final control over their election, were sometimes willing, in the interests of diplomacy, to meet the wishes of the Russian princes. We may assume, though for lack of evidence we cannot assert, that most metropolitans of Kiev in the pre-Mongol period were citizens of the empire; but there are at least two noteworthy exceptions. In 1051 Hilarion, a native Russian priest, was appointed to the see of Kiev by prince Yaroslav and an assembly of Russian bishops. The interest of this appointment is heightened by the fact that he was a distinguished scholar and writer. Most modern historians believe that it was made in defiance of Byzantium's wishes; some go as far as to argue that the Russian ruler attempted by this action to assert the independence of his church from Byzantine control. The latter view is based on no convincing evidence, is at variance with what we know of the policy and behaviour of both Yaroslav and Hilarion, and does not tally with the prevailing Russian attitude to Byzantium at the time. It is not impossible that the Russians elected their native candidate without consulting the Byzantine authorities. It is likely however—and circumstantial evidence can be found to support this view—that the patriarchate was persuaded to ratify the choice either before or after Hilarion's appointment.

The second well-authenticated case of an election of a native metropolitan occurred a century later, in quite different political circumstances. This time it did amount to a revolt against the right of the patriarch to appoint the primate of Russia. The country by that time was divided into several virtually independent principalities, each contending for political supremacy. The attempts of the Emperor Manuel Comnenus to draw them into the net of his intricate European diplomacy directed against Hungary and the Normans of Sicily caused the main Russian principalities to align themselves in the conflict, some on the side of and others against Byzantium. Prince Izyaslav of Kiev, a relative of Géza II of Hungary, was hostile to the empire. In 1147, without any recourse to Constantinople, he persuaded an assembly of Russian bishops to elect as metropolitan the learned monk Clement, a native of Smolensk. This arbitrary action provoked a storm within the Russian Church, envenomed the strife among the princes of the land and led to a schism between the metropolitanate of Kiev and the patriarchate which, save for a brief interlude, lasted for nine years. An influential minority of the bishops, most of them Byzantine citizens, held that Clement's election was uncanonical and invalid; and the same view was professed by those Russian princes who were either allies of the empire or for other reasons opposed to Izyaslav. It was only after the latter's death in 1154 that the Kievans accepted a metropolitan sent from Constantinople. The schism, though now formally healed, left an aftermath of bitterness: in 1164 Rostislav, the prince of Kiev, refused to recognize a new primate whom the patriarch had appointed without consulting him, and in the presence of the Byzantine ambassador threatened to enact a new law enabling the metropolitan to be elected and consecrated by the bishops of the realm by command of the senior prince. This ill-tempered outburst must have caused grave scandal to many law-abiding Russians, who revered both the emperor's authority and the mother church of Constantinople; and their prince's disrespectful words were subsequently erased from every manuscript save one of the contemporary Russian chronicle which records this event. It required all the diplomatic skill of the Emperor Manuel and several Byzantine embassies to persuade the Russian ruler to accept the patriarch's nominee. The idea that the metropolitan of Kiev could be elected by the local bishops did not die out in Russia: it was put forward again by Andrew Bogolyubsky, the powerful prince of Vladimir in North-East Russia (1157–74), whose autocratic behaviour resembles more closely the policy of the future Muscovite rulers than that of his Kievan predecessors. But Andrew was unwilling to press this contentious issue to a point of open rupture with the Byzantine Church; and his alternative plan of securing a separate metropolitanate in Vladimir, independent of Kiev and subject only to Constantinople, was dropped in the face of adamant Byzantine opposition.

The Russian attack of 1043 proved to be, except for a minor clash on the lower Danube in 1116, the last military encounter between Russia and the empire. Of their political relations during the next hundred years we know relatively little. It was not until the 1140s that the Russians began once more to play an important role in the empire's northern diplomacy. This role was to a large extent determined by the facts of their country's political development. By the middle of the twelfth century Russia was no longer a single state ruled by the prince of Kiev. The principality of Kiev, now reduced mainly to the area west of the middle Dnieper, still retained a prominent position, based on the historic prestige of its capital city and the presence within it of the primate of the Russian Church. But its political power and economic prosperity had greatly declined. To a large extent this was due to military reasons. A fresh series of assaults on Russia's southern borderlands began in 1061. New nomadic invaders, the Cumans (whom the Russians called the Polovtsy), became during the next few years masters of the steppe. They proved to be an even greater menace to Kievan Russia than the Pechenegs. In the course of the next century and a half they launched some fifty major attacks upon the middle Dnieper valley. Cities in this area were periodically sacked; the last Russian bridgeheads in the steppe, including the distant outpost of Tmutorokan', were lost to the nomads by the late eleventh century; and after about 1150 the southern part of the Baltic–Black Sea river route, which now ran through Cuman territory, was seldom available to Russian trade for more than brief periods, despite heroic attempts to keep it open. The virtual severance of the lower Dnieper route by the Cumans imperilled Kiev's links with Byzantium; and the exhausting border warfare which the South Russians were forced to wage in the twelfth century against this pagan foe stunted the growth of their political institutions and compelled them to retreat step by step from the fringes of the steppe towards the remoter forest areas. By the 1140s Kiev had begun to yield its political and economic dominance in Russia to two new centres, both situated on the periphery of the country. In the north-east, between the upper Volga and the Oka, a branch of the princely family descended from Vladimir Monomakh built up a powerful realm based successively on the cities of Rostov, Suzdal' and, in the second half of the twelfth century, Vladimir. This area, part of which was still a frontier district, was later to become the nucleus of medieval Muscovy. At the opposite, south-western, extremity of the land, in the valleys of the Dniester and the Prut and on the eastern slopes of the Carpathians, as far as the estuary of the Danube, lay the wealthy principality of Galicia, with its main city of Galich, then ruled by a senior branch of Yaroslav's descendants. Its geographical position, contiguous to the imperial theme of Paristrion and astride the trade route from the lower Danube to the Baltic, goes far to explain the fact that Galicia, of all the twelfth century Russian principalities, had the closest links with Byzantium.

Each of these principalities, Kiev, Suzdal' and Galicia, pursued in this period its own policy towards the empire. These different policies were determined mainly by the political rivalry of the princes and by the largely successful efforts of the Byzantine government to use them as pawns on the intricate chessboard of its European diplomacy.

The foreign policy of the Emperor Manuel Comnenus, whose aim was to restore Byzantium's hegemony over the former lands of the *imperium Romanum* and who strove, in the end without success, to build up a coalition of European states directed against his enemies—first the Normans of Sicily and later the Emperor Frederick Barbarossa—has been mentioned in relation to his ambitions in Hungary. As a further means of achieving his aims Manuel sought to draw the Russian princes into a military alliance against Hungary, a country with which the empire between 1150 and 1167 was almost continuously at war.

In the late 1140s three princes were competing for hegemony in Russia: Izyaslav of Kiev (a grandson of Vladimir Monomakh), his uncle Yury Dolgoruky of Suzdal' and his cousin Vladimirko of Galicia. The first was an ally of Hungary and an enemy of Byzantium; the latter two supported the empire, and it is noteworthy that the contemporary Byzantine historian who records this fact describes the prince of Suzdal' as the emperor's "ally" (*symmachos*), and the princes of Galicia as his "vassal" (*hypospondos*).[28] This suggests that at least the latter may have formally acknowledged Manuel as his overlord. To have on the eastern borders of Hungary a vassal principality whose ruler was devoted to imperial interests was naturally a boon to the emperor; but the position in this area took a sudden turn for the worse after 1152, when Vladimirko's successor Yaroslav began to move out of the Byzantine orbit and to make advances to Géza II of Hungary. Almost simultaneously, however, the empire's position improved in Kiev: after Izyaslav's death in 1154, Manuel's ally Yury of Suzdal' seized control of the city, and the ecclesiastical schism that had followed Clement's appointment as metropolitan was brought to an end. Relations between Constantinople and Kiev became tense once more after Yury's death in 1157. Prince Rostislav supported the deposed metropolitan Clement and visibly chafed under the domineering policy of the Byzantine patriarchate, which provoked him in 1164 to the angry outburst which has been noted above. The years 1164–5 spelled grave peril to the whole of Manuel's policy in Russia. His cousin Andronicus, the future emperor, whom he had imprisoned for plotting, escaped from Constantinople and fled to the court of Yaroslav of Galicia. The emperor, faced with the frightening prospect of an alliance between Galicia and Hungary with a view to placing Andronicus on the Byzantine throne, was forced to beat a diplomatic retreat: he gave a free pardon to his turbulent cousin, who was persuaded to return to Constantinople (1165). In the same year he sent a high-ranking Byzantine official, his relative and namesake, to Russia on an important diplomatic mission: the envoy—if we can believe the Byzantine historian who recorded his exploits—accomplished his task brilliantly. Rostislav of Kiev was induced to sign a treaty with the empire, undertaking to supply it with auxiliary troops and to accept the Byzantine candidate as metropolitan of Kiev; in return he received unspecified gifts, and probably the promise that he or his successor would be consulted before the next primate of the Russian Church was appointed. From Kiev the Byzantine ambassador travelled to Galicia, where he persuaded Yaroslav to renounce his Hungarian alliance and to pledge loyalty to the empire.

This burst of diplomatic activity between Russia and the empire in the mid-twelfth century remained unparalleled, if we may judge from the silence of the sources, for the next two hundred years. After 1165 and until the mid-fourteenth century we hear of no conflict between the two; it seems safe to assume that their relations remained friendly and, at least until the capture of Constantinople by the armies of the Fourth Crusade, fairly close. Manuel I's diplomacy had consolidated Byzantium's political influence over the more important Russian principalities. The effective sovereignty of their rulers was not thereby impaired: none of them of course was either appointed or removed from office by the emperor, as was the case with the early princes of Serbia. Yet, as members of the ideal "family" of princes over which the emperor presided in a double capacity, as *paterfamilias* and vicegerent of God, they owed a theoretical allegiance to him Nor was the emperor's sovereignty over Russia invariably confined to the purely ideal realm; in Manuel Comnenus' time, we have seen, it could also be expressed in more concrete terms: in the obligation assumed by the Russian princes to supply troops for the Byzantine armies; and in the status and duties of an imperial vassal, accepted by at least one prince of Galicia. It was in this principality that the tradition of political loyalty to the empire was most deeply rooted in the twelfth century. About the year

1200 Roman, the powerful prince of Galicia, invaded and devastated the home of the Cumans who, in alliance with the Bulgarians, were then advancing across Thrace towards Constantinople. A contemporary Byzantine writer acknowledged that the salvation of Byzantium was due on this occasion to "the most Christian nation of the Russians" whose "God-mustered phalanx" relieved the pressure on the imperial capital. It is worth noting that he ascribed this happy event partly to the "admirable devotion" which the Russians had for the Byzantines, and partly to the influence exerted upon them by the metropolitan of Kiev;[29] and it is not without significance that the Russians thus demonstrated their loyalty to the empire only a few years after the Bulgarians and the Serbs had rebelled against it and asserted their political independence.

5 BYZANTIUM AND THE VARANGIANS

The last type of relationship between Byzantium and an East European people to be considered here differs greatly from those examined above. The Varangian Northmen who served as mercenaries in Constantinople or in the field armies of the empire were neither permanently settled on its territory nor did they form a stable ethnic group within the Byzantine Commonwealth. Yet their encounter with the Byzantines is for several reasons germane to the theme of this book. It provides some evidence of the impact which the empire's wealth, power and civilization had on the imagination of its more primitive neighbours; it illustrates, often very vividly, the role which differences in national temperament and in social ideals could play in the relations between Byzantium and the "barbarians"; it adds to our knowledge of the methods used by the Byzantines to control and exploit groups and individuals who had been thrust into their empire's orbit; and it forms a brief but important episode in the history of the Byzantine Commonwealth, owing to the role which the Varangians played as intermediaries between the empire and early medieval Russia.

It was in the triple guise of raiders, merchants and mercenaries that the Byzantines came to know the Varangians between 850 and 1050, when contact between them was closest. Members of the military retinue of the Russian princes of Kiev; auxiliary troops levied by the latter in Scandinavia; Swedish adventurers seeking their fortune in Constantinople, the fabulous Mikligard of the Nordic sagas: all these Northmen who, in war and in peace, were drawn into the orbit of Byzantium, had come south in search of employment, booty or renown in a protracted movement of migration which a modern historian has termed *'un long glissement vers le soleil'*.[30] Though they often appeared in Constantinople simultaneously under various guises—the Russo-Byzantine treaty of 911 shows them as raiders, merchants and imperial mercenaries—it is broadly true that the Varangians came to represent in the eyes of the Byzantines these three types in succession. As late as 1043, it is true, they formed the spearhead of the Russian attack on Constantinople, reviving the memories of the earlier Viking invaders whom their terrified victims had so uncritically identified with Gog and Magog. On the whole, however, the Byzantines had grown accustomed by the late tenth century to think of Varangians above all as highly expert mercenary troops. They had taken part in the naval expeditions against Crete in 911 and 949, and served as auxiliaries in the Arab war in Asia Minor. In 988, it will be remembered, Vladimir of Kiev sent an expeditionary corps of six thousand Varangians to the aid of the Emperor Basil II. From that time onwards the existence of a standing service unit, consisting of Northmen and periodically replenished by fresh contingents from Russia and Scandinavia, can be traced in Byzantium for almost a hundred years. Some of these Varangians were organized in separate detachments within the imperial armies. During the first half of the eleventh century we find them on active service in Syria, Armenia, Bulgaria, Apulia and Sicily. Others, stationed in the capital, formed the celebrated Varangian Guard, entrusted with the duty of defending the emperor's person. These stalwarts, armed with heavy axes and two-edged swords, provoked a good deal of curiosity and comment in Constantinople, with the result that we know more about them than about their compatriots in the field. Yet the latter undoubtedly played the more important role in the empire's military history.

These Scandinavian mercenaries were not always an unmixed blessing to the emperors and to the princes of Kiev. About 980, according to the *Russian Primary Chronicle*, Vladimir was faced with an incipient revolt of the Varangians in his own city; furious at the prince's refusal to pay them adequate wages, they demanded that "he show them the way to the Greeks". Before dispatching them to Constantinople, Vladimir sent an embassy to the emperor with the following message: "Behold, Varangians are on the way to your city: do not keep them there, or they will cause you as much trouble as they have done here, but disperse them in various places; and do not let a single one of them return here".[31]

This curious story is almost certainly of Varangian origin. It is not hard to believe that it was told, and possibly invented, by these disgruntled retainers who, instead of the expected military preferment in Constantinople, were sent off to serve in the empire's provincial armies and who blamed their misfortune on the avarice and treachery of their Russian paymaster: he had not only cheated them of their wages, but slandered them in the emperor's eyes. This is not the first example we have encountered of a story retold by the Russian chronicler which probably goes back to a Varangian source. In this case the facts may well be authentic. Even in the eleventh century, when the Byzantines had learnt to appreciate the loyalty of their Viking guardsmen in Constantinople, they were wary of their turbulence and suspicious of their motives. In the second half of the century a Byzantine author wrote a treatise in which he offered sound advice to the emperor on the way to treat foreigners in Constantinople. Much of it undoubtedly refers to the Varangians:

Foreigners [the author writes] unless they are of royal stock in their own country, you should not promote to high rank nor entrust with great offices of state; for you will by so doing make a fool of yourself and of your own Byzantine high officials. ... If foreigners serve [only] for clothing and bread, be assured that they will serve you loyally and wholeheartedly, looking to the bounty of your hands for trifling sums of money and for bread. If you were to honour a foreigner with a rank higher than that of a *spatharocandidatus*, he would then become disdainful and would not serve you well. Inquire and learn, my lord, how many difficulties fell to the lot of previous emperors—of the Lord Basil the Porphyrogenitus [i.e. Basil II], his father, grandfather, great-grandfather and emperors of still earlier times. But why mention the ancient ones? Neither the Lord Romanus Argyrus [i.e. Romanus III, 1028–34], nor any of the above-mentioned emperors of blessed

304

memory promoted a Frank or a Varangian to the rank of *patricius*, nor . . . [to that of] *hypatus* or *stratiotophylax;* at most [they made] him a *spatharius.* Yet all these [foreigners] served them for bread and clothing.

And the author goes on to cite approval the example of the greatest Varangian of them all, Harold Hardrada who, "though a young man, wished to come and do homage to the Emperor Michael of blessed memory" [i.e. Michael IV, 1034–41], and who, though he was the son of a king, was well content to be made a guardsman.[32]

Our author's advice conformed to the traditional Byzantine practice of keeping close watch on all foreigners resident in Constantinople; this policy of caution seems to have been successful: for the Varangians played little part in the numerous palace revolutions of the eleventh century. They do not appear to have been greatly interested in the internal politics of the empire. Their attitude to Byzantium and its citizens was complex and probably, like that of many East European peoples, ambivalent. The differences in temperament and social behaviour between the Byzantines and the Northmen were no doubt too great for real mutual understanding. Some impression of these differences can be obtained by comparing the Greek sources with the Old Norse sagas which, for all their legendary elements, still retain much of the authentic spirit of the Viking age. The cult of cold and self-controlled intelligence and the distrust of reckless conduct, so characteristic of the Byzantine ideal of human behaviour, could hardly find favour in the eyes of the high-spirited, impulsive and sometimes chivalrous Northmen; nor did their often over-bearing manner, quarrelsome nature, fondness for the heady wines of Constantinople and inclinations to spin most improbable yarns about their military deeds, greatly commend them to their paymasters. Anna Comnena, who had a high regard for the faithfulness and the military qualities of the Varangians, observed characteristically that, for all their courage in battle, their behaviour was marred by "inexperience and heat".[33] Yet despite these temperamental differences, the Byzantines and the Northmen did, it seems, come to appreciate each other. The emperors had reason to be grateful for the loyalty of their Varangian Guard; while the Varangians, apart from the material advantages they gained from their employment, could not but marvel at the beauties and wealth of

Mikligard, whose emperor they were proud to serve. There is poetic exaggeration, but nothing historically improbable, in these words of a Varangian leader addressed to the emperor, as reported in the *Saga of St. Olaf*: "Although there were burning fire in front of me, yet would I and my thegns leap into it, if I knew that your pleasure, O King, could so be purchased".[34]

Apart from the role they played, together with the Slavs, in the development of the Russian state, the main contribution of the Varangians to the history of Eastern Europe was to provide a bridge between several of its constituent parts. To the culture of this area their direct contribution was slight: the scarcity of Scandinavian loan-words in the Russian language, mainly confined to the vocabulary of administration and trade, is probably a fairly reliable index of their influence on the social and cultural life of the Eastern Slavs. But their constant journeyings and far-flung political ambitions made them unrivalled carriers of ideas and objects belonging to other cultures; and for this reason the cosmopolitan civilization that flourished in the early Middle Ages along the river route from Scandinavia to Byzantium owes not a little to their role of professional middlemen. Nowhere is this role more clearly apparent than in the astonishing career of Harold Hardrada. Its different stages mark out the highways of trade, diplomacy and war which in the eleventh century linked Western, Northern and Eastern Europe to the Mediterranean within a vast network of communications woven by the Vikings. We see him successively fighting for his half-brother St. Olaf, king of Norway; a commander in the armies of Yaroslav, prince of Kiev; arriving in Constantinople with five hundred warriors about 1034; employed for nine years by three Byzantine emperors, whom he served both as captain of the Varangian Guard and in campaigns in Asia Minor, Sicily and Bulgaria; leaving Byzantium secretly, after Constantine IX had refused his request to be allowed to return to Norway; back in Russia during the winter of 1042–3, where he married Yaroslav's daughter Elizabeth, whom he had wooed for long; proclaimed king of Norway where, we are assured by a Byzantine writer, he "retained his loyalty and love for the *Rhomaioi*" and still took pride in the rank of guardsman and in the title of *spatharocandidatus* he had received in the emperor's service;[35] finally as prospective conqueror of England, where he met his death at the battle of Stamford Bridge in 1066. His role as a transmitter of Byzantine cultural influence to Northern Europe is attested fairly reliably in the field of numismatics: the appearance of a series of strikingly accurate imitations of contemporary Byzantine coin types on Danish coins of the mid-eleventh century was almost certainly due to the arrival in Scandinavia of the vast treasure which Harold Hardrada is known to have accumulated while in imperial service.

The Norman conquest of England, which extinguished Harold's last ambition, proved a turning point in the history of the Varangian Guard in Constantinople. In the 1070s Anglo-Saxon refugees began to migrate to Byzantium and to serve in the emperor's army; and by the end of the century, it seems, his bodyguard had come to consist mainly of Englishmen. It was then that the Northmen, now well on the way to being assimilated by the Slavs in Russia, started to fade away from the horizon of the Byzantines.

NOTES

1 *The Itinerary of Benjamin of Tudela*. Critical text, transl. and commentary by M. N. Adler (London, 1907), p. 11.
2. John Cinnamus, *Historia*, v, 8, ed. A. Meineke (Bonn, 1836), p. 223.
3. C. Dawson, *The Making of Europe* (London, 1939), p. 84.
4. E. Condurachi, I. Barnea, P. Diaconu, "Nouvelles recherches sur le *Limes* byzantin du Bas-Danube aux Xe-XIe siècles", *Proceedings of the XIIIth International Congress of Byzantine Studies* (London, 1967), pp. 179–82.
5. See Plate 31.
6. Scylitzes-Cedrenus, ii, p. 530.
7. H. Gelzer, "Ungedruckte und wenig bekannte Bistümerverzeichnisse der orientalischen Kirche", *Byzantinische Zeitschrift*, ii (1893), pp. 40–66; *FHB*, xi, pp. 40–7.
8. Scylitzes-Cedrenus, ii, pp. 581–7.
9. Ibid., pp. 654–7.
10. L. Bréhier, *Vie et mort de Byzance* (Paris, 1948), p. 277.
11. Anna Comnena, *Alexiad*, xiv, 7, ed. B. Leib, iii (Paris, 1945), p. 180.
12. Theophylact of Ohrid, *Epistolae*, PG 126, cols. 308–557.
13. Idem, *De iis quorum Latini incusantur*, ibid., cols. 221–49.
14. Ibid., cols. 308–9, 508.

15. Michael Choniates (Acominatus), *Works*, ed. Sp. Lambros, ii (Athens, 1880), p. 44.

16. Theophylact of Ohrid, *Epistolae*, ibid., cols. 405, 409–16.

17. Ibid., col. 425.

18. *Vita S. Clementis*, ii: Milev, pp. 78–98.

19. George Acropolites, *Historia*, 44, ed. A. Heisenberg, i (Leipzig, 1903), pp. 76–7.

20. *DAI*, ch. 32, p. 160.

21. P. Kehr, "Papsturkunden in Rom", *Nachrichten von der Königl. Gesellschaft der Wissenschaften zu Göttingen, philolog.-histor. Klasse*, 1900, p. 148.

22. Cinnamus, *Historia*, vi, II, pp. 287–8; Nicetas Choniates, *De Manuele Comneno*, v, 4, p. 207.

23. *Povest'*, p. 95; Cross, p. 130. Cf. Isaiah, i, 6.

24. Agapetus, *Expositio capitum admonitoriorum*, xxi, *PG* 86 (1), col. 1172.

25. Michael Psellus, *Chronographie*, xc, ed. E. Renauld, ii (Paris, 1928), p. 8.

26. *Povest'*, pp. 115–16; Cross, p. 149.

27. *Das Paterikon des Kiever Höhlenklosters*, ed. D. Tschižewskij (Chizhevsky) (Munich, 1964), p. 68; G. P. Fedotov, *A Treasury of Russian Spirituality* (London, 1950), p. 43.

28. Cinnamus, *Historia*, iii, 11, p. 115; v, 12, p. 235.

29. Nicetas Choniates, *Historia*, pp. 691–2.

30. M. Bloch, *La Société féodale. La formation des liens de dépendance* (Paris, 1949), p. 62.

31. *Povest'*, p. 56; Cross, p. 93.

32. *Cecaumeni strategicon et incerti scriptoris de officiis regiis libellus*, ed. B. Wassiliewsky and V. Jernstedt (St. Petersburg, 1896), pp. 95–7. German transl. H.-G. Beck: *Vademecum des byzantinischen Aristokraten* (Graz, 1956), pp. 138–9, 140–1.

33. Anna Comnena, *Alexiad*, iv, 6, ed. Leib, i (Paris, 1937), p. 160.

34. *Saga of St. Olaf: Flateyjarbok*, ii (*Christiania*, 1862), p. 380; cited in R. M. Dawkins, "Greeks and Northmen", *Custom is King: Essays Presented to R. R. Marett* (London, 1936), p. 41.

35. Cecaumenus, p. 97; Beck, p. 141.

18 The *Codex Assemanianus*, one of the earliest known Glagolitic manuscripts, is believed to have been written in Macedonia in the eleventh (or perhaps the tenth) century. It is a Gospel lectionary, followed by a *menologion*.

19 The Cyrillic *Codex Suprasliensis*, dating from the eleventh century, is the longest of the extant Old Church Slavonic manuscripts. It is believed to have been written in Eastern Bulgaria, and contains a *menologion* for the month of March.

20 (above) The frescoes at Nerezi, near Skopje (1164), were executed by a team of painters: the Lamentation over the Dead Christ was the work of the master painter, who probably came from Constantinople.

21 (below) The paintings in St Sophia, Ohrid, were probably executed about 1040. They include this somewhat severe and formal representation of St Basil celebrating the liturgy.

22 Elegance, refinement and love of picturesque detail, characteristic features of Byzantine art in its final phase, are apparent in these portraits of three military saints at Manasija (1406-18).

23 The Dormition of the Virgin at Sopoćani (1263-8) has some claims to be considered the finest extant work of East European art of the thirteenth century.

24-26 The frescoes in two towers of St Sophia in Kiev illustrate the Russians' interest in the games and contests of the Hippodrome in Constantinople, and exalt the Byzantine emperor's supra-national sovereignty. The scene on the wall of the south-west tower (24) shows the Kathisma Palace on the east side of the Hippodrome, with spectators in the galleries, and the haloed emperor, attended by two courtiers, in the imperial box. Paintings in the north-west tower show (25) a warrior fighting a masked man, and (26) an oriental-looking musician. These frescoes were probably commissioned by the Kievan ruler Vladimir Monomakh (1113-25), whose mother belonged to the imperial family of Byzantium.

27 *Our Lady of Vladimir* This celebrated Byzantine panel was brought
from Constantinople to Russia in
the mid-twelfth century and became
the palladium of the Russian state.
Only the faces are original.

28 The traditions of Palaeologan
painting and individual artistry are
combined in this fresco, painted by
Theophanes the Greek in the
Church of the Transfiguration in
Novgorod (1378). Outward serenity
and inner dynamism are apparent in
the austere and spiritualised face of
this Stylite saint. The dramatic effect
is heightened by the treatment of the
drapery and the remarkable use of
high-lights.

29 In Rublev's icon of the Trinity, painted *c*. 1411 in memory of St Sergius of Radonezh, a traditional theme is treated with true theological insight and artistic refinement. Abraham's three visitors (Genesis xviii) represent the persons of the Holy Trinity: the central angel is probably the
Son, with the Father on the left and the Holy Spirit on the right. The composition is governed by
the motif of the circle, symbol of eternity.

30 *St Constantine-Cyril* This painting in the lower church of San Clemente in Rome is usually dated to the second half of the ninth century, and is believed by many authorities to represent St Constantine-Cyril, the Apostle of the Slavs. It may thus be a contemporary, or near contemporary, portrait.

31 *St Clement of Ohrid* This wooden high relief, 141 by 33 centimetres in size, dates from the fourteenth century. Clement's shoulders are covered by a bishop's *omophorion*, and the book he holds symbolises his educational work.

32 *St Sava*
Remarkable for its
spirituality and psy-
chological subtlety,
this portrait of the
greatest churchman in
Serbia's history was
painted *c.* 1234 in the
narthex of the monas-
tery church of Mile-
ševa, which became the
centre of St Sava's cult.

33 *St Sergius of Radonezh* Russia's greatest
monastic saint (*d.* 1392)
prepared himself for
his life as a teacher of
men by a period of sol-
itary ascetic training in
the forests north of
Moscow. According to
his medieval biog-
rapher he was visited
by animals and gained
the friendship of a
bear. The story is illus-
trated in this miniature
from a late sixteenth or
early seventeenth cen-
tury Russian manu-
script of his life.

8

Byzantium and
Eastern Europe
in the Late Middle Ages

Two events in the first half of the thirteenth century weakened the bonds of the Byzantine Commonwealth, already loosened by the successful revolt of the Bulgarians and the Serbs. The first was the capture of Constantinople by the armies of the Fourth Crusade in 1204; as a result, most of the imperial lands in the Balkans—Thrace, Macedonia, Thessaly, Boeotia, Attica and the Peloponnese—were partitioned among Frankish barons; the more important Greek islands and ports were seized by the Venetians; and the Byzantines, deprived of their capital, were forced to assemble the broken fragments of their empire on the periphery of the Greek-speaking world, in Epirus, in North-Western Asia Minor and in remote Trebizond. In 1261 Michael VIII Palaeologus, operating from Nicaea, recaptured Constantinople, thus bringing to an end the short-lived and parasitical Latin Empire of Romania; and during the next twenty years, for the last time in history, the restored Byzantine Empire was able to pursue in Europe and the Near East a "great power" policy, whose imperialist aims recalled the programme of Manuel Comnenus. But Michael's efforts to revive the universalist claims of Byzantium were short-lived and in the end unsuccessful. The southern part of the Balkan peninsula, except for the Peloponnese, was now—save for a brief period in the first half of the fourteenth century—lost to the empire; further north, the restored kingdoms of Serbia and Bulgaria were hostile, and their rulers, who had not lifted a finger to help Byzantium when it was attacked by the crusaders, proved

Map 8   Eastern Europe, *c.* 1350

only too ready to join the coalition organized against Michael VIII by Charles of Anjou. With its economic and military resources sadly depleted and its foreign trade now controlled by the Venetians and the Genoese, the Palaeologan Empire soon lost its position as a world power. After Michael VIII's death in 1282 it became in effect a minor Balkan state, fighting for its existence against the attacks of its neighbours. In terms of power politics, the Byzantine Commonwealth had no longer any effective centre.

The second blow to its political coherence was dealt by the Mongol invasion of Russia. The conquest of the Russian principalities between 1237 and 1240 by the armies of Batu, Chingis Khan's grandson, which culminated in the capture of Kiev in 1240, made the country a political dependency of the Tatar khans of the Golden Horde. For the next 240 years the princes of Central and Northern Russia paid tribute to and ruled by the grace of the sovereign of a Turko-Mongol empire whose capital was on the lower Volga. Preoccupied first by the need to build up the administration and economy of their devastated lands and to find a *modus vivendi* with their conquerors, and later by their own political struggles, these princes lived, between 1250 and 1350, in a world remote from Byzantium. Only in the mid-fourteenth century, after the princes of Moscow, relying on a policy of subservience to the Horde, had embarked on the task of "gathering" the Russian principalities under their sway, were the central and northern areas of the country drawn once again into the empire's political orbit.

And yet, however much the political links between the different parts of the commonwealth were loosened in the thirteenth century, neither the Fourth Crusade nor the Mongol conquest of Russia was able to break them completely. The channels of communication between the Greek and the Slav worlds were kept open by the Orthodox Church. In the first half of the thirteenth century, it is true, Byzantine Christianity seemed to be in full retreat before the Roman Church, whose leaders were quick to take advantage of the new situation which the rise of the Latin Empire of Constantinople had created in Eastern Europe. In 1204 the Bulgarian ruler Kaloyan was crowned king by a Roman cardinal, pledging in exchange his and his church's loyalty to the pope. This

agreement was preceded by five years' negotiation with Innocent
III, conducted in an atmosphere of mutual suspicion and make-
believe, the pope mindful of Boris' defection from the Roman
Church in 870, and Kaloyan pretending against all evidence that
Innocent had granted him the imperial title and a patriarchal
status to his archbishop. Yet this settlement, though hedged in
with evasion and equivocation (in the voluminous correspondence
between Innocent and Kaloyan there is not the slightest allusion
to any doctrinal difference between the Western and the Eastern
Churches),[1] was destined to last longer than Boris' concordat
with Nicholas I. Nor were the Serbs slow to realize that the decline
of Byzantine power required a rapprochement with the West, the
more so since their country was still open to the influence of Latin
Christianity spreading inland from the Adriatic coast. About the
year 1200 Stephen, Nemanja's son and successor, divorced his Byzantine bride, the emperor's daughter; he later married the granddaughter of Enrico Dandolo, the formidable Doge of Venice who,
more than any other leader of the Fourth Crusade, was responsible
for the sack of Constantinople. Then, at the time when Kaloyan
was beginning his discussions with Rome, Stephen too approached
Innocent III, promising to place Serbia under the jurisdiction of
the Holy See, and requesting a royal crown. Agreement was
reached, and in 1217 Stephen was crowned by a papal legate. To
his own people he became known henceforth as "the First
Crowned" (*Prvovenčani*). Even the Russians, who, despite earlier
frictions with Constantinople over the manner of appointing the
metropolitans of Kiev, had shown the most consistent loyalty to
the Byzantine Church, were not immune to the attractions of
Rome. In an attempt to shake off the yoke of the Tatars, and
pinning his hopes on the crusade against them that was being
planned in Rome, Daniel, prince of Galicia and Volynia, offered to
acknowledge papal supremacy. In 1253 he was crowned king with
a crown sent by Innocent IV. The failure of the crusade to materialize, and the reimposition of Tatar control over Daniel's lands
ended this short-lived attempt to bring Western Russia into the
orbit of Latin Christendom.

However, despite these tactical manoeuvres, the prospects of the
Roman Church in Eastern Europe, as events were soon to show,
were less good than they appeared to be in the opening years of the

thirteenth century. The Latin Empire of Constantinople proved unable to enforce its hegemony over the Balkans: it never wholly recovered from its defeat at the hands of Kaloyan at the battle of Adrianople in 1205. As for the Slav nations, their willingness to accept papal jurisdiction was due to political motives, and neither the Bulgarians nor the Serbs nor the West Russians seem to have been seriously disposed to renounce the Orthodox faith which their ancestors had received from Constantinople. The fact that not a single doctrinal issue appears to have been raised in the course of their rulers' negotiations with the papacy suggests that for them at least, in a Christendom that was still felt to be a single body, a change of allegiance from the Greek to the Latin Church was a matter of ecclesiastical jurisdiction, not of theological belief. The Byzantine patriarchate, the traditional guardian of Orthodoxy, had been expelled from Constantinople; but it had found refuge in Nicaea, whose rulers regarded themselves as the lawful successors of the emperors of Byzantium. And it was towards Nicaea that, in the decades following the fall of Constantinople, the ecclesiastical policy of the Slav rulers of Eastern Europe was increasingly orientated. For their part, the Greek patriarchs of Nicaea welcomed, and possibly instigated, these *démarches*; and the fact that the Russians, the Serbs and the Bulgarians eventually recognized them as the legitimate leaders of the Orthodox Church greatly helped their secular sovereigns, the emperors of Nicaea, to vindicate their claim to the political heritage of Byzantium. It was in the Nicaean period (1204–61) that these three nations obtained ecclesiastical privileges which in different degrees increased the autonomy of their respective churches. There can be little doubt that these were concessions extorted through diplomatic pressure from a weakened empire in exile; yet these privileges, which helped to strengthen the loyalty of these churches to the patriarchate at a time when the combined pressure of the papacy and of the Latin crusading states threatened to disrupt the unity of Orthodox Christendom, are also examples of the realism and diplomatic skill displayed by the Byzantine authorities in their dealings with the nations of Eastern Europe.

The most modest of these privileges was that accorded to the Russian Church. About 1250 the Russian monk Cyril, sent to Nicaea by Prince Daniel of Galicia for consecration as metropolitan of Kiev, returned, duly consecrated, to Russia. The appointment of a native candidate, though not without precedent, was unusual: a hundred years earlier, it will be remembered, the Russians had vainly tried to persuade the Byzantine authorities to adopt this practice. And the fact that for more than a century after 1250 the metropolitan see of Kiev was, with complete regularity, occupied by Byzantines and Russians in turn bears out the statement made by a Byzantine writer that a formal agreement was concluded between the two countries, stipulating that every other incumbent of this see was to be a native Russian.

The most generous of Nicaea's concessions was made to Bulgaria. Roman jurisdiction seems to have weighed lightly on the shoulders of Kaloyan's successor Boril (1207–18). This may be inferred from the fact that the council convened by him in Trnovo to deal with the powerful revival of Bogomilism in his realm followed the procedure of the Eastern and not the Western Church. It was his successor John Asen II (1218–41) who finally repudiated Bulgaria's ecclesiastical dependence on Rome. In 1235, in Gallipoli, he signed a treaty of alliance with the Nicaean Empire, by which the Bulgarian Church was recognized as an autonomous patriarchate, under the largely nominal primacy of the patriarch of Nicaea. The main reason for the granting of this privilege, unprecedented since the recognition of the Bulgarian patriarchate by Byzantium between 927 and 971, was almost certainly political: the Nicaean Emperor John III Vatatzes needed an ally in the Balkans in his struggle not only with the Latin Empire but also with the Greek principality of Epirus which was still a rival claimant to the Byzantine heritage. It is likely that similar considerations prompted the concessions which his predecessor, Theodore I Lascaris, made to the church of Serbia, and which in scope fell somewhere between those granted to the Russians and to the Bulgarians.

The position of the Serbian Church, nominally subject to Rome after 1217, in fact still under the jurisdiction of the archbishop of Ohrid, whose see lay within the borders of the principality of Epirus, was an impossibly ambiguous one. It would seem that Sava, who had returned to Serbia from Mount Athos in 1208 at the request of King Stephen, disapproved of his brother's pro-Roman policy. By c. 1217 he was back on the Holy Mountain. In

1219, probably at Stephen's request, he travelled to Nicaea where he petitioned the emperor to permit the establishment of an independent Serbian Church. Theodore I, welcoming any move that would weaken his Epirot rival, persuaded his patriarch to agree to Sava's request. Sava was consecrated archbishop of Serbia and returned home to build and administer his autocephalous Orthodox Church. His work of setting up new dioceses and monastic schools—the most famous were at Studenica, his father's foundation, and at Žiča, the centre of his archdiocese—was interrupted by two more journeys to the Near East. The first took him again to Nicaea, where he succeeded in confirming the autonomy of the Serbian Church against the claims of its former superior, the archbishop of Ohrid. It was either then or on his previous visit in 1219 that he obtained from the Nicaean authorities the further concession that the archbishops of Serbia were in future to be consecrated by the local bishops, without recourse to the patriarch. The independence of the Serbian Church was limited only by the requirement (also imposed on the Bulgarians in 1235) that the patriarch's name be given precedence in liturgical commemoration. On his last journey abroad, in 1235, Sava died in Trnovo. His posthumous cult, in which his personal holiness, his signal services to his church and nation, and his family ties with the founders of the Nemanja dynasty were given equal prominence, raised him—alongside his father—to an unrivalled position among the saints and heroes of the Serbian people.

The concessions granted by the Nicaean government to Serbia, Bulgaria and Russia counteracted the centrifugal forces which, in the thirteenth century, threatened to dissolve the Byzantine Commonwealth. The fact that all these concessions were ecclesiastical is significant: neither then nor in the future (with the brief exception of the period between 1261 and 1282, when Michael VIII reigned in Constantinople) was the empire able again to pursue in Eastern Europe a policy of hegemony by military, political or diplomatic means. But, in striking contrast to the growing impotence of the government's foreign policy, the Byzantine Church came to assume, in the last two centuries of the empire's history, the role of chief spokesman and instrument of the imperial traditions of East Rome. It was largely thanks to the oecumenical

315

patriarchate that the commonwealth retained a tangible structure during the late Middle Ages. The patriarchate fostered the continuing prestige and influence of Byzantine civilization throughout Eastern Europe; worked, on the whole successfully, to maintain the loyalty of the Slav Orthodox Churches to Constantinople; propounded, particularly in the second half of the fourteenth century, the view that the bishop of Constantinople was the spiritual overlord of all Christians; restated, sometimes in forcible terms, the doctrine of the emperor's universal authority; and succeeded in this period in extending its jurisdiction over the Rumanian lands north of the Danube. The role of the church as a unifying force, holding together the different parts of the Orthodox community, can best be illustrated by surveying the relations between Byzantium and the countries of Eastern Europe in the thirteenth and fourteenth centuries.

I BYZANTIUM AND BULGARIA

The Second Bulgarian Empire reached the zenith of its military and political power in the reign of John Asen II (1218–41). His victory over the ruler of Epirus at the battle of Klokotnitsa (in Thrace) in 1230 eliminated the latter as a serious claimant to Constantinople, indirectly weakened the Latin Empire, and established Bulgaria as the leading power in the Balkans. Well could the Bulgarian monarch boast of his military exploits in these words, engraved on one of the columns in a church at Trnovo:

> I, John Asen, in Christ God faithful tsar and autocrat of the Bulgarians . . . went out to wage war in Romania, defeated the Greek army and captured the Emperor Lord Theodore Comnenus himself and all his *boyars*. And I occupied all the land from Adrianople to Dyrrachium—Greek, Albanian and Serbian alike. Only towns in the vicinity of Constantinople and the city itself are held by the Franks; but they too have submitted to my imperial authority, for they have no other emperor but me; only thanks to me do they survive, for thus God has ordained.[2]

The last of these claims was over-sanguine: the Latins had another thirty years to rule in Constantinople; and the real beneficiary of the battle of Klokotnitsa proved to be the Nicaean emperor. But John Asen II did control most of Thrace and

Epirus; and his desire to seize Constantinople, as well as his conquests on the Adriatic seaboard, recalled the ambitions and achievements of Symeon. The resemblance between these two Bulgarian monarchs did not stop there. Like his tenth century predecessor, John Asen II lived in the world of Byzantine political ideas; his agreement with Nicaea in 1235 showed his attachment to Eastern Christianity; and he too dreamed of a Slavo-Greek universal empire centred in Constantinople, with himself as its sovereign. In two charters issued in 1230 he styled himself "Emperor (Tsar) of the Bulgarians and the Greeks".[3] The first part of this title, though not of course the second, seems to have been recognized by the authorities of Nicaea. In one respect, however, he differed from Symeon, and indeed from his own uncle Kaloyan: their aggressive policy had fanned the hatred between Greeks and Slavs (Kaloyan, in revenge for the past misdeeds of Basil II the "Bulgar-slayer", went so far as to call himself "slayer of *Rhomaioi*"); John Asen, by contrast, tempered his imperialist ambitions with a broadminded tolerance that endeared him to some at least of his Greek contemporaries. The Nicaean statesman and historian George Acropolites gave him a testimonial that is surely unparalleled among the extant Byzantine judgements on foreign Balkan monarchs:

> He never raised the sword against his own people, nor did he stain himself with the murder of Byzantines, as the former rulers of Bulgaria had done. For this he was loved not only by the Bulgarians, but also by the Byzantines and by other peoples. . . . Among the barbarians he was the best of men.[4]

After John Asen II's death Bulgaria rapidly lost her dominant position in the Balkans. For a brief period the initiative passed to the Byzantines. Michael VIII, hoping, it seems, to restore the empire's authority over Bulgaria and Serbia and to revive the Balkan policy of Basil II, subjected their autonomous churches to the jurisdiction of the archbishopric of Ohrid (1272). In 1279 his armies invaded Bulgaria, reached the vicinity of Trnovo, and advanced to the lower Danube. But Michael's ecclesiastical policy was wrecked by the opposition provoked in Eastern Christendom by his sponsorship of the short-lived union with the Roman Church, concluded at Lyons (1274); the Slav Churches regained their independence; and the Byzantine troops, who for the last time in history had penetrated north of the Balkan mountains, withdrew. Neither the empire nor the Bulgarians were able thereafter to play an active role in Balkan power politics. The decline of Bulgaria was hastened by the Mongol invasions, as a result of which the country paid tribute to the Golden Horde during the second half of the thirteenth century, and by the separatist tendencies of its constituent provinces, which led to the break-away of the West Bulgarian principality of Vidin (1281–1323). By the early fourteenth century effective power in the Balkans had passed to the Serbs; and their victory over the Bulgarians at the battle of Velbuzhd in 1330 transformed it into virtual hegemony.

Yet, despite the country's political eclipse, its rulers continued to regard themselves as heirs to the imperial traditions of John Asen II. The influence of Byzantium on the Bulgarian state and society reached its peak in the late thirteenth and fourteenth centuries. The charters issued by the tsars of the "Second Empire" show, in their terminology and legal concepts, the extent to which their country had adopted the empire's administrative and fiscal system. Titles and privileges of the nobility, immunities granted to monasteries, obligations of dependent peasants, taxes and penalties, reveal not merely a correspondence in terminology, but in most cases an essential identity, with their Byzantine models. In the field of culture as well, fourteenth century Bulgaria was in many respects a Byzantine province, dependent on the religious, literary and artistic centres of Constantinople, Thessalonica and Mount Athos. Political ideologists in Constantinople and Trnovo shared the belief that their two countries belonged to a single, supranational community, though they sometimes differed in their assessment of their relative status within it. The Constantinopolitan authorities, while acknowledging the title of the *basileus* of Trnovo, underlined the latter's subordinate position by the traditional device of describing him as the "spiritual son" of the *autocrator* of Byzantium.[5] The Bulgarians were apt at times to reverse the relationship and to claim for their sovereign an oecumenical authority. In its most consistent and grandiloquent form this claim was advanced by the Tsar John Alexander (1331–71), who styled himself "Emperor and Autocrat of all Bulgarians and Greeks". This title occurs on his coins, in his charters, in the writings of his subjects and in two famous manuscripts commissioned by him, which were copied and painted in Trnovo in the mid-fourteenth century. The first is a Church Slavonic translation of the Byzantine world chronicle of Constantine Manasses; a miniature of this manuscript, which is now in the Vatican Library, depicts John Alexander with crown and sceptre, the imperial scarlet boots on his feet and a golden halo round his head; the divine origin of his sovereignty is symbolized by the figure of Christ, who stands on his right, and by an angel flying down from heaven and placing a second, smaller crown over his imperial diadem. The same details, so characteristic of the Byzantine theory of imperial sovereignty, recur in another miniature of the same manuscript, in which the Bulgarian tsar—perhaps in imitation of a portrait of Manuel Comnenus which was probably in the original Greek manuscript—stands beside King David.[6] The second of the two manuscripts, a Gospel Book now in the British Museum, has a painting of John Alexander in full regalia, with his wife and two sons.[7] These finest surviving examples of Bulgarian manuscript illumination show how thoroughly the tradition of Byzantine imperial portraiture had been assimilated by the Balkan Slavs in the late Middle Ages.

John Alexander's claim to sovereignty over "all Bulgarians and Greeks" suggests at first sight an imperialist programme identical with that of Symeon and John Asen II; and there is no doubt that the view that the tsar of Bulgaria had a warrant from heaven to rule over Byzantium had its roots in a tradition whose origins can be traced back to the early tenth century. There is, however, a significant difference between the views of John Alexander and of his predecessors as to how this supranational sovereignty was to be achieved. Symeon and John Asen II both strove to capture Constantinople. In the fourteenth century, for all the weakness of the Byzantine Empire, the Bulgarians could not hope to accomplish this military feat. Trnovo, not Constantinople, was now to become, in their universalist dreams, the centre of the Orthodox Commonwealth. The point is clearly made by John Alexander's court translator, in two glosses which he inserted into his Slavonic version of the chronicle of Constantine Manasses. This twelfth century Byzantine author had been the leading exponent of the idea that Constantinople was the New Rome which, as the seat of the true universal emperor, had superseded in the divine plan the

319

"Old" and fallen Rome of the West. Constantine's account of the sack of Rome by the Vandal Gaiseric in 455 is followed by this classic exposition of the theory of the *renovatio imperii*:

> And this is what became of the older Rome. But our Rome flourishes and increases, grows strong and younger. May she grow until the end—yea, thou Emperor who rulest over all—she who has such a resplendent and light-bearing emperor, the very great sovereign lord, countless times victorious, Manuel Comnenus. . . . May ten thousand suns measure his dominion.[8]

The Bulgarian translator gave a literal rendering of this high-flown Byzantine panegyric, except for two passages: for the words "our Rome" [i.e. Constantinople] he substituted "our New Constantinople" (*novyi Tsar'grad*) [i.e. Trnovo], and replaced the name Manuel Comnenus by that of "Alexander, the most gentle and merciful, the lover of monks and protector of the poor, the great tsar of the Bulgarians".[9] The significance of these glosses is clear: the seat of eternal Rome, the focus and symbol of the authority of the emperor who "rules over all", which—as all the Eastern Christian world believed—once migrated from the banks of the Tiber to the shores of the Bosphorus, had now forsaken its second abode and moved north, to the capital of the Bulgarian tsars. This concept of the eternal, migrating Rome had its roots in the idea of the *translatio imperii* by which the Byzantines attempted in the Middle Ages to find legal and historical support for the earlier and simpler theory of the empire's *renovatio*. The Bulgarians merely carried it a step further. This vision of a universal Christian polity had once impelled two Bulgarian rulers to attempt the building of a Graeco-Slav empire, centred in Constantinople; now that physical means of achieving this aim were lacking, the ideologists of John Alexander fell back on the wishful thought that the centre of the "renovated" empire had been transferred to Trnovo. From one point of view this notion of the Bulgarian capital as the "New Constantinople" was a breach—the first recorded one—in the East European conception of the Byzantine *oikoumene*. But in another sense this fourteenth century Slav version of the *translatio imperii* provides evidence of how, in an East European world far removed from modern political thinking, the consciousness of the supranational Byzantine Commonwealth still exercised mastery over the minds of men.

These imperialist dreams had little practical effect on the relations between Bulgaria and the empire. In the second half of the fourteenth century both were faced with sterner and more immediate realities. The Ottoman Turks, established in Europe since the middle of the century, rapidly overran most of what remained of Byzantine territory, defeated the Serbs in two great battles on the Maritsa (1371) and on Kosovo Polje (1389), and invaded Bulgaria. On 17 July 1393 Trnovo fell to the armies of the Sultan Bāyezīd I. The Second Bulgarian Empire ceased to exist, and before the end of the century the whole country was in the hands of the Turks. For nearly five hundred years Bulgaria was to remain a province of the Ottoman Empire. Yet this last attempt of its ideologists to reconcile their loyalty to the supranational Orthodox Commonwealth with their country's aspiration to play the leading role within it was not forgotten in Eastern Europe. A century and a half later, after the Byzantine Empire itself had fallen to the Turks, the Russian panegyrists of the principality of Moscow made use of the Bulgarian claims to the political heritage of Constantinople to develop their own more celebrated theory of "Moscow the Third Rome".

2 BYZANTIUM AND SERBIA

The decline of Byzantine power in the Balkans affected the relations between the empire and Serbia in two ways. During most of the thirteenth century Serbian foreign policy oscillated uncertainly between the competing interests of its more powerful neighbours: alliances were concluded, sometimes with Epirus or Nicaea, sometimes with Hungary and the Angevins of Sicily and Naples. Culturally, too, Serbia retained in the thirteenth century its intermediate position between the Latin and the Greek worlds, a position typified by Nemanja's double baptism and by his son's simultaneous acquisition of a royal crown from Rome and an autonomous church from Nicaea. Byzantine influence, which spread from neighbouring Bulgaria and especially from Macedonia up the Vardar, was strongest in the Ibar river basin and in the plain of Kosovo, the historic nuclei of the principality of Raška. Relations with the West were maintained through the

Serbian towns on or near the Adriatic, especially Bar (Antibari), and through coastal cities outside the country like Dubrovnik and Dyrrachium which had close contacts with Italy. In this period the Serbian ruling classes, in their foreign policy, their economic interests and their cultural life, looked to the West as much as to the Greek world. This situation began to change in the late thirteenth century, when the expansion of the Serbian state south-eastward into Macedonia led to the annexation of Byzantine territory and brought it within striking distance of the imperial cities on the Aegean coast. This expansion, which culminated in the mid-fourteenth-century conquests of Stephen Dušan, brought the country into an intimate relationship with the Greek-speaking world. Henceforth and until the Turkish conquest, the Serbs, without severing their contacts with their western neighbours, remained within the orbit of Byzantium.

In the thirteenth century Byzantine influence on Serbia was exerted mainly through the church. The Serbian archdiocese, with its administrative autonomy and close association with crown and nation, followed the pattern accepted in Eastern Christendom far more closely than that of the Latin world, where national churches had long been a thing of the past. The posthumous cult of St. Sava helped to keep Serbian Christianity in contact with the religious centres which he himself had visited: Mount Athos, Jerusalem, Constantinople and Trnovo. From the Bulgarian capital, where he died, his body was brought back to Serbia, to the royal monastery of Mileševa (1237). His cult, of which this shrine became the centre, acquired in the late Middle Ages an international importance even beyond the frontiers of the Orthodox Slav world; and it was probably at his tomb in Mileševa that Tvrtko I, the Catholic ruler of Bosnia, in a belated attempt to restore the almost defunct Serbian realm, was crowned king (1377). In the centuries to come the veneration of "the illuminator of Serbia", transmuted into legend and poetry, did much to maintain his people's devotion to the Orthodox Church and to their other national institutions; the strength of this popular cult was demonstrated time and again in Serbian history, not least in 1595, when the Turkish occupants felt obliged to remove St. Sava's body from Mileševa and to burn it.

The impact of Byzantine culture upon thirteenth century Serbia was diminished not only by the geographical remoteness of inland Raška, but also by the rival appeal of Western trade and Latin religious influence, and by the continued strength of native Slav traditions. Of the latter, it is true, we know little. The absence of a permanent royal residence, and the habit displayed by the Serbian kings, like the Hungarian and German rulers of the Middle Ages, of constantly moving from one castle or monastery to another, must have made it harder for them to build their court and chancellery on the Byzantine model and, like the tsars of Preslav and Trnovo, to adorn their capitals in imitation of Constantinople. Until the late thirteenth century the court of the Serbian *kralj* was a pretty simple and primitive establishment. The one native institution of the time, apart from the church, on which we have some information is the national assemblies. These had already developed, in a manner reminiscent of the early Frankish assemblies, in the maritime region of Dioclea in the tenth and eleventh centuries. Later we find them in Raška, consisting of representatives of the aristocracy, government officials and the clergy, convened by the king on formal occasions, such as a royal coronation or an abdication, the issue of new laws, the enthronement of an archbishop or the foundation of a monastery. These consultative *sabori* owed much to the earlier Dioclean councils; the extent of their debt to Byzantine representative assemblies, which they resemble in some respects, is less clear. Their political importance appears to have been in inverse proportion to the solemnity and frequency of their deliberations. No Serbian sovereign convened them so often, and with such pomp and ceremony, as Stephen Dušan; yet, whereas the early rulers of the Nemanja dynasty seem to have genuinely consulted with their assemblies on matters of state, in the reign of the all-powerful Dušan they were stripped, in accordance with Byzantine autocratic traditions, of all political prerogatives save that of ratifying the monarch's decisions.

Serbia's cultural relations with the West were most clearly apparent in the sphere of art. These will be discussed in a later chapter. In the economic and religious fields these links were still very close in the thirteenth century: and they explain the peripheral position occupied by thirteenth century Serbia within the Byzantine world. An important Western element in its medieval society were the "Saxon" miners (*Sasi*) who came to the country probably from Hungary and worked the rich mines of silver, lead, copper and iron which, in the second half of the century, were beginning to make Serbia's fortune: the most famous were in Novo Brdo, to the east of Kosovo Polje, and in Rudnik, in the north of the country. The mining towns founded by the "Saxons" developed a form of municipal administration which, it has recently been argued, may well have been borrowed by other medieval cities of Serbia, many of which enjoyed autonomous privileges unknown in Byzantine cities.

The growth of the Serbian mining industry caused a rapid development of the country's foreign trade. Very little of this trade with the Byzantium. The products of the mines were mostly exported by sea to Western Europe. The intermediaries in this trade were merchants from the Adriatic coast, mainly from Kotor and Dubrovnik. Kotor, which belonged to the Serbian realm from 1186 to 1371, provided its rulers with finance and customs officials, and with diplomatic agents for foreign missions. Dubrovnik, a Byzantine dependency until 1205, then under Venetian sovereignty until 1358, a part-Latin, part-Slav city with autonomous institutions, extensive possessions in Southern Dalmatia and a long tradition of maritime trade, was compelled in the thirteenth century by the pressure of Venetian competition to seek an outlet for its commercial activity in the interior of the Balkans. As a result, the Ragusans became the principal entrepreneurs in the Serbian mining industry and the middlemen in the country's export trade. The trade routes that linked inland Serbia to the coast were regularly used by merchants and craftsmen from Dubrovnik and Kotor, who helped to bring the Serbian economy into the European commercial circuit and to acquaint the towns and monasteries of the interior with Western culture, especially with Romanesque art.

Religion, as well as industry and trade, provided a link between medieval Serbia and the West. Alongside the Serbian Orthodox Church whose archiepiscopal see was transferred in the mid-thirteenth century from Žiča to Peć, a number of Latin bishoprics in the land owed allegiance to Rome. Situated on or near the Adriatic coast, they were divided administratively into three groups: the archbishopric of Bar, directly subject to the Holy See, together with its suffragan sees; the bishopric of Kotor, which had jurisdiction over the Latins of the Serbian interior (including the mining "Saxons") and was dependent on the see of Bari in Apulia; and the bishoprics of Trebinje and Zahumlje (Herzegovina), subject to the archbishopric of Ragusa (whose see lay outside Serbian territory). Many Benedictine abbeys existed in these Serbian maritime districts. The religious dualism shown by the coexistence of Orthodox and Roman dioceses in the country was also manifest in the ecclesiastical policy of the Serbian monarchs, most of whom, while remaining faithful to the Orthodox Church, cultivated good relations with the papacy: of the ten members of the Nemanja dynasty who ruled Serbia between *c.* 1168 and 1371, one was baptized by a Roman priest, one was crowned by a papal legate, one was influenced by the Catholic loyalties of his French wife, one joined the Roman Church (it is true, after his abdication) and three, without taking this final step, expressed a readiness to recognize the pope's authority. In some of these overtures there was no doubt a strong element of political opportunism: not least in the cases of Stephen the First Crowned, whose profession of loyalty to the Roman Church coincided with the collapse of Byzantium after the Fourth Crusade, and Stephen Dušan, who was willing to acknowledge papal supremacy in exchange for being appointed "captain of all Christendom" against the Turks. Yet some at least of these Serbian rulers seem to have been genuinely convinced that acceptance of the pope's jurisdiction was not incompatible with loyalty to the traditions of the Orthodox Church; and this belief, shared, as we have seen, by several Bulgarian monarchs of the time, provides some evidence that at least among the Balkan converts of Byzantium there was, even in the late Middle Ages, little or no consciousness of a definitive schism in the body of Christendom.

A new period in the history of Serbo-Byzantine relations began in the reign of King Stephen Uroš II Milutin (1282–1321), Nemanja's great-grandson. The south-eastern boundary of the Serbian kingdom, where it abutted on Byzantine Macedonia, had scarcely shifted since Nemanja's time: only his son Stephen had annexed a narrow strip of territory, bringing the frontier to the Šar Mountains. In the early years of Milutin's reign the Serbian armies crossed this range and occupied a large part of Northern Macedonia, up to and including Debar, Veles and Štip. The centre of

the conquered area was the city of Skoplje. This move had two
important consequences. By crossing the mountains the Serbs, for
the first time in their history, passed over the watershed between
the Danube and the Aegean Sea and, by occupying the Tetovo-
Polog basin, gained control of the upper reaches of the Vardar:
the way was now open for further expansion to the south-east
down that river towards Thessalonica; and the policy of the Serbian state from now on became definitely orientated towards the
Byzantine Empire. Secondly, by capturing Skoplje the Serbs acquired at last a city whose strategic position, admirable
fortifications and ancient renown equipped it to serve as a national
capital; a city which, owing to its central situation in the Balkan
peninsula astride the Morava-Vardar trade route and to its largely
Greek population, seemed destined to become the metropolis of a
united Balkan empire. Milutin's expansion into Macedonia, made
possible by his country's economic development through mining
and trade and by the swollen resources and ambitions of its landed
aristocracy, not only established his kingdom as a major power in
the Balkans: it also resulted in the deep involvement of Serbia in
the empire's politics, and ensured that her late medieval culture
was to bear, in all its essential traits, the imprint of Byzantium.

This imprint soon became visible in the country's social life.
Two Byzantine embassies which visited Serbia in the thirteenth
century recorded their impressions of its royal court. The
difference between the two accounts is striking. In 1266 the envoys
of Michael VIII travelled to the residence of Uroš I in an attempt
(which proved unsuccessful) to arrange a marriage between the
emperor's daughter and the Serbian king's son Milutin. They were
not impressed by what they saw. They found the royal court
"plain and paltry", and were shocked to find the king's daughter-
in-law shabbily dressed and bent over her spindle. The unfavourable impression was mutual, for the Serbian monarch was
scandalized by the luxury of the ambassador's retinue and com-
mented ironically on the unfamiliar spectacle of the eunuchs who
formed the cortège of the Byzantine princess.[10] Some thirty
years later Theodore Metochites, the distinguished statesman and
scholar, went to Serbia on another matrimonial mission, as ambassador of Andronicus II. His task was to persuade King Milutin
to marry the emperor's five-year-old daughter Simonis. The mar-

riage was arranged (and duly solemnized!) in 1299, and a treaty was concluded by which Milutin's conquests in Macedonia were handed over to him as a dowry. Metochites paints a picture of the Serbian royal residence very different from the impressions gained by the embassy of 1266: Milutin's ceremonial dress, he tells us, was studded with pearls and precious stones, and the luxury of his court, he noted with approval, was quite Byzantine.[11] Serbia's political orientation towards Byzantium was already so strong that several of its writers in close touch with official circles explicitly acknowledged the emperor's universal sovereignty. Thus King Milutin's court panegyrist, the future Archbishop Danilo II, referred to the *basileus* of Constantinople as "the universal emperor of New Rome"; and a pupil of Danilo described him in the same vein as "the orthodox universal emperor, the Lord Andronicus".[12]

It was not only in the ceremonies of its court and in the political thinking of its educated classes that Serbia began to display in Milutin's crucial reign the growing influence of Byzantium. As it annexed more and more Byzantine territory in Macedonia, its rulers became more familiar with the administrative, legal and fiscal institutions of the empire and adopted them on an increasing scale. After 1300 increasing numbers of new names for court titles, offices of state, taxes and legal concepts, all borrowed from Byzantium, are mentioned in Serbian documents; some occur in their Greek form, others in Slavonic translation. A notable instance was the introduction of the Byzantine system of land tenure. The old structure of the themes had broken down after Basil II's death in 1025. By the second half of the eleventh century, in the place of the free peasant-soldier commune, two types of land holding had become prevalent in the Byzantine Empire: on the one hand the large hereditary estate of the civil or military magnate and, on the other, crown property handed out to eminent Byzantines or foreigners to administer, usually in return for military service, free of state taxation. The latter system was called *pronoia* (literally, "care"), and its recipient was termed *pronoiarios* ("the one who has care" over the property).[13] The grant of *pronoia* differed from a gift of land of the first type in that it was held for a limited time, usually until the recipient's death, and was, until the second half of the thirteenth century, inalienable. From the time of Michael VIII, however, *pronoiarioi* were allowed to bequeath their estates and revenues to their heirs, though they could not be other-wise alienated, and the obligation of service remained. The heredi-table *pronoia* closely resembles the West European fief; whether or not we may think it legitimate to speak of "Byzantine feudal-ism"—and the point should at least be made that the *pronoia* system was indigenous to Byzantium and not a Western import-ation—there is no doubt that this system, founded on the double relationship between land tenure and military service and between the lord of the manor and the peasants (*paroikoi*) economically dependent on him, was an essential element in that process of "feu-dalization" which, in the later Byzantine Empire, so greatly in-creased the power of the landed military aristocracy at the expense of the central administration.

The spread of the *pronoia* system in the late eleventh and in the twelfth centuries to Thrace and Macedonia has already been noted. Very probably it also existed in the Second Bulgarian Empire, though because of the penury of sources relating to the social and economic history of the North-Eastern Balkans in this period this cannot be stated with certainty. It is, however, well attested in Serbia; local social and economic factors, which made conditional land ownership under the control of the state accept-able to the Serbian aristocracy, no doubt facilitated its spread. But the institution as such was certainly borrowed from the Byzantine Empire. It is significant that the earliest evidence of a *pronoia* in Serbia is found in an immunity charter issued by King Milutin in 1299–1300 to a monastery near Skoplje, a region he had recently acquired from the Byzantines.[14] Dušan's conquests resulted in a considerable extension of this type of land holding in Serbia. The Serbian *pronoia* followed the Byzantine model (including its newly acquired heritable character), except in two comparatively minor respects: while the Byzantine *pronoiarioi* served no one but the crown, there are some cases of Serbian ones owing service to mon-asteries; and where as the Byzantine peasants paid their dues in money, the Serbian *paroikoi* paid their lord mainly in labour. These differences may be explained, in the first case by the By-zantine view of the emperor as the source of all law and military authority, and in the second by the fact that Serbia had a far less developed money economy than the empire.

If the first three stages in the history of the relations between

328

medieval Serbia and Byzantium were marked by Nemanja's and Sava's recourse to Greek models for the organization of their church, by the uneasy equilibrium between East and West that characterized Serbian policy and culture in the thirteenth century, and by the growing Byzantine influence on Serbian society in the reign of Milutin, the fourth stage was reached in the reign of Stephen Dušan (1331–55). The policy of this most powerful of all Serbian monarchs aimed at the conquest of Byzantium. In this he nearly succeeded. Taking advantage of the military decline of Bulgaria after the battle of Velbuzhd and of the civil wars which rent the empire, he annexed in the space of some fifteen years the whole of Macedonia (except Thessalonica), Albania, Epirus and Thessaly. By 1350 the Serbian realm extended to the River Nestos and to the Gulf of Patras. Byzantium had been shorn of half of its territory, and Serbia had doubled its size. Without much exaggeration Dušan could describe himself, in a letter to the republic of Venice, as "lord of almost the whole Roman Empire".[15]

Once again, however, the two main cities in the Balkans, Constantinople and Thessalonica, eluded the grasp of a Slav monarch bent on achieving mastery over South-Eastern Europe. Shortly before his death Dušan had come to realize that, like Symeon in the tenth century, he could not hope to conquer Byzantium without a fleet. While he belatedly prepared to build one, he sought to legitimize his past conquests and to arm himself for future ones by resorting to ideological weapons; having spent much of his childhood, until the age of thirteen, in Constantinople, he could be expected to choose the very weapons which had already been used by Bulgarian rulers who, like him, had acquired their political education in a world dominated by Byzantine universalist ideas. In 1345 Dušan proclaimed himself "Emperor and Autocrat of Serbia and Romania" (the Slavonic form of the title was "Tsar of the Serbs and the Greeks"). But his claim to the supreme position within the commonwealth required the sanction of the church; and this, according to Byzantine legal concepts, meant coronation by a patriarch. Shortly afterwards he raised the Serbian archbishop to the rank of "Patriarch of the Serbs and the Greeks", a transaction for which he secured the approval of the highest ecclesiastical dignitaries within the boundaries of his realm (these included the archbishop of Ohrid and representatives of the

Athonite monasteries), as well as that of the patriarch of Bulgaria. On Easter Sunday, 16 April 1346, at a national assembly at Skoplje, Dušan was crowned emperor by his newly appointed patriarch of Peć. The Byzantine authorities reacted sharply to this double act of usurpation. The Serbian monarch's claim to sovereignty over the "Greeks" was denounced, though in recognition of his conquests his title of "Emperor of the Serbs" was acknowledged in Constantinople. Graver sanctions were applied in the ecclesiastical sphere: the oecumenical patriarch Callistus a few years later excommunicated the tsar and his religious leaders, not only for the unlawful creation of the Serbian patriarchate, but also on account of Dušan's title and his conquest of Byzantine territory.

Dušan's imperial coronation gave a further impetus to the Byzantinization of his country's administrative machinery; this indeed became a practical necessity as the Serbian realm annexed one Byzantine province after another. It was after his first major territorial acquisition—the city of Serres in Eastern Macedonia—in 1345 that his charters began to conform more closely to the traditions of Byzantine diplomatic. Many of them were composed in Greek. To solve the administrative and social problems posed by the transformation of the Serbian kingdom into a Graeco-Serbian empire, Dušan issued his celebrated legal code, the *Zakonik* (in 1349 and, in an enlarged form, again in 1354), which combined Byzantine jurisprudence with Serbian customary law: here, too, he imitated the legal activity and prerogatives of the East Roman emperors. In his wholesale introduction of Byzantine titles and offices into the hierarchy of court and into the structure of government, Dušan went much further than any of his predecessors; and it is worth noting that some of the titles which the tsar bestowed on his relatives, those of Caesar, despot and *sebastocrator*, were by tradition in the exclusive patronage of the emperor.

It would be a mistake, however, to think of Dušan's realm as merely an administrative replica of fourteenth century Byzantium. In the words of a contemporary Byzantine writer Dušan, "having proclaimed himself emperor of the Romans, exchanged the barbarian ways for the Roman manners", let his son rule over the lands to the north of Skoplje and the Vardar "according to the customs of the Serbians", and kept for himself "the Roman country and cities" from Skoplje to the defile of Christoupolis (north of the Gulf of Kavalla), to be governed "according to the custom of the Romans".[16] This division of authority was more apparent than real: for Dušan was too much of an autocrat to relinquish the supreme power over any part of his realm; and his son was in any case but a child at the time. But it is interesting to observe this dualism between the northern part of Dušan's realm, the original kernel of the Serbian state, where local customary law and the political traditions of the former kings were still in force, and the recently acquired Greek and Albanian lands, from the Šar Planina to the Aegean and to the Gulf of Patras, which retained their earlier Byzantine administration. Conditions changed little in the latter areas, except that in some places the local Greek bishops and high civil officials were replaced by Serbs. In all other respects Dušan resolved to rule over these lands, which he clearly regarded as the more important part of his realm, as the "successor (nastavnik) of the great and holy Greek emperors".[17]

The political historian may wonder whether, in Dušan's terminology, the term "successor" was intended to apply solely to the former imperial lands now held by the tsar, or to the whole Byzantine Empire, whose sovereignty he had seemingly and from a distance usurped. A precise answer to this question is hardly possible; and it may well be that the term was intentionally ambiguous. But some light on the problem is shed by two contemporary documents which tell us something about the tsar's view of his constitutional relationship to the Byzantine emperor. The first one, dated November 1345, is a chrysobull or imperial charter, issued by the Serbian monarch to the monasteries of Mount Athos.[18] Dušan had requested the monks, as a token of their recognition of his newly acquired sovereignty over the Holy Mountain, to institute the regular liturgical commemoration of his name. The monasteries agreed to this, but on condition that the name of the Byzantine emperor be always commemorated before that of the Serbian ruler. The opening clause of Dušan's chrysobull makes it clear that he accepted this condition: this proves that a few months before his imperial coronation he formally recognized that his own position within the commonwealth was subordinate to that of its supreme head, the emperor of Byzantium.

331

Our second piece of evidence is more significant still, for it shows that even after his coronation as "Emperor of Serbia and Romania" Dušan was still prepared at least implicitly to subscribe to the traditional view that the *basileus* in Constantinople was the sole legitimate overlord of the Orthodox community of nations. In July 1351 the Emperor John V issued a chrysobull confirming the privileges of the monastery of Chilandar on Mount Athos. The document states that the emperor issued it at the request "of the sublime emperor of Serbia, his beloved . . . Lord Stephen".[19] The fact that Dušan made this request on behalf of a Serbian monastery situated in a region that was part of his realm cannot have been due to simple politeness. And if we remember that the privilege of issuing chrysobulls was regarded in Byzantium as a visible sign of the emperor's authority, and their acceptance by the recipient as a mark of his submission to it, we may be prepared to conclude that, despite his high-flown pretensions to universal sovereignty, the "Emperor of the Serbs and the Greeks" still accepted as axiomatic the view that he who reigns in Constantinople is the legitimate master of the Christian Commonwealth.

After Dušan's death in 1355 his empire fell into rapid decline. His son and successor, the Tsar Uroš, was unable to prevent his multinational realm from breaking up into a number of independent principalities. One of them, whose historical importance has only recently been fully appreciated, continued for the next sixteen years to embody Dušan's programme of Serbian-Greek collaboration. The brief life span of this principality inaugurates the final period in the history of Serbo-Byzantine relations. It comprised most of Eastern Macedonia, from the Vardar to the Nestos and from the defiles of the Strymon to the Aegean coast. It included the Chalcidice peninsula with Mount Athos, but not Thessalonica nor the coastal cities between the Strymon and the Nestos estuaries. Its territory thus coincided almost exactly with that of the former Byzantine theme of Strymon; and its capital was, likewise, Serres. In its government and administration the principality of Serres was more closely modelled on Byzantium than even Dušan's empire had been. The friendly relations established with Constantinople by its ruler, the Despot John Uglješa, made possible the lifting of the anathemas against the Serbian Church and the restoration of communion with the oecumenical patriarchate, first in the principality of Serres (1368) and a few years later in Serbia as a whole. The astonishing vitality of the Byzantine tradition, which survived every military clash and political dispute between the empire and its Balkan neighbours, had thus, on the eve of the Turkish conquest, reasserted itself once more.

This tradition could now indeed be invoked as a means of strengthening the bonds of the commonwealth against the enemy. To the Slavs as well as to the Greeks Byzantium appeared in those years as the bulwark of the Orthodox faith. A Bulgarian chronicler, in his almost contemporary account of the defeat of the Ottoman forces by the Mongols at Ankara in 1402, reflected on the providential destiny of Constantinople: "by the grace of God", he wrote, "the Holy City has been delivered until now from all foreign enemies".[20] This sense of solidarity was shared by several prominent Byzantines. The former Emperor John Cantacuzenus, in a conversation with the legate of Pope Urban v in 1367, declared that, for all the occasional bouts of hostility, the Bulgarians, the Serbs "and their like" "are our brothers in faith (*homopistoi*)".[21] And in the previous year the distinguished writer and statesman Demetrius Cydones referred more explicitly still to the ties that united his compatriots to the Balkan Slavs. He set little store, it is true, by any military pact with them, and preferred to pin his hopes upon an alliance with the Latin powers. Yet he too admitted that the Bulgarians and the Serbs "are people similar (*homoious*) to us, devoted to God, who on many occasions have shared many things in common with us".[22]

These belated dreams of saving the Byzantine Commonwealth by a common effort of the Christian powers of South-Eastern Europe were soon dispelled by the Turkish victories in the Balkans. In 1393 the Bulgarian capital fell to the sultan's troops. In two major battles the Serbs lost the remnants of their medieval empire. Their defeat on the Maritsa in 1371 ended the independent existence of the principality of Serres; and after the battle of Kosovo Polje (1389), which later tradition was to transmute into poetry and myth, the north Serbian principality, between the Šar Planina, the Morava and the Danube, became a vassal state of the sultan. Its rulers maintained political and cultural links with Constantinople and, as their investiture by the emperor with the high-ranking Byzantine title of despot shows, kept their loyalty to the head of the commonwealth. One of them, George Branković (1427–56), lived to see the greater part of his country occupied by the Turks. His great fortress of Smederevo on the Danube, the last stronghold of Serbian independence, fell in 1459 to the armies of Mehmet II.

3 BYZANTIUM AND THE RUMANIAN LANDS

The plain between the lower Danube, the Carpathians and the Prut offered, almost from the foundation of the East Roman Empire, a passage or temporary home to invaders from the Eurasian steppes whose relations with Byzantium, in war and in peace, were recorded in the early chapters of this book. It is not before the late Middle Ages that we find evidence of stable societies and organized political life in this region. In the fourteenth century, when the impenetrable mist that envelops the earlier history of this area begins to clear and the historian finds himself on more solid ground, he can detect the outlines of two Rumanian states: Wallachia, between the Transylvanian Alps and the lower Danube; and Moldavia, between the Eastern Carpathians and the Prut. In both regions the development of local institutions and the beginnings of an organized political life seem to have been linked with the successful struggle of their princes to shake off Hungarian rule: this was achieved by Wallachia in 1330, and by Moldavia in 1365. It was only then, after they had acquired enough power, ambition, independence and wealth, that these Rumanian rulers were impelled to increase their prestige at home and status abroad by cementing links with the empire. They had no need to look for examples in the behaviour of East European rulers of the past to know that the first step along this desirable road was to obtain a church organization under Byzantine auspices.

The Byzantines, for their part, had at least three reasons for being interested in the Rumanian principalities. The first was trade. In the late Middle Ages Constantinople relied heavily on the raw materials, particularly food supplies, imported from lands bordering on the Black Sea: Wallachian and Moldavian wheat was shipped to Constantinople from Vicina near the estuary of the

Danube and from Akkerman at the mouth of the Dniester; in 1360–1 honey, wax and wine are also mentioned among the commodities exported to the Constantinopolitan suburb of Pera from the port of Chilia at the mouth of the Danube. Further evidence of commerce between the empire and the lower Danubian lands in the fourteenth century is provided by a large hoard of Byzantine coins recently discovered in the Northern Dobrudja. Though the benefit it brought to the Byzantines was reduced by the fact that the Black Sea trade was then controlled by the Genoese, and to a lesser extent by the Venetians, there is no doubt that the empire welcomed and promoted these commercial relations with Wallachia and Moldavia.

The second reason for the more active Byzantine policy north of the Danube in this period was the ambition of the oecumenical patriarchate to consolidate and extend its hegemony in Eastern Europe. It is likely that Byzantine Christianity had already been spreading for some time from Bulgaria to the neighbouring lands between the Danube and the Carpathians. But this, however probable, is no more than a hypothesis, and the first well-attested date in the history of the Rumanian Church is 1359. In that year a metropolitan of Wallachia was appointed by the Byzantine authorities, with his see in Argeş, the new princely capital in the southern foothills of the Transylvanian Alps. Similar status was achieved by the church of Moldavia in 1401 when, after a lengthy dispute with Constantinople over the manner of appointing its incumbent, the Rumanian candidate was recognized by the patriarchate as metropolitan in Suceava, the residence of the Moldavian princes. The creation of these two metropolitanates of "Oungrovlachia" and "Moldovlachia", as they were called by the Byzantine chancellery, was something of a triumph for the oecumenical patriarchate which, at a time when the empire was sinking to its final ruin, was able to establish its authority between the lower Danube and the southern boundaries of Poland. The Rumanians, for their part, by acquiring two organized churches under Constantinopolitan jurisdiction, gained an international status comparable to that of their East European neighbours, and secured their belated entry into the Byzantine Commonwealth. There is little reliable information on the political connections of the court of Argeş and Suceava with Byzantium; but, though

335

present-day scholars are inclined to attribute to them no more than a marginal importance, there seems little doubt that at least Mircea the Old of Wallachia (1386–1418) and Alexander the Good of Moldavia (1400–31) maintained relations with Constantinople that were not only ecclesiastical. As for Byzantine influences on Rumanian culture, which will be discussed in a later chapter, and which were stronger in Wallachia than in Moldavia, they were exerted not so much directly as through the medium of the Balkan Slav countries: the clearest proof of this is the fact that Church Slavonic remained the liturgical language of the Rumanian Church until the late seventeenth century.

The third reason which made the empire interested in the Rumanian lands was a military one; and it was the most urgent of all. In the late fourteenth century and in the first half of the fifteenth the Byzantines had only one serious hope of saving their capital from the Turkish menace; and it rested on the Hungarian crown. Wallachia and to a lesser extent Moldavia had close links with the neighbouring Hungarian province of Transylvania, and could be expected to play their part in the anti-Turkish crusades planned in Buda. Thus Mircea of Wallachia accompanied King Sigismund on the campaign which led to the disastrous defeat of the Christians at Nicopolis on the Danube (1396). And it was a Transylvanian soldier of genius, John Hunyadi, who together with his Hungarian sovereign captained the Christian forces which, after a victory over the Turks in Serbia, were defeated at the battle of Varna in 1444. The failure of the "Crusade of Varna" sealed the fate of South-Eastern Europe. Wallachian resistance to the Ottomans rapidly crumbled after the country's invasion in 1462 by Mehmet II, the conqueror of Constantinople. Moldavia retained its independence for another half century, thanks to its ruler Stephen the Great, a patron of monasteries, learning and art, whose victories over the Turks and successful defence of the Danube frontier caused the pope to address him as "*Athleta Christi*". After his death in 1504 Moldavia became a vassal state of the Ottoman Empire, and the last surviving fragment of the Byzantine Commonwealth in South-Eastern Europe lost its independent existence.

In the late Middle Ages Russia was probably of greater importance to Byzantium than at any time since the tenth century. There were three main reasons for this. Now that the Byzantines, faced with the financial ruin of their state, were increasingly driven to rely on foreign aid, raw materials and contributions of money from Russia could be seen as essential to the empire's economy. In the second place, to maintain friendly political relations with the Russians, in a world in which the diminished empire, beset by enemies in the Balkans, was fighting for its life, must have seemed to the statesmen in Constantinople to be a matter of plain common sense. Finally, the Byzantine patriarchate, striving to compensate for the empire's political impotence by extending its own international jurisdiction, could not but view the Russian Church with its numerous flock as the pivot of its ecclesiastical policy in Eastern Europe. The Russians, for their part, despite several crises which threatened to undermine their loyalty to Byzantium, still looked to Constantinople as to the spiritual and administrative centre of the Orthodox Christian world. This convergence of mutual interests, as well as a common attachment to the same religious and cultural tradition, continued in the fourteenth and the first half of the fifteenth century to ensure that Russia retained her place within the Byzantine Commonwealth.

Trade relations between the empire and Russia, after a temporary eclipse due to the Mongol invasion and to the Latin conquest of Constantinople, revived in the fourteenth century. The role played in this revival by the Genoese colonies of Caffa and Soldaia on the South Crimean coast has already been noted. Through them furs from Central and Northern Russia, and probably wax and honey as well, were shipped to Constantinople, and Byzantine cloths, together with weapons and paper from Italy, were exported to Muscovy. The principal trade route from Moscow to Constantinople in this period followed the Don to the port of Tana (Azov) at its estuary, crossed the Sea of Azov to Caffa or Soldaia and then cut across the Black Sea to Sinope and thence to the Bosphorus. In 1379 a Muscovite embassy completed this journey in two and a half months. An alternative route led from Novogorod and other cities of North-Western Russia across Lithuanian territory to Akkerman and thence by sea to Byzantium. These routes were used extensively not only by merchants and diplomatic missions, but also by Russian pilgrims on their way to Constantinople and other holy places that lay beyond it, such as Mount Athos and Jerusalem. At a time when the imperial treasury, as a fourteenth century Byzantine scholar observed with erudite sarcasm, contained nothing but "air, dust and Epicurean atoms",[23] Russian money was clearly as necessary to Byzantium as Russian raw materials. In 1346 part of the structure of St. Sophia, weakened by recent earthquakes, collapsed. The ruler of Muscovy sent a large sum of money for the repair of the building.[24] A further sum was sent in 1398 to the aid of Constantinople, blockaded at that time by the Turks: a donation intended, in the words of a contemporary Russian chronicler, as "alms for those who are in such misery".[25] Both these gifts were obtained through the good offices of the primate of the Russian Church. In 1400 this prelate received an urgent request from his superior, the Byzantine patriarch, to start another fund-raising campaign; he was to assure his Russian flock that it was more meritorious to contribute money for the defence of Constantinople than to build churches, to give alms to the poor, or to redeem prisoners: "for this Holy City", wrote the patriarch, "is the pride, the support, the sanctification and the glory of Christians in the whole *oikoumene*".[26]

The imperial government's efforts to enlist the support—if only financial—of the Russians by using its principal ecclesiastical agent in the country were, of course, fully in keeping with the past traditions of Byzantine diplomacy. In the fourteenth century, however, the new and complex political situation in Russia presented the imperial statesmen with an awkward dilemma. In the Russian lands, which around 1300 had formed a cluster of petty principalities virtually independent of each other and subject to the formidable power of the Golden Horde, two political structures had now emerged, competing for the allegiance of the Eastern Slavs: the grand duchy of Lithuania and the principality of Moscow. The former had been expanding from its original nucleus round Vilna and on the middle Niemen eastward and south-eastward, gradually absorbing the former territory of Western Russia. By about 1362 the grand dukes of Lithuania had replaced the Tatars as overlords of the middle Dnieper valley; by the end of the century they had advanced their frontier to the Black Sea and, in the east, to within a hundred miles of Moscow. Muscovy, still the smaller of the two states, was emerging as the unquestioned leader of the central Russian principalities and was claiming with growing conviction and authority to embody the political and cultural traditions of Kievan Russia. The metropolitan-primate was a powerful symbol of this continuity. His residence, it is true, had been moved from Kiev to Vladimir (1300), and thence to Moscow (1328); but these successive migrations had as yet no legal significance, and this prelate retained until the mid-fifteenth century his traditional title of "metropolitan of Kiev and All Russia". In practice the fourteenth century metropolitans, whether they were native Russians or Byzantine citizens, tended to identify themselves with the policies and aspirations of the princes of Moscow. Granted extensive privileges by the khans of the Golden Horde who showed some religious tolerance by exempting the Russian Church from taxation and by protecting its property, the metropolitans placed their considerable moral authority at the disposal of the Muscovite rulers in their efforts to achieve political dominance in Central and North-Eastern Russia. The church's role in supporting the growing belief that the prince of Moscow was alone strong enough to stand up to the Tatars and achieve one day the liberation of the country is less clearly attested. This belief seemed to be vindicated in 1380, when the Russian troops commanded by Dimitri, prince of Moscow, defeated a large Tatar army at Kulikovo; and although the role played by the church in preparing the psychological ground for this first significant Russian victory over their Asian masters may have been exaggerated by fifteenth century panegyrists, who hailed it as a signal triumph for Muscovy and the Christian faith, it is likely that some ecclesiastical leaders gave their blessing to this new policy of national resistance.

The Byzantine government was well aware of these changes which were affecting the balance of power between the upper Volga, the Baltic and the Black Sea. More particularly, it had become clear by the early fourteenth century that the grand dukes of Lithuania, Moscow's rivals for political hegemony over Russia, hoped to deprive their opponents of the considerable advantages derived from the presence within their city of the chief bishop of

339

the Russian Church; and that their best hope lay in persuading the Byzantine authorities either to transfer the seat of the metropolitan to Lithuania, or at least to set up a separate metropolitanate in their country. The dilemma which faced the Byzantines was the following: could the authority of the patriarchate best be maintained by the traditional policy of keeping the Russian Church under the power of a single prelate, appointed from Constantinople? And if so, should he reside in the historic see of Kiev, which from about 1362 was on Lithuanian territory, or in Moscow? Or, on a realistic assessment of the power structure in Eastern Europe, should there now be two separate metropolitanates, one in Moscow, and the other in Kiev? The choice between these alternatives was not an easy one. Tradition, administrative convenience, and the respect for the power and financial resources of the princes of Moscow prompted a pro-Muscovite solution. Yet there were cogent arguments, too, on the opposite side. In the fourteenth century the Lithuanian ruling classes were still predominantly pagan; but they had the tiresome habit of trying to blackmail the Byzantines by the threat of going over to the Roman Church. If they could be won over to Orthodox Christianity the authorities of Constantinople could expect to revive the great missionary traditions of the patriarchate and to incorporate a large new area of Eastern Europe into the Byzantine Commonwealth. The struggle between the pro-Lithuanian and the pro-Muscovite parties in Constantinople, each of them urged on by promises, threats, or financial bribes by their protégés in the field, lasted through most of the century; and with bewildering and unedifying frequency the patriarchs of Constantinople set up separate metropolitanates for Lithuania (and often for Galicia as well) only to abolish them a few decades, or years, later. Matters came to a head in 1354: in June of that year the Muscovite candidate Alexius was appointed "metropolitan of Kiev and All Russia" by the Emperor John IV Cantacuzenus and the Patriarch Philotheus; a few months later, after Cantacuzenus' abdication, the new Patriarch Callistus consecrated as metropolitan Roman, the candidate of the Lithuanian ruler Olgerd, in terms, it would seem, ambiguous enough to enable him and his secular patron to claim jurisdiction over the whole of Russia. A year or two later a veritable auction seems to have taken place in Constantinople between the two rival prelates, at which Moscow gained a partial victory: Roman's jurisdiction was confined to Lithuania, and Alexius retained his title of "metropolitan of Kiev and All Russia". This vacillating policy, which ended only in 1408 when the Lithuanian dioceses were finally subjected to Moscow, was not calculated to enhance the popularity of the Byzantine authorities in either Lithuania or Muscovy. The pagan Olgerd is said to have declared with understandable pique that he preferred the worship of the sun to that of the demon of cupidity, to whom the patriarchs of Constantinople had surrendered, and to have abandoned his intention of converting his nation to Byzantine Christianity.[27] Any remaining hopes the Byzantines may have entertained of attaching Lithuania to the Commonwealth were dashed in 1386, when Olgerd's son Jagiello was baptized into the Roman Church and married the queen of Poland. Through this marriage Lithuania was united with the Polish Kingdom and, although it included a large Russian Orthodox population within its borders, moved outside the orbit of Byzantium.

Nor were the Muscovites, though they proved the winners in the end, any more satisfied by these dubious manoeuvres. In 1375 the Patriarch Philotheus, with the same lack of canonical decorum which his predecessor Callistus had displayed in 1354, and again in deference to Olgerd's wishes, consecrated the latter's candidate Cyprian as "metropolitan of Kiev, Lithuania, and Russia" in the lifetime of Alexius, the lawful incumbent of two of these three sees. The Russians felt deeply humiliated by this affront to their popular metropolitan; and even the Byzantines were impressed by the "great tumult" and the "attitude of revolt" which this affair provoked all over Russia.[28] Indignation grew stronger still after Alexius' death in 1378, when the patriarchate, heavily bribed by the Russian envoys who had gone beyond their brief, appointed as his successor one of these envoys, whose name was fraudulently substituted on the deed of investiture for that of the genuine candidate who had died on the way. The confusion which this disreputable deal created in the affairs of the Russian Church ended only in 1390, when the Muscovites accepted Cyprian as metropolitan of Russia.

The rulers of Moscow, who on several occasions in the second half of the fourteenth century found themselves the victims of these machinations of Byzantine diplomacy, could hardly have been expected to entertain feelings of goodwill towards the authorities of Constantinople, and especially towards the emperor, whose influence on the appointment of the Russian metropolitans was usually only too apparent. It is not surprising that their loyalty to Byzantium was at times strained to breaking point. Some time between 1394 and 1397 Antony IV, patriarch of Constantinople, sent a letter to Prince Basil I of Moscow, rebuking him for having caused his metropolitan to omit the emperor's name from the commemorative diptychs of the Russian Church. The patriarch further reprimanded the Muscovite ruler for having made disparaging remarks about the *basileus*. He took a particularly grave view of Basil's statement: "We have the church, but not the emperor." To acknowledge the authority over Russia of the patriarch but not of the emperor is, Antony points out, a contradiction in terms: for "it is not possible for Christians to have the church and not to have the empire. For church and empire have a great unity and community; nor is it possible for them to be separated from one another". And, in an attempt to make the Russian sovereign see the grievous error of his ways, and in pursuance of his own duty as "universal teacher of all Christians", the patriarch solemnly reiterated the basic principle of Byzantine political philosophy. "The holy emperor," he writes, "is not as other rulers and governors of other regions are. ... He is anointed with the great myrrh, and is consecrated *basileus* and *autocrator* of the Romans—to wit, of all Christians." These other rulers, "who are called kings promiscuously among the nations", exercise a purely local authority; the *basileus* alone is "the lord and master of the *oikoumene*", the "universal emperor", "the natural king" whose laws and ordinances are accepted in the whole world. His oecumenical sovereignty is made manifest by the liturgical commemoration of his name in the churches of Christendom; and, as the patriarch's letter pointedly implies, the prince of Moscow by discontinuing this practice within his realm had deliberately rejected the very foundations of Christian law and government.[29]

There are few documents which express with such force and clarity the basic theory of the medieval Byzantine Commonwealth. The Patriarch Antony's letter is a classic exposition of the doctrine of the universal East Roman empire, ruled by the

342

basileus, successor of Constantine and vicegerent of God, supreme law-giver of Christendom, whose authority was held to extend, at least in a spiritual and "metapolitical" sense, over all Christian rulers and peoples. The fact that this solemn and defiant profession of faith was made from the capital of a state that was facing political and military collapse, only emphasizes the astonishing strength and continuity of this political vision which pervades the entire history of Byzantium and had hitherto been accepted implicitly by the nations of Eastern Europe. "The doctrine of one oecumenical emperor," a distinguished Byzantinist has written, "had never been laid down more forcibly or with more fiery eloquence than in this letter which the patriarch of Constantinople sent to Moscow from a city blockaded by the Turks."[30]

What significance should we attach to the refusal of a Muscovite sovereign to recognize, in the late fourteenth century, the universalist claims of the emperor? This question can best be answered by considering how far, and in what sense, these claims were acknowledged in Russia before and after the reception of the patriarch's letter by Basil I. The evidence provided by medieval Russian service books is unfortunately insufficient to determine whether the emperor's name was consistently commemorated. Some grounds, however, for believing that Russian princes of the early Middle Ages accepted the emperor's supreme position in Orthodox Christendom have already been cited. Direct evidence on this point is not abundant, and for good reason: these rulers, however genuine their respect for the city of Constantinople and for its supreme authorities, were always careful to safeguard their own political prerogatives, and anxious, within the limits allowed them by their Mongol overlords in the thirteenth and fourteenth centuries, to be seen to exercise their national sovereignty. Some indication of their attitude to the emperor has nevertheless been preserved in late medieval documents. At the turn of the thirteenth century a Russian ruler is stated to have borne the Byzantine court title "steward of the imperial table"—a sign at least of his recognition of the emperor's right to bestow such titles on client princes; and the same ruler is said to have conveyed his "reverent homage" to the Emperor Andronicus II.[31] Although the servility of this form of address may reflect the wishful thinking of the Byzantine author who records this event, the authenticity of the title need not perhaps be questioned. Our next piece of evidence comes from the mid-fourteenth century. In a letter to Symeon, the grand prince of Moscow, dated September 1347, the Emperor John Cantacuzenus wrote: "Yes, the empire of the Romans, as well as the most holy great church of God [i.e. the patriarchate of Constantinople] is—as you yourself have written—the source of all piety and the teacher of law and sanctification."[32] This clearly implies the existence of an earlier, not extant, letter written by the Russian sovereign to the Byzantine authorities, in which he explicitly acknowledged the emperor's legislative authority over Russia. And in 1452, a year before the fall of Constantinople, the grand prince of Moscow, Basil II, wrote to the last emperor of Byzantium, Constantine XI, in these terms: "You have received your great imperial sceptre, your patrimony, in order to confirm all the Orthodox Christians of your realm and to render great assistance to our Russian dominion and to all our religion."[33] The idea that the emperor enjoys certain prerogatives in Russia, though veiled in diplomatic language, is clearly apparent in these two texts. The nature of these prerogatives was not specified in any treaty or agreement. But their substance was defined in the Byzantine collections of canon and imperial law which enjoyed great authority in Russia, and indeed throughout Eastern Europe, in the Middle Ages; and the primates of the Russian Church, who were the guardians and interpreters of this law, could be expected, especially when they were Byzantine citizens, to instil in their flock not only a reverence for the "oecumenical church" (as the patriarchate of Constantinople was called by the Russians of the time)[34] but also a respect for the emperor's supreme position in Christendom. Precise constitutional notions, it has already been pointed out, cannot helpfully be used to define the political relations of the different parts of the Byzantine Commonwealth to its centre in Constantinople. In practice the Russian sovereigns would certainly never have tolerated, except in ecclesiastical matters, any direct interference of the emperor in the internal affairs of their principalities; and their relationship to the *basileus* was something different from their very tangible allegiance to the khans of the Golden Horde who, between 1240 and 1480, imposed tribute and conferred investiture upon them. At the

344

same time there are strong grounds for believing that from the conversion of Russia to Christianity to the fall of Byzantium, the Russian authorities, with the sole exception of Basil I of Muscovy, acknowledged, at least tacitly, that the emperor was the head of the Christian Commonwealth, that as such he possessed by divine right a measure of jurisdiction over Russia, and that, in the words of the Patriarch Antony, "it is not possible for Christians to have the church and not to have the empire".

We have no direct knowledge of the effect which the patriarch's letter had on Basil I. It is likely that the emperor's name was restored before long to the diptychs of the Russian Church; for already in 1398 the Muscovite government sent a large sum of money to the Emperor Manuel II for the defence of Constantinople. And the deference with which, as we have seen, Basil I's successor addressed the *basileus* strongly suggests that, so long as Constantinople remained in Christian hands, the Russians never again revolted against the ordered hierarchy of the Byzantine Commonwealth.

This survey of Russo-Byzantine relations in the late Middle Ages will have indicated that the attitude of the Russians to Byzantium was in this period markedly ambiguous: their resentment at the discreditable methods to which the Byzantine authorities resorted in the appointment of the Russian metropolitans did not inhibit them from contributing generous sums of money for the architectural and military needs of Constantinople; and Basil I's ill-tempered gesture of bravado against the emperor's authority should not obscure the fact that his predecessors and his successor recognized the oecumenical jurisdiction of the *basileus*. This emotional polarity in the Russian image of "the Greeks", this complex amalgam of attraction and repulsion, can be traced through the entire history of Russia's relations with the empire. Some of its earlier symptoms have already been described. A curious later example is provided by a bilingual glossary and phrase book compiled in the fifteenth century by an anonymous Russian traveller who recorded some of his impressions of the strange Byzantine environment. He had nothing but respect for "the wise Greek language" which he was trying so hard to learn; but on the whole, he noted, the Greeks "are difficult people, unfriendly and unloving".[35]

Yet in Russia, as in the other countries of the commonwealth, the accumulated legacy of political distrust and the personal antipathy which the Byzantines so often inspired paled before the vision of what Byzantium stood for in the things of the mind and the spirit. The immensity of the debt which these countries owed to its civilization was everywhere apparent. Religion and law, literature and art, bore witness to the fact that the East European nations had been and still were the pupils of East Rome. Nowhere outside the empire was reverence for the city of Constantinople more deeply or widely felt than in medieval Russia. Nowhere as movingly as in the writings of the Russian pilgrims who journeyed there in the late Middle Ages was the belief revealed that this city was the fountainhead of the true faith.[36]

This vision of Constantinople as the New Jerusalem was tarnished and partially obscured in Russia as a result of the Council of Florence, which marks a turning point in the relations between Muscovy and Byzantium. On 6 July 1439 this council proclaimed the union between the Eastern and the Western Churches. By signing—with one dissentient voice—the Act of Union, the Greek delegation, headed by the Emperor John VIII and comprising several distinguished theologians, formally committed the Byzantine Church to the acceptance of those Roman doctrines, including that of papal supremacy, which had hitherto been rejected in Eastern Christendom. There is no doubt that their readiness to subscribe to them was partly motivated by the hope of securing military aid in the West against the growing Turkish threat to Constantinople. The Council of Florence was also attended by a Russian delegation, led by Isidore, metropolitan of Kiev and All Russia, who three years earlier had been appointed by the patriarch to the Muscovite see. In 1441 Isidore, an enthusiastic supporter of the union and now a cardinal and apostolic legate, returned to Moscow. His liturgical commemoration of Pope Eugenius IV exacerbated the Muscovites' anger at their metropolitan's behaviour at the council, which they condemned as a betrayal of the Orthodox faith. By order of the Grand Prince Basil II, Isidore was arrested and imprisoned. A year later he escaped abroad, perhaps with the connivance of the Russian government. Muscovy thus openly rejected the Union of Florence.

To the Muscovites, who consistently opposed doctrinal agree-

346

ment with the Latin Church, the acceptance of the Florentine Union by the highest authorities of Byzantium came as a severe shock. Four and a half centuries of unwavering loyalty to the church of Constantinople had left them unprepared for the sudden discovery that, as the Russian primate expressed it tersely in 1451, "the emperor is not the right one, and the patriarch is not the right one".[37] Their embarrassment was increased by the urgent need to find a successor to the deposed Isidore; and so, once again, the question of the metropolitan see of All Russia became the crucial issue in the relations between Russia and Byzantium.

After Isidore's flight from Moscow three courses of action were open to the Russians: they could break off canonical relations with the patriarch, on the grounds that by accepting the Union of Florence he had become a heretic, and proceed to elect a new primate themselves; or they could take the latter action without rejecting the patriarch's jurisdiction, in the hope that the Byzantine authorities could eventually be induced to sanction the election; or else they could play for time, pretend to ignore the union between the Greek and Latin churches, and meanwhile seek permission from Constantinople to elect and consecrate their metropolitan in Russia, in the hope that the anti-unionist party in Byzantium, known to be on the ascendant, would soon secure control of the government. The first course was too revolutionary for the conservative and law-abiding Muscovite churchmen, and there is no evidence to suggest that the Russians in 1441 seriously contemplated a move which would have cast them adrift from their mother church. In fact they resorted to the third, and later to the second, course of action. In 1441 Basil II wrote a letter to the patriarch, saluting him as the supreme head of Orthodox Christians and asking, with courtesy and diffidence, for a written authorization to have a metropolitan elected in Russia by a national council of bishops. And at the end of his skilfully argued letter the Russian sovereign declared his intention to maintain the close relations which had always existed between Christian Russia and "the holy emperor" and to continue to recognize the patriarch's jurisdiction.[38]

The fate of his letter is unknown; indeed there is no certainty that it was even sent. For the next seven years Russia remained without a metropolitan. For Basil these were difficult years: he had a civil war on his hands, and for several months in 1445 he was a prisoner of the Tatars. The next move to end the impasse was made in December 1448, when a council of Russian bishops, convoked by Basil II, elected the native Bishop Iona as metropolitan of All Russia.

The die was cast; Iona's consecration was a direct challenge to the patriarch's authority. It seems that the Russians, even at this late hour, were extremely perturbed by the consequences of their own audacity. An influential minority in Muscovy held that Iona's appointment was uncanonical. For more than three years the Russians awaited the Byzantine response in anxious silence. Finally, in 1452 Basil II wrote a last letter to Constantinople, addressed to the Emperor Constantine XI. It was as respectful in tone as his letter of 1441: indeed, he went as far as to acknowledge that the emperor possessed by virtue of his office a degree of authority over Russia. But, behind the now expert phraseology of Muscovite diplomacy, two new notes are sounded in this letter: self-justification for what was felt to be, even in Russia, an act of ecclesiastical insubordination; and an allusion, veiled but pointed, to the fact that a considerable section of Byzantine society remained strongly opposed to the government's unionist policy:

> We beseech your Sacred Majesty not to think that what we have done we did out of arrogance, nor to blame us for not writing to your Sovereignty beforehand; we did this from dire necessity, not from pride or arrogance. In all things we hold to the ancient Orthodox faith transmitted to us, and so we shall continue to do . . . until the end of time. And our Russian Church, the holy metropolitanate of Russia, requests and seeks the blessing of the holy, oecumenical, catholic, and apostolic church of St. Sophia, the Wisdom of God, and is obedient to her in all things according to the ancient faith; and our father, the Lord Iona, metropolitan of Kiev and All Russia, likewise requests from her all manner of blessing and union, except for the present recently appeared disagreements.[39]

This final attempt of the Russians to square the circle by reconciling their traditional loyalty to the church and emperor of Byzantium with their unwillingness to remain dependent on a unionist patriarch, was soon rendered obsolete by rapidly moving events. On 5 April 1453 Mehmet II laid siege to Constantinople, and on 29 May the city fell. The Union of Florence, never popular with the majority of its citizens, collapsed with the Byzantine

348

Empire, and the Greek Church reverted to Orthodoxy. Basil II's letter remained unsent in the state archieves of Moscow. The theological obstacle to Russia's dependence on the see of Constantinople had disappeared, only to be replaced by a political one, which in the eyes of the power-conscious Muscovite rulers proved the more insuperable of the two: its church was now in the power of a Muslim state, and its patriarch received his investiture from the Ottoman sultan. And so the Russian Church retained the autonomous status it had acquired *de facto* in 1448, a status which in 1589, by common consent of the other Orthodox churches, was converted to that of an autocephalous patriarchate.

This final chapter in the history of Russo-Byzantine relations, which covers the twelve years preceding the empire's fall, will have illustrated their remarkable solidity. Of all the East European peoples who owed allegiance to the church of Constantinople, the Muscovites were by far the most hostile to Latin Christianity; they would never have countenanced those diplomatic flirtations with Rome to which the Bulgarian and Serbian rulers periodically resorted. The Greeks, by signing the Union of Florence, had in their view betrayed Orthodoxy. Yet even then, the Russians did everything in their power to avoid breaking their canonical dependence on the patriarchate and continued to ascribe even to a unionist emperor the pre-eminent position in Christendom. The Byzantines had done their work in Russia very thoroughly: through all the strains and stresses which imperilled the relations between Moscow and Constantinople, the Russians retained, so long as the empire existed, their loyalty to the commonwealth.

Yet this picture requires some qualification. Something undoubtedly changed after the Council of Florence in the Russians' traditional attitude to Byzantium. During the next twenty years a new interpretation of Russia's relationship to the empire slowly developed in Moscow. Its precise antecedents are obscure, and it was consciously formulated only after the fall of Constantinople; yet the historical myth which sustained it seems to have acquired body and substance between 1441 and 1453. The premises of this myth were simple in the extreme: the Greeks, by signing the Decree of Florence on terms imposed by the pope, betrayed the Orthodox faith, and the emperor and the patriarch fell into heresy; the main cause of this regrettable lapse was the Greeks' fondness for money, for they were shamelessly bribed by the pope; by contrast, the Orthodox faith is preserved in Russia, thanks to Basil II, who exposed the traitor Isidore and confirmed the true religion of his ancestors. The contrast between the tragic inconstancy of the Byzantines and the inspired faithfulness of the Russians enabled the historical myth to be carried a step further: for it was tempting to assume that Moscow and not Constantinople was now the providential centre of the true Christian faith. We do not know when this step was first taken, and when the Muscovites evolved this new conception of Russia, no longer on the periphery of the Byzantine Commonwealth, but now the very centre and heart of Orthodox Christendom. As we shall see later, this view, which was closely linked with the development of post-medieval Russian nationalism, was to provide the ideological foundation for the theory of "Moscow the Third Rome". But it must be emphasized that the Muscovite ideologues of Basil II were not yet ready to draw these conclusions from their interpretation of the Greek sell-out at Florence and from their belief in the historic destiny of their own nation.

NOTES

1. The pope's letters to Kaloyan, to the archbishop of Trnovo and to other Bulgarian officials: *PL* 214, cols. 825, 1113–15, 1116–18; 215, cols. 156–8, 277–87, 292–4, 295–6, 705–6, 1162. Kaloyan's letters to the pope: *PL* 214, cols. 1112–13; 215, cols. 155–6, 287–8, 290–2, 551–3.

2. V. N. Zlatarski, *Istoriya na bŭlgarskata dŭrzhava prez srednite vekove*, iii (Sofia, 1940), pp. 587–96.

3. I. Dujčev, *Iz starata bŭlgarska knizhnina*, ii (Sofia, n.d.), pp. 40–2, 320–30.

4. George Acropolites, *Historia*, ed. A. Heisenberg, i (Leipzig, 1903), pp. 43, 64.

5. Ostrogorsky, *Staatenhierarchie*, p. 51, n. 16; F. Dölger, *Byzanz und die europäische Staatenwelt* (Ettal, 1953), pp. 156–7.

6. I. Dujčev, *The Miniatures of the Chronicle of Manasses* (Sofia, 1963), pl. 1, 33.

7. B. Filov, *Miniatyurite na Londonskoto evangelie na Tsar' Ivan Aleksandra* (Sofia, 1934), pl. 136.

8. Constantine Manasses, *Compendium Chronicum*, verses 2546–2552, ed. I. Bekker (Bonn, 1837), pp. 110–11.

9. *Die slavische Manasses-Chronik*, nach der Ausgabe von J. Bogdan (Munich, 1966), pp. 99–100.

10. George Pachymeres, *De Michaele Palaeologo*, v, ed. I. Bekker, i (Bonni 1835), pp. 350–2.

11. K. N. Sathas, Μεσαιωνικὴ Βιβλιοθήκη, i (Venice, 1872), p. 173.

12. Archbishop Danilo, *Životi kraljeva i arhiepiskopa srpskih*, ed. Dj. Daničić (Zagreb, 1866), pp. 126, 141, 164, 168.

13. See above, p. 281.

14. G. Ostrogorsky, *Pour l'histoire de la féodalité byzantine* (Brussels, 1954), pp. 187–97.

15. K. Jireček, *Geschichte der Serben*, i (Gotha, 1911), p. 386, n.3.

16. Nicephorus Gregoras, *Byzantina historia*, xv, 1, vol. ii, p. 747.

17. A. V. Soloviev, *Odabrani spomenici srpskog prava* (Belgrade, 1926), p. 128.

18. A. Soloviev and V. Mošin, *Grčke povelje srpskih vladara* (Belgrade, 1936), pp. 28–34.

19. "Actes de Chilandar, publiés par L. Petit", *Vizantiisky Vremennik*, xvii (1911), p. 292.

20. J. Bogdan, "Ein Beitrag zur bulgarischen und serbischen Geschichtschreibung", *Archiv für slavische Philologie*, xiii (1891), p. 534.

21. J. Meyendorff, "Projets de concile oecuménique en 1367", *DOP*, xiv (1960), pp. 170–1.

22. Demetrius Cydones, *Oratio pro subsidio Latinorum*, PG 154, col. 972.

23. Nicephorus Gregoras, *Hist. Byz.*, xv, 11, vol. ii, p. 790.

24. Gregoras, *Hist. Byz.*, xxviii, 34–36, vol. iii, pp. 198–200.

25. *Polnoe Sobranie Russkikh Letopisey*, xi (Moscow, 1965), p. 168.

26. *Acta Patriarchatus Constantinopolitani*, ed. F. Miklosich and I. Müller, is, (Vienna, 1862), p. 361.

27. Gregoras, *Hist. Byz.*, xxxvi, 41, vol. iii, p. 521.

28. *Acta Patriarchatus Constantinopolitani*, ii, p. 14.

29. Ibid., pp. 188–92; Engl. transl. E. Barker, *Social and Political Thought in Byzantium* (Oxford, 1957), pp. 194–6.

30. Ostrogorsky, *History of the Byzantine State*, p. 554.

31. H. Haupt, "Neue Beiträge zu den Fragmenten des Dio Cassius", *Hermes*, xiv (1879), p. 445.

32. *Acta Patriarchatus Constantinopolitani*, i, p. 263.

33. *Russkaya Istoricheskaya Biblioteka*, vi (St. Petersburg, 1880), col. 577.

34. For the expression "oecumenical Church" see F. von Lilienfeld, "Russland und Byzanz im 14. and 15. Jahrhundert", *Proceedings of the XIIIth International Congress of Byzantine Studies*, p. 110.

35. M. Vasmer, *Ein russisch-byzantinisches Gesprächbuch* (Leipzig, 1922), p. 25, ll. 341–2, p. 26, ll. 376–9, p. 27, l. 384; L. S. Kovtun, *Russkaya leksikografiya epokhi srednevekov'ya* (Moscow–Leningrad, 1963), pp. 326–89.

36. *Itinéraires russes en Orient,* French transl. B. de Khitrowo, I, i (Geneva, 1889).

37. *Russkaya Istoricheskaya Biblioteka,* vi, col. 559.

38. Ibid., cols. 525–36.

39. Ibid., cols. 583–4.

9

Factors in Cultural Diffusion

The reader of the preceding chapters will now be familiar with the multiform and changing relations which bound the East European countries to the Byzantine Empire during the Middle Ages. The time has come to draw together the scattered threads of our study, and to look more closely at the Byzantine Commonwealth as a whole. We must consider its structure and function, the forces which kept its different parts together, and the strains and stresses which at times diminished its cohesion. The political links between its peripheral areas and its centre in Constantinople will continue to receive attention. But the emphasis from now on will be mainly on cultural factors. For it is in the realm of culture that the nature and vitality of this international society, with its relatively unified outlook and rich diversity of historical experience, can be most clearly perceived.

If an educated citizen of Byzantium had been asked to define the foundations of his empire's hegemony over the peoples of Eastern Europe, he would have pointed without hesitation to two: the Orthodox Church and the emperor's universal sovereignty. If, furthermore, he were concerned with foreign policy or international relations, and thus familiar with the political philosophy contained in *The Book of Ceremonies*, he might have elaborated these points by referring to the existence of a hierarchy of subordinate states revolving in obedient concord round the throne of the supreme autocrat in Constantinople, whose authority, in its rhythm and order, reproduced the harmonious movement given to the universe by its Creator. His idea of the Byzantine *oikoumene* would have had strong religious overtones: for, as the emperor was

353

God's vicegerent on earth, and the empire the pattern and prefiguration of the heavenly kingdom, so was this supranational Christian community the God-appointed custodian of the one true Orthodox faith, destined to fulfil this role until the last days and the coming of Antichrist. The modern historian can detect in these ideas, which provided the ideological basis and moral justification for Byzantium's foreign policy, the threefold influence of Rome, Hellenism and Christianity. The egocentric phantasy entertained by so many Byzantines that their empire was, in principle, co-extensive with the civilized universe, was borrowed from the Romans, and the name *Rhomaioi*, which they proudly applied to themselves, epitomized their claim to the exclusive heritage of the Roman imperial tradition. So firmly rooted was this concept of the universal empire, centred in Constantinople, that Byzantium's bitterest enemies in Eastern Europe implicitly accepted it: it shaped, we have seen, the imperialist designs of Symeon of Bulgaria, who styled himself "Emperor of the Bulgarians and the Romans"; and the analogous title of "Emperor of Serbia and Romania", usurped by Stephen Dušan, was based on the same axiom that there could be but one Orthodox Empire in Christendom. It is not surprising that the imperial title assumed by the German kings was treated in Byzantium with angry contempt. In 968, according to Liutprand of Cremona, when the papal legates came to Constantinople bearing a letter addressed to "the emperor of the Greeks", in which the pope referred to Otto I as "the august emperor of the Romans", the Byzantines could not contain their indignation:

> "The audacity of it" they cried, "to call the universal emperor of the Romans, the one and only Nicephorus, the great, the august 'emperor of the Greeks', and to style a poor barbaric creature 'emperor of the Romans'! O sky! O earth! O sea! What shall we do with these scoundrels and criminals?"[1]

The offensive epithet "barbaric" applied by the Byzantines to the German emperor leads us into a different world of ideas. The barbarians were in their eyes those tribes and nations which dwelt in outer darkness beyond the confines of the empire, and whose culture, religion and way of life placed them outside the *oikoumene*. The attitude of the Byzantines to these lesser breeds without the law contributed as much to the theory that underlay their

354

foreign policy as the Roman doctrine of the empire's universality. For the very existence of the barbarians was a scandalous breach of the emperor's sovereignty. And so the Byzantines, with their characteristically Greek tendency to rationalize natural phenomena, were driven to explain and justify these limitations of the emperor's universal authority: the barbarians, they argued, may today be outside the empire's hegemony, or in revolt against it; but ideally and potentially they were still its subjects; if their lands remained outside the *oikoumene*, this was the result of God's permissive will, of the Divine *oikonomia*, and some day they would be induced to pay homage to their legitimate sovereign.

This notion of the "barbarian", and the very word, are Greek in origin. In the classical period the Greeks applied the term *barbaroi* to the people who spoke alien and incomprehensible tongues and whose way of thinking and behaving was un-Greek. In the Hellenistic age that term acquired a new emphasis, designating those who lived outside the community of Greek culture. It was in this cultural context that the Byzantines adopted the concept of "barbarian". The East Roman Empire was made up of too many different races for any meaningful distinction to be possible on ethnic grounds between the *Rhomaios* and the barbarian. The Byzantines, it is true, still called the non-Greek languages "barbarian"; and often affected to despise them for their uncouthness and cacophony. But the distinctive mark of the *Rhomaios* was membership of the Orthodox Church and allegiance to the emperor. The barbarian was now the pagan, neither directly subject to the emperor's laws nor, through membership of the Byzantine Commonwealth, indirectly to his sovereignty. The pagan who accepted Orthodox Christianity ceased, in theory, to be a barbarian. This, according to a seventh century writer, was the case of the Bulgar ruler Kovrat;[2] and a Byzantine hagiographer, writing about the year 1300, made this point still clearer: "The Lord who has created being out of nothing and has called forth the children of Abraham from stones can also out of a barbarian make a saint."[3] But even this theoretical acceptance of Christianity's redeeming power sometimes proved too explicit for the arrogant pharisaism of the Byzantines: not only was the Western emperor, the pope's "beloved spiritual son", denounced by them as a "bar-

355

barian"; they occasionally applied this term even to Orthodox peoples, especially when they so far forgot their duty of obedience to the emperor as to make war upon him, as the Russians did in 1043. In an endeavour, perhaps, to reconcile their belief in the inherent superiority of the Greek-speaking *Rhomaioi* with the accepted doctrine that all Christian peoples are equal in the sight of God, the Byzantines sometimes used the term "semi-barbarians" (*mixobarbaroi*) to describe those nations and individuals whose origins or behaviour showed that they were imperfectly assimilated into the East Roman cultural community. The word could be applied either to Byzantine citizens who were forgetting their civilized habits and becoming contaminated by contact with real "barbarians", or to foreigners who had gone some way towards absorbing Greek civilization. As an example of the first type we could cite the imperial frontier troops on the lower Danube in the eleventh century; a likely example of the second type is Symeon of Bulgaria, whose diligent studies in Constantinople earned him the nickname of "the half-Greek".

The Roman idea of the universal empire and the Greek, or rather Hellenistic, concept of "barbarians" were combined in Byzantium's foreign policy with a third element which gave this policy a sense of purpose and a moral foundation. This element was derived from the Judaeo-Christian tradition. The Byzantines believed that the political organization of this world is part of God's universal plan and is closely bound up with the history of man's salvation. As the universal structure of the Roman Empire had providentially paved the way for the victorious advance of the Christian faith, so were the *Rhomaioi*, the chosen people dedicated to the service of Christ by the Emperor Constantine, to reap where the First Rome had sown, and to bring the teaching of the Gospel to all the nations of the earth. So the *pax Romana* was equated with the *pax Christiana*, and the empire's foreign policy became intimately associated with the missionary work of the Byzantine Church. Of this association we have already encountered many examples; and it is seldom possible to tell, in any given instance, whether the missionaries sent from Constantinople were acting primarily as agents of East Roman imperialism, and how far they were capable of subordinating the empire's political interests to the spiritual welfare of their barbarian converts:

doubtless this distinction would have seemed to them, and to those who sent them, quite unreal.

These basic principles of Byzantium's foreign policy were implemented through a programme of diplomacy whose intricate and recurrent pattern we have learnt to recognize: to defend the empire's borders by nipping in the bud the attacks of the barbarians from beyond the Danube; to extend as far as possible the boundaries of Byzantium's political and cultural hegemony by creating beyond the borders a chain of client states, whose loyalty would be ensured by acceptance of the religion and of the political supremacy of the emperor in Constantinople; these were surely the unchanging aims of Byzantine policy in Eastern Europe. As for the methods used to induce the barbarians to associate themselves with the empire, they varied according to circumstances. The simplest, and one frequently used until the financial crisis of the eleventh century, was money. In the belief that every man has his price, the imperial governments from Justinian I to Basil II paid out considerable sums to their East European neighbours. In many cases this money was undoubtedly tribute, extorted by the barbarians at the point of the sword. But the Byzantines, seeking perhaps to exorcize the bitter humiliation caused by their military failures, preferred to regard these contributions as a form of imperial bounty bestowed as a reward for services which its recipients had rendered, or would render, to the empire. Thus tribute became a further means of associating the barbarians with the empire. This association was also expressed by the bestowal upon their rulers of titles taken from the hierarchy of the imperial court. This policy had three principal aims: to flatter the vanity of the satellites of Byzantium; to bind them politically to the empire; and to determine, to the satisfaction of the protocol-minded Byzantines, the rank occupied by a particular ruler and his people within the commonwealth. Other methods, such as the permission occasionally granted to barbarians to settle on actual or putative imperial territory, and the bestowal of Byzantine brides and insignia upon their rulers, had a similar aim.

On the home front no effort was spared to impress the barbarian rulers, or their envoys, with the power and majesty of the empire. The high officials who directed the Empire's foreign affairs—the master of the offices and, after the eighth century, the master of

357

ceremonies and the logothete of the course—knew how to combine elaborate pageantry with the requirements of military security. Historians are understandably fond of citing Liutprand's famous description of an imperial audience in the palace in 949: the immense throne which by some hidden mechanism would suddenly levitate to the ceiling, with the emperor upon it; the gilded tree with its singing birds of bronze; the mechanical lions which roared and beat the ground with their tails.[4] It may well be that this display of Byzantine technological skill overawed the envoys of the less sophisticated nations of Eastern Europe. But the evidence suggests that they were at least as impressed when shown the buildings in Constantinople, and especially the church of St. Sophia.

We have encountered in the course of this study a number of technical terms used by Byzantine writers to describe the status of various East European peoples associated with the empire. The Russians, after their first conversion in the 860s, were termed *hypekooi* ("subjects") and *proxenoi* ("public friends") of Byzantium.[5] In the twelfth century the Russian princes of Suzdal' and Galicia were designated respectively as the emperor's *symmachos* ("ally") and *hypospondos* (literally "under a treaty");[6] the term *symmachos* (plural *symmachoi*) was also applied to the Russians and the Uzes in the eleventh century, to the Hungarians in the twelfth, and to the Bulgarian ruler in the thirteenth;[7] while the word *hypospondos* (plural *hypospondoi*) was likewise used in respect of the Caucasian Tzani in the sixth century, and of Bulgaria after its conquest by Basil II.[8] Three other terms were used in a similar context: *enspondos* ("ally", cf. *spondai*, "a solemn treaty"), applied to the Crimean Goths in the sixth century and to the Bulgarian ruler who is also termed *symmachos*;[9] its equivalent *misthoforos* ("mercenary"), applied to the ruler of the Utigurs in the sixth century;[10] and *katekoos* ("obedient", plural *katekooi*), used of the Tzani in the sixth century, and of the Serbs in the twelfth.[11]

All these technical terms, when considered within their context, seem to have much the same significance. At least three of them, *enspondoi*, *hypospondoi* and *symmachoi*, were applied by writers of the early Byzantine period to the *foederati* and the *socii populi Romani*, autonomous subjects of the Roman Empire who, by virtue of a treaty (*foedus*) concluded with Rome, guarded its fron-

358

tiers in exchange for a regular subsidy, imperial protection and the right of self-government.[12] It may be unwise, in view of the linguistic conservatism of the Byzantines, to attach too much constitutional importance to the recurrence of these terms. Yet, if the essential continuity of Romano-Byzantine institutions is borne in mind, it will surely appear significant that the Byzantines, when faced with the problem of defining the status of their East European satellites, could do no better than to resort to the old terminology of Roman administration. This being so, the position occupied by these client peoples within the Byzantine Commonwealth may to some extent at least be understood in the light of the Roman concept of *foederatio*, which defined the status of the empire's subject-allies. This concept had the advantage of enabling Byzantium to safeguard its universalist claims, without being obliged to press them too far; while the "barbarians", gaining a new prestige from their legal association with the empire, could still preserve their political autonomy.

The Roman notion of *foederatio* is thus a more helpful criterion for viewing the relations between Byzantium and the peoples of Eastern Europe than either the Western medieval concept of suzerainty and vassalage, or the modern distinction between sovereign and dependent states. In the last resort, however, any attempt to define these relations in precise legal terms will probably oversimplify and distort their true nature. One may suggest that the difficulty which some historians have experienced of explaining how the political independence of the medieval peoples of Eastern Europe could be reconciled with their recognition of the emperor's supremacy will appear less intractable if their links with the empire are viewed not from the standpoint of modern interstate relations, nor in terms of a conflict between "nationalism" and "imperialism", but in the context of the Byzantine Commonwealth, that supranational community of Christian states of which Constantinople was the centre and Eastern Europe the peripheral domain.

II

The centre and the periphery of this area were connected by the routes of communication and trade which were described in the

359

first chapter of this book. The Byzantine Empire, which was a sea-power during much of its history, inherited the trade relations which since remote antiquity had linked the Mediterranean with Asia and continental Europe. Destined—or condemned—by its geographical position, astride the great arteries of commerce and migration, to play the role of a world power, Byzantium was faced with the inescapable fact that these ancient trade routes opened into the Eastern Mediterranean. Naturally, therefore, in response to the northward and eastward flow of trade from the Black Sea, the Aegean and the Adriatic, the continental peoples of Europe and Asia used these channels to advance towards the Mediterranean; and if, as often happened, they controlled the inland extremities of these trade routes, they were tempted to possess themselves of their points of exit into the sea. Thus a recurrent theme in the history of the Balkans, in medieval and modern times, has been the effort of invaders from Central Europe and of the slavs from the northern part of the peninsula to descend the valleys of the Maritsa, the Strymon and the Vardar, and to seize control of the mouths of these rivers on the Aegean coast. Similarly the Vikings in the early Middle Ages used the Baltic–Black Sea river route as a highway of expansion towards the Mediterranean, and the Eastern Slavs later fought to retain control of the lower Dnieper in order to keep open the main channel of communication with Byzantium. These migrations of peoples were, we have seen, followed by a reverse movement from south to north, instigated by the statesmen in Constantinople with the aim of taming and civilizing them. The alternate movements of commodities, men and ideas to and from the Mediterranean world, which have been compared to the rhythmic pulsations of the living heart,[13] brought the periphery of this world into close contact with its centre on the Bosphorus, and carried the civilization of Byzantium up rivers, across plains and over seas to the farthest borderlands of Eastern Europe.

The analogy between the alternating current flowing to and from the Mediterranean and the beating of a heart may help us to understand better the nature of this process of cultural diffusion. For their part, the East European peoples were usually not content merely to invade Byzantine territory, nor even to send their merchants and goods to the empire's maritime cities. As well as land

and objects of luxury, they often sought to acquire the empire's civilization. Their willingness to "reach out" for it shows that the process of borrowing was seldom, if ever, a passive one. Thus the conversion of many an East European nation was not just the result of the empire's missionary and diplomatic initiative: often it was preceded by the dispatch of envoys to Constantinople, with the aim of gathering information on Byzantine Christianity or of negotiating the terms of its acceptance on behalf of their pagan sovereign. The story of the embassies sent by Vladimir of Russia to verify the religious claims of his neighbours, however fictional some of its details may be, illustrates vividly the barbarians' active quest for a higher form of culture. Furthermore, however strong the initial impulse to accept *in toto* a culture associated with superior strength, wealth and intellectual eminence, and loaded with prestige, the East European societies never absorbed Byzantine civilization wholesale. In every case it was adapted in its new peripheral environment to local needs and conditions, through a process of selection whereby its various elements were accepted, rejected or transformed. This process, which cultural anthropologists call diffusion or acculturation (according to whether they consider the migration of individual cultural traits or the first-hand contact between cultures as a whole), is one of singular complexity, and the historian, with the evidence and methods available to him, can scarcely hope to grasp and define it in its entirety. The documents at his disposal are seldom unambiguous. Societies are usually so immersed in their own traditions that they notice the differences between themselves and their neighbours much more than they do the similarities; except for conspicuous features, such as religion, they tend to play down and soon to forget the foreign source of their culture: and so it is not surprising that they frequently fail to record their cultural borrowings. Only too often, as Fernand Braudel has observed of the history of cultural diffusion, we lack the addresses and the labels, and sometimes the contents and the wrapping as well.[14] For the present, we must be content to note the creative role which the "receiving" countries of Eastern Europe played in the diffusion of Byzantine civilization; and attempt to identify, whenever possible in concrete instances, some of the factors involved in this process of creative borrowing.

The most obvious of these factors is the antecedent culture of the borrower. For example, the ethnic dualism which was still manifest in Bulgaria and Russia prior to their conversion to Christianity undoubtedly affected the speed with which Byzantine culture was transplanted to these countries. In both cases the ruling minority, the Turkic Bulgars and the Vikings, were attached to their pagan religion, and the subject people, the Slavs, had for some time been subjected to the influence of Christianity. Yet if this racial dichotomy retarded the Christianization of Bulgaria, it probably hastened Russia's; for the Old Bulgar society, conservative and continental in outlook, had far more affinity with the life of the Eurasian steppes than with that of the Mediterranean, and hence remained for long refractory to the influence of Byzantium; while the outward-looking, seafaring and commercially minded Vikings, constantly travelling between Novgorod, Kiev and Constantinople, soon became carriers of Byzantine ideas and customs. Thus the Varangian community in Kiev already included many Christians some fifty years before Russia's official conversion. By contrast, in ninth century Bulgaria the Old Bulgar Turkic clans formed the spearhead of the militant anti-Christian movement.

These carriers, agents of cultural diffusion, are another factor to be considered when studying the transmission of this civilization to the peoples of Eastern Europe. The Vikings serving in the retinue of the princes of Kiev and in the Varangian Guard in Constantinople did not merely, in the course of their journeys, carry luxury goods and religious beliefs from Byzantium to Russia. They also brought with them the elements of an articulate heroic tradition, not unlike that of the Norse sagas, which may well have partly originated in the Mediterranean world. Significant traces of this tradition have been preserved in the *Russian Primary Chronicle*.[15] Other examples of cultural intermediaries have been encountered in the course of this study: the Slavs of Macedonia, long exposed to cultural influences spreading north from Thessalonica, as well as the Byzantine prisoners of war captured by the khans, did much to acquaint the Bulgarians with Greek Christianity; and the cities of Dalmatia, which effectively until the eleventh century and to a limited extent until the late twelfth ensured the empire's presence on the Adriatic coast, played the same role in relation to the Serbs and Croats of the interior. Maritime cities such as these played an important part as cultural intermediaries. In the seaports of Eastern Thrace—Mesembria, Anchialus, Develtus and Sozopolis—, in the Greek cities of the Southern Crimea, above all in the cosmopolitan centres of Constantinople and Thessalonica, the peoples of Eastern Europe came into direct contact with the religion, art and literature of Byzantium. This was equally true of the international monastic foundations of the empire, especially Mount Athos and Mount Olympus in Bithynia, where monks from many East European lands read, copied and translated works of Byzantine religious and secular literature, which were then transmitted to their countrymen at home.

The study of cultural intermediaries can help to bring out the importance of the geographical factor in this process of diffusion. Seas, plains, river valleys and mountain passes were the channels through which the centres of Byzantine civilization sent out, like great searchlights, their beams of light to the most distant corners of Eastern Europe. These beams radiated from Constantinople up the Maritsa valley to Northern Thrace and the Bulgarian hinterland; from Thessalonica up the Vardar into Macedonia; from Dalmatia up the Zeta river to Southern Serbia, and up the Neretva to Herzegovina and Bosnia; up the Dnieper and its affluents to the Russian cities. The speed with which they travelled, and their intensity, were affected by distance and by physical barriers, by the latter more than the former. So long as the society and culture of the empire's northern neighbours remained on a primitive level, Byzantine influence was exerted upon them mainly at short range, across a frontier which, though never entirely closed, was still a frontier. But as the East European nations developed more complex and sophisticated cultures of their own, especially after the ninth century, distance began to play a diminishing role, and Byzantine cultural traits were carried directly or through intermediaries across large intervening expanses of land and sea. They were halted far more effectively by mountain barriers. Many a community that dwelt in or behind the more inaccessible mountains of the Balkan peninsula remained for centuries scarcely affected by their influence; and in these cases the diffusion of Byzantine civilization, especially when it was further slowed down or interrupted by the resistance of these peoples, resembled less the continuous beam of a searchlight than the faint glimmering of a distant star. The Pindus and the Rhodopes, for instance, were far less affected in the Middle Ages by Byzantine influences than the faraway city of Novgorod in Northern Russia.

The student of cultural diffusion must also take into account the social, political and economic conditions prevalent in the "receiving" countries. In the case of Eastern Europe the evidence of the sources is often slender, especially in the early phases of their encounter with Byzantium. We know little, for instance, about the immediate effects of their migrations upon the social and economic life of the peoples concerned. The Hungarians became a largely agricultural nation soon after their arrival in Central Europe, and this no doubt facilitated their conversion to Christianity. A similar transition from pastoral nomadism to a farming economy can be observed among the Bulgars after their migration from the South Russian steppes to the Balkans; and it is probable that this fundamental change of life weakened their society's resistance to the impact of Byzantium. A significant comment on their conversion was made by a tenth century Byzantine author: "the Bulgarians", he stated, "had become the adopted sons of our God, and had ... unlearnt the life of the waggon-dweller and nomad and had learnt instead the Gospel of Grace".[16] The empire's missionaries, at least, knew from experience that it was much harder to convert nomadic than settled peoples; and it is perhaps partly for this reason that the nomad always remained for the Byzantines the archetypal barbarian.

There is no doubt, furthermore, that Byzantine civilization was assimilated most rapidly and effectively in those countries which had evolved or were evolving a centralized form of government. The fragmented and politically inchoate *Sklaviniae* of the Balkans, and the East Slavonic tribes scattered over the territory that was later united by the Russian princes, were but faintly touched by its influence. But Boris of Bulgaria and Vladimir of Russia both ruled over realms with relatively well developed monarchical traditions, and were able therefore to impose new cultural and religious patterns upon their subjects by personal example and the use of force. Similarly, Byzantine Christianity began to have a strong impact on Hungary after its unification under the Árpád dynasty. As for Serbia, the Byzantinization of its culture and institutions acquired momentum only after the country had achieved political unity under a strong government in the late twelfth century, in the reign of Stephen Nemanja.

The relationship between the growth of monarchical institutions and conversion to Christianity was a complex and, in most of the cases cited above, a reciprocal one. For not only did political centralization pave the way for Byzantinization: the reverse was equally true. Christianity, together with the social ideology and material trappings that came with it, enabled the East European monarchs of the early Middle Ages to claim divine sanction for their sovereignty, to unite their subjects by the common profession of an exclusive faith, to exalt their own status by royal dress and state ceremonial modelled on the ritual of the imperial court, and through their newly gained association with Byzantium to increase their international prestige. Moreover, it was only by borrowing an ideology and a pattern of culture from abroad that they could hope, like the leaders of "developing countries" of today, to carry out the desired modernization of their societies. To implement their programme of reform these rulers were driven to rely not on the traditional aristocracies, whose archaic structures, tribal exclusiveness and conservative views made them unfit to serve as an instrument of change, but on other groups consisting of men open to the new ideas and devoted to their princes' policies. The resultant change in the governing élites and the increase in social mobility, which occurred in a number of East European countries in the early Middle Ages, can be detected most clearly in racially heterogeneous societies. In Bulgaria, for instance, Boris' conversion was followed by a repression of the Old Bulgar aristocracy and an attempt to entrust public offices to Slavs, the former subject-race, who had long been exposed to the influence of Byzantine Christianity. Similarly in Hungary the Slavs seem to have played an important role in the transformation of the Finno-Ugrian Magyars from nomads into farmers and in the religious conversion of the country.

As for the aristocracy of the newly converted countries, their attitude to the social changes which came with Byzantine cultural influences seems to have been ambivalent. On the one hand, the new religion threatened to strike at the root of their ancient privileges which had their origin and justification in the pagan way of life. On the other hand, the importation of goods from the empire satisfied their growing consumer needs and fondness for the luxuries of life, and enabled them to share with their sovereign in the social prestige attendant on greater wealth and education.

This ambiguous attitude to Byzantium and its exports is also apparent in another factor of great importance in the process of cultural diffusion: the human one. Unless we are prepared to give this factor its full weight, the process will appear abstract and mechanical, and we might be tempted to ascribe the desire of the East European élites to acquire the fruits of Byzantine civilization solely to self-interest. Such a conclusion would distort our understanding of a complex phenomenon, whose interwoven threads and dramatic overtones are of considerable historical interest. Yet it is not easy to disentangle these threads; and even if he is successful in this task, the historian may find himself in the end with a series of disconnected facts which have little meaning when viewed separately. He may wonder whether so subtle and elusive a phenomenon as the attitudes—emotional, moral, intellectual—of the East European peoples to Byzantium can ever be truly apprehended by the method of plucking individual threads from a rich and varied texture. But if he wishes to understand this phenomenon, he has, initially, no alternative to the method of analysis: he must consider specific instances of the reaction of these peoples to Byzantium, and attempt to classify them in the hope that a comprehensive picture will emerge at the end.

It is not surprising that Byzantine civilization, as it spread to the empire's neighbours, encountered some resistance. The social and moral values which it brought with it were often quite alien to the patterns of their inherited culture, and could hardly fail to provoke the distrust and fear of the traditionalists. On the basic plane of human feeling, this hostility was partly caused by the personal dislike which the Byzantines—the "Greeks", as the Slavs invariably called them—often provoked by their attitudes and behaviour. The exasperating self-righteousness of their foreign policy, and their pharisaic belief in the boundless superiority of the *Rhomaios* over the "barbarian" which their representatives abroad, such as Archbishop Theophylact of Ohrid, did so little to conceal, were not made to endear them to their East European proselytes. Their ecclesiastical policy was not always marked by the wise forbearance which prompted several emperors, notably in the Macedonian and Nicaean periods, to grant the Slavonic Churches a measure of self-government. Boris of Bulgaria turned to Rome because the patriarch of Constantinople had shown himself unresponsive to the aspirations of the Bulgarian Church. Even the Russians, who were far more respectful pupils of East Rome than the Balkan Slavs, came to resent the rigidness with which the patriarchs insisted on selecting their own candidates to the see of Kiev when they felt strong enough to do so, and to despise the ease with which, whenever the empire was weak, the Byzantine authorities yielded on this issue to Russian political or financial pressure. Byzantium's "great power" diplomacy, pursued with ruthless cunning, caused bitter resentment, not least among its victims in the Eurasian steppe. It is hardly surprising that the superior skill and dubious methods of its diplomatists instilled in its East European neighbours a suspicion of Byzantine motives and a conviction that the Greeks were political intriguers and not to be trusted. The aphorism "the Greeks have remained deceivers to the present day",[17] coined by a Russian chronicler of the eleventh or early twelfth century, was no doubt frequently and pointedly quoted, not only in medieval Russia.

A curious example of the distrust provoked by the Byzantines in Eastern Europe can be found in the constitution of the monastery of Bachkovo. This famous house was founded in 1083 in the Rhodope Mountains, south of Philippopolis, by a Georgian expatriate, Gregory Pacurianus (son of Bakuriani). A close associate of the Emperor Alexius Comnenus, Gregory had risen to the highest ranks in his service; in 1086, as commander-in-chief of the Byzantine armies in Europe, he was killed in a battle against the Pechenegs and the Paulicians. Yet this Caucasion immigrant seems to have had little affection for the citizens of the empire which he served with such distinction and which rewarded him so handsomely. His monastery's constitution, which was drawn up in Greek, Georgian, and perhaps also in Armenian, specified that Georgians were to be given preference over all other nationals seeking admission; more particularly, no Byzantine was to be admitted into the community, except for one secretary responsible for the monastery's relations with the local authorities: for the *Rhomaioi*, Gregory warns, "are violent, cunning and grasping men" who, given the chance would soon take possession of the monastery; "such things," he declares, "have often happened because of the simplicity and innocence of our nation. If this were not so, we [Georgians] would not have followed them [the Byzantines] as our teachers in the faith".[18]

On a deeper level of consciousness, the forceful introduction of Byzantine patterns into the pagan societies of Eastern Europe sometimes created an explosive situation, in which the accumulated anxieties provoked by the threat to the old ways of life were apt to erupt in sudden panic or despair. These anxieties may be observed in three successive stages of these societies' surrender to the impact of Byzantine civilization. At first this impact is perceived as a remote menace, as yet incapable of destroying the cherished traditions of the past: vigilance and occasional resort to social pressure are sufficient to keep it at bay. A situation of this kind seems to be implied in the words ascribed in the Russian chronicle to Prince Svyatoslav of Kiev, whom his mother Olga was trying to persuade to become a Christian: "How could I alone accept another religion? My retainers will laugh at me."[19] The fear of ridicule was in this case a strong enough weapon in the hands of the prince's military retinue to enforce his conformity to the old pagan way of life.

In the second stage of the encounter between the old and the new order the situation is more critical. The invasion of the traditional culture has already taken place; the pagan cults and beliefs have been outlawed by the newly converted rulers, and an intensive campaign of re-education has been started by the local authorities and their Byzantine advisers, with the avowed aim of replacing them by a new set of values: these, as we know from Boris' questions to the pope, could range over a considerable area of human belief and conduct, from Christian theology and marriage laws to details of dress and personal hygiene. At this point, when the old traditions, though in full retreat, still retain their appeal and the new imports have not yet been assimilated, the society is threatened with disaffection or schism. The adherents of the old culture, if unwilling to renounce it, can do one of two things: they can either stake their lives on a desperate bid to destroy the new order and its representatives; or sink into a state of passive despondency, in fruitless regret for bygone days. The

368

leaders of the Old Bulgar clans, who soon after Boris' baptism and decision to impose Greek Christianity on all his subjects tried to assassinate him and replace him by their own nominee, opted for the first alternative. They themselves had just been baptized, no doubt forcibly; and in the months, or perhaps weeks, that followed they rose in defence of their cherished beliefs, privileges and customs. Boris' own account of this event, which has survived in the pope's reply to his letter of 866, shows that they rebelled not only against the Christian religion, but against the whole Byzantine fabric in which it had been imposed on their country. An example of the second type of hostile reaction is found in the sequel to the Russian chronicler's story of how Prince Vladimir, immediately after his conversion and the baptism of his subjects, had the children of the leading families of Russia conscripted for purposes of education. He was not the first nor the last to realize that the building of a new social order and ideology requires a planned indoctrination of the young, and that this can best be achieved by removing them from the influence of their parents. The reaction of the pupils' families to these state schools was predictable. The Russian chronicler records with characteristic irony: "The mothers of these children wept over them, for they were not yet strong in the faith, and mourned for them, as though they were dead."[20] Though the absence of any reference to the fathers' reactions may be due to the monastic chronicler's anti-feminine prejudice, it seems more likely that he was implying that the menfolk of the Russian aristocracy had already been won over to the new Christian order and supported their ruler's educational campaign. It is the women who appear in this story as the sorrowful and powerless representatives of family tradition and of the old dying culture.

The last stage in the confrontation between Byzantine civilization and the pre-Christian culture of Eastern Europe leads us away from the limelight of royal courts and large cities, where change is often rapid and dramatic, to the obscure and seemingly motionless life of remote village communities. The nation has now been officially Christian for several decades; its ruling and urban classes, the first to adopt the new faith, are striving to imitate, at least in their public lives, their Byzantine mentors: court ceremonial and dress are modelled on those of Constantinople; public buildings, ecclesiastical and secular, are constructed on the Byzantine architectural pattern; artists and craftsmen from Constantinople have been invited to decorate them; a tradition of literature and learning is growing up in the cities; and very slowly, through the work of the missionaries and the growing administrative centralization, this urban and aristocratic culture has begun to spread to the pagan countryside. There the immemorial customs, sacrificial offerings of food and animals, magical rites of fertility, the cult of fire and other natural elements, the wild ecstasy of popular feasts and the social prestige enjoyed by soothsayers and shamans, come under severe pressure from the invading culture. Ancient holy places and popular idols are profaned and overthrown, and Christian churches are built on the sites where they stood. Only in comparatively rare and harmless cases does the Christian clergy, native or Byzantine, show willingness to adapt pagan beliefs and customs to the imperious demands of the new religion. Resistance is either crushed or forestalled by the military power of the state. The resultant shock is so severe that these primitive communities, whose social life has been centred on the now proscribed customs and values, gradually sink into hopelessness. In such a case it needs but a further blow to their wellbeing, a famine, a drought, or the confiscation of their lands for the benefit of the church, to bring their frustration to boiling point. And if at this juncture a prophet arises among them who promises to release them from their bondage and bring back the good old days by supernatural means, they will rally round him with the courage of despair.

Such revivalist movements were common among the Indian tribes of North America in the nineteenth century. Several striking instances of the same phenomenon were recorded in eleventh century Russia. The main centres of unrest were on the periphery of the land, the forest zone between the upper Volga and the Oka, including Rostov and Suzdal', and the remote Beloozero in the far north: frontier districts where the Eastern Slavs were intermingled with Finnic tribes. The story of these various revolts, as told by the *Russian Primary Chronicle*, followed a similar pattern.[21] "Magicians" of local peasant origin, operating in famine-stricken districts, persuaded their followers to massacre members of the wealthy landowning aristocracy on the grounds that they were hoarding food. Militantly anti-Christian (on one occasion they murdered a priest), they claimed to possess secret knowledge, supernatural powers and the gift of prophecy. The Russian secular authorities dealt ruthlessly with these shamans: some were executed or banished (1024); another group, who murdered rich women, were lynched by order of the prince of Kiev's tax collector (c. 1071). These movements, pagan and peasant in character, were directed against the new religious and social order that was being imposed by the combined power of church and state. How dangerous they could be to both is instanced by two episodes which occurred about 1071 and which show that these revivalist movements were not confined to the backward and rural districts of Russia. One of these "magicians" came to Kiev, where he rallied his supporters by prophesying that in four years' time the Dnieper would start to flow backwards and Byzantium and Russia would exchange places, "so that the Greek land would be where Russia was, and Russia where the Greek land was".[22] Despite the obscurity of this oracular utterance, it is probably not too fanciful to interpret it as an expression of the obsessive fear of Byzantium and all its works which must have gripped the heart of more than one half-defeated pagan leader in eleventh century Russia. Another shaman appeared at that time in Novgorod, "pretending to be a god, and he led almost the entire city astray, claiming to foresee all things, reviling the Christian faith, and saying that he would walk across the Volkhov [river] in the sight of all".[23] The rebellion was finally quelled, but not before the whole population of the city, except the bishop, the prince and his retinue, had espoused the prophet's cause. The wholesale apostasy of the second most important city in Russia shows that the future of Byzantine Christianity was still far from assured nearly a hundred years after the country's official conversion.

Two of these "magicians" made a remarkable confession of faith. Questioned after their arrest about their views on the way man was created, they replied:

God washed himself in a bath and, having perspired, dried himself with a rag and threw it from heaven down to earth. And Satan began to argue with God as to who would create man out of it. And the Devil created man, and God placed a soul in him. This is why, whenever a man dies, his body goes to the earth, and his soul to God.[24]

This curious doctrine is traceable to two different sources. The first part of the confession echoes a popular legend which was still current among Finnic tribes between the Oka and the middle Volga in the nineteenth century. The second part is, in substance and even terminology, unmistakably Bogomil.

The channels through which a basic tenet of this neo-Manichaean sect was carried from the Balkans to Northern Russia are unknown. No explicit reference to any native form of Bogomilism can be found in the Russian sources; and it is probably safe to assume that this movement never really took root in the country. However, the abundant apocryphal literature of Greek origin which circulated in Slavonic translation in medieval Russia under the name of "Bulgarian fables" contains more than a trace of dualistic views; and it is by no means impossible that Bogomil missionaries, who were famed for their zealous and far-flung proselytism, made their way from the Byzantine Empire or Bulgaria to Russia.[25] All that can be stated with assurance is that North Russian shamans, in their attempt to revive the pagan culture of their ancestors, made use in the eleventh century of a teaching ultimately derived from the Balkan Bogomils. We may suppose that this infusion of a dualistic current of thought into a pagan revivalist movement gave the latter a firmer doctrinal foundation, and perhaps helped to relieve the despondency and misery of the peasants of Northern Russia by offering them a persuasive solution to the problem of the origin of human suffering. In the Balkan Slav lands, and to a more limited extent in Russia, Bogomilism, which became a popular movement of dissent fighting against the theological, ethical and social teaching of a state-supported church, offers a striking example of native resistance to the intrusive civilization of Byzantium.

These examples will have shown that Byzantine civilization, as it spread to the countries of Eastern Europe, encountered in different classes of the population a resistance that was sometimes extensive and powerful. In view of this, one may wonder why these countries borrowed so much and so readily from Byzantium. Part of the answer to this question has been given earlier in this chapter: particular cultural traits were adopted because of their functional usefulness in solving a social problem or satisfying a material need; thus Christianity could help to overcome internal frictions due to racial diversity within the "receiving" country; the Byzantine doctrine of the divine origin of political authority sustained the local monarch's ambition to increase his power over his subjects; ability to tap the springs of Byzantine technological skill enabled him to carry out difficult engineering projects, such as the building of bridges and fortresses; while commercial and ecclesiastical links with the empire satisfied the ruling classes' appetite for objects of luxury, impressive buildings and education. The craving for beauty and learning and for the prestige attendant on their possession provided, as we shall see, the strongest of incentives for the acquisition of Byzantine literature, law and art.

In the last resort, however, the factor which helped the most to overcome local resistance to Byzantine civilization was the unrivalled prestige which it came to enjoy throughout Eastern Europe. Until the twelfth century no other European country could hope to compete with the Byzantine Empire, whether in wealth, power or cultural achievements. To be associated with it was an eagerly sought honour. Constantine Porphyrogenitus, who was well aware of the attitude of foreigners to the empire which he ruled, complained of the "importunate demands and brazenly submitted claims" of "the nations of the northerners", among whom he listed the Khazars, the Hungarians and the Russians.[26] These nations, he explained, craved especially for Byzantine crowns, robes of state and marriage alliances with the imperial family. In no small measure, too, did the empire's prestige rest on its military power and technology. Its notorious secret weapon, the Greek fire, which its seafaring foes had learned to dread, exerted an understandable fascination; and Constantine tells us in the same passage that he has received frequent demands from East European nations for samples of this priceless commodity.

Byzantine prestige was, of course, also closely linked with the appeal of the Christian religion. Modern historians tend to stress, and rightly so, the political and social motives which brought medieval rulers to the baptismal font. Yet we should not dismiss too lightly the interpretation placed on these events by contemporary chroniclers and hagiographers for whom the driving force of personal belief was the decisive factor. It would be rash to regard the conversion of Boris of Bulgaria, Gyula of Transylvania or Vladimir of Russia as no more than far-sighted acts of worldly statesmen, prompted by self-interest. What we know of their lives after baptism is at least compatible with the view that their conversions were genuine and that their Christian beliefs were held with sincerity. The precise nature and scope of these beliefs can hardly be determined, for lack of reliable evidence. In some cases the Gospel teaching, with its message of spiritual and moral regeneration, must have had a real impact. At other times the beauty of liturgical worship, perceived through eye and ear, softened and held captive men's hearts. And within the ruling societies of Eastern Europe, whose religious and social preoccupations had centred hitherto on family, clan, tribe or kingdom, there must have been not a few to whom the universal perspective of the Christian religion offered a new and deeply exciting experience.

Although some East European monarchs, notably those of Bulgaria and Serbia, accepted for a while the spiritual authority of Rome, and other nations, such as Hungary and Croatia, gradually moved out of the Byzantine orbit, the majority of the countries remained faithful to the mother church of Constantinople. However much their rulers may have chafed under the sometimes overbearing authority of the oecumenical patriarchs, they and their subjects never seriously questioned, at least until the fifteenth century, the role of the Byzantine Church as the centre and arbiter of the Orthodox faith. In or about 1347 King Magnus Eriksson of Sweden sent an embassy to Novgorod to propose to its archbishop and citizens a disputation on the respective merits of the Catholic and Orthodox religions. The Russian reply to the king is recorded as follows: "If you wish to know whose faith is better, ours or yours, you should send [envoys] to Constantinople, to the patriarch, for it is from the Greeks that we received the Orthodox faith".[27]

If, on the higher levels of society, the East European peoples regarded the Byzantines as their mentors in matters of doctrine, the attitude of the simpler folk was more instinctive and spontaneous. It found striking expression in their reverence for the city of Constantinople which in their language the Slavs called *Tsargrad*, the Imperial City. For the whole of Eastern Christendom Constantinople was a holy city, not only because it was the seat of the emperor and his spiritual counterpart, the oecumenical patriarch. Its principal claim to holiness lay in the supernatural forces believed to be present within its walls: the memorials of Christ's passion and the innumerable relics of saints; the churches and monasteries, repositories of prayer and famed shrines of Christendom; above all, the patronage of its heavenly protectors, the Divine Wisdom, whose temple was St. Sophia, and the Mother of God, whose robe, preserved in the church of Blachernae, was venerated as the city's palladium. In the aura of sanctity that surrounded it, Constantinople could be rivalled only by Jerusalem: indeed, it was often thought of as the New Jerusalem. The East European pilgrims and travellers who visited Constantinople in the Middle Ages displayed before the number of its relics and the holiness of its sanctuaries the same open-eyed wonder and religious awe which they reveal in their descriptions of the Holy Land. More than one of them dwells on the breath-taking beauty of the church of St. Sophia and on the loveliness of the liturgical chanting therein: "a chant", declared Antony, the future archbishop of Novgorod who visited the city in 1200, "like that of the angels".[28] In his and other accounts which medieval Russian pilgrims have left us, we sometimes catch an echo of the same excitement with which the envoys of Vladimir of Russia reported to their sovereign their impressions of the public worship in Constantinople: "We knew not whether we were in heaven or on earth." For the nations of the Byzantine Commonwealth Constantinople was not only "the eye of the faith of the Christians", but also "the city of the world's desire".[29]

NOTES

1. Liutprand, *Relatio de Legatione Constantinopolitana*, xlvii, pp. 200–1. English transl. Wright, pp. 263–4.
2. See above, p. 89.
3. Constantine Acropolites, Λόγος εἰς τὸν ἅγιον Βάρβαρον, *Analekta Hierosolymitikes Stakhyologias*, i (St. Petersburg, 1891), p. 406.
4. Liutprand, *Antapodosis*, vi, 5, pp. 154–5; Wright, pp. 207–8.
5. See above, p. 242.
6. See above, p. 300.

7. Scylitzes-Cedrenus, ii, p. 465; ibid., p. 657; Cinnamus, p. 299; Nicetas Choniates: Sathas, *Bibl. gr. medii aevi*, i, p. 95.

8. Agathias, *Hist.* v, 1, ed. Keydell, p. 164; *Byz. Zeitschrift*, ii (1893), p. 44.

9. Procopius, *De aedificiis*, iii, 7, p. 101; Nicetas Choniates, loc. cit.

10. Agathias, *Hist.* v, 24, p. 195.

11. Agathias, v, 1, p. 164; Cinnamus, pp. 236, 299.

12. D. Obolensky, "The Principles and Methods of Byzantine Diplomacy", *Actes du XIIe Congrès International d'études byzantines*, i (Belgrade, 1963), pp. 56–8.

13. F. Braudel, *La Méditerranée et le monde méditerranéen à l'époque de Philippe II* (Paris,1949), p. 556.

14. Braudel, *La Méditerranée*, 2nd ed., ii (Paris, 1966), p. 98.

15. A. Stender-Petersen, *Die Varägersage als Quelle der altrussischen Chronik* (Aarhus–Leipzig, 1934).

16. Jenkins, "The Peace with Bulgaria", *Polychronion*, pp. 290–1, 294.

17. *Povest'*, p. 50; Cross, p. 88.

18. "Typikon de Grégoire Pacourianos pour le monastère de Pétritzos (Bačkovo) en Bulgarie", *Viz. Vremennik*, xi, suppl. no. 1 (1904), pp. 44–5; *FHB*, xiv, p. 56.

19. *Povest'*, p. 46; Cross, pp. 83–4.

20. *Povest'*, p. 81; Cross, p. 117.

21. *Povest'*, pp. 99–100, 116–21, 141; Cross, pp. 134–5, 150–4, 173.

22. *Povest'*, p. 116; Cross, p. 150.

23. *Povest'*, p. 120; Cross, p. 154.

24. *Povest'*, p. 118; Cross, pp. 151–2.

25. D. Obolensky, *The Bogomils* (Cambridge, 1948), pp. 277–83.

26. *DAI*, ch. 13, p. 66.

27. *Novgorodskaya pervaya letopis'* (Moscow–Leningrad, 1950), p. 359.

28. *Puteshestvie Novgorodskogo Arkhiepiskopa Antoniya v Tsar'grad*, ed. P. Savvaitov (St. Petersburg, 1872), col. 93; *Itinéraires russes en Orient*, p. 97.

29. L. Sternbach, "Analecta Avarica", *Rozprawy* of the Academy of Cracow, xv (1900), p. 304; E. Legrand, "Description de l'Eglise des Saints-Apôtres", *Revue des Etudes Grecques*, ix (1896), p. 38.

IO

Religion and Law

The geographical and political framework within which Byzantine civilization was transmitted to Eastern Europe has been described in earlier chapters. An attempt has also been made to explain the reasons which led the peoples who lived in this area to accept, despite local resistances, its values and products. The time has come to consider the results of this process of diffusion, to single out the more important features of the Byzantine tradition which were borrowed by the East European nations, and to see what became of them in their adopted homes. Our inquiry will be concentrated on four of these features—religion, law, literature and art. In all these fields the East European countries proved to be willing and often eager pupils of Byzantium. Yet the adoption of Byzantine civilization by their educated classes was no mere passive borrowing or slavish imitation. Instances have already been cited when some of its traits were modified and adapted to local needs by contact with the native cultural and social environment, by the action of intermediaries and by the facts of geography. The selective, and to some extent creative, character of this borrowing could hardly fail to give rise, within the Byzantine cultural area, to local peculiarities and variations, some of them indigenous, others due to later developments. To identify, let alone describe, these "original" traits is often exceedingly difficult, partly owing to the inadequacy of the sources available to the historian and partly because he still lacks those criteria for the comparative study of cultures which are today being gradually evolved by anthropologists and sociologists. The problem is perhaps least intractable in the field of literature: here the relative abundance of the sources, particularly in Russia, allows precise conclusions to be drawn both about the types of Byzantine writings selected for

377

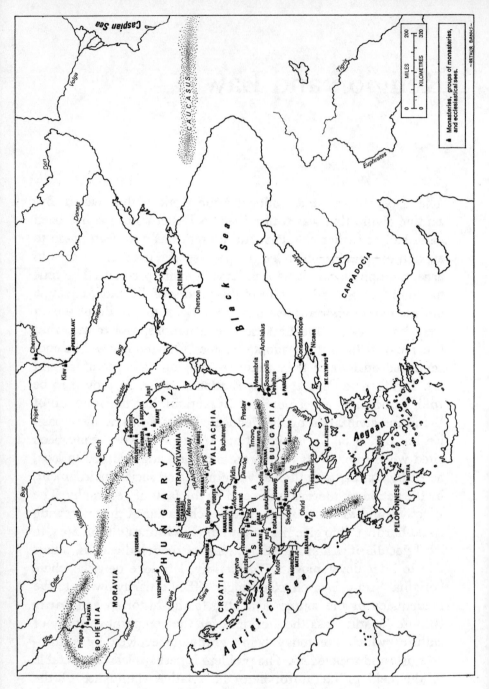

Map 9   Cultural centres of the Commonwealth I

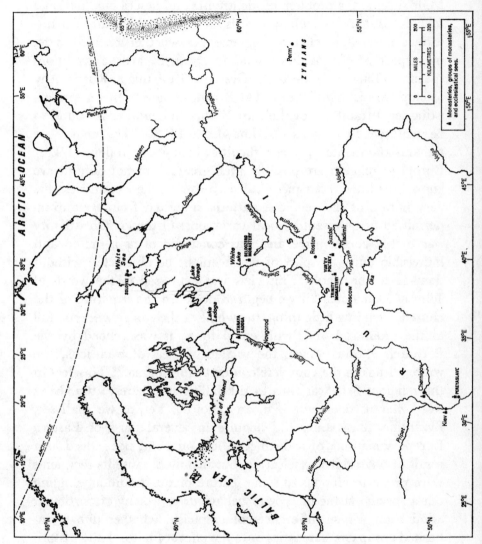

Map 10   Cultural centres of the Commonwealth II

translation and about the views held by East European authors on their own countries' relationship to Byzantium. In the realm of art where, except in Russia, the extant monuments are nowhere sufficient for a continuous tradition to be traced right through the Middle Ages, the problem of identifying and describing "national schools" is more difficult; and it is hardly surprising that art historians have still reached no agreement on whether it is legitimate, in respect of the Middle Ages, to speak of artistic traditions specific to Bulgaria or Serbia or Greece or Rumania or Russia. Any attempt to distinguish imported Byzantine law from the pre-existing legal traditions of the East European countries is bound to be tentative so long as our knowledge of Slav customary law remains rudimentary. The difficulties facing the student of East European religion are possibly even greater: for not only do we know very little about medieval paganism in these countries; the very nature of the religious patterns inherited from Byzantium permitted of no essential local variations: Orthodox Christianity was highly conservative and was conceived of as a sacred and indivisible unity, no part of which might be abstracted without damage to the whole. This view was expressed in the words of John of Damascus: "if we begin to demolish the structure of the church, even in a little thing, the whole of the edifice will soon fall to the ground";[1] and, with equal force, it was echoed by the Patriarch Photius: "even the smallest neglect of traditions," he wrote, "leads to the complete contempt for dogma."[2] To select in the religious field was thus to risk falling into heresy; the Greek word *hairesis* does indeed mean "choice". Yet, as we shall see, Byzantine Christianity did acquire in several parts of Eastern Europe something of a distinctive local flavour, not indeed as a result of any arbitrary selection, but mainly because its recipients were prone to emphasize some feature of this tradition, singling out a specific virtue or type of behaviour as worthy of particular admiration. These differences of emphasis, whether due to inherited group characteristics or to the effect of natural and historical environment, or to both, are worth investigating in the four fields here selected for special study. One of the aims of this and the following chapter will be to show that an attempt to identify and describe the local "recensions" which Byzantine civilization underwent in various parts of Eastern Europe is, like the recognition of style in art, a legitimate undertaking, however imperfect and tentative its outcome may be. And it will be suggested that these local variations are, from the historian's viewpoint, less significant than the common pattern of values, beliefs and intellectual and aesthetic experience which, in the course of the Middle Ages, the Bulgarians, the Russians, the Serbs and the Rumanians acquired from Byzantium.

I RELIGION

The work of East Roman missionaries, and the administrative build-up of territorial churches that followed it, resulted in the transplantation of the Christian Orthodox tradition of Byzantium to the countries of Eastern Europe. Nowhere perhaps is the wholesale nature of this borrowing more apparent than in the field of monasticism. The slight variations of type which can be detected in the early Middle Ages between the monasteries of the different East European areas are far less significant than the underlying unity of formal structure and spiritual experience which they reveal; and these differences become even less perceptible after 1300, when a new current of asceticism and spirituality, which originated in the leading monasteries of the Byzantine Empire, further strengthened the ties that bound together the various local branches of East European monasticism. However, alongside this increasingly unified monastic tradition, different forms of secular and popular religion developed on indigenous ground, particularly in Russia and Serbia; but these blendings of Byzantine and local traditions, exemplified in the religious cult of national kings and princes, are more apparent in earlier periods. It seems a justifiable inference from the sources to suggest that, at least in the field of religion, the Byzantine tradition in Eastern Europe became during the Middle Ages increasingly homogeneous.

Together with a veneration for the monastic life and its followers, which greatly increased after the defeat of Iconoclasm in 843, the peoples of this area inherited from Byzantium a threefold ascetic tradition. It was represented first by the eremitical life which, though no longer of central importance in Eastern Christendom, was still practised on Mount Athos and elsewhere

381

and was sustained by the highly popular accounts of the early anchorites of Egypt and Palestine—the *Historia Monachorum*, the *Lausiac History* of Palladius and the *Pratum Spirituale* of John Moschus. These works were translated into Slavonic in the early Middle Ages. The second type, intermediate between the eremitical and the organized community system, was that of the *lavra*, consisting of a group of hermits who lived separately though under the direction of an abbot and met on Sundays for the common celebration of the Eucharist. It, too, existed on Mount Athos, and was propagated in Eastern Europe through the Slavonic translation of the lives of the Palestinian monks, written in the sixth century by Cyril of Scythopolis. The third form of Byzantine monasticism found the most ready acceptance and had the longest history. It was typified by the coenobitic monastery, a highly organized and centralized community whose members, living together in the same building, owning no personal property, were subject to the identical discipline of prayer and work under the authority of an abbot. Coenobitic monasticism, developed in Upper Egypt in the fourth century by St. Pachomius, was organized by St. Basil of Caesarea, and was given its definitive form in the early ninth century by St. Theodore the Studite. The monastery of Studios in Constantinople, of which he was abbot, played during the early Middle Ages a role in Eastern Europe comparable in some degree to the position occupied in Western Christendom by the abbey of Cluny. The austerity of its rules on corporate worship, manual work and study was tempered by a moderation in the practice of asceticism which on the whole was characteristic of Byzantine coenobitic monasticism. Some of the brethren acted as spiritual directors to Constantinopolitan families. The monastery performed works of charity, ran a school and had a famed *scriptorium*. In the liturgical field Studios set a pattern for the whole of Eastern Christendom, and many hymns still in current use in the Orthodox Church were composed during the ninth century within its walls. Its constitution claimed to be, in the words of its preamble, "the best and the most royal rule which indeed avoids both extravagance and inadequacy".[3]

In the second half of the tenth century the Studite Rule was introduced on Mount Athos. Near the southern tip of the peninsula a large coenobitic monastery was founded in 963 by St. Athanasius and richly endowed by the Emperor Nicephorus Phocas. The Great Lavra, as it was called, was the first of the foundations of the Studite type on the Holy Mountain, a remote area of great natural beauty which soon became the leading centre of East Christian monasticism, with houses belonging to nations from the farthest periphery of the Byzantine world, from Georgia to Amalfi. They were soon joined by the Slavs. The Bulgarian monastery of Zographou is attested on Mount Athos by the mid-tenth century. The Russians had a monastery of their own on the peninsula by 1016, and in 1169 they obtained a second one, that of St. Panteleimon. The Serbian monastery of Chilandar was, we have seen, founded on Mount Athos by Stephen Nemanja and St. Sava at the close of the twelfth century. These three Slav houses—Zographou, St. Panteleimon and Chilandar—which still exist, became flourishing literary centres, where Byzantine religious writings were translated into Slavonic, to be carried thence to the medieval monasteries and towns of Eastern Europe. The analogy, suggested earlier, between the alternating current of men and ideas flowing to and from the Mediterranean and the pulsations of a living heart, finds a further illustration in the role of Mount Athos, drawing to itself men from all over Eastern Europe who sought training in the monastic life, and then sending back, through these Slav monasteries founded on its soil, the results of their labours and learning to their native lands.

The beginnings of Bulgarian monasticism antedate the international importance of Mount Athos. The first monasteries in that country, founded around 900, mainly in and near Ohrid and Preslav, probably owed their existence to the influence of Thessalonica and Constantinople. They seem to have been mostly royal foundations, patterned on the Byzantine houses endowed by emperors and wealthy individuals with the aim of ensuring for themselves a place of burial and perpetual prayer for the repose of their souls. A more specifically Bulgarian form of monasticism can be detected several decades later; its heyday may be tentatively dated to the period from 950 to 1150. Its two most marked features were the desire to combine the cult of the hermit's life with the institutional need for coenobitic monasteries, and a tendency for new houses to cluster in the mountains of Northern Macedonia.

This earliest important centre of South Slav monasticism lay between the upper valleys of the Strymon and the Vardar, more particularly in the mountain areas of Vitosha (south of Sofia), Rila and Osogovo (the latter range intersects the present Bulgarian-Yugoslav frontier). These three regions, which lie in the centre of the Balkan peninsula, are all associated with the ascetic feats of St. John of Rila, the patron saint of Bulgaria. He spent the greater part of his life (c. 880–946) as a hermit, striving to penetrate ever deeper into the wild mountains and to escape the worldly consequences of his growing fame as a holy ascetic and a miracle-working healer. Only at the end of his life, in deference to the many disciples who had gathered round him, did he consent to forgo his search for solitude and to found a coenobitic monastery in his last abode, in the recesses of the Rila Mountains. His posthumous fame and cult spread to Serbia, Hungary, Russia and Byzantium; one of his biographies was written in the twelfth century by a high-ranking Byzantine official. In his own country John has always been venerated as a hermit and as the founder of the Rila monastery, Bulgaria's most hallowed shrine. His earliest extant Old Slavonic *Vita*, though far from independent of Byzantine hagiographical patterns, reveals in the homeliness of some of its details and in the unassuming poetry of its language the influence of a more popular local tradition.[4]

The same blending of the solitary and coenobitic traditions, and the same geographical area, are associated with the cult of three other North Macedonian hermits, Prochorus of Pšinja, Gabriel of Lesnovo and Joachim of Osogovo. Their Slavonic biographies tell us little about their natural lives; all three seem to have lived in the eleventh century. But the close link with the cult of St. John of Rila is unmistakable: their ascetic feats were performed in the Osogovo Mountains, where John had received the tonsure; and each of them is associated with the foundation, or revival, of a medieval monastic community: the most famous of these is Lesnovo, rebuilt and decorated with remarkable paintings after the Serbian conquest of the fourteenth century. By promoting the cult of their founders, whose relics they zealously preserved, these Macedonian monasteries became nurseries of a popular devotion which spread to the surrounding countryside.

The coenobitic house, founded in a remote, usually mountainous, place by a contemplative hermit, seems to have remained the characteristic form of Bulgarian monasticism in the Middle Ages. By contrast, the earliest Russian monasteries were nearly always situated near towns; moreover, of the seventy or so attested in Russia before the thirteenth century about two-thirds were princely foundations. The main exception was the Kiev monastery of the Caves, the leading monastic house of the pre-Mongol period. It had no secular founder, and no original patron or initial endowment. One of its early brethren, reflecting with pride on its spontaneous rise, wrote: "Many monasteries have indeed been founded by emperors and nobles and wealthy men, but they are not such as those founded by tears and fasting, by prayer and vigils."[5] Of all the non-Greek East European monasteries of the early Middle Ages it is the only one of which detailed historical records have survived; and although much of this evidence is hagiographical, it permits a fairly full and accurate picture to be drawn of the impact of the Byzantine ascetic tradition on eleventh- and twelfth-century Russia.

The origins of the monastery are associated with the name of Antony, a Russian who travelled to Mount Athos in the early eleventh century and there became a monk. "Go back to Russia", the abbot who professed him is said to have declared, "and may the blessing of the Holy Mountain be with you, for many will become monks because of you." Antony returned to Kiev and there, on the outskirts of the city, settled in a cave overlooking the Dnieper. His fame as a holy hermit spread throughout the land, and by the middle of the century disciples had gathered round him in sufficient numbers to make it necessary to dig a larger cave on the same site, to house them all.[6] Two features of this story, told in the *Russian Primary Chronicle*, are worth noting. In the first place, Antony was a recluse by choice, and his eremitical ideal shaped the early history of the monastery. Secondly, his foundation is described as an offshoot of Athonite monasticism, and upon it, as the chronicle repeatedly stresses, rested "the blessing of the Holy Mountain". The next stage in the monastery's history is associated with his Russian disciple Theodosius, its abbot from *c.* 1062 to 1074. He is the central figure in the history of early Russian monasticism. He introduced two important reforms, moving the monastery above ground and sending one of his monks to Constantinople with instructions to obtain a copy of the Studite Rule. This *typicon*, which was drawn up in Constantinople in the eleventh century and was probably a slightly modified version of the original rule, became the constitution of the monastery of the Caves, and the principles of a strictly ordered community life thus supplanted, without altogether eliminating, the more individualistic, eremitical ideal of St. Antony.

St. Theodosius' eleventh-century biographer, despite his copious borrowings from Greek hagiographical writings, especially from Cyril of Scythopolis, draws a lifelike portrait of the founder of Russian coenobitic monasticism.[7] The impression we gain is of a man of deep and unassuming humility, balanced moderation in the practice of asceticism, and considerable moral authority. The latter quality was manifest in his relations with the princes and nobles of the land, as well as with his own monks. Attempts have been made to ascribe original Russian features to Theodosius' spirituality, and also to contrast his gentleness, humaneness and voluntary self-humiliation with the more sombre and heroic kind of asceticism practised by St. Antony and his hermits.[8] These efforts are not convincing. It may be that the virtues attributed to St. Theodosius by medieval Russian writers were those which most commended themselves to his compatriots. But they were not less prized in Byzantine spirituality, and were often indeed singled out as models of behaviour in the common patrimony of Christendom. It is true that Theodosius' coenobitic ideal seems, at first sight, to have little in common with the portraits of some hermits of his monastery which survive in the Russian Chronicle[9] and also in an early thirteenth century account[10]—awesome recluses who mortified their passions by superhuman efforts, waging grim battles against ubiquitous temptation in a demon-haunted world. In this, too, the monastery of the Caves reflected the traditions of Byzantine asceticism with its tension, never fully resolved, between the contemplative calling in which man can attain to the vision of God by mastering his passions, and the life in community, where he may gain salvation by obedience and charity shown to the other members of the monastic brotherhood. Yet in Kiev, as in Byzantium, the two types of monastic life had points of contact. Neither Antony nor Theodosius were exclusively committed to their respective ideals of asceticism: and the latter was a devoted and much-esteemed pupil of the former, a relationship which in East Christian monasticism is the most sacred of human bonds. In the monastery of the Caves, as in Studios and in other Byzantine coenobitic houses, provision was often made for the recluse to live, temporarily or permanently, in or near the precincts of the monastery. In Russia as in Byzantium (at least after the sixth century) it was generally recognized that, though the solitary life was suited for men of high spiritual calibre and experience, it was full of pitfalls for the average monk and that the corporate ideal still provided the safe and royal way to sanctification. This was the view of Bishop Simon of Vladimir, a former monk of the monastery of the Caves, who wrote: "All that you do in your cell is of little importance: whether you read the Psalter, or chant the Twelve Psalms—all this cannot compare with a single 'Lord, have mercy', sung in congregation."[11]

The unrivalled prestige enjoyed by the monastery of the Caves in Kievan Russia, and the personal influence exerted by several of its abbots on the ruling circles of the country, go far to explain the considerable role it played in the early Middle Ages. Bishop Simon in the early thirteenth century counted some fifty members of the community who, during the past century and a half, had been appointed bishops. Some at least of them must have felt at times like echoing the nostalgia with which, writing from his distant see in North-East Russia, this prelate voiced his devotion to his *alma mater*:

> I tell you truly [he wrote to a member of the community] that I would straightway set at naught all this honour and glory, if only I could be one of the stakes in the fence standing beyond the monastery gates, or if I could lie as a bit of dirt in the monastery of the Caves, so that men would trample upon me, or if I could become one of the poor, begging by its gates.[12]

The history of this house, at least until the Mongol invasion, shows how rapidly and thoroughly the Byzantine monastic tradition could be assimilated: the three basic elements in this tradition—the writings of the early Egyptian and Palestinian monks, the eremitical practices of Mount Athos, and the Constantinopolitan Studite Rule—combined to shape the life of the leading monastery in early medieval Russia.

It may seem surprising that the monastic movement which developed in Macedonia between 950 and 1150 appears to have had little or no direct impact upon Serbia. This was perhaps due to several reasons: many of the monasteries were founded at a time when Macedonia was a Byzantine province and when direct contacts between it and Serbia do not appear to have been very close; Serbian monasticism began to develop in the second half of the twelfth century, when Raška, its centre, was orientated mainly towards the Adriatic coast; finally the North Macedonian area, where these early South Slav monasteries had arisen, was acquired by the Serbs only in the late thirteenth century, by which time their monasticism had already evolved its characteristic features. Outwardly the great Serbian monasteries of the Middle Ages differed from the type that prevailed in Bulgaria and in the Byzantine Empire: in these countries rural monastic houses tended to cluster in mountainous regions, as on Athos, on Bithynian Olympus, in Cappadocia and in Northern Macedonia. In Serbia the monasteries were mostly isolated and self-contained communities, often built, like the Cluniac and Cistercian abbeys of Central Europe, in wooded valleys whose position testifies to their founders' sense of natural beauty. This is true above all of the great royal foundations (*zadužbine*), many of which are renowned for the paintings in their churches: Studenica, the burial place of Stephen Nemanja; Žiča, founded by Stephen the First-Crowned, the first centre of the Serbian archdiocese; and Sopoćani, built by Uroš 1 between 1260 and 1265; all three were situated in or near the valley of the Ibar, the original nucleus of the principality of Raška. Equally famous were the royal monasteries of Mileševa on a tributary of the Lim, the focus of St. Sava's cult, Gračanica near Kosovo Polje and Dečani in the plain watered by the upper Drim; the first was founded in the thirteenth century, the latter two in the fourteenth. Outside Constantinople, no other area of Eastern Europe could boast of so many monasteries of central importance in its national life. These royal *zadužbine* cemented that close partnership of church and state which is a distinguishing mark of Serbian medieval history. They were richly endowed with land and property, and their abbots, chosen and invested by the king, advised him on important matters of state.

Whatever local features these monasteries may have acquired through their association with public life, there is no doubt that the structure and ordering of Serbian Orthodox monasticism owed virtually everything to Byzantine models. This was due in large measure to St. Sava. He introduced Byzantine monastic patterns into his country in three stages: first he adopted as the constitution of the Chilandar monastery on Mount Athos the *typicon* of the Constantinopolitan monastery of Our Lady *Evergetis,* itself a variant of the Studite Rule; then, on his return to Serbia, he introduced the same rule into the monastery of Studenica, of which he became abbot; finally, after a journey to the Holy Land, Sava, now archbishop of Serbia, brought to Studenica some elements of the liturgical *typicon* of the monastery of St. Sabas (Sava) in Palestine, which had already been adopted in part by many communities in Constantinople. The constitution of Studenica became the model for all the other royal monasteries of the land; and Serbian monasticism, in its organization, discipline, liturgical practice and spirituality, was thus stamped by the same three traditions, derived from Mount Athos, Constantinople and Palestine, which shaped the ascetic life of Eastern Europe in the Middle Ages.

A new period in the history of East European monasticism began about 1330, when a great Byzantine ascetic, St. Gregory of Sinai, founded a community in the remote region of Paroria, in the Strandzha Mountains of South-Eastern Bulgaria. In contrast to the Western ideal of monastic stability, he had acquired his ascetic training in numerous travels which took him to the monasteries and hermitages of Cyprus, Sinai, Crete, Mount Athos, Mytilene and Constantinople. Gregory's reputation as a master of the spiritual life soon attracted disciples from the Byzantine Empire, Bulgaria and Serbia; and during the next twenty years the monastery of Paroria played a leading part in a revival of contemplative monasticism which spread in the late Middle Ages through the whole of Eastern Europe. This revival is associated with a movement known to modern historians as Hesychasm. The term is derived from the Greek word *hesychia* ("quietude"), used by East Christian mystics to describe the state of recollection and inner silence which follows man's victory over his passions and leads him, through the practice of contemplative prayer, to the knowledge of God. This "prayer of the heart" had gradually become linked with the frequent repetition of the "Jesus prayer" ("Lord Jesus Christ, Son of God, have mercy upon me") and with certain bodily exercises (such as the regulation of breathing), designed to aid spiritual concentration. Gregory of Sinai, one of the foremost teachers of Hesychasm, was certainly no innovator. His theology, rooted in the Greek patristic tradition, owed a special debt to St. John of the Ladder (died between 670 and 680) and to St. Symeon the New Theologian (949–1022), the great Constantinopolitan mystic. This "method" of contemplative prayer resembles that practised in the late thirteenth century by Nicephorus the Hesychast on Mount Athos, though it seems that Gregory learned it before his visit to the Holy Mountain. In essence, however, it goes back to the traditions of fifth century Christian ascetism, if not earlier still. Gregory played a central role in this late medieval monastic movement. Until his death in 1346 his monastery of Paroria was, next to Mount Athos, the foremost centre of Hesychasm in the Balkans. His Slav and Greek disciples who received their monastic training there included highly educated men who later rose to prominent positions in the churches of their respective lands; and through them their master's writings and oral teaching spread through the monasteries and royal courts of Eastern Europe. Byzantium, Bulgaria, Serbia, Rumania and Russia were all affected by this new cosmopolitan movement: monks, churchmen, writers and artists, travelling from country to country—"wandering for the sake of the Lord", as a fourteenth century writer put it[13]—found themselves in a similar spiritual and cultural environment; and through this "Hesychast International",[14] whose influence extended far beyond the ecclesiastical sphere, the different parts of the Byzantine Commonwealth were, during the last hundred years of its existence, linked to each other and to its centre perhaps more closely than ever before.

The Hesychast movement had, at least in the second half of the fourteenth century, a further characteristic: many of its leaders were men of intellectual distinction who had personal links with one another. Most had been trained as monks either on Mount Athos or in Paroria, sometimes in both places. One of them was the Bulgarian, St. Theodosius of Trnovo. He learned the technique of asceticism and the practice of mystical prayer under

Gregory in Paroria. After his master's death he, too, wandered for a while between Byzantine and Bulgarian monasteries; finally, about 1350, he settled in Kilifarevo on the northern slopes of the Balkan Mountains, not far from Trnovo; there, with the help of the Tsar John Alexander, he founded a monastic community modelled on the now defunct Paroria house. His reputation soon made Kilifarevo a Hesychast centre of international renown; in the words of his medieval hagiographer, "no sooner had he settled in the mountainous place called Kilifarevo than rumour flew all around, not only to the Bulgarian people, but also to the Serbs and the Hungarians and the Rumanians and to those who live around Mesembria".[15] Theodosius' practice of *hesychia* did not prevent him from actively intervening in public affairs: he is reported to have played the leading part in suppressing a fresh outbreak of Bogomilism in Bulgaria; and his role in the ecclesiastical politics of his time is striking evidence of the international solidarity that existed between the Hesychast groups of Eastern Europe and of their loyalty to their Byzantine mentors. The Bulgarian patriarchate, established in 1235, was, it will be remembered, placed under the nominal supremacy of the Byzantine Church. The outward sign of this primacy was the obligation incurred by the head of the Bulgarian Church to commemorate liturgically the patriarch of Constantinople and to apply to him for the chrism used in the churches of his country. In the mid-fourteenth century the Bulgarian primate discontinued these practices, thus claiming in effect complete independence from his Byzantine colleague. The Patriarch Callistus protested. He was an ardent Hesychast and had been trained in Paroria by Gregory of Sinai. Theodosius, his friend and fellow-pupil, rallied to his support: he condemned the action of his own ecclesiastical superior, the Bulgarian patriarch, and endorsed Callistus' efforts to enforce the authority of the Oecumenical See over the church of Bulgaria. Towards the end of his life Theodosius, with several disciples, left Kilifarevo for Constantinople, where the patriarch placed at his disposal a suburban monastery in which he could devote himself to the contemplative life. He died there in 1363.

The monasteries of Paroria and Kilifarevo became the nurseries for the propagation of Hesychasm in Eastern Europe. One of the disciples of Theodosius who accompanied him to Constantinople was Euthymius, his principal assistant at Kilifarevo. He later became patriarch of Bulgaria and was to play the central role in the Graeco-Slav literary movement of the late Middle Ages. Another leading Hesychast was St. Romil (or Roman) of Vidin (*d.* 1375), a pupil both of Gregory and Theodosius. He ended his life in Northern Serbia where, together with his "Sinaite" companions from the Bulgarian *hesychasteria,* he brought the ascetical and mystical tradition of his master into late medieval Serbian monasticism.

Unlike other East European countries, Serbia seems to have been touched by the Hesychast tradition only late in the Middle Ages and, if we can judge from the silence of the sources, somewhat superficially at that. This has sometimes been ascribed to the influence of St. Sava and to the highly organized monasticism, in close contact with court and government circles, which he imposed upon his country. There is some danger of over-simplification in this view. It is true that the Serbian *zadužbine* resembled in their public and cultural activity the great abbeys of Central and Western Europe more than they did the hermitages of Mount Athos, the North Macedonian monasteries of the early Middle Ages, or the later Bulgarian *hesychasteria.* Yet the mystical tradition had its impact on Serbian monasticism: St. Sava had experienced it on Mount Athos; and some of the royal foundations, such as Studenica, had attached to them groups of cells where chosen monks, living in *lavrai,* could devote themselves to the contemplative life. Moreover, a notable revival of interest in mystical theology can be observed in fourteenth century Serbia. Not only was the work of St. John of the Ladder, one of the leading precursors of the Hesychast movement, frequently copied at that time; more significantly still, about the middle of the century some of the writings of St. Gregory Palamas, the leading Hesychast theologian, were translated into Slavonic in Serbia. St. Gregory (1296–1359), archbishop of Thessalonica, was known for his teaching on the Uncreated Light, the ineffable grace that illumines him who is spiritually transformed through the ceaseless practice of the "prayer of the heart". This light, which he identified with the light that shone on Mount Tabor during the Transfiguration, is, he believed, one of the "energies" or "operations" of God, distinct from His essence, yet capable of uniting man to the Divine Nature. Palamas' teaching, which owes much to Maximus the Confessor, was after some controversy proclaimed as Orthodox by various synods in Constantinople, in 1341, 1347, 1351. It was eventually accepted, through the influence of the disciples of Gregory of Sinai, in all East European countries; not least in Serbia, whose powerful monarch, Stephen Dušan, met Palamas on Mount Athos in 1347. Yet on the whole Serbian monasticism remained until the last quarter of the fourteenth century faithful to the pattern into which the kings of the Nemanja dynasty had moulded it. It was only after the arrival of the monks from Paroria and Kilifarevo that Serbian monasteries, rising in remote areas of the country, became primarily devoted to the contemplative life. There, in the wooded highlands by the lower Morava, Serbian monasticism, espousing the mystical theology and the interior prayer of the Hesychasts, was finally absorbed into the late medieval Byzantine tradition and, on the eve of the Turkish conquest, clung in the face of a society in turmoil to its vision of the Uncreated Light, capable of transfiguring the world.

It was mainly from Kilifarevo, and probably from Paroria as well, that Hesychasm spread to the Rumanian principalities. Another source of this influence was Mount Athos, one of whose monasteries, Koutloumousiou, was placed (c. 1371) under the patronage of a Wallachian prince. In 1372 its abbot Chariton became metropolitan of "Oungrovlachia". But the central figure in the transmission of Hesychasm to Wallachia was the monk Nicodemus (d. 1406). Born of a Greek father and a Serbian mother, he received his training on Mount Athos, and is believed to have enjoyed the esteem of Philotheus, the Hesychast patriarch of Constantinople. Two famous Wallachian monasteries owe their foundation to him: Vodiţa (c. 1374) and Tismana (c. 1385). With his Byzantine, Serbian, Rumanian and Bulgarian connections (he corresponded on theological matters with Euthymius, patriarch of Trnovo), Nicodemus of Tismana is a living image of that cosmopolitan culture which, centred in Byzantium and cemented by Hesychasm, linked together the monasteries of Eastern Europe in the late Middle Ages. His friend, the Serbian monk Isaiah, was another Hesychast of international standing. As abbot of the Russian monastery of St. Panteleimon on Mount Athos (a post to which he was appointed by Stephen Dušan), he headed a delegation sent about 1375 by Prince Lazar of Serbia to Constantinople which persuaded the Patriarch Philotheus to revoke the excommunication levelled by his predecessor Callistus against the Serbian Church. Before long Hesychasm penetrated still further north, to Moldavia. Neamțu, the country's leading medieval monastery, was founded in the late fourteenth century, probably by one of Nicodemus' disciples. The spiritual interests of its monks may be glimpsed in the fact that among the manuscripts copied at Neamțu in the following century were the works of John of the Ladder and Gregory of Sinai.[16]

We know little about the formal organization of the Balkan and Rumanian monasteries of the late Middle Ages. The Hesychasts might have been expected to favour the eremitical or semi-erematical life, as more conducive to the practice of interior prayer. This, at least, seems to have been true of some of their leaders. Certainly a number of *hesychasteria* belonged to the *lavra* type of settlement, in which the monks lived in separate huts, though under the guidance of a spiritual director or abbot, and met only for the periodic celebrations of the liturgical office. But, paradoxically enough, Hesychasm contributed to the revival of coenobitic monasticism in Eastern Europe. One reason for this was the dislike felt by many leading Hesychasts for the individualism and laxity which were then affecting some of the Athonite foundations and which produced, in the late fourteenth century, a new type of "idiorrhythmic" monastery whose monks were allowed to acquire property and to free themselves from the abbot's authority. Only the restoration of the strict community life, it was felt, could arrest these aberrant tendencies. Secondly, the *koinobion*, or coenobitic monastery, was regarded in Hesychast circles as a necessary school for the monk who, having been trained in its rigorous discipline, was later called, either definitively or for a time, to devote himself to the solitary practice of "the prayer of the heart". That is why many a *koinobion*, particularly in this period, was associated with a group of secluded monks forming a dependent *lavra*. This connection between coenobitic and semi-eremitical monasticism was particularly close in late medieval Russia.

The fact that so many of the early Russian monasteries were situated in or near towns made them vulnerable to the attacks of the Mongols. A large number were sacked and destroyed during the invasion of 1237–40. Only in the second quarter of the fourteenth century did Russian monasticism begin to revive. This new movement, as the earlier one, derived its spiritual and organizational principles from Byzantium; but it differed from the earlier Russian model in several respects. Its leaders, moved by the desire for solitude and silence, were drawn to the vast virgin forests that stretched north of Moscow, over the upper reaches of the Volga, as far as the White Sea. But these hermits were seldom allowed to enjoy their solitude for long: disciples, attracted by their reputation for holiness, would join them, and gradually the recluse's wooden hut, or his abode in the hollow of a tree, was transformed into a society of the *lavra* type. The monks would clear the forest, sow crops and build a village in which peasants from the neighbourhood would settle. Gradually this semi-eremitical group grew into a large *koinobion*, owning lands donated by the state or bequeathed by individuals, and the original anchorite would become its often unwilling abbot. Not infrequently one of the brethren, with the permission of his spiritual father, would leave the now rich and bustling monastery and strike out alone into the forest further north, and the whole process would be repeated. This flight "into the desert", as it was called by contemporary writers, led to the rise of many new foundations, large and small, in Northern Russia; and the fourteenth and fifteenth centuries, during which this movement gathered momentum, became the golden age of Russian monasticism. The central figure in this monastic revival was St. Sergius of Radonezh, the founder of the Trinity monastery, seventy-one kilometres north of Moscow (in what is today Zagorsk). The ascetic and spiritual features of this most revered of all Russian saints, as portrayed by his contemporaries, remind one of St. Theodosius of Kiev. In two respects, however, the revival reflected contemporary trends in Byzantine monasticism. The gradual transition from the semi-eremitical to the coenobitic life was due in part to local geographical and economic causes: the *lavrai* scattered in the forest clearings of Northern Russia, living in rigorous frontier conditions, could best hope to survive by organizing themselves into working agricultural communities. The increased value placed in this period on coenobitic monasticism by the Byzantines undoubtedly accelerated this process. About 1354 St. Sergius was visited by envoys from the Patriarch Philotheus urging him to introduce a community rule into his monastery. After some hesitation, he complied with this request: and the Trinity Monastery, by adopting the Studite Constitution, became the model for all other late medieval Russian *koinobia*. Secondly, the monastery's close links with Constantinople facilitated the spread of Hesychasm to Central and Northern Russia. Some evidence of this is perhaps provided by St. Sergius' disciple and biographer Epiphanius, who describes his master's mystical experiences in terms which may suggest an analogy with Palamas' teaching on the Uncreated Light; however, the theological implications of his account are not specific enough for this connection to be traced with any certainty. More explicit evidence is provided by the library of the Trinity monastery which contained in the fourteenth and fifteenth centuries Slavonic translations of some of the classics of Hesychast spirituality.

Through the numerous sister and daughter houses of the Trinity monastery Hesychast influences spread in the late fourteenth and early fifteenth centuries to the far north of Russia. By 1400 a great centre of monastic settlement had arisen north of the upper Volga, between the Sheksna, the Sukhona and the Kostroma rivers. The most famous of these houses was founded by St. Cyril (*d.* 1427) near Beloozero (the White Lake). It was a strict and wealthy *koinobion*. In 1429 one of its monks settled on an island in the White Sea, laying the foundation of the monastery of Solovki: East Christian monasticism had reached the confines of the Arctic Ocean.

This late medieval monastic movement, which carried the Byzantine ascetic and spiritual tradition almost as far as the Arctic Circle, was not without its inner tension and conflicts. The new coenobitic foundations, including the Trinity monastery, soon began to acquire land and wealth. This enabled them to engage in works of charity, to recruit members of the aristocracy, and to develop that ornate and elaborate liturgical rite which became a distinguishing mark of the post-medieval Russian Church; but it also immersed them in the affairs of the world, and sometimes led to a decline in monastic discipline. The contemplative tradition often burned with a brighter flame in the smaller forest *lavrai*, called *skity* in Russia, whose monks came increasingly to believe that landowning was incompatible with the monastic estate. The leading representative of this movement was St. Nil (Nilus) Sorsky (*c.* 1433–1508). His teaching stressed the value of the semi-ere-mitical life in the *skit* as the "royal" or "middle" way between solitary and coenobitic monasticism, enabling the monk to combine obedience to his superior with dedication to perpetual prayer. He was more deeply influenced than any of his Russian contemporaries by Byzantine Hesychasm. In one of his writings he tells us of his visit to Mount Athos and "the lands of Constantinople" where he observed small groups of monks living together and practising *hesychia.*[17] On his return to Russia he founded a *skit* near the Beloozero *koinobion*, where he had received the tonsure. Though he seems unfamiliar with the writings of Gregory Palamas, he owes a considerable debt to the other teachers of Hesychasm: by far the most numerous of his quotations from the Church Fathers are (in this order) from John of the Ladder, Isaac the Syrian, Symeon the New Theologian and Gregory of Sinai.[18] Nil seems to have been the first spiritual teacher in Russia to have instructed his disciples to combine the practice of the "Jesus Prayer" with the psychosomatic methods used by the Balkan Hesychasts. He was the last outstanding representative of late Byzantine spirituality in medieval Russia.

This survey of East European monasticism will have shown that all the essential features of its ascetic and spiritual tradition and of its organization were borrowed from the leading monastic centres of the Byzantine Empire, above all from Mount Athos, Constantinople, and to a lesser extent from Thessalonica. In the variety of their formal structure and in the unity of their religious experience the East European monasteries of the Middle Ages faithfully reflected the ideals and achievements of their Byzantine models. It is not to monasticism that we must look for evidence of any significant deviation from Byzantine religious patterns.

There is perhaps only one field in which such a deviation may be seen. In several East European countries there developed a cult of national rulers for which no model can be found in Byzantium. The Byzantines, to be sure, endowed their emperors with sacred attributes. The *basileus*, whose sovereignty was held to be the earthly reflection of God's monarchy in heaven, was by virtue of his office raised high above the level of ordinary men. The epithets by which he was described—*isapostolos* ("equal of the apostles"), *hagios* ("holy"), even (until the ninth century) *theios* ("divine")—, the imperial "liturgy" which was the focus of the court ceremonial and resembled so closely that of the church, and the anointing which, from the twelfth century, formed part of the coronation ceremony, all emphasized his "holiness". Yet the Byzantine emperor lacked one feature which sustained the sovereignty of many European monarchs of the Middle Ages: despite his exalted status, he never became the centre and embodiment of a national community. The reasons for this are many and complex: among them was the racial diversity of the empire which, at least until the fourteenth century, prevented the growth of any sense of ethnic solidarity; the absence of a law of imperial succession, despite the growth of the idea of legitimacy after the ninth century and the stability of several imperial dynasties, of which the Macedonian, which reigned from 867 to 1056, was by far the most popular; above all, perhaps, the idea, which the Byzantines took over from the Romans and never wholly abandoned, that the imperial throne was the gift of providence and its violent seizure by revolutionary methods could be justified by their very success. The frequency of forced abdications and *coups d'état* in the history of the empire suggests that, despite their veneration for the imperial office, the Byzantines—except in the Macedonian period—seldom felt a strong emotional bond with their sovereign.

It was otherwise in several countries of Eastern Europe. There, particularly in Slavonic lands, native traditions of kingship, whose roots probably went back at least as far as the barbarian migrations, had established the ruler as the military leader of his people and the natural focus of their ethnic and religious loyalties. The coming of Christianity may have divested his sovereignty of some of its divine or magical attributes, and superimposed upon it the more distant and shadowy suzerainty of the emperor in Constantinople. But the blessing of the church gave a new spiritual dimension to his authority, and a stronger cultural and political unity to his people. As the baptiser of his nation and ruler by divine right, he too could now claim the title "equal of the apostles"; and his descendants, by fostering the cult of their saintly ancestor, could bring their country a step forward on the road to national self-determination and increase its international prestige. The holy kings and princes of Eastern Europe resemble in this respect the royal saints of the early Germanic kingdoms far more than they do the few emperors and empresses of Byzantium who were canonized for their services to the church. There is little evidence of a widespread cult of native ruler in medieval Bulgaria; but in Russia, and especially in Serbia, it had a long and remarkable history.

The Russian people's cult of some of their medieval rulers owed much to the fact that they all belonged to the same family. Both in the Kievan and the early Muscovite periods the princes were all descended from a common ancestor. Neither the multiplication of the princely branches nor, after the mid-eleventh century, the political fragmentation of the realm ever destroyed that bond between the ruler and his subjects which caused the dynasty to be regarded as a personification of the state and as a symbol of its continuity. Some of these princes were venerated by the people and canonized by the Russian Church for their evangelical zeal: above all the "apostolic" rulers Olga and Vladimir. Others owed their canonization to their outstanding services to church and nation: foremost among these was Alexander Nevsky (*c.* 1220–63), prince of Novgorod and later grand prince of Vladimir, who defeated the Swedes and the Teutonic Knights and humbled himself before the Tatars to save his subjects from their depredations. His medieval biographer compared him to Samson, Solomon and the Emperor Vespasian.[19] His *Vita*, despite the author's half-hearted attempt to cast it into a hagiographical mould, is in effect a tale of military valour. A third group of holy princes were victims of political assassination or, like the Greek "neo-martyrs" of the Ottoman period, gave their lives for the Christian faith. The most famous of these was Prince Michael of Chernigov, executed by the Tatars in 1246 for refusing to bow down before an idol of Chingis Khan.

The literary form of these princely *vitae* followed, more or less, the hagiographical pattern which their Russian authors borrowed from Byzantium. But their viewpoint was largely non-Byzantine. The concept they expressed of the holy ruler, linked to his people by language and blood, supernatural protector and patron of his nation, is much more akin to the image of the sacred monarch we find in biographies stemming from the Slav lands of Central and Eastern Europe. It was in medieval Serbia, however, that the cult of the holy king reached its fullest development.

Like the Russians, the Serbs during a large part of their medieval history were ruled by a single native dynasty. From the mid-twelfth century, when their country's political centre was transferred from maritime Zeta to inland Raška, and until 1371 every ruler of Serbia belonged to the family of Stephen Nemanja. The devotion which this dynasty inspired in the Serbian people, as well as the personal deserts of its members, have no doubt been exaggerated by its medieval and modern apologists: yet, allowing for this idealization, the extent to which the Nemanjids became identified in the eyes of their subjects with the achievements and aspirations of their nation remains impressive. The purpose of this ruler-cult, fostered by the princes themselves and by generations of court panegyrists, was doubtless in some measure political: it was to consolidate the legitimacy of the Nemanjids of Raška (at first perhaps against the rival claims of Zeta) and thus to increase the unity and cohesion of the realm. Its origins must be sought partly in the persistence of the ancient tribal ethos with its worship of dead ancestors; but it was primarily the influence of the church that endowed the Nemanjids with a sacred aura that exceeded the veneration paid to any other royal family in Eastern Europe. Here again it was St. Sava who laid the foundations on which his compatriots were to build. It was he who *c.* 1208 brought his father's body back from Chilandar to Serbia and fostered the belief, so central to Serbian medieval thought, that the welfare of the state is dependent on its possession of the miracle-working relics of its holy founder. In his celebrated biography of Nemanja, Sava created the image of the medieval Serbian king, patron of the church, founder of monasteries, friend of the emperor, redoubtable in battle, ruler by divine grace, who brought peace and renown to his realm and restored and enlarged his "inheritance";[20] and it is worth noting that this political "inheritance" (*dedina*) is conceived as something at once more tangible and restricted than the cosmic "inheritance" (*kleronomia*) claimed by the Byzantine emperors in their charters. This stylized pictures, free on the whole from hagiographical *clichés*, provided the model for future writers who continued, until the fall of the medieval Serbian realm, to record the exploits, secular and religious, of an unbroken line of holy kings. Together with the *Vitae* of the archbishops of Serbia, including those of St. Sava, these royal biographies, the best of which were written in the thirteenth and early fourteenth centuries, are the principal contribution made by the Serbs to the literature of medieval Europe.[21] They were probably influenced to some degree by Byzantine secular biography, whose most distinguished products were the Life of Basil I by his grandson Constantine Porphyrogenitus, and the story of Alexius I's exploits by his daughter Anna Comnena. But the strong impact of native traditions can be detected in their peculiar blend of family chronicle, hagiographical and monastic ideals and political concepts derived from the charters of medieval Serbian kings.

The East European cult of national rulers had one feature which deserves special mention, partly for its intrinsic interest and partly because it reveals a striking independence of Byzantine hagiographical and political models. It found expression in the posthumous veneration of princes who were victims of political murder and whose death was held to be a voluntary sacrifice, made in conscious imitation of Christ's sacrificial death. They were regarded as martyrs, not in the sense that they were killed for the Christian faith, but because, by their act of non-resistance, they chose to die as innocent and voluntary victims in imitation of Him who, by laying down His life for mankind, became the supreme prototype of all martyrs. Traces of this belief can be found in medieval Scandinavia: one of the versions of the death of St. Olaf, King of Norway (*d.* 1030), states that he was murdered by his subjects "and, since he did not resist, was put to death and crowned with martyrdom".[22] But it is in Slavonic countries that this cult of "martyred" princes found the widest scope for its development. The first of them was St. Wenceslas (Václav) of Bohemia. This Czech duke was put to death in 929 by order of his brother Boleslav, who coveted his throne. His earliest biographer, who wrote in Old Church Slavonic towards the middle of the tenth century, draws a patent analogy with Christ's death; and in his subsequent *Vitae*, composed during the hundred years that followed his murder, Wenceslas is glorified as a martyr.[23]

This cult of non-violence was carried a stage further in the biography of the Serbian prince John Vladimir of Dioclea. It is included in a Latin chronicle written in the twelfth century by an anonymous priest from Antibari (Bar) on the Adriatic coast.[24] An ally and probably a vassal of the Emperor Basil II, John Vladimir was forced to surrender himself and his lands to Samuel of Bulgaria. His imprisonment was cut short by romance. Samuel's daughter Kosara fell in love with him, and the Dioclean prince was restored to his throne, with Kosara as his queen. In 1016, two years after Samuel's death, he was treacherously lured to Prespa by the Bulgarian Tsar John Vladislav, and murdered. St. John Vladimir is depicted by his biographer as a Christ-like figure, who sacrificed himself for his people, and sought and gained a martyr's crown. His memory was kept throughout the Middle Ages on the South Adriatic coast from Lake Scutari to Dyrrachium, by Serbs, Greeks and Albanians; and his relics may still repose in the Albanian monastery of Shën-Gjin near Elbasan, named after him. In the interior of Serbia, however, his cult was soon forgotten, probably for political reasons: the rulers of Raška, who claimed an exclusive right over all Serbian lands and strove to establish the prerogatives of the Nemanja dynasty, no doubt sought to obliterate the memory of the patron saint of Dioclea-Zeta, whose kings had once held sway over most of the Serbian tribes. Yet the cult of "martyred" princes was not unknown in the late medieval Serbian kingdom: King Stephen Uroš III, deposed and murdered in 1331 at the instigation of his son Stephen Dušan, was held by the second half of the fourteenth century to be a martyr; and his official biographer, Gregory Tsamblak, abbot (c. 1400) of Dečani, his foundation, in an attempt to provide a rational basis for this belief, observed that "there is more than one road leading to martyrdom".[25]

The belief that the innocent victim of assassination can be regarded as a martyr, especially if he refuses to resist his murderers, found the widest and readiest acceptance in medieval Russia. It achieved its most articulate and popular expression in the cult of Boris and Gleb, the sons of St. Vladimir, killed in 1015 for political reasons by their elder brother Svyatopolk. The two princes were canonized by the Russian Church soon after their death. Their cult, fostered by successive rulers of Russia in the eleventh and twelfth centuries, naturally enhanced the prestige of the ruling dynasty and, to that extent at least, acquired political significance. Yet there is reason to believe that the manner of their death had an immediate and powerful impact upon their compatriots at large, and that people of all classes and stations of life soon became convinced that the murdered princes were numbered among the saints of God. We have striking testimony of this in three biographies written in Russia during the hundred years that followed their death. One of them, entitled *The Tale and Passion and Eulogy of the Holy Martyrs Boris and Gleb*, became—to judge from the numerous manuscripts of it that have survived—one of the most popular works of medieval Russian literature.[26] No doubt this was partly due to its literary merits: the story of the two murders is told with a fine command of dramatic tension, enhanced by the author's stress on the pitiful helplessness of the young princes. Both are afraid to die and cling desperately to their last moments on earth. Confronted with his assassins, Gleb pleads for mercy in terms reminiscent of folk laments: "Have mercy on my youth, have mercy, my lords! ... Do not reap me from my life that has not ripened, do not reap the unripe ear of corn. Do not cut down the vine that has not grown to maturity. ... This is no murder, but a cutting of unseasoned wood."[27] But the terror and the pity which the story aims to instil in the reader do not mask the spiritual significance of the death of Boris and Gleb. The author of the Tale might eschew conventional heroics, yet he makes it clear that the two brothers, faced with a decision between resistance and death, chose the latter deliberately, in conscious imitation of Christ and His martyred disciples.

There is some evidence that the national cult of these princely "passion-sufferers", as they were called in their country, was at first viewed by the Byzantines with a certain distrust. As late as 1072, the Greek metropolitan of Kiev is said to have disbelieved in their sanctity.[28] But the evidence of miracles recorded beside their graves, and perhaps diplomatic considerations as well, persuaded the patriarchate to give way. Not surprisingly, the memory of Boris and Gleb was venerated in Bohemia, where a portion of their relics was preserved in the eleventh century in the abbey of Sázava; the similarity between their death and that of St. Wenceslas is repeatedly pointed out in Russian medieval texts; and in the wake of the fairly close cultural relations which then existed between Bohemia and Kiev, the cult of the Czech saint spread to Russia.

The veneration of these murdered princes was fostered in Bohemia, in Russia and among the Serbs by the state authorities, hagiographers and recipients of the saints' posthumous favours. The conviction, widely held in the Middle Ages in France and England, that the king possesses in his life-time certain healing powers, has no parallel either in Byzantium or in the other lands of Eastern Europe. But in several Slavonic countries within the Byzantine Commonwealth the power to cure disease was ascribed posthumously to these murdered princes, who, it was believed, had earned a martyr's crown by the way in which they met their death. Members of their countries' ruling dynasties, these champions of non-violence became the patrons and supernatural protectors of their respective nations, in peace and in war. Though their cult has no analogy in the Byzantine tradition, the admiring devotion they inspired in their compatriots may serve to measure the impact which at least one teaching of the Christian Gospel had upon the minds of several peoples of Central and Eastern Europe.

2 LAW

The acceptance of Byzantine law by the countries of the East European Commonwealth may be viewed in the context of two wider historical phenomena: the diffusion of Byzantine civilization in those lands; and the "reception" of Roman law in medieval Europe as a whole. The second of these problems does not directly concern us here. Yet its obvious relevance to the theme of this section should not be overlooked. Byzantine law, however often reformulated and interpreted in the course of the empire's history, remained firmly based on Justinian's codification of Roman law. This same body of law, which remained dominant in Eastern Europe throughout the Middle Ages and in some areas survived the fall of Constantinople, continued to operate in Italy, Spain and Southern France during the "Dark Ages", and in the twelfth and thirteenth centuries became the common heritage of

Western civilization. But whereas in the West, after the fall of Rome, the history of this law was, in Vinogradoff's phrase, "a ghost story", its maintenance and diffusion in Eastern Europe were assured by the continued existence of the Eastern Roman Empire, whose political and administrative tradition never lost touch with its Roman origins. And in the lands of Eastern Europe that lay beyond the borders of the empire, ruling classes emerged in the early Middle Ages, ready and indeed anxious to "receive" the laws of Byzantium. There were several reasons for their interest in these laws. The first was purely practical: as these barbarian states acquired more developed institutions, the growing complexity of social and economic relations created legal problems which could no longer be solved by recourse to traditional customary law; the gaps between changing life and immutable custom could most conveniently be filled by borrowings from Byzantine legislation. This occurred most naturally in the Balkans, where the traditions of Romano-Byzantine law, antedating the Slav invasions, survived in the towns and among the clergy. The second reason was political: for the more ambitious monarchs of Eastern Europe who sought to increase their power and centralize their realms, Romano-Byzantine law, with its notion of the state lording it over individuals and classes, provided a welcome opportunity to ensure their ascendancy over all their subjects, great and small. The third reason was a religious one: adoption of Christianity made it necessary to obtain collections of canon law, which set forth the principles of church organization and prescribed a code of Christian discipline and behaviour. The *Nomocanones*, as these Byzantine collections were known, contained not only ecclesiastical legislation, but also imperial decrees on church matters. The "reception" of Roman law was thus bound up with the adoption of canon law. In Eastern no less than in Western Europe the saying was valid: *Ecclesia vivit sub iure Romano*. A fourth reason which facilitated the diffusion of Byzantine law was a cultural one. It lay in the immense prestige which the empire's legal tradition enjoyed in the eyes of its neighbours. No barbarian code could ever compete in this respect with the wisdom and perfection ascribed to the Byzantine law books, especially to those of Justinian whose authority in legislative matters was regarded as sacred both in Byzantium and in the lands of its commonwealth.

Two conclusions may be drawn from these preliminary remarks on the "reception" of Byzantine law. Firstly, it was a phenomenon closely connected with the development of new social and political structures in the "receiving" countries. Secondly, the active, creative role played in this transmission by the societies of these countries was often considerable. Selective borrowing and adaptation to local conditions were, we have seen, inherent in the process of diffusion of Byzantine civilization. This is clearly apparent in the field of law. The medieval lawyers of the East European countries outside the empire never acquired the necessary degree of reflection and juridical maturity to compose extensive glosses or to create schools of law. In this respect they fell far behind their Italian colleagues of the twelfth century. But they, or their political masters, proved able to select those handbooks of Byzantine law which were of greatest practical use; to commission their translation into Slavonic, often adapting the originals by adding or suppressing phrases or whole articles; and sometimes to insert into these Slavonic versions of Byzantine law items derived from Latin sources. For Eastern Europe, no less than for the West, we may accept the truth of Vinogradoff's statement: "The way in which the light of Roman legal lore was transformed while breaking through the many-coloured panes of local custom was most varied."[29]

Selective borrowing of a foreign culture implies the capacity of the "receiving" society to reject those of its aspects which, for one reason or another, it cannot or will not assimilate. In some cases particular features of Byzantine legislation encountered in their land of adoption a stubborn, and sometimes successful, resistance from local custom. The agents of this resistance were often aristocratic groups, reluctant to surrender their social or economic privileges to the Roman principle of equality of all citizens before the law. The fear of losing these privileges was, we have seen, the motive force behind the revolt of the Bulgar nobles against the decision of their ruler Boris to impose Christianity on his people in 865. In his letter to the pope, Boris asserted that the rebellious *boyars* had accused him of "giving them a law that is not good".[30] A curious instance of a successful resistance of Slavonic customary law to Byzantine legislation is recorded in the *Russian Primary Chronicle*. St. Vladimir, soon after his conversion, was faced with an outbreak of brigandage in his realm. Traditional custom required that murderers be punished by a system of "compositions", or monetary fines. The Byzantine bishops at the prince's court demanded that the death penalty be imposed on the criminals. Vladimir at first refused, but later agreed to the execution of those found guilty of robbery. Soon, however, it became apparent that the abolition of monetary fines for this offence was depriving the state of a much needed source of revenue. These economic considerations appear to have persuaded the clergy to drop their insistence on applying the Byzantine penal code. In the words of the chronicle, "the bishops and the elders [of the city] said: 'We have many wars; if we had the fines, we could use them to buy weapons and horses.' Vladimir said 'Let it be so'. And Vladimir lived [henceforth] according to the customs of his father and his grandfather." The chronicler attributes the prince's refusal to have the robbers executed to pious motives: "I fear sin", he is said to have declared to his bishops.[31] Whatever may be thought of this explanation, the story undoubtedly reflects the successive stages of a conflict between Slavonic customary law, which at that time did not recognize capital punishment by the state, and the more severe penal sanctions of Byzantine criminal law. The latter, as the story shows, suffered a rebuff. A similar case was recorded in Serbia, where capital punishment was likewise unknown until the mid-fourteenth century. In 1308 the senate of Ragusa requested King Milutin of Serbia to impose the death penalty on those of his subjects who were guilty of the murder of Ragusan citizens, on the grounds that this punishment is "*justicia quae Deo et hominibus et toti mundo amabilis est*". The king replied that he had sworn at his coronation not to spill the blood of his subjects, had no intention of doing so now and preferred to abide by the old Serbian custom of imposing fines for murder.[32] This, however, did not prevent him a few years later from having his eldest son blinded, in accordance with the time-honoured Byzantine method of disposing of political rivals.

In assessing the impact of the Byzantine legal tradition upon the countries of Eastern Europe, a distinction should be made between ecclesiastical and secular law. The distinction, it is true, is valid only in part, for Byzantine canon law included imperial legislation, and in many parts of the commonwealth the church enjoyed a measure of extra-ecclesiastical jurisdiction over the whole of society. Nevertheless the *Nomocanones* and the secular Byzantine law books had somewhat different fates in medieval Eastern Europe. The former were accepted unquestioningly and without change. The oldest of them, attributed to John Scholasticus, patriarch of Constantinople (565–77), was translated into Slavonic in the ninth century, probably by St. Methodius. It must have served the needs of the Cyrillo-Methodian mission in Moravia, and of the early Bulgarian Church. A little later, probably in tenth century Bulgaria, a second Slavonic version of the *Nomocanon* was made. The original, for long erroneously ascribed to the Patriarch Photius, was based on a seventh century Byzantine collection, containing the so-called apostolic canons, the rulings of the first four oecumenical councils and of some local synods, precepts of the Fathers of the Church, and imperial decrees on ecclesiastical matters. It was used in Bulgaria and Russia at least until the early thirteenth century. Finally about 1219 St. Sava, soon after his consecration as archbishop of Serbia, translated (or transcribed an earlier Slavonic version of) "Photius' Nomocanon", with commentaries by medieval Greek canonists, adding to it a complete translation of the *Procheiron* (a late ninth century code of Byzantine civil and public law) and of several edicts of Justinian and Alexius Comnenus. This work, which he carried out in Thessalonica, on his way home from Nicaea, provided the Slav peoples of the Byzantine Commonwealth with a single authoritative manual of canon and secular law. St. Sava's *Nomocanon*—known to the Slavs as the *Book of the Pilot*—became the basic constitution of the Serbian, Bulgarian and Russian churches.

The impact of Byzantine secular legislation on the lands of Eastern Europe is harder to measure. Only if we knew the extent of its influence on local custom could we hope to define this impact with any precision. Few medieval codes of customary law have, however, survived from these areas. From Bulgaria and Rumania we have none. Bulgarian medieval sources are notoriously scarce. It is virtually certain, however, that from 1018 to 1185 the lands between the lower Danube, the Adriatic and the Black Sea, annexed to the empire by Basil II, were administered by East Roman law: the code then in force in Byzantium was the *Basilica*, a revised version of the Justinian *Codex* issued by Leo VI (886–912).

The earliest evidence of Rumanian secular law dates from the fifteenth century: it was then purely Byzantine. In Serbia, as we shall see, some features of customary law survived in the country's late medieval legislation. It is only in Russia that medieval documents of indigenous law have survived in any number; but their relationship to the imported Byzantine law books is seldom clear. Little more can be attempted here than to trace the history of the Byzantine secular codes on East European soil, and to examine, whenever possible, their impact on native customary law.

The earliest Byzantine law book to be "received" in Eastern Europe offers something of a historical paradox. This was the *Ecloga*, issued in 726 by the Iconoclast emperors Leo III and Constantine V. It is a brief summary of the main rulings of private and criminal law then current, with the main emphasis on family law. Its avowed aims were to make Justinian's legislative work, the *Institutes*, the *Digest*, the *Codex* and the *Novels*, more intelligible, especially to provincials, and to revise it in the direction of "greater humanity". The *Ecloga* retained great influence in the empire until the 870s, when Basil I condemned it, on account of its Iconoclast origins, as "the annulment of good law".[33] But curiously enough, though it was largely discredited in Byzantium, it remained in its Slavonic versions the most popular Byzantine law book in the East European lands of the commonwealth until the fourteenth century.

There were two Slavonic versions of the *Ecloga*. One is a fairly faithful translation, probably done in tenth century Bulgaria. In several respects, however, it deviates from the original, in a manner suggesting a deliberate attempt to adapt the norms of Byzantine jurisprudence to the conditions of an early medieval Slav society. The most important of these changes is the omission of the chapter concerned with the lease of landed property: these Byzantine legal provisions could hardly have been applicable to the more primitive economy of the Slavonic countries, where large landed estates were still practically unknown. The other Slav version is of greater interest to the legal historian. Although it consists of relatively brief excerpts from the *Ecloga*, its deviations from the original are more significant. Its title is *Judicial Law for Laymen*. Its Bulgarian origin, for long accepted by most scholars, is now seriously questioned; persuasive arguments have been put forward to link it with ninth century Moravia; and it seems probable that it was compiled by Constantine or by his disciples for the aims of his mission among the Slavs of Central Europe. Of its thirty-two articles ten are literal translations, and nineteen are adaptations, of the *Ecloga*; the remaining three are not to be found in the original. Much of the book is concerned with criminal law. The adaptations reveal two tendencies: to substitute, in the case of serious offences, enslavement of the guilty party for the mutilation (blinding or cutting off the nose) decreed by the Byzantine text; and to impose, in addition to the secular penalties prescribed in the original, ecclesiastical punishment in the form of lengthy fasts. These fasts, accompanied by public penance, are the subject of those clauses for which no model can be found in the Greek *Ecloga*. The penitential discipline for which they provide corresponds more closely to contemporary Latin, rather than Byzantine, canon law, and points therefore to Moravia as the probable origin of at least this part of the *Judicial Law for Laymen*.

This Slavonic adaptation of the *Ecloga* was current in medieval Bulgaria. In Russia, where it has survived in many manuscripts, it was probably accepted in the pre-Mongol period; by 1280 at the latest it formed part of the *Nomocanon* used by the Russian Church, and so remains to the present day. It was not until the fourteenth century that the East European peoples acquired another collection of Byzantine law of comparable importance in their legal history. This was the *Syntagma*, compiled in Thessalonica in 1335 by the monk Matthew Blastares. It was intended as a handbook for the use of the clergy, and included material from the *Nomocanon* and from secular law books, such as the *Procheiron* and the *Basilica*. Translated into Slavonic in Serbia at the behest of Stephen Dušan, it enjoyed great authority there, as well as in Bulgaria, Russia and Rumania.

What effect did the "reception" of Byzantine law have on native legislation in Eastern Europe? For reasons already explained, this question can only be answered, and that very tentatively, in respect of Russia and Serbia. The first indigenous Russian code was the *Pravda Russkaya* ("The Russian Law"), whose earliest version was compiled in the eleventh century. It is not so much a systematic code as a collection of juridical notes and comments, and is essentially a handbook of customary, and particularly penal, law. Though its promulgation, first by Prince Yaroslav of Kiev, may have been due to his desire to imitate the emperors' legislative activity, and though scholars have detected in it some influence of the *Ecloga* (through the *Judicial Law for Laymen*), the *Pravda Russkaya*, taken as a whole, shows little evidence of being based on a Byzantine model. The sanction it accords to blood feuds, the absence of state-imposed capital punishment, its elaborate system of monetary "compositions" for many kinds of offence and its imposition of the blood-wite for murder, are far removed from the principles of Byzantine jurisprudence. On the other hand, these and other features of its penal prescriptions reveal some striking analogies with Frankish and Anglo-Saxon law. Nor has any Byzantine influence been detected in the late medieval Russian codes, the most notable of which are the "charters" of Pskov and Novgorod. Only one Russian legal document is patently based on Byzantine sources: the *Church Statute* of St. Vladimir. Although the extant text has suffered alteration, there is little doubt that it was issued in something like its present form soon after Russia's conversion to Christianity. It lists the various categories of people—ecclesiastics and persons dependent on the church—who are exempt from the jurisdiction of the civil courts; and the decision to publish these regulations was made, Vladimir states, after he had "consulted the Greek *Nomocanon*".[34] One feature of Vladimir's "statute" is, however, definitely non-Byzantine: the prince decreed that one-tenth of the revenue of his realm should be earmarked for the endowment of his royal church of Our Lady in Kiev. The church tithe was unknown in Byzantium, and the origin of this clause has consequently aroused much speculation: it is commonly (but not universally) believed that this practice was borrowed by Vladimir from the Western Church, where it was well established at the time.

If Russian secular jurisprudence shows little sign of direct Byzantine influence, late medieval Serbian legislation is deeply permeated by it. In 1349 the Tsar Stephen Dušan published his celebrated Code (*Zakonik*), and in 1354 he re-issued it in an enlarged form. In all the extant manuscripts the earlier version is preceded by the text of two Byzantine law-books in Slavonic translation: a shortened form of the *Syntagma* of Blastares, and a collection obscurely named *Justinian's Law*, thought to be an abridgment of the *Farmer's Law*, a code issued for provincial use in the late seventh or early eighth century, probably by Justinian II. The significant fact is that the *Zakonik* makes no attempt to duplicate the enactments of these East Roman codes, but supplements them in many ways. Further proof that Dušan intended to base the administration of his Serbo-Greek Empire on Byzantine law is found in the words of the charter by which he announced the publication of his code: its aim, he states, is to "establish the laws of the most true Orthodox faith appropriate to the holy Apostolic Church, to the lands and cities".[35] This aim was required by the very nature of his empire, in which Greeks outnumbered Serbs, and in whose newly-annexed provinces—Southern and Eastern Macedonia, Thessaly, Albania and Epirus—town people, landowners, monasteries and peasants had long lived by the norms of Byzantine law.

The *Zakonik*, which represents in essence the contribution made by Dušan's lawyers to his tripartite *Codex*, has certainly some basis in Serbian customary law. However, the old nationalistic and Romantic view that the *Zakonik* embodies the quintessence of the Serbian native traditions has now been generally abandoned. Many of its clauses, formerly thought to embody ancient Slav custom, have been shown to be derived from Byzantine law: among them are the articles which deal with the rules of legal procedure, extend state protection to the poor and the persecuted, and establish the principle of a realm transcending the interests of individuals and classes and ruled by a sovereign himself subject to the laws he has promulgated. In the last resort, Dušan's Code provides clear evidence of the strength which the Byzantine legal tradition still commanded in Eastern Europe in the late Middle Ages.

It will be evident from the foregoing account that the reception of East Roman law by the nations of Eastern Europe strengthened the bonds of the Byzantine Commonwealth. Its transmission could not fail to have political overtones. The public law of Byzantium rested on the axiom that the emperor was the source of all legislation and that his ordinances had universal validity throughout the Christian *oikoumene*. And the rulers of the East European lands, by accepting the imperial law books as mandatory within their own realms, implicitly subscribed to this belief. The fact that, at least in Russia and in Serbia, they issued codes of their own does not invalidate this conclusion. It merely underlines—andtheir political relations with the empire will already have demonstrated this—that in matters of state administration they regarded themselves as fully sovereign within their domains. This sovereignty was, in the intellectual climate of the Middle Ages, fully compatible with the universal, meta-political, authority conceded to the emperor, the supreme law-giver in Christendom. The degree to which this authority was specifically recognized in the field of law no doubt varied from country to country. Byzantine secular legislation seems to have been most readily accepted by the Balkan Slavs and the Rumanians. In Russia its influence was felt mainly through the medium of canon law. The Byzantine *Nomocanones* contain a number of statements in which the emperor's position in Christendom is clearly defined: not the least explicit of them is found in the preface to the sixth Novel of the Emperor Justinian, issued in 535:

> The greatest blessings which God's philanthropy, coming from on high, has conferred upon mankind are the priesthood and the imperial authority (*basileia*). The priesthood ministers to things divine; the imperial authority presides and watches over things human; but both proceed from one and the same source, and both adorn the life of man.[36]

Such texts, included in the law books which the East European nations borrowed from the empire, not only underline the status of the Byzantine emperor, the highest authority on earth; they also express that constantly sought for, though seldom realized, ideal of the harmonious, "symphonic" relationship between church and state which was yet another legacy of Byzantium to the countries of Eastern Europe.

NOTES

1. John of Damascus, *De imaginibus oratio II*, PG 94, col. 1297; English transl. E. Barker, *Social and Political Thought in Byzantium* (Oxford, 1957), p. 87.
2. Photius, ep. 13, *PG* 102, col. 724. See above, p. 127.
3. *Descriptio Constitutionis Monasterii Studii*, PG 99, col. 1704.

4. Ed. I. Ivanov, *Godishnik na Sofiiskiya Universitet, ist.-filol. fak.*, xxxii, 13 (1936), pp. 28–37.

5. *Povest'*, p. 107; Cross, p. 141.

6. *Povest'*, pp. 105–6; Cross, pp. 139–40.

7. *Das Paterikon des Kiever Höhlenklosters*, ed. D. Tschiżewskij (Munich, 1964), pp. 20–78; English transl. G. P. Fedotov, *A Treasury of Russian Spirituality* (London, 1950), pp. 15–49.

8. See G. P. Fedotov, *The Russian Religious Mind*, i (Cambridge, Mass., 1966), pp. 110–31.

9. *Povest'*, pp. 126–31; Cross, pp. 159–64.

10. *Das Paterikon*, pp. 124–8, 134–49, 155–71, 179–89: German transl. in *Russische Heiligenlegenden*, ed. E. Benz (Zurich, 1953), pp. 180–243.

11. *Das Paterikon*, p. 99.

12. Ibid., p. 103.

13. P. Devos, "La version slave de la Vie de S. Romylos", *Byzantion*, xxxi (1961), p. 176.

14. A. Elian, "Byzance et les Roumains à la fin du Moyen Age", *Proceedings of the XIIIth International Congress of Byzantine Studies* (London, 1967), p. 199.

15. *Zhitie i zhizn' prepodobnago otsa nashego Feodosiya*, ed. V. N. Zlatarski, *Sbornik za Narodni Umotvoreniya, Nauka i Knizhnina*, xx (1904), pp. 22–3.

16. E. Turdeanu, *La littérature bulgare du XIVe siècle et sa diffusion dans les pays roumains* (Paris, 1947), p. 12.

17. F. von Lilienfeld, *Nil Sorskij und seine Schriften* (Berlin, 1963), p. 254.

18. Ibid., pp. 124–6.

19. V. Mansikka, *Zhitie Aleksandra Nevskogo* (St. Petersburg, 1913), p. 2.

20. *Spisi sv. Save*, ed. V. Ćorović (Belgrade, 1928), pp. 151–75. German transl. and commentary, S. Hafner, *Serbisches Mittelalter* (Graz, 1962), pp. 27–61.

21. Stephen the First-Crowned, *Life of St. Symeon* (Stephen Nemanja): *Svetosavski Zbornik*, ii (Belgrade, 1939), pp. 15–76; German transl. and commentary, S. Hafner, *Serbisches Mittelalter*, pp. 65–129; Archbishop Danilo and others, *Životi kraljeva i arhiepiskopa srpskih*, ed. Dj. Daničić (Zagreb, 1866); Domentijan, *Život sv. Simeuna i sv. Save*, ed. Daničić (Belgrade, 1865); Teodosije, *Život sv. Save*, ed. Daničić (Belgrade, 1860).

22. Adam of Bremen, *Gesta Hammaburgensis Ecclesiae Pontificum, MGH, Scriptores rerum Germanicarum in usum scholarum*, ed. B. Schmeidler (Hanover, 1917), schol. 41 (42), p. 120; English transl. F. J. Tschan, *History of the Archbishops of Hamburg–Bremen* (New York, 1959), p. 96.

23. *Fontes Rerum Bohemicarum*, i, pp. 125–39, 146–90, 199–227.

24. *Letopis popa Dukljanina*, ed. F. Šišić (Belgrade, 1928), pp. 331–41.

25. Gregory Tsamblak, *Život Stefana Dečanskoga, kralja srbskoga: Arkiv za Povjestnicu Jugoslavensku*, iv (Zagreb, 1857), p. 21.

26. *Zhitiya svyatykh muchenikov Borisa i Gleba*, ed. D. I. Abramovich (Petrograd, 1916), pp. 27–66; *A Historical Russian Reader*, ed. J. Fennell and D. Obolensky (Oxford, 1969), pp. 21–51.

27. *Zhitiya*, p. 41.

28. Ibid., p. 56.

29. P. Vinogradoff, *Roman Law in Mediaeval Europe* (London, 1909), pp. 18–19.

30. *Resp.* 17, *PL* 119, col. 988.

31. *Povest'*, pp. 86–7; Cross, p. 122.

32. *Liber Statutorum Civitatis Ragusii*, liber viii, cap. 58: *Monumenta historico-juridica Slavorum meridionalium*, ix (Zagreb, 1904), pp. 201–2.

33. I. and P. Zepos, *Jus graecoromanum*, ii (Athens, 1931), p. 116.

34. *Pamyatniki Russkogo Prava*, ed. S. V. Yushkov, i (Moscow, 1952), pp. 237–44.

35. *Zakonik Stefana Dušana*, ed. S. Novaković (Belgrade, 1898), p. 5.

36. *Novella 6, praefatio: Corpus Iuris Civilis*, iii, pp. 35–6.

I I

Literature and Art

I LITERATURE

In an earlier chapter, in which some of the agents affecting the spread of Byzantine civilization to Eastern Europe were discussed in general terms, emphasis was laid on the role of intermediaries. The importance of this factor is nowhere so apparent as in the realm of literature. Here the East European peoples were provided, at the time of their conversion to Christianity, with a channel which ensured a regular flow of cultural influence from the Greek-speaking world, and were thus able to build up rapidly a literary tradition based on Byzantine models. This channel, which was to prove of great cultural potency, was the Old Church Slavonic language. The rise of this language, which owes its existence to the translation by Constantine-Cyril and his collaborators of the Greek New Testament and liturgical offices into a Slavonic dialect of Southern Macedonia, has already been described. Its role as a cultural intermediary was assured by its peculiar relationship to medieval Greek on the one hand, and to the spoken languages of the Slav peoples on the other. It also owed much of its success to the skill of the early translators who developed it into a refined and supple instrument.

In its earliest phase Old Church Slavonic was shaped by the struggle to render into a tongue innocent of any literary heritage the rich variety of Byzantine Greek. This struggle with the tradition of Greek prose and poetry varied in difficulty. The relatively simple and straightforward Greek of the New Testament offered few formidable difficulties to the translators; the liturgical texts, with their poetic texture, florid syntax and larger number of abstract terms for which there was often no exact equivalent in

416

Slavonic, presented more of a problem. The hardest to render were the Greek patristic writings, whose style, often ornate and involved, was steeped in the traditions of classical rhetoric. We can judge of the quality of the first translations by the earliest extant manuscripts in Old Church Slavonic, written in the eleventh (in some cases perhaps in the late tenth) century, and also from a fragment of Constantine's preface to his Slavonic Gospel lectionary. In this work the inventor of Glagolitic script and creator of Old Church Slavonic explains the principles and methods he has adopted in his translation: he has attempted, he says, to give as literal a rendering as possible of this most sacred of all Christian texts; yet the differences between Greek and Slavonic are such that a word-for-word translation was not feasible for reasons of accuracy and style: "for we have need not of words or terms, but of the meaning".[1] In his translations, and notably in his Gospel lectionary, Constantine proved as good as his word: he rendered the different shades of meaning of the same Greek term by several Slavonic words, paraphrased the original when a literal translation would have obscured its sense, and sometimes devised Slav equivalents for Greek turns of phrase. His achievement, applauded by modern philologists, was to safeguard the essential qualities of the Slavonic vocabulary and syntax, while enriching the new language with loan words, semantic calques and syntactical and stylistic devices borrowed from Greek. The imprint of the Greek language upon Old Church Slavonic, and thus upon the literature of medieval Eastern Europe, proved indelible.

The relationship between Old Church Slavonic and the spoken languages of the Slav world was more complex. In the ninth century, at the time of the Cyrillo-Methodian mission, the Slavonic idioms were still very close to each other, the differences between them being far less marked than those which divide the various German and Italian dialects of today. The Slavs in this period were still conscious of speaking the same tongue. The South Macedonian dialect, used by Constantine for his translations, was intended not just for the Moravians, but for all the Slavs. Two centuries later, however, the situation had altered. The growing number of Byzantine writings translated into Old Church Slavonic had made this language at once richer and more complex. The neologisms and semantic calques introduced from Greek to express notions new to the Slavs, and the increasing use of devices borrowed from Byzantine prose and alien to the syntactical structure of Slavonic—especially the coining of compound words—tended to elevate Old Church Slavonic above the level of ordinary speech and to endow it with a hieratic and learned quality. This process was not yet far advanced in the eleventh century: to the Bulgarians and the Russians, for example, Old Church Slavonic must have seemed at that time merely a superior form of their own spoken tongue. Yet it was felt to be a sacred idiom, the proper vehicle for the dialogue between God and man, and the only language fit for the higher forms of literature. It was not, however, the only written language used by the Slavs. In Russia, for instance, the spoken vernacular was already employed in the eleventh century both for private correspondence and for the codes of local customary law, such as the *Pravda Russkaya*—a fact all the more noteworthy since the Byzantine law books circulated only in Old Church Slavonic versions, and were never translated into the vernacular. The same dichotomy between two written languages, the literary and the non-literary, can be observed in other medieval Slav countries. But the two not infrequently overlapped. The fact that Church Slavonic retained throughout the Middle Ages a close relationship to the spoken vernacular of the different Slav countries made possible a degree of interpenetration between the literary and the spoken idioms for which we find no parallel in the history of medieval Latin in the West. The capacity for hybridization shown by Church Slavonic is one of the secrets of its profound and lasting influence upon the Slav languages of Eastern Europe, not least upon modern Russian.

An intermediary can be a screen as well as a bridge. The very success of Old Church Slavonic as a literary language made it unnecessary for most educated people in Eastern Europe to learn Greek. Some of them undoubtedly did, notably in the upper ranks of the clergy and in royal chancelleries. But an extensive knowledge of the language seems to have been somewhat rare, particularly in medieval Russia. The Byzantine writings translated into Slavonic were mostly ecclesiastical in character. The combined effect of these two facts was to inhibit the Orthodox Slavs from gaining access to the literature and thought of classical Greece. This was undoubtedly a loss, and it must be recognized

418

that Old Church Slavonic was responsible for restricting the range of Greek culture accessible to the Slavs. Some elements of this culture did, however, filter through in the Slavonic versions of Greek writings which, as we shall see, were acquired by the Slavs in the early Middle Ages: these included Byzantine patristic works and the Christian hymnography of the Empire, which owe much to the traditions of classical rhetoric. It is true nonetheless that the secular and pagan elements in Byzantine literature had far less impact upon the thought-world of the Orthodox Slavs, and that—with the possible exception of Vladimir's educational establishments in Russia—the non-Greek-speaking countries of Eastern Europe do not seem to have taken over the state-sponsored schools, which were so important a feature of Byzantine urban culture from the early tenth century onwards. On the other hand, by providing the Slavs with a literary medium which was close to their spoken vernacular, Old Church Slavonic greatly increased the number of educated persons in Eastern Europe capable of acquiring this culture, albeit partially and indirectly.

One further general point regarding the Church Slavonic linguistic tradition must be made. The summit of its achievement, in terms of the quality of literary output, stands at the very beginning of its long history, in the first two generations of translators, i.e. between 862 and approximately 910. This was partly due, no doubt, to the prestige which Old Church Slavonic came to enjoy immediately after its creation, and which caused medieval Slav writers to regard the language of Cyril and Methodius as a divine legacy which might be imitated, but never surpassed. Thus, whereas the unsophisticated Greek of the New Testament must have seemed to the Byzantines, on linguistic grounds, greatly inferior to classical Greek which remained for them the literary ideal, Old Church Slavonic, whose vocabulary and syntax were modelled on the classicizing medieval Greek, appeared vastly superior to the primitive Macedonian dialect on which it was based. Moreover, Old Church Slavonic was particularly well served by its earliest users. Few, if any, of the subsequent translations into that language equalled those of Cyril and Methodius and of their immediate disciples, carried out in Constantinople, Moravia and Macedonia. A decline in quality seems to have set in already in the first half of the tenth century, traceable to the Bulgarian school of

Preslav. With some conspicuous exceptions, translations tended to become more mechanical, and the Greek syntax was followed more slavishly, in a manner often far removed from Constantine-Cyril's profound philological and literary insight. The subsequent history of Old Church Slavonic was determined by the remarkable fact that it reached the peak of its achievement as a literary language during the formative years when it was struggling to reconcile the peculiar qualities of the Slavonic tongue with the linguistic tutelage of Greek, and thus to acquire its identity.

No comprehensive account can be given here of the later development of Church Slavonic, nor of the literature written in that language during the Middle Ages. Our inquiry must be confined to two distinct periods in the history of East European literature: the first extends from the late ninth century to approximately the year 1100, the second covers the fourteenth and the early fifteenth centuries. It is instructive to consider the similarities, and the differences, between the writings of these two periods: such a comparison may help us to understand better the character and the dynamics of Byzantium's cultural influence upon Eastern Europe.

The first period is marked by several striking characteristics. In the first place, Slavonic literature before 1100 was still remarkably homogeneous. It retained an organic link with the Cyrillo-Methodian tradition, and was based on a common Old Church Slavonic language. This language was used by writers in Moravia, Bohemia, Croatia, Bulgaria and Russia. So uniform was this literary tradition that it is often exceedingly difficult to identify on linguistic grounds the origin of Old Church Slavonic texts written during this period in these various countries. It was only in the twelfth century that this linguistic unity began to break up, and Old Church Slavonic, under growing pressure from the different forms of the national vernacular, started to give way to local recensions of what philologists term "Church Slavonic".

The homogeneity of the Old Church Slavonic literary tradition explains another of its characteristics. The writings—translations and original works—composed within the area over which it spread should be regarded as creations of a single, supranational literature. The nationalistic point of view of earlier literary historians, who treated works written in ninth century Macedonia, tenth century Bohemia and eleventh century Kiev as products of separate

34-36 Piety, divinely-sanctioned authority and care for the well-being of the Church were three attributes of the Byzantine emperor's sovereignty. They are illustrated in 34 (above) the late ninth-century mosaic in the narthex of St Sophia, depicting Leo VI in adoration before Christ; 35 (right) the ivory relief (c. 945) showing Constantine VII Prophyrogenitus being crowned by Christ; and 36 (below) the votive mosaic panel (probably executed in 1118) in the south gallery in St Sophia, representing the Virgin and Child between John II Comnenus and the Empress Irene, who in a ritual gesture offer a bag of money and a diploma.

37 *King Vladislav* (*c.* 1234-43). This contemporary portrait of the founder of Mileševa, remarkable for its expressiveness and lack of idealisation, may well have been painted from life.

38 (below left) *Nemanja's Family Tree*. In the fourteenth century, the custom arose of depicting the apotheosis of the Serbian dynasty in this schematic form, inspired by the iconography of the Tree of Jesse. Portrayed as the monk Symeon, Stephen Nemanja, flanked by his sons Sava and Stephen, upbears his descendants, while Christ hovers over them, making a symmetrical gesture of blessing (Dečani).

39 (below) Miniature from a Gospel Book (copied in 1356) in the British Museum, shows the Bulgarian Tsar with his wife and two sons.

40 (above) About 1045 Prince Yaroslav had himself and his family painted in the central nave of his cathedral in Kiev. Portrayed were the prince (presenting a model of St Sophia to Christ), his wife, his five sons and his five daughters. Less than half of the composition has survived. Three of Yaroslav's daughters—who may be the ones depicted here—became respectively queens of Norway, France and Hungary.

41 In this votive fresco (painted in 1488) in the monastery church of Voroneţ in Bucovina, the monastery's founder, Stephen the Great of Moldavia, followed by his family, offers a model of his church to Christ. Their vigorous and realistically portrayed faces contrast with the more abstract features of Christ and St. George. The princely clothes, and the treatment of the subject, are purely Byzantine.

42-43 *The Iconoclast Crisis.* The condemnation of Iconoclasm strengthened the Empire's powers of expansion and enabled its religious art to spread throughout Eastern Europe. Two opposite phases of the conflict are depicted in these miniatures: 42 (left) to implement the decrees of the Iconoclast Synod of 815, an image of Christ is being daubed with whitewash (Barberini Psalter); 43 (below) the Iconodule Patriarch Nicephorus (806-15) is treading on the prostrate Iconoclast Patriarch John the Grammarian (837-43) (Chludov Psalter).

44-45 (above) *Igor's naval campaign against Byzantium* (941) A Byzantine and a Russian view of the decisive encounter. In the Greek Scylitzes manuscript (44) six Byzantine warships are attacking five Russian ones, three of which are sinking. The Russian version (Radziwill) shows Igor's navy about to be destroyed by Greek fire (45). The details are fanciful, for the Greek fire was discharged from ships.

46 The Emperor's triumph over his enemies was a traditional theme of Byzantine imperial iconography. Probably painted to celebrate the conquest of Bulgaria in 1018, this miniature portrays the Emperor Basil II in parade armour, crowned by Christ, his diadem and spear held by two archangels, while at his feet Bulgarian chieftains grovel in the dust (Venice Psalter).

47-48 Christian rulers of Eastern Europe and of Caucasian lands often rendered honour or homage to the emperor. (47) and (48) The audience granted by Constantine Porphyrogenitus to Olga of Kiev is here seen through Byzantine and Russian eyes. (47) In the Scylitzes manuscript Olga, attended by a lady-in-waiting, stands respectfully before the seated emperor. (48) In the Russian version she sits conversing with her imperial godfather, whose servants bring her precious gifts (Radziwill).

49 (below) The entry of a nation into the Byzantine Commonwealth was usually achieved through the conversion of its ruler to Greek Christianity. The Baptism of Bulgaria (865): the Emperor Michael III and the Empress hold out their arms in a symbolical gesture to receive their godson Boris, who is being christened by the Patriarch. Behind the latter stands a group of Boris' nobles waiting to be baptised (Manasses).

50 (above) In some areas of Eastern Europe Christianity and the patterns of Byzantine culture that went with it had to be imposed by force. The axe and the cross, borne by prince and bishop, are about to lay low the leader of a pagan revolt in Novgorod (c. 1071). (Radziwill)

51 Byzantine diplomacy was not always successful. The imperial government's negotiations with Symeon in 913 did not save the Empire from further Bulgarian attacks. Above, Symeon, seated on the left, is entertained at a state banquet in the Blachernae Palace by Constantine VII (on his left) and the Patriarch Nicholas (in the centre). One detail at least is fictitious: for Constantine was eight years old at the time: nor is it certain that Symeon was ever allowed into Constantinople. (below) Symeon at the head of his troops is attacking the Byzantines, whose emperor engages in spirited rear-guard action. In fact there is no record of the emperor taking the field in person against Symeon's armies (Manasses).

2 To most Europeans he Byzantine Emperor ust have seemed a emote yet sacred fig- re. In this late medi- val Russian miniature e Emperor Heraclius ears a wholly fanciful own. By contrast his o courtiers wear oth hats identical ith the head-dress of edieval Russian inces (Radziwill).

53 and 54 The siege of Constantinople in 1453. Details from a sixteenth-century painting in the monastery church of Moldoviţa in Bucovina emphasises the military valour and the piety of the Byzantines in the face of the Turkish onslaught.

Bulgarian, Czech and Russian literatures, though still entrenched in the textbooks, is being gradually abandoned by modern scholars. One of them has aptly described this literary tradition as the Slavonic recension of Byzantine culture. The history of this common literature has yet to be written, and until we have a detailed comparative study of its principal works all conclusions regarding it must remain tentative. There is little doubt, however, that its supranational character admirably equipped it for the role of a cultural intermediary, both between Byzantium and the Slavs and between the various countries of Eastern Europe. Cultural intercourse between the different parts of the commonwealth was promoted by a brisk circulation of Old Church Slavonic manuscripts. From Moravia Cyrillo-Methodian writings were carried to Bohemia, Croatia and Bulgaria; from Bulgaria a large part of the corpus of translations done by native scholars travelled to Russia; the Russians also borrowed and absorbed into their own literature works produced in Moravia and Bohemia. These constant migrations of texts, which were formerly thought to result from successive waves of reciprocal national "influences", should be seen rather as the circulation within a single international community of one body of literature regarded as its common preserve. The instigators, agents and beneficiaries of these cultural exchanges were mostly churchmen and scholars who were transferred, or moved of their own free will, from country to country: these itinerant *literati*, Byzantines as well as Slavs, contributed much to the cosmopolitan culture of the East European world of the early Middle Ages. The inter-Slav character which some of these texts acquired in the process of migration was, in other cases, imprinted on them from the start: in more than one cultural centre scholars from several Slavonic countries, sometimes no doubt assisted by Byzantines, produced translations by a common effort; such international centres were Constantinople, Thessalonica, Mount Athos, Ohrid, Preslav, the abbey of Sázava in Bohemia and Kiev. In the latter city, the *Russian Primary Chronicle* tells us, Prince Yaroslav in 1037 assembled many scribes who translated books from Greek into Slavonic.[2] The traces of several Slavonic languages apparent in some translations current in Russia at the time suggest that Yaroslav's scribes may have formed a kind of international commission.

The translation of Greek works into Slavonic was, of course, part of the wider process of Byzantine cultural diffusion. We may thus expect to find in this literary activity the social overtones which, we have seen, existed in the encounter between the Byzantine Empire and a number of medieval Slav societies, all of them in a state of rapid development, whose ruling classes had reasons of their own for wishing to adopt some at least of the empire's civilization. The fact that this civilization could now be clothed in a native literary garb made the prospect doubly attractive. It is hence not surprising to find the East European rulers actively "reaching out" for the literature of Byzantium; furthermore, following a pattern we have observed in other fields, particular aspects of this literature were selected to meet specific needs of the "receiving" countries, and the selected products were adapted in their new homes to local requirements. The selection, it is true, was sometimes done by the Byzantines, though more often by their Slav pupils. This occurred, at least in the beginning, with the translations of the Byzantine service books. This work, performed by Cyril and Methodius for the needs of the Moravian mission, and continued by their disciples in Bulgaria, provided the medieval Slav Churches with virtually the whole corpus of Greek liturgical texts. Medieval Greek liturgical poetry, which is the greatest creation of Byzantine verbal art, has not ceased to the present day to exert a powerful influence upon the mind and emotions of the Orthodox Slavs. Its effect in the Middle Ages even on the less educated converts of Byzantium must have been overwhelming. Recent studies of the earliest Slavonic liturgical manuscripts have shown that the first translators, and especially Constantine-Cyril who was himself an accomplished Greek poet, succeeded in adapting the metrical forms and structures of the originals to the syllabic requirements of Slavonic speech in a manner which combined respect for the traditional text with creative originality. And together with translations of Greek liturgical books the Slavs received in this period the melodies used for the sung parts of the services. The earliest systems of Byzantine musical notation have not yet been deciphered; but it is clear that the basic principles of Byzantine chant, its structural organization and melodic vocabulary, were adopted at the outset by the Slavonic Orthodox churches. This was done with the same combination of accuracy and freedom which marked Constantine's translation of the Gospel lectionary: while fidelity to the meaning of the original remained the primary aim, the translators of the musical manuscripts chose to paraphrase the text rather than to give a literal rendering whenever this was needed to reproduce the syllabic structure of the Byzantine melody.

Next to the Bible, the provision of liturgical books—the most important were the texts of the liturgies of St. John Chrysostom, of St. Basil of Caesarea and of the Presanctified, the *Euchologion*, the *Horologion*, the *Triodion*, the *Pentekostarion*, the *Heirmologion* and the *Oktoechos*—was the first prerequisite for setting up the new Slavonic churches. The next stage was to provide these churches with a means of consolidating and spreading the new faith and of defending it against paganism and heresy. The Byzantine missionaries and their Slav converts found this instrument in Greek patristic literature. The choice they made in this immense body of writing is instructive: the great majority of the Greek fathers whose works were translated in this period *in extenso* or in anthologies belonged to the golden age of patristics, the fourth and the fifth centuries; among them were Athanasius, the three Cappadocians—Basil, Gregory of Nazianzus and Gregory of Nyssa—, John Chrysostom, Isidore of Pelusium and Theodoret of Cyrus. It is noteworthy that, at least before the thirteenth century, many more writings of these early Greek Fathers were translated into Slavonic than works of contemporary Byzantine literature. One of the reasons for this was no doubt a practical one: the patristic corpus, with its coherent body of Christian doctrine, its compendious exegesis of the Scriptures and its sermons which could be used for many occasions, offered theoretical and practical guidance to East European churchmen who, like their fourth and fifth century predecessors, strove to impose Christianity upon a troubled and still semi-pagan world. Several of these Fathers, moreover, enjoyed a unique authority in Eastern Christendom: in the late tenth century the Bulgarian priest Cosmas urged his country's clergy to "imitate the holy Fathers and bishops who performed their duties before you—I mean Gregory, Basil, John and the others, the mere mention of whose names is enough to strike fear into the demons".[3]

Next to the Scriptures, the liturgical books and patristic works, the Slavs borrowed most readily from Byzantium the Lives of the Saints. The greater part of the official hagiographical corpus of the Greek Church was translated into Slavonic in this period. These *Vitae*, which either circulated singly or were collected in *menologia* by months of the ecclesiastical year, extolled the virtues of Christian heroism, and often satisfied the craving of the medieval man for the wonderful and the miraculous. Apart from monastic hagiography, which has been discussed in the preceding chapter, a notable favourite was the *Life of St. Alexius*, translated into Slavonic in the tenth century. It tells the story of a young Roman nobleman who left his wife on his wedding night and, after many years spent in prayer and fasting in distant lands, returned to die in his parents' home, unrecognized by anyone. The Byzantine hagiographical tradition, to which the Slavs began to make their own contribution as early as the ninth century, soon became the common patrimony of the East European peoples: its international character is nowhere more apparent than in the cult of St. Demetrius of Thessalonica, whose posthumous defence of his city against the attacks of the Slavs is extolled by his Greek biographers, and who became one of the most popular saints in the medieval Slav world.

The study of this hagiography is of interest to the literary historian because it shows that some Byzantine works appealed to the Slavs not only on account of their spiritual content, but also for their narrative value. Sometimes indeed the edifying and the picturesque were scarcely distinguished: this is true of *Barlaam and Josaphat*, a Christian version of an Indian story of the Buddha, translated in this period. Other writings, of a more explicitly secular character, were obviously selected for their literary qualities or informative value. Among them were Flavius Josephus' *History of the Jewish War* and the *Romance of Alexander* by the Pseudo-Callisthenes, works which introduced the Slav reader to the world of antiquity, the *Physiologus* and the *Christian Topography* of Cosmas Indicopleustes, which provided them with a smattering of natural history and geography, and the epic poem *Digenis Akritas*, which describes the wars waged against the Arabs by the Byzantines on the Eastern frontier. All these works were translated from Greek into Slavonic not later than the twelfth century, and some of them at least a hundred years earlier.

Of the secular works translated in this period the most influential were the Byzantine chronicles. The historiography of the East Roman Empire was of two kinds. On the one hand there was the ordered account of events by writers who strove to imitate the ideas and style of the Greek classical historians, Herodotus and Thucydides. They aimed at objectivity, polished presentation and the discovery of causal relations between events. Of the twenty or so distinguished practitioners of this art, between the sixth and the fifteenth century, the majority were lay scholars, high military or civil officials, or members of the imperial family. They naturally wrote for the educated classes of society. These writings were generally known as histories. On the other hand there were the chronicles, popular works with a conception of history less sophisticated and more explicitly Christian. They were usually written by monks or priests in homely and unadorned language, and were intended for the less educated reader. Their theme was world history, from Adam to the writer's time, and their purpose was to illustrate the role played by the Christian Empire of Byzantium in the story of man's salvation, traceable through the destiny of the Jewish and Greek peoples, the Hellenistic monarchies of the Near East, and Rome. Their authors were interested less in the causal relationship between events than in their sequence, which could be used to show that the Byzantines, the people of the New Covenant, were the divinely appointed guardians of the Orthodox faith for whose triumph the earlier states and societies of mankind had providentially paved the way.

It is a striking fact that, whereas not one of the Byzantine histories seems to have been translated into Slavonic during the Middle Ages, Slav versions were made of most of the chronicles. Some scholars have attempted to explain it by arguing that the histories were too difficult to translate because of their classicizing language, and that their contents, concerned solely with Byzantine events, would have held no interest for Slavonic readers. These arguments are unconvincing. The Slavonic translators, as we have seen from the examples of liturgical and patristic texts, were perfectly capable of grappling with the most intractable specimens of Greek; while the repeated use made by East European writers of material relating to Byzantine history contained in the chronicles shows that they were extremely interested in the events of this

425

history. Their preference for the chronicles can be attributed more satisfactorily to the religious interpretation of history contained therein: to the belief, in particular, that human affairs are controlled by supernatural forces which manifest themselves in earthquakes, comets and eclipses; that the destiny of individuals and of nations is a stake in the never-ending struggle between God and Satan; and that the unfolding of the divine plan in history is furthered by the conversion of nations to the Christian faith. These ideas, which are expressed much more forcibly and vividly in the chronicles than in the histories, could be put to practical use both by the Byzantine missionaries, and by those recently baptized Slavs who sought to understand the significance of what had happened to themselves and their countries. This conception of history had the added advantage of being incomplete: the Kingdom of Heaven and its earthly counterpart, the Christian Commonwealth, were ever capable of expansion; and the story left unfinished in the Byzantine chronicles could now be taken up and carried on by the Slavs: which, as we shall see, they were not slow to do.

Two of these works may be singled out for their influence on the religious and historical thought of the medieval Slavs. The Chronicle of John Malalas, written in the sixth century, ranges from the Creation to the last years of Justinian's reign. Fastidious scholars have judged its weaknesses severely: in a recent work it is condemned for its "undisciplined narrative", "gross inaccuracies", and "slipshod style".[4] Yet to the Slavs of the Middle Ages it brought some knowledge both of ancient history and Greek mythology. Its Slavonic translation, done in Bulgaria in the tenth century, was known in Russia by the late eleventh, and was later brought to Serbia. The ninth century Chronicle of George the Monk (or *Hamartolos*, "the sinner") proved even more popular, to judge from the fact that it was twice translated into Slavonic: in the eleventh century (probably in Kiev), and again in the fourteenth (in Bulgaria). The translation combined the original version, a universal history from Adam to 842, with a sequel which carried Byzantine events to the year 948. Together, these two chronicles greatly enlarged the geographical horizon of the Slavs, and provided them with an outline of world history down to the middle of the tenth century and with a framework for their own independent historical research.

426

A survey of the main types of literature translated from Greek into Slavonic in the early Middle Ages will help to identify another characteristic of Byzantine cultural diffusion in this period. A number of these translated works, especially the secular ones, underwent a gradual change in their adopted countries. This change was caused partly by the impact of their new cultural environment, and partly by renewed influences from their original Byzantine home. These influences, which were due to the efforts of editors and copyists to bring these texts back closer, in form and content, to their Greek prototypes, and which tended to offset the effect of natural development, were exerted mainly in the late Middle Ages. In the earlier period with which we are at present concerned, the translated works, by a process of adaptation, were apt to acquire fresh features and to develop local variants. This suggests an analogy between literary "translation" and the botanical process of "transplantation", in the light of which it may be said that the writings so transplanted from Byzantium to Eastern Europe brought forth creative offshoots which continued to live and grow in their new soil. Transplantation was thus accompanied by changes in the borrowed product, and this process was indeed possible only because the society and the culture of the "receiving" country were at that time in a state of rapid change. In this process the translated works not only acquired new traits, but also stimulated, by a kind of cultural osmosis, the growth of "original" literature in different parts of the Slavonic world.

The "originality" of this literature was, of course, relative. The early medieval writers of Moravia, Bulgaria, Russia and Serbia were, for their literary conventions and for much of their subject matter, deeply indebted to Byzantine literature. But their imitation of it was in many cases far from slavish. One instance already cited—the medieval biographies of Slav rulers—will have shown with what freedom the Greek hagiographical patterns could be used. A few other examples will serve to illustrate the creative adaptability displayed by the more gifted Slavonic writers in this period.

Two of the earliest works written in Old Church Slavonic were, from this viewpoint, among the most successful. They are the biographies of Constantine-Cyril and of Methodius, written in Moravia towards the end of the ninth century.[5] The *Vita Constantini,*

427

composed before the end of 882 at the instigation and probably with the help of Methodius, is particularly remarkable for the elegance and lucidity of its style. Both biographies, which record in some detail the missionary activities and cultural achievements of the two brothers, reflect with vivid accuracy the various facets of ninth century Byzantine life: the provincial administration, the programme of education, the revival of secular learning, the religious controversies, the range of the empire's foreign policy, the belief in the emperor's universal sovereignty and more homely details such as the beauty contests and the vogue for falconry in Byzantium. At the same time, they are imbued with a strong and at times emotional commitment to the Slavonic language and letters, for the advancement of which Cyril and Methodius laboured with such devotion and success. It proved important for the subsequent development of Old Church Slavonic literature that two of its earliest original works reflect that cosmopolitan universalism which the church and empire of Byzantium preached to the newly converted nations of Europe.

The same Cyrillo-Methodian spirit breathes in the early works produced in Bulgaria and Russia. At the turn of the ninth century a disciple of the two brothers, Constantine of Preslav (who later became bishop of that city) composed his celebrated acrostic *Alphabetical Prayer*. This Old Church Slavonic poem, written in lines of twelve syllables in imitation of the Byzantine dodecasyllabic metre, is a lyrical encomium of the Slavonic letters. The author declares his devotion to the memory of their creator, his master and namesake, and touches on a theme of central importance in Cyrillo-Methodian literature: the Slavonic version of the Scriptures and of the liturgy is a manifestation of the Divine Word, which has made it possible for the Slavs to be numbered among the peoples of God.[6] This idea that the Slavs, through their conversion to Christianity and by acquiring sacred books in their own language, have become members of the universal Christian family, was voiced with equal force by Russian writers of the eleventh century. The earliest of these to be known by name was Hilarion, metropolitan of Kiev. His *Sermon on Law and Grace*, composed about 1050, is an encomium of Prince Vladimir, who is extolled in rhetorical terms for his work of implanting the true Byzantine religion in his country.[7] It reveals the author's wide familiarity with Greek patristic and apologetic literature, and its form shows the influence of Byzantine imperial panegyrics. Hilarion's devotion to his native land is combined with a keen sense of the universality of Christendom of which the Russians are now part: this fusion of local patriotism with what would be called today an "oecumenical" outlook was characteristic of the writers of the Cyrillo-Methodian tradition whose works came to typify the Slavonic "recension" of Byzantine culture.

The most ambitious attempt to place the new Slav culture within a universal framework was made in the *Russian Primary Chronicle*. Next to the biographies of Cyril and Methodius, this is the masterpiece of early medieval Slavonic literature. Its central theme is the history of the Russian people from the mid-ninth century to the year 1116. The story of the gradual elaboration of its text, despite the painstaking research of generations of Russian scholars, is still uncertain. On the following points, however, there is now fairly general agreement: the chronicle owes its origin to the desire of Prince Yaroslav of Kiev (1019–54) to provide a historical foundation for his policy of unifying and centralizing his realm; the successive recensions of the text were carried out partly in the princely court, but more often by monks, especially in the Kiev monastery of the Caves; in its present form it owes most of all to one of these monks, Nestor, who about 1113 carried out a thorough revision of his predecessors' work, and by incorporating much new material, particularly of Byzantine origin, greatly enlarged the chronicle's scope. Although the central—and probably the original—core of the work is the story of Russia's conversion to Christianity, secular events loom large in its subject-matter. Not least of these are the campaigns of the Russians against Byzantium, and their age-long struggle against the nomads of the steppe. But the national events are consciously placed against a wider background. In a lengthy introduction, based largely on the Slavonic translations of the chronicles of George Hamartolos and John Malalas, the story is told of the division of the earth among the sons of Noah after the Flood, and of the dispersal of the nations after the building of the Tower of Babel.[8] This excursion into the remote past of mankind, in accordance with Byzantine models, is made by the Russian chronicler with deliberate intent: by claiming that one of the seventy-two nations which were scattered from the Tower of Babel were the Slavs, he gives a new and universal dimension to the history of his own people. Not content, however, with this fanciful attempt to graft the Russians on to mankind's genealogical tree, he took a further step in order to discover a more restricted, yet culturally more precise, unit within which their history could be made intelligible. He found this unit in the community of Slav peoples. In another digression into the past, based this time on Moravian sources, he gives an account of the work of Cyril and Methodius, emphasizing the "power" and "intelligibility" of the Slavonic letters which have become the patrimony of the entire Slav world. The Russians, he claims, who speak the same Slav language, have now in their turn become the spiritual heirs of this tradition.[9]

The debt which this way of thinking owes to Byzantine historiography is evident. The translated chronicles provided their Russian imitators not only with factual material but with the very framework of universal history. The authors of the *Russian Primary Chronicle* may have delighted in recounting the military exploits of their compatriots against the overbearing and perfidious "Greeks"; yet they were aware that the history of the "Greek tsardom" had a special relevance to the fate of the Russian people; it is significant that the dated section of the chronicle (including its sequel to the year 1118) opens and closes with an event of Byzantine history: the accession of Michael III and the death of Alexius I. At the same time, the skill and ingenuity with which the Russian chronicler built up his narrative, moving from the universal (the migration of the tribes of the earth) through the general (the cultural community of the Slav peoples) to the particular (the history of his own nation), and his inference that the Cyrillo-Methodian tradition is the spiritual bridge between Byzantium and Russia, show with what creative originality he was able to adapt Byzantine historical thought to the now articulate national consciousness of his own people. In its grasp of disparate material, in its sense of the importance of central events, in the vividness and pungency of its language—a combination of Old Church Slavonic with elements of the spoken vernacular—the *Russian Primary Chronicle* is a work of outstanding merit, superior in many respects to the Byzantine chronicles on which it was partly modelled. Next to art, it was in the field of historiography that the Russians made their greatest contribution to the culture of the Byzantine Commonwealth. The numerous chronicles composed in Russia in the later Middle Ages sought to imitate the first of the country's historical works; they never equalled it in quality.

Several references have been made on the preceding pages to the "Cyrillo-Methodian tradition". This expression has been used to designate the body of writings, translated and original, produced in the Old Church Slavonic language between the late ninth and the early twelfth centuries, and also a particular outlook, part religious and part political, which served to determine the place occupied by the Slavs within the Christian community. This outlook needs to be defined more closely. It was based on the belief that a language which serves as a medium for the Christian liturgy becomes thereby a sacred language, and that the nation which speaks it is raised to the status of a people consecrated to God. For all tongues are equal in His sight; and it is through man's most intimate possession, his mother tongue, that He can come into closest contact with the human soul. Hence every Christian nation with a native liturgical language and culture has its own particular mission and legitimate place within the universal family of Christian peoples. These ideas were never expressed, at least in the Middle Ages, in so general and abstract a manner. But the constituent elements of this outlook, applied to the Slavs, are scattered in the writings of the Cyrillo-Methodian school. One of these elements is joy and pride in the newly acquired Slavonic letters, seen as a bountiful manifestation of the Divine Word. This idea, already present in the *Alphabetical Prayer*, is expressed with particular eloquence in another Old Church Slavonic poem, the *Prologue* to the full text of the Gospels, also written in regular Byzantine dodecasyllables, and variously ascribed to St. Cyril or to Bishop Constantine of Preslav. The author compares people without sacred books in their own language to a naked body and to a dead soul, and laments the misery of those who, deprived of letters, can neither hear the peal of thunder nor smell the scent of flowers. And, turning to his compatriots, the poet triumphantly exclaims: "Hear you, the whole Slavonic people! Hear the Word, for it came from God, the Word that nourishes human souls, the Word that strengthens heart and mind, the Word that prepares all men to know God!"[10] It is perhaps worth noting that this poetic eulogy of the vernacular language has a parallel in a passage written almost simultaneously at the other end of Europe, though in sober prose: "It seems better to me," wrote King Alfred of England, "for us also to translate some books which are most needful for all men to know into the language which we can all understand."[11]

Another element in this concept of ethnic self-determination was the belief, frequently voiced by writers of the Cyrillo-Methodian tradition, that the Slavs, converted to Christianity and provided with their own letters, have become "a new people". Their late entry into the Christian Commonwealth was no sign of inferiority: rather was it to be viewed in the light of Christ's parable, related by St. Matthew (xx, 1–16), of the householder who went out to hire labourers for his vineyard: those who were hired at the eleventh hour received the same salary as those who had from the beginning "borne the burden and heat of the day". The Slavs, late comers as they were, shared in the spiritual rebirth of nations capable of praising God in their own languages. This rebirth was interpreted in Biblical terms: the appearance of the Slavonic liturgy and books was held to be an extension of the miracle of Pentecost, by which the Holy Spirit descended upon the apostles in tongues of fire; and this new Pentecost, like the first one, by furthering the unity of all mankind in Christ, rescinded the ancient confusion of tongues which sprang from the Tower of Babel. This idea was not an invention of medieval Slav writers: the contrast between Babel and Pentecost, and the belief that the latter has cancelled the former, are emphasized in the Byzantine offices of Whitsunday, and can be found in the writings of several Greek Fathers; but to apply them to Slav vernacular Christianity required a fairly sophisticated capacity for adaptation. Here again the Cyrillo-Methodian tradition proved itself a creative cultural force.

A final example may be cited to illustrate the vitality and emotive power of this tradition. Not content to emphasize the role of the Slavs within the Christian community, and of the Cyrillo-Methodian heritage in the economy of man's salvation, several medieval writers went so far as to exalt this heritage in metaphysical terms. They applied to the discovery and spread of the Slavonic letters the words of the Prophet Isaiah (xxix. 18, xxxv. 6, Septuagint version): "In that day shall the deaf hear the words of a book, and the tongue of the dumb shall be clearly heard". The idea that "the divine shower of letters", sent down upon the Slav nations, has its part to play in preparing the transfiguration of the created world and the advent of the Kingdom of God did not seem strange to the writers of the Cyrillo-Methodian school. For this sense of cosmic triumph is powerfully conveyed in the opening verses of the thirty-fifth chapter of the Book of Isaiah, the very verses from which they quoted to describe the bounty of the Slav vernacular tradition:

> The wilderness and the dry land shall be glad, the desert shall rejoice and blossom; like the crocus it shall blossom abundantly, and rejoice with joy and singing. . . . Then the eyes of the blind shall be opened, and the ears of the deaf shall be unstopped. Then shall the lame man leap as a hart, and the tongue of the dumb shall be clearly heard. . . . They shall see the glory of the Lord, the splendour of our God.

The fervour and enthusiasm lavished on the Slav vernacular tradition by these early medieval authors, which touch their writings with the excitement of a cultural springtime, began to wane in the twelfth century. The achievements of the two Byzantine apostles to the Slavs were not forgotten in Eastern Europe, least of all in Russia where most of the extant manuscripts of their biographies have been preserved. The work of St. Cyril became the object of renewed interest in the late fourteenth century. But in the literary field the Cyrillo-Methodian school was by then showing signs of obsolescence. The linguistic and cultural situation in the Slav countries had altered greatly since the ninth century. The unity of the Slavonic tongue had been broken, and the spoken dialects of the different parts of the Slav world had now developed into distinct languages. Old Church Slavonic, once the *lingua franca* of this world, had undergone a complex evolution: on the one hand, it had absorbed elements of the local vernaculars and had thus also lost something of its pristine unity; on the other hand, this Church Slavonic (as it is termed in its new phase), still used for the "higher" forms of literature in Bulgaria, Serbia and Russia, had retained much of its original grammatical and syntactical structure, and was by then out of touch with the spoken idioms of those countries: by the late fourteenth century it was well on the way to becoming a dead language. These two features of Church Slavonic—its lack of unity and its divorce from the vernacular Slav tongues—have a direct bearing on a remarkable literary movement which originated in fourteenth century Bulgaria and spread during the last century of the Middle Ages throughout Eastern Europe.

The originator of this movement was Euthymius, patriarch of Trnovo from 1375 to 1393. A Bulgarian by birth, he joined the monastic community of Kilifarevo, where he became the leading disciple of St. Theodosius. Owing to his personal abilities and to his close spiritual links with his master, he became the outstanding representative, in its third generation, of the Slavonic Hesychast school founded by St. Gregory of Sinai. Much of his adult life, like that of the other leaders of this movement, was peripatetic: he spent eight years in the monasteries of Constantinople and Mount Athos, practising *hesychia* and working in a Graeco-Slav environment as a copyist of manuscripts and a writer. By 1371 he was back in Bulgaria, and before long was elected primate of his Church. As patriarch he became noted for his prolific writing, his championship of Hesychasm and his courageous behaviour in the face of the growing Turkish menace. The capture of Trnovo by the armies of the Sultan in 1393 marked the end of the independent Bulgarian church and state: and the final picture (drawn by a disciple) of Euthymius, walking to his exile through the streets of the capital, bathed in tears and lamented by his flock, is a fitting memorial to this last great prelate in the medieval history of the Balkan Slavs.

It was in the realm of scholarship that Euthymius' international renown and influence proved the greatest. His main legacy to posterity was a wholesale revision of the liturgical texts, based on a consistent and clearly thought-out linguistic programme. This programme, to judge from the evidence of his disciples and from Euthymius' own writings, involved a thorough reassessment of the role of Church Slavonic and of its relationship to Greek. Its starting point was the conviction that public welfare and morality, as well as the purity of the Orthodox faith, were dependent on the accuracy and literary qualities of the sacred books. In the judgement of Euthymius and his collaborators these books were sadly deficient in both respects. Earlier translators from the Greek had either through ignorance misunderstood the originals or through literary boorishness rendered them in coarse and inelegant language. Later copyists, through error and lack of coordination, had made matters worse: things had got to a point where, to quote one of Euthymius' disciples, "if one were to assemble a hundred books, one could not find two identical in orthography and language".[12] This state of affairs was doubly regrettable: it pointed to a sad decline in the standards of writing, and the errors and discrepancies in the sacred texts were plainly conducive to heresy. The latter danger was felt to be particularly acute: several heretical movements were recorded in fourteenth century Bulgaria, and St. Theodosius himself, we have seen, took part in his church's struggle against the Bogomil sect.[13]

Euthymius proposed two remedies: to return to the grammar, orthography and punctuation of the original translations of Cyril and Methodius; and to remodel the morphology and syntax of Church Slavonic as closely as possible on Greek. The theoretical basis and practical implications of this reform are described by his disciple at one remove, Constantine of Kostenets. Having studied under one of Euthymius' pupils in the monastery of Bachkovo in Bulgaria, he moved to Serbia where *c.* 1418 he wrote his celebrated treatise *On Letters*.[14] It is the work of a poor historian and of a linguistic pedant. He believed that the language of Cyril and Methodius was basically Russian, with an admixture of six other Slav tongues; that sacred languages form a family, in which Hebrew, Greek and the Slav ones are respectively the father, the mother and the children; and that Slavonic writing must in all respects follow Greek models. Not only did he insist on a completely literal translation of the Greek texts, readily sacrificing clarity of sense to the desire to achieve exact equivalence between words, and even separate letters, in the two languages; he also urged that spelling should conform to the orthography of the earliest Slavonic texts on the one hand, and to the accentual conventions of Greek on the other.

Constantine's linguistic programme, which was probably a starker version of the literary reforms of Euthymius of Trnovo, may seem to us undiluted pedantry. In several respects, however—notably in its idealization of the Old Church Slavonic past and in its appeal to the authority of Byzantine models—it was symptomatic of the outlook and strivings of East European intel-

435

lectuals of the late Middle Ages. In the troubled world of Balkan politics, the victories of the Turks could be seen to be a result of the spiritual disunity and moral decline of the Christians. A sense of impending doom and a despondent belief that the present times were inferior to the glorious past were then fairly widespread in Byzantium. The notion that the corruption of morals was a result of a corruption in the spelling of manuscripts may seem far-fetched to the modern mind: but when these manuscripts contained the sacred texts of the Christian religion, and faulty transcriptions could be held responsible for doctrinal error, this inference did not sound so extravagant to the medieval man. There was some logic in the contention of Euthymius and his followers that the purity of the Orthodox faith could be restored and safeguarded if the national varieties of Church Slavonic could overcome their disparity and return to their common source, the language of Cyril and Methodius. And, believing that their cultural heritage could be saved by literary standardization, they turned for guidance to another source, the very one which had given form and substance to the Cyrillo-Methodian mission to the Slavs: the Greek language and the sacred texts of the Byzantine Church. The translations and original writings of Euthymius and his school, which were carried from Bulgaria to Serbia, Rumania and Russia, and prompted local writers in those countries to imitate them, thus laid the foundations for a new literary movement. This movement had several features in common with the earlier, Cyrillo-Methodian, one: it was international in character; it made use of the Slavonic literary tradition as a channel for the diffusion of Byzantine civilization; and it was closely associated with, and to some extent based on, a specific ideology. This ideology was no longer shaped by the Cyrillo-Methodian ideas of ethnic self-determination. Its roots lay in the outlook of the late Byzantine world.

There are cogent reasons for believing that one of the sources of Euthymius' linguistic and literary reforms was Hesychasm. Euthymius himself was an ardent Hesychast, and had close personal connections with other members of this religious school on Mount Athos, and in Constantinople, Rumania and Russia. The emphasis he and his disciples laid on ritual purity and strictness, and their anxiety to conform to Greek models, were in full accord with the programme of the Hesychasts who strove to renew and purify liturgical life and championed the primacy of the Byzantine Church in matters of faith and ecclesiastical discipline. In the abundant crop of new translations which grew out of Euthymius' reforms and became the common property of the East European peoples, pride of place was accorded to the ascetic and spiritual writings popular in Hesychast circles, such as the works of John of the Ladder, Symeon the New Theologian, Gregory of Sinai and Gregory Palamas. Euthymius' own hagiographical writings were patterned, in content and form, on the *Vitae* written by the Hesychast patriarchs of Constantinople, Callistus I and Philotheus; he, too, used the lives of saints to extol the ideal of *hesychia*;[15] and he borrowed from his Greek models the new style of hagiographical and panegyrical writing, which was to enjoy great vogue in Eastern Europe during the next hundred years: a style ornate, rhetorical and emotional, with a tendency to interweave the narrative with theological reflections and to reduce the concrete and factual material to a minimum, with the aim of raising the subject-matter above the level of historical contingency to a timeless and universal plane.

Another feature of the new movement was its antiquarianism. In the early Middle Ages, we have seen, the Cyrillo-Methodian tradition generated fresh creative energies in the Slav countries of Eastern Europe. The nascent Christian cultures of these countries responded to the impact of Byzantine civilization, channelled through this tradition, by developing local features which may be compared to the native offshoots of a transplanted body. The "forward-looking" character of this process explains the vitality and "youthfulness" apparent in the early Old Church Slavonic literature. By contrast, the writers of the late medieval, "Euthymian" tradition had, in the main, their eyes fixed on the past. In a world in turmoil, where true culture was felt to be declining, the Orthodox faith was threatened by heresy, and even the integrity of the Christian Commonwealth was no longer assured, they pinned their hopes on a return to a golden age: an age epitomized by the pristine tradition of Cyril and Methodius and by the unquestioned authority of the Byzantines, which their ancestors had accepted with such benefit to themselves. To restore, preserve and purify this cultural legacy became their professed aim. This obsession with the past explains two important features of this movement: the literalness and servility with which the Byzantine texts were rendered into Slavonic, and which contrast with the boldness and originality of the early Cyrillo-Methodian translations; and the birth at this time of a new historical consciousness, manifest both in the interest shown by Muscovite writers in the culture of Kievan Russia, and in the belief entertained by statesmen and ideologists of Bulgaria and Serbia that their respective countries were destined to assume the political heritage of the Byzantine Empire. In this tendency to idealize the past we may detect the seeds of an outlook which was later to bear fruit in the European Renaissance.

A further contrast is worth noting between the East European literary movements of the early and the late Middle Ages. The former, dominated by the missionary ideals of Cyril and Methodius, aimed at bringing the religion and civilization of Byzantium to as wide a circle of Slav converts and pupils as possible. The fact that Old Church Slavonic was then close to the spoken vernacular tongues greatly facilitated its diffusion. Indeed, the early writers of the Cyrillo-Methodian tradition regarded the intelligibility of the Slavonic letters as their greatest asset. The late medieval movement was strikingly different in this respect. Its leaders, in encouraging the use of archaic and elaborate turns of phrase and of Greek semantic and phraseological calques, were consciously trying to dissociate the sacred and educated language from the vulgar spoken tongue. They largely succeeded in this task. The Church Slavonic which they developed and wrote was rich in vocabulary and florid in syntax; but it was hardly intelligible to the untutored. This esoteric language, and the literature which it sustained, became the preserve of an ecclesiastical and learned coterie, of an East European mandarinate. It was a far cry from the triumphant belief of the early disciples of Cyril and Methodius that the invention of the Slavonic letters had fulfilled Isaiah's prophecy that the dumb would speak and the deaf hear "the words of a book".

Several factors facilitated the spread of this late medieval, "Euthymian", recension of Byzantine culture. One of them was literary collaboration, particularly active in the fourteenth century, between Slav and Greek monks in the principal religious and cultural centres of the Byzantine world. This collaboration was stimulated by the Hesychast tradition, which attracted men from many lands to these famed nurseries of the spiritual life. There manuscripts were copied and collated, and Greeks, Serbs, Bulgarians, Rumanians and Russians exchanged literary works and translated Byzantine texts into Church Slavonic. Such centres were the monasteries of Constantinople (especially Studios), Mount Athos, Thessalonica, the Meteora monasteries of Thessaly and the Bulgarian *hesychasteria* of Paroria and Kilifarevo. Another factor which made this movement truly international was a reverse process, which scattered men and manuscripts over Eastern Europe. Many of these monks who returned home, their visit or their training completed, were joined by refugees, some of them distinguished churchmen or scholars, seeking to escape from the Turkish invasion. This northward movement gathered momentum after the battle of Kosovo (1389) and the capture of Trnovo (1393). Bulgarian disciples of Euthymius migrated to Northern Serbia; Serbs to the Rumanian principalities; Greeks and Balkan Slavs to Russia.

The role played by these learned refugees in spreading Byzantine civilization in its late medieval Slavonic form has sometimes been overstressed by historians who persisted in viewing the Eastern European world of that time as a collection of separate national cultures. To judge this role in proper perspective, it should be recognized that these scholars moved within the same cultural area, whose unity, already apparent in the ninth and tenth centuries, had recently been strengthened by the spread of Hesychasm and of Euthymius' literary reforms. In migrating from one part of the Byzantine Commonwealth to another, they faced no formidable problems of adaptation: they expected to find, and generally did, similar conditions for their scholarly or ecclesiastical work. Some of them were men of intellectual eminence who contributed much to the cultural life of their adopted countries; but it is important to realize that they were not so much innovators as heirs to one and the same international tradition of religion and letters.

The role of these immigrants can be illustrated in the cultural history of Rumania. Such a man as Nicodemus of Tismana, whose monastic activity in Wallachia has already been noted, was a typical produce of this fourteenth century cosmopolitan culture.[16] He and other immigrants from Bulgaria, Serbia and Mount Athos, who carried the teachings of Hesychasm and the writings of the Euthymian school north of the Danube, contributed much to the growth of Slavonic literature in fifteenth century Wallachia and Moldavia. But the foundation for this growth was laid earlier. The Slavonic literature is believed to have spread from Bulgaria to the lands between the lower Danube and the Carpathians as early as the tenth century. But it was only in the fourteenth that Church Slavonic literature began to develop in the two principalities, under the patronage of the princely courts of Argeş and Suceava, and of the young Rumanian Church. Until the second half of the fifteenth century this literature consisted almost wholly of translations from the Greek and of writings obtained from the Balkan Slavs. Its first independent work of any significance was the chronicle compiled at the court of Stephen the Great of Moldavia (1457–1504). Church Slavonic was to remain the official language of the church and the princely chancelleries in Rumania until the late seventeenth century. Its social status and prestige were enhanced by the fact that, except as a liturgical language, it was incomprehensible to the uneducated. During the whole of this period it was apparently also spoken at times, like French in eighteenth century Europe, at the Rumanian court, in learned circles, and by the nobility. It remained as a living token of that aristocratic, cosmopolitan culture which served as a channel for the diffusion of Byzantine civilization in the late Middle Ages.

The contribution of the Balkan emigrants to the cultural life of Russia was particularly notable. One of them was the Bulgarian monk Cyprian Tsamblak. He had the usual impeccable Hesychast antecedents: they included periods of monastic training at Kilifarevo under St. Theodosius, as well as in Constantinople and on Mount Athos, and a life-long friendship with Euthymius of Trnovo. In 1375 he was appointed to the see of Kiev and played an active part in the politics of the Byzantine patriarchate in Lithuania and Muscovy. From 1390 to 1406 he was metropolitan of Moscow and All Russia. As head of the Russian Church he stimulated the flow of South Slavonic manuscripts into Russian monastery libraries, and took the initiative in the compilation of the first comprehensive Muscovite chronicle, which included historical material collected from different parts of the country. His editorial work on this chronicle, which stressed the role of Moscow as the centre of national unity and the relevance of the ancient Kievan heritage to its history, shows that this Bulgarian prelate was well attuned to the ideological and political preoccupations of the rulers of his adopted country.

The same adaptability to local conditions was shown by another distinguished expatriate, the Serb Pachomius. He spent some fifty years in Russia, and died there about 1484. His political sympathies were variously engaged in the service of his Novgorodian and Muscovite patrons. Most of his writings were new redactions, in the current "Euthymian" rhetorical style, of existing *Vitae* and panegyrics of Russian saints.

This new manner of writing, which Russian literary historians have dubbed "the second South Slav influence" (to distinguish this movement from the earlier wave of Bulgarian "influence" exerted on their country in the tenth and eleventh centuries), had already found a distinguished native practitioner. The Russian monk Epiphanius, nicknamed the Wise, wrote between 1396 and *c.* 1420 two remarkable *Vitae*, devoted to Stephen of Perm' and Sergius of Radonezh.[17] Stephen was a Russian monk who in the late fourteenth century evangelized the Zyrians, or Komi (a people related to the Finns), in the remote north-eastern part of the country, by inventing an alphabet for them and translating the liturgical books into their language. Epiphanius draws a parallel between his achievement and that of St. Cyril, the apostle of the Slavs, suggesting with more than a touch of Muscovite chauvinism that St. Stephen's merit was the greater, for whereas Cyril was assisted by his brother Methodius, Stephen had no help save from God. But Epiphanius, who had a sound knowledge of Greek, did more than slavishly copy the literary conventions of the South Slavonic school. Building to some extent on earlier traditions of Russian literature, he developed this style, for which he coined the singularly apt term "word-weaving", to a degree of sophistication and technical artistry unknown to his Balkan models. Its mannered ornateness, repetitiveness and emphatic diction hold little appeal for the modern reader; but he may still learn to appreciate, especially in the *Life of St. Stephen*, the author's balanced construction, rhythmic prose, euphonic effects and subtle play on words. Epiphanius' writings illustrate most faithfully several basic characteristics of the Church Slavonic literature in the late Middle Ages: its aristocratic refinement, its tendency to view concrete events *sub specie aeternitatis*, and its longing to transmute the contingent phenomena of this world into a vision of ordered spiritual beauty.

The outlook and careers of the leading protagonists of this movement will have revealed a further trait, typical of the cosmopolitan Slavo-Byzantine world in which they lived. Dispersed throughout Eastern Europe, they remained in close touch with each other. Many shared a common loyalty to a spiritual *alma mater*, such as Mount Athos or Kilifarevo. Most of them were personally linked with Euthymius of Trnovo, who dominated this movement with the same authority which Cyril and Methodius and their immediate disciples had enjoyed among the Slavs of the early Middle Ages. And, whether through Euthymius or directly, they retained contact with the religious and cultural life of Constantinople, whose hagiographical literature and Hesychast spirituality remained models for the whole of Eastern Europe.

The career of one of the leading disciples of Euthymius may be mentioned in conclusion, for it shows the astonishing range of this international movement of men. Gregory Tsamblak, nephew of the Metropolitan Cyprian, was a Bulgarian by birth. After spending several years on Mount Athos, he became at the very end of the fourteenth century abbot of the monastery of Dečani in Serbia, where he wrote, in the prescribed literary manner, a biography of King Stephen Uroš III. Between 1401 and 1406 he was in Moldavia, working as a priest. He then went to Lithuania, where he was used by the country's ruler who wished to set up a separate Orthodox Church in his realm, with its main see in Kiev. In the hope of persuading the Russian and the Byzantine authorities to agree to this plan, Gregory travelled to Moscow and Constantinople. The patriarchate, under strong pressure from the Muscovite government, refused to sanction the partition of the Russian Church, and excommunicated him. Ignoring the interdict, Gregory returned to Lithuania, where he was consecrated metropolitan of Kiev by the local bishops (1415). Three years later he made a notable appearance in the West as a delegate of his Lithuanian sovereign to the Council of Constance, charged with

442

the duty of negotiating a union with the Roman Church. However, though he is said to have kissed the pope's foot, he declined to subscribe to his teachings. This was the last well-attested adventure of this ambitious and learned prelate. He died about 1420.

2   ART

The history of Byzantine art in the East European countries begins with their conversion to Christianity. Byzantine architects and painters followed closely in the wake of imperial missionaries and diplomats, and were sent, often no doubt at the request of the newly converted princes, to build and decorate the churches of their realms. The process began in the second half of the ninth century. Byzantine art, slowly recovering from the prohibitions of the Iconoclast age when all corporeal images had been banned from places of worship, was then embarking on one of its greatest periods. This phase, which spans the tenth and eleventh centuries, is often described after the name of the dynasty which ruled in Constantinople from 867 to 1056 as the "Macedonian Renaissance". The churches of the period were built and decorated in accordance with definite formal principles. Their shape—mostly a cube surmounted by a dome—imitated the popular notion of the structure of the universe. The idea that the church is an image of the cosmos also underlay the system of internal decoration. Compositions in mosaic—a material particularly favoured in this period—formed a carefully ordered group of pictures, disposed in a descending hierarchy which symbolized God's universal kingdom of heaven and earth: Christ the All-Ruler, enthroned in majesty and escorted by his angels, in the cupola; his Mother, interceding for the human race, in the conch of the apse; scenes of Christ's earthly life, selected in accordance with the liturgical sequence of the main ecclesiastical festivals, in the niches and squinches lower down; and, in the third and lowest zone, single figures of the saints. This topographical symbolism, which formed the ideal iconographical scheme of a Byzantine church of the tenth and eleventh centuries, expressed the cosmic nature of the Christian religion, bore witness to the theology of the Incarnation as restated by the opponents of Iconoclasm, and emphasized the liturgical function of the building, in which the drama of man's redemption was re-enacted through the celebration of the eucharist. The same iconographical pattern was reproduced, wholly or in part, in most of the churches built within the Byzantine Commonwealth in the early Middle Ages. In the style of their paintings they reflected the two contrasting traditions which shaped the art of the Macedonian Renaissance: the elegant, academic and classical manner which had its roots in the Hellenistic traditions cultivated in the great cities of the empire; and the more austere, hieratic and transcendental style associated with the monasteries, which stemmed from Syria and Anatolia. The relationship between these two traditions—the courtly and the monastic—varied throughout the history of Byzantine and East European art. In some of its masterpieces, such as the mosaics of Daphni near Athens (c. 1100), they were blended with perfect mastery.

The last creative age of Byzantine art was during the fourteenth and early fifteenth centuries. The mural paintings of this period reveal a new blend of the classical and the monastic styles whose distinguishing marks are an emotional treatment of the subjects, an increased sense of rhythm and dramatic tension, elegance of design, and a taste for descriptive scenes and picturesque detail. It has recently become clear, however, that this "Palaeologan Renaissance" had its roots in twelfth-century Comnenian art. One of the masterpieces of this art, the Deesis mosaic in the south gallery of St. Sophia in Constantinople, with its delicate modelling and the tenderness and dignity of its figures, foreshadows a number of features formerly regarded as late medieval innovations. Palaeologan art, whose main products are religious in character, spread from Constantinople and Thessalonica to the farthest confines of the Byzantine Commonwealth. Except for the paintings in the church of the Chora (the Kariye Camii) in Constantinople and at Mistra in the Southern Peloponnese, its greatest surviving works are in the Balkan Slavonic countries, in Rumania and in Russia. As much as the monastic and literary movements of the time, this art imprinted a unified and cosmopolitan stamp upon the late medieval culture of Eastern Europe.

Another general problem relevant to a discussion of East European art is that of patronage. The building and decoration of

444

the churches and secular buildings were mostly commissioned by local rulers, nobles, prelates and abbots of the great monasteries. In the early Middle Ages, when it was necessary to rely on the services of imported Byzantine artists and craftsmen, few of these patrons, except the princes, were rich enough to pay the high fees undoubtedly charged by these foreign masters. The fees were not lessened by the rulers' desire to increase their own prestige through sumptuous decoration and lavish display. Their ability to meet the costs depended on their political power, and the latter on the degree of centralization of their realms. Hence, in the field of art, we observe the same phenomenon which we encountered when studying the diffusion of other aspects of Byzantine civilization: the powers of penetration of this culture were in direct proportion to the growth, within the "receiving" country, of a luxury-loving, courtly society and of centralized political institutions. Furthermore, princely patronage often determined the selection of artistic programmes. While local ecclesiastical authorities naturally favoured themes extolling the spiritual and ascetic life, secular rulers were not always content to express their religious fervour by having the churches of their realms decorated with paintings testifying to the truth of the Christian religion: they were apt, on occasion, to choose subjects for their political or national significance. This use of art for partly secular reasons may be illustrated by two examples. The cathedral of St. Sophia in Kiev, whose foundation stone was laid *c.* 1037 and whose date of consecration is still in dispute, contains a number of frescoes: one cycle, in the central nave, painted about 1045, depicted Prince Yaroslav and his family, thus glorifying the Russian ruling dynasty in the eyes of all the faithful; another, more unusual, theme appears on the walls and vaults of the two tower staircases leading to the galleries where, in all probability, the prince, his relatives and his courtiers attended divine service. Several of these paintings, which have been dated to the first quarter of the twelfth century, represent scenes enacted in the hippodrome of Constantinople: acrobats, jugglers and jousters disport themselves in the arena, charioteers are poised to begin their race, while the emperor, seated on his throne in the imperial box, watches the games. In another scene the emperor, wearing the crown and seated on a white charger, is depicted riding in triumph. One fresco of this

445

cycle, depicting a warrior fighting a masked man, has been taken by some scholars to portray an episode from the "Gothic Games", a kind of ritual dance performed before the emperor seated at table, in the presence of representatives of the circus parties of Constantinople, on the ninth day after Christmas. In view of the determined opposition of the clergy in medieval Eastern Europe to any kind of profane "games", their depiction inside a church may seem astonishing. But if it is remembered that the games of the Byzantine hippodrome and the ceremonies of the palace were regarded as a symbolic exaltation of the emperor's sovereignty and as part of the "imperial liturgy" which visibly expressed it, the representation of these scenes in twelfth-century Kiev will be seen to have political and cultural significance. These frescoes testify to the spread of the imperial art of Constantinople to the periphery of the Byzantine Commonwealth, illustrate the spell cast on the imagination of the Russians by the distant glories of Constantinople, and—when it is observed that the head of the emperor in these paintings is surrounded by a nimbus, whereas that of Yaroslav in the nave was unnimbed—may provide pictorial evidence of their princes' recognition of the emperor's ideal supremacy.

The second example of how religious art could be made to serve the interests of the East European ruling classes comes from Serbia. In the thirteenth century the practice arose of including among the paintings in the Serbian churches scenes depicting episodes in the lives of members of the Nemanja dynasty. The earliest instances are two cycles of paintings in Studenica (c. 1235) and Sopoćani (1263–8) representing Stephen Nemanja's departure for Mount Athos, his reception on the Holy Mountain, his death, and the transfer of his relics to Studenica. Recent study of these much damaged frescoes has shown that their subject-matter was inspired by Nemanja's biography and by the liturgical office in his honour, both written by St. Sava. Several other monastic churches contain similar historical compositions: they depict the death of St. Sava, the translation of his relics to Mileševa, the investiture of Serbian rulers at national assemblies, and their final moments on earth. The best known of these thirteenth-century paintings portrays Queen Anne, the mother of Uroš 1, on her death-bed, surrounded by members of the Serbian ruling family. These royal pictures, which aim to convey the spiritual significance of political

446

power and to glorify individual rulers and their dynasty, were probably modelled on the collective portraits of members of the imperial family which, we know from written documents, existed in Byzantium in the Comnenian age. But their warm and unaffected piety stems from a native, and by now deeply felt, devotion to Nemanja's dynasty. The thirteenth century was the heyday of these historical compositions. In the following century they gave way to more abstract and schematic representations of the royal family: in the churches of Gračanica, Peć and Dečani its members were portrayed in a vast genealogical diagram, patterned on the Tree of Jesse; and in one case—in the monastery of Matejče in Macedonia, painted *c.* 1355—the Nemanjids are grafted on to the family tree of the emperors of Byzantium, in pictorial illustration of Dušan's claim to the political inheritance of the empire.

A third general problem is of special relevance to our present theme. How far did Byzantine art, as it spread through Eastern Europe, assume local features? And, assuming that these can be identified, do they warrant the use of the term "national schools" to describe the artistic products of the different regions of the Byzantine Commonwealth? These are difficult and still controversial problems. In this brief survey no claim can be made to resolve them: little more can be attempted here than to place them in a historical perspective.

One obstacle encountered by those who would answer these questions is national and cultural prejudice. It has led many East European scholars to exaggerate the originality or to widen unduly the radius of activity of their country's art, and some Byzantinists to regard these local products as provincial forms, not to say servile imitations, of Constantinopolitan art. Another difficulty is the destruction suffered by works of art. This was nowhere so widespread in the Middle Ages as in Bulgaria. Byzantines and Russians in the tenth century, Turks in the fourteenth and fifteenth, were responsible for the disappearance of many religious and secular buildings in that country. The sack of Preslav by John Tzimisces in 971, and that of Kiev by the Mongols in 1240, have deprived us of many outstanding monuments. By contrast Serbia and Moldavia, comparatively sheltered from foreign conquest at the time of their most vigorous artistic activity, have preserved many more works of art. Enough, however, has survived in Eastern Europe as a whole to demonstrate the predominance in that area, during the whole of the Middle Ages, of the tradition and art forms derived from Constantinople and other cultural centres of the Byzantine Empire. This tradition reflected both the continuity and the changing patterns of Byzantine art from the early Macedonian to the late Palaeologan periods. Its lasting appeal and the geographical range of its expansion are equally remarkable. Byzantine art, which freely crossed all political frontiers, remained the basic international idiom from the Southern Peloponnese to the confines of the Arctic Ocean, and from the Northern Adriatic to the Caucasus, until the end of the Middle Ages. In many of these areas its influence survived well beyond that time.

It is obvious that this artistic tradition could not have remained uniform over so vast an area. Apart from the renewals which this art frequently experienced in its homeland, it was no less immune than the other aspects of Byzantine culture to the impact of local environment. The patronage of princes and prelates, we have seen, was usually required for the creation of works of monumental art. Most of these seem to have owed their origin, at least indirectly, to the initiative of the local political authorities. Hence the programme which these rulers imposed on the artists under their control tended to be circumscribed within the boundaries of their respective national states. Thus local patronage tended in some degree to offset the cosmopolitanism of Byzantine art forms and to create conditions potentially favourable to the rise of "national" schools.

It may be doubted, however, whether this process ever advanced very far in medieval Eastern Europe. In the first place, the boundaries of the different states which comprised the Byzantine Commonwealth were, particularly in the Balkans, exceedingly unstable. It is clearly impossible, during much of the Middle Ages, to differentiate on national grounds between East Serbian and West Bulgarian art; while Macedonia, a favourite hunting ground for nationalistically-minded Balkan art historians, was occupied at various times in the Middle Ages by Bulgarians, Byzantines, Serbs and Turks. More importantly, the embryonic "national" tendencies nearly always proved unstable and ephemeral. Some, such as the Serbian school of painting of the thirteenth century, lost a

448

measure of their identity by receiving a fresh injection of Byzantine influence; others, like the ornamental sculptures on the façades of the twelfth- and early thirteenth-century churches of North-Eastern Russia, or the late medieval frescoes of Northern Serbia, represent traditions that were cut short by foreign conquest. In the last resort it is safer to ascribe the variations which Byzantine art displays in different regions of Eastern Europe not to ethnic peculiarities or national propensities, but to the effect of local workshops operating singly or in groups and in close contact with their secular or ecclesiastical patrons. These workshops, whose durability and radius of activity varied greatly, employed techniques and executed programmes which were ultimately derived from Byzantine models. The differences between their products were less marked than, for instance, those between the various schools of Italian painting in the thirteenth and fourteenth centuries. They were certainly far less significant than their common affiliation to the artistic tradition of Byzantium which, in the words of a distinguished modern scholar, formed in Eastern Europe "local dialects rather than separate languages".[18]

It may be helpful to keep in mind these general points when considering some of the more important works produced by artists who worked within this tradition in the Balkans, in Rumania and in Russia.

1 The Balkans

Apart from a painting in ceramic of a saint (probably St. Theodore) discovered during the excavations of Preslav, and probably dating from the tenth century, the earliest outstanding examples of medieval Balkan art are the frescoes in the church of St. Sophia in Ohrid (c. 1040). This Macedonian city was then the seat of the archdiocese set up by the Byzantines after Bazil II's conquest of the Central and Northern Balkans. The paintings, which include a rare representation of St. Basil of Caesarea celebrating the liturgy, are severe and somewhat archaic in manner. They have been attributed to the influence of a workshop in Thessalonica, a city closely linked to the Macedonian hinterland by the valley of the Vardar. The next cycle of monumental paintings in Macedonia belongs to

449

a different epoch and tradition. The little church of Nerezi near Skopje, built and decorated in 1164, was commissioned by a member of the imperial family; and it is very likely that the master painter came from Constantinople. More gentle and delicate in execution than the work in St. Sophia, the frescoes are remarkable for the expressiveness of the faces and the dramatic tension of the scenes. These qualities are particularly evident in the two poignant representations of the Descent from the Cross and of the Lamentation of the Virgin. The paintings of Nerezi are in the mainstream of twelfth century Byzantine art.

The next stage in the history of Balkan painting is marked by the emergence in the thirteenth century of a recognizably Serbian school. One of its earliest products are the frescoes of the monastery church of Mileševa in Western Serbia. Commissioned by King Vladislav, it was built and decorated about 1234. Its painters, who were probably Serbs, had mastered the Byzantine iconographic programme, but were forced to modify it in places in view of the considerable, and un-Byzantine, height of the building: the architecture of Mileševa, like that of other thirteenth century Serbian churches, represents a blending of Byzantine elements with Romanesque influences from Dalmatia. The origins of the Mileševa paintings are still not altogether clear. The differences of style which they reveal may to some extent be explained in terms of the dualism, characteristic of medieval Byzantine art, between the courtly and the monastic traditions: the former is exemplified by the paintings in the main body of the church, with human figures vigorously modelled in the classical manner against a golden background imitating mosaic, such as the well-known Angel of the Resurrection and the portrait of the donor, King Vladislav; the monastic style is represented by the pictures of monks and hermits in the narthex. Yet this dichotomy should not be pressed too far: the ascetic paintings in the narthex include one of St. Sava, the donor's uncle, which is wholly in the tradition of Hellenistic portraiture.

Chronologically the next masterpiece of Balkan art is the small church of Boyana, near Sofia. It contains one of the very few comprehensive cycles of medieval paintings to have survived in Bulgaria. As far as we can judge, medieval art in that country deviated very little from the Byzantine tradition, and displayed

450

few of the local peculiarities of thirteenth century Serbian art, whose more eclectic character was partly due to contacts with Dalmatia and Italy. The main decoration at Boyana was executed in 1259, in the refined manner of Constantinopolitan art of the eleventh and twelfth centuries. Its outstanding items, which bear the mark of an individual genius with a taste for realistic detail, are several representations of Christ, and four portraits depicting the tsar and tsaritsa of Bulgaria, as well as the founder of the church and his wife.

Serbian art, meanwhile, was advancing to full maturity. It achieved its triumph in the mural paintings of the monastery church of Sopoćani in Central Serbia, founded by King Uroš I. Executed between 1263 and 1268, they are the supreme masterpiece of Balkan Slavonic art. They are notable for the majesty and solemn rhythm of the compositions, the monumental dignity of the draped figures, and the distinctive colouring, with its blending of purple, green, blue and ochre. They include a celebrated panel of the Dormition of the Virgin, in which the apostles, in the garb of ancient philosophers, are grouped round Our Lady's dead body, while Christ, bathed in a transcendental light, prepares to carry her soul to heaven. In no other extant work of art of the thirteenth century was the classical tradition, in its Byzantine interpretation, so successfully channelled into the service of Christianity as in the paintings of Sopoćani.

It is likely that the masters of Sopoćani were in touch with a workshop in Thessalonica, even if they were not trained in that city. The influence of Thessalonica on Serbian painting increased in the early fourteenth century with Serbia's expansion into Macedonia, and the resultant orientation of the country's cultural life towards Byzantium. After 1300 Serbian monumental painting began to lose its distinctive traits and to adopt the conventions and techniques of the cosmopolitan Palaeologan art which originated in Constantinople. This internationalization of Serbian art was part of a wider movement, whose impact on religion, law and literature has already been discussed, and which imposed a more unified Byzantine pattern on the East European culture of the fourteenth century. The historian of medieval Serbian art is well equipped to study this process of cultural diffusion: for whereas the earlier Comnenian style was transplanted ready-made on to

451

Serbian soil, Palaeologan art was still developing at the time when its conventions were adopted in that country, and local artists made a significant contribution to its growth. One ruler and two painters played the leading role in this process. King Milutin provided the secular patronage; while the new artistic programme was carried out by a couple of artists whose names have recently come to light: Michael and Eutychius. Their origin and nationality are unknown; they seem to have formed a mobile workshop which operated between 1295 and 1321 in Macedonia and Raška, in close touch with the artistic centres of Thessalonica and Constantinople; the paintings it produced—St. Clement of Ohrid (1295) and the royal chapel at Studenica (1313–14) are outstanding examples—illustrate the different variants of the picturesque and narrative Palaeologan style which reached its peak in the fourteenth century mosaics and frescoes of the Kariye Camii in Constantinople.

These painters of the "Milutin School", who worked on both sides of the Byzantine-Serbian frontier, were faced with the difficult problem of reconciling their desire to multiply descriptive scenes (in accordance with the prevalent Palaeologan manner) with the extensive architectural proportions which many Serbian churches had borrowed from the West. They tried to solve it by dividing the surface of the walls and vaults into a large number of relatively small panels. This fragmentation, which we find at Staro Nagoričino (1317) and Gračanica (1318–21), tended to create a monotonous effect and to destroy the balance between the decoration and the architectural framework. This tendency became even more pronounced after Milutin's death (1321), when Serbian art entered upon a period of decline which lasted for some fifty years. The curious fact that this decline coincided with the age of Serbia's greatest political and military power has never been satisfactorily explained. The tendency to multiply narrative scenes in a vast pictorial encyclopaedia reached its climax in the decoration of Dečani (1335–50). The fact that the Dečani frescoes were painted by artists from Kotor on the Adriatic who worked in "the Greek manner" is evidence that Byzantine-Serbian relations in the field of art were then at a low ebb.

Medieval Serbian art was still to experience its Indian summer. In the northern part of the country, between the Šar Planina and the Danube, in a diminished realm which after 1389 owed allegiance to the Turks, a refined and cosmopolitan culture, still inspired by Byzantium yet in increasingly close contact with Central Europe, flourished for the last time in the Balkans. The rulers of this principality, Stephen Lazarević and George Branković, were internationally-minded patrons of the arts. Thanks to the comparative prosperity of their despotate, increased by the exploitation of the silver and copper mines of Rudnik, they were able in the last quarter of the fourteenth century and in the early fifteenth to commission a number of lavishly decorated churches. This artistic revival owed much to their relations with Byzantium, and to the fact that Northern Serbia lay astride one of the routes, the Morava valley, which was followed by monks, scholars and artists who migrated northward to escape the Turkish advance. The finest paintings of the "Morava School" are in the monastery churches of Ravanica (c. 1378), Kalenić (1413–17), and Manasija (or Resava: 1406–18). The conventions of Palaeologan art were still dominant here, though by contrast with the Serbian painters of the previous period the artists avoided overloading their iconographic programmes, and restored the balance between architecture and decoration. The painters of Manasija were probably trained in Thessalonica. By contrast with the monumental tradition of thirteenth century Serbian painting and the narrative style of the fourteenth, the frescoes of the Morava School are executed in a decorative and somewhat sentimental manner. In their ability to portray the physical grace of the aristocratic warrior and the disembodied grandeur of the ascetic, they illustrate two features of this late medieval Serbian culture: its courtly refinement, and its endeavour, on the eve of the final Turkish conquest, to transmute the harsh realities of life into a dream-like vision of spiritual beauty.

2 Rumania

The early history of Rumanian art confirms the view, expressed above, that a coherent artistic tradition could arise in an East European country only when its political and ecclesiastical institutions were sufficiently developed to provide the artists with a continuous and adequately endowed patronage. Moldavia and Wallachia reached that stage in the mid-fourteenth century. It was then that the two principalities acquired a degree of administrative centralization, a measure of economic prosperity, and a church organization dependent on the Byzantine patriarchate. It was then, too, that the first medieval monuments arose in those lands. At first these were mainly concentrated in Wallachia. The churches of Cozia and of St. Nicholas at Curtea-de-Argeş are the two outstanding works of fourteenth century Rumanian art. The former closely follows the architectural pattern of contemporary North Serbian churches. Curtea-de-Argeş, completed between 1364 and 1377, was attached to the court of the Wallachian princes and was built as their place of burial. Its frescoes are the most complete cycle of Byzantine Palaeologan painting on Rumanian soil. Several of them, it has recently been proved, were directly inspired by the mosaics of the Kariye Camii in Constantinople.[19] Moldavia developed a fully articulate artistic tradition only in the second half of the fifteenth century, in the reign of Stephen the Great. Its products are more original and historically significant than those of Wallachian art. The fortresses (now in ruins) and the numerous churches and monasteries (most of them still standing) which Stephen commissioned mark the highest achievement of medieval Rumanian architecture. In painting the Moldavians made their most notable contribution to European art in the sixteenth century. The external walls of churches had occasionally been decorated with pictures in several Balkan countries before then; but the practice of covering the entire external surface of the walls with elaborate cycles of paintings seems to have been an invention of Moldavian artists. The earliest example of this technique is on the church of St. George in Suceava (1522). It was followed by the external decorations at the monasteries of Humor (1535), Moldovita (1537), Voroneţ (c. 1547), and Sucevita (c. 1600). Despite their late date, these celebrated paintings are still faithful to the Byzantine Palaeologan tradition, which is only slightly diluted by the admixture of realistic and lyrical elements derived from local popular art.

The first clearly defined period in the history of Russian art begins with the country's conversion to Christianity in the late tenth century and ends with the Mongol invasion. In terms of significant extant works, it covers the two centuries between the foundation of the stone church of St. Sophia in Kiev *c.* 1037 and the completion of the cathedral of Yur'ev Pol'sky in North-Eastern Russia in 1234. The geographical distribution of the monuments reflects fairly accurately the changing pattern of the country's political and economic life: in the eleventh century, in conformity with the urban and cosmopolitan character of Russia's early medieval culture, they were concentrated in the cities on the main and lateral branches of the great commercial river route which led from the Baltic to the Black Sea; in the twelfth and early thirteenth centuries, when Kiev and the other South Russian cities were losing their commanding position, many buildings, especially churches, arose in the new centres of power on the north-eastern and western periphery of the land. Most of the important works created in this period were grouped within three areas, centred on the cities of Kiev, Novgorod and Vladimir.

It was Prince Yaroslav who made Kiev the artistic centre of eleventh century Russia. Among the five major buildings he caused to be erected in his capital, the church of St. Sophia held pride of place. Its very name, as well as the fact that it became the court church, the main cathedral of the realm and the seat of the metropolitan-primate of the Russian Church, suggest that he intended it to be, in function if not in appearance, a copy of St. Sophia of Constantinople. Architecturally, it conformed fairly closely to the prevailing Byzantine plan. Yet several features, which are not found in extant Byzantine churches, show that Yaroslav's builders adapted this plan to local tastes and requirements: they include an increased number of apses (five instead of the normal three), two tower staircases, and thirteen cupolas. Its mosaics, almost certainly executed by Constantinopolitan artists, are good examples of eleventh century Byzantine art: they include the bust medallion of Christ Pantokrator in the dome, flanked by four archangels; beneath them, the twelve apostles in the drum of the central cupola; the massive standing figure of the Virgin in the conch of the main apse, interceding with raised arms for the human race; the Communion of the Apostles just beneath; the Fathers of the Church, in the lower part of the apse; and the two figures of the Annunciation on the spandrels of the triumphal arch. These mosaics, and other Christological and Marian scenes painted in the aisles and transepts, offer one of the most complete examples of the descending hierarchy of heaven and earth which the painters of the Macedonian Renaissance were accustomed to depict on the walls of a church. They are the purest specimens of Byzantine monumental art preserved on Russian soil.

The second artistic centre of pre-Mongol Russia was in the north of the country. The stone cathedral of Novgorod, built between 1045 and 1050 to replace an earlier wooden church, is a simplified version of St. Sophia of Kiev, with the admixture of Romanesque elements in its architecture. Its helmet-shaped cupolas were to become typical of the architectural landscape of early medieval Russia. In the twelfth century a number of churches in that region were decorated with highly accomplished wall paintings. The artists were probably native Russians, who had assimilated the technique and iconographic programmes of their Byzantine teachers. One of them was responsible for the frescoes (c. 1167) in the church of St. George in Staraya Ladoga, near the shores of Lake Ladoga: this was the furthest point reached hitherto by the Byzantine artistic tradition in its northward expansion. Another group of painters decorated in the same tradition, though with an admixture of Romanesque and local elements, the celebrated church of the Saviour Nereditsa in Novgorod (1199). Before their destruction in the Second World War, the austere, solemn and monumental paintings of Nereditsa offered one of the best examples in Eastern Europe of a complete cycle of decorations, covering most of the available surface of the interior walls of a church.

If the twelfth-century paintings in the Novgorod area, for all their basically Byzantine iconography and technique, reveal several local provincial features, this cannot be said of the art of North-Eastern Russia. The churches built during the second half of this century and in the first decades of the thirteenth in Suzdal', Vladimir and the surrounding region display in their architecture,

456

and sometimes in their painting, a monumentality and refinement which go back to the earlier Kievan traditions on the one hand and to Byzantine Comnenian art on the other. The reasons for this were economic and political. The security which North-Eastern Russia then enjoyed from attacks by the steppe nomads, the colonization of virgin lands, the development of novel agricultural techniques, the exploitation of large domains by a usually docile aristocracy, the growth of new towns, the increase of foreign trade down the Volga and up the rivers leading into the Baltic—all these factors had combined by the third quarter of the twelfth century to make the princes of these lands the richest in Russia. This once remote region was, moreover, developing international connections. Vladimir, the capital of Prince Andrew Bogolyubsky (1157–74), was visited, we are told by a contemporary chronicler, by "merchants from Constantinople ... from [other parts of] Russia, and from the Latin countries."[20] Culturally, however, this frontier district was by comparison with Kiev and Novgorod still a backwater. Andrew, in order to make good his claim to the inheritance of the former princes of Kiev, and to enhance the status of his principality, was compelled to look to Byzantium for his models. This he did by combining an ecclesiastical policy with an artistic programme. He made, as we have seen, an abortive attempt to persuade the patriarch to set up a separate metropolitanate in Vladimir; instituted within the churches of his domains a new feast, that of the Protective Veil (*Pokrov*) of Our Lady, unknown to the Byzantines, yet based on an episode in the Greek *Vita* of his namesake St. Andrew, the Constantinopolitan "Fool for Christ's sake"; and, in an attempt to demonstrate that the Mother of God, the heavenly defender of Constantinople, had now extended her protection to the principality of Vladimir (and indeed to the whole of Russia), brought to his capital a highly venerated icon of the Virgin, painted in Constantinople probably shortly before 1150. Our Lady of Vladimir, as this celebrated panel painting came to be called, was, until recent times, perhaps the most widely revered sacred object in Russia: in time of national danger, particularly during the Mongol invasions, it was regarded as the country's palladium.

The belief, fostered by Andrew Bogolyubsky, that his principality was placed under the special protection of the Mother of

God is further instanced in the fact that the churches which he founded were all consecrated to Marian feasts. Among them were the cathedral of the Dormition in Vladimir (1158–60), and the exquisite little church on the river Nerl', dedicated to the new feast of Our Lady's Protective Veil. A remarkable feature of these churches is the stone carvings on their external walls. These sculptures became more profuse and luxurious on the later churches of North Eastern Russia, the cathedral of St. Dimitri in Vladimir (1194–7) and that of St. George in Yur'ev Pol'sky (1230–4). Except in the latter building, their content is predominantly secular, and their function apotropaic: the lions, griffins, centaurs and birds, interspersed with religious scenes, were intended to protect the church from evil forces. Two themes are given special prominence: King David, with crown and harp, and the ascension to heaven of Alexander the Great; both these subjects, in Byzantine art, symbolized the apotheosis of royal and imperial power. The artistic origin of these carvings has been much debated. They certainly owe something to Romanesque influences which probably came from Germany. Their basic features, however, it has recently been suggested, are derived from Byzantine secular art. Although no sculptures of this kind have survived on the territory of the Byzantine Empire, similar carvings, made in 1250–65, exist on the upper part of the western façade of St. Mark's in Venice, and analogous themes grouped in the same manner have been detected in the mosaics, probably dated 1160–70, of the Norman Stanza in the royal palace at Palermo.[21] The almost simultaneous appearance in Sicily, Venice and North-Eastern Russia of works belonging to the same tradition of secular art, which doubtless stemmed from Constantinople, is not only a strong argument pointing to the Byzantine origin of the carvings of the Vladimir churches; it also shows that the study of a particular cultural trait, encountered on the periphery of the Byzantine sphere of influence, can help to reconstruct a whole artistic tradition which arose in its centre.

The century between 1250 and 1350, in the history of Russian art, is an almost total blank. The Mongol invasion of 1237–40 resulted in an immense loss of life, the destruction of cities and a general impoverishment of the whole country. The princes who ruled over lands which, owing to the increasing political fragmentation, had mostly diminished in size, and who were obliged to pay a large tribute to their Tatar overlords, had no longer the resources to commission major works of art. It was only in the second quarter of the fourteenth century that this situation began to change. A new focus of wealth and artistic patronage was emerging in Novgorod. Thanks to its remote position, the city had escaped the Mongol invasion. Though nominally subject to the Golden Horde, and politically dependent most of the time upon the princes of North-Eastern Russia, it had gradually strengthened its municipal institutions, and by 1300 had become in effect an autonomous republic. The extensive lands it had acquired in the far north, as far as the White Sea, the Arctic Ocean and the Urals, supplied the city with furs, fish, salt, copper and other valuable raw materials; and its merchants and land-owning nobility grew rich from the transit trade which made Novgorod the main emporium for goods from North-Eastern Russia and from the towns of the Hanseatic League. Its local church, though canonically dependent on the metropolitans of Moscow, maintained direct links with Constantinople. For these reasons, when the new Palaeologan art began to spread northward from Byzantium in the first half of the fourteenth century, it was readily accepted in Novgorod. Between 1350 and 1450, owing to the patronage of its rich merchants, nobles and churchmen, this city became the foremost artistic centre in Russia and the leading northern outpost of late medieval Byzantine art. As early as 1338 a Byzantine master was commissioned by the archbishop of Novgorod to paint one of the churches of the city.[22]

The art of wall painting in Novgorod reached its peak in the second half of the fourteenth century. The history of this local tradition is not altogether clear. Of its Byzantine origin there can be no doubt. The Novgorodians, who were highly sensitive to every novelty coming from Constantinople, regarded the art of the fresco as a "Greek" art. They were not averse, however, to adapting it to local tastes, and as a result the Palaeologan tradition produced several off-shoots on this northern soil. The paintings in the monastery church of Kovalevo (1380) displayed, in the technique of modelling, the classicism of the figures, and their sense of movement and of the picturesque, the relatively undiluted influence of Balkan (either Constantinopolitan or, more probably,

Serbian) art. But in the church of Volotovo (painted in the 1380s) a very different manner is apparent. In its frescoes (destroyed, with those of Kovalevo, in the Second World War), remarkable for their colours and sense of rhythm, a search for an "expressive ugliness", reminiscent of late medieval Gothic painting, was substituted for the antique conception of human beauty.

The Volotovo frescoes have a stylistic affinity with the work of a great master, Theophanes the Greek. He was one of those Byzantine emigrants who, we have seen, contributed much to the cultural life of Eastern Europe in the late Middle Ages. After working in Constantinople and the Crimea, he moved to Russia, where he lived for some thirty years, first in Novgorod and later in Moscow, where he died between 1405 and 1415. He is said to have painted more than forty churches; in only two of them—the church of the Transfiguration in Novgorod, and the cathedral of the Annunciation in Moscow—has his work been preserved. His Novgorod frescoes (1378) show how the traditions of pure Constantinopolitan art could be adapted to local tastes and requirements. They combine the style of early Palaeologan painting with some of the local experiments carried out by the master of Volotovo. They also reflect the genius of a highly individual artist, whose portraits of Old Testament prophets and Christian saints, with their austere spirituality, pathos and rhythm, brought a new visionary stream into Russian art. The seven panels he painted on the iconostasis of the Moscow cathedral are in the same manner. Their monumental size (over two metres high) represents a turning-point in the history of the iconostasis. It was in late medieval Russia (and to a lesser extent in fourteenth century Macedonia) that the screen separating the sanctuary from the nave, which in Byzantine churches was usually no more than a row of columns joined by a parapet, an architrave and two or three tiers of icons, gradually grew in compactness, to become in the sixteenth and seventeenth centuries a solid wall, covered with paintings. Theophanes' enlarged panels mark an early stage in the development of the lofty and monumental iconostasis which was later, in the post-Byzantine period, exported from Muscovy to Mount Athos, and from there to the Balkan Orthodox countries.

For all his ability to adapt his style to the tastes of his Russian patrons, Theophanes seems to have remained in the mainstream of

Byzantine Palaeologan art. We do not know whether he ever revisited his native land. But a well-authenticated story shows that the memories of Constantinople continued to live in the mind of this Greek expatriate. Epiphanius, the Russian hagiographer, met the old master in Moscow and came to admire his learning and enjoy his conversation. One day he begged him to paint on the frontispiece of a book which he, Epiphanius, was writing, a picture of the church of St. Sophia in Constantinople. Whereupon, he tells us, Theophanes "boldly took his brush and rapidly painted a likeness of a church, in the image of the one in Constantinople, and gave it to me". This picture, he goes on to say, enjoyed a great vogue in Moscow: "from that leaf great benefit accrued to the other Muscovite painters, for many copied it, competing with each other and borrowing it one from the other".[23]

Theophanes may well have been in Constantinople at the time of the Synods of 1341 and 1351 which vindicated the doctrines of Gregory Palamas. It has been suggested that the influence of Hesychast theology can be detected in his paintings. He was beyond doubt a highly educated man, and the fact that both in Byzantium and Russia he moved in circles in which Hesychast ideas were current makes this connection seem plausible. In practice, however, it is very hard to prove. The wider question of the influence of Hesychasm on Palaeologan art has been raised by several modern scholars. Their attempts to demonstrate this influence are ingenious but, in the present writer's opinion, inconclusive. Only one of their arguments seems specific enough to carry weight. It relates to the theme and iconography of the Transfiguration. This theme figures prominently in Hesychast theology; and Gregory Palamas, it will be remembered, identified the radiance which emanated from Christ when He was transfigured on the mountain in the presence of His disciples with the Uncreated Light which illumines the man to whom is vouchsafed the vision of divine glory. It has been observed that the number of churches dedicated to the Transfiguration increased in Eastern Europe in the fourteenth and early fifteenth centuries. Moreover, this period witnessed a certain change in the iconography of this scriptural event. The glory that enveloped Christ at that moment was commonly depicted in the form of an elliptical mandorla; the figures of Moses and Elias appeared sometimes within, sometimes outside it.

The three apostles in the scene were traditionally represented as either having just awoken from their sleep (Luke ix, 32) or "falling on their face" down the mountain, terrified by the vision (Matthew xvii, 6). In Palaeologan paintings the two prophets are generally placed outside the mandorla, to emphasize that Christ alone irradiates what Palamas described as "the inaccessible light, in which God dwells and which clothes Him as with a mantle". Similarly in the fourteenth century the apostles are usually depicted falling headlong from a precipitous mountain: in this way, too, the transcendence of the transfigured Christ is safeguarded and stressed. In the last resort, however, this iconographic argument is probably insufficient to prove the dependence of late Byzantine painting on Hesychast theology. All that can safely be said is that Palaeologan art, an art primarily religious in content, is unlikely to have escaped the influence of the contemporary and equally cosmopolitan Hesychast movement which had so profound an impact on East European culture in the late Middle Ages.

Theophanes' influence on the tradition of wall-painting in Novgorod was short-lived. In the fifteenth century the local artists turned increasingly to another medium, in which they achieved a degree of excellence seldom equalled in medieval Russian art. The Novgorod icons of this period offer one of the best examples of how the most refined traditions of Byzantine painting could be assimilated and adapted to local conditions. The differences between the Novgorodian and the Byzantine panel-paintings have sometimes been exaggerated. It remains true, however, that the fifteenth century Novgorod icons have a quintessence of their own which, with the necessary experience, can be easily recognized. It lies partly in the choice of themes. In addition to the classical subjects of East Christian iconography, the Novgorodian painters showed a particular devotion to certain saints, whose supernatural protection was sought for specific local needs: among them were St. George, the warrior-horseman, the holy couple Florus and Laurus, protectors of horses, Elijah who waters the earth with rain, Blasius who watches over cattle, Paraskeve the guardian saint of merchants, Nicholas the help of mariners, and Anastasia who presides over childbirth. Such specialization in the charitable functions of saints was not unknown in Byzantine art; but nowhere in the East Christian world of the Middle Ages was it so consistently developed as in the iconography of fifteenth-century Novgorod. This presupposes in both artist and patron a sensitivity to the needs and tastes of an agricultural and mercantile society, and an ability to reflect creatively on the function of the icon as an intermediary between the material and spiritual worlds. In style these icons have equally well marked characteristics. To contrast their joyful optimism with the alleged severity of Byzantine panel-paintings is, no doubt, to underestimate the variety of the latter and to over-simplify the picture. Yet the Novgorod icons of this period have several features which we do not find so often nor in such close conjunction in their Byzantine or South Slav counterparts. Among these qualities are a simplicity and economy of composition; a mastery of line and a skill in inserting figures into a nar-rowly defined space; a serene, poetic yet powerful expressiveness; above all, perhaps, a marvellously rich palette, in which vermilion, green and golden colours predominate. It may fairly be claimed that the Novgorod icons of the fifteenth century represent, together with the Serbian wall paintings of the thirteenth, the outstanding contribution made by the Slav peoples of Eastern Europe to the art of the Byzantine Commonwealth.

Only one reference has been made so far to Muscovite art. Few of its early works, from before 1400, have survived. The first monumental buildings, such as the cathedrals of the Kremlin, arose in the last quarter of the fifteenth century and in the early years of the sixteenth; they fall outside the chronological bound-aries of this book. The history of Muscovite art really begins, and this survey of medieval Russian art may conveniently be brought to an end, with the name of the greatest Russian painter of all time, Andrew Rublev. Born about 1370, he became a monk, and in 1405 was commissioned together with Theophanes to paint the iconostasis of the Moscow cathedral of the Annunciation. How far Rublev was trained by the old Byzantine master remains uncer-tain. Although there are considerable differences of style between them, it seems probable that it was Theophanes who introduced his young Russian colleague to the traditions of Palaeologan painting, which were to leave a profound imprint upon the latter's mature work. A few years later Rublev was chosen by the grand prince of Moscow to decorate the cathedral of the Dormition in Vladimir, and about 1425 he painted part of the iconostasis for the newly built cathedral in the monastery of the Holy Trinity. He died in 1430. Which of the extant paintings in these churches are due to his brush is not known for certain: those which can be attributed to him with some probability reveal a classical balance and a graceful rhythm which are in the pure Constantinopolitan manner. To them he added a clarity of composition and a suave tranquillity of mood peculiarly his own. All these qualities are present in the highest degree in the only work which can with certainty be ascribed to him: the icon of the Holy Trinity. Never before or since did the Byzantine tradition reach such mature perfection on Russian soil as in the figures of the three angels, symbolizing the triune God, seated in total stillness round the eucharistic table, expressing in a subtle rhythm the idea of harmony and mutual love. It is with good reason that this masterpiece of medieval Russian painting has been called "a Greek hymn upon a Slavonic tongue".[24]

NOTES

1. A. Vaillant, "La Préface de l'Evangéliaire vieux-slave", *Revue des Etudes Slaves*, xxiv (1948), p. 8.

2. *Povest'*, pp. 102–3; Cross, pp. 137–8.

3. Popruzhenko, p. 79; Puech and Vaillant, p. 127.

4. F. Dölger in *The Cambridge Medieval History*, iv, 2 (Cambridge, 1967), p. 234.

5. See above, chapter 3, note 1.

6. Ed. R. Nahtigal, "Rekonstrukcija treh starocerkvenoslovanskih izvirnih pesnitev", *Akademija Znanosti in Umetnosti v Ljubljani, Razprave filoz.-filol.-histor. razreda*, i (1943), pp. 56–7.

7. L. Müller, *Des Metropoliten Ilarion Lobrede auf Vladimir den Heiligen und Glaubensbekenntnis* (Wiesbaden, 1962); *A Historical Russian Reader*, pp. 1–20.

8. *Povest'*, pp. 9–11; Cross, pp. 51–2.

9. *Povest'*, pp. 21–3; Cross, pp. 62–3.

10. A. Vaillant, "Une poésie vieux-slave: la Préface de l'Evangile" *Revue des Etudes Slaves*, xxxiii (1956), pp. 7–25; R. Jakobson, "St. Constantine's Prologue to the Gospel", *St. Vladimir's Seminary Quarterly*, vii (1963), pp. 14–19.

11. *King Alfred's West-Saxon Version of Gregory's Pastoral Care*, ed. H. Sweet, i (London, 1934), p. 6.

12. V. Jagić, *Rassuzhdeniya yuzhnoslavyanskoy i russkoy stariny o tserkovno-slavyanskom yazyke* (St. Petersburg, 1896), p. 108.

464

13. See above, p. 391.

14. Jagić, *Rassuzhdeniya*, pp. 95–199.

15. E. Kałużniacki, *Werke des Patriarchen von Bulgarien Euthymius* (Vienna, 1901).

16. See above, p. 393.

17. *Zhitie sv. Stefana, episkopa Permskogo*, ed. V. Druzhinin (The Hague, 1959) (reprint); *Die Legenden des Heiligen Sergij von Radonež*, ed. N. Tikhonravov (Munich, 1967) (reprint).

18. A. Grabar in *The Cambridge Medieval History*, iv, 2, p. 348.

19. P. A. Underwood, *The Kariye Djami*, i (London, 1967), pp. 117–24.

20. *Ipat'evskaya Letopis'*, s.a. 1175: *Polnoe Sobranie Russkikh Letopisey*, ii (Moscow, 1962), col. 591.

21. A. Grabar, "Svetskoe izobrazitel'noe iskusstvo domongol'skoy Rusi i *Slovo o polku Igoreve*", *Trudy Otdela Drevnerusskoy Literatury*, xviii (1962), pp. 233–71.

22. *Novgorodskaya Pervaya Letopis'*, ed. A. N. Nasonov (Moscow-Leningrad, 1950), p. 348.

23. V. N. Lazarev, *Feofan Grek i ego shkola* (Moscow, 1961), pp. 113–14.

24. C. R. Morey, *Mediaeval Art* (New York, 1942), p. 167.

EPILOGUE

The capture of Constantinople by the troops of the Sultan Mehmet II on 29 May 1453 brought the history of the Byzantine Commonwealth to a close. Its political bonds, as we have seen, had greatly loosened since the late thirteenth century; yet they were not completely broken, despite the decay of the Byzantine state and the growing power of several East European nations in the late Middle Ages. The patriarchate of Constantinople remained a centralizing force, working for political as well as religious unity. The doctrine propounded by its leaders that "it is not possible for Christians to have the church and not to have the empire"[1] still commanded widespread acceptance in Eastern Europe. And neither the political ambitions of the Balkan rulers nor the shock produced in Russia by the Greek "betrayal of Orthodoxy" at the Council of Florence dispelled the ancient belief that the centre of the Christian *oikoumene* was in Constantinople. This belief was indeed reinforced by the new and stronger cultural ties which bound the East European lands to Byzantium during the last century of the empire's existence.

It is hence not surprising that the fall of Constantinople aroused in these countries immediate feelings of horror and dismay. Greeks, Slavs and Rumanians reacted to this event by composing laments, in poetry and prose, for the captured and stricken city. A Greek popular poem, probably composed in the second half of the fifteenth century, describes an imaginary scene of the last liturgy celebrated in St. Sophia in the presence of the emperor and the patriarch, which was interrupted by the arrival of the infidels: as tears were seen in the eyes of the Virgin on the church's icons, the clergy was commanded by a voice from heaven to send the cross, the Gospel book and the holy table to Western Europe, lest they be profaned by the Turks.[2] In another version of the story, as the

Turks broke into St. Sophia a priest bearing the chalice left the building through a door which miraculously closed behind him: on the day the Greeks recapture their city, he will re-emerge to complete the unfinished liturgy.[3] A contemporary Serbian lament on the fall of Constantinople forms part of a panegyric of the Serbian ruler George Branković (d. 1456) who rebuilt at his own expense a section of its walls.[4] Another dirge on the capture of the "Great City", composed soon after the event by the Greek writer John Eugenicus, was soon translated into Russian, and became part of Muscovite literature. It mourns "the glorious and much-longed-for City, the mainstay of our race, the splendour of the *oikoumene*"; the church of St. Sophia, "that heaven on earth, that second paradise"; the schools and libraries now destroyed; and the citizens of Byzantium, "the holy nation", "the people of the universe", driven from their homes and scattered like autumn leaves; the magnitude of these disasters invited comparison with the great calamities of mankind: the destruction of Jerusalem by the Romans, Christ's death upon the cross, and the last days of the world.[5]

Gradually, as the emotional shock wore off, this apocalyptic view of the destruction of the Christian Empire was superseded by another. The contrast, which the Muscovite ideologues had begun to draw after the Council of Florence, between the religious inconstancy of the Greeks and the Russians' fidelity to Orthodoxy could hardly fail to suggest that Moscow, not Constantinople, was now the centre of the true Orthodox faith. In the years immediately following the fall of Byzantium Russian churchmen began openly to voice this conclusion. In 1460 the metropolitan of Moscow declared that the fall of Constantinople was God's punishment for the Greek betrayal of Orthodoxy at Florence;[6] and in 1492 another primate of the Russian Church described Moscow as "the new Constantinople".[7] On this ideological ground was constructed, in the following decades, the celebrated theory of "Moscow, the Third Rome". Its leading exponent, the Russian monk Philotheus, contrasted the sorrowful fate of the First Rome, which had long ago forfeited its claim to world dominion by falling into heresy, and of the Second Rome, now in the hands of the infidels, with the providential destiny of the Muscovite realm: Moscow, the capital of the only remaining independent Orthodox state in the world, was now the guardian of the true faith and the heir to the Roman imperial traditions. In a letter addressed to his sovereign, the grand prince of Moscow Basil III (1505–33), Philotheus wrote:

> Know ye, most pious tsar, that all the empires (tsardoms) of the Orthodox Christian religion have come together into your tsardom: thou art the only tsar of the Christians in the whole world. . . . All the Christian tsardoms have been gathered into thy tsardom. After this we await the Kingdom (tsardom) of which there shall be no end. . . . Two Romes have fallen, but the third stands, and a fourth there will not be.[8]

This philosophy, which ascribed to the Russian sovereigns religious and political pre-eminence in the Christian world and saw in their realm the immediate precursor of the Kingdom of God, is sometimes cited in support of the view that the sixteenth century rulers of Muscovy deliberately took over the imperial traditions of Byzantium. Some modern historians have gone further still in their endeavour to trace the impact of Russia's "Byzantine heritage" down the centuries: this legacy, they contend, can be seen both in the authoritarian nature of Russian political institutions of more recent times, and in the conviction, expressed by successive rulers of the Soviet Union, that the doctrines of the Communist Party of the U.S.S.R. are destined to overcome Christianity, capitalism and liberal democracy and supplant them throughout the world. In these brief concluding remarks the author can do little more than declare his belief that this reading of Russian history is at best one-sided, and that the concept of a direct continuity between Byzantine and post-medieval Russian political ideas and institutions finds little support in the history of Muscovy during the century and a half that followed the fall of Constantinople.

Historians who have argued in favour of this continuity have usually ascribed great importance to the following facts: the marriage, concluded in 1472, between Ivan III of Moscow and Zoe Palaeologina, the niece of the last Byzantine emperor; the adoption by her husband—as yet unofficially—of the title tsar (the Slavonic equivalent of *basileus*), and its formal assumption by his grandson Ivan IV in 1547; the similarities between the Muscovite and the Byzantine coronation rites; and the re-statement of Philotheus' theory of "Moscow the Third Rome" in the Act instituting the patriarchate of Moscow in 1589. None of these facts, however, provide convincing proof that the Russians in this period deliberately sought to revive and lay claim to the political heritage of Byzantium. Neither Ivan III nor any of his successors ever claimed that the marriage with Zoe gave them a right to this heritage. It is true that after his marriage Ivan III began to use the Byzantine two-headed eagle on his seals, a practice adopted increasingly by his successors. It should be remembered, however, that—although it appears as an emblem of sovereignty on imperial portraits from the end of the thirteenth century—the two-headed eagle was never the official coat-of-arms of the Byzantine Empire. Furthermore, Ivan III was not the first East European monarch to make political use of this emblem: as early as the thirteenth and fourteenth centuries it appears as a badge of sovereignty in different lands of the Byzantine Commonwealth—in Serbia, Bulgaria, Rumania and in Russia itself. The title of tsar, which the Russians applied in the Middle Ages both to the Byzantine emperor and to the khan of the Golden Horde, was first assumed by Ivan III after Russia's liberation from Tatar rule in 1480; furthermore, Ivan IV in 1576 instructed his ambassadors to the court of the Western emperor to claim the right to this title because he had conquered the Tatar "tsardoms" of Kazan' and Astrakhan'.[9] The coronation rites of the Russian tsars of the sixteenth and seventeenth centuries, for all their similarities to the Byzantine imperial coronation, were far from identical with the latter: the Muscovite "tsars and autocrats of all Russia", to judge from these rites, were endowed with less exalted attributes than the former emperors of Byzantium, and were considered to derive their sovereignty from their princely ancestors as well as from God. Finally, the creation of the patriarchate of Moscow, to which the highest authorities of the Eastern Church gave their approval, in no way implied that Russia possessed ecclesiastical supremacy: for Moscow was given the lowest rank in the hierarchy of patriarchates, after Constantinople, Alexandria, Antioch and Jerusalem.

These negative arguments may be reinforced by a consideration of the motives and aims of Russia's foreign policy in the late fifteenth and in the sixteenth centuries: these, too, strongly suggest that the political implications of the theory of "Moscow the Third Rome" were not taken too seriously by the governments of the time. Russian diplomatic documents of this period clearly show that, in place of the medieval conception of a hierarchy of states, presided over by the Byzantine emperor, Ivan III and his successors were guided by the notion of a family of European nations whose sovereigns were equal in status. This post-medieval idea of the Great Powers resembled neither the Christian universalism of Byzantium nor Philotheus' notion of a world supremacy exercised by the Muscovite tsardom. Furthermore, the aims of Russia's foreign policy in this period were directly opposed to the view that its sovereigns were the heirs of Byzantium. The most important of these aims, and the one most consistently pursued, was to regain the western lands which had formed part of Kievan Russia and had been annexed by the Lithuanians in the fourteenth century. This policy, unsuccessful until the second half of the seventeenth century, involved Muscovy in a series of wars with Lithuania and Poland. To implement a "Third Rome" programme the Russians would have had to pursue a policy of expansion in the Balkans; and this sooner or later would have led to a conflict with the Ottoman Empire. A war on two fronts would have seriously jeopardized Russia's irredentist ambitions in the West; while a friendly sultan, it was hoped, could restrain his vassal, the Tatar khan of the Crimea, from attacking Muscovy from the south. This explains why in 1582 Ivan IV declared to the papal envoy, Antonio Possevino: "we do not want the realm of the whole universe";[10] and why all the attempts of western powers to entice the sixteenth century tsars into an alliance against the Turks were studiously ignored in Moscow. While the pope, the Holy Roman Emperor, the Venetians and the Greeks themselves were urging the Russians, as their price for this alliance, to demand Constantinople as their historic heritage, the Muscovite rulers turned a deaf ear to these blandishments, and confined themselves to claiming the inheritance of the Russian lands over which their Kievan forebears had ruled. "Moscow the Second Kiev", not "Moscow the Third Rome" was the hall-mark of their foreign policy.

Even on the ideological plane, Philotheus' attribution of universal sovereignty to the Muscovite ruler failed to win general assent. Russian political thought in the Middle Ages had been influenced, we have seen, by a treatise written in the sixth century by the Byzantine deacon Agapetus. The Russians showed a special fondness for the following passage of this treatise: "In the substance of

470

his body, the emperor is like any man, but in the power of his office he is like God, the Master of all men: for there is on earth no higher than he."[11] In medieval Russia this quotation was invariably taken to refer to the Byzantine emperor. It was not until the early sixteenth century that Agapetus' definition of the divine nature of the monarch's prerogatives began to be applied to the tsar of Muscovy. But the implication, contained in this definition, this his sovereignty is universal was now played down by the Russians. It was clearly with this intention that a Muscovite author, writing between 1533 and 1563, adapted another passage from Agapetus' treatise. In the original the emperor is compared to a pilot who sees that "the ship of the universal commonwealth (*pankosmiou politeias*) does not founder beneath the waves of iniquity". In the Russian version the words "universal commonwealth" are replaced by "his great realm".[12] This anonymous panegyrist of Muscovite autocracy was evidently thinking in purely national terms. He would surely have subscribed to Ivan IV's view that the Russian tsardom could lay no claim to "the realm of the whole universe".

The theory of "Moscow the Third Rome" was not, however, wholly devoid of historical significance. There is no doubt that the panegyrists of "Holy Russia" welcomed the idea that the centre of the Orthodox faith and the seat of Christian sovereignty had migrated to Moscow after the fall of Constantinople. But the great majority of them were churchmen, and the theory which they borrowed from the monk Philotheus seems to have remained in this period a preserve of ecclesiastics. It had no effect upon government policy. Philotheus' views were strongly tinged with eschatological elements: the Third Rome was for him but a prelude—possibly a brief one—to "the kingdom of which there shall be no end". It is noteworthy that his doctrine was embraced by the schismatic Old Believers, who in the second half of the seventeenth century endured persecution because of their refusal to accept the liturgical reforms of the Patriarch Nikon. Amid the turmoil caused by these reforms in the whole of Russia, they had even more reason to believe that the end of time was near. And, along with these apocalyptic stirrings, this last significant resurgence of the "Third Rome" ideology displayed another feature characteristic of sixteenth and seventeenth century Russian

471

culture: its overt nationalism. The Old Believers on the stake and in the tsar's torture chambers were, in the name of Holy Russia, protesting against Nikon's efforts to impose upon his church the scriptural texts and the liturgical practice of the Greeks; to their great indignation he had declared: "I am a Russian ... but my faith and religion are Greek".[13]

A similar type of nationalism inspired the policy of the rulers of Russia, especially after 1480. The ideological basis of this policy, developed in the self-contained and power-conscious society of sixteenth century Muscovy, was far narrower than the political philosophy which had guided the Byzantine statesmen of the Middle Ages. It is in the *Realpolitik* of Ivan III, Basil III and Ivan IV that we can detect the clearest signs of Russia's "turning away" from the political heritage of Byzantium. And it is significant that this process, which began in the late fifteenth century, coincided with the growth of the country's diplomatic and cultural relations with the West. Two and a half centuries later, after the westernizing reforms of Peter the Great, Russia became—as she had been in the eleventh and twelfth centuries—an integral part of the European state system.

The changes that have transformed Russia's cultural and social life during the past three hundred years—the influence of Polish education and manners in the seventeenth century, the acceptance by the intelligentsia of French literature and German philosophy, the impact of the Industrial Revolution, the spread of Socialism and Marxism—did not, to be sure, erase all traces of the country's Byzantine past. Thus the theocratic idea of the sacred monarch, ruling his realm in harmony with the church—an idea widely accepted in sixteenth and seventeenth century Muscovy and which owed much to Byzantine influence—was not wholly eradicated by Peter the Great's efforts to subject the ecclesiastical order to the power of the state, in accordance with Lutheran models and western concepts of the natural law. The Orthodox Christian tradition, which until recently retained the loyalty of the great majority of its population, remains the principal legacy of Byzantium to modern Russia. The nature and force of this legacy cannot be discussed here. It may be suggested, however, that the secularization of the upper class culture caused by Peter's reforms and its consequent divorce from the beliefs and way of life of the peasantry brought the effective influence of Byzantine cultural patterns on Russian society as a whole to an end in the early eighteenth century.

In the Balkans, despite—and in some respects because of—the Turkish rule this influence survived longer. Several institutions current in Byzantium and the Balkan countries in the late Middle Ages—notably the fiscal system—were taken over by the Ottoman Empire. The early sultans strove to appear in the eyes of their Christian subjects as the heirs of the emperors of East Rome. Mehmet II, the conqueror, had large numbers of Greeks moved from different parts of his empire to the depopulated city of Constantinople, now renamed Istanbul. The Christians in the Ottoman Empire, though accorded a low status in society, were organized in a *millet*, or "nation", and were allowed to retain their laws and customs. Their strongest link with the past was the patriarch of Constantinople: this dignitary was not only granted the privileges and immunities enjoyed by his Byzantine predecessors; he was also recognized by the sultan as the secular, as well as the spiritual, head of all his Christian subjects. As "ethnarch" of the Christian *millet*, with civil authority over it, he held the rank of a high Ottoman official and was responsible only to the sultan. His vestment was adorned with the old imperial double-headed eagle, and his coursts dispensed justice in accordance with Byzantine law. All the Orthodox peoples of the Balkans—with the temporary exception of the Serbs, who were granted religious autonomy between 1557 and 1766—were in effect under his ecclesiastical jurisdiction. Far more than in the late Byzantine period, the patriarchs of Constantinople were thus able, under Turkish rule, to vindicate their ancient title of "oecumenical".

Next to the patriarchate, two social groups preserved and fostered the Byzantine traditions in South-Eastern Europe: the Greek merchant aristocracy of Constantinople, and the Rumanian princes of the sixteenth and seventeenth centuries. The former, who came to be known as the Phanariots because many of them resided near the patriarchate in the Phanar quarter, exerted a growing influence upon the Church's organs of administration. Some of them, like the Cantacuzeni, claimed descent from Byzantine imperial families. Others, like Alexander Mavrocordato

473

(*d.* 1709), rose to the highest ranks in the Ottoman administration. Many were highly educated men and devotees of Greek culture, which they actively promoted in the patriarchal academy in Constantinople. And although their outlook became increasingly tinged with the secular humanism which they imbibed largely from the university of Padua, the Phanariots, by their financial support of the patriarchate's educational efforts, by their cosmopolitan upbringing, and by their cult of Hellenism, did much to keep alive among the Greek subjects of the sultan a consciousness of their Byzantine heritage.

This sense of a continuing Byzantine tradition was equally strong in the Rumanian principalities. The rulers of Wallachia and Moldavia, having submitted voluntarily to the sultan, were allowed to preserve their autonomy. Though they were vassals of the Porte, and were usually, after the middle of the sixteenth century, appointed to their thrones by the sultan, they were conscious of their position as the sole remaining Christian rulers in South-Eastern Europe. Their considerable wealth, derived from the trade in native corn and livestock, enabled them to support and patronize the churches of Constantinople, Alexandria and Jerusalem, as well as the monasteries of Mount Athos. In this and other respects they saw themselves as the heirs of the emperors of Byzantium; and they were sometimes acknowledged as such by the foreign recipients of their princely munificence. Copying the ceremonial of the former imperial court, fostering Greek literature, scholarship and theology in their capitals of Bucharest and Iasi, these Rumanian *Domni* steeped themselves in the political and cultural traditions of Byzantium to a far greater extent than their Russian contemporaries, the Muscovite tsars; and under their patronage, which was acknowledged throughout much of South-Eastern Europe and in the Christian communities of the Near East, a miniature Byzantium, which a Rumanian historian has described as "Byzance après Byzance",[14] began to take shape north of the Danube. The most remarkable of these neo-Byzantine rulers was Basil Lupu (the Wolf), prince of Moldavia from 1634 to 1653. He managed the finances of the patriarchate; presided, in the best traditions of the Byzantine Emperors, over a council of the Orthodox Church convened in 1642 in Iași, his capital, at which the sees of Constantinople and Kiev were represented;

474

and is even said to have planned his own imperial coronation. In the second half of the seventeenth century these two neo-Byzantine movements, sponsored by the Phanariots and the Rumanian princes, achieved a measure of fusion. In search of land in which they could invest their wealth and of a territorial base from which they could work for the restoration of Byzantium, the Phanariots began to migrate to Wallachia and Moldavia. Before long they secured for themselves the thrones of the two principalities. During the next century and a half the princes of Wallachia and Moldavia belonged to half a dozen or so prominent Greek families: some of them, like the Cantacuzeni, acquired large estates in the principalities and intermarried with the local Rumanian nobility; others, like the Mavrocordatos and Ghikas (the latter a Hellenized Albanian family), were appointed by the sultan from among the Phanariots of Constantinople. These princes, many of whom were men of wide culture, maintained close links with the Greeks of Constantinople and were thus able to provide an intellectual foundation to the Rumanian dream of a revived Byzantium.

Yet there were in the outlook of the eighteenth century Phanariots inherent contradictions which undermined and eventually destroyed the cogency of these neo-Byzantine aspirations. Most of them were sincere Christians and devoted to the Orthodox Church. At the same time, they fell increasingly under the sway of the new rationalist and humanist philosophy current in Western Europe. Moreover, while continuing to pay lip-service to the cosmopolitan legacy of Byzantium, these Phanariots tended, also under Western influence, to stress the principle of nationality. This led them to promote a policy of active and often aggressive Hellenization, of which the Slav churches in the Balkans were the victims, and to work for the rebirth of the Greek nation: a programme which resulted in the national rebellion of 1821 and the war of independence. These new ideas and programmes, which determined the intellectual and political development of the modern Greek state, were not compatible in the long run with the survival of the Byzantine tradition. Its decline, in South-Eastern Europe, caused by the impact of the ideas of the Enlightenment and of modern nationalism, may be dated to the late eighteenth century; and during the following decades the force of this tradition was finally spent.

"The death of Byzantium", of course, never wholly came about in the Balkans, any more than it did in Russia. For a century after 1821 the imagination of the Greek people and their statesmen continued to be haunted by the "Great Idea" of restoring the Byzantine Empire by the recapture of Constantinople. These ambitions were finally wrecked by the Asia Minor disaster of 1921–2. But the heritage of Byzantium has not been obliterated from the cultural life of South-Eastern Europe. In the remoter monasteries and village communities of the mainland and on the islands, in the private faith and corporate worship of peasants and townfolk who have remained true to the religion of their forefathers, above all perhaps in the celebration of the Eucharist, that symbolic drama of man's salvation re-enacted without essential change since the early days of the Christian Empire, the Orthodox people of Eastern Europe preserve to this day a living contact with their Byzantine past.

NOTES

1. See above, p 342.
2. N. G. Polites, Ἐκλογαὶ ἀπὸ τὰ τραγούδια τοῦ ἑλληνικοῦ λαοῦ, 3rd ed. (Athens, 1932), no. 2, pp. 12–13.
3. N. G. Polites, Παραδόσεις (Athens, 1904), no. 35, p. 23.
4. I. Dujčev, "La conquête turque et la prise de Constantinople dans la littérature slave contemporaine", Byzantinoslavica, xvii (1956), pp. 277–8.
5. Τοῦ νομοφύλακος Ἰωάννου διακόνου τοῦ Εὐγενικοῦ μονῳδία ἐπὶ τῇ ἁλώσει τῆς μεγαλοπόλεως, ed. S. P. Lambros, Νέος Ἑλληνομνήμων, v. 2–3 (1908), 219–26; cf. D. Obolensky, "Byzantium and Russia in the Late Middle Ages" in Europe in the Late Middle Ages, ed. J. R. Hale and others (London, 1965), pp. 274–5.
6. Russkaya Istoricheskaya Biblioteka, vi (St. Petersburg, 1880), cols. 648–9.
7. Ibid., col. 799.
8. V. Malinin, Starets Eleazarova monastyrya Filofey i ego poslaniya (Kiev, 1901), pp. 50–5.
9. Pamyatniki diplomaticheskikh snosheniy drevney Rossii s derzhavami inostrannymi, i (St. Petersburg, 1851), cols. 604–5.
10. Ibid., x, col. 301.
11. See above, p. 292.

12. I. Ševčenko, "A Neglected Byzantine Source of Muscovite Political Ideology", *Harvard Slavic Studies*, ii (1954), pp. 159–62.

13. W. Palmer, *The Patriarch and the Tsar*, ii (London, 1873), p. 175.

14. N. Iorga, *Byzance après Byzance* (Bucharest, 1935).

BIBLIOGRAPHY

This is not a systematic bibliography, but a list of works for further reading. Books and articles in East European languages are cited only when they are of special importance or when no work on the subject appears to exist in a West European tongue. Further references and detailed bibliographies will be found in the following works: Gy. Moravcsik, *Byzantinoturcica*, i, 2nd ed. (Berlin, 1958); H.-G. Beck, *Kirche und Theologische Literatur im byzantinischen Reich* (Munich, 1959); I. Dujčev, "Les Slaves et Byzance", *Etudes historiques à l'occasion du XIe Congrès International des Sciences Historiques*, Stockholm (Sofia, 1960), pp. 31-77; *The Cambridge Medieval History*, iv, 1 and 2, ed. J. M. Hussey (2nd ed., Cambridge, 1966-7); G. Ostrogorsky, *History of the Byzantine State* (2nd ed., Oxford, 1968).

CHAPTER I: THE GEOGRAPHICAL SETTING

The geography and the historical geography of the Balkans

J. Cvijić, *La Péninsule Balkanique* (Paris, 1918).

J. Ancel, *Peuples et nations des Balkans*, 2nd ed. (Paris, 1941).

——, "L'unité balkanique", *Revue Internationale des Etudes Balkaniques*, i (Belgrade, 1934), pp. 117-39.

Geographical Handbook Series (Naval Intelligence Division, London): *Greece*, 3 vols. (1944-5); *Jugoslavia*, 3 vols. (1944-5); *Albania* (1945).

A. Philippson, *Das byzantinische Reich als geographische Erscheinung* (Leiden, 1939).

F. Braudel, *La Méditerranée et le monde méditerranéen à l'époque de Philippe II*, 2nd ed., 2 vols. (Paris, 1966). English transl., 2 vols. (London, 1972-3).

J. J. Wilkes, *Dalmatia* (London, 1969).

The Greek colonies on the northern coast of the Black Sea

E. H. Minns, *Scythians and Greeks* (Cambridge, 1913).

M. Rostovtzeff, *Iranians and Greeks in South Russia* (Oxford, 1922).

479

The Dobrudja

La Dobroudja (Bucharest, 1938).

Din istoria Dobrogei, i, by D. Pippidi and D. Berciu (Bucharest, 1965); ii, by R. Vulpe and I. Barnea (Bucharest, 1968).

Constantinople: its site and monuments

A. Van Millingen, *Byzantine Constantinople: the Walls of the City and Adjoining Historical Sites* (London, 1899).

Die Landmauer von Konstantinopel, i, by F. Krischen (Berlin, 1938), ii, by B. Meyer-Plath and A. M. Schneider (Berlin, 1943) [*Denkmäler antiker Architektur*, vi and viii].

E. Mamboury, *The Tourists' Istanbul* (Istanbul, 1953).

R. Janin, *Constantinople Byzantine*, 2nd ed. (Paris, 1964).

D. Talbot Rice, *Constantinople, Byzantium–Istanbul* (London, 1965).

M. Maclagan, *The City of Constantinople* (London, 1968).

Thessalonica

O. Tafrali, *Topographie de Thessalonique* (Paris, 1913).

——, *Thessalonique au XIVe siècle* (Paris, 1913).

A. E. Vakalopoulos, *A History of Thessaloniki* (Thessalonica, 1963).

The Belgrade–Constantinople highway

K. Jireček, *Die Heerstrasse von Belgrad nach Constantinopel und die Balkanpässe* (Prague, 1877).

The Via Egnatia

T. L. F. Tafel, *De via militari Romanorum Egnatia, qua Illyricum, Macedonia et Thracia iungebantur* (Tübingen, 1842). Reprinted, London, 1973.

"Via Egnatia": in Pauly-Wissowa, *Real–Encyclopädie der Classischen Altertumswissenschaft*, v (1905), cols. 1988–93.

P. Collart, *Philippes, ville de Macédoine, depuis ses origines jusqu'à la fin de l'époque romaine* (Paris, 1937).

Routes from the Adriatic coast into the interior

K. Jireček, *Die Handelsstrassen und Bergwerke von Serbien und Bosnien während des Mittelalters* (Prague, 1879).

The Crimea

G. I. Brătianu, *Recherches sur le commerce génois dans la Mer Noire au XIII⁰ siècle* (Paris, 1929).

A. A. Vasiliev, *The Goths in the Crimea* (Cambridge, Mass., 1936).

A. L. Yakobson, *Srednevekovy Krym* [Medieval Crimea] (Moscow–Leningrad, 1964).

M. Nystazopoulou-Pélékidis, "Venise et la Mer Noire du XIᵉ au XVᵉ siècle", *Thesaurismata*, vɪɪ (Venice, 1970), pp. 15–51.

Eurasian Nomads

R. Grousset, *L'empire des steppes* (Paris, 1939).

S. V. Kiselev, *Drevnyaya istoriya yuzhnoy Sibiri* [The Early History of Southern Siberia] (Moscow, 1951). Reviewed by B. Rubin, "Das neue Bild der Geschichte Eurasiens", *Jahrbücher für Geschichte Osteuropas*, ii (1954), pp. 89–120.

A. Toynbee, *Constantine Porphyrogenitus and his World* (London, 1973), pp. 411–60.

Russia

W. H. Parker, *An Historical Geography of Russia* (London, 1968).

CHAPTER 2: BARBARIANS IN THE BALKANS

General

The Byzantine sources concerned with the Balkan Slavs are being published by the Bulgarian and the Serbian Academies of Science: *Fontes historiae bulgaricae*, i, iii, vi, viii, ix, xi, xiv (Sofia, 1954–) (in Greek and Bulgarian); *Fontes byzantini historiam populorum Jugoslaviae spectantes*, i, ii, iii (Belgrade, 1955–) (in Serbo-Croat).

D. Obolensky, "The Empire and its Northern Neighbours, 565–1018", *The Cambridge Medieval History*, iv, 1 (1966), pp. 473–518.

The Slavs and their invasions of the Balkans

L. Niederle, *Manuel de l'antiquité slave*, i (Paris, 1923).

K. Jażdżewski, *Atlas to the Prehistory of the Slavs*, 2 parts (Łódź, 1948–9).

P. Lemerle, "Invasions et migrations dans les Balkans depuis la fin de l'époque romaine jusqu'au VIIIᵉ siècle", *Revue Historique*, ccxi (1954), pp. 265–308.

F. Dvornik, *The Slavs: Their Early History and Civilization* (Boston, 1956).

The Antes

G. Vernadsky, "On the Origins of the Antae", *Journal of the American Oriental Society*, lix (1939), pp. 56–66.

F. Dvornik, *The Making of Central and Eastern Europe* (London, 1949), pp. 277–86.

V. Beševliev, *Zur Deutung der Kastellnamen in Prokops Werk "De Aedificiis"* (Amsterdam, 1970).

The Avars

H. H. Howorth, "The Avars", *Journal of the Royal Asiatic Society*, xxi (1889), pp. 721–810.

L. Hauptmann, "Les rapports des Byzantins avec les Slaves et les Avares pendant la seconde moitié du VIᵉ siècle", *Byzantion*, iv (1927–8), pp. 137–70.

E. Darkó, "Influences Touraniennes sur l'évolution de l'art militaire des Grecs, des Romains et des Byzantins", *Byzantion*, x (1935), pp. 443–69, xii (1937), pp. 119–47.

A. Kollautz, "Die Awaren. Die Schichtung in einer Nomadenherrschaft", *Saeculum*, v (1954), pp. 129–78.

G. László, "Etudes archéologiques sur l'histoire de la société des Avars", *Archaeologia Hungarica*, xxxiv (1955).

Avaro-Slav sieges of Thessalonica

A. Tougard, *De l'histoire profane dans les actes grecs des Bollandistes* (Paris, 1874).

P. Lemerle, "La composition et la chronologie des deux premiers livres des Miracula S. Demetrii", *Byzantinische Zeitschrift*, xlvi (1953), pp. 349–61.

F. Barišić, *Čuda Dimitrija Solunskog kao istoriski izvori* [*Les Miracles de St. Démétrius comme source historique*] (Belgrade, 1953). [With a summary in French.]

The Avar siege of Constantinople in 626

F. Barišić, "Le siège de Constantinople par les Avares et les Slaves en 626", *Byzantion*, xxiv (1954), pp. 371–95.

A. N. Stratos, *Byzantium in the Seventh Century*, i (Amsterdam, 1968), pp. 173–96, 370–5.

The Slav occupation of Greece

M. Vasmer, *Die Slaven in Griechenland* (Berlin, 1941). [*Abhandlungen der Preussischen Akademie der Wissenschaften*, philos.-hist. kl., xii.]

P. Charanis, "The Chronicle of Monemvasia and the Question of the Slavonic Settlements in Greece", *DOP*, v (1950), pp. 139–66.

——, "On the Slavic Settlement in the Peloponnesus", *Byzantinische Zeitschrift*, xlvi (1953), pp. 91–103.

——, "Ethnic Changes in the Byzantine Empire in the Seventh Century", *DOP*, xiii (1959), pp. 23–44.

A. Bon, *Le Péloponnèse byzantin jusqu'en 1204* (Paris, 1951).

P. Lemerle, "Une province byzantine: le Péloponnèse", *Byzantion*, xxi (1951), pp. 341–54.

——, "La Chronique improprement dite de Monemvasie: le contexte historique et légendaire", *Revue des Etudes Byzantines*, xxi (1963), pp. 5–49.

R. Jenkins, *Byzantium and Byzantinism* (Cincinnati, 1963).

S. Hood, "Isles of Refuge in the Early Byzantine Period", *The Annual of the British School at Athens*, no. 65 (1970), pp. 37–45.

Samo

J. Mikkola, "Samo und sein Reich", *Archiv für slavische Philologie*, xlii (1929) pp. 77–97.

G. Vernadsky, "The Beginnings of the Czech State", *Byzantion*, xvii (1944–5) pp. 315–28.

G. Labuda, *Pierwsze państwo słowiańskie* [The First Slav State] (Posnań, 1949). [With a summary in French].

Onogurs and Bulgars

V. N. Zlatarski, *Istoriya na bŭlgarskata dŭrzhava prez srednite vekove* [A history of the Bulgarian State in the Middle Ages], i, 1 (Sofia, 1918).

S. Runciman, *A History of the First Bulgarian Empire* (London, 1930).

Gy. Moravcsik, "Zur Geschichte der Onoguren", *Ungarische Jahrbücher*, x (1930), pp. 53–90. Reprinted in the same author's *Studia Byzantina* (Amsterdam, 1967), pp. 84–118.

CHAPTER 3: THE BALKANS IN THE NINTH CENTURY: THE
BYZANTINE RECOVERY

General

F. Dvornik, *Les Slaves, Byzance et Rome au IXe siècle* (Paris, 1926).

——, "Byzantium, Rome, the Franks, and the Christianization of the Southern Slavs", *Cyrillo-Methodiana*, ed. M. Hellmann and others (Cologne-Graz, 1964), pp. 85–125.

M. Spinka, *A History of Christianity in the Balkans* (Chicago, 1933).

D. Obolensky, "The Empire and its Northern Neighbours, 565–1018", loc. cit.

A. P. Vlasto, *The Entry of the Slavs into Christendom* (Cambridge, 1970).

P. Lemerle, *Le Premier Humanisme Byzantin* (Paris, 1971).

Slav Revolts in the Peloponnese

P. Charanis, "Nicephorus I, the Savior of Greece from the Slavs (810 AD)", *Byzantina-Metabyzantina*, i (1946), pp. 75–92.

D. A. Zakythinos, *Le Despotat Grec de Morée*, ii (Athens, 1953).

R. J. H. Jenkins, "The Date of the Slav Revolt in Peloponnese under Romanus I", *Late Classical and Mediaeval Studies in Honor of A. M. Friend, Jr.* (Princeton, 1955), pp. 204–11.

Establishment of themes in the Balkans

P. Lemerle, *Philippes et la Macédoine orientale à l'époque chrétienne et byzantine* (Paris, 1945).

J. Ferluga, *Vizantiska uprava u Dalmaciji* [*L'Administration Byzantine en Dalmatie*] (Belgrade, 1957). [With a summary in French.]

H. Glykatzi-Ahrweiler, "Recherches sur l'administration de l'Empire Byzantin aux IXᵉ-XIᵉ siècles", *Bulletin de Correspondance Hellénique*, lxxxiv (1960), pp. 1–111.

Re-hellenization of Greece

See the works cited above, under Chapter 2, *The Slav occupation of Greece*, and: D. A. Zakythinos, Οἱ Σλάβοι ἐν Ἑλλάδι (Athens, 1945).

Bulgaria in the ninth century

V. N. Zlatarski, *Istoriya na bŭlgarskata dŭrzhava*, i, 1, 2 (Sofia, 1918, 1927).

S. Runciman, *A History of the First Bulgarian Empire* (London, 1930).

I. Sakâzov, *Bulgarische Wirtschaftsgeschichte* (Berlin–Leipzig, 1929).

Old Bulgarian inscriptions

V. Beševliev, *Die Protobulgarischen Inschriften* (Berlin, 1963).

——, "Les inscriptions protobulgares et leur portée culturelle et historique", *Byzantinoslavica*, xxxii (1971), pp. 35–51.

Photius' letter to Boris

I. Dujčev, "Au lendemain de la conversion du peuple bulgare", *Mélanges de Science Religieuse*, viii (1951), pp. 211–26. Reprinted in the same author's *Medioevo Bizantino-Slavo*, i (Rome, 1965), pp. 107–23.

Nicholas I's letter to Boris

I. Dujčev, "Die *Responsa Nicolai I. Papae ad consulta Bulgarorum* als Quelle für die bulgarische Geschichte", *Festschrift des Haus-, Hof- und Staatsarchivs*, i (Vienna, 1949), pp. 349–62. Also in *Medioevo Bizantino-Slavo*, i, pp. 125–48.

R. E. Sullivan, "Khan Boris and the Conversion of Bulgaria: A Case Study of the Impact of Christianity on a Barbarian Society", *Studies in Medieval and Renaissance History*, iii (Lincoln, Nebraska, 1966), pp. 53–139.

M. Kusseff, "St. Clement of Ochrida", *The Slavonic and East European Review*, xxvii (1948), pp. 193–215.

I. Snegarov, "Les sources sur la vie et l'activité de Clément d'Ochrida", *Byzantinobulgarica*, i (Sofia, 1962), pp. 79–119.

P. Gautier, "Clément d'Ohrid, évêque de Dragvista", *Revue des Etudes Byzantines*, xxii (1964), pp. 199–214.

Climent of Ohrid, ed. Lj. Isaiev (Skopje, 1968).

Kliment Okhridski, ed. D. Angelov and others (Sofia, 1968).

The ninth century conversion of the Serbs

G. S. Radojičić, "La date de la conversion des Serbes", *Byzantion*, xxii (1952), pp. 253–6.

I. Dujčev, "Une ambassade byzantine auprès des Serbes au IXe siècle", *Zbornik Radova Vizantološkog Instituta*, vii (1961), pp. 53–60. Also in *Medioevo Bizantino-Slavo*, i, pp. 221–30.

Croats in the ninth century

F. Šišić, *Geschichte der Kroaten*, i (Zagreb, 1917).

S. Guldescu, *History of Medieval Croatia* (The Hague, 1964).

N. Klaić, *Povijest Hrvata u ranom srednjem vijeku* [The History of Croatia in the Early Middle Ages] (Zagreb, 1971).

CHAPTER 4: THE BALKANS IN THE TENTH CENTURY:
THE CRISIS OF IMPERIALISM

General

In addition to the works of Zlatarski, Runciman and Obolensky, cited above:

G. Ostrogorsky, "Die byzantinische Staatenhierarchie", *Annales de l'Institut Kondakov*, viii (1936), pp. 41–61.

F. Dölger, *Byzanz und die europäische Staatenwelt* (Ettal, 1953), pp. 140–96.

The literary movement in tenth-century Bulgaria

G. Soulis, "The Legacy of Cyril and Methodius to the Southern Slavs", *DOP*, xix (1965), pp. 19–43. [Includes references to recent works on the subject.]

The Bulgaro-Byzantine War of 894–6

G. I. Brătianu, "Le commerce bulgare dans l'Empire byzantin et le monopole de l'empereur Léon VI à Thessalonique", *Sbornik Nikov: Izvestiya na Bŭlgarskoto Istorichesko Druzhestvo*, xvi–xviii (1940), pp. 30–6.

S. Runciman, *The Emperor Romanus Lecapenus and his Reign* (Cambridge, 1963).

G. Ostrogorsky, "Die Krönung Symeons von Bulgarien durch den Patriarchen Nikolaos Mystikos", *Actes du IVe Congrès International des Etudes Byzantines*, i (Sofia, 1935), pp. 275–86.

F. Dölger, "Bulgarisches Zartum und byzantinisches Kaisertum", *Byzanz und die europäische Staatenwelt*, pp. 140–58.

R. J. H. Jenkins, "The Peace with Bulgaria (927) celebrated by Theodore Daphnopates", *Polychronion, Festschrift Franz Dölger zum 75. Geburtstag* (Heidelberg, 1966), pp. 287–303.

Byzantine influences on the culture and institutions of tenth-century Bulgaria

P. Mutafchiev, "Der Byzantinismus im mittelalterlichen Bulgarien", *Byzantinische Zeitschrift*, xxx (1929–30), pp. 387–94.

D. Angelov, "Die gegenseitigen Beziehungen und Einflüsse zwischen Byzanz und dem mittelalterlichen Bulgarien", *Byzantinoslavica*, xx (1959), pp. 40–9.

The Paulicians

S. Runciman, *The Medieval Manichee* (Cambridge, 1947).

N. G. Garsoïan, *The Paulician Heresy* (The Hague, 1967).

The Bogomils

D. Obolensky, *The Bogomils. A Study in Balkan Neo-Manichaeism* (Cambridge, 1948).

A. Schmaus, "Der Neumanichäismus auf dem Balkan", *Saeculum*, ii (1951), pp. 271–99.

D. Angelov, *Bogomilstvoto v Bŭlgariya*, 2nd ed. (Sofia, 1969).

The Russo-Byzantine War of 970–1

G. Schlumberger, L'*épopée byzantine à la fin du Xe siècle*, i (Paris, 1896); and the articles cited in the *Cambridge Medieval History*, iv, 1 (1966), pp. 963–4.

Byzantium and Samuel's realm

G. Schlumberger, L'*épopée byzantine*, ii (Paris, 1900).

CHAPTER 5: BYZANTIUM AND EAST-CENTRAL EUROPE

Cyril and Methodius and the Moravian Mission

The sources and the considerable bibliography of modern works relating to Cyril and Methodius are listed in: G. A. Il'insky, *Opyt sistematicheskoy Kirillo-*

Mefod'evskoy bibliografii [An attempt at a systematic Cyrillo-Methodian biblio-graphy] (Sofia, 1934); M. Popruzhenko and S. Romanski, *Kirilometodievska bibliografiya za 1934–40 (Sofia, 1942).*

A number of primary sources are published in *Constantinus et Methodius Thessalonicenses. Fontes,* ed. F. Grivec and F. Tomšič (Zagreb, 1960) and in A. Vaillant, *Textes vieux-slaves,* i: *textes et glossaire* (Paris, 1968). The main Old Church Slavonic documents, the *Vita Constantini and the Vita Methodii,* have been translated into Latin (*Ibid.,* pp. 169–238), into French (F. Dvornik, *Les Légendes de Constantin et de Méthode vues de Byzance,* Prague, 1933, pp. 349–93; A. Vaillant, *Textes vieux-slaves,* ii: *traductions et notes* (Paris, 1968), pp. 1–25, 34–43) and German (J. Bujnoch, *Zwischen Rom und Byzanz,* Graz, 1958).

F. Dvornik, *Les Slaves, Byzance et Rome au IXe siècle.*

——, *Les Légendes de Constantin et de Méthode vues de Byzance.*

——, *Byzantine Missions among the Slavs. SS. Constantine-Cyril and Methodius* (New Brunswick, 1970).

F. Grivec, *Konstantin und Method, Lehrer der Slaven* (Wiesbaden, 1960).

A. P. Vlasto, *The Entry of the Slavs into Christendom* (Cambridge, 1970).

The eleven-hundredth anniversary of the Moravian mission, in 1963, gave rise to a number of international symposia and commemorative volumes. To the reader unfamiliar with the languages of Eastern Europe the following may be specially recommended:

Cyrillo-Methodiana, ed. M. Hellmann and others (Cologne–Graz, 1964).
DOP, xix (1965), pp. 1–87, 257–65.

Great Moravia

Magnae Moraviae Fontes Historici, i (Prague-Brno, 1966), ii (Brno, 1967), iii (Brno, 1969).

Ríša vel'komoravská [The Great Moravian Empire], ed. J. Stanislav (Prague, 1935).

J. Poulík, "The Latest Archaeological Discoveries from the Period of the Great Moravian Empire", *Historica,* i (Prague, 1959), pp. 7–70.

C. Parrott, "Great Moravia in the Light of Recent Archaeological Excavations", *Oxford Slavonic Papers,* xii (1965), pp. 1–20.

J. Pošvář, "Die byzantinische Währung und das Grossmährische Reich", *Byzantinoslavica,* xxvi (1965), pp. 308–17.

K. Bosl, "Das Grossmährische Reich in der politischen Welt des 9. Jahrhunderts", *Sitzungsberichte der Bayerischen Akademie der Wissenschaften,* phil.-hist. Klasse (1966), vii.

Das Grossmährische Reich, ed. F. Graus and others (Prague, 1966).

I. Boba, *Moravia's History Reconsidered* (The Hague, 1971).

Old Church Slavonic and its alphabets

V. Jagić, *Entstehungsgeschichte der kirchenslavischen Sprache,* 2nd ed. (Berlin, 1913).

N. S. Trubetskoy, *Altkirchenslavische Grammatik. Schrift-, Laut- und Formensystem* (Vienna, 1954).

G. Nandriş and R. Auty, *Handbook of Old Church Slavonic*, 2 vols. (London), 1959, 1965).

Vernacular translations of the liturgy in Eastern Christendom

C. Korolevskij, *Liturgie en langue vivante* (Paris, 1955).

I. Dujčev, "Il problema delle lingue nazionali nel medio evo e gli Slavi", *Ricerche Slavistiche*, viii (1960), pp. 39–60.

The Slavonic Liturgy in Moravia

A. Dostál, "The Origins of the Slavonic Liturgy", *DOP*, xix (1965), pp. 67–87.

The Cyrillo-Methodian tradition in Bohemia

R. Jakobson, "The Kernel of Comparative Slavic Literature", *Harvard Slavic Studies*, i (1953), pp. 37–55.

K. Onasch, "Der Cyrillo-Methodianische Gedanke in der Kirchengeschichte des Mittelalters", *Wissenschaftliche Zeitschrift der Martin-Luther-Universität Halle-Wittenberg*, vi (1956–7), pp. 27–39.

Magna Moravia. Commentationes ad memoriam missionis Byzantinae ante XI saecula in Moraviam adventus editae (Prague, 1965) [*Opera Universitatis Purkynianae Brunensis, facultas philosophica*, 102].

The Cyrillo-Methodian tradition in Poland

K. Lanckorońska, "Studies on the Roman-Slavonic Rite in Poland", *Orienaliat Christiana Analecta*, clxi (1961).

T. Lehr-Spławiński, "Nowa faza dyskusji o zagadnieniu liturgii słowiańskiej w dawnej Polsce" [A new stage in the discussion of the problem of the Slavonic liturgy in Old Poland], in the same author's *Od piętnastu wkieów* (Warsaw, 1961), pp. 51–67.

The Cyrillo-Methodian tradition in Croatia and Dalmatia

V. Novak, "The Slavonic-Latin Symbiosis in Dalmatia during the Middle Ages", *The Slavonic and East European Review*, xxxii (1953–4), pp. 1–28.

J. Hamm, "Der Glagolismus im mittleren Balkanraum", *Die Welt der Slaven*, i (1956), pp. 265–75.

S. Smržík, *The Glagolitic or Roman-Slavonic Liturgy* (Cleveland, 1959).

N. Klaić, "Historijska podloga hrvatskoga Glagoljaštva u X i XI stoljeću" [The historical basis of the Croat Glagolitic movement], *Slovo*, xv–xvi (Zagreb, 1965), pp. 225–81. [With a summary in German.]

I. Ševčenko, "Three Paradoxes of the Cyrillo-Methodian Mission", *Slavic Review*, xxiii (1964), pp. 220–36.

D. Obolensky, "Cyrille et Méthode et la christianisation des Slaves", *Settimane di studio del Centro italiano di studi sull' alto medioevo*, xiv (Spoleto, 1967), pp. 587–609.

Khrabr's treatise

A. Vaillant, *Textes vieux-slaves*, i, pp. 57–61, ii, pp. 47–9 (Paris, 1968).

A. Dostál, "Les origines de l'Apologie slave par Chrabr", *Byzantinoslavica*, xxiv (1963), pp. 236–46.

V. Tkadlčík, "Le moine Chrabr et l'origine de l'écriture slave", *Byzantinoslavica*, xxv (1964), pp. 75–92.

Early history of the Magyars

B. Hóman, *Geschichte des ungarischen Mittelalters*, i (Berlin, 1940).

Gy. Moravcsik, "Byzantine Christianity and the Magyars in the Period of their Migration", *The American Slavic and East European Review*, v, 14–15 (1946), pp. 29–45.

C. A. Macartney, *The Magyars in the Ninth Century* (Cambridge, 1968).

I. Boba, *Nomads, Northmen and Slavs. Eastern Europe in the Ninth Century* (The Hague, 1967).

Byzantine civilization in medieval Hungary

E. von Ivánka, "Griechische Kirche und griechisches Mönchtum im mittelalterlichen Ungarn", *Orientalia Christiana Periodica*, viii (1942), pp. 183–94.

Gy. Moravcsik, "The Role of the Byzantine Church in Medieval Hungary", *The American Slavic and East European Review*, vi, 18–19 (1947), pp. 134–51.

I. Kniezsa, "Zur Frage der auf Cyrillus und Methodius bezüglichen Traditionen auf dem Gebiete des alten Ungarn", *Cyrillo-Methodiana*, ed. M. Hellmann and others (Cologne-Graz, 1964), pp. 199–209.

Political relations between Byzantium and medieval Hungary

Gy. Moravcsik, "Pour une alliance byzantino-hongroise (seconde moitié du XIIᵉ siècle)", *Byzantion*, viii (1933), pp. 555–68.

——, "Hungary and Byzantium in the Middle Ages", *The Cambridge Medieval History*, iv, 1 (1966), pp. 566–92.

——, *Byzantium and the Magyars* (Amsterdam, 1970).

F. Dölger, "Ungarn in der byzantinischen Reichspolitik", in the same author's Παρασπορά (Ettal, 1961), pp. 153–77.

R. Browning, "A New Source on Byzantine-Hungarian Relations in the Twelfth Century", *Balkan Studies*, ii (1961), pp. 173–214.

E. Darkó, "Die ursprüngliche Bedeutung der unteren Teiles des ungarischen Heiligen Krone", *Annales de l'Institut Kondakov*, viii (1936), pp. 63–77.

M. Bárány-Oberschall, "The Crown of the Emperor Constantine Monomachos", *Archaeologia Hungarica*, xxii (1937).

Gy. Moravcsik, "The Holy Crown of Hungary", *The Hungarian Quarterly*, iv (1938–9), pp. 656–67.

P. J. Kelleher, *The Holy Crown of Hungary* (Rome, 1951). [*Papers and Monographs of the American Academy in Rome*, xiii].

J. Deér, "Die Heilige Krone Ungarns", *Denkschriften der Österreichischen Akademie der Wissenschaften*, xci (1966).

CHAPTER 6: THE BLACK SEA COAST, THE EURASIAN STEPPE
AND RUSSIA

General

D. Obolensky, "The Empire and its Northern Neighbours", *The Cambridge Medieval History*, iv, 1.

A. P. Vlasto, *The Entry of the Slavs into Christendom*.

Byzantium and the Turks of Central Asia

S. Vailhé, "Projet d'alliance turco-byzantine au VIᵉ siècle", *Echos d'Orient*, xii (1909), pp. 206–14.

N. V. Pigulevskaya, "Vizantiiskaya diplomatiya i torgovlya shelkom v V–VII vv." [Byzantine diplomacy and the silk trade in the Vth to VIIth centuries], *Vizantiisky Vremennik*, n.s., i (1947), pp. 184–214.

D. Sinor, "The Historical Role of the Turk Empire", *Cahiers d'Histoire Mondiale* i (1953), pp. 427–34.

The Crimea in the early Middle Ages

A. A. Vasiliev, *The Goths in the Crimea*.

I. Stratonov, "Die Krim und ihre Bedeutung für die Christianisierung der Ostslaven", *Kyrios*, i (Königsberg, 1936), pp. 381–95.

A. L. Yakobson, *Srednevekovy Krym*.

Byzantium and the Khazars

A bibliography of sources and modern works relating to the Khazars will be found in "The Khazars", *Bulletin of the New York Public Library*, xlii, 9 (1938), pp. 695–710, lxiii, 5 (1959), pp. 237–41.

See also I. Sorlin, "Le problème des Khazares et les historiens soviétiques dans les vingt dernières années", *Travaux et Mémoires du Centre de Recherche d'Histoire et Civilisation Byzantines*, iii (Paris, 1968), pp. 423–55.

D. M. Dunlop, *The History of the Jewish Khazars* (Princeton, 1954).

M. I. Artamonov, *Istoriya Khazar* [*A History of the Khazars*] (Leningrad, 1962).

The ecclesiastical province of Gothia

V. A. Moshin, " 'Επαρχία Γοτθίας v Khazarii v VIII-m veke" [The Eparchy of Gothia in Khazaria in the eighth century], *Trudy IV-go s'ezda Russkikh Akademicheskikh Organizatsy za granitsey*, i (Belgrade, 1929), pp. 149–56.

Gy. Moravcsik, "Byzantinische Mission im Kreise der Türkvölker an der Nordküste des Schwarzen Meeres", *Proceedings of the XIIIth International Congress of Byzantine Studies*, Oxford, 1966 (London, 1967), pp. 21–4.

Byzantium and Abasgia

V. Latyshev, "K istorii Khristianstva na Kavkaze" [A contribution to the history of Christianity in the Caucasus], *Sbornik arkheologicheskikh statey, podnesennyi gr. A. A. Bobrinskomu* (St. Petersburg, 1911), pp. 169–98.

Byzantium and the Alans

Yu. Kulakovsky, "Khristianstvo u Alan" [Christianity among the Alans], *Vizantiisky Vremennik*, v (1898), pp. 1–18.

V. Grumel, "La date de la conversion des Alains et l'archevêché d'Alanie", *Echos d'Orient*, xxxiii (1934), pp. 57–8.

The origins of the Russian State

V. Thomsen, *The Relations between Ancient Russia and Scandinavia and the Origin of the Russian State* (Oxford, 1877).

G. Laehr, *Die Anfänge des russischen Reiches* (Berlin, 1930) [*Historische Studien*, clxxxix].

H. Paszkiewicz, *The Origin of Russia* (London, 1954), pp. 109–32.

Varangian Problems, in *Scando-Slavica*, Supplement i (Copenhagen, 1970).

Russian attacks on Constantinople

A. Vasiliev, *The Russian Attack on Constantinople in 860* (Cambridge, Mass., 1946).

G. Ostrogorsky, "L'expédition du prince Oleg contre Constantinople en 907", *Annales de l'Institut Kondakov*, xi (1940), pp. 47–62.

A. Vasiliev, "The Second Russian Attack on Constantinople", *DOP*, vi (1951), pp. 161–225.

M. V. Levchenko, *Ocherki po istorii russko-vizantiiskikh otnosheny* [An Outline of the History of Russo-Byzantine Relations] (Moscow, 1956), pp. 128–71.

S. Mikucki, "Etudes sur la diplomatique russe la plus ancienne. I. Les traités byzantino-russes du Xe siècle", *Bulletin international de l'Académie Polonaise des Sciences et des Lettres, cl. de philol., d'hist. et de philos.*, vii (Cracow, 1953), pp. 1–40.

I. Sorlin, "Les traités de Byzance avec la Russie au Xe siècle", *Cahiers du monde russe et soviétique*, ii (1961), 3, pp. 313–60, 4, pp. 447–75.

Olga's conversion and visit to Constantinople

G. Laehr, *Die Anfänge des russischen Reiches*, pp. 103–6.

G. Ostrogorsky, "Vizantiya i Kievskaya knyaginya Ol'ga" [Byzantium and Olga, princess of Kiev] *To Honor Roman Jakobson* (The Hague, 1967), pp. 1458–73.

Byzantium and Vladimir of Russia

G. Vernadsky, *Kievan Russia* (New Haven, 1948), pp. 56–65.

Canonical status of Vladimir's church

V. Laurent, "Aux origines de l'Eglise russe. L'établissement de la hiérarchie byzantine", *Echos d'Orient*, xxxviii (1939), pp. 279–95.

E. Honigmann, "The Foundation of the Russian Metropolitan Church according to Greek Sources", *Byzantion*, xvii (1944–5), pp. 128–62.

L. Müller, *Zum Problem des hierarchischen Status und der jurisdiktionellen Abhängigkeit der russischen Kirche vor 1039* (Cologne, 1959).

The Slavonic liturgy in tenth century Russia

D. Obolensky, "The Heritage of Cyril and Methodius in Russia", *DOP*, xix (1965), pp. 45–62.

CHAPTER 7: THE BONDS OF THE COMMONWEALTH

Albanians

L. von Thallóczy, *Illyrisch-Albanische Forschungen*, 2 vols. (Munich–Leipzig, 1916).

M. von Šufflay, *Städte und Burgen Albaniens, hauptsächlich während des Mittelalters* (Vienna, 1924).

G. Stadtmüller, "Forschungen zur albanischen Frühgeschichte", *Archivum Europae Centro-Orientalis*, vii (Budapest, 1941), pp. 1–196.

M. Gyóni, "La transhumance des Vlaques balkaniques au Moyen Age", *Byzantinoslavica*, xii (1951), pp. 29–42.

E. Stănescu, "Byzantinovlachica", *Revue des Etudes Sud-Est Européennes*, vi (1968), pp. 407–38.

Byzantium and Bohemia

M. Paulová, "Die tschechisch-byzantinischen Beziehungen und ihr Einfluss", *Byzantinoslavica*, xix (1958), pp. 195–205.

Early history of the Rumanians

A. D. Xénopol, *Histoire des Roumains de la Dacie Trajane*, i (Paris, 1896).

N. Iorga, *Histoire des Roumains et de la Romanité orientale*, 5 vols. (Bucharest, 1937).

R. W. Seton-Watson, *A History of the Roumanians* (Cambridge, 1934).

Tmutorokan'

N. Bănescu, "La domination byzantine à Matracha (Tmutorokan), en Zichie, en Khazarie et en 'Russie' à l'époque des Comnènes", *Bulletin de la section historique de l'Académie Roumaine*, xii (1941).

A. V. Soloviev, "Domination byzantine ou russe au nord de la Mer Noire à l'époque des Comnènes?", *Akten des XI. Internationalen Byzantinisten-Kongresses* (Munich, 1960), pp. 569–80.

G. G. Litavrin, "A propos de Tmutorokan", *Byzantion*, xxxv (1965), pp. 221–34.

Byzantine policy in Bulgaria in the eleventh and twelfth centuries

V. N. Zlatarski, *Istoriya*, ii (Sofia, 1934).

G. G. Litavrin, *Bolgariya i Vizantiya v XI–XII vv.* [Bulgaria and Byzantium in the XIth and XIIth centuries] (Moscow, 1960).

D. Angelov, "Die bulgarischen Länder und das bulgarische Volk in den Grenzen des byzantinischen Reiches im XI.-XII. Jahrhundert (1018–1185)", *Proceedings of the XIIIth International Congress of Byzantine Studies* (London, 1967), pp. 149–66.

A. Dostál, "Les relations entre Byzance et les Slaves (en particulier les Bulgares) aux XIe et XIIe siècles du point de vue culturel", *Proceedings*, pp. 167–75.

The archbishopric of Ohrid

H. Gelzer, *Der Patriarchat von Achrida* (Leipzig, 1902).

I. Snegarov, *Istoriya na Okhridskata arkhiepiskopiya* [A History of the Archbishopric of Ohrid], i (Sofia, 1924).

C. Neumann, *Die Weltstellung des byzantinischen Reiches vor den Kreuzzügen* (Leipzig, 1894); French translation by Renauld and Kozlowski (Paris, 1905).

N. Svoronos, "Société et organisation intérieure dans l'empire byzantin au XIᵉ siècle: les principaux problèmes", *Proceedings of the XIIIth International Congress of Byzantine Studies*, pp. 373–89; see the comments on this paper by H. Evert-Kappesowa and E. Stănescu, ibid., pp. 397–408.

Byzantine position on the lower Danube in the eleventh century

E. Stănescu, "La crise du Bas-Danube byzantin au cours de la seconde moitié du XIᵉ siècle", *Zbornik Radova Vizantološkog Instituta* (Belgrade), ix (1966), pp. 49–73.

E. Condurachi, I. Barnea, P. Diaconu, "Nouvelles recherches sur le *Limes* byzantin du Bas-Danube aux Xᵉ–XIᵉ siècles", *Proceedings of the XIIIth International Congress of Byzantine Studies*, pp. 179–93.

Byzantium and the Pechenegs

V. G. Vasil'evsky, *Vizantiya i Pechenegi* [Byzantium and the Pechenegs], in the same author's *Trudy*, i (St. Petersburg, 1908), pp. 1–175.

P. Diaconu, *Les Petchénègues au Bas-Danube* (Bucharest, 1970).

The pronoia and the "feudalization" of the Balkans

G. Ostrogorsky, *Pour l'histoire de la féodalité byzantine* (Brussels, 1954).

——, *Quelques problèmes d'histoire de la paysannerie byzantine* (Brussels, 1956).

The Old Church Slavonic tradition in the Balkans in the eleventh and twelfth centuries

W. K. Matthews, "Sources of Old Church Slavonic", *The Slavonic and East European Review*, xxviii (1949–50), pp. 466–85.

Origin of the "Second Bulgarian Empire"

R. L. Wolff, "The 'Second Bulgarian Empire'. Its Origin and History to 1204", *Speculum*, xxiv (1949), pp. 167–206.

Ostrogorsky, *History of the Byzantine State*, p. 404, n. 1.

Croatia in the eleventh century

F. Šišić, *Geschichte der Kroaten*.

S. Guldescu, *History of Medieval Croatia*.

N. Klaić, *Povijest Hrvata u ranom srednjem vijeku*.

S. Ćirković, *Istorija Srednjovekovne Bosanske Države* [History of the medieval Bosnian State] (Belgrade, 1964).

The Serbs in the eleventh and twelfth centuries

K. Jireček, *Geschichte der Serben*, i (Gotha, 1911).

Dj. S. Radojičić, "Srpsko Zagorje, das spätere Raszien", *Südost-Forschungen*, xvi (1957), pp. 259–84.

M. Dinić, "The Balkans, 1018–1499", *The Cambridge Medieval History*, iv, 1 (1966), pp. 519–22.

Istorija Crne Gore [The History of Montenegro], ed. M. Ćurović and others, i (Titograd, 1967), pp. 381–444.

Agapetus' treatise and its Slavonic versions

F. Dvornik, *Early Christian and Byzantine Political Philosophy*, ii (Washington, D.C., 1966), pp. 712–15.

I. Ševčenko, "A Neglected Byzantine Source of Muscovite Political Ideology", *Harvard Slavic Studies*, ii (1954), pp. 141–79.

——, "On Some Sources of Prince Svjatoslav's *Izbornik* of the year 1076", *Orbis Scriptus, Festschrift für Dmitrij Tschiżewskij zum 70. Geburtstag* (Munich, 1966), pp. 723–38.

The Russo-Byzantine war of 1043

G. Schlumberger, *L'Epopée Byzantine*, iii (Paris, 1905), pp. 460–76.

G. Vernadsky, "The Byzantine-Russian War of 1043", *Südost-Forschungen*, xii (1953), pp. 47–67.

G. G. Litavrin, "Psell o prichinakh poslednego pokhoda russkikh na Konstantinopol' v 1043", [Psellus' evidence concerning the reasons for the last Russian campaign against Constantinople in 1043], *Vizantiisky Vremennik*, xxvii (1967), pp. 71–86.

A. Poppe, "La dernière expédition russe contre Constantinople", *Byzantinoslavica*, xxxii (1971), pp. 1–29, 233–63.

Vladimir Monomakh

See his autobiography in *Povest'*, i, pp. 153–63; Cross, pp. 206–15.

Russian foreign marriages

N. de Baumgarten, "Généalogies et mariages occidentaux des Rurikides russes", *Orientalia Christiana*, ix, 35 (1927), pp. 1–95.

B. Leib, *Rome, Kiev et Byzance à la fin du XIe siècle* (Paris, 1924), pp. 143–78.

E. Golubinsky, *Istoriya russkoy tserkvi* [A History of the Russian Church], i, 1, 2nd ed. (Moscow, 1901).

D. Obolensky, "Byzantium, Kiev and Moscow: A Study in Ecclesiastical Relations", *DOP*, xi (1957), pp. 21–78.

A. Poppe, *Państwo i Kościół na Rusi w XI wieku* [Church and State in eleventh century Russia] (Warsaw, 1968). [With a summary in English.]

——, "Le prince et l'Eglise en Russie de Kiev depuis la fin du Xe siècle jusqu'au début du XIIe siècle", *Acta Poloniae Historica,* xx (1969), pp. 95–119.

Political relations between Byzantium and the Russian principalities

G. Vernadsky, "Relations byzantino-russes au XIIe siècle", *Byzantion,* iv (1927–8), pp. 269–76.

M. V. Levchenko, *Ocherki,* pp. 386–497.

O. Jurewicz, "Aus der Geschichte der Beziehungen zwischen Byzanz und Russland in der zweiten Hälfte des 12. Jahrhunderts", *Byzantinistische Beiträge,* ed. J. Irmscher (Berlin, 1964), pp. 333–57.

Byzantium and the Varangians

A. Stender-Petersen, *Die Varägersage als Quelle der altrrussischen Chronik* (Aarhus-Leipzig, 1934).

——, *Varangica* (Aarhus, 1953).

V. G. Vasil'evsky, *Varyago-russkaya i varyago-angliiskaya druzhina v Konstantinopole XI i XII vekov* [The Varangian–Russian and the Varangian–English Guard in Constantinople in the eleventh and twelfth centuries], *Trudy,* i (1908), pp. 176–401.

R. M. Dawkins, "Greeks and Northmen", *Custom is King: Essays presented to R. R. Marett* (London, 1936), pp. 35–47.

——, "The Later History of the Varangian Guard", *The Journal of Roman Studies,* xxxvii (1947), pp. 39–46.

A. Vasiliev, "The Opening Stages of the Anglo-Saxon Immigration to Byzantium in the Eleventh Century", *Annales de l'Institut Kondakov,* ix (1937), pp. 39–70.

S. Blöndal, "The Last Exploits of Harald Sigurdsson in Greek Service", *Classica et Mediaevalia,* ii (1939), pp. 1–26.

——, "Nabites the Varangian", ibid., pp. 145–67.

P. Grierson, "Harold Hardrada and Byzantine Coin Types in Denmark", *Byzantinische Forschungen,* i (1966), pp. 124–38.

B. S. Benedikz, "The Evolution of the Varangian Regiment in the Byzantine Army", *Byzantinische Zeitschrift,* lxii (1969), pp. 20–4.

General

M. Spinka, *A History of Christianity in the Balkans* (Chicago, 1933).

F. Dölger, "Die mittelalterliche Kultur auf dem Balkan als byzantinisches Erbe", *Byzanz und die europäische Staatenwelt*, pp. 261–81.

F. Dvornik, *The Slavs in European History and Civilization* (New Brunswick, 1962).

M. Dinić, "The Balkans, 1018–1499", *The Cambridge Medieval History*, iv, 1 (1966), pp. 519–65.

Michael VIII's policy in the Balkans

D. J. Geanakoplos, *Emperor Michael Palaeologus and the West* (Cambridge, Mass., 1959).

Byzantine influences on the "Second Bulgarian Empire"

D. Angelov, "Die gegenseitigen Beziehungen und Einflüsse zwischen Byzanz und dem mittelalterlichen Bulgarien", *Byzantinoslavica*, xx (1959), pp. 40–9.

M. Lascaris, "Influences byzantines dans la diplomatique bulgare, serbe et slavo-roumaine", *Byzantinoslavica*, iii (1931), pp. 500–10.

The theory of the Translatio imperii

F. Dölger, "Rom in der Gedankenwelt der Byzantiner", in *Byzanz und die europäische Staatenwelt*, pp. 70–115.

Serbia in the thirteenth and fourteenth centuries

K. Jireček, *Geschichte der Serben*, i.

——, "Staat und Gesellschaft im mittelalterlichen Serbien", *Denkschriften der Kaiserlichen Akademie der Wissenschaften in Wien, philos.-histor. Kl.*, lvi (1912), lviii, 2 (1914).

——, *La civilisation serbe au Moyen Age* (Paris, 1920).

M. Laskaris, *Vizantiske princeze u srednjevekovnoj Srbiji* [Byzantine Princesses in medieval Serbia] (Belgrade, 1926).

A. Schmaus, "Zur Frage der Kulturorientierung der Serben im Mittelalter", *Südost-Forschungen*, xv (1956), pp. 179–201.

Dj. Slijepčević, *Istorija srpske pravoslavne crkve* [History of the Serbian Orthodox Church], i (Munich, 1962).

Serbian national assemblies

N. Radojčić, *Srpski državni sabori u srednjem veku* [The Serbian state assemblies in the Middle Ages] (Belgrade, 1940).

Mining industry in Serbia

M. Dinić, *Za istoriju rudarstva u srednjevekovnoj Srbiji i Bosni* [The History of Mining in medieval Serbia and Bosnia], 2 vols. (Belgrade, 1955–62).

Ragusan trade

K. Jireček, *Die Bedeutung von Ragusa in der Handelsgeschichte des Mittelalters* (Vienna, 1899).

B. Krekić, *Dubrovnik (Raguse) et le Levant au Moyen Age* (Paris–The Hague, 1961).

Byzantium and Stephen Dušan

In addition to the works of K. Jireček, cited above:

M. Dinić, "Dušanova carska titula u očima savremenika" [Dušan's imperial title in the eyes of contemporaries], *Zbornik u čast šeste stogodišnjice Zakonika Cara Dušana*, i (Belgrade, 1951), pp. 87–118.

G. Soulis, "Tsar Stephen Dušan and Mount Athos", *Harvard Slavic Studies*, ii (1954), pp. 125–39.

——, "Byzantino-Serbian Relations", *Proceedings of the XIIIth International Congress of Byzantine Studies*, pp. 57–61.

Byzantine influences on medieval Serbian administration

V. Mošin, "Vizantiski uticaj u Srbiji u XIV veku" [Byzantine influence on fourteenth-century Serbia], *Jugoslovenski Istoriski Časopis*, iii (1937), pp. 147–60.

F. Dölger, "Die byzantinische und die mittelalterliche serbische Herrscher-kanzlei", *Actes du XIIe Congrès International d'Etudes Byzantines*, i (Belgrade, 1963), pp. 83–103.

The principality of Serres

G. Ostrogorsky, *Serska Oblast posle Dušanove smrti* [*La Principauté serbe de Serrès*] (Belgrade, 1965).

——, "Problèmes des relations byzantino-serbes au XIVe siècle", *Proceedings of the XIIIth International Congress of Byzantine Studies*, pp. 41–55.

The Turkish conquest of Serbia

S. Novaković, *Srbi i Turci XIV i XV veka*, new ed. S. Ćirković (Belgrade, 1960);

German transl. K. Jezdimirović, *Die Serben und Türken im XIV. und XV. Jahrhundert* (Semlin, 1897).

N. Radojčić, "Die griechischen Quellen zur Schlacht am Kosovo Polje", *Byzantion*, vi (1931), pp. 241–6.

M. Braun, *Kosovo, die Schlacht auf dem Amselfelde in geschichtlicher und epischer Überlieferung* (Leipzig, 1937).

Byzantium and the Rumanian principalities

A. Elian, "Les Rapports Byzantino-Roumains", *Byzantinoslavica*, xix (1958), pp. 212–25.

——, "Moldova și Bizanțul în secolul al XV-lea", in *Cultura moldovenească în timpul lui Ștefan cel Mare*, ed. M. Berza (Bucharest, 1964), pp. 97–179 [with copious bibliography].

——, "Byzance et les Roumains à la fin du Moyen Age", *Proceedings of the XIIIth International Congress of Byzantine Studies*, pp. 195–203.

Byzantium and Russia in the Late Middle Ages

D. Obolensky, "Byzantium and Russia in the Late Middle Ages", in *Europe in the Late Middle Ages*, ed. J. R. Hale and others (London, 1965), pp. 248–75.

F. von Lilienfeld, "Russland und Byzanz im 14. und 15. Jahrhundert", *Proceedings of the XIIIth International Congress of Byzantine Studies*, pp. 105–15.

Muscovy and Lithuania in the fourteenth century

G. Vernadsky, *The Mongols and Russia* (New Haven, 1953).

J. L. I. Fennell, *The Emergence of Moscow, 1304–1359* (London, 1968).

Byzantine ecclesiastical policy towards Muscovy and Lithuania

I. Ševčenko, "Russo-Byzantine Relations after the Eleventh Century", *Proceedings of the XIIIth International Congress of Byzantine Studies*, pp. 93–104.

J. Meyendorff, "Alexis and Roman: a Study in Byzantino-Russian Relations (1352–1354)", *Byzantinoslavica*, xxviii (1967), pp. 278–88.

Russian attitudes to Byzantium after the Council of Florence

I. Ševčenko, "Intellectual Repercussions of the Council of Florence", *Church History*, xxiv (1955), pp. 291–323.

M. Cherniavsky, "The Reception of the Council of Florence in Moscow", ibid., pp. 347–59.

G. Alef, "Muscovy and the Council of Florence", *The American Slavic and East European Review*, xx (1961), pp. 389–401.

D. Obolensky, "Byzantium and Russia in the Late Middle Ages", pp. 266–75.

The Byzantine concept of the hierarchy of nations

G. Ostrogorsky, "Die byzantinische Staatenhierarchie", loc. cit.

——, "The Byzantine Emperor and the Hierarchical World Order", *The Slavonic and East European Review*, xxxv (1956–7), pp. 1–14.

F. Dölger, *Byzanz und die europäische Staatenwelt.*

A. Grabar, "God and the 'Family of Princes', presided over by the Byzantine Emperor", *Harvard Slavic Studies*, ii (1954), pp. 117–23.

Byzantine attitudes to "barbarians"

K. Lechner, *Hellenen und Barbaren im Weltbild der Byzantiner* (Munich, 1954).

The mixobarbaroi

E. Stănescu, "Les 'mixobarbares' du Bas-Danube au XIᵉ siècle", *Nouvelles Etudes d'Histoire publiées à l'occasion du XIIᵉ Congrès des Sciences Historiques, Vienne, 1965* (Bucharest, 1965), pp. 45–53.

Byzantine diplomacy

D. Obolensky, "The Principles and Methods of Byzantine Diplomacy", *Actes du XIIᵉ Congrès International d'Etudes Byzantines*, i (Belgrade, 1963), pp. 45–61. Reprinted in the same author's *Byzantium and the Slavs: Collected Studies* (London, 1971).

Cultural diffusion and acculturation

"L'acculturation": *XIIᵉ Congrès International des Sciences Historiques, Rapports I: Grands Thèmes* (Vienna, 1965), pp. 7–102.

Heresy and social dissent

Hérésies et sociétés dans l'Europe pré-industrielle, 11ᵉ-18ᵉ siècles, ed. J. Le Goff (Paris–The Hague, 1968).

Constantinople as a holy city

N. H. Baynes, "The Supernatural Defenders of Constantinople", *Analecta Bollandiana*, lxvii (1949), pp. 165–77; reprinted in the same author's *Byzantine Studies and Other Essays* (London, 1955), pp. 248–60.

P. Sherrard, *Constantinople, Iconography of a Sacred City* (London, 1965).

Byzantine monasticism

H.-G. Beck, *Kirche und theologische Literatur im byzantinischen Reich* (Munich, 1959), pp. 120–40.

J. M. Hussey, "Byzantine Monasticism", *Cambridge Medieval History*, iv, 2 (1967), pp. 161–84.

Mount Athos

P. Sherrard, *Athos, the Mountain of Silence* (London, 1960).

Le Millénaire du Mont Athos 963–1963. *Etudes et Mélanges*, 2 vols. (Chevetogne, 1963–4 [with exhaustive bibliography].

Monasticism in Bulgaria

P. Slankamenac, "Legende o južnoslovenskim anahoretima" [Legends of South Slav Anchorites], *Glasnik Skopskog Naučnog Društva*, i (1925), pp. 215–33.

I. Dujčev, *Rilskiyat svetets i negovata obitel* [The Saint of Rila and his Monastery] (Sofia, 1947).

Kh. Khristov, G. Stoikov and K. Miyatev, *The Rila Monastery* (Sofia, 1959).

Russian monasticism

V. O. Klyuchevsky, "St. Sergius: the Importance of his Life and Work", *The Russian Review*, ii, 3 (London, 1913), pp. 45–59. [Translated text of a speech delivered in 1892]; reprinted in *Readings in Russian History*, ed. S. Harcave, i (New York, 1962), pp. 153–64.

L. K. Goetz, *Das Kiever Höhlenkloster als Kulturzentrum des vormongolischen Russlands* (Passau, 1904).

A. Soloviev, "Histoire du monastère russe au Mont-Athos", *Byzantion*, viii (1933), pp. 213–38.

N. Zernov, *St. Sergius, Builder of Russia* (London, n.d.).

V. Mošin, "Russkie na Afone i russko-vizantiiskie otnosheniya v XI-XII vv." [Russians on Mount Athos and Russo-Byzantine relations in the eleventh and twelfth centuries], *Byzantinoslavica*, ix (1947–8), pp. 55–85.

I. Smolitsch, *Russisches Mönchtum. Entstehung, Entwicklung und Wesen, 988–1917* (Würzburg, 1953).

R. P. Casey, "Early Russian Monasticism", *Orientalia Christiana Periodica*, xix (1953), pp. 372–423.

F. von Lilienfeld, *Nil Sorskij und seine Schriften* (Berlin, 1963).

G. P. Fedotov, *The Russian Religious Mind*, ii (Cambridge, Mass., 1966), pp. 195–315.

N. Iorga, "Le Mont Athos et les pays roumains", *Bulletin de la section historique de l'Académie Roumaine*, ii (1914), pp. 149–213.

Ortodoxia, v, 2 (Bucharest, 1953).

E. Turdeanu, "Les premiers écrivains religieux en Valachie: l'hégoumène Nicodème de Tismana et le moine Philothée", *Revue des Etudes Roumaines*, ii (Paris, 1954), pp. 114–44.

P. Ş. Năsturel, "Aperçu critique des rapports de la Valachie et du Mont Athos des origines au début du XVIᵉ siècle", *Revue des Etudes Sud-Est Européennes*, ii (1964), pp. 93–126.

Monasticism in Serbia

V. Marković, *Pravoslavno monaštvo i manastiri u srednjevekovnoj Srbiji* [Orthodox Monasticism and Monasteries in Medieval Serbia] (Sremski Karlovci, 1920).

A. E. Tachiaos, "Le monachisme serbe de Saint Sava et la tradition hésychaste athonite", *Recueil de Chilandar*, i, ed. G. Ostrogorsky (Belgrade, 1966), pp. 83–9.

D. Bogdanović, *Jovan Lestvičnik u vizantijskoj i staroj srpskoj književnosti* [*Jean Climaque dans la littérature byzantine et la littérature serbe ancienne*] (Belgrade, 1968) [with a summary in French].

Hesychasm

Monk Vasily (Archbishop Basil Krivocheine), "The Ascetic and Theological Teaching of Gregory Palamas", *The Eastern Churches Quarterly*, iii (1938), pp. 26–33, 71–84, 138–56, 193–214 (reprinted separately 1954).

J. Meyendorff, *Introduction à l'étude de Grégoire Palamas* (Paris, 1959).

H.-G. Beck, "Humanismus und Palamismus", *Actes du XIIᵉ Congrès International d'Etudes Byzantines*, i, pp. 63–82.

F. von Lilienfeld, "Der athonitische Hesychasmus des 14. und 15. Jahrhunderts im Lichte der zeitgenössischen russischen Quellen", *Jahrbücher für Geschichte Osteuropas*, vi (1958), pp. 436–48.

A. E. Tachiaos, Ἐπιδράσεις τοῦ ἡσυχασμοῦ εἰς τὴν ἐκκλησιαστικὴν πολιτικὴν ἐν Ῥωσίᾳ, *1328–1406* (Thessalonica, 1962).

G. M. Prokhorov, "Isikhazm i obshchestvennaya mysl' v Vostochnoy Evrope v XIV v." [Hesychasm and Social Thought in Eastern Europe in the Fourteenth Century], *Trudy Otdela Drevnerusskoy Literatury*, xxiii (1968), pp. 86–108.

P. Syrku, *K istorii ispravleniya knig v Bolgarii v XIV v.* [The History of the Correction of Books in fourteenth century Bulgaria], i, 1 (St. Petersburg, 1898), pp. 61–71, 148–61, 167–247. Reprinted, London, 1972.

V. S. Kiselkov, "Srednovekovna Paroriya i Sinaitoviyat monastir'" [Medieval Paroria and the Monastery of Gregory of Sinai], *Sbornik v chest' na Vasil N. Zlatarski* (Sofia, 1925), pp. 103–18.

G. Ayanov, "Stari monastiri v Strandzha" [The Old Monasteries in the Strandzha], *Bulletin de l'Institut Archéologique Bulgare*, xiii (1939), pp. 253–64 [with a summary in French].

Theodosius and the Kilifarevo Monastery

P. Syrku, *K istorii ispravleniya knig*, pp. 166–7, 240–411.

V. S. Kiselkov, *Sv. Teodosy Trnovski* (Sofia, 1926).

Romil of Vidin

F. Halkin, "Un ermite des Balkans au XIVe siècle. La Vie grecque inédite de Saint Romylos", *Byzantion*, xxxi (1961), pp. 111–47.

P. Devos, "La version slave de la Vie de S. Romylos", ibid., pp. 149–87.

The medieval cult of Russian princes

N. Serebryansky, "Drevne-russkie knyazheskie zhitiya" [Old Russian Princely Vitae], *Chteniya v Imperatorskom Obshchestve Istorii i Drevnostey Rossiiskikh pri Moskovskom Universitete*, 1915, 3.

G. P. Fedotov, *The Russian Religious Mind*, ii, pp. 149–85.

Alexander Nevsky

A. M. Ammann, "Kirchenpolitische Wandlungen im Ostbaltikum bis zum Tode Alexander Newski's", *Orientalia Christiana Analecta*, cv (1936), pp. 279–308.

The medieval cult of Serbian Kings

Dj. S. Radojičić, "Die politischen Bestrebungen in der serbischen mittelalterlichen Geschichtsschreibung", *Südost-Forschungen*, xix (1960), pp. 87–102.

S. Hafner, *Studien zur altserbischen dynastischen Historiographie* (Munich, 1964).

Byzantine imperial biographies

P. J. Alexander, "Secular Biography at Byzantium", *Speculum*, xv (1940), pp. 194–209.

The cult of the murdered ruler in Eastern Europe

K. Górski, "La naissance des états et le 'roi-saint'. Problème de l'idéologie féodale", in *L'Europe aux IXᵉ–XIᵉ siècles. Aux origines des Etats nationaux*, ed. T. Manteuffel and A. Gieysztor (Warsaw, 1968), pp. 425–32.

The cult of St. Wenceslas in Bohemia and Russia

The early biographies of St. Wenceslas: *Fontes Rerum Bohemicarum*, i (Prague, 1873).

R. Jakobson, "Some Russian Echoes of the Czech Hagiography", *Annuaire de l'Institut de Philologie et d'Histoire orientales et slaves*, vii (1939–44), pp. 155–80.

D. Čyževśkyj (Chizhevsky), "Anklänge an die Gumpoldslegende des hl. Václav in der altrussischen Legende des hl. Feodosij und das Problem der 'Originalität' der slavischen mittelalterlichen Werke", *Wiener Slavistisches Jahrbuch*, i (1950), pp. 71–86.

The cult of Boris and Gleb

F. von Lilienfeld, "Die ältesten russischen Heiligenlegenden. Studien zu den Anfängen der russischen Hagiographie und ihr Verhältnis zum byzantinischen Beispiel" in: *Aus der byzantinistischen Arbeit der Deutschen Demokratischen Republik*, i (Berlin, 1957), pp. 237–71.

G. P. Fedotov, *The Russian Religious Mind*, i, pp. 94–110.

L. Müller, "Neuere Forschungen über das Leben und die kultische Verehrung der heiligen Boris und Gleb", *Slawistische Studien zum V. Internationalen Slawistenkongress in Sofia 1963*, ed. M. Braun and E. Koschmieder (Göttingen), pp. 295–317 [with bibliography].

Byzantine law in Eastern Europe

K. Kadlec, *Introduction à l'étude comparative de l'histoire du droit public des peuples slaves* (Paris, 1933).

A. Soloviev, "L'influence du droit byzantin dans les pays orthodoxes", *Relazioni del X Congresso Internazionale di Scienze Storiche (Roma, 1955)*, vi (Firenze), pp. 599–650.

——, "Der Einfluss des byzantinischen Rechts auf die Völker Osteuropas", *Zeitschrift der Savigny-Stiftung für Rechtsgeschichte*, Romanistische Abteilung, lxxvi (1959), pp. 432–79.

Slavonic translations of the Nomocanones

F. Dvornik, "Byzantine Political Ideas in Kievan Russia", *DOP*, ix–x (1956), pp. 78–91.

The Ecloga

Text in J. and P. Zepos, *Jus graecoromanum*, ii (Athens, 1931), pp. 1–62; French transl. and commentary C. A. Spulber, *L'Éclogue des Isauriens* (Cernauţi, 1929); English transl. and commentary E. H. Freshfield, *A Manual of Roman Law: the Ecloga* (Cambridge, 1926).

The Slavonic version of the Ecloga

M. Andreev, "Le droit romain et l'Eclogue slave (Quelques considérations sur les écarts de l'Eclogue slave du droit romain)", *Bartolo da Sassoferrato, Studi e documenti per il VI centenario (Univ. di Perugia)*, i (Milan, 1962), pp. 107–29.

E. E. Lipshits, *Ekloga* (Moscow, 1965), p. 21 and *passim*.

The "Judicial Law for Laymen"

Text: *Zakon Sudny lyudem kratkoy redaktsii*, ed. M. N. Tikhomirov (Moscow, 1961).

J. Vašica, "Origine Cyrillo-Méthodienne du plus ancien code slave dit 'Zakon Sudnyj Ljudem'", *Byzantinoslavica*, xii (1951), pp. 154–74.

V. Ganev, *Zakon Soudny lyud'm* (Sofia, 1959).

V. Procházka, "Le Zakon Sudnyj' Ljud'm et la Grande Moravie", *Byzantinoslavica*, xxviii (1967), pp. 359–75, xxix (1968), pp. 112–50.

Pravda Russkaya

Pravda Russkaya, ed. B. D. Grekov, i (Moscow–Leningrad, 1940): text, ii (1947): commentaries; English transl. of the text in G. Vernadsky, *Medieval Russian Laws* (New York, 1947), pp. 26–56.

Vladimir's Church Statute

Text in *Pamyatniki Russkogo Prava*, ed. S. V. Yushkov, i (Moscow, 1952), pp. 235–54; English transl. G. Vernadsky, "The Status of the Russian Church during the first half-century following Vladimir's Conversion", *The Slavonic and East European Review*, xx (1941), p. 306; French transl. M. Szeftel, *Documents de droit public relatifs à la Russie médiévale* (Brussels, 1963), pp. 229–45.

Stephen Dušan's Zakonik

Text: *Zakonik Stefana Dušana, Cara Srpskog*, ed. S. Novaković (Belgrade, 1898); English transl. and notes by M. Burr, "The Code of Stephan Dušan", *The Slavonic and East European Review*, xxviii (1949–50), pp. 198–217, 516–39.

A. Soloviev, *Zakonodavstvo Stefana Dušana* [Stephen Dušan's Legislation] (Belgrade, 1928).

——, "Le droit byzantin dans la codification d'Etienne Douchan", *Revue historique de droit français et étranger*, 4e série, vii (1928), pp. 387–412.

N. Radojčić, "Dušanov Zakonik i vizantisko pravo" [Dušan's *Zakonik* and Byzantine law], *Zbornik u čast šeste stogodišnjice Zakonika Cara Dušana*, i, pp. 45–77.

Byzantine Law in Rumania

V. A. Georgesco, "La réception du droit romano-byzantin dans les Principautés roumaines (Moldavie et Valachie)", *Mélanges Henri Lévy-Bruhl* (Paris, 1959), pp. 373–91.

G. Cronţ, "La réception des Basiliques dans les pays roumains", *Nouvelles Etudes d'Histoire, publiées à l'occasion du XIIe Congrès des Sciences Historiques, Vienne, 1965* (Bucharest, 1965), pp. 171–80.

P. J. Zepos, "Byzantine Law in the Danubian Countries", *Balkan Studies*, vii (1966), pp. 343–56.

CHAPTER II: LITERATURE AND ART

The relationship of Old Church Slavonic to Greek

M. Weingart, "Le vocabulaire du vieux-slave dans ses relations avec le vocabulaire grec", *Studi Bizantini e Neoellenici*, v (1939), pp. 564–77.

A. Dostál, "Die Widerspiegelung der byzantinischen Welt in der ältesten Periode der slawischen Sprachen", *Aus der byzantinistischen Arbeit der Tschechoslowakischen Republik*, ed. J. Irmscher and A. Salač (Berlin, 1957), pp. 36–47.

K. Schumann, *Die griechischen Lehnbildungen und Lehnbedeutungen im Altbulgarischen* (Wiesbaden, 1958).

The Cyrillo-Methodian translation of the Gospels

O. Grünenthal, "Die Übersetzungstechnik der altkirchenslavischen Evangelienübersetzung", *Archiv für slavische Philologie*, xxxi (1910), pp. 321–66, xxxii (1911), pp. 1–48.

E. Berneker, "Kyrills Übersetzungskunst", *Indogermanische Forschungen*, xxxi (1912–13), pp. 399–412.

A. Vaillant, "La Préface de l'Evangéliaire vieux-slave", *Revue des Etudes Slaves*, xxiv (1948), pp. 5–20.

K. Horálek, "La traduction vieux-slave de l'Evangile: sa version originale et son développement ultérieur", *Byzantinoslavica*, xx (1959), pp. 267–84.

B. O. Unbegaun, "La formation des langues littéraires slaves: problèmes et état des questions", *Actes du VIIIe Congrès de la Fédération Internationale des Langues et Littératures Modernes* (Liège, 1961), pp. 135–49.

——, "L'héritage cyrillo-méthodien en Russie", *Cyrillo-Methodiana*, ed. M. Hellmann and others (Cologne–Graz, 1964), pp. 470–82.

——, "Le russe littéraire est-il d'origine russe?", *Revue des Etudes Slaves*, xliv (1965), pp. 19–28.

The Old Church Slavonic literary tradition

R. Jakobson, "The Kernel of Comparative Slavic Literature", *Harvard Slavic Studies*, i (1953), pp. 37–55.

Slavonic translations of:

(1) *Byzantine liturgical texts:*

R. Jakobson, "The Slavic Response to Byzantine Poetry", *Actes du XIIe Congrès International d'Etudes Byzantines*, i, pp. 249–67.

M. Velimirović, "The Influences of the Byzantine Chant on the Music of the Slavic Countries", *Proceedings of the XIIIth International Congress of Byzantine Studies*, pp. 119–40. Cf. the comments on his paper by D. Stefanović, ibid., pp. 141–7.

(2) *Greek patristic writings*

I. Dujčev, "Les rapports littéraires byzantino-slaves", *Actes du XIIe Congrès International d'Etudes Byzantines*, i, pp. 411–29.

(3) *Byzantine hagiography*

I. Dujčev, "Les rapports hagiographiques entre Byzance et les Slaves", *Proceedings of the XIIIth International Congress of Byzantine Studies*, pp. 363–70.

(4) *Byzantine secular tales and romances*

I. Dujčev, "Les rapports littéraires byzantino-slaves", loc. cit.

G. Soulis, "The Legacy of Cyril and Methodius to the Southern Slavs", *DOP*, xix (1965), pp. 36–7 [with a bibliography].

(5) *Byzantine Chronicles*

M. Weingart, *Byzantské Kroniky v literatuře církevněslovanské* [Byzantine Chronicles in Church Slavonic Literature], 2 vols. (Bratislava, 1922–3).

I. Dujčev, "Übersicht über die bulgarische Geschichtsschreibung", in *Antike und Mittelalter in Bulgarien*, ed. V. Beševliev and J. Irmscher (Berlin, 1960), pp. 51–69.

Local off-shoots of translated Byzantine literature

D. S. Likhachev, "The Type and Character of the Byzantine Influence on Old Russian Literature", *Oxford Slavonic Papers*, xiii (1967), pp. 16–32.

The Vita Constantini

N. van Wijk, "Zur sprachlichen und stilistischen Würdigung der altkirchen-slavischen *Vita Constantini*, *Südost-Forschungen*, vi (1941), pp. 74–102.

Constantine of Preslav's Alphabetical Prayer

A. Vaillant, *Textes vieux-slaves*, i, pp. 68–70, ii, pp. 54–7.

F. Grivec, *Konstantin und Method*, pp. 215–17.

Hilarion's Sermon on Law and Grace

L. Müller, *Des Metropoliten Ilarion Lobrede auf Vladimir den Heiligen und Glau-bensbekenntnis* (Wiesbaden 1962).

The Russian Primary Chronicle

Povest', ii: an historical and literary study, and a commentary by D. S. Li-khachev. Cross, pp. 3–50, 220–95.

The ideological basis of the Cyrillo-Methodian tradition

R. Jakobson, "The Beginnings of National Self-Determination in Europe", *The Review of Politics*, vii (1945), pp. 29–42.

D. Obolensky, "The Heritage of Cyril and Methodius in Russia", *DOP*, xix (1965), pp. 47–65.

——, "Cyrille et Méthode et la christianisation des Slaves", *Settimane di Studio del Centro Italiano di Studi sull'alto medioevo*, xiv (Spoleto, 1967), pp. 602–9.

The Prologue to the Holy Gospel

A. Vaillant, *Textes vieux-slaves*, i, pp. 65–8.

F. Grivec, *Konstantin und Method*, pp. 217–21.

R. Jakobson, "The Slavic Response to Byzantine Poetry", loc. cit., pp. 264–7.

The Patriarch Euthymius and his school

E. Kałużniacki, *Werke des Patriarchen von Bulgarien Euthymius (1375–1393)* (Vienna, 1901). Reprinted, London, 1971.

——, *Aus der panegyrischen Litteratur der Südslaven* (Vienna, 1901). Reprinted, London, 1971.

V. Kiselkov, *Patriarkh Evtimy* (Sofia, 1938).

É. Turdeanu, *La littérature bulgare du XIVe siècle et sa diffusion dans les pays rou-mains* (Paris, 1947).

K. M. Kuev, *Konstantyn Kostenecki w literaturze bulgarskiej i serbskiej* [Constantine of Kostenets in Bulgarian and Serbian Literature] (Cracow, 1950).

The East European literary movement of the late Middle Ages

K. Onasch, "Renaissance und Vorreformation in der byzantinisch-slawischen Orthodoxie", *Aus der byzantinistischen Arbeit der Deutschen Demokratischen Republik*, i (Berlin, 1957), pp. 288–302.

R. Picchio, "'Prerinascimento esteuropeo' e 'Rinascita slava ortodossa'", *Ricerche Slavistiche,* vi (1958), pp. 185–99.

——, "Die historisch-philologische Bedeutung der kirchenslavischen Tradition", *Die Welt der Slaven*, vii (1962), pp. 1–27.

D. S. Likhachev, "Nekotorye zadachi izucheniya vtorogo yuzhnoslavyanskogo vliyaniya v Rossii" [Some problems involved in the study of the second South-Slavonic influence in Russia], in *Issledovaniya po slavyanskomu literaturovedeniyu i fol'kloristike: doklady Sovetskikh uchenykh na IV Mezhdunarodnom s'ezde slavistov* (Moscow, 1960), pp. 95–151.

——, "Predvozrozhdenie na Rusi v kontse XIV—pervoy polovine XV veka" [The Pre-Renaissance in Russia at the end of the fourteenth and in the first half of the fifteenth centuries], in *Literatura epokhi Vozrozhdeniya i problemy vsemirnoy literatury* (Moscow, 1967), pp. 136–82.

V. Mošin, "O periodizatsii russko-yuzhnoslavyanskikh literaturnykh svyazey X–XV vv." [The periodisation of the Russian–South Slav literary relations between the tenth and the fifteenth centuries], *Trudy Otdela Drevnerusskoy Literatury*, xix (1963), pp. 28–106.

I. Dujčev, "Tsentry vizantiisko-slavyanskogo obshcheniya i sotrudnichestva" [The centres of contact and collaboration between the Byzantines and the Slavs], ibid., pp. 107–29.

The Metropolitan Cyprian

L. A. Dmitriev, "Rol' i znachenie mitropolita Kipriana v istorii drevnerusskoy literatury" [The role and significance of the Metropolitan Cyprian in the history of medieval Russian literature], ibid., pp. 215–54.

Epiphanius

D. Čiževskij (Chizhevsky), *History of Russian Literature from the Eleventh Century to the End of the Baroque* (The Hague, 1960), pp. 167–80.

M. Dane, "Epiphanius' Image of St. Stefan", *Canadian Slavonic Papers*, v (1961), pp. 72–86.

G. P. Fedotov, *The Russian Religious Mind*, ii, pp. 195–245.

Gregory Tsamblak

A. I. Yatsimirsky, *Grigory Tsamblak* (St. Petersburg, 1904).

É. Turdeanu, *La littérature bulgare du XIVe siècle et sa diffusion dans les pays roumains* (Paris, 1947), pp. 149–55.

Byzantine church decoration

O. Demus, *Byzantine Mosaic Decoration* (London, 1947).

G. Mathew, *Byzantine Aesthetics* (London, 1963).

The "Palaeologan Renaissance" in art

P. A. Underwood, *The Kariye Djami*, 3 vols. (London, 1967).

D. Talbot Rice, *Byzantine Painting, the Last Phase* (London, 1968).

Art et Société à Byzance sous les Paléologues. Actes du Colloque organisé par l'Association Internationale des Etudes Byzantines à Venise en septembre 1968 (Venice, 1971).

Princely patronage and the frescoes of St. Sophia in Kiev

A. Grabar, "Les fresques des escaliers à Sainte-Sophie de Kiev et l'iconographie impériale byzantine", *Annales de l'Institut Kondakov*, vii (1935), pp. 103–17.

——, *L'empereur dans l'art byzantin* (Paris, 1936), pp. 62–74.

V. N. Lazarev, "Novye dannye o mozaikakh i freskakh Sofii Kievskoy. Gruppovoy portret semeistva Yaroslava" [New data concerning the mosaics and frescoes of St. Sophia in Kiev. The group portrait of Yaroslav's family], *Vizantiisky Vremennik*, xv (1959), pp. 148–69.

——, *Old Russian Murals and Mosaics* (London, 1966), pp. 20–9, 47–65, 236–41.

Historical compositions in Serbian medieval painting

S. Radojčić, *Portreti srpskih vladara u srednjem veku* [Portraits of medieval Serbian rulers] (Skopje, 1934).

D. Winfield, "Four Historical Compositions from the Medieval Kingdom of Serbia", *Byzantinoslavica*, xix (1958), pp. 251–78.

V. Djurić, "Istorijske kompozicije u srpskom slikarstvu srednjega veka i njihove književne paralele" [*Compositions historiques dans la peinture médiévale serbe et leurs parallèles littéraires*], *Zbornik Radova Vizantološkog Instituta*, viii, 2 (1964), pp. 69–90, x (1967), pp. 121–48, xi (1968), pp. 99–127 [with a summary in French].

International and local traditions in East European art

A. Grabar, *L'art du moyen age en Europe orientale* (Paris, 1968).

Serbian medieval painting

R. Hamann-MacLean and H. Hallensleben, *Die Monumentalmalerei in Serbien und Makedonien, vom 11. bis zum frühen 14. Jahrhundert* (Giessen, 1963).

S. Radojčić, *Staro srpsko slikarstvo* [Old Serbian painting] (Belgrade, 1966).

Mileševa

S. Radojčić, *Mileševa* (Belgrade, 1963) [with a summary in English].

Boyana

A. Grabar, *L'église de Boïana* (Sofia, 1924).

——, *La peinture religieuse en Bulgarie au moyen age* (Paris, 1928).

K. Miyatev, *Rospis' Boyanskoy Tserkvi* [The paintings of the Boyana Church] (Dresden–Sofia, 1961).

Sopoćani

V. Djurić, *Sopoćani* (Belgrade, 1963) [with a summary in English].

Serbian and Macedonian painting of the first half of the fourteenth century

V. R. Petković and Dj. Bošković, *Manastir Dečani* (Belgrade, 1941).

S. Radojčić, *Majstori starog srpskog slikarstva* [The Masters of Old Serbian Painting] (Belgrade, 1955).

H. Hallensleben, *Die Malerschule des Königs Milutin* (Giessen, 1963).

V. Djurić, "L'art des Paléologues et l'état serbe. Rôle de la cour et de l'église serbes dans la première moitié du XIVᵉ siècle", in *Art et Société à Byzance sous les Paléologues*, pp. 177–91.

The "Morava School" of painting

S. Stanojević, L. Mirković and Dj. Bošković, *Manastir Manasija* (Belgrade, 1928).

Late medieval painting in Rumania

I. D. Ştefănescu, *L'évolution de la peinture religieuse en Bucovine et en Moldavie depuis les origines jusqu'au XIXᵉ siècle*, 2 vols. (Paris, 1928).

——, *La peinture religieuse en Valachie et en Transylvanie depuis les origines jusqu'au XIXᵉ siècle*, 2 vols. (Paris, 1930–32).

P. Henry, *Les églises de la Moldavie du nord, des origines à la fin du XVIᵉ siècle* (Paris, 1930).

Rumania: Painted Churches of Moldavia (UNESCO World Art series, n.d.).

M. A. Musicescu and G. Ionescu, *The Princely Church of Curtea de Argeş* (Bucharest, 1967).

G. Nandriş, *Christian Humanism in the Neo-Byzantine Mural-Painting of Eastern Europe* (Wiesbaden, 1970).

Medieval Russian Art

D. Ainalov, *Geschichte der russischen Monumentalkunst der vormoskovitischen Zeit* (Berlin–Leipzig, 1932).

G. H. Hamilton, *The Art and Architecture of Russia* (London, 1954).

V. N. Lazarev, "La méthode de collaboration des maîtres byzantins et russes", *Classica et Mediaevalia*, xvii (1956), pp. 75–90.

St. Sophia of Kiev

O. Povstenko, *The Cathedral of St. Sophia in Kiev* (New York, 1954).

V. N. Lazarev, *Mozaiki Sofii Kievskoy* [The Mosaics of St. Sophia of Kiev] (Moscow, 1960).

——, *Old Russian Murals and Mosaics*, pp. 31–65.

G. N. Logvin, *Sofiya Kievskaya* (Kiev, 1971).

Nereditsa

V. K. Myasoedov, *Freski Spasa-Nereditsy* [The Frescoes of the Church of the Saviour Nereditsa] (Leningrad, 1925).

Twelfth- and thirteenth-century architecture in the Vladimir–Suzdal' area

N. N. Voronin, *Zodchestvo severo-vostochnoy Rusi XII–XV vekov* [The Architecture of North-Eastern Russia in the twelfth to fifteenth centuries], 2 vols. (Moscow, 1961–2).

Our Lady of Vladimir

N. P. Kondakov, Ikonografiya Bogomateri [The Iconography of the Mother of God], 2 vols. (St. Petersburg–Petrograd, 1914–15).

A. I. Anisimov, *Our Lady of Vladimir*, transl. N. G. Yaschwill and T. N. Rodzianko (Prague, 1928).

N. N. Voronin, "Iz istorii russko-vizantiiskoy tserkovnoy bor'by XII v." [Aspects of Russo-Byzantine ecclesiastical strife in the twelfth century], *Vizantiisky Vremennik*, xxvi (1965), pp. 190–218.

Kovalevo

V. N. Lazarev, *Iskusstvo Novgoroda* [The Art of Novgorod] (Moscow–Leningrad, 1947), pp. 85–91.

Volotovo

L. Matsulevich, *Tserkov' Uspeniya Presvyatoy Bogoroditsy v Volotove* [The Church of the Dormition of the Mother of God in Volotovo] (St. Petersburg, 1912). Lazarev, *Iskusstvo Novgoroda*, pp. 79–84.

Theophanes the Greek

V. N. Lazarev, *Feofan Grek* (Moscow, 1961). German translation: *Theophanes der Grieche und seine Schule* (Vienna and Munich, 1968).

The early development of the iconostasis

V. N. Lazarev, *Feofan Grek*, pp. 86–94.

A. Grabar, "Deux notes sur l'histoire de l'iconostase d'après des monuments de Yougoslavie", *Zbornik Radova Vizantološkog Instituta*, vii (1961), pp. 13–22.

Hesychasm and Palaeologan painting

G. Millet, *Recherches sur l'iconographie de l'Evangile aux XIVᵉ, XVᵉ et XVIᵉ siècles* (Paris, 1916), pp. 216–31.

L. Bréhier, "La rénovation artistique sous les Paléologues et le mouvement des idées", *Mélanges Charles Diehl*, ii (Paris, 1930), pp. 1–10.

M. Vasić, "L'hésychasme dans l'Eglise et l'art des Serbes du Moyen Age", in *L'Art Byzantin chez les Slaves. Recueil dédié à la mémoire de Théodore Uspenskij*, i (Paris, 1930), pp. 110–23.

L. Ouspensky (Uspensky) and V. Lossky, *The Meaning of Icons*. (St. Vladimir's Seminary Press, New York 1982).

L. Uspensky, "Isikhazm i 'Gumanizm': Paleologovsky Rastsvet" [Hesychasm and Humanism: the Palaeologan flowering], *Messager de l'Exarchat du Patriarche Russe en Europe Occidentale* (Paris), lviii (1967), pp. 110–27; "Isikhazm i rastsvet russkogo iskusstva" [Hesychasm and the flowering of Russian art], ibid., lx (1967), pp. 252–70.

N. K. Goleizovsky, "Isikhazm i russkaya zhivopis' XIV–XV vv." [Hesychasm and Russian painting of the fourteenth and fifteenth centuries], *Vizantiisky Vremennik*, xxix (1969), pp. 196–210.

Fifteenth-century Novgorod icons

V. N. Lazarev, *Iskusstvo Novgoroda*, pp. 106–22.
——, *Novgorodian Icon-Painting* (Moscow, 1969) [text in Russian and English].

Rublev

J. A. Lebedewa, *Andrei Rubljow und seine Zeitgenossen* (Dresden, 1962).
V. N. Lazarev, *Andrey Rublev i ego shkola* [Andrew Rublev and his school] (Moscow, 1966).

General

N. Iorga, *Byzance après Byzance* (Bucharest, 1935); new edition, Bucharest, 1971.

I. Dujčev, "Byzance après Byzance et les Slaves", in the same author's *Medioevo Bizantino-Slavo*, ii (Rome, 1968), pp. 287–311.

Laments on the fall of Constantinople

G. Megas, "La prise de Constantinople dans la poésie et la tradition populaires grecques", in: *1453-1953. Le cinq-centième anniversaire de la prise de Constantinople* (Athens, 1953), pp. 125–33.

I. Dujčev, "La conquête turque et la prise de Constantinople dans la littérature slave contemporaine", *Byzantinoslavica*, xiv (1953), pp. 14–54, xvi (1955), pp. 318–29, xvii (1956), pp. 276–340.

V. Grecu, "La chute de Constantinople dans la littérature populaire roumaine", ibid., xiv (1953), pp. 55–81.

D. Obolensky, "Byzantium and Russia in the Late Middle Ages", in *Europe in the Late Middle Ages*, pp. 273–5.

The theory of Moscow the Third Rome

G. Olšr, "Gli ultimi Rurikidi e le basi ideologiche della sovranità dello Stato russo", *Orientalia Christiana Periodica*, xii (1946), pp. 322–73.

D. Obolensky, "Russia's Byzantine Heritage", *Oxford Slavonic Papers*, i (1950), pp. 37–63; reprinted in *Readings in Russian History*, ed. S. Harcave, i (New York, 1962), pp. 93–117.

W. K. Medlin, *Moscow and East Rome* (Geneva, 1952).

D. Stremooukhoff, "Moscow the Third Rome: Sources of the Doctrine", *Speculum*, xxviii (1953), pp. 84–101.

H. Schaeder, *Moskau das dritte Rom*, 2nd ed. (Darmstadt, 1957).

N. Andreyev, "Filofey and his Epistle to Ivan Vasil'yevich", *The Slavonic and East European Review*, xxxviii (1959–60), pp. 1–31.

The two-headed eagle

A. V. Soloviev, "Les emblèmes héraldiques de Byzance et les Slaves", *Annales de l'Institut Kondakov*, vii (1935), pp. 119–64.

The title tsar in sixteenth-century Russia

V. Savva, *Moskovskie tsari i vizantiiskie vasilevsy* [The Muscovite Tsars and the Byzantine basileis] (Kharkov, 1901).

M. Cherniavsky, "Khan or Basileus: An Aspect of Russian Mediaeval Political Theory", *Journal of the History of Ideas*, xx (1959), pp. 459–76.

Coronation ceremonies of the Muscovite rulers

G. Olšr, "La Chiesa e lo Stato nel cerimoniale d'incoronazione degli ultimi sovrani Rurikidi", *Orientalia Christiana Periodica*, xvi (1950), pp. 267–302.

Byzantine influences on Ottoman institutions

B. Cvetkova, "Influence exercée par certaines institutions de Byzance et des Balkans du Moyen Age sur le système féodal ottoman", *Byzantinobulgarica*, i (1962), pp. 237–57.

The patriarchate of Constantinople under Ottoman rule

T. H. Papadopoullos, *The History of the Greek Church and People under Turkish Domination* (Brussels, 1952).

S. Runciman, *The Great Church in Captivity* (Cambridge, 1968).

The Phanariots

N. Iorga, *Byzance après Byzance*.

S. Runciman, *The Great Church in Captivity*, pp. 360–84.

The decline of the Byzantine tradition in Greek lands

J. Campbell and P. Sherrard, *Modern Greece* (London, 1968), pp. 19–43.

INDEX

Aachen, treaty of (812), 136
Abasgia, as Byzantine client state, 234–5, 262; mentioned, 52–3, 229, 262
Abasgians, 46, 52–3, 219
Abbasid Khalifate, 101
Abkhazia, *see* Abasgia
Abydus, battle of (989), 255
Achaia, 310
Achelous, battle of (917), 151
Acroceraunian Mountains, 18, 40
Acropolites, George, 317
Actium, battle of (31 B.C.), 108–9
Adrianople, geographical position of, 18, 29–31, 100, 310; strategic importance of, 36, 96; on Belgrade-Constantinople highway, 37, 93, 177; Slav attacks on, 68; capital of Theme of "Macedonia", 108; captured by Bulgarians (914), 150; mentioned, 69, 115, 174, 316
Adrianople, battle of (1205), 313
Adriatic Sea, coastline of, 20, 21, 42, 80, 96, 182, 312, 378; and communications with Balkan peninsula, 24, 25–6, 36; and port of Dyrrachium, 18, 33, 40, 69, 100, 278, 310, 322, 402; and Via Egnatia, 40; and Byzantine strategic position, 104, 107, 136–7, 141, 177, 179, 287, 288, 362–3; theme system, 107, 108–9, 141; Narentani settlements on, 134, 135–6; Symeon of Bulgaria's invasions of seaboard of, 151, 317; trade routes across,

182, 324, 360; Venetian influence in, 287; cultural centres on, 132, 448, 452; mentioned, 77, 79, 86, 267, 268, 291, 388, 402, 408
Aegean Sea, geographical position of, 18, 27, 29, 100, 182, 219, 268, 310, 378; Byzantine strategic position in, 33–4, 104, 107, 246; and Belgrade-Constantinople highway, 36; trade in, 65, 182, 360–2; and theme system, 107, 108; mentioned, 42, 77, 79, 163, 177, 178, 322, 326, 331–2
Afghanistan, 225
Agapetus, Deacon, 292, 470
Agathias, 71
agriculture in lowlands of Balkan peninsula, 27; in Moesian plain, 28–9; practised by Slavs, 81–2, 100, 116, 208; practised by Magyars 208–9, 364, 365; and famines, 277; in Russia, 395, 457; mentioned, 24, 54, 88
Ajtony, Hungarian leader, 210
Akathistos hymn, 79
Akkerman, 310, 335, 338
Alania, 235
Alans, 46, 53, 72, 152, 219, 234–5
Albania, geographical position of, 18, 21, 26, 310; coastal regions of, 26, 40; highlands of, 80, 141; Byzantine influence in, 104–5; Samuel of Bulgaria's occupation of, 176; invaded by Normans, 289; expansion of Serbian state into, 329,

517

Nicephorus Phocas' campaigns against, 173; wars against Turks, 225; and relations with Russians, 238; John Curcuas' wars against, 246; and *Digenis Akritas*, 424; mentioned, 24, 34, 52, 53, 86, 177, 255, 303

Aral Sea, 222

Arcadiopolis, geographical position of, 18, 100; and Belgrade–Constantinople highway, 37; capital of Theme of Thrace, 107

architecture, 443–5, 448–50, 452–8, 460–1, 463

Arctic Ocean, 379, 396, 448, 459

Argeş, 310, 335, 378, 440

Argos, 100, 112

Aristotle, 142

Armenia, geographical position of, 43, 219, 269; Byzantine vassal states in, 52; as source of conscripts, 83–4; Constantine V's victories in, 94; Paulician sect in, 163, 282; Varangian mercenaries employed in, 303; mentioned, 88, 235, 246, 275, 367

Armenians, as conscripts in Byzantine army, 83–4; as missionaries, 88; mentioned, 226

Arnulf, King of Germany, 133

Árpád (Magyar ruler), 205, 206, 209; dynasty of, 214, 364

Arsenius, Abbot, 129

art, and Byzantine tradition, 157, 211–13, 318, 364, 443–64; Bulgarian, 318–19, 380, 447–51; Serbian, 323, 324, 380, 446–53, 463; Romanesque traditions, 324, 450, 456, 458; Rumanian, 335, 380, 444, 449, 453–4; Russian, 345, 379, 380–1, 444–9, 455–64; process of cultural diffusion, 364, 374, 379–81, 443–64; "Macedonian Renaissance", 443, 448, 456; "Palaeologan Renaissance", 444, 448, 452–4, 459–63; and patronage, 444–8, 450–60, 463; "Milutin" school of,

452; "Morava" school of, 453; mentioned, 13, 24–5; *see also* Architecture; Mosaics; Paintings

Asen I, Tsar of Bulgaria, 286

Asia Minor, geographical position of, 43, 219; trade routes in, 47–8; Byzantine control over, 52, 309; Persian advance across (626), 77; Arab-Byzantine border warfare in, 101; and the theme system of administration, 106–7; Paulician sect in, 163; monasteries in, 185, 193; Iconophile refugees in, 230; Russian invasions of, 240; Bardas Phocas' activities in, 255; Byzantines defeated in (1071), 280; Varangians employed as mercenaries in, 302–3, 306; mentioned, 56, 77, 218, 225, 275, 476

Askold, Varangian leader, 239, 241, 242

Asparuch, Bulgar Khan, 90–3, 114, 176, 179

Astrakhan, 469

Athens, geographical position of, 18, 100, 268; capital of Theme of Hellas, 107; metropolitanate of, 111; Basil II's visit to (1018), 178–9; Michael Choniates as metropolitan of, 285; Catalan Duchy of, 310; as cultural centre, 378, 444; mentioned, 80, 81, 106, 202, 242

Athos, Mount, 291, 293, 310, 314, 318, 322, 331–2, 338, 363, 378, 381–97, 434–46, 460, 474

Attica, migration of Albanians to, 23; Avaro-Slav invasion of (587), 75–6; Byzantine influence re-established in, 104–5; and theme system of administration, 107, 141; Samuel of Bulgaria's occupation of, 177; Magyar invasion of (936), 206; Frankish barons in, 309

Attila, ruler of the Huns, 49, 64, 73, 183

Augustae, 18, 69

Augustus, Emperor, 108

in *De Administrando Imperio*, 45; captured by Béla III of Hungary, 215; Peter Delyan's rebellion in (1040), 277; mentioned, 64, 131, 142, 214; *see also* Singidunum

Belisarius, 68

Beloozero, 219, 239, 370, 396; *see also* White Lake

Beloozero Monastery, 379, 396, 397

Benedictines, 211, 325

Benjamin of Tudela, 271

Berezan', 43, 62, 247

Bertinian Annals, 239

Beşiktaş, *see* St. Mamas

Bessarabia, geographical position of, 18; Antes' settlements in, 66, 72; Onogur settlements in, 90; Magyar settlements in, 145; mentioned, 87, 91

Bithynia, 219, 235, 246, 363, 388

Bitolj, 18, 40

Black Sea, and communications with Balkan Peninsula, 24–5, 27–9, 36, 38, 42–6; geographical position of, 18, 100, 182, 219, 266, 269, 310, 360; trade in, 29, 50–9, 93–4, 145, 225, 227–8, 334, 337; and communications with Mediterranean, 33, 360; and Baltic–Black Sea waterway, 43, 59–62, 65, 238–9, 243, 259, 273, 299, 360, 455; colonized by Greeks, 51, 80; Bulgar settlements on coast, 90–1, 92, 117, 176; Russian influence in, 200, 247; Byzantine strategic position on coast, 218–21, 234, 247; Khazar settlements on coast, 229–30, 234; Lithuanian rule on shores of, 338–9, 340; mentioned, 25, 26, 87, 157, 408

Blastares, Matthew, 410–12

Boeotia, geographical position of, 18; migration of Albanians to, 23; Byzantine influence re-established in, 104–5; and theme system, 107, 141; Samuel of Bulgaria's occupation of, 177; Frankish barons in, 309

Bogas, John, military governor of Cherson, 150

Bogomilism, 164–72, 281–2, 314, 372, 391, 435

Bohemia, Avar settlements in, 73–4, 85; Slav settlements in, 85; geographical position of, 182, 184, 268, 310; monasteries in, 196, 208, 403; Cyrillo-Methodian tradition in, 196–200, 266, 267, 271; Russia's relations with, 260, 267; cultural centres in, 378; literature of, 420, 421; mentioned, 174, 401; *see also* Czechs

Bojana, River, 100, 134

Bokhara, 225

Boleron, Theme of, 110

Boleslav, Duke of Bohemia, 401

Bonus, Byzantine commander, 78

Book of Ceremonies, 158, 213, 228, 234, 248, 262, 353

Book of the Pilot, 408; *see also* Nomocanones

Boril, King of Bulgaria, 314

Boris I, Bulgarian Khan, 116–34, 142–4, 154, 159, 162, 184, 192, 250, 286, 312, 364–9; 373, 406

Boris II, Tsar of Bulgaria, 176

Boris, Russian prince, St., 402–3

Bořivoj, Duke of Bohemia, 196

Bosna, River, 100, 136

Bosnia, geographical position of, 18, 22, 268, 287, 310; isolation of, 22, 287; and growth of Bosnian kingdom, 40–1, 287–8; Bogomilism in, 170–1; as part of Byzantine Commonwealth, 287–8; under the rule of Tvrtko I, 322

Bosphorus, geographical position of, 18, 30, 43, 100; and fortifications of Constantinople, 31, 32–3, 157; trade routes through, 51, 62, 182, 244, 337, 360; Persians encamped by (626), 77; and Russian attacks on Constantinople (860), 240; (941), 246; Bardas Phocas' invasion of (988), 255; Third Crusade ar-

art and architecture in, 447–51; mentioned, 20, 21, 36, 39, 40, 41, 57, 68, 82, 100, 103, 175, 219, 235, 257, 349; *see also* Volga Bulgars

"Bulgarian fables", 372

Burgas, Gulf of, 93–6, 141

Butua, 77; *see also* Budva

Byron, Lord, 24, 26

Byzantine Church, East European peoples' recognition of primacy of, 13, 14, 316–21; liturgy of, 78, 102–3, 130–31, 188–9; and hegemony of Byzantine Commonwealth, 87–9, 114–15, 148, 155–6, 311–21, 330–4, 342–61, 466–7, 472–6; and defeat of Iconoclasm, 101–2, 200, 229–30, 381; conversion of Slavs to Christianity by, 111–12, 116, 130–3, 362, 365; and Bulgarian Church, 116–33, 151, 160–72, 276, 283–6, 313–21, 370; and theory of the pentarchy, 120, 122; split with Roman Church over "*filioque*", 121, 127–8, 193–4; split with Roman Church over papal supremacy, 120; conversion of Serbs to Christianity by, 134–6, 290–91; conversion of Croats to Christianity by, 136–8; and Paulicianism, 163–6, 169, 170, 281–2; and Bogomilism, 164–72, 281–2, 314; and divine origin of emperor's power, 172, 291–3, 353–6, 397–9; and Moravian mission, 184–201, 202, 207; and question of Slavonic liturgy, 185–204, 260–1, 283; and "three languages" heresy, 191, 203; and *Nomocanones*, 196, 405–13; influence in Hungary of, 205–15, 364; attempts to evangelize Khazars, 229–34; conversion of Alans to Christianity by, 234–5; and Russian attack on Constantinople (860), 240–42; conversion of Russia to Christianity, 242, 247–67, 292–3, 362; conversion of Rumanians to Christianity by, 272, 273; and

Russian Church, 260–2, 292, 295–7, 300–1, 312–16, 337–50, 367–8, 375, 377, 467–73; and Serbian Church, 313–16, 321–3, 324–5, 328–32; and Rumanian Church, 335–6; and Council of Florence, 346–7, 350; and revivalist movements, 370–72; mentioned, 104

Byzantine Commonwealth, concept of, 13–18, 117–18, 141–60, 211–13, 266–73, 309–21, 330–4, 342–61, 466–76

Caffa, geographical position of, 43, 50, 310; as trading centre, 337; *see also* Theodosia

Calabria, geographical position of, 100, 268; Byzantine reconquest of, 109; mentioned, 270

Callistus I, Patriarch of Constantinople, 330, 340, 391, 394, 437

Camaterus, Petronas, 232

Campulungu, 178

Cantacuzeni family, 473, 475

Capet, Margaret, 216

Capidava, 268, 278

Cappadocia, 241, 378, 388, 423

Carolingian Empire, 113, 116–17

Carpathian Mountains, geographical position of, 18, 27, 43, 46, 54, 58, 85, 181–2, 266, 268, 310; and Slav migrations, 64–5, 272; crossed by Magyars (896), 146, 205; Magyar settlements in, 207–8, 209, 219; Rumanians in, 272, 334, 335; cultural centres in, 378, 440; mentioned, 95, 197, 299

Carsium, 268, 278

Carthage, 66

Časlav, Prince of Serbia, 159–60

"Caspian Gates", 53

Caspian Sea, geographical position of, 43, 59, 219, 220, 269, 310, 378; and trade routes, 52–3, 222–4, 228; and kingdom of the Huns, 64; Khazar settlements, 231; mentioned, 57

Catalans, 310

Cathar movement, 170

Caucasian lands, seaboards of, 48, 52; settlements of Huns in, 87–90; Byzantine influence in, 225, 227–8, 236, 267; mentioned, 234–5, 241, 358, 367

Caucasus Mountains, geographical position of, 43, 46–7, 59, 88–90, 218–20, 266–9, 310, 378; mentioned in *De Administrando Imperio*, 46, 51–2; and trade routes, 47, 222–4; passes in, 51, 52, 53; Byzantine interests in, 53, 57, 159, 262; arrival of Avars in (550s), 72; as source of conscripts, 83; Khazar settlements in, 227–9, 231, 232; Alan settlements in, 235; mentioned, 185, 205, 448

Caves, Monastery of the, 296, 386–7, 429

Central Asian Turks, 72, 221–5

Cephalonia, 100, 108

Cetina River, 100, 134, 136

Chalcedon, 77

Chalcidice, 18, 34, 310, 332

Chariton, Metropolitan of Wallachia, 393

Charlemagne, destruction of Avar empire by, 95, 113; relations with Byzantium, 149

Charles Martel, 228

Charles the Simple, King of France, 246

Charles of Anjou, 311

Chernigov, 269, 296, 378, 379

Cherson, geographical position of, 43, 45, 48–9, 219, 269; fortifications of, 48–9; Justinian II's exile in, 92, 226; Pope Martin I's exile in, 225; Iconophile refugees in, 230; Theme of, 232; Bishopric of, 234; and relations with Pechenegs, 235, 237; Vladimir of Russia's relations with, 253–6, 258–9; mentioned, 50, 227, 240, 247, 293; *see also* Chersonesus

Chersonesus, 24, 25, 48; *see also* Cherson

Chilandar Monastery, 291, 332, 383, 389, 400

Chilia, 335

China, silk trade, 48, 50, 52, 221–4

Chingis Khan, 311, 399

Choeroboscus, George, 143

Choerosphactes, Leo, 146

Choniates, Michael, 202, 285

Christian Topography (by Cosmas Indicopleustes), 424

Christoupolis, defile of, 310, 331

Chronicle of George the Monk, 426, 429

Chronicle of John Malalas, 426, 429

Chronicle of Monemvasia, 83

Chrysopolis, battle of (988), 255

Cicero, 25

Cilicia, 173

Cimmerians, 46, 47, 56

Circassians, 46

Cistercians, 388

Clement I, Pope, St., 192

Clement of Ohrid, St., 131–2, 142, 161, 171, 196, 198, 283, 285, 452

Clement, Metropolitan of Kiev, 297, 300

Clovis, Frankish King, 82

Cluny, Abbey of, 382

Codex Assemanianus, 284

Codex Eninensis, 284

Codex Suprasliensis, 284

Colchis, *see* Mingrelia

communism, 468

Conrad III, King of Germany, 38

Constance, *see* Council of Constance

Constans II, Emperor, 85, 105, 225

Constantine I the Great, Emperor, birthplace of, 36; and system of military defence, 69–70; and foundation of Constantinople University, 102–3; mentioned, 119, 256

Constantine IV, Emperor, 90

Constantine V, Emperor, 94–5, 114, 163, 229, 409

Constantine VII Porphyrogenitus, Emperor, and *De Administrando Imperio*, 45, 85–6, 200, 236, 256; relations with Bulgaria, 147–52,

Constantinople, Church of, *see* Byzantine Church

Corfù, geographical position of, 18; strategic importance of, 26

Corinth, geographical position of, 100; capital of the Peloponnesian Theme, 108; metropolitanate of, 111, 112; mentioned, 80, 81, 106

Corinth, Gulf of, geographical position of, 18, 24; mentioned, 152

Corinth, Isthmus of, fortifications of, 69; Slav invasions of, 79; Samuel of Bulgaria's invasion of, 177

Corippus, 73

Coron, 310

Corsica, 66

Cosmas, Bulgarian priest, 165–72, 423

Council of Constance, 442

Council of Florence, 346–50, 466, 467

Cracow, 182, 197

Cres, 100, 109

Crete, Venetian trade with, 26; Slav raid on (623), 79; Arab control over, 101; captured by Nicephorus Phocas, 173; Byzantine expeditions against (911), 245; (949), 303; monasteries in, 389; mentioned, 270

Crimea, Greek colonies in, 24, 47–50, 363; Venetian colonies in, 26, 51; geography and climate, 43, 47–51, 59, 219, 269, 310; under Byzantine sovereignty, 45–53, 87–8, 175, 205, 218–21, 225–38, 247, 272–3; *limes Tauricus* in, 49; economy of, 49–51; Justinian II's exile in, 92, 226–7; Turkish invasion of (576), 223; Pope Martin I's exile in, 225; under Khazar sovereignty, 226–32; Iconophile refugees in, 229–30; Russian invasions of, 240, 253–5, 258; and Christianization of Russia, 259–60; Genoese colonies in, 337; as cultural centre, 363, 460; Tatar occupation of, 470; mentioned, 33, 192, 267, 358

Croatia and Croats, origins of, 85–6; migration to Balkans of, 85–6; geographical position of, 85–6, 136–8, 182, 268, 310, 378; Christianization of, 86–7, 137, 287–8, 364, 375; subjects of Frankish Empire, 96, 136–7; growth to nationhood, 99, 110; and Byzantine Commonwealth, 114, 137–8, 141, 179, 183, 214, 287; political institutions of, 136–8; culture of, 197–8; and union with Hungary (1102), 137, 287; relations with Bulgaria, 155; use of Slavonic liturgy in, 196–8; literature in, 420, 421; mentioned, 109, 193, 363; *see also* Dalmatian Croatia; Pannonian Croatia; "White Croatia"

Crusades, First, 38, 280; Second, 38; Third, 38, 290; and Belgrade–Constantinople highway, 37–8; Fourth, 31, 42, 301, 309, 311, 325; mentioned, 41

Csanád, *see* Marosvar

Cumans (Polovtsy), in South Russian Steppes, 56–7, 280, 299; and destruction of Pechenegs (1091), 281; relations with Byzantium, 281, 282; mentioned, 21, 32, 286, 302

Curcuas, John, 246

Curtea-de-Argeş, 454

Cydones, Demetrius, 333

Cyprian, Metropolitan of Kiev, Lithuania and Russia, 341, 440, 442

Cyprus, Venetian trade with, 26; captured by Nicephorus Phocas, 173; Iconophile refugees in, 229; monasteries in, 389

Cyril, Metropolitan of Kiev, 313–14

Cyril of Scythopolis, 382, 386

Cyril of Thessalonica, *see* Constantine (Cyril) St., of Thessalonica

Cyrillic script, 187–8, 199, 284

Czechs, early medieval culture of, 14, 196–7, 271, 421; and martyrdom of St. Wenceslas, 401, 403; mentioned, 273; *see also* Bohemia

Dnieper – *contd*

Slav settlements on, 64, 66, 238, 360; Magyar settlements on, 146; Khazar settlements on, 228; Viking settlements on, 233–4, 238, 239, 241, 242, 246; Cuman settlements on, 298–9; mentioned, 50, 59, 90, 222, 247, 253, 338, 363, 371, 385

Dnieper Rapids, 43,.61–2, 175

Dniester, River, geographical position of, 24, 43, 45, 65, 182, 219, 268, 310, 378; Bulgar settlements on, 91, 95; mentioned, 24, 58, 299, 335

Dobrudja, geographical position of, 18, 28, 310; Slav occupation of, 65; Avar occupation of, 72, 74; Bulgar occupation of, 90, 91; Magyar invasion of (895), 146; Russian invasion of (967), 173; fortifications in, 278; mentioned, 69, 335; *see also* Little Scythia

Dölger, Franz, 15

Don, River, geographical position of, 43, 58, 59, 219, 269, 310, 378; mentioned in *De Administrando Imperio*, 45–6; as boundary of "Old Great Bulgaria", 90; Magyar settlements on, 146, 205; Khazar settlements on, 231, 232; Pecheneg settlements on, 235; Cuman settlements on, 280; mentioned, 24, 50, 52, 55, 67, 70, 228, 337

Donets, River, geographical position of, 43, 219, 269, 310, 378; Antes' settlements on, 66

Doros, geographical position of, 43, 49, 219; Crimean Goths in, 226; bishopric of, 230, 231

Dorostolon, 18, 69; *see also* Silistria

Drava, River, 18, 19, 86, 100, 136, 181, 182, 197, 268, 270, 310, 378

Drin, River, geographical position of, 18, 100; mentioned, 21, 134, 388

Drina, River, 100, 134, 287

Dubrovnik, geographical position of, 18, 100, 310; as merchant republic, 26; and theme system of administration, 109; Arab siege of (867), 109, 136; and contacts with Italy, 322; as trading centre, 324; under Venetian sovereignty (1205–1358), 324; as cultural centre, 378; mentioned, 26, 77, 134; *see also* Ragusa

Ducas, Constantine, 147

Duks, monk, 143

Durazzo, *see* Dyrrachium

Dvina, River, 379

Dyje, River, 182, 184

Dyrrachium, geographical position of, 18, 100, 310; and Via Egnatia, 33, 40; Slav attack on (548), 67–8; fortifications of, 69; Theme of, 108, 110, 271, 287; captured by Bulgarians (997), 177; Albanian settlements near, 271; captured by Peter Delyan (1040), 277; and contacts with Italy, 322; mentioned, 77, 111, 151, 288, 316, 402

Ecbatana, 221

Ecloga, 196, 409–11

Edessa, 18, 40

Edirne, *see* Adrianople

Egypt, Umayyad Khalifate's control over, 101; anchorites in, 382, 387; mentioned, 153

Elbasan, geographical position of, 18, 40; as cultural centre, 378; cult of St. John Vladimir in, 402

Elbe, River, Slav settlements on, 85; geographical position of, 182, 268, 310, 378; mentioned, 65

Elizabeth, Princess (daughter of Yaroslav of Kiev, wife of Harold Hardrada), 306

emperor of Byzantium, concept of universal sovereignty of, 13–15, 117–20, 148–60, 211–16, 261–3, 292–3, 318–21, 327, 329–34, 342–8, 353–9, 397–401, 466–72

England, and reconquest of the *Danelaw*, 246; and relations with

Russia, 295; battle of Stamford Bridge (1066), 306–7; Norman conquest of, 307; mentioned, 404

Enravotas, 115

Epiphanius the Wise, 396, 441–2, 461; *see also Life of St. Stephen of Perm'*

Epirus, geographical position of, 18, 26, 310; system of fortifications in 69; Avaro-Slav invasion of (587), 75–6; Slav occupation of, 79, 80, 274; Byzantine influence in, 104–5; Theme of, 77; Samuel of Bulgaria's occupation of, 176; and Nicaean Empire, 314–15; and battle of Klokotnitsa (1230), 316; relations with Serbia, 321, 329, 412; mentioned, 309

Erzerum, 163

Erzgebirge, 266, 268

Eskeje Pass, 110

Euboea, migration of Albanians to, 23; geographical position of, 18, 100, 268, 310; Avaro-Slav invasion of (587), 75–6; Straits of, 107; mentioned, 284

Euchologion, 423

Euchologium Sinaiticum, 284

Eudoxia, Princess (niece of Isaac II Angelus), 290

Eugenicus, John, 467

Eugenius IV, Pope, 346

Eumathius, 95

Euphrates, River, Paulician strongholds on, 163; and silk route, 221; geographical position of, 269, 310, 378; mentioned, 67

Euthychius, painter, 452

Euthymius, Patriarch of Trnovo, 392, 393, 434–42

Ezeritae, 110, 274

Fallmerayer, J. P., 112

Farmer's Law, 412

feudalism, 161, 281, 328

Finland, 43

Finnic peoples, 58, 228, 239, 273, 441

Finland, Gulf of, geographical position of, 43, 219, 220, 266–8, 310, 379; and Baltic–Black Sea waterway, 60, 239

Florence, *see* Council of Florence

France, Albigensian movement in, 170; Magyar campaigns in, 206; and relations with Russia, 295, 472; mentioned, 47, 246, 404

Franks, contact with Albanians, 23; Christianity, 83; Croats as subjects of, 96, 136–7; relations with Bulgaria, 116–17, 120, 123; relations with Byzantium, 158, 256–7, 267, 309; relations with Moravia, 184, 186, 188–97, 199, 207; opposition to Slavonic liturgy of, 203; relations with Hungary, 209; relations with Russians, 239–40; and Fourth Crusade, 309; and occupation of Balkans, 309; and occupation of Constantinople (1204), 316; and national assemblies, 323; legal system of, 411; mentioned, 85, 95, 305

Frederick I Barbarossa, Western emperor, 38, 214, 290, 300

Gabriel of Lesnovo, 384

Gaiseric, King of the Vandals, 320

Galata Peninsula, 243

Galich, 268, 299, 378

Galicia, geographical position of, 85, 182, 268, 299, 310; relations with Byzantium, 299–301, 340, 358; Tatar control over, 312; mentioned, 65, 205, 313

Gallipoli, geographical position of, 18, 310; Slav invasions of, 67; Kutrigur invasion of (559), 68; mentioned, 314

"Gates of Trajan", 37, 177

Genoa, and Black Sea trade, 25, 29, 50–1, 335, 337; mentioned, 311

George Branković, Despot of Serbia, 334, 453, 467

Georgia and Georgians, geographical position of, 43, 219; Byzantine diplomacy in, 53; Khazar invasion of, 228; Iconophiles in, 230; as Byzantine client state, 262; and Bachkovo monastery, 367; on Mount Athos, 383

Gepids, 64, 73, 77

Gerard of Csanád, St., 211

Germanus, Patriarch of Constantinople (715–30), 79

Germany and Germans, and Roman Church, 117, 184–5; and destruction of Moravian state, 205; Magyar campaigns in, 205–6, 207; influence in Hungary of, 209, 210; relations with Russia, 249–50, 472; relations with Czechs, 271; empire of Frederick Barbarossa, 214, 290; and Third Crusade, 290; mentioned, 253, 257–8, 323, 354, 417

Géza I, King of Hungary, 212

Géza II, King of Hungary, 214, 297, 300

Géza, Prince of Hungary, 209

Ghika family, 475

Glagolitic script, 187–8, 197–9, 284, 417

Gleb, Russian prince, St., 402–3

Gnosticism, 166

Godfrey of Bouillon, 38

Golden Horde, 51, 56, 57–8, 310, 311, 318, 338–9, 344, 459, 469; see also Mongols

Golden Horn, and fortifications of Constantinople, 30, 31, 32–3, 147; as natural harbour, 33; and siege of Constantinople (626), 77–8; and siege of Constantinople (813–14), 96; and Russian attack on Constantinople (907), 243–4; and Russian attack on Constantinople (941), 246; mentioned, 153, 250

Gorazd, 196

Gordas, 87–8

Gorzovium, see Gurzuf

Gothia in Crimea, 230–4

Goths, Valens defeated by, 31; Crimean, 49, 51, 219, 221, 226–7, 230, 272, 358; Arian, 49; in south Russian steppes, 65; influence of Christianity on, 83, 201; mentioned, 27, 32, 34–6, 56, 70, 181

Gotland, geographical position of, 43; and Baltic–Black Sea waterway, 60

Grabar, André, 15

Gračanica Monastery, 378, 388, 447, 452

Grammos Mountains, 271

"Great Fence" of Thrace, 96

Great Lavra Monastery, 383

"Great Moravia", area covered by, 182, 184, 199; see also Moravia

"Great Portage", 60

"Greek fire", 95, 101, 158, 175, 246–7, 294, 373

Greek folk songs, 23, 467

Greek language, as official imperial language, 84, 112, 354–5; as a liturgical language, 112, 186–96, 202–4, 260–1, 283, 422; used in Bulgaria, 115, 119, 130, 133, 143, 153, 198; and literature, 142, 157, 285, 319, 372, 416–29, 434–6, 438–41, 466–7, 474; spoken at Hungarian court, 210–11; spoken in southern Crimea, 272; used in Russia, 292, 345; used in Serbia, 327, 330; mentioned, 15, 37, 81, 148, 227, 274, 293, 309, 367

Gregory VII, Pope, 287, 288

Gregory, Bishop of Nin, 197

Gregory Palamas, St., Archbishop of Thessalonica, 392, 396, 397, 437, 461

Gregory of Sinai, St., 389–94, 397, 434, 437

Gurzuf, geographical position of, 43; fortifications of, 49

Gytheion, 274

Gyula, Hungarian leader, 207, 208, 373

Hadrian II, Pope, 128, 192–4
Hadrian, Emperor, 69
Haemimontus, 37, 69
Haemus Mountains, *see* Balkan Mountains
Halys, River, 378
Hanseatic League, 459
Harold Hardrada, Varangian leader, King of Norway, 305–7
Harold, King of England, 295
Hebrew language, 191, 194, 203, 231, 233, 435
Hebrus, River, *see* Maritsa, River
Heirmologion, 423
Helen, Empress (wife of Constantine VII), 248
Hellas, Theme of, 100, 107; Slav settlements in, 274
Henry I, King of France, 295
Heraclea, geographical position of, 18, 219; and Belgrade–Constantinople highway, 37
Heraclea Pontica, 246
Heraclius, Emperor, 77, 78, 80, 85–7, 88–9, 96, 133, 134, 183, 220, 227
Herodotus, 425
Herzegovina, geographical position of, 18, 22, 134; Zachlumi settlements in, 287; mentioned, 325, 363; *see also* Zachlumia, Zahlumje
Hesychasm, 389–97, 434–42, 461–2
Hexaemeron (St. Basil the Great), 143
Hierotheus, Bishop of Hungary, 207–8
Hilarion, Metropolitan of Kiev, 296–7, 428–9; *see also Sermon on Law and Grace*
Himerius, Admiral, 245
Hincmar, Archbishop of Rheims, 117
Historia Monachorum, 382
History of the Jewish War (Josephus), 424
Hlm, 134; *see also* Herzegovina; Hum
Hohenstaufen dynasty, 16
Holmgardr, *see* Novgorod
Horologion, 423
Hum, 134; *see also* Herzegovina; Hlm
Humor Monastery, 378, 454

Hungary, location of, 54, 65, 73; Bulgar settlements in, 95; foundation of kingdom of, 146; natural resources of, 174; relations with Byzantium, 181, 204–16, 236, 266, 271–2, 289–90, 297–302, 336, 358, 373–4; area covered by, 182, 268, 310; Avar settlements in, 183; monasticism in, 197, 210–11, 391; and Crown of Constantine Monomachus, 211; and Holy Crown of Hungary, 212–13; and union with Croatia (1102), 287; relations with Russia, 295, 297, 300–1; relations with Serbia, 321, 324; relations with Rumania, 334–5; economy of, 364, 365; cultural centres in, 378; cult of St. John of Rila in, 384; mentioned, 14, 19, 26, 137, 250, 323; *see also* Magyars
Huns, Balkans invaded by, 35, 36, 181; Crimea occupied by, 48–9, 87–9; illiteracy of, 55; in south Russian steppes, 56, 64, 88–90; and creation of "Old Great Bulgaria", 90; relations with Khazars, 231; mentioned, 21, 28, 32, 65
Hunyadi, John, Voivode of Transylvania, 336
Hvar, 100, 134, 182, 198

Iași, 474
Ibar, River, 18, 39, 100, 134, 182, 289, 310, 321, 378, 388
Iberians, *see* Georgians
Iconoclasm, 101–3, 200, 229–30, 381, 409, 443
Ignatius, Patriarch of Constantinople, 128, 242
Igor, prince of Kiev, 246–8
Illyrians, 22, 80, 83, 271
Illyricum, invaded by Bulgars, 67; Slav occupation of, 81, 83; Avar occupation of, 85–6; arrival of Croats in, 86; arrival of serbs in 86;

Illyricum – *contd*
ecclesiastical jurisdiction over, 128
Il'men, Lake, geographical position of, 43; and Baltic–Black Sea waterway, 60
Indians (North American), 370
Indicopleustes, Cosmas, 424; *see also Christian Topography*
Inn, River, 268
Innocent III, Pope, 312
Innocent IV, Pope, 312
Iona, Metropolitan of Kiev and All Russia, 348
Ionian Islands, geographical position of, 18, 26; Byzantine navy in, 33; and theme system, 108, 141
Ionian Sea, geographical position of, 100, 268, 310; Byzantine strategic position in, 104–5, 107; Norman activities in, 289
Iorga, Nicholas, 15
Iran and Iranians, 56, 59, 66
Irene, Empress, 105
Irene (Piroska) of Hungary, wife of John II, 213
Irene, Tsaritsa of Bulgaria, *see* Maria Lecapena
Iron gate, geographical position of, 18, 19, 182; mentioned, 205
Isaac II Angelus, Emperor, 215–16, 286, 290
Isaiah, Serbian monk, 393
Isidore, Metropolitan of Kiev and All Russia, 346, 350
Isidore of Seville, 80
Iskŭr, River, geographical position of, 18; and Belgrade–Constantinople highway, 36; mentioned, 21
Islam, 57, 101, 225, 227, 229, 231, 233, 252, 349
Istanbul, 473; *see also* Constantinople
Istria, geographical position of, 18, 26, 136, 137, 141, 268, 270
Italy, and close connections with Dalmatia, 21–2; and communications with Balkan peninsula, 25, 26, 65; and Corfu, 26; and trade in

Black Sea, 29; and trade with Serbia, 41; and trade with Bulgaria, 41; and connections with Crimea, 47–8, 50–1, 337; Justinian I's conquests in, 66, 76; Lombard invasion of (568), 73; Byzantine reconquests in, 109, 141; Albigensian movement in, 170; Magyar campaigns in, 206; Byzantines defeated in (1071), 280; mentioned, 18, 157, 182, 229, 404, 406, 417, 449, 451
Itil', 219, 228, 231
Ivan III, Grand Prince of Moscow, 468, 469, 470, 472
Ivan IV, Tsar of Russia, 55, 468, 469, 470, 471, 472
Izyaslav, Prince of Kiev, 295, 297, 300

Jader, 77; *see also* Zadar
Jagiello, Grand Duke of Lithuania, 341
Jannina, 141
Jaxartes, River, 222; *see also* Syr Daria
Jerusalem, Iconophile refugees in, 230; pilgrimages to, 338; patriarchate of, 469; mentioned, 120, 240, 322, 346, 375, 467, 474
Jews, 132, 425
Joachim of Osogovo, 384
John VIII, Pope, 193–5
John I Tzimisces, Emperor, 174–7, 210, 275, 278, 447
John II Comnenus, Emperor, 213
John III Vatatzes, Emperor, 314
John V Palaeologus, Emperor, 332
John VI Cantacuzenus, Emperor, 333, 340, 344
John VIII Palaeologus, Emperor, 346
John Alexander, Tsar of Bulgaria, 318, 319, 320, 391
John Asen II, Tsar of Bulgaria, 314, 316–19
John of Ephesus, 75
John the Exarch, 143, 144

John of Gothia, 230
John the Orphanotrophus, 277
John of Rila, St., 384
John of Salisbury, 16
John Scholasticus, Patriarch of Constantinople, 408
John Uglješa, Despot of Serres, 332
John Vladimir, St., Prince of Dioclea, 402
John Vladislav, Tsar of Bulgaria, 402
Josephus, Flavius, 424; *see also History of the Jewish War*
Judaism, 228, 229, 231, 233, 252
Judicial Law for Laymen, 409, 410, 411
Justin I, Emperor, 67
Justin II, Emperor, 73, 221
Justinian I, Emperor, and struggle for Danubian *limes*, 28, 68–72; and fortification of Belgrade, 35–6; and fortification of Cherson, 48–9; and *limes Tauricus*, 49, 218, 220; and fortification of Petra, 53; and dealings with Kutrigurs, 55, 67–8; 70–71; imperial design of, 66–7; and Slav invasions, 67–72; Italian conquests of, 66, 76; diplomacy of, 70–2, 85–7, 220, 229; and relations with Utigurs, 223; and codification of Roman law, 404, 405, 408, 413; and *Chronicle of John Malalas,* 426; mentioned, 19, 133, 214, 221, 226, 292, 357
Justinian II, Emperor, 85, 92, 93, 105, 226–7, 412
Justinian's Law, 412
Justiniana Prima, 39

Kalenić Monastery, 378, 453
Kalokyros, 173
Kaloyan, King of Bulgaria, 311–14, 317
Kanalites, 134
Kardutsat, Bishop, 88
Kariye Camii (Church of the Chora), 444, 452, 454

Kashgar, 221
Kavalla, 100, 109, 330–1
Kazakhstan, 222
Kazan', 56, 469
Kegen, Pecheneg leader, 279
Kerch, Straits of, geographical position of, 43, 46, 51, 218; presence of Khazars on, 226, 231; mentioned, 273
Khazars, in south Russian steppes, 56–7, 90, 92, 201, 219–20, 238; and alliance with Byzantium, 57, 103–4, 185, 227–34; Justinian II's relations with, 226–7; in Crimea, 226–32; diminished power of, 234–5; mentioned, 46, 51, 52, 226, 227, 228, 229, 231, 232, 237, 241, 252, 254, 273, 373
Khorasan, 225
Khortitsa, 62; *see also* St. Gregory, Island of
Khrabr, monk, 143, 203
Kiev, geographical position of, 43, 58, 219, 269, 310, 379; as trading centre, 60–62, 362; besieged by Pechenegs (968–9), 174; baptism of Andrew I of Hungary in, 211; as capital of Russia, 238–9, 241–3, 245–62, 291–9; metropolitanate of, 299–302, 312–14, 339–41, 367, 403, 440–2, 474; Varangian mercenaries in, 302–4, 306, 362; captured by Mongols (1240), 311, 447; as cultural centre, 378, 379, 420, 421, 426, 429, 441, 445–7, 455–7; pagan revolt in, 371–2; monasteries in, 385–7; tithe system in, 411; mentioned, 173, 175, 368, 371, 404, 470
Kievan Russia, 57, 219, 238–62, 273, 291–9, 339, 387, 399, 438, 470
Kilifarevo Monastery, 378, 391–3, 434, 439, 440, 442
Kleidion Pass, geographical position of, 18, 39; mentioned, 178
Klis, 18, 41, 137
Klokotnitsa, battle of (1230), 310, 316

474–5; in Old Church Slavonic, 416–21, 427–33, 435–8; classical Greek, 418–19; in Church Slavonic, 433–42; "Euthymian" tradition, 434–41; French, 472; mentioned, 13, 131, 132

Lithuania, geographical position of, 310; trade routes across, 337–8; political structure of, 338; territorial expansion of, 338–9, 470; Christianity in, 339–41, 440, 442

Little Preslav, 100, 173, 178

Little Scythia, 28, 69; see also Dobrudja

Liutprand, Bishop of Cremona, 142, 257, 354, 358

Ljes, 77, 100; see also Lissus

Ljudevit, Prince of Croatia, 136–7

Lombards, and occupation of Pannonian plain, 64; invasion of Italy by (568), 73; struggle in Italy against Byzantines, 73, 76

London, 246

Lošinj, 100, 109

Louis VII, King of France, 216

Louis the German, King of the East Franks, 117, 120, 184, 190, 191, 193, 194, 199

Louis the Pious, Western emperor, 239

Lovat', River, geographical position of, 43, 59, 219, 268, 310, 379; and Baltic–Black Sea waterway, 60

Lower Moesia, 28–9, 69, 91

Ludmila, St., of Bohemia, 196

Lüleburgaz, see Arcadiopolis

Lutheranism, 472

Lyons, Council of (1274), 317

Macedonia, geographical position of, 18, 20, 21, 100, 182, 268; "Campania", 27, 34, 105; Vlakhs in, 22; terrain of, 27, 33, 39; and Via Egnatia, 33; Kutrigur invasion of (559), 68; system of fortifications in, 69; Slav settlements in, 75, 79, 81, 85, 105, 108, 130, 187, 189, 362; Byzantine Empire's northern borders in, 101; Byzantine control over, 104–5, 178; and theme system, 108, 109, 110, 141, 275; bishoprics in, 111; expansion of Bulgarian state into, 130, 141, 145, 151, 176; St. Clement's activities in, 131–2, 142; Bogomilism in, 170; use of Slavonic liturgy in, 197, 199; Magyar invasions of (934–61), 206; invaded by Uzes (1064), 279–80; pronoiai in, 281, 328; literature in, 283–4; as leading centre of Slavo-Byzantine civilization, 286; Frankish barons in, 309; expansion of Serbian state into, 321–2, 325–30, 332, 412; monasteries in, 160, 383, 388, 392; Slavonic dialect of, 187, 416–20; art and architecture in, 447–52, 460; mentioned, 34, 36, 40, 41, 95, 133, 289, 367, 398

"Macedonian Renaissance", 443, 448, 456

Maeotis, Lake of, see Azov, Sea of

Maglić, 18, 39

Magnus Eriksson, King of Sweden, 374

Magyars, in south Russian steppes, 56, 219; foundation of kingdom of Hungary, 146, 209; relations with Byzantium, 159, 183, 204–16; allied with Svyatoslav, 174; destruction of Moravian state, 196, 199, 200; Byzantine cultural influence on, 205, 210; conversion to Christianity of, 206–12; economy of, 208–9, 365; political institutions of, 209; and relations with Khazars, 232; attacked by Pechenegs, 146, 235, 236; mentioned, 32, 145, 152, 262, 272; see also Hungary

Makrolivada, 96, 100

Maku, Bishop, 88

Malamir, Khagan, 115

Malea, Cape, 106, 274

Michael VII Ducas, Emperor, 212
Michael VIII Palaeologus, Emperor, 309, 315, 317, 326, 327
Michael, St., Prince of Chernigov, 399
Michael, Prince of the Zachlumi, 151-2
Michael, King of Zeta, 288
Michael, painter, 452
Mileševa Monastery, 322, 378, 388, 446, 450
Milutin, King of Serbia, *see* Stephen Uroš II Milutin
"Milutin" school of painting, 452
Mingrelia, 51
Mircea the Old, Prince of Wallachia, 336
Mislav, Prince of Croatia, 137
Mistra, 378, 444
Mljet, 100, 134
Modon, 310
Moesia, Kutrigurs' invasion of (559), 68; Bulgar occupation of, 91-2, 145; mentioned, 29, 36; *see also* Lower Moesia; Upper Moesia
Mojmir, Prince of Moravia, 184
Moldavia, geographical position of, 310; as Rumanian principality, 334-6, 394, 474-5; culture of, 440, 442, 447, 454; monastic movement in, 394; mentioned, 272
Moldoviţa Monastery, 378, 454
monasteries and monasticism, in Bulgaria, 160-1, 171-2, 281-2, 285, 317, 378, 382-6, 388-93, 435; in Hungary, 196, 210-11, 378, 391; in Crimea, 229-30; in Russia, 296, 378, 381-3, 385-7, 390, 393-7, 428; in Serbia, 314-15, 322-5, 328-32, 378, 381-3, 388-94, 400; in Rumania, 335, 378, 390-4, 454; and process of cultural diffusion, 363, 428-9; *lavra*, 382, 394-6; coenobitic, 382-7, 394-7; anchorites and eremitical, 381-2, 384-7, 394-7; and Hesychast movement, 389-97, 434-43, 461-2; idio-

rrhythmic, 394; in Albania, 402; monastic tradition in art, 443-54, 459-60, 463-4; mentioned, 13, 229, 291, 367-8, 412, 424, 474-6
Monemvasia, geographical position of, 100; mentioned, 80, 106, 112
Mongolia, Turkish settlements in, 221; mentioned, 49, 55
Mongols, Russia invaded by (1237-40), 311, 337, 343, 395, 447, 455-6; Bulgaria invaded by, 318; and battle of Ankara (1402), 333; mentioned, 21, 50, 51, 72, 294-6, 385, 387, 410; *see also* Tatars
Monophysites, 88
Montenegro, geographical position of, 18, 22; coastal regions of, 26, 134; and Via de Zenta, 40-1; mountains of, 134, 288; mentioned, 141
Morava, River in the Balkans, geographical position of, 18, 69, 100, 268, 310, 378; and Belgrade-Constantinople highway, 33-6; and Morava-Vardar highway, 39-41, 45, 79, 145, 326; Slav settlements on, 83; Stephen Nemanja's defeat on (1190), 290; mentioned, 134, 333, 393, 453
Morava, River in Central Europe, 65, 182, 184
"Morava" school of painting, 453
Moravane, 83
Moravia, Slav settlements in, 85, 131, 184; Cyrillo-Methodian mission to (863), 103, 131, 183-201, 202-3, 207, 260, 267, 408, 410, 417, 422; geographical position of, 181, 182, 184, 268, 310; and kingdom of "Great Moravia", 184-201, 260; and destruction of Moravian state, 196-7, 199, 200; culture of, 378, 419, 420, 421, 427, 430; mentioned, 14, 132
"Moravian Gate", 65, 182
Moschus, John, 382; *see also Pratum Spirituale*
Moscow, geographical position of,

Moscow — *contd*
310, 379; as trading centre, 337; seat of the primate of the Russian Church, 338–42, 346–50, 440, 442, 459, 467; as cultural centre, 459, 460–1, 463; as "the Third Rome", 321, 467–72; patriarchate of, 468, 469, 474; mentioned, 311, 395; *see also* Muscovy

Mosynopolis, 100, 109; *see also* Komotini

Murad I, Sultan, 31

Musala, 20

Muscovy, area covered by, 310; relations with Byzantium, 338–50; political and cultural development of, 338, 438, 440–1, 442, 460, 463, 467; cult of national rulers in, 399; and "Byzantine heritage", 468–73, 474; mentioned, 298, 299; *see also* Moscow

Myriocephalon, battle of (1176), 215

Mytilene, 389

Nagoričino, *see* Staro Nagoričino

Naissus, geographical position of, 18; and Belgrade–Constantinople highway, 36; fortifications of, 69; mentioned, 39; *see also* Niš

Naples, 310, 321

Narenta, River, *see* Neretva, River

Narentani, 83, 134, 136, 151

Narses, 67

nationalism, 15–16, 144, 350, 360–1, 412, 420, 472, 475

Naum, St., 132, 142, 196, 198, 283

Naupactus, 100, 111

Neamţ Monastery, 378, 394

Neapolis, 109

Nemanja dynasty, 325, 400, 402, 446–7

Neretva, River, geographical position of, 18, 22, 41, 100, 134, 378; Narentani settlements on, 83; mentioned, 109, 287, 363

Nerl', River, 458

Nestor, chronicler, 429

Nestos, River, 100, 109, 310, 329, 332

Neva, River, 60

Nicaea, 309, 310, 313–17, 321, 378, 408

Nicaean Empire, 286, 313–17, 321, 367

Nicephorus I, Emperor, 95, 106

Nicephorus II Phocas, Emperor, 173–4, 257–8, 354, 383

Nicephorus III Botaneiates, Emperor, 212

Nicephorus the Hesychast, 390

Nicholas I, Pope, 117, 120–9, 191, 192, 194, 312

Nicholas Mysticus, Patriarch of Constantinople, 147–54, 156, 159, 235

Nicodemus of Tismana, 393–4, 439–40

Nicomedia, 219, 246

Nicopolis, geographical position of, 100, 268; Theme of, 108; captured by Peter Delyan (1040), 277; mentioned, 111

Nicopolis ad Haemum, geographical position of, 18; roads through, 38; fortifications of, 69

Nicopolis on Danube, battle of (1396), 310, 336

Niemen, River, 43, 58, 64, 219, 268, 310, 338, 379

Nikon, Patriarch of Moscow, 471–2

Nikon the Penitent, St., 112

Nil Sorsky, St., 397

Nin, 137, 182

Niš, geographical position of, 18, 100, 182, 268; and Belgrade–Constantinople highway, 36, 38, 68; and Via de Zenta, 40–1; Slav occupation of, 79; captured by Béla III of Hungary, 215; captured by Peter Delyan (1040), 277; Frederick Barbarossa's visit to (1189), 290; mentioned, 145, 279, 289; *see also* Naissus

Nišava, River, geographical position of, 18; and Belgrade–Constan-

Polybius, 31–2, 76
polygamy among pagan Bulgars, 119, 126
Poreč, 182, 198
Possevino, Antonio, 470
Poti, *see* Phasis
Prague, bishopric of, 250; mentioned, 197
Pratum Spirituale (John Moschus), 382
Pravda Russkaya, 410–11, 418
Preslav, geographical position of, 100, 182; as capital of Bulgaria, 133, 142, 144, 158, 322; as trading centre, 145; captured by Svyatoslav (969), 174; sacked by John Tzimisces (971), 174–5, 176, 447; captured by Basil II, 178; school of Slavonic letters in, 142–3, 198–9, 419–20, 428; as cultural centre, 378, 421, 449; monasteries in, 383; mentioned, 132, 146, 158
Prespa, Lake, 100, 130, 176, 182
Prespa, town in Macedonia, 402
Preveza, peninsula of, 108
Prima signatio, 256
Princes' Islands, 240
Pripet, River, 378, 379; marshes, 64
Priscus, Byzantine commander, 76
Prizren, 268, 288
Procheiron, 408, 410
Prochorus of Pšinja, 384
Procopius, and comments on Alans, 53; and comments on Utigurs, 55, 223–4; and comments on Slavs, 67, 82; and comments on Justinian's strategy and diplomacy, 68, 71–2
Prologue to the Holy Gospel, 431
pronoia system, 281, 327–8
Prut, River, geographical position of, 43, 65, 182, 219, 268, 310, 378; Rumanian settlements on, 334; mentioned, 58, 299
Psalterium Sinaiticum, 284
Psellus, Michael, 284, 293
Psiol, River, 43, 58, 219
Pskov Charter, 411
Pula, 182, 198

Rab, 100, 109
Ragusa, geographical position of, 18; as merchant republic, 26; and Balkan trade routes, 41; archbishopric of, 325; mentioned, 77, 324, 407; *see also* Dubrovnik
Ras, 18, 289–91, 378
Rascia, *see* Raška
Raška, geographical position of, 18, 134, 268, 323; as nucleus of medieval Serbian kingdom, 39, 134, 287, 289–91, 400, 402; national assemblies held in, 323; art and architecture in, 452; mentioned, 321, 388
Rastislav, Prince of Moravia, 184–5, 186–93, 199, 201
Rastko of Serbia, *see* Sava, St.
Ravanica Monastery, 378, 453
Regensburg, 120, 182, 207
Resava Monastery, *see* Manasija Monastery
Rhine, River, 64
Rhodes, 18
Rhodope Mountains, geographical position of, 18, 21, 27–9, 34; Vlakh settlements in, 22; and Belgrade–Constantinople highway, 37; Bulgarian settlements in, 110, 141, 160, 281; mentioned, 80, 364
Riga, Gulf of, geographical position of, 43; and Baltic–Black Sea waterway, 60
Rijeka, 182, 198
Rila Fragments, 284
Rila Monastery, 378, 384
Rila Mountains, geographical position of, 18, 20, 29; and Belgrade–Constantinople highway, 37; monasteries in, 160; mentioned, 384
Rollo, Norman Duke, 246
Roman, Prince of Galicia, 302
Roman, Metropolitan of Lithuania, 341
Roman Church, Christianization of Croatia, 86–7; Christianization of

542

Russia and Russians – *contd*
(860), 240–1; treaty with Byzantium (874), 242; attack on Constantinople (907), 243–4; treaty with Byzantium (911), 244–8, 303; attack on Constantinople (941), 246–7; treaty with Byzantium (944), 247–8; under rule of Vladimir, 251–63; relations with Bohemia, 260, 267; status within Byzantine Commonwealth, 261–3, 273, 291–4, 300–4, 337–50, 358; Russian Church, 259–61, 292, 295–7, 300–1, 312–15, 338–50, 367, 373–5, 399, 442; and Tmutorokan', 273; Cuman settlements in, 280, 298–9; war with Byzantium (1043), 293–4, 298, 303, 356; rise of principality of Suzdal', 299–301, 358; rise of principality of Galicia, 299–301, 358; Mongol invasion of (1237–40), 311, 337; rise of principality of Muscovy, 338–50; Union of Florence rejected by, 346–50, 446; influence of Byzantine culture in, 362–4, 368; revivalist movements in, 370–3; cult of St. John of Rila in, 384; cult of national rulers in, 399, 402–4; application of Romano-Byzantine law in, 406–13; Old Church Slavonic used in, 417–21; literature in, 420, 421, 426–39, 441–2; art and architecture in, 444–9, 455–64; and fall of Constantinople (1453), 467; and "Byzantine heritage", 468–73, 474, 475–6; mentioned, 14, 31, 43, 50, 51, 87, 103, 174–6, 195, 200, 225, 268–9, 278, 379; *see also* Kievan Russia *and* Muscovy

"The Russian Law", *see Pravda Russkaya*

Russian Primary Chronicle, 60, 239, 243, 252, 256, 292, 304, 362, 370, 385–6, 406–7, 421, 429–31

Ryurik, Viking leader in Novgorod, 239, 292

Sabiri, 53, 72, 88
Saga of St. Olaf, 306
St. Aitherios, *see* Berezan'
St. Anastasia, 462
St. Andrew, the Fool for Christ's sake, 211
St. Athanasius, 143, 382–3, 423; *see also Discourse against the Arians*
St. Basil of Caesarea, 143, 382, 423, 449; *see also Hexaemeron*
St. Blasius, 462
St. Clair-sur-Epte, treaty of, 246
St. Cosmas, 212
St. Damian, 212
St. Demetrius of Thessalonica, 79, 85, 211–12, 424
St. Elijah, 462
St. Florus, 462
St. George, 212, 462
St. Gregory, Island of, *see* Khortitsa
St. Gregory of Nazianzus, 423
St. Gregory of Nyssa, 423
St. Isaac the Syrian, 397
St. Isidore of Pelusium, 423
St. John the Baptist, 210
St. John Chrysostom, 143, 189, 201, 423
St. John of Damascus, and Iconoclasm, 101, 102; mentioned, 143, 380
St. John of the Ladder, 390, 392, 394, 397, 437
St. Laurus, 462
St. Ludmila, 196
St. Mamas, suburb of Constantinople, 244, 247
St. Mark, Republic of, *see* Venice
St. Michael, 399
St. Nicholas, 462
St. Nikon the Penitent, 112
St. Pachomius, 382
St. Panteleimon Monastery, near Preslav in Bulgaria, 132, 142
St. Panteleimon, Russian Monastery on Mount Athos, 383, 393
St. Paraskeve, 462
St. Paul, 164, 191

Serbia and Serbians – *contd*
in, 327–8; and *Zakonik*, 330; Turkish occupation of, 333–4, 336, 473; cult of national rulers in, 399–404; and cult of St. John Vladimir, 402; application of Romano-Byzantine law in, 407–9, 410–13; art and architecture in, 446–53, 463; and fall of Constantinople (1453), 467; relations with Ottoman Empire, 473; mentioned, 20, 38, 39, 69, 96, 136, 137, 142, 156, 176, 302, 312–313, 316, 364, 401, 441, 448, 449, 450, 460, 469; *see also* "White Serbia"

Serdica, geographical position of, 18, 268; and Belgrade–Constantinople highway, 36, 37; fortifications of, 69, 95, 96; captured by Bulgars, 95, 96; besieged by Basil II (986), 177; captured by Peter Delyan (1040), 277; mentioned, 279; *see also* Sofia

Sergius, Patriarch of Constantinople, 78

Sergius, St., of Radonezh, 395–6, 441

Sermon on Law and Grace (Hilarion), 428–9

Serres, geographical position of, 18, 39, 100, 310; capital of Theme, 109, 332–3; captured by Serbs (1345), 330; mentioned, 333

Severi, 92

Sheksna, River, 379, 396

Shën-Gjin Monastery, 402

Shipka Pass, 18, 38

Shkumbi, River, 18, 40

Šibenik, 182, 198

Siberia, 56, 89

Sicily, Arab conquest of, 101; geographical position of, 268, 310; Norman occupation of, 297, 300; Varangian mercenaries employed in, 303, 306; Angevin control of, 321; art and architecture in, 458; mentioned, 14, 66, 270

Sigismund, King of Hungary, 336

Silesia, 85

Silistria, 100, 145, 146, 158, 173, 175, 268, 275, 278; *see also* Dorostolon

Silzibul, Khan, 221

Simon, Bishop of Vladimir, 387

Simonis, Princess (daughter of Andronicus II; wife of Milutin, King of Serbia), 326–7

Sinai, 389

Singidunum, 18, 36, 39, 69, 74; *see also* Belgrade

Sinj, 18, 41

Sinope, 310, 337

Sirmium, geographical position of, 18, 182, 268; surrendered to Avars (582), 74, 183; cult of St. Demetrius in, 211; Theme of, 275, 287; mentioned, 193, 214, 224

Sklaviniae, 83, 85, 91, 97, 105–11, 274, 364

Sklavini, as ancestors of Balkan Slavs, 65; raids into Byzantine territory, 68, 70, 74

Skoplje, Skopje, geographical position of, 18, 20, 182, 268, 310; captured by Byzantines (1004), 210; centre of the Theme of Bulgaria, 275, captured by Peter Delyan (1040), 277; occupied by Serbs, 326, 328–31; mentioned, 39

Skopska Crna Gora, Mountains, 105

Slav language, and Slavonic Liturgy, 130–3, 142–3, 160, 185–204, 260–1, 272, 283, 336, 428–33; as official language of Bulgaria, 133; original literature in, 143, 260–1, 319–20, 372, 420–1, 427–42; and Glagolitic script, 187–8, 197–9, 284, 417; and Cyrillic script, 187–8, 198–9, 284; and Old Church Slavonic, 189, 196, 260, 283–4, 384, 401–2, 416–21, 427–34, 435–9; literature translated into, 382, 392, 396, 406–12, 416–28, 434–41; and spoken vernacular, 416–22, 430–5, 438; and Church Slavonic, 433–42; mentioned, 155, 157, 274, 285, 292, 327, 329, 468

Taygetus Mountains, 106, 268, 274
Tempe, Vale of, 100, 177
Terbouniotes, 134
Terek, River, geographical position of, 43, 46, 219, 269; Sabiri settlements on, 53; Khazar settlements on, 231, 233
Termács, Magyar chieftain, 206
Tervel, Khagan, 92-3, 114, 226
Tetovo, 310, 326
Tettenhall, battle of (910), 246
Teutonic Knights, 310, 399
Thames, River, 246
Theme system of administration, 100, 106-13, 141, 232, 270-1, 275, 327, 332
Theoderic, King of the Ostrogoths, 82
Theodora, wife of Justinian II, 226
Theodora Comnena (sister of Manuel I), 215
Theodore I Lascaris, Emperor, 314-15
Theodore the Studite, St., 382
Theodosia, 24, 50; see also Caffa
Theodosius II, Emperor, 32-3
Theodosius III, Emperor, 93
Theodosius of Kiev, St., 296, 385-7, 395
Theodosius of Trnovo, St., 390-91, 434, 435, 440
Theophanes, protovestiarius under Romanus I, 246
Theophanes the Greek, painter, 460-3
Theophilus, Emperor, 102, 187, 231-2, 239
Theophylact, Archbishop of Ohrid, 202, 284-5, 366
Theophylact Lecapenus, Patriarch of Constantinople, 162-4, 170, 172, 207
Thermopylae, and Kutrigur invasion (559), 68; fortifications of, 69; mentioned, 18, 177
Thessalonica, geographical position of, 18, 21, 33, 100, 182, 268, 310; as chief city of "Campania", 27, 34;

and Via Egnatia, 33; as a citadel, 34; as centre of international communications, 34, 39-41; mentioned in De Administrando Imperio, 45; Avar and Slav attacks on, 75, 77-81, 85, 105-6; capital of Theme, 108, 110, 185; as trading centre, 144; Bulgarian attacks on, 147, 177, 277; St. Demetrius as patron saint of, 79, 211, 424; as cultural and artistic centre, 318, 362, 378, 421, 439, 444, 449-53; monastic centre in, 383, 392, 397, 439; mentioned, 19, 111, 130, 141, 185, 187, 285, 326, 329, 332, 410
Thessaly, Vlakhs in, 22, 271; Albanians in, 23; geographical position of, 18, 268, 310; Kutrigur invasion of (559), 68; system of fortifications in, 69; Avaro-Slav invasion of (587), 75-6; Slav occupation of, 79, 80, 105-6; Byzantine influence in, 104-5; bishoprics in, 111; and Theme system, 141; Samuel of Bulgaria's occupation of, 176, 177; Peter Delyan's invasion of (1040), 277; Frankish barons in, 309; annexed by Serbia, 329, 412; Meteora monasteries of, 439
Thrace, geographical position of, 18, 21, 27, 29-41, 100, 182, 268, 310; Slav invasions of, 22, 67-9, 75, 79-80; Vlakhs in, 22; Kutrigurs in, 55, 68, 70; Avar designs on, 72; Bulgar invasions of, 67, 93-6, 115, 141, 145-7, 150-52, 154, 174, 177; Byzantine Empire's northern borders in, 101, 113; Theme of, 107, 110, 141; Paulicians in, 163, 282; Magyar invasions of (934-61), 206; Pecheneg invasions of (1048-53), 279; invasion by Uzes (1064), 279; pronoiai in, 281, 328; Cuman invasion of (1200), 302; Frankish barons in, 309; cultural life in, 363; mentioned, 32, 83, 90, 104, 117, 157, 178, 294, 316

549

91; battle of (1444), 336
Vatika Bay, 274
Vatopedi Monastery, 291
Velbuzhd, battle of (1330), 310, 318, 329
Veles, 105, 310, 325
Venice, close connections with Dalmatia, 21–2, 26, 42, 287; geographical position of, 18, 182, 268, 310; Crimean colonies of, 25, 50; occupation of Corfù, 26; and Black Sea trade, 29, 335; assault on Constantinople by (1204), 31; and Balkan trade routes, 40–1, 42, 135–6; as Byzantine dependency, 109, 141, 287; Constantine and Methodius' visit to (867), 191, 194, 201–2; art and architecture in, 458; Republic of St. Mark, 287; and Fourth Crusade, 309, 312; relations with Serbia, 329; mentioned, 14, 33, 132, 195, 203, 324, 470
Veregava Pass, 92
Vespasian, Emperor, 399
Veszprém, 182, 210, 378
Via Egnatia, 18, 33, 34, 40; military importance of, 41; and Theme of Strymon, 109
Via de Zenta, 40
Vicina, 334
Vidin, 100, 178, 182, 210, 310, 318, 378
Vikings, 57–60, 157, 174, 220, 232; and Russia, 238–48, 249–61, 293–4; and Byzantium, 303, 306; as carriers of Byzantine ideas and customs, 360–62; see also Varangians
Vilna, 310, 338
Viminacium, geographical position of, 18; and Belgrade–Constantinople highway, 36; fortifications of, 69
Vinogradoff, Sir P., 405, 406
Visegrád, 182, 211, 378
Visigoths, 29

Vistula River, 64, 65, 182, 197, 219, 268, 310, 378
Vita Constantini, 427
Vitichev, 43, 61
Vitosha, Mount, 36, 378, 384
Vladimir, city of, 269, 298–9, 310, 339, 379, 399; centre of art, 455, 457–8, 463
Vladimir, St. Prince of Russia, 251–63, 292, 303–4, 361, 364, 369, 373, 375, 399, 402, 406–7, 428; Church Statute of, 411
Vladimir, Bulgarian ruler, 132–3
Vladimir Monomakh, Prince of Kiev, 294–5, 299, 300
Vladimirko, Prince of Galicia, 300
Vladislav, King of Bohemia, 271
Vladislav, King of Serbia, 450
Vlakhs, origins of, 22, 270, 271, 272; mentioned, 286
Vlastimir, Prince of Serbia, 134
Vodiţa Monastery, 378, 393
Vojvodina, 181
Volga, River, situation of, 43, 46, 58, 219, 220, 266, 269, 310, 378, 379; Byzantine vassal states on, 52; and Baltic–Black Sea waterway, 60; Khazar settlements on, 90, 227–8, 230–1; Pecheneg settlements on, 235; Viking trade on, 238; and Golden Horde, 311; mentioned, 50, 59, 223, 252, 299, 339, 370, 372, 395–6, 457
Volga Bulgars, 252, 254
Volkhov, River, geographical position of, 43, 59, 219, 268, 379; and Baltic–Black Sea waterway, 60; mentioned, 371
Volos, 268, 277; see also Demetrias
Volotovo, church of, 460
Volynia, 310, 312
Voroneţ, Monastery, 378, 454
Vrbas, River, 100, 136
Vychegda, River, 379

Wallachia, historical geography of,